The New Chess Player

Le Nouveau Joueur d'Échecs

Der neue Schachspieler

De Nieuwe Schaakspeler

Den nye Schackspelaren

Il Nuovo Giocatore di Scacchi

El Nuevo Ajedrecista

Новый Шахматист

3

1978

C

PITMAN

PITMAN PUBLISHING LIMITED
39 Parker Street, London WC2B 5PB

Associated Companies
Copp Clark Limited, Toronto
Fearon-Pitman Publishers Inc., Belmont, California
Pitman Publishing New Zealand Ltd., Wellington
Pitman Publishing Pty Ltd., Melbourne

Distributed in Italy by
Edizioni Scolastiche APE SpA
Via Tanaro 14, 20128 Milano

© The Chess Player Ltd 1979

First published in Great Britain 1979

Printed and bound in England by
Billing & Son Ltd., Guildford

ISBN 0 273 01287 8

Contents

+ =   white stands slightly better   les blancs ont jeu un peu meilleur   Weiss steht etwas besser   wit staat er iets beter voor vit står något bättre   il bianco sta un po' meglio   el blanco está algo mejor белые стоят немного лучше

= +   black stands slightly better   les noirs ont jeu un peu meilleur   Schwarz steht etwas besser   zwart staat er iets beter voor svart står något bättre   il nero sta un po' meglio el negro está algo mejor   черные стоят немного лучше

±   white has the upper hand   les blancs ont le meilleur jeu   Weiss steht besser   wit staat beter   vit står bättre   il bianco sta meglio   el blanco está mejor   белые стоят лучше

∓   black has the upper hand   les noirs ont le meilleur jeu   Schwarz steht besser zwart staat beter   svart står bättre   il nero sta meglio   el negro está mejor черные стоят лучше

+ −   white has a decisive advantage   les blancs ont un avantage décisif   Weiss hat entscheidenden vorteil   wit heeft een beslissend voordeel   vit har avgörande fördel il bianco è in vantaggio decisivo   el blanco tiene una ventaja decisiva   белые имеют решающее преимущество

− +   black has a decisive advantage   les noirs ont un avantage décisif   Schwarz hat entscheidenden vorteil   zwart heeft een beslissend voordeel   svart har avgörande fördel   il nero è in vantaggio decisivo el negro tiene una ventaja decisiva   черные имеют решающее преимущество

=   the game is even   le jeu est égal   das Spiel ist ausgeglichen   de stellingen zÿn gelÿkwaardig   spelet är jamnt   giuoco pari   el juego está equilibrado   игра равна

≈   approximately equal   plus où moins égal ungefähr gleich   ongeveer gelÿkwaardig narmelsevis jämnt   piu o meno eguale más o menos igual   приблизительно равно

∝   the position is unclear   le jeu est incertain das Spiel ist unklar   de posities zÿn onduidelÿk   ställningen är oklar   il giuoco è poco chiaro   la posición no es clara неясная позиция

!   a very good move   un tres bon coup ein sehr guter Zug   een zeer goede zet ett bra drag   una buona mossa   una jugada muy buena   очень хороший ход

!!   an excellent move   un excellent coup ein ausgezeichneter Zug   een uitstekende zet   ett utmärkt drag   una mossa ottima una jugada excelente   отличный ход

?   a mistake   un coup faible   ein schwacher Zug   een fout   ett dåligt drag   una mossa debole   una mala jugada   плохой ход

??   a blunder   une grave erreur   ein grober Fehler   een ernstige fout   ett grovt fel un grave errore   un gran error   грубая ошибка

!?   a move deserving attention   un coup qui mérite l'attention   ein beachtenswerter Zug   een zet die de aandacht verdient ett drag som fortjäner uppmärksamhet una mossa degna di considerazione   una jugada que merece atención   ход, заслуживающий внимания

?!   a dubious move   un coup d'une valeur douteuse   ein Zug von zweifelhaftem wert   een dubieuze zet   ett tvivelaktigt drag   una mossa dubbia   una jugada de dudoso valor   ход, имеющий сомнительную ценность

Δ   with the idea . . .   avec l'idée . . .   mit der Idee . . .   met het idee om . . .   med idén . . .   con l'idea . . .   con idea . . . с идеей...

N   a novelty   une innovation   eine Neuerung   een nieuwtje   en nyhet   un'innovazione   una novedad   новинка

Contributors

		? Lysenko	
		R. Maric	IM
		E. Mednis	IM
R. Bellin	IM	A. Miles	GM
G. Botterill	IM	N. Povah	
W. Browne	GM	K. Pytel	IM
A. Filipowicz	IM	Z. Ribli	GM
D. Friedgood		D. Sahovic	GM
F. Gheorghiu	GM	G. Sigurjonsson	GM
S. Gligoric	GM	L. Shamkovich	GM
E. Gufeld	GM	J. Speelman	IM
E. Haag	IM	A. Suetin	GM
V. Hort	GM	S. Taulbut	IM
Z. Ilic		J. Timman	GM
G. Iskov	IM	M. Tseitlin	IM
A. Kapengut		W. Uhlmann	GM
G. Kasparov		D. Velimirovic	GM
J. Konikowski		S. Webb	IM
B. Larsen	GM	K. Wicker	

Journals

Ajedrez, British Chess Magazine, Butlleti D'Escacs, Ceskoslovensky Sach, Chess, Chess Bulletin (Canada), Chess in Australia, Chess Life and Review, Deutsche Schachblatter, Deutsche Schachzeitung, Europe Echecs, Fernschach, Jaque, Jaque Mate, Le Courrier Des Echecs, L'Italia Scacchistica, Magyar Sakkelet, Modern Chess Theory, Revista Romana de Sah, Rochade, Sahovski Glasnik, Scacco, Schaakbulletin, Schach, Schach-Echo, Schack nytt, Schakend Nederland, Shahmat, Shakhmatna Mis'l, Skakbladet, South African Chessplayer, Suomen Shakki, Szachy, Tidskrift for Schack, 64 Шахматы Шахматный Бюллетень Шахматы в СССР

Bulletins

1977: Baku, Beltsi, Kallithea, USA Final, USSR-Jugoslavia
1978: Alicante, Bagneux, Beersheva, Bydgoszcz, Chiburdanidze-Kushnir, DDR Final, Groningen, Hallsberg, Herzlia, Israel Final, Jugoslavia Final, Jurmala, Kiel, Lodz, Lvov, Malaga, Mexico, Minsk, Niksic, Osijek, Quito, Ribe, Roskilde, Sao Paulo, Silva-Durao, Sinaia, Smed.Palanka, Titovo Uzice, USSR Womens Final

Novelties

4	Miles	—	Timman
5	Magerramov	—	Sturua
8	A.Petrosian	—	Kapengut
10	Rashkovsky	—	Alburt
48	Knaak	—	Nogueiras
49	Sturua	—	Vladimirov
55	Ilic	—	Pinkas
57	F.Portisch	—	Ree
63	Palatnik	—	Kuzmin
64	Beljavsky	—	Farago
87	Miles	—	Browne
99	Adamski	—	Lehmann
110	Sahovic	—	Ligterink
144	Kayumok	—	Semeniuk
146	Byrne	—	Timman
147	Volovik	—	Rundquist
148	Velimirovic	—	Kurajica
153	Haag	—	Szlovak
159	Mednis	—	Byrne

Combinations

3	Ogaard	—	Larsen
5	Magerramov	—	Sturua
21	Miles	—	Mestrovic
33	Lukacs	—	Mihalchishin
43	Browne	—	Formanek
46	Gheorghiu	—	Hebert
52	Gheorghiu	—	Arnason
55	Ilic	—	Pinkas
57	F.Portisch	—	Ree
64	Beljavsky	—	Farago
73	Tseitlin	—	Antonov
81	Kuzmin	—	Ree
102	Farago	—	Ftacnik
110	Sahovic	—	Ligterink
123	Vadasz	—	Adorjan
144	Kayumov	—	Semeniuk
147	Volovik	—	Rundquist
150	Marcinkiewicz	—	Kocur

163	Dorfman	—	Tukmakov
167	Kavalek	—	Byrne
173	Knox	—	Curtin
175	Saharov	—	Banstatis
182	Donchev	—	Semkov
186	Klovan	—	Mochalov
190	Bronstein	—	Lanka
191	Kapengut	—	Mishuchkov
203	Gufeld	—	Klovan
222	Shamkovich	—	Benko
227	Marczell	—	Saharov
246	Vitolins	—	Mihalchishin
284	Sveshnikov	—	Kochiev
285	Lutikov	—	Lanka
287	Grospeter	—	Sinkovits
292	Westerinen	—	Sahovic
316	Peresipkin	—	Alburt
323	Hulak	—	Vukic
324	Ree	—	Palatnik
335	Ostermeyer	—	Botterill
336	Grospeter	—	Mednis

152	Uhlmann	—	Ljubojevic
157	Haag	—	Molnar
162	Parma	—	Hamann
170	Vakhrushev	—	Soloviev
173	Knox	—	Curtin
178	Brummer	—	Gheorghiu
180	Velimirovic	—	Ivanovic
183	Gufeld	—	Zaichik
191	Kapengut	—	Mishuchkov
194	Sigurjonsson	—	Ogaard
195	Soloviev	—	Lysenko
197	Mihalchishin	—	Taborov
203	Klovan	—	Gufeld
222	Shamkovich	—	Benko
239	Egorovsky	—	Gusikov
247	Rantanen	—	Kaiszauri
287	Grospeter	—	Sinkovits
291	Filipowicz	—	Rajna
302	Velimirovic	—	Uhlmann
319	Velimirovic	—	Kovacevic

Theory

1 c4 e5 2 ♘c3 ♘f6
2...d6 3 g3 f5 4 d4! ♗e7 N (4...e4 5 f3 ♘f6 6 ♗g2 exf3 7 ♘xf3 g6 8 0-0 ♗g7 Toran-Tal, Oberhausen 1961, 9 d5!; 4...exd4 5 ♕xd4 ♘c6 6 ♕d2! ♘f6 7 b3 g6 8 ♗b2 ♗g7 9 ♗g2 0-0 10 ♘h3 ♘e5 11 0-0± Etruk-Arulaid, Tallinn 1962) 5 dxe5 dxe5 6 ♕xd8+ ♗xd8 7 ♗g2 ♘f6 8 b3 c6 9 ♗b2 ♘bd7 10 ♘f3 0-0 11 0-0 ♖e8 12 ♖ad1 ♗c7 13 ♘h4!? ∝/+= Taimanov-Vaganian, Leningrad 1977

3 ♘f3 ♘c6 4 g3
a) 4 d4 exd4 5 ♘xd4 ♗b4 6 ♗g5 h6 7 ♗h4 g5? 8 ♘xc6 N (8 ♗g3 d6 9 ♘xc6! bxc6 10 ♕a4!±) 8...bxc6 9 ♗g3 ♗xc3+ 10 bxc3 d6 11 f3 ♕e7 12 e4± Rube-Keiler, Eggesin 1978;

b) 4 d4 e4 5 ♘d2 ♗b4 6 e3 0-0 7 ♕c2 ♖e8 8 ♘d5 N (8 a3 ♗xc3 9 ♕xc3 d5 10 b3 ♗f5 11 ♗b2 ♘e7 12 h3 c6 13 ♗e2 a5 14 b4!± Riumin-Ragozin, USSR 1942) 8...d6 9 ♘xb4 ♘xb4 10 ♕c3 a5 11 d5 c6 12 dxc6 bxc6 13 a3 ♘a6 14 b3 c5 15 ♗b2± Pytel-Ostojic, Bagneux 1978;

c) 4 e4 ♗c5 5 ♘xe5 ♘xe5 6 d4 ♗b4 (6...♘xe4 N 7 ♘xe4 ♗b4+ 8 ♘c3 ♘g6 9 ♗d3 0-0 10 0-0 ♕h4 11 ♘e4 ♗e7 12 f4± Stepak-Manevich, Israel Final 1978) 7 dxe5 ♘xe4 8 ♕d4 ♘xc3 9 bxc3 ♗e7 10 ♕g4 g6 N 11 ♗h6 ♗f8 12 ♕f4 ♗xh6 13 ♕xh6 ♕e7 14 ♗d3 ♕f8 15 ♕f4± Skalkotas-Nevrakis, Kallithea 1977

4...♗b4
a) 4...♘d4 5 ♗g2 ♘xf3+ 6 ♗xf3 ♗b4 7 0-0 0-0 8 ♕c2 ♖e8 Δ c6, d5= Smejkal-Korchnoi, Palma 1972

b) 4...♘d4 5 ♘xe5!? ♕e7 6 f4 d6 7 ♘d3 ♗f5 8 e3 ♗g4 9 ♗e2 ♘xe2 10 ♘xe2 ♕e4 11 ♘f2 ♕xc4 12 ♘xg4

♘xg4 13 ♘d4 ♘f6 14 ♕e2= Rivas-Barri, USSR 1978;

c) 4...♘d4 5 ♘h4!? N g5!? 6 ♘f3 ♘xf3+ 7 exf3 ♗c5 8 ♕e2 Botterill-Botto, England 1977, 8...d6=

5 ♗g2 0-0 6 0-0 e4
a) 6...♘xc3 7 dxc3 e4 8 ♘e1 h6 9 ♘c2 d6 10 ♘e3 ♖e8 11 ♕c2! b6 12 h3 a5 13 ♔h2 ♗d7 Rogoff-Portisch, Biel 1976, 14 ♘d5 Δ ♗e3, ♖ae1, f3 +=;

b) 6...♖e8 7 ♘e1! d6 8 ♘c2 ♗xc3 9 dxc3 ♗e6 10 ♘e3 ♘a5!? N (10...♕c8 11 ♘d5! ♘d7 12 e4±) 11 b3 ♗g4! 12 ♘d5 (12 ♘c2) 12...c6 13 ♗b4 f5 14 e4 Averbakh-Passerotti, Reggio-Emilia 1977/78, 14...fxe4 15 ♗xe4 ♕d7 16 ♗g2 ♘f6!? 17 ♗g5!? ♖ad8!?∝

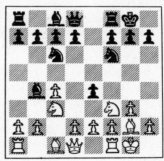

7 ♘e1
7 ♘g5 ♗xc3 8 bxc3 ♖e8 9 ♕c2 ♕e7 10 d3 exd3 11 exd3 b6 12 ♗d2 ♗b7 13 ♖ae1 ♕f8 14 ♗f4+= Holmov-Kapengut, Beltsi 1977

7...♗xc3 8 dxc3 h6! 9 ♘c2 ♖e8 10 ♘e3 b6
10...d6 11 ♕c2 ♖e5= Polugaevsky-Savon, USSR Final 1973

11 ♕c2 ♗b7 12 ♖d1!
12 ♗d2 ♘e5 13 ♖ad1 ♕e7 14 h3? ♕e6 15 b3 ♘f3+!∓ Hernandez-Olafsson, Tallinn 1975

12...♘e5 13 h3 d6 14 b3 ♕d7 15

♘d5= Averbakh-Martorelli, Reggio Emilia 1977/78

1 c4 ♘f6 2 ♘f3 c5 3 d4 cxd4 4 ♘xd4 e6 5 ♘c3

a) 5 g3 ♕a5+ 6 ♘d2 ♕b6 7 e3 ♘c6 8 ♘xc6 bxc6 9 ♗g2 ♗e7 10 0-0 0-0= Coppini-Averbakh, Reggio Emilia 1977/78,

b) 5 g3 d5 6 ♗g2 e5 7 ♘b3 ♗b4+ 8 ♘c3 dxc4 9 ♕xd8+ ♔xd8 10 ♘d2 ♘c6 11 ♘xc4 ♘d4!? 12 ♔f1! ♘d7 13 ♘d5 ♗f8 14 ♗d2!± Zaitsev-Garcia, Quito 1978

5...♘c6

a) 5...♗b4 6 g3 ♘e4 7 ♕d3 ♕a5 8 ♘c2 ♗xc3+ 9 bxc3 f5 10 ♗g2 ♘c6 11 ♗a3 b6 12 0-0 += Karasev-Nebolisin, Beltsi 1978;

b) 5...♗b4 6 ♘b5 a6 7 ♘d6+ ♔e7 8 ♘xc8+ ♕xc8 9 ♕b3 ♘c6 10 ♗d2 d6 11 e3 ♖d8= Minev-Grigorov, Bulgaria Final 1976;

c) 5...♗b4 6 ♘b5 0-0 7 a3 ♗xc3+ 8 ♘xc3 d5 9 e3 ♘c6 10 ♗e2 dxc4 11 ♗xc4 ♕xd1+ N (11...♘e5 12 ♗e2 ♗d7) 12 ♔xd1 e5 13 f3 ♖e8 14 ♗d2 += Kovacs-Valenti, Reggio Emilia 1977/78

6 g3 ♕b6

6...♗c5 7 ♘b3 ♗b4 8 ♗g2 d5 9 cxd5 ♘xd5 10 a3! ♗xc3+ 11 bxc3 0-0 12 ♕c2 ♕c7 13 c4 ♘e5 14 c5 N (14 ♘d2 b5 15 c5 ♗b7 16 0-0 ♖ac8 17 ♘b3 a5 18 e4 += Korchnoi-Spassky 1977) 14...b6 15 0-0 ♗b7 16 ♗b2 ♘d7 17 ♖ac1 ♖ac8= Mortensen-Parma, Kiel 1978

Diagram

7 ♘b3

a) 7 ♘db5 ♘e5! 8 ♗g2 a6 9 ♗e3 ♕a5 10 ♗f4 axb5 11 ♗xe5 bxc4∓ D.Byrne-Geller, USA-USSR 1955;

b) 7 ♘db5 ♗c5?! N 8 ♗g2 ♗xf2+! 9 ♔f1 ♘g4 10 ♕d6! ♖b8? 11 ♘a4! ♕a5 12 ♗d2! 1-0 Lipinski-Schinzel, Warsaw 1977

7...♗b4

7...♘e5 8 e4 ♗b4 9 ♕e2 a5 10 ♗e3 ♕c7 11 f4 ♘eg4 12 ♗d2 a4 13 ♘d4 ♕b6 14 ♘db5± Grinberg-Greenfeld, Herzlia 1978

8 ♗g2 ♕a6

8...0-0 9 0-0 ♗xc3 10 c5 ♕c7 11 bxc3 b6 12 ♗f4 e5 13 ♗g5 ♘e8 14 cxb6 axb6 15 ♗e7 +− Mihalchishin-Valenti, Rome 1977

9 ♘d2

9 c5 N ♘a5 10 ♗f4 0-0 11 ♗d6 ♖e8 12 0-0 ♗xc3 13 bxc3 ♘c6 14 ♘d4 += Schmidt-Joksic, Vrnjacka Banja 1978

9...♗xc3 10 bxc3 0-0 11 c5 N

11 ♕b3 N d5! 12 ♕b5 (12 0-0 ♘a5 13 ♕a3 b6 14 cxd5 exd5 15 c4 ♘xc4 16 ♘xc4 ♕xc4 17 ♗b2 ♘e4∓ Tatai-Ostojic, Rome 1977) 12...♕a5 13 ♕xa5 ♘xa5 14 cxd5 exd5 15 0-0 ♖e8 16 ♖e1 ♗d7= Firnhaber-Parma, Kiel 1978

11...b6 12 cxb6 axb6 13 0-0 b5 14 ♘b3 d5 15 a4!? bxa4 16 ♘c5 ♕b5=+ Bagirov-Gulko, Lvov 1978

Slav

1 d4 d5 2 c4 c6 3 ♘f3

8

a) 3 cxd5 cxd5 4 ♘c3 ♘c6 5 ♘f3 ♘f6
6 ♗f4 e6 7 e3 ♗d6 8 ♗g3 0-0 9 ♘e5
♗xe5 10 dxe5 ♘d7= Silva-Durao,
1978;

b) 3 ♘c3 e6 4 e4 dxe4 5 ♘xe4 ♗b4+
6 ♗d2 (6 ♘c3 c5 7 ♗e3 ♘f6 N [7...
♕a5?! 8 ♘e2 cxd4 9 ♗xd4 ♘f6 10 a3
♗e7 Alekhine-Junge, Salzburg 1942,
11 b4! ♕d8 12 ♗e3±] 8 dxc5 ♕xd1+
9 ♖xd1 ♘a6 10 ♘e2 ♗d7 11 a3
♗xc5 12 ♗xc5 ♘xc5 13 b4 +=
Azmayparashvili-Andrianov, USSR
1978) 6...♕xd4 7 ♗xb4 ♕xe4+ 8 ♗e2
c5 9 ♗xc5 ♕xg2 10 ♗f3 ♕g5 11
♗e3 ♕a5+ 12 ♗d2 ♕c7 13 ♘e2 ♘c6
14 ♘c3 N (14 ♗c3 ♘e5 15 ♘d4 ♗d7
16 ♕e2 ♘f6∓ Kovacs-van Scheltinga,
Amsterdam 1954) 14...♘ge7 15 0-0
0-0 16 ♘b5 ♕b8 17 c5 b6 18 ♖c1
♖d8∓ Douven-Berg, Ribe 1978

3...♘f6 4 ♘c3 dxc4

4...e6 5 ♗g5 dxc4 6 e4 b5 7 e5 h6
8 ♗h4 g5 9 ♘xg5 hxg5 10 ♗xg5
♘bd7

a) 11 g3 ♕a5 12 exf6 b4 13 ♘e4 ♗a6
14 ♕f3 ♕d5 15 ♗e3 0-0-0 16 ♗e2
♗b7 17 0-0 ♖g8 18 ♖fc1 c5 19 ♘d2
♘xf6 N (19...cxd4= Flohr) 20 ♕xd5
exd5 21 dxc5 ♘d7∝ Fodor-Tompa,
Corres 1977;

b) 11 ♕f3 ♗b7 12 ♗e2 ♕b6! 13
♗xf6 c5 14 ♘e4 ♖h6!? N (14...♖g8
15 ♕f4 cxd4 16 ♘h5 ♘c5 17 ♗xf7+
♔d7 18 ♘xc5 ♗xc5 19 0-0-0 ♗d5∓
Zollner-Junge, Warsaw 1942) 15 ♗g5
♖g6 16 ♕f4 cxd4 17 h4≈ Hamann-
Schramm, Kiel 1978;

c) 11 exf6 ♗b7 12 g3 ♕b6 (12...c5
13 d5 ♘e5!?∝ N) 13 ♗g2 0-0-0 14 0-0
♘e5?! 15 dxe5! ♖xd1 16 ♖axd1 ♗c5
(16...c5 17 ♗xb7+ ♔xb7 8 ♖fe1
a6 19 ♘e4± Hollis-Jovcic, Corres
1975) 17 ♘e4 ♗d4 18 ♘d6+± Hollis-
Baumbach, corres 1977

5 a4 ♗f5

a) 5...♘a6;

b) 5...♗g4 6 ♘e5 ♗h5 7 g3 e6 8 ♗g2
♗b4 (8...a5 9 0-0 ♘a6 10 h3 ♗b4 11
♘xc4 ♗e7 12 ♕d2?! ♘d7 Δ ♘b6=
Nemet-Kovacevic, Virovitica 1977)
9 ♘xc4 0-0 10 0-0 ♘a6 N (10...a5
11 h3 ♘bd7 12 g4 ♗g6 13 ♗g5+=
Euwe) 11 h3 ♕e7 12 g4 ♗g6 13
♗g5 ♖fd8 14 e3 ♘c5 15 ♘e5±
Bleiman-Birnboim, Beersheva 1978

6 ♘e5

6 e3 e6 7 ♗xc4 ♗b4 8 0-0 0-0 9 ♕e2
♘bd7 10 ♖d1 N!? ♘e4 11 ♘a2 ♗e7
12 b3 a5 13 ♗b2 ♕b6 14 ♘c3 ♖fd8
15 ♘xe4 ♗xe4 16 ♘d2 ♗c2 17 ♖dc1
♗g6 18 f3 ♗g5∓ Uhlmann-Starck,
Eggesin 1978

6...e6 7 f3 ♗b4 8 e4

a) 8 ♘xc4 ♘d5 9 ♗d2 ♕h4+ 10 g3
♕xd4 11 e3 ♕f6 12 ♘a2?! N (12 e4
♘xc3 13 ♕b3 ♗xe4 14 ♗xb4 ♕d4 15
fxe4 ♕xe4+ 16 ♔f2± Mikenas-Feigin,
Kemeri 1939) 12...♗xd2+ 13 ♕xd2
0-0 14 e4 ♗g6 15 exd5 exd5 16 ♘a3
♕xf3 ∝/∓ Kolpakov-Kosikov, Beltsi
1978

b) 8 ♘xc4 ♘bd7 9 ♕b3 (9 e4!) 9...a5
10 e4 ♗g6 11 ♗g5 ♕b8 12 ♗e2 0-0
13 0-0 b5! 14 axb5 cxb5 15 ♘e3 e5
16 d5 ♕b6 17 ♔h1 += Keene-
Birnboim, Beersheva 1978

8...♗xe4! 9 ♘xf7?! N

9 fxe4 ♘xe4 10 ♕f3 ♕xd4 11 ♕xf7+ ♔d8 12 ♗g5+ ♘xg5 13 ♕xg7 ♗xc3+ 14 bxc3 ♕xc3+ 15 ♔e2 ♕c2+ 16 ♔e1 ♕c3+ ½-½ Beljavsky-Steinberg, USSR 1971

9...♔xf7 10 fxe4 ♘xe4 11 ♕h5+ g6 12 ♕f3+ ♘f6 13 ♗d2 ♗xc3!

13...♕xd4 14 0-0-0 ♕g4 15 ♕f2 ♕f5 16 ♕h4

14 bxc3 ♕d5! 15 ♕g3 ♘bd7∓
Beljavsky-Peresipkin, USSR Final 1977

Benko Gambit

1 d4 ♘f6 2 c4 c5 3 d5 b5 4 cxb5 a6 5 e3

5 bxa6 g6 6 ♘c3 (6 a7!? N ♖xa7 7 ♘c3 ♗a6 8 ♘f3 ♗g7 9 ♘d2 0-0 10 e4 ♗xf1 11 ♘xf1 ♕a5 Karasev-Chekhov, Beltsi 1978) 6...♗xa6 7 e4 (7 g3 d6 8 ♗g2 ♗g7 9 ♘f3 0-0 10 0-0 ♘bd7 11 ♖e1 ♕a5 12 e4 ♖fb8!? [12...♘g4! 13 h3 ♘ge5 14 ♘xe5 ♗xe5 15 ♗f1= Mista-Spiridonov, Cienfuegos 1972] 13 e5 dxe5 14 ♘xe5 ♗xe5 15 ♖xe5 ♖a7 16 ♖e3 ♘e8 17 ♖e4 ♘d6≈ Magrin-Formanek, Reggio Emilia 1977/78) 7...♗xf1 8 ♔xf1 d6 9 ♘ge2?! (9 ♘f3 ♗g7 10 g3 0-0 11 ♔g2 ♕a5 12 ♖e1 Tarjan-Webb, Hastings 1977/ 78, 12...♘bd7 Δ ♖fb8, ♘e8, ♘c7) 9...♗g7 10 h3 0-0 11 ♔g1 ♘bd7 N (11...♕b6 12 ♖b1 ♘a6 13 ♗e3 ♖b8 14 ♔h2 ♘d7 15 ♕d2 ♕a5 16 ♗g5 += Enklaar-Ree, Netherlands Final 1972) 12 ♖b1 ♕a5 13 ♗e3 ♖fb8 14 ♕c2 ♘e8 15 ♔h2 ♘c7 16 b3 ♘b5 =/=+ Fedder-Webb, Roskilde 1978

5...g6

5...e6 6 ♘c3 exd5 7 ♘xd5 axb5 8 ♗xb5 ♗b7 9 ♗c4! ♗e7 10 ♘e2 ♘xd5 11 ♗xd5 ♗xd5 12 ♕xd5 ♕a5+ 13 ♗d2 ♕a6 14 0-0± Tukmakov-Bednarski, Decin 1977

6 ♘c3 ♗g7 7 ♘f3

7 ♕b3!? (Korchnoi) 7...d6 8 a4 ♘bd7 9 ♖a3 0-0 10 ♘f3 Donner-Miles, Amsterdam 1977, 10...♗b7!=; 10 ♗c4 axb5 11 axb5 ♗b7 12 ♘ge2 ♘b6 13 e4 ♘fd7= Baumbach-Grunberg, Erfurt 1973

7...d6

a) 7...0-0 8 a4!? e6!? 9 e4 exd5 10 exd5 ♖e8+ 11 ♗e2=; 9 bxa6 ♘xa6 10 ♗c4 ♘b4 11 0-0 exd5 12 ♘xd5 ♘fxd5 13 ♗xd5 ♖b8 14 ♖a3 ♗a6 15 ♖e1 c4∓ Reinhardt-Szmetan, Buenos Aires 1977;

b) 7...0-0 8 a4!? axb5 9 ♗xb5 d6 10 0-0 ♘a6 11 ♖a3 ♘c7 12 ♗d2 ♘d7 13 ♗xd7 ♗xd7 14 ♘c4 ♖a6 15 e4 += Petrosian-Alburt, USSR Final 1977

8 a4 0-0 9 e4

a) 9 ♖a3! ♘bd7 10 e4 ♕c7 11 ♗e2 axb5 12 ♘xb5 ♕b8 13 ♕c2 ♗a6 14 0-0± Razuvaev-Tukmakov, USSR Final 1975;

b) 9 ♖a3! e6!? N 10 ♗c4! axb5 11 ♗xb5 exd5 12 ♗xd5 ♘xd5 13 ♕xd5 ♖a6 14 0-0 ♗e6 15 ♕d3 d5 16 ♕c2 ♖c6 17 ♖d1 +=/∞ Panno-Garcia, Buenos Aires 1977

9...♘bd7?!

9...e6 10 dxe6 fxe6 11 e5! ♘g4! 12

10

♕xd6 ♗b7!≈ Farago-Filipowicz, Polanica Zdroj 1977
10 ♗d2 ♘e8 11 ♗e2 ♘c7 12 0-0 ♗b7 13 ♖b1 axb5 14 axb5 ♕h8 15 b4 ♖a3 16 ♕c1 ♕a8 17 b6! cxb4 18 ♖xb4 ♘e8 19 ♘d4± Farago-Gaprindashvili, Dortmund 1978

Nimzo-Indian

1 d4 ♘f6 2 c4 e6 3 ♘c3 ♗b4 4 e3
a) 4 a3 ♗xc3+ 5 bxc3 c5 (5...♘e4 6 ♕c2 f5 7 e3 b6 8 ♗d3 ♗b7 9 ♘e2 ♕h4 10 0-0 0-0 11 f3 ♘g5 12 ♗d2 ♘c6 13 ♘g3 ♘a5 14 ♗e1 ♕h6= Starck-Bruggemann, Eggesin 1978) 6 f3 (6 e3 b6 7 ♘e2 ♘a6 8 ♘g3 ♕c7 9 e4 cxd4 10 cxd4 ♗xc4 11 ♕c2!± Vaganian) 6...d5 (6...♘c6 7 e4 d6 8 ♗e3 ♕a5 9 ♕d2 b6 10 ♗d3 cxd4 11 cxd4 ♕xd2+ 12 ♔xd2 ♘a6 13 ♖b1 e5 14 ♘e2 0-0= Gutman-Savon, USSR 1977) 7 cxd5 ♘xd5 8 dxc5 f5 9 e4 (9 ♕c2!) fxe4 10 ♕c2 ♕h4+ 11 g3 ♕f6 12 fxe4 0-0 13 ♗d3 ♘c7!? N (13...♕xc3+ 14 ♕xc3 ♘xc3 15 ♗f4! ± Hollis-Kauranen, corres 1977) 14 ♘h3 e5 15 ♘g5 g6 16 ♗e3 ♕e7 17 h4 h5 18 ♗c4+ ♔g7 19 0-0-0± Giffard-Ostojic, Bagneux 1978;
b) 4 ♕c2 c5 (4...0-0 5 a3 ♗xc3+ 6 ♕xc3 b6 7 ♗g5 ♗b7 8 ♘f3 [8 e3 d6 9 f3! ♘bd7 10 ♗d3 c5 11 ♘e2 cxd4 12 ♕xd4!± Forintos-Eperjesi, Hungary 1974] 8...d6 9 e3 ♘bd7 10 ♕c2 ♗xf3!? 11 gxf3 c5 12 ♖d1! ♖c8 13 ♗e2!± Nogueiras-Vitolins, Jurmala 1978) 5 dxc5 0-0 6 ♘f3 (6 a3 ♗xc5 7 ♘f3 b6 8 ♗g5 ♗b7 9 e3 ♗e7 10 ♖d1 N [10 ♗e2 h6 11 ♗h4 d5 12 ♗xf6 ♗xf6 13 cxd5 ♗xc3+ 14 ♕xc3 ♗xd5= Boleslavsky-Taimanov USSR Final 1957] 10...♘a6 11 ♗e2 ♘c5 12 ♖d4 d6 13 0-0 a6 14 b4 += Farago-

Spassov, Moscow 1977) 6...♘a6 7 a3?! ♗xc3+ 8 ♕xc3 ♘xc5 9 b4 ♘ce4 10 ♕c2 a5 11 ♗d2 ♗xf2 12 ♔xf2 ♘g4+ 13 ♔g3 ♘e3 N (13...f5 14 ♗b3 ♕c7+ 15 ♗f4 e5 16 ♗g5 d5 −+ Honfi-Gipslis, Pecs 1964) 14 ♕b3 ♕g5+ 15 ♔f3 ♘g4∓ Agzamov-Ivanov, Vilnius 1978;
c) 4 ♘f3 c5 5 g3 ♘e4 (5...cxd4 6 ♘xd4 ♘e4 7 ♕d3 ♕a5 8 ♕c2!? ♗xc3+ 9 bxc3 ♘c5 10 ♕d4! 0-0 11 ♗a3 d6 12 0-0-0!?∝ Banas-Lerner, Stary-Smokovec 1977) 6 ♕d3 cxd4 7 ♘xd4 ♕a5 8 ♘b3 ♘xc3 9 ♗d2 ♘e4 10 ♕xe4! ♗xd2+ 11 ♘xd2 0-0 12 ♗g2 ♖d8 N (12...♘c6 13 ♕e3 d5 14 0-0 d4 15 ♕d3 ♖d8 16 a3 ♕h5 17 f4 += Tukmakov-Fernandez, Decin 1977) 13 ♕f4 d5 14 cxd5 exd5 15 0-0 ♘c6 16 ♘b3 ♕b6 17 ♖fd1 ♗e6 18 ♖d2 += Lombardy-Zuckerman, USA Final 1978
4...b6
a) 4...c5 5 ♘e2 d5 6 a3 ♗a5 7 dxc5 dxc4 8 ♕xd8+ ♔xd8 9 ♗d2 e5 (9...♘bd7 10 ♘g3 ♘xc5 11 ♗xc4 ♘c7 12 ♖d1 += Ivkov-Donner, Amsterdam 1971) 10 ♘g3 N (10 ♘e4 ♘c6 11 ♘2g3 ♘xe4 12 ♘xe4 ♗xd2+ 13 ♔xd2 ♘a5 14 ♔c3 ♗e6 15 ♘d6± Hort-Garcia, Leipzig 1973) 10...♗e6 11 ♘ce4 ♗xd2+ 12 ♔xd2 ♘xe4 13 ♘xe4 ♔e7 14 ♖c1? ♖d8+ 15 ♔c3 ♗d5!∓ Ghitescu-Schneider, Roskilde 1978;
b) 4...c5 5 ♗d3 ♘c6 6 ♘f3 ♗xc3+ 7 bxc3 d6 8 0-0 (8 e4 e5 9 d5 ♘e7 10 ♘g1 N ♕a5 11 ♘e2 ♗g4 12 f3 ♗d7 13 a4 0-0-0= Ogaard-Csom, Kiel 1978) 8...e5 9 ♘d2 0-0 N 10 d5 ♘e7 11 e4 ♘e8 12 ♕c2 ♘g6 13 g3 += Gligoric-Andersson, Niksic 1978;
c) 4...c5 5 ♗d3 0-0 6 ♘f3 d5 7 0-0 ♘c6 8 a3 ♗xc3 9 bxc3 dxc4 (9...♕c7 10 cxd5 exd5 11 ♘h4 ♖e8 12 f3

11

b6 N 13 ♖a2 a5 14 ♖e2 ♗b7 15 ♗b2 ♖ad8 16 ♕e1 g6 17 g4± Portisch-Hort, Niksic 1978) 10 ♘xc4 ♕c7 11 ♖e1 e5 12 d5 ♘a5 13 d6 ♕d8 14 ♘xe5 ♘xc4 15 ♘xc4 ♗e6 16 ♕d3 ♘g4! N (16...♗xc4 17 ♕xc4 ♕xd6= Milic-Matanovic, Jugoslavia 1954) 17 ♖e2 ♗xc4 18 ♕xc4 ♕xd6 19 g3 ♘e5 20 ♕a2 ♕g6∓ O.Rodriguez-Olafsson, Las Palmas 1978;

d) 4...d5 5 ♕a4+ ♘c6 6 ♘f3 ♗d7 7 ♕c2 a6 8 a3 ♗d6 9 c5 ♗f8 10 ♗d3 g6 11 e4 dxe4 12 ♘xe4 ♘xe4 13 ♗xe4 ♗g7= Giffard-Pytel, Bagneux 1978

5 ♗e2
5 ♗d3 ♗b7 6 ♘f3 ♘e4 7 0-0 ♘xc3?! (7...♗xc3 8 bxc3 f5 9 ♕c2 N [9 d5 ♘c5 10 ♗a3 ♘ba6 11 ♗c2 0-0 12 ♘d4 ♖f6 13 f3 ♖h6?! 14 ♕e2 ♕f6 15 ♖ae1 ♖e8 16 ♗c1± Gligoric-Cafferty, Teesside 1972] 9...0-0 10 ♘d2 ♕h4 11 f3 ♘xd2 12 ♗xd2 ♘c6 13 ♖ab1 d6 14 ♖fe1± Lukacs-Skrobek, Lodz 1978) 8 bxc3 ♗xc3 9 ♖b1 ♘c6 10 ♖b3 ♗a5 11 e4 h6 N (11...♘e7 12 d5 ♘g6 13 ♗d4± Gligoric-Larsen, Lugano 1970) 12 d5 ♘e7 13 ♗b2 0-0 14 ♘e5 ♘g6 15 ♘g4 ♕e7 16 f4 f5 17 exf5 exf5 18 ♘xh6+ +− Balashov-Romanishin, Lvov 1978

5...♗a6 6 ♗g3
6 a3 ♗xc3+ 7 ♘xc3 d5 8 b4 ♗xc4 9 ♗xc4 dxc4 10 ♕e2 c5 11 dxc5 bxc5 12 ♕xc4 ♘bd7 N (12...cxb4 13 axb4 0-0 14 ♗b2 += Portisch-Kluger, Budapest 1961) 13 0-0 0-0 14 bxc5 ♕a5= Najdorf-Evans, Sao Paulo 1978

Diagram

6...0-0 7 e4 ♘c6
7...d5 8 cxd5 ♗xc3+ 9 bxc3 ♗xf1 10 ♔xf1 exd5 11 e5 ♘e4 12 f3 ♘xg3

13 hxg3 f6 N (13...f5 14 exf6 ♕xf6 15 ♖h5 c6 16 ♕d3 += Gligoric-Hecht, Berlin 1971) 14 ♕d3 g6 15 ♗a3 ♖e8 16 ♖e1 fxe5 17 dxe5± Knaak-Raitza, Eggesin 1978

8 ♗d3 e5 9 d5
9 0-0 ♗xc3 10 bxc3 d6 11 ♗e3 ♘a5 12 ♕e2 ♘d7 13 f4± Donner-Andersen, Busum 1968

9...♗xc3+ 10 bxc3 ♘e7 N
10...♘a5= Taimanov

11 ♗g5 ♘e8 12 c5!? ♗xd3 13 d6!? cxd6 14 cxd6 ♘xd6 15 ♕xd3 ♗b7 16 ♖d1 d6 ∞/=+ Knaak-Ligterink, Jurmala 1978

Grunfeld

1 d4 ♘f6 2 c4 g6 3 ♘c3 d5 4 cxd5
4 ♘f3 ♗g7

a) 5 cxd5 ♘xd5 6 e4 ♘xc3 7 bxc3 c5 8 ♗e2 ♗g4 N 9 ♖b1 0-0 10 0-0 cxd4 11 cxd4 ♗xf3 12 ♗xf3 ♗xd4 13 ♗h6 ♖e8 14 ♖xb7 ♘c6= Commons-Tarjan, USA Final 1978;

b) 5 ♕b3 dxc4 6 ♕xc4 0-0 7 e4 ♗g4 (7...♘a6 8 ♗f4 c5 9 ♖d1 cxd4 10 ♖xd4 ♕b6 11 e5 ♗e6 12 ♕b5 ♘d7 N [12...♘h5 13 ♗e3 ♕xb5 14 ♗xb5 f6 15 ♖a4 ♘c7 16 ♘d4 += Portisch-Timman, Wijk aan Zee 1972] 13 ♘d5 ♗xd5 14 ♖xd5 ♘dc5 15 ♕xb6 axb6= Danielsen-Fedder, Roskilde

1978) 8 ♗e3 ♘fd7 9 ♕b3 ♘b6 10 ♖d1 ♘c6 11 d5 ♘e5 12 ♗e2 ♘xf3+ 13 gxf3 ♗h5 14 ♖g1 ♕c8!? N 15 ♘b5 c6!? 16 ♘xa7 ♖xa7 17 ♗xb6 ♖a8 18 a4± Ljubojevic-Jansa, Titovo Uzice 1978;
c) 5 ♕a4+ c6 6 cxd5 ♘xd5 7 e4 ♘xc3 8 bxc3 0-0 9 ♗a3 ♖e8 N (9...b6 10 ♗e2 c5 11 0-0 cxd4 12 cxd4 ♗b7= Lilienthal-Simagin, USSR 1955) 10 ♗e2 ♘d7 11 ♖d1 e5!? 12 dxe5 ♕b6 13 0-0 ♘xe5 14 ♘d4 += Garcia-Beljavsky, Leningrad 1977

4...♘xd5 5 e4 ♘xc3 6 bxc3 ♗g7 7 ♗c4 c5

a) 7...0-0 8 ♘e2 b6 9 h4 ♘c6 10 h5 ♘a5 11 ♗d3 e5 12 dxe5 N (12 hxg6 fxg6 13 ♗e3 ♗b7 14 ♕d2 ♕e7= Larsen) 12...♗xe5 13 hxg6 fxg6 14 ♗h6 ♗g7 15 ♗xg7 ♔xg7 16 ♕d2± Mohring-Uhlmann, Eggesin 1978;
b) 7...0-0 8 ♘e2 ♕d7 9 0-0 b6 10 ♗e3 ♗a6!? N (10...♗b7 11 ♗d3 e6 12 ♕d2 c5 13 ♖ad1 cxd4 14 cxd4 ♘c6= Petkevich-Tseitlin, USSR 1972) 11 ♗d5 ♘c6 12 ♕a4 ♗b7 13 ♘f4 ♖ad8 14 ♕c2 e6 15 ♗b3 ♘a5 =+ Gligoric-Gulko, Niksic 1978

8 ♘e2 ♘c6 9 0-0 0-0 10 ♗e3 cxd4

a) 10...♘a5 11 ♗d3 b6 12 ♖c1 N (12 ♕d2 ♗b7 13 ♗h6 e6 14 ♗xg7 ♔xg7 15 ♖ad1 += Tarjan-Garcia, Wijk aan Zee 1974) 12...cxd4 13 cxd4

e6 14 e5 ♗b7 15 ♘f4 ♕d7= Bagirov-Tukmakov, Lvov 1978;
b) 10...♗g4 11 f3 ♘a5 12 ♗d5!? N ♗d7 13 ♖b1 ♕c8 14 dxc5 e6 15 ♗b3 ♗b5= Hort-Timman, Niksic 1978

11 cxd4 ♗g4

11...♘a5 12 ♗d3 b6 13 ♖c1 e6 14 ♕d2 N (14 e5! ♗b7 15 ♘f4 ♕e7 16 ♕g4 ♘c6 17 h4 += Gligoric-Tukmakov, Jugoslavia-USSR 1975) 14...♗b7 15 h4 ♕e7 16 ♗g5 f6 17 ♗f4 e5 18 dxe5 fxe5 19 ♗g5± Knaak-Heinig, Eggesin 1978

12 f3 ♘a5 13 ♗d3

13 ♖c1 ♘xc4 14 ♖xc4 ♗d7 15 ♕b3 a6 16 ♘c3 b5 17 ♖c5 e6 TN (17...♖c8 18 ♖d1 e6 19 d5 ♕e7∝ Balashov-Savon, USSR 1971) 18 ♖fc1 ♕a5 19 ♘e2 ♖fc8= Rosenlund-Webb, Roskilde 1978

13...♗e6 14 d5

14 ♖c1 ♗xa2 15 d5 ♗b3 16 ♕e1 e6 17 ♕b4 exd5 18 ♖c5 dxe4 TN (18...♗c4 19 ♗xc4 ♘xc4 20 ♖xd5= Shamkovich) 19 ♗xe4 ♕e7 20 ♕xa5 f5 21 ♖c7 ♕e6 22 ♗d4 ♗h6 ∝/± Foisor-Tonoli, Groningen 1978

14...♗xa1 15 ♕xa1 f6 16 ♕b1

16 ♖d1?! TN ♗f7 17 ♕b2 ♖c8 18 ♗xa7 ♘c4 19 ♕xb7 ♖c7∓ Kozlovskaya-Melashvili, USSR Final 1978

16...♗d7 17 ♖h6 ♛c7?! N
17...♖e8!? △ ♛b6∓ Hartston
18 ♖c1 ♛d6 19 ♗xf8 ♚xf8 20 ♛b2
+= Anikaev-Kalinskaya, Beltsi 1978

1 d4 ♞f6 2 c4 g6 3 ♞c3 d5 4 ♗f4
a) 4 ♗g5 ♞e4 5 ♗h4 ♞xc3 6 bxc3 dxc4
7 e3 ♗e6 8 ♞f3 f6 9 ♖b1 b6 10 ♞d2
c6 11 a4 ♗g7 12 ♞xc4 ♞d7 13 ♗d3
0-0 14 0-0 += Rodzikowska-Vokralova,
Bydgoszcz 1978;
b) 4 ♞f3 ♗g7 5 ♗g5 ♞e4 (5...dxc4
6 e4 c5 7 ♗xc4 N cxd4 8 ♛xd4
♛xd4 9 ♞xd4 ♞c6 10 ♞xc6 bxc6 11
0-0 += Dorfman-Smyslov, Lvov 1978)
6 cxd5 ♞xc3 7 bxc3 ♛xd5 8 e3 c5
(8...♗g4 9 ♗e2 ♞d7 N [9...♞c6 10
♗h4 0-0 11 0-0 ♖fe8 12 ♗g3 e5 13
h3± Simagin-Korchnoi, USSR Final
1968] 10 ♗f4 ♛a5 11 0-0 0-0 12
♖b1 b6 13 ♛c2 c6 14 ♖b4!? ♞f6=
Rosenlund-Danielsen, Roskilde 1978)
9 ♗b5+ ♗d7 10 c4 ♛f5 N (10...♞e4
11 0-0 ♗xb5! 12 cxb5 ♞d7 13 ♖c1 b6
14 dxc5 ♞xc5= Gipslis) 11 ♖b1 cxd4
12 exd4 ♗xb5 13 ♖xb5 ♛e6+ 14 ♛e2
♛xe2+ 15 ♚xe2 += Haik-D.Roos,
Bagneux 1978

4...♗g7 5 e3 0-0
5...c5 6 dxc5 ♛a5
a) 7 ♛a4+ ♛xa4 8 ♗xa4 ♞a6 9 cxd5
[9 ♞f3 ♗d7 10 ♞c3 dxc4 11 ♗xc4
♞xc5 12 0-0 0-0 13 ♖fd1 ♖ac8 14
♗e5 Smejkal-Uhlmann, Leningrad
1973, 14...♗e6!=] 9...♞xd5 10 ♗b5+
♗d7 11 ♗xd7+ N [11 c6 ♗xc6=
Petrosian-Bronstein, Moscow 1971]
11...♚xd7 12 0-0-0 ♚c6 13 ♞f3
♞xc5= Haik-Schmidt, Bagneux 1978;
b) 7 ♖c1 ♞e4 8 cxd5 ♞xc3 9 ♛d2
♛xa2 10 bxc3 ♛a5 11 ♗c4 ♞d7 12
♞e2 ♞xc5 N (12...♞e5 13 ♗a2
Petrosian-Fischer 1971, 13...♛xc5 =+)
13 0-0 b5 14 ♖a1 ♛b6 15 ♖fb1

♗d7 16 ♞d4 ♞e4 17 ♛d3 ♞xf2!≈
Dorfman-Gulko, Lvov 1978

6 cxd5 ♞xd5 7 ♗xd5 ♛xd5 8 ♗xc7
♗f5
8...♞c6!? 9 ♞e2 ♗g4 10 f3 ♗xf3
11 gxf3 ♛xf3 12 ♖g1 ♖ac8 N (12...
♛xe3 13 ♗f4 ♛e4 14 ♗g2 ♛f5 15
♗xc6! bxc6 16 ♛d2± Kyschukow-
Saligo, corres 1968) 13 ♗g2 ♛h5 14
♗g3 e5 15 ♗xc6 ♖xc6 16 d5± Fedder-
Rajna, Roskilde 1978
9 ♞e2 ♖c8!? N
a) 9...♞a6 10 ♞c3 ♛e6! 11 ♗xa6 ♛xa6
12 f3 ♖ac8 13 ♗g3 ♖fd8 14 ♛e2 ♗d3
15 ♛d2 ♗h6 16 f4 e5!∓ Hester-
Portisch, Adelaide 1971;
b) 9...♞a6 10 ♞f4 ♛d7 11 ♗a5 ♛d6!
12 ♗xa6 ♛xa6 13 ♞c3 g5 14 ♞d5
♛d6 15 ♞b4 a5 16 ♞d3 b5= Sokolov-
Pioch, corres 1974/75
10 ♞c3 ♛c6 11 ♗g3
11 ♗a5 e5 12 d5 ♛c5 Gipslis

Diagram

11...♞a6 12 a3 e5! 13 d5
13 dxe5 ♖d8 △ ♞c5
13...♛b6 14 e4 ♖xc3! 15 bxc3 ♗xe4
16 f3?!
16 ♗xa6 ♛xa6 17 f3 ♗d3∓
16...♛e3+ 17 ♗e2 ♛xc3+ ∓/-+
Tamme-Gulko, Parnu 1978

14

King's Indian

1 d4 ♘f6 2 c4 g6 3 ♘c3 ♗g7 4 e4 d6 5 f3

a) 5 ♘f3 0-0 6 ♗e2 e5 7 ♗e3 ♘g4 8 ♗g5 f6 9 ♗c1 ♘c6 10 h3 exd4 11 ♘xd4 ♘xd4 (11...♘ge5 12 ♘xc6 bxc6!? 13 f4 ♘d7 14 0-0 ♖b8 15 ♕c2 += Sahovic-Gufeld, Jurmala 1978) 12 ♕xd4 ♘e5 13 ♕d5+ ♔h8 14 ♗e3 f5 15 exf5 ♗xf5 16 0-0 += Hort-Sigurjonsson, Reykjavik 1978;

b) ♘f3 0-0 6 ♗e2 ♘bd7 7 0-0 e5 8 ♖e1 c6 9 ♗f1 a5 10 ♖b1 exd4 11 ♘xd4 ♖e8 12 b3!? N ♘g4 13 ♕xg4 ♗xd4 14 ♕g3 ♕f6 15 ♗b2 ♘c5 =+ Liebert-Knaak, Eggesin 1978

5...0-0

5...♘bd7 6 ♘h3′ c5 7 d5 0-0 8 ♘f2 a6 9 ♗e2 N (9 a4 ♘e8 10 ♗e2 e5 11 0-0 h6 12 ♕d2 ♔h7 13 a5± Liberzon-Kislov, USSR 1970) 9...♕c7 10 0-0 e6 11 a4 cxd5 12 cxd5 ♖e8 13 ♗e3 += Gligoric-Tringov, Osijek 1978

6 ♗e3

6 ♗g5 ♘bd7 7 ♕d2 c5 8 d5 a6 9 ♘ge2 ♖b8 10 ♘c1 TN (10 ♘g3 ♖e8 11 ♗e2 ♕a5 12 a4 ♕b4 13 0-0 ♘e5 14 ♘d1 += Lilienthal-Shamkovich, USSR Final 1953) 10...♖e8 11 ♗e2 ♘b6 12 0-0 e6 13 a4 exd5 14 cxd5± Beljavsky-Ermenkov, Alicante 1978

6...♘c6

6...e5 7 d5 c5 8 ♗d3 ♘h5 9 ♘ge2 f5 10 exf5 gxf5 11 ♕d2 N (11 ♕c2 e4! 12 fxe4 f4 13 e5 ♘xe5 14 ♗xh7+ ♔h8 15 ♗f2 ♘d7∝ Velimirovic) 11...a6 12 a4 ♘d7 13 ♗g5 ♕e8 14 0-0 += Hort-Gligoric, Niksic 1978

7 ♘ge2

7 ♗d3 a6 8 ♘ge2 e5 9 d5 ♘b4 10 ♗b1 a5 11 ♕d2 ♘e8 12 0-0 c6 13 dxc6 bxc6 14 a3 ♘a6 15 c5!± Silva-Durao 1978

7...♖b8 8 ♕d2 a6 9 h4 h5 10 ♗d5 TN

10 0-0-0 ♖e8 11 ♗h6 b5 12 g4 bxc4 13 ♘g3 e5 14 ♗xg7 ♔xg7 15 dxe5 ♖xe5 16 g5 ♘d7 17 f4± Gheorghiu-Westerinen, Torremolinos 1974

10...♘h7 11 ♗h6 ♗xh6 12 ♕xh6 e6 13 ♘e3 ♕f6 14 0-0-0 b5≈ Ghitescu-Westerinen, Roskilde 1978

Sicilian

1 e4 c5 2 ♘f3 ♘c6 3 ♗b5 e6

a) 3...♕b6 4 ♘c3 e6 5 0-0 ♘ge7 6 ♖e1 ♘d4 7 a4 N a6 8 ♗c4 ♘g6 9 d3 ♘xf3+ 10 ♕xf3 ♗d6 11 ♕h5 += Inkiov-Helmers, Lodz 1978;

b) 3...♘f6 4 e5 ♘d5 5 0-0 e6 6 ♘c3!? N ♘xc3 7 dxc3 ♕c7 8 ♖e1 b6 9 ♗f4

♗e7 10 ♕e2 ♗b7 11 a4 0-0-0=
Kaspret-Franzoni, Groningen 1978;

c) 3...g6 4 0-0 ♗g7 5 c3 ♘f6 6 ♖e1
0-0 7 d4 cxd4 8 cxd4 d5 9 e5 ♘e4
10 ♘c3 ♘xc3 11 bxc3 ♘a5 12 ♕a4
a6 13 ♗d3 N (13 ♗f1 ♗g4 14 ♘d2
♖c8 15 ♘b3 += Sax-Janosevic,
Madonna di Campiglio 1974) 13...
♗d7 14 ♕b4 b5 15 h4 += Ivanov-
Kapengut, Beltsi 1978;

d) 3...g6 4 0-0 ♗g7 5 ♖e1 e5 6 c3
♘ge7 7 d4!? cxd4 8 cxd4 exd4 9 ♗f4
a6! 10 ♗f1!? N (10 ♗c4 d6 11 ♘g5
0-0 12 ♕b3 d5! 13 ♗xd5 ♘xd5 14
exd5 ♘a5= Botvinnik-Veresov, USSR
1963) 10...d6 11 ♘bd2 0-0 12 ♘b3
♗g4∓ Stein-Kagan, Israel Final 1978)

e) 3...g6 4 0-0 ♗g7 5 ♖e1 ♘f6 6 e5
♘d5 7 ♘c3 ♘c7 8 ♗xc6 dxc6 9 ♘e4
♘e6 10 b3 (10 d3= Biyiasas-Kagan,
Petropolis 1973) 10...0-0 11 ♗a3 b6
12 c3 ♘f4 13 d4 ♗g4 =+ Enders-
Liebert, Eggesin 1978

4 0-0 ♘ge7 5 ♖e1 a6

5...♘g6 6 c3 a6 7 ♗f1 d6 8 d4 ♗e7
9 ♘a3 0-0 10 ♘c2 e5 11 dxc5 dxc5
12 ♘e3 += Lutikov-Kirpichnikov,
Jurmala 1978

6 ♗f1

6 ♗xc6 ♘xc6 7 ♘c3 ♗e7 8 d4 cxd4
9 ♘xd4 0-0 10 ♘xc6 bxc6 11 ♕g4
e5 12 ♕g3 d6 13 ♗h6 ♗f6= Stein-
Birnboim, Israel Final 1978

6...d5 (= Keres) **7 exd5 ♕xd5**

7...♘xd5 8 a4 ♗e7 9 ♘a3 0-0 10
♘c4 b6 11 b3 ♗f6 12 ♘ce5 ♗b7 13
♗b2 ♕c7 14 ♕c1 += Ostojic-Seret,
Bagneux 1978

**8 ♘a3 ♕d8 9 ♘c4 ♗f5 10 a4 ♗d6
11 d3 ♗c7 12 g3 0-0 13 ♗g2 ♖b8
14 ♘g5 ♘a5 15 ♕h5 h6 16 ♘e4 +=**
Hulak-Sax, Osijek 1978

**1 e4 c5 2 ♘f3 ♘c6 3 d4 cxd4 4 ♘xd4
♘f6 5 ♘c3 e5 6 ♘db5 d6 7 ♗g5**

a) 7 a4 a6 8 ♘a3 ♗e7 (8...♗e6 9
♘c4 ♖c8 10 ♗d3 ♘b4 11 ♘e3 ♗e7
12 0-0 0-0 13 ♖e1 ♕c7 14 ♗e2 ♕c5=
Gufeld-Filipenko, USSR 1978) 9 ♗e3
♗e6 10 ♘c4 ♘xe4!? 11 ♘xe4 d5 12
♘b6 dxe4 13 ♘xa8 ♕xa8 14 c3 0-0
15 a5 f5 16 ♕a4 ♔h8 17 ♗c4±
Sakharov-Timoshenko, USSR 1978;

b) 7 ♘d5 ♘xd5 8 exd5 ♘e7 9 c4 ♘f5
10 ♗d3 ♗e7 11 0-0 0-0 12 f4 ♘d4=
Holmov-Vasyukov, Zalaegerszeg 1977

7...a6 8 ♘a3 b5 9 ♗xf6

a) 9 ♘d5 ♗e7 10 ♘xe7 ♘xe7 11
♗xf6 (11 ♗d3 ♗b7 12 ♗xf6 gxf6
13 c4 bxc4 14 ♘xc4 d5! 15 exd5
♕xd5 16 ♘d6+ ♔f8 17 ♗e4 ♕a5+ =
Smyslov-Sveshnikov) 11...gxf6 12 ♕f3
f5 13 exf5 ♗xf5 14 ♗d3 ♗xd3 (14...
♗e6 15 0-0 d5 16 ♖fd1 f5 17 ♕h5
♗f7 16 ♕h6 e4 19 ♘xb5! ♗g6 20
♗f1!± Tringov-Georgadze, Varna
1977) 15...♕xd3 d5 16 c3 ♕b6 17
0-0 f5 18 ♖ae1 e4 19 ♕e3 ♕f6 20 f3
0-0 21 ♘c2 ♖ae8 22 fxe4 dxe4 23
♘d4± Gipslis-Jasnikowski, Hradec
Kralove 1978;

b) 9 ♘d5 ♗e7 10 ♗xf6 ♗xf6 11 c3
(11 h4? ♗xh4 12 ♖xh4 ♕xh4 13
♘c7+ ♔e7 14 ♘xa8 ♕xe4+ 15 ♕e2
♕b4+ 16 c3 ♕a5 17 ♕e3 ♗e6∓
Chandler-Kouatly, Philippines 1977)

11...♘g5 (11...0-0 12 ♘c2 ♗g5 [12... ♖b8 13 ♗e2 ♗g5 14 0-0 ♗e6 15 ♕d3 a5 16 ♖fd1 ♕d7 17 ♕g3 += Balashov-Dvoretsky, USSR Final 1976] 13 a4 bxa4 14 ♖xa4 a5 15 ♗c4 ♔h8! 16 0-0 f5 17 exf5 ♗xf5= Geller-Sveshnikov, USSR Final 1978) 12 ♘c2 ♖b8 13 a4! bxa4 14 ♘cb4! ♗d7 15 ♗xa6 0-0 16 ♖xa4 f5 17 exf5 e4 18 h4!± Sorokin-Gutman, USSR 1978

9...gxf6 10 ♘d5 f5 11 ♗d3
11 ♕d3!? fxe4 12 ♕xe4 ♗g7 13 ♘f6+ (13 ♘e3?! d5! 14 ♕xd5 ♕xd5 15 ♘xd5 0-0 16 c3 ♗b7 17 ♘c2 ♖fd8 =/=+ Kapengut-Kalinichev, USSR 1978) 13...♗xf6 14 ♕xc6+ ♗d7 15 ♕xd6 ♕e7 16 0-0-0 ♕xd6 17 ♖xd6 ♗e7 18 ♖d5 f6 19 ♖d2 ♗e6≈ Muratov-Timoshenko, USSR 1978
11...♗e6 12 ♕h5
12 c4!? ♕a5+ 13 ♔f1 ♗xd5!? (13... fxe4 14 ♗xe4 ♗g7∝ Balashov-Geller, USSR Final 1978) 14 cxd5 ♘e7! N (14...♘d4 15 ♘c2 fxe4 16 ♗xe4 ♘xc2 17 ♕xc2 += Tseshkovsky-Suradiradja, Albena 1977) 15 exf5 ♗g7 16 ♗e4 ♕b4 17 ♕e2 ♖c8 18 g3 ♘g8! Δ ♘f6, ♗h6= Suetin-Gurgenidze, USSR 1978
12...♗g7 13 0-0 f4 14 c4!? N bxc4
14...0-0 15 cxb5 ♘d4∝

15 ♗xc4 0-0 16 ♖ac1 ♖b8 17 b3 ♗xd5?
17...♔h8
18 ♗xd5± Stean-Sax, Las Palmas 1978

1 e4 c5 2 ♘f3 d6 3 d4 cxd4 4 ♘xd4 ♘f6 5 ♘c3 a6 6 ♗g5
a) 6 g3 e5 7 ♘de2 ♗e7 8 ♗g2 ♘bd7 9 0-0 0-0 10 ♘d5 ♘xd5 11 ♕xd5 ♖b8 12 a4 b5= Kagan-Gruenfeld, Israel Final 1978;
b) 6 f4 g6 7 ♘f3 ♗g7 8 e5 ♘h5?! N (8...♘g4 9 h3 ♘h6 10 ♗c4 0-0 11 g4 ♘c6 12 ♗e3 dxe5 13 fxe5 ♗e6 14 ♗xe6± Ghizdavu-Ghitescu, Timisoara 1972) 9 ♗c4 0-0 10 ♘g5 e6 11 g4 +− Kavalek-Byrne, USA Final 1978)
c) 6 f4 ♕c7 7 ♗e2 (7 ♗d3 g6 8 0-0 ♗g7 9 ♔h1 ♘bd7 10 ♕e1 b5 11 ♘f3 e5 12 fxe5 dxe5 13 ♗g5 ♗b7 14 a4!± Tseshkovsky-Savon, Sochi 1975; 7 a4!?) 7...e5 8 ♘b3 (8 ♘f3 ♗e6 9 f5 ♗c4 10 ♗g5 ♘bd7 11 ♕d2 ♗xe2 12 ♕xe2 ♖c8 =+ Szabo-Petrosian, Stockholm 1952) 8...b5 9 ♗f3 ♗b7 10 0-0 ♘bd7 11 a3 exf4 12 ♗xf4 ♘e5 13 ♘d4 g6 14 ♔h1! (Δ ♘xb5) ♖d8 15 ♗g5 ♗e7 16 ♗h6± Tseshkovsky-Tukmakov, Lvov 1978
6...e6 6...♘c6 7 ♗xf6!? gxf6 8 ♘b3 f5 9 exf5 ♗xf5 10 ♗d3 ♗xd3 11 cxd3 ♗g7 12 0-0 0-0 13 f4 += Velimirovic-Diesen, Osijek 1978

Diagram

7 f4 ♗e7
a) 7...h6 8 ♗xf6 ♕xf6 9 ♕d2 ♕d8 10 0-0-0 ♗e7 11 ♘f3 ♘c6 12 ♔b1 ♗d7 13 g4 ♕c7= Nevrakis-Pytel, Kallithea 1977;
b) 7...b5 8 e5 dxe5 9 fxe5 ♕c7 10

17

♕e2 ♘fd7 11 0-0-0 ♗b7 12 ♘xe6 fxe6 13 ♔g4 ♕xe5 14 ♗d3 ♗e7 15 ♗xe7 ♔xe7 16 ♖he1 h5! N 17 ♕b4+ ♔c5 18 ♕h4+ ♘f6= Olafsson-Polugaevsky, Reykjavik 1978;

c) 7...♕b6 8 ♘b3 ♗e7 9 ♕f3 ♘bd7 10 0-0-0 ♕c7 11 ♗h4 b5 12 a3 ♖b8 13 g4 h6= Lederman-Stean, Beersheva 1978;

d) 7...♕b6 8 ♕d2 ♕xb2 9 ♖b1 ♕a3 10 ♗xf6 gxf6 11 ♗e2 h5!? 12 0-0 ♘d7 13 ♔h1 ♘c5?! 14 ♖f3 N (14 e5!± Spassov-Tukmakov, Ybbs 1968) 14...♕a5 15 ♘b3 ♕c7 16 ♘xc5 dxc5 17 f5∝ Velimirovic-Tringov, Osijek 1978;

e) 7...♕b6 8 ♕d2 ♕xb2 9 ♖b1 ♕a3 10 f5 ♘c6 11 fxe6 fxe6 12 ♘xc6 bxc6 13 e5

1) 13...♘d7 14 ♗e2 d5 15 ♖b3 N (15 0-0 ♗e7 16 ♗e3 ♗c5 17 ♔h1 ♗xe3 18 ♕xe3 ♕c5 19 ♔h3 += Platonov-Kudishevich, Ukraine Final 1970) 15...♕a5 16 0-0 ♕c7 17 ♘a4± Tatai-Lederman, Beersheva 1978;

2) 13...♘d5 14 ♘xd5 cxd5 15 ♗e2 dxe5 16 0-0 ♖a7! 17 c4 ♕c5+ 18 ♔h1 d4 19 ♗h5+ g6 20 ♗d1 ♗e7! N (20...♗d6 21 ♕f2 ♖f8 22 ♗a4+ ♖d7 23 ♕h4 +- Petrushin-Dementiev, USSR 1972) 21 ♗a4+ ♔d8 22 ♖f7 h6! 23 ♗xh6 e4!∝ Heemsoth-Weber, Corres 1978, 24 ♖e1!;

3) 13...dxe5 14 ♗xf6 gxf6 15 ♘e4 ♗e7 16 ♗e2 h5 17 ♖b3 ♕a4 18 ♘xf6+! (18 c4 f5 19 0-0 fxe4 20 ♔h1 c5 21 ♕c3 ♕c6 22 ♕xe5 ♖f8 23 ♗xh5+ ♔d8 24 ♖d1+ ♗d7 25 ♗g6 N ♗d6!∓ Espig-Helmers, Lodz 1978) 18...♗xf6 19 c4 ♗h4+ 20 g3 ♗e7 21 0-0 ♗d7 N ∝ Timman-Ribli, Niksic 1978

8 ♕f3 ♕c7 9 0-0-0 ♘bd7 10 ♗d3

a) 10 g4 h6 11 ♗xf6 gxf6!? N 12 ♗g2 ♘c5 13 ♖he1 ♗d7 14 ♘f5 ♗f8 15 ♘d5!? exd5 16 exd5+ ♔d8 17 ♕c3± Kosokin-Imanaliev, USSR 1978;

b) 10 g4 b5 11 ♗xf6 gxf6 12 f5 ♘e5 13 ♕h3 ♗d7 14 g5! b4 15 fxe6 fxe6 16 gxf6 bxc3 17 fxe7± Maryasin-Litvinov, Minsk 1978

d) 10 ♕g3 h6 11 ♗h4 g5 12 fxg5 ♘h5 13 ♕e3 ♕c5 14 ♕d2! N (14 ♔b1 hxg5 15 ♗f2 ♘e5 16 ♕d2 ♕c7 17 ♘f3 b5 N [17...♘xf3 18 gxf3 ♗d7= Kupreichik-Beljavsky, USSR Final 1974] 18 ♘xg5 ♖b8 19 ♘f3!?∝ Liberzon-Bleiman, Beersheva 1978) 14...hxg5 15 ♗f2 ♕c7 16 ♗e3 g4 17 ♗e2 ♘e5 18 ♗g5 f6 19 ♗h4 ♗d7 20 h3 gxh3 21 ♖xh3 0-0-0 22 ♗xh5 ♖xh5 23 ♘f5!± Ernst-Beckemeyer, Ribe 1978

10...b5
10...h6 11 ♕h3 ♘b6 12 f5 e5 13 ♘de2 ♗d7 14 ♗e3 N ♘c6 15 ♗xb6?!

♕xb6 16 g4 d5!∓ Neumann-
Hamann, Kiel 1978
**11 ♖he1 ♗b7 12 ♘d5 ♘xd5 13 exd5
♗xg5 14 ♘xe6+?! fxe6 15 ♕h5+
♔d8?**
15...♔f8 16 fxg5 ♘e5 17 ♗xh7 ♕c4!∓
Misevic-Masic, Vrsac 1973
16 ♕xg5+ ♘f6 17 ♖xe6 N
17 dxe6 ♖e8 18 ♗xh7 ♖e7 19 ♗g6
♖c8 Poliakov-Golunov, USSR 1976,
20 ♖d2!±
**17...♖e8 18 ♗xh7 ♖xe6 19 dxe6
♕e7∓** Aseev-Novikov, USSR 1978

**1 e4 c5 2 ♘f3 ♘c6 3 d4 cxd4 4 ♘xd4
♘f6 5 ♘c3 d6 6 ♗g5 e6**
a) 6...♗d7 7 f4 ♕b6 8 ♘b3 ♕e3+ N
(8...♘g4! 9 ♕e2 ♘d4 10 ♕d2 ♘xb3
11 axb3 ♕e3+ 12 ♕xe3 ♘xe3 13
♔d2 ♘xf1+ 14 ♖hxf1 e6 =+
Polugaevsky-Suetin, USSR Final 1968)
9 ♕e2 ♕xe2+ 10 ♗xe2 a6 11 ♗xf6
gxf6 12 ♘d5 ♖c8 13 0-0-0 ♗e6 14
♔b1 f5= Durao-Silva, Portugal Final
1978
b) 6...♗d7 7 ♕d2 ♖c8 8 0-0-0 ♘xd4
9 ♕xd4 ♕a5 10 f4 ♖xc3 11 bxc3
e5 12 ♕b4 ♕xb4 13 cxb4 ♘xe4 14
♗h4 g5 15 fxg5 ♗e7 16 ♗c4 N (16
♖e1 d5 17 ♗d3 h6 18 ♗xe4 dxe4
19 ♖xe4 += Boleslavsky) 16...h6 17
♖hf1 ♗e6 18 ♗xe6 fxe6 ∝/+=
Kulikova-Ioseliani, USSR Women
Final 1978;
c) 6...♗d7 7 ♕d2 ♖c8 8 f4 ♘xd4 9
♕xd4 ♕a5 10 e5 dxe5 11 fxe5 e6
12 0-0-0 ♖xc3 13 ♗d2 ♕xa2 14
♗xc3 g6 15 b4! N ♘d5 16 ♗c4 ♗h6+
17 ♖d2 ♕a3+ 18 ♗b2± Beljavsky-
Ubilava, USSR 1978

Diagram

7 ♕d2 a6 8 0-0-0 ♗d7 9 f4 ♗e7

a) 9...b5 10 e5!? N dxe5 11 fxe5 ♘xe5
12 ♕e1 ♕c7 13 ♔b1 b4 14 ♘e4 ♗e7
15 ♘xf6+ gxf6 16 ♗f4∝ Vitolins-
Schneider, Jurmala 1978;
b) 9...b5 10 ♗xf6 gxf6 11 ♘xc6 (11
♔b1 ♕b6 12 ♘xc6 ♗xc6 13 ♗d3 b4
N [13...h5 14 ♖hf1 0-0-0 15 f5±
Krogius-Geller, USSR Final 1960]
14 ♘e2 h5 15 ♖hf1 a5 16 c3 +=
Holmov-Lukin, USSR 1978) 11...
♗xc6 12 ♕e3 ♕e7 13 a3 (13 ♗d3
♕a7 14 ♕h3 b4 15 ♘e2 ♕c5 16 f5
e5= Ljubojevic-Gheorghiu, Manila
1976) 13...h5 14 ♗d3 ♕a7 15 ♕h3
♗h6 16 ♖hf1 ♕c5 17 ♔b1 a5 18
e5∝ Westerinen-Ermenkov, Jurmala
1978;
c) 9...b5 10 ♗xf6 gxf6 11 g3 N ♕b6
12 ♘ce2 ♕a5 13 ♕xa5 ♘xa5 14
♗g2 ♖c8 15 c3 ♗e7 16 f5 e5 =/=+
Murei-Stean, Beersheva 1978
10 ♘f3 b5 11 ♗xf6 gxf6
11...♗xf6 12 ♕xd6 ♗e7 13 ♕d2 b4
14 ♘e2 ♖a7 15 ♘ed4 ♕b6 16 ♘xc6
♕xc6 17 ♕d4!± Vogt-Suetin,
Budapest 1976

Diagram

12 g3
a) 12 ♗d3 ♕b6 N 13 ♔b1 0-0-0 14
f5 ♔b8 15 ♖hf1 a5 16 g3 +=
Timoshenko-Arhipkin, USSR 1978;

b) 12 f5 ♕b6 13 ♔b1 0-0-0 14 g3
♔b8 15 fxe6 N fxe6 16 ♗h3 ♗c8 17
♕h6 ♕c5∓ Beljavsky-Tal, Leningrad
1977

**12...♕b6 13 ♗h3 0-0-0 14 f5 ♘b8
15 fxe6 fxe6 16 ♘e2?** N 16 ♔b1 ♗c8
17 ♕e1!± Karpov-Liberzon, Bad
Lauterberg 1977

**16...♘e5! 17 ♘fd4 ♘c4 18 ♕d3 f5!
19 exf5 e5!∓** Mautlovic-Ivanovz,
Jugoslav Final 1978

**1 e4 c5 2 ♘f3 e6 3 d4 cxd4 4 ♘xd4
♘f6 5 ♘c3 a6 6 ♗e2 d6 7 0-0 ♗e7 8
f4 0-0**

8...♕c7 9 ♗e3 ♘c6 10 ♔h1 ♗d7 11
♕e1 b5 12 a3 0-0 13 ♕g3 ♘xd4 14
♗xd4 ♗c6 15 ♖ae1 ♕b7 16 ♗d3
b4 17 axb4 [17 ♘d1!? g6 18
♘f2 bxa3 19 bxa3 d5 20 e5
♘e4 21 ♗xe4 dxe4 22 ♘g4 ♖fd8 23
♘h6+± Sznapik-Smejkal, Sandomierz
1976] 17...♕xb4 18 ♘e2 ♕b7 19
e5 ♘h5 20 ♕h3 g6 21 ♘g3 dxe5 22
♗xe5 ♘g7 23 ♗c3 += Sax-Jansa,
Budapest 1976

Diagram

9 ♔h1
a) 9 ♗e3 ♘c6 10 ♕e1 ♘xd4 11 ♗xd4
b5 12 ♗f3 ♗b7 13 ♖d1 ♕c7 14 e5
dxe5 15 ♗xb7? N (15 fxe5 ♘d7 16

♗xb7 ♕xb7 17 ♘e4± Tseshkovsky-
Petrushin, USSR 1973) 15...exd4!
16 ♗xa8 dxc3 17 ♗e4 cxb2 18 f5?
♘g4 −+ Alekhina-Belavenets, USSR
Women Final 1978;
b) 9 ♗e3 ♘c6 10 ♕e1 ♗d7 11 ♕g3
♘xd4 12 ♗xd4 ♗c6 13 ♖ae1 b5 14
a3 ♕d7 15 ♗d3 a5 16 ♕h3 e5!=∓
Gajic-Schmidt, 1978
9...♕c7
9...♘c6 10 ♗e3 ♗d7 11 ♘f3 ♕c7
12 a3 b5 13 ♗d3 ♖fb8 14 e5
♘g4 15 exd6 ♕xd6 16 ♗g1 += Ostojic-
Peters, Bagneux 1978
10 ♕e1 b5 11 ♗f3 ♗b7 12 e5 ♘e8!!
TN
12...dxe5 13 fxe5 ♘fd7 14 ♗xb7
♕xb7 15 ♕g3 ♕c7 16 ♗f4 ♔h8 17
♘e4 ♘c6 18 ♘f3 ♘b4 19 ♘f6±
Klovan-Pribyl, Hungary 1970
**13 ♕g3 ♘d7 14 exd6 ♗xd6 15 ♘e4
♖c8! 16 c3 ♘c5 17 ♘xc5 ♗xc5 18
♗xb7 ♕xb7 19 ♗e3 ½-½** Klovan-
Ermenkov, Jurmala 1978

**1 e4 c5 2 ♘f3 e6 3 d4 cxd4 4 ♘xd4
a6 5 ♗d3**

5 ♘c3 ♕c7 6 ♗d3 ♘f6 7 0-0 ♘c6 8
♗e3 ♘e5 9 h3 b5 10 ♕e2 (10 f4
♘c4 11 ♗xc4 ♕xc4 12 ♕d3 ♗b7
13 a4 ♕xd3 14 cxd3 b4 15 ♘ce2±
Tal-Kochiev, Leningrad 1977) 10...
♗b7 N (10...b4 11 ♘b1 d5 12 ♘d2

20

dxe4 13 ♘xe4 ♘d5!?∝ Duckstein-
Taimanov, Copenhagen 1965) 11 f4
♘xd3 12 cxd3 d6 13 ♖ac1 ♛d8 14
♛f2 ♗e7 15 g4 0-0 =+ Bodach-Heinig,
Eggesin 1978

5...♘c6

a) 5...g6 6 c4 ♗g7 7 ♗e3 ♘e7 8 ♘c3
0-0 9 0-0 d5 10 exd5 exd5 11 ♖c1±
Weinstein-Christiansen, USA Final
1978;

b) 5...♗c5 6 ♘b3 ♗a7 7 ♛e2 (7 ♘c3
♘c6 8 ♛e2 ♘ge7 9 ♗e3 0-0 10 ♗xa7
♖xa7 11 f4 += Sokolowski-Kardys,
Bydgoszcz 1978) 7...♘c6 8 ♗e3 ♗xe3
9 ♛xe3 ♛c7 10 ♘c3 ♘f6 11 f4 d6
12 g4?! ♘xg4 13 ♛g3 f5 14 exf5
exf5 15 ♘d5∝ Romm-Stepak, Israel
Final 1978;

c) 5...♘f6 6 0-0 d6 7 c4 (7 a4!? N
b6 8 ♘d2 ♗b7 9 a5 bxa5 10 ♛e2
♘c6 11 ♘xc6 ♗xc6 12 ♘c4 a4 13
e5 ♘d5 14 ♖d1 ♗e7 15 ♛g4± Kuzmin-
Gheorghiu, Leningrad 1977) 7...♘bd7
8 ♘c3 b6 9 ♖e1 ♗b7 10 ♘d5!? ♘e5
11 f4 ♘xd3 12 ♛xd3 ♗e7 13 ♘xe7
♛xe7 14 e5 dxe5 15 fxe5 ♘d7 =+
Okrajek-Hesse, Eggesin 1978

6 ♘xc6 dxc6 7 f4

a) 7 0-0 e5 8 a4 ♗d6 9 ♘d2 ♘f6 (9...
♘e7 10 ♘c4 ♘g6 11 ♘b3 0-0 12 ♗e3
♘f4 13 f3 ♗e6 14 ♗xe6 ♘xe6= Geller-
Polugaevsky, USSR 1959) 10 ♘c4

♗c7 11 a5 ♗e6 12 ♛e1 0-0 13 ♖a3
♘h5 14 ♘e3 ♘f4∝ Kagan-Stepak,
Israel Final 1978;

b) 7 ♘d2 e5 8 ♛h5 ♗d6 9 ♘c4 ♘f6
10 ♘xd6+ N (10 ♛g5 0-0 11 0-0
♗c7= Larsen-Kavalek 1970) 10...♛xd6
11 ♛e2 ♗e6 12 0-0 ♘d7 13 ♖d1 ♛e7
14 b3 0-0 15 a4 a5 16 ♗a3± Jansa-
Cebalo, S. Palanka 1978

7...e5 8 f5 ♘f6 9 ♗e3?

9 ♛f3 ♗e7 10 ♗e3 b5 11 0-0 c5 12
♖d1 ♛c7 13 c4 b4 14 ♘d2 ♗b7=
Arnason-Miles, Reykjavik 1978

**9...♗xe4! 10 ♛g4 ♘f6 11 ♛f3 ♛d5
12 ♛xd5 cxd5** −+ Gajic-Cebalo,
S. Palanka 1978

1 e4 c5 2 ♘f3 e6 3 d4 cxd4 4 ♘xd4
♘f6 5 ♘c3 ♘c6 6 ♘xc6 bxc6 7 e5
♘d5 8 ♘e4 ♛c7!?

8...f5 9 exf6 ♘xf6 10 ♘d6+ ♗xd6 11
♛xd6 ♗a6 12 ♗xa6 ♛a5+ 13 ♗d2
♛xa6 14 ♗b4 ♔f7 15 ♘c3 ♖ad8 16
a3 ♖hf8 17 0-0-0 ♔g8 18 ♖he1 ♛b5
19 f3 c5 20 ♖e5 ♘d5 21 ♖dxd5!±
Dolmatov-Arnason, Groningen 1978

9 f4 c5! N

9...f5 10 exf6 ♘xf6 11 ♘xf6+ gxf6
12 ♛h5+ ♔d8 13 ♗d2 d5 14 0-0-0
♖b8 15 ♛h4 ♗e7 16 ♘c3 ♖f8 17
g3± Kurajica-Rossolimo, Montilla
1972

10 c4 ♗b4 11 a3
11 g3 ♗b7 12 ♗g2 ♖d8! 13 0-0 d5
14 exd6 ♗xd6 15 ♕e2 0-0 16 ♗e3
♗e7 17 a3 ♘c6!= Jakobsen-
Rosenlund, Roskilde 1978; 11 ♗e2!
**11...♘c6 12 ♗d3 ♘d4 13 0-0 ♗b7
14 ♗e3 ♘f5 15 ♗f2 ♖d8 16 ♕c2
d6 17 b4±** Schneider-Rosenlund,
Roskilde 1978

**1 e4 c5 2 ♘f3 e6 3 d4 cxd4 4 ♘xd4
♘f6 5 ♘c3 d6 6 g4 a6**
a) 6...e5 7 ♗b5+ ♗d7 8 ♗xd7+ ♕xd7
9 ♘f5 h5 10 ♗g5!? ♘h7 N (10...♘xg4
11 h3!± Keres) 11 ♗d2 hxg4 12
♕xg4 g6 13 ♘e3 ♗h6 14 0-0-0 ♘c6≈
Liberzon-Murei, Beersheva 1978)
b) 6...♘c6 7 g5 ♘d7 8 ♗e3 ♗e7 9 ♖g1
0-0 10 ♕h5!? ♖e8 11 0-0-0 a6 12
♔b1 ♗f8 13 ♖g3± Ermenkov-Jansa,
Titovo Uzice 1978
7 g5 ♘fd7 8 ♗e3
8 f4 N ♘c6 9 ♗e3 ♗e7 10 h4 h6 11
♕f3 ♘xd4 12 ♗xd4 hxg5 13 hxg5
♖xh1 14 ♕xh1 e5≈ Beljavsky-Hort,
Leningrad 1977
8...b5 9 a3
9 a4 b4 10 ♘a2 ♗b7 11 ♗g2 ♘c5
12 ♘xb4 ♗xe4 13 ♕g4 d5 14 ♘d3
♗e7 15 h4 += Smyslov-Hort,
Leningrad 1977
9...♗b7
9...♘b6 10 ♖g1 ♘8d7 11 f4 ♗b7 12
f5 e5 13 ♘e6! N (13 ♘b3 += Balashov-
Malich, Leipzig 1973) 13...fxe6 14
♕h5+ g6 15 fxg6 ♔e7 16 gxh7 ♗g7
17 0-0-0 ♕e8 18 g6 ♘f6 19 ♕xe5!
+− Shamkovich-Benko, USA Final
1978
10 h4 ♘b6 N
10...♘c6 11 ♕e2 ♘de5 12 0-0-0 +=
Alexander-Lundholm, Corres 1972
**11 h5 ♘8d7 12 ♖h3 ♗e7 13 g6 ♘f6
14 ♕g4 ♕e7 15 gxf7+ ♔xf7 16 0-0-0±**

Pokojowczyk-Sznapik, Lodz 1978

**1 e4 c5 2 ♘f3 e6 3 d4 cxd4 4 ♘xd4
♘f6 5 ♘c3 d6 6 g4 h6 7 ♗g2**
a) 7 ♖g1 ♘c6 8 h4 d5 9 ♗b5 ♗d7 10
exd5 ♘xd5 11 ♘xd5 exd5 12 ♕e2+
♗e7 13 ♘f5± Liberzon-Formanek,
Beersheva 1978;
b) 7 g5 hxg5 8 ♗xg5 ♘c6 9 ♕d2 ♕b6
10 ♘b3 ♘e5 (10...a6 11 0-0-0 ♕c7
N 12 ♗g2 ♘e5 13 f4 ♘c4 14 ♕d4
♗e7 15 e5 ♘h7 16 exd6 ♘xd6≈
Chiburdanidze-Kushnir, 1978) 11 ♕e2
♗d7 N (11...♕c7 12 h4 ♗d7 13 0-0-0
♖c8 14 h5 ♘c4 15 ♖h3± Gipslis-
Sax, Amsterdam 1976) 12 0-0-0 ♖c8
13 h4 a6 14 ♖h3 ♕c7 15 f4 ♘c4 16
♖hd3 ♘h7 17 e5!± Lanka-Knaak,
Jurmala 1978
7...♘c6 8 ♘b3
8 g5 hxg5 9 ♗xg5 ♗e7 10 ♘xc6
bxc6 11 e5 ♘d5 12 ♗xe7 ♕xe7 13 ♕g4
0-0 14 exd6 ♕xd6 15 0-0-0 += Stepak-
Djindjihashvili, Israel Final 1978

8...a5 9 a4 ♗e7 N 9...d5 10 exd5
♘b4!≈ Boleslavsky
**10 h3 e5 11 ♗e3 ♘b4 12 ♕d2 ♗e6
13 0-0 ♖c8 14 f4 exf4 15 ♖xf4
♗xb3 16 cxb3 ♘d7 17 ♖f5±** Lutikov-

Knaak, Jurmala 1978

Caro Kann

**1 e4 c6 2 d4 d5 3 ♘c3 dxe4 4 ♘xe4
♘f6 5 ♘xf6+**
5 ♘g3 c5 6 ♘f3 ♘c6 7 dxc5 N ♛xd1+
8 ♚xd1 ♗g4 9 ♗e3 0-0-0+ 10 ♚c1
♗xf3 11 gxf3 e6 12 a3 ♘d5 13 b4
a5∝ Enders-Starck, Eggesin 1978
5...exf6 6 ♗c4
a) 6 c3 ♗d6 7 ♗d3 0-0 8 ♛c2 ♖e8+
9 ♘e2 g6 10 h4 ♘d7 11 h5 ♘f8 12
♗h6! [12 hxg6 fxg6 13 ♚f1!? N
♗e6 14 ♗h6 ♛e7∝ Gurgenidze-
Mohring, H.Kralove 1977/78] 12...
♛c7 13 0-0-0 ♗e6 14 c4 ♖ad8 15
hxg6 fxg6 16 c5 ♗e7 17 ♘f4 ♗f7
18 ♗c4 +− Kavalek-Andersson 1978;
b) 6 ♘f3 ♗e6 7 ♗d3 ♘a6 8 c3 ♘c7
9 0-0 b5? 10 ♖e1 ♗d6 11 ♛c2 ♚f8
12 ♘h4 ♛d7 13 ♘f5 h5 14 a4±
Mihaljcisin-Duric,   USSR-Jugoslavia
1978
6...♛e7+ 7 ♛e2
7 ♗e2 ♛c7 8 ♘f3 ♗d6 9 0-0 0-0 10
♗e3 ♘d7 11 c4 ♖e8 12 ♛d2 ♘f8 13
h3 += Vogt-Mohring, Eggesin 1978
7...♗e6
7...♗g4 8 ♛xe7+ ♗xe7 9 ♗f4 N ♘d7
10 f3 ♗e6 11 ♗d3 ♘b6 12 a3 0-0
13 ♘e2 += Jovcic-Radojcic, Titovo
Uzice 1978
8 ♗d3 c5 N
8...♛c7 9 ♛f3 ♗d6 10 ♘e2 0-0 11
♘g3 ♖e8 12 0-0 ♘d7 13 ♗d2 ♗d5!∝
Hort

Diagram

**9 dxc5 ♛xc5 10 ♘f3 ♘c6 11 0-0 ♗d6
12 h3 0-0 13 ♗e3 ♛a5 14 ♗d2 ♛h5
15 ♘d4 ♛xe2 16 ♘xe2 ♗e5** =+ Jovcic-
Andersson, Titovo Uzice 1978

**1 e4 c6 2 d4 d5 3 ♘c3 dxe4 4 ♘xe4
♘f6 5 ♘xf6+ gxf6 6 ♗c4**
a) 6 ♘e2 ♘d7 7 ♘g3 ♘b6 8 c3 ♛d5
9 ♛h5 ♛xh5 10 ♘xh5 ♗g4 11 ♘g3
e5 12 ♘e4 ♗e7= Lazzarato-Vilmaz,
Groningen 1978;
b) 6 ♘f3 ♗f5 7 ♗e2 ♛c7 8 0-0 ♘d7
9 ♗e3 e6 10 c4 0-0-0 11 ♛a4 ♚b8
12 b4± Groszpeter-Pasman, Groningen 1978;
c) 6 c3 ♗f5 7 ♘f3 (7 ♘e2 h5 8 ♘g3
♗g6 9 h4 e6 10 ♗e2 ♛a5 11 a3 ♗d6
12 b4 ♛c7 13 ♘xh5± Zatulovskaya-
Semenova, Lvov 1977) 7...♛c7 (7...e6
8 ♗d3 [8 ♗f4 ♘d7 9 ♗e2 ♘b6 10 0-0
♘d5 11 ♗g3 ♗h6 12 c4± Boleslavsky-
Flohr, USSR Final 1944] 8...♗xd3
9 ♛xd3 ♛c7 10 0-0 ♘d7 11 a4 0-0-0=
H.Riemsdyk-D.Riemsdyk, Sao Paulo
1978) 8 g3 ♘d7!? 9 ♗g2 0-0-0 10
0-0 h5 11 ♖e1 e5 12 ♛a4 ♚b8 13
dxe5 ♘c5 14 ♛f4 ♗g6 15 e6±
Tavdidishvili-Greenfeld, Herzlia 1978;
d) 6 ♗f4?! ♛b6!? (6...♗f5 7 ♗c4 e6
8 ♘f3 ♗d6 9 ♗g3 ♗g4 N 10 c3 ♛c7
11 0-0 h5 12 ♗e2 h4∝ Thomson-
Carlsson, Hallsberg 1977/78) 7 b3?!
N (7 ♘f3!? ♛xb2 8 ♗d3∝ Poulsen-
Larsen, Copenhagen 1973) 7...e5! 8
dxe5 fxe5 9 ♛e2 ♗b4+ 10 ♗d2 ♗e6
11 ♘f3 ♘d7 12 ♗xb4 ♛xb4+ 13 ♛d2

a5 14 ♘g5 ♕xd2+ 15 ♔xd2 ♗d5= Baczynsky-Basman, London 1978

6...♗f5 7 ♗f4

7 ♘f3 (7 c3 e6 8 ♗f4 ♘d7 9 g4 ♗e4 10 f3 ♗d5 11 ♗xd5 cxd5 12 ♕a4 ♕b6 13 0-0-0 ♖c8= Shachar-Greenfeld, Herzlia 1978) 7...♕c7 8 c3 e6 9 ♘h4 ♗g6 10 ♕f3 ♘d7 11 ♗f4 ♗d6 12 ♗g3 0-0-0 13 0-0 f5 14 ♗xd6 ♕xd6 15 ♖fe1 += Formanek-Pasman, Beersheva 1978

7...e6 8 ♘f3 ♗d6 9 ♗g3 ♕c7 10 ♕e2!? 10 ♘h4!

10...♗g4 11 0-0-0 ♘d7 12 d5! cxd5 13 ♗xd5 ♗f4+ 14 ♔b1 ♗xg3 15 hxg3 0-0-0? 16 ♗xb7+! +− Westerinen-Rosenlund, Roskilde 1978

1 e4 c6 2 d4 d5 3 ♘c3 dxe4 4 ♘xe4 ♘d7 5 ♘f3

a) 5 ♘e2!? N ♘gf6 6 ♘2g3 e6 7 ♗f4 ♘xe4 8 ♘xe4 ♘f6 9 ♘xf6+ ♕xf6 10 ♕d2 ♗e7 11 0-0-0 0-0 12 h4 ♕f5 13 ♗e5 f6 14 ♗d3± Grinfeld-Ignatieva, USSR Women's Final 1978;

b) 5 ♗c4 ♘gf6 6 ♘xf6+ ♘xf6 7 ♘f3 ♗f5 8 0-0 e6 9 ♕e2 ♗e7 10 ♗g5 0-0= Kagan-Bleiman, Israel Final 1978

5...♘gf6 6 ♘xf6+ ♘xf6 7 ♗c4

7 ♘e5 e6 N 8 c3 ♗e7 9 ♗d3 0-0 10 0-0 ♘d7 11 ♗f4 ♘xe5 12 ♗xe5 ♗f6 13 ♕e2 += Parma-Radulov, Kiel

1978

7...♗f5

7...e6 8 0-0 ♗e7 9 ♕e2 0-0 10 c3 b6 11 ♗f4 ♗b7 12 ♖ad1 += Lein-Benko, USA Final 1978

8 0-0 e6 9 c3

9 h3 ♗d6 10 ♕e2 ♕c7 11 c3 h6 12 ♘e5 ♗xe5 13 dxe5± Rohde-Hernando, Alicante 1978

9...♗g4 10 a4 a5 11 h3 ♗h5 12 ♗e2 ♗xf3 13 ♗xf3 ♗e7 14 ♕b3 += Kagan-Lederman, Beersheva 1978

1 e4 c6 2 d4 d5 3 exd5 cxd5 4 c4

4 ♘c3 ♗f5 5 ♘f3 e6 6 ♗b5+ ♘c6 7 ♘e5 ♖c8 N 8 0-0 ♗d6 9 ♗xc6+ bxc6 10 ♖e1 ♘e7 11 ♗f4 ♘g6 12 ♘xg6 hxg6 13 ♗xd6 ♕xd6 14 g3 += Mohring-Starck, Eggesin 1978

4...♘f6 5 ♘c3 ♘c6 6 ♘f3

6 ♗g5 ♕b6 7 cxd5 ♘xd4 8 ♘ge2 (8 ♗e3 e5 9 dxe6 ♗c5 10 exf7+ ♔e7 11 ♗d3?! [11 ♗c4±] 11...♖d8 12 ♖c1 ♗g4 13 ♕d2 ♖ac8 14 h3 Schubert-Pasman, Groningen 1978, 14...♗h5!∓) 8...♘xe2 9 ♗xe2 ♕xb2 10 ♘b5 ♕e5 N (10...♘e4 11 ♖b1 ♕xa2 12 ♘c7+ ♔d8 13 ♘e6+! +−) 11 f4 ♕e3 12 ♘c7+ ♔d8 13 ♘xa8 +− Liberzon-Pasman, Beersheva 1978

6...♗g4 7 cxd5 ♘xd5 8 ♕b3 ♗xf3 9 gxf3 ♘b6 10 ♗e3 e6 11 ♖g1! N

11 0-0-0 ♖c8 12 ♔b1 ♕c7 13 ♘b5 ♕b8 14 ♘xa7 +− Sisniega-Grosspeter, Innsbruck 1977
11...♖c8 12 ♖d1 g6 13 d5 ♘xd5 14 ♕xb7 ♗b4∞ Velimirovic-Nikolac, Jugoslav Final 1978

1 e4 c6 2 ♘c3 d5 3 ♘f3 ♗g4 4 h3 ♗h5
4...♗xf3 5 ♕xf3 ♘f6 6 d4 (6 exd5 cxd5 7 ♗b5+ ♘c6 8 0-0 e6 9 ♘e2 ♖c8 10 ♘d4 ♗e7 11 ♘xc6 bxc6 12 ♗a6 ♖b8 13 c3 c5= Mestrovic-Vukic, Jugoslav Final 1978) 6...e6 7 ♗d3 dxe4 8 ♘xe4 ♕xd4 9 ♗e3 ♕e5 10 0-0-0 ♘bd7 11 ♗f4 ♕a5 12 ♔b1 ♗e7 13 ♘d6+ ♗xd6 14 ♗xd6 0-0-0∞ Villarreal-Shamkovich, Mexico City 1978
5 exd5 cxd5 6 ♗b5+ ♘c6 7 g4 ♗g6 8 ♘e5 ♖c8 9 d4
9 ♕f3 N e6 10 d3 f6?! 11 ♗xc6+ bxc6 12 ♘xg6 hxg6 13 ♕e3 ♕d7 14 ♘e2 ♗d6= Malzman-Perm, Israel Final 1978
9...e6 10 ♕e2 10 h4?! f6 11 ♘xg6 hxg6 12 ♕d3 ♔f7 13 h5 gxh5 14 gxh5 ♘e7 15 ♗e3 ♘f5 16 ♗xc6 ♖xc6 17 0-0-0 N (17 ♘e2 =+ Fischer-Smyslov, Candidates 1959) 17...♗b4 18 ♘e2 ♕a5∓ Durao-Silva, Portugal Final 1978

10...♗b4 11 h4 ♘e7 12 h5 ♗e4 13 f3 0-0! 14 ♗xc6

14 fxe4 ♘xd4 15 ♕d3 dxe4 Δ ♖xc3∓
14...♘xc6 15 ♘xc6 ♖xc6 16 0-0
16 ♔f1 f5 17 fxe4 fxe4+ 18 ♔g2 ♗xc3 19 bxc3 ♖xc3 20 ♗d2 ♖cf3∓ Ivanov-Efimov, USSR 1978
16...♗xc3 17 bxc3 ♖xc3 18 ♗d2! ♖xc2 19 fxe4 dxe4 ½-½ Durao-Silva, Portugal Final 1978

1 e4 c6 2 d4 d5 3 ♘c3 dxe4 4 ♘xe4 ♗f5 5 ♘g3
5 ♘c5 b6 6 ♘b3 ♘f6 N 7 ♘f3 ♘bd7 8 g3 a5 9 ♗g2 e6 10 0-0 a4 11 ♘bd2 ♗e7 12 ♘e5± Bronstein-Lutikov, Jurmala 1978
5...♗g6 6 h4
a) 6 ♗c4 e6 7 ♘1e2 ♘f6 8 h4 h6 9 ♘f4 ♗h7 10 ♘b3 ♗d6 11 ♘fh5 0-0 12 ♗e3 ♘bd7 13 ♕e2 b5= Lazzarato-Grosspeter, Groningen 1978;
b) 6 ♘f3 ♘d7 7 ♗d3 e6 8 0-0 ♘gf6 9 b3 ♗e7 10 ♗b2 0-0 11 c4 a5 12 ♗c3 N ♗b4= Weinstein-Shamkovich, USA Final 1978;
c) 6 ♘h3 ♘f6 7 ♘f4 e5 8 ♘xg6 hxg6 9 dxe5 ♕a5+ N (9...♕xd1 10 ♔xd1 ♘g4 11 ♘e4 ♘xe5 12 ♗e2 f6 13 c3 ♘bd7 14 ♗e3 += Fischer-Foguelman, Buenos Aires 1960) 10 ♗d2 ♕xe5+ 11 ♕e2 ♕xe2+ 12 ♗xe2 ♘bd7 13 0-0-0 ♗c5 14 f4 0-0 15 f5 += Tseshkovsky-Bagirov, Lvov 1978
6...h6 7 ♘f3 ♘d7 8 h5 ♗h7 9 ♗d3 ♗xd3 10 ♕xd3 e6 11 ♗d2 ♕c7 12 0-0-0
12 ♕e2 ♘gf6 13 0-0-0 (13 ♖h4 0-0-0 14 ♘e5 ♘xe5 15 dxe5 ♘d7 16 f4 ♗e7 17 ♖h3 ♘c5 18 0-0-0 += Matulovic-Nikolac, Jugoslav Final 1978) 13...♘d6!? 14 ♘f5 ♗f4 15 ♗xf4 ♕xf4+ 16 ♘e3 b5 (16...0-0-0 17 ♔b1 ♖he8 18 ♖d3 ♘d5 19 ♘c4 ♕c7 20 ♖a3 ♔b8 21 g3 += Ivanovic-Nikolac, Jugoslav Final 1978) 17

♖dg1 0-0-0 18 c4 a6 19 ♔b1 ♔b7 20 ♖c1 ♖c8 21 a4! += Ivanovic-Vukic, Jugoslav Final 1978

12...♗d6 13 ♘e4 ♗f4 14 ♕a3 ♘gf6 15 ♖h4 ♘xe4 16 ♗xf4 ♕d8 17 ♗e5 ♘ef6 18 ♘d2 b5 19 ♕g3 △ ♗c7, ♗d6± Timman-Ivanovic, Niksic 1978

Spanish

1 e4 e5 2 ♘f3 ♘c6 3 ♗b5 a6 4 ♗xc6 dxc6

4...bxc6!? 5 0-0 d6 6 d4 f6 7 ♘h4!? ♗e6 8 b3 g6 9 g3 ♘h6 10 c4 ♗g7= Pavlovic-Knezevic, Nis 1977

5 0-0 ♕d6

a) 5...♕e7 6 d4 exd4 7 ♕xd4 ♗g4 8 ♗f4! ♗xf3 9 gxf3 ♘f6 10 ♘c3 ♘h5 11 ♗g3 ♖d8= Dvoretsky-Smyslov, USSR 1974)

b) 5...♕e7 6 d3 ♗g4 7 ♘bd2 f6 8 ♘c4 ♗h5 9 a4 ♘h6 10 ♖xh6 gxh6 11 ♘e3 0-0-0 12 ♘f5 ♕e8 13 ♕e2 ♖g8= Padevsky-Djuric, Vrnjacka-Banja 1978;

c) 5...♘e7 6 d3 ♗g6 7 ♗e3 ♗d6 8 d4 ♗g4 9 h3 ♗xf3 10 ♕xf3 0-0 11 dxe5 ♗xe5= Martinovic-Nikolac, Vrnjacka Banja 1978;

d) 5...♗d6 6 d4 exd4 7 ♕xd4 f6 8 ♘bd2 (8 ♖d1!? Westerinen) 8...♗e6 (8...♘h6! 9 ♘c4 ♘f7 10 b3 0-0 11 h3

b5! =+ Karaklaic-Gligoric, Manila 1975; 10 ♘xd6+ cxd6 11 ♗f4=) 9 b3 ♘h6 10 ♘c4 ♘f7 11 ♗xd6 cxd6 12 ♘d2 c5 13 ♕e3 0-0= Schussler-Rantanen, Stockholm 1978;

e) 5...f6 6 d4 (6 d3!? ♗g4 7 ♗e3 c5 8 ♘bd2 ♕d7 9 a3 ♗d6 10 ♕b1 a5 11 c3 ♘e7 12 h3 ♗h5 =+ Kagan-Djindjihashvili, Israel Final 1977/78) 6...exd4 7 ♘xd4 c5 8 ♘b3 ♕xd1 9 ♖xd1 ♗g4!? (9...♗d7 10 ♗f4 0-0-0 11 ♘c3 g5 N [11...♗e6 12 ♖xd8+ ♔xd8 13 a4! += Schmitt-Kalinski 1971] 12 ♗g3 h5 13 ♘d5 ♗d6 14 ♗xd6 cxd6 15 ♖d2 += Passerotti-Kovacs, Reggio Emilia 1977/78) 10 f3 ♗e6 11 ♗e3 b6 12 ♘c3 (12 a4 ♗d6 13 a5 0-0-0 14 ♘c3 ♔b7= Adorjan-Ivkov, Skopje 1976) 12...♗d6 13 a4 ♔f7! 14 a5 c4 15 ♘d4 b5 16 ♘xe6 N (16 ♘f5? ♗xf5 17 exf5 ♘e7 18 g4 h5∓ Timman-Korchnoi 1976) 16...♔xe6 17 ♘d5 ♘e7 18 ♘xe7 ♔xe7= Evans-Biyiasas, New York 1977

6 d4

a) 6 d3 f6 7 ♗e3 c5 N (7...♗g4! 8 ♘bd2 ♕d7! Ghinda-Ciocaltea, Rumania Final 1975) 8 ♘bd2 ♗e6 9 ♕e2 ♘e7 10 ♘b3 b6 11 c3 ♕c6 12 ♘fd2 ♘g6= Ristic-Mihaljcisin, Vrnjacka Banja 1978;

b) 6 ♘a3 ♕e6!? (6...b5 7 c4 ♗g4!)
7 b3 (7 d4 ♗xa3 8 bxa3 exd4 9 ♕xd4
♘f6 10 ♗b2 0-0 11 ♘e5 b6 12 f4
c5 13 ♕e3 ♗b7 14 f5 += Evans-Lein,
New York 1977) 7...♘e7 8 ♘c4 f6
9 d4 ♘g6 10 dxe5 fxe5 11 ♘g5 ♕f6
12 ♕h5 ♗e7 13 ♘f3 ♗d6 14 ♗b2 0-0
15 ♘cxe5± Gruchacz-Lombardy, Lone
Pine 1978

6...exd4 7 ♕xd4 f6
7...♗d7 8 ♗e3 0-0-0 (8...c5! Euwe)
9 ♘d2 ♕g6 N (9...♘h6 10 h3 ♕g6
11 ♕f3 f5≈ Larsen-Portisch 1977)
10 ♕e2 f5 11 ♘xf5 ♗xf5 12 exf5
♕xf5 13 ♕f3 ♘e7 14 c4 g6=
Makropoulos-Mestrovic, Kallithea
1977
**8 ♗e3 ♗d7 9 c4 0-0-0 10 ♘c3 ♕e5
11 f4 ♕e8 12 ♕f3 ♔b8 13 ♖ad1 +=**
Kagan-Kraidman, Beersheva 1978

**1 e4 e5 2 ♘f3 ♘c6 3 ♗b5 a6 4 ♗a4
d6 5 0-0**
a) 5 c3 f5 (5...♗d7 6 d4 g6 7 ♗e3
♗g7 8 ♘bd2 ♕e7 N 9 d5 ♘b8 10
c4 ♘f6 11 c5 0-0 12 ♖c1± Beljavsky-
Medina, Alicante 1978) 6 exf5 ♗xf5
7 0-0 ♗d3 8 ♖e1 e4 9 ♖e3 (9 ♗c2
♗e7? [9...♗xc2 10 ♕xc2 ♘f6 11
♘g5 ♕d7 12 d3 0-0-0 13 dxe4 d5∝]
10 ♗xd3 exf3 11 ♕xf3 ♘f6 12 ♗c2
0-0 13 d4± Taulbut-Upton, Groningen
1978; 9 ♕b3 b5? 10 c4 ♘ge7 11 cxb5
axb5 12 ♗xb5 ♗xb5 13 ♕xb5 ♖a5
14 ♕c4 +− Reyner-Yensen, USSR
1978) 9...♗e7 10 ♘e1 ♗g5 11 ♖h3
♘h6!? 12 ♘xd3 exd3 13 ♕e1+ N (13
♖xd3 0-0≈ Shagalovich-Shianovsky,
USSR 1960) 13...♔d7 14 ♖xd3 ♖e8
15 ♕f1 ♖e4! 16 ♖d4! ♖xd4 17 cxd4
b5 18 d5 ♘d4 19 ♗d1 b4 20 ♗a4+±
V. Zagorovsky-Nun, corres 1978;
b) 5 ♗xc6+ bxc6 6 d4 f6 7 ♗e3 ♘e7
8 ♘c3 (8 c4 exd4 9 ♗xd4 c5 10 ♗c3

♗e6 11 ♘bd2 ♘c6 12 0-0 ♗e7 13
♘h4 ♕d7 14 ♕h5+ ♗f7 15 ♕e2±
Ivanov-Muchamedeyanov, Beltsi 1978)
8...♘g6 9 h4 h5 10 ♕d3 ♗e7 11
0-0-0 ♗d7 12 ♔c4 ♕b8 13 dxe5 fxe5
14 ♘g5 ♗xg5 15 ♗xg5 ♕b7=
Formanek-Tatai, Beersheva 1978
5...♗d7 6 d4
6 c4 ♘f6 7 ♘c3 ♗e7 8 d4 ♘xd4 9
♘xd4 exd4 10 ♕xd4 ♗xa4 11 ♘xa4
0-0 12 ♘c3 += Ermenkov-Medina,
Alicante 1978

6...b5
6...♘ge7 7 d5 ♘b8 8 c4 ♘g6 9 ♗e3
♗e7 10 ♘bd2 0-0 11 b4 ♗xa4 N
(11...c5 12 bxc5 dxc5 13 ♗xd7 ♘xd7
14 a4± Geller-Bondarevsky, USSR
1963) 12 ♕xa4 ♘d7 13 ♕c2 ♘f6
14 h3 += Martin-Medina, Alicante
1978
7 ♗b3 exd4 8 c3 dxc3 9 ♕d5 N
9 ♕d3 ♘f6 10 ♗g5 ♗e7 11 a4 ♘a5
12 ♗c2 ♘c4 13 ♖a2 h6 14 ♗h4 +=
Tal-Ciocaltea, Kizlovodsk 1964
**9...♕e7 10 ♘xc3 ♘f6 11 ♕d3 ♕d8
12 e5! ♘xe5 13 ♘xe5 dxe5 14 ♗g5
♗c6 15 ♕e2 ♗b4 16 ♖ad1 ♗d6 17
f4 e4 18 ♘xe4±** Kristiansen-
Westerinen, Roskilde 1978

**1 e4 e5 2 ♘f3 ♘c6 3 ♗b5 a6 4 ♗a4
♘f6 5 0-0 ♘xe4 6 d4 b5 7 ♗b3 d5 8**

dxe5 8 ♘xe5 ♘xe5 9 dxe5 ♗e6?!
10 ♘d2 N (10 c3 ♗c5 11 ♕e2 0-0
12 ♗e3± Keres) 10...♘c5 11 f4 ♕d7
12 ♕f3 ♘xb3 13 ♘xb3 ♗f5 14 ♕f2
♗e7= Hobusch-Walther, Eggesin 1978

8...♗e6 9 c3

a) 9 ♗e3 g6 N 10 ♘bd2 ♗g7 11 ♘xe4
dxe4 12 ♗xe6 ♕xd1 13 ♗xf7+ ♔xf7
14 ♘g5+ ♔e7 15 ♖axd1 +− Parma-
Brendel, Kiel 1978;

b) 9 ♘bd2 ♗c5 10 c3 (10 ♕e2 ♗e7
11 c3 0-0 12 ♘d4 ♘b8?! 13 ♗c2
♕d7 14 b4 ♘b7 15 f4± Hamann-
Brendel, Kiel 1978) 10...♘xb3? (10...
g6 11 ♗c2 ♗g7 12 ♘d4! ♘xe5 13 f4
♘c4 14 f5 ♘e3 15 ♕f3 ♘xf1 16
fxe6 ♗xd4+ 17 cxd4 ♘xe6 18 ♘xf1
♘xd4∓ Neumann-Brendel, Kiel 1978;
10...d4! 11 ♗xe6 N ♘xe6 12 ♘b3
dxc3 13 ♕c2 ♘b4 14 ♕xc3 ♕d3=
Mednis-Tarjan, USA Final 1978) 11
♘xb3 ♗e7 12 ♘fd4! (12 ♘bd4 ♘xd4
13 cxd4 0-0 14 ♕d3 f6 15 exf6 ♖xf6
16 ♘e5 += Chiburdanidze-Alekina,
Lvov 1977) 12...♘xe5 13 ♖e1 ♗g6 14
♘xe6 fxe6 15 ♘d4 ♘f8 16 ♕g4 h5 17
♕xg7 +− Kuzmin-Beljavsky, Baku
1978;

c) 9 ♕e2 ♗e7 10 ♖d1 0-0 (10...♘c5
11 ♘c3 ♘xb3 12 cxb3 ♘a5 N 13
♘d4 0-0 14 ♘xe6 fxe6 15 ♕g4 +=
Matulovic-Ostojic, Jugoslav Final
1978) 11 c4 (11 c3 ♕d7 12 ♗e3 f5
13 ♘bd2 ♘a5 14 ♘d4 c5= Kurajica-
Diesen, Osijek 1978) 11...bxc4 12
♗xc4 ♗c5 13 ♗e3 ♗xe3 14 ♕xe3 ♕b8
15 ♗b3 ♘a5 16 ♘e1 ♘xb3 17 axb3
f5! N 18 f3 f4 19 ♕d4! c5 20 ♕d3
♘g5 21 ♕c2 Oechslein-Preinfalk, BRD
1978, 21...♕b6! △ ♗f5, ♘e6∓

Diagram

9...♗c5

9...♘c5 10 ♗g5 ♕d7 11 ♗c2 ♗g4
12 ♖e1 ♘e6 13 ♗h4 Kayomov-Lanka,
Beltsi 1978, 13...♗c5!=

10 ♘bd2 0-0 11 ♗c2 ♗f5

11...♘xf2 12 ♖xf2 f6 13 exf6 ♗xf2+
14 ♔xf2 ♕xf6 15 ♘f1 ♘e5 16 ♗e3
♖ae8 17 ♗c5 ♘xf3 (17...♖f7 18 ♘g3
♗g4= Wittmann-Esnaola, corres 1974)
18 gxf3 ♖f7 19 ♔g2 h5 20 ♕d3 ♕g5+
21 ♔h1± Kupreichik-Shereshevsky,
Minsk 1978

**12 ♘b3 ♗g4 13 ♘xc5 ♘xc5 14 ♖e1
♖e8 15 ♗f4 d4≈** Balashov-Beljavsky,
Leningrad 1977

**1 e4 e5 2 ♘f3 ♘c6 3 ♗b5 a6 4 ♗a4
♘f6 5 0-0 ♗e7 6 ♖e1 b5 7 ♗b3 d6 8
c3 0-0 9 h3 ♘a5 10 ♗c2 c5 11 d4
♘c6**

a) 11...♘d7 12 d5 ♘b6 13 b3 N [13
g4 h5 14 ♘h2 hxg4 15 hxg4 ♗g5

28

16 ♘d2 g6 =∓ Fischer-Keres, Curacao 1962] 13...f5 14 exf5 ♗xf5 15 ♘a3 ♕d7 16 c4 b4 17 ♗xf5 ♕xf5= Hulak-Ostojic, Jugoslav Final 1978;
b) 11...♘d7 12 ♘bd2 cxd4 13 cxd4 ♗f6 14 d5 ♘b6 15 ♘f1 ♗d7 16 b3 ♘b7 17 ♗e3 N (17 ♗d2 ♕c7 18 ♘e3 ♖fc8 19 ♕e2 += Ostojic-Ciocaltea, Skopje 1969) 17...♘c5 18 a4 bxa4 19 b4 ♘b3 20 ♗xb3 axb3 21 ♕xb3 ♕b8= Savon-Dorfman, Lvov 1978;
c) 11...♕c7 12 ♘bd2 ♘c6 (12...♗b7 13 d5 ♖fb8 14 ♘f1 ♘c4 15 ♘3h2 [15 ♘g3 ♗c8 16 a4 bxa4 17 ♖a2 ♘b6 18 ♗xa4 ♘xa4 19 ♕xa4 g6= Matulovic-Jovcic, Titovo Uzice 1978] 15...♗c8 16 ♘g3 ♗f8 17 ♕e2 ♖a7 18 ♖f1 ♔h8 19 ♔h1 ♖ba8 20 f3 ♘g8 21 ♘g4± Jansa-Jovcic, Titovo Uzice 1978) 13 d5 (13 dxc5 dxc5 14 ♘f1 ♖d8 15 ♕e2 ♗e6 16 ♘e3 c4 17 ♘f5 h6! N [17...♘d7 18 ♘g5±] 18 ♘3h4 ♗f8 19 ♕f3 ♗d7 20 ♗e3 += Silva-Durao 1978) 13...♘d8 (13...♘a7?! 14 ♘f1 ♗d7 15 g4 ♘c8 16 ♘g3 g6 17 ♔h2 ♘e8 18 ♗h6 += Klovan-Schneider, Jurmala 1978) 14 a4 ♖b8 15 b3 N (15 b4 c4 16 ♘f1 ♘e8 17 axb5 axb5 18 ♘3h2 f6 19 f4 += Karpov-Spassky, USSR Final 1973) 15...♘e8 16 ♕e2 g6 17 ♗d3 ♗d7 18 axb5 axb5 19 ♗b2 f6 20 ♖a2 ♘f7 21 ♖ea1 += Velimirovic-Matanovic, Jugoslav Final 1978;
d) 11...♕c7 12 ♘bd2 cxd4 13 cxd4 ♗d7 (13...♘c6 14 ♘b3 [14 a3 ♗d7 15 d5 ♘a5 16 ♘f1 ♖fc8 17 ♗d3 ♗d8 18 ♘g3 ♕a7 19 ♖f1 ♗b6= Tseshkovsky-Dorfman, Lvov 1978] 14...a5 15 ♗e3 a4 16 ♘bd2 ♘b4 17 ♗b1 ♗d7 18 a3 ♘c6 19 ♗d3± Matulovic-Kovacevic, Titovo Uzice 1978) 14 ♘f1 ♖ac8 (14...♖fc8 15 ♗d3 ♘c6 16 ♗e3 ♕d8 N 17 ♘g3 ♕e8 18 a3 ♗f8 19 ♕d2±

Parma-Hamann, Kiel 1978) 15 ♘e3 ♖fe8 16 b3 ♘c6 N 17 ♗b2 ♗d8 18 ♖c1 ♕a7 19 dxe5 dxe5 20 ♘d5± Westerinen-Rajna, Roskilde 1978
12 ♘bd2
12 d5 ♘a7 13 ♘bd2 ♗d7 14 ♘f1 ♘c8 15 ♘e3 ♕c7 16 b3 ♘b6= Vitolins-Klovan, Jurmala 1978
12...cxd4 13 cxd4 exd4?! 14 ♘b3 d3 15 ♗xd3 ♗b7 16 ♗d2 ♖e8 17 a4 ♗f8= Geller-Romanishin, Lvov 1978

1 e4 e5 2 ♘f3 ♘c6 3 ♗b5 a6 4 ♗a4 ♘f6 5 0-0 ♗e7 6 ♖e1 b5 7 ♗b3 d6 8 c3 0-0 9 h3 ♘b8
a) 9...♘d7 10 d4 ♘b6 (10...♗f6 11 ♗e3 ♖e8 N 12 ♘bd2 ♘a5 13 ♗c2 c5 14 d5 ♘f8 15 b4 ♘b7 16 a4 += Georgiev-Lazzarato, Groningen 1978) 11 ♘bd2 exd4 12 cxd4 d5 13 ♗c2 ♗e6 14 e5 ♕d7 15 ♘f1 N (15 ♘b3 ♘a4 16 ♗g5 f6 17 exf6 ♗xf6 18 ♕b1 h6 Δ ♘e7, ♗f5= Darga) 15...♘b4 16 ♗b1 ♗f5 17 ♗g5 ♗xb1 18 ♕xb1 f6 19 ♗h4! += Hulak-Nikolac, Jugoslav Final 1978;
b) 9...h6 10 d4 ♖e8 11 ♘bd2 ♗f8 12 ♘f1 (12 ♗c2 ♗d7 13 ♗d3 N ♕b8 14 b3 g6 15 ♗b2 ♗g7 16 d5 ♘d8 17 c4 ♘h5= Savon-Geller, Lvov 1978) 12...♗d7 (12...♗b7 13 ♘g3 ♘a5 14 ♗c2 g6 15 a4 ♘c4 N [15...♕d7 16 b3 ♗g7= Korchnoi-Smyslov, Zagreb 1970] 16 ♗d3 d5!?∞ Georgiev-Rohde, Students Final 1978) 13 ♘g3 ♘a5 14 ♗c2 c5 15 b3 cxd4 (15...♘c6 16 d5 ♘e7 17 ♘h4 N [17 ♗e3 ♕c8 18 ♕d2 ♔h8 19 a4 += Jansa-Geller, Hungary 1970] 17...g5?! 18 ♘hf5 += Grunfeld-Malzman, Israel Final 1978) 16 cxd4 ♘c6 17 ♗b2 ♖c8 18 a3 ♕c7 N [18...♕b6 19 b4 a5 20 d5 ♘e7 21 ♗c1 += Janosevic-Geller, Belgrade 1969] 19 ♖c1 ♕b8 20 ♕d2

29

g6 21 d5 ♘a7 22 ♗c3± Petrushin-Faibisovich, Beltsi 1978

10 d4
10 a4 ♗b7 11 d3 ♘bd7 12 axb5 axb5 13 ♖xa8 ♗xa8 14 ♘a3 ♗c6 15 ♗g5 ♘c5 16 ♗c2 N (16 ♗a2 ♗d7 17 ♘c2 ♗e6=) 16...♖e8 17 d4 exd4 18 ♘xd4 ♗xe4= Matulovic-Matanovic, Jugoslav Final 1978

10...♘bd7 11 ♘bd2
11 c4 c6 12 ♘c3 b4 13 ♘a4 c5 14 dxc5 dxc5 15 ♗c2 ♕c7 16 b3 ♗b7= Kuzmin-Smejkal, Leningrad 1977

11...♗b7 12 ♗c2 ♖e8 13 ♘f1 ♗f8 14 ♘g3 g6 15 a4 c5
15...♗g7 16 ♗d3 c6 N (16...d5?! 17 ♗g5! dxe4 18 ♗xe4 ♗xe4 19 ♘xe4 exd4 20 ♘xd4 c5 21 ♗xf6!± Karpov-O'Kelly, Caracas 1970) 17 ♗d2 ♘b6 18 b3 ♘bd7 19 ♕c2 d5= Kavalek-Lombardy, USA Final 1978

16 d5 ♘b6
a) 16...c4 17 ♗g5 h6 18 ♗e3 ♘c5 19 ♕d2 ♔h7 20 ♘h2 ♖b8 N 21 ♖f1 ♕e7 22 f3 ♗g7 23 ♖f2 ♘g8 24 axb5 axb5 25 ♖af1± Timoshenko-Zhukovitsky, Beltsi 1978;
b) 16...c4 17 ♗e3 ♘c5 18 ♕d2 ♘fd7 19 ♘h2 N (19 h4 h5 20 ♘g5 ♕e7 21 ♖a3 ♗h6 22 ♖ea1 ♘b6= Jansa-Holmov, Sochi 1974) 19...♗g7 20 ♘g4 ♖f8 21 ♗g5± Damjanovic-Durao, Malaga 1978

17 ♕e2 ♘xa4 18 ♗xa4 bxa4 19 ♖xa4 ♗c8 20 ♗g5 N
a) 20 ♗d2 Tal-Vogt, Leningrad 1977, 20...♖b8;
b) 20 b3 ♖e7 21 ♗g5 ♗g7 22 ♕e3 ♕f8= Balashov-Smejkal, Leningrad 1977

20...h6 21 ♗e3 ♖b8 22 ♖ea1 ♘h7 23 ♕c2 h5 24 ♘d2 ♗e7 25 ♘c4±
Geller-Romanishin, USSR 1978

Scotch

1 e4 e5 2 ♘f3 ♘c6 3 d4 exd4 4 ♘xd4
a) 4 c3 d5 5 exd5 ♕xd5 6 cxd4 ♗b4+ 7 ♘c3 ♗g4 8 ♗e2 ♗xf3 9 ♗xf3 ♕c4 10 ♗xc6+ (10 ♕b3!?) 10...♕xc6? (10...bxc6 11 ♕e2+ ♕xe2+ 12 ♔xe2 0-0-0 13 ♗e3 ♘e7 14 ♖hd1 ♖he8 15 ♖d3 ½-½ Emma-Vogt, Skopje 1972) 11 0-0 ♘e7 12 ♕b3 ♗xc3 13 bxc3 0-0 14 ♖e1 N (14 c4± Penrose-Barden, London 1958) 14...♖fe8 15 c4 ♘f5 16 ♗b2 ♖e4∓ Morales-Acevedo, Mexico City 1978;
b) 4 c3 dxc3 5 ♘xc3 d6 6 ♗c4 ♘f6 7 ♘g5?! N ♘e5 8 ♗b3 h6 9 f4 hxg5 10 fxe5 ♘g4 11 ♕d4 dxe5 12 ♕xe5+ ♕e7 13 ♕xe7+ ♗xe7 14 ♗xg5 ♗d6!∓ Mariotti-Smejkal, Leningrad 1977

4...♗c5 5 ♘b3
5 ♗e3 ♕f6 6 c3 ♘ge7 7 g3!? d5! 8

♗g2 ♘xd4 (8...♗xd4 9 cxd4 dxe4 10 ♘c3 0-0 11 ♘xe4 ♕g6 12 0-0 ♗e6! △ ♗d5 =∓ Kupreichik-Parma, Dortmund 1975) 9 cxd4 ♗b4+ 10 ♘c3 dxe4 N (10...♗xc3+ 11 bxc3 dxe4 12 ♗xe4 ♘h3!?∝) 11 ♗xe4 c6 12 0-0 0-0 13 a3 ♗xc3 14 bxc3 ♗f5 15 ♗g2 ♖ad8 16 ♕b3 ♖d7 =∓ Cibulka-Kluger, R.Sabota 1977

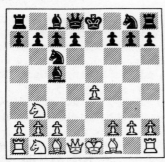

5...♗b6 6 ♘c3 ♘ge7
6...♕f6 7 ♕e2 ♘ge7 8 h4 h6 9 ♘d5 ♘xd5 10 exd5+ ♘e7 11 ♖h3 N (11 g4 d6 12 g5 ♕f5 13 gxh6 gxh6 14 c4 ♗d7 15 ♗d2 0-0-0 =∓ Kupreichik-Klovan, Kirovabad 1973) 11...d6 12 ♖f3 ♕g6 13 ♖f4 f5 14 ♗d2 0-0 15 c4 ♖e8 16 h5 ♕f7 17 ♗e3 g5∓ Bellon-Tatai, Rome 1977
7 ♗g5 0-0 8 ♕d2
8 a4 f6 9 ♗h4 a6 10 ♘c4+ ♔h8 11 0-0 d6 12 ♔h1 ♘e5 13 ♗e2 ♘5g6= Reinert-Nielsen, Ribe 1978
8...d6 9 0-0-0 f6 10 ♗h4 ♗e6 11 f4 ♘g6 12 ♗f2 f5 13 g3 ♘ge7 14 ♗g2 =∓ Radulov-Cording, Hamburg 1977

French

1 e4 e6 2 d4 d5 3 e5 c5 4 c3
4 dxc5 ♘c6 5 ♗f4 ♗xc5 6 c3 f6 7 ♘f3 fxe5 8 ♘xe5 ♘f6 9 ♗d3 ♗b6 10 ♘d2 0-0 11 ♕e2 e5 12 ♗g3 +=

Kosanski-Marovic, Osijek 1978
4...♘c6 5 ♘f3 ♕b6
5...♗d7 6 a3 ♖c8 7 b4 cxd4 8 cxd4 ♕b6 9 ♗b2 a6 10 ♗e2 ♘h6 11 0-0 ♗e7 12 ♘c3 += Pasman-Tatai, Beersheva 1978
6 a3
6 ♗d3 ♗d7 7 0-0 cxd4 8 cxd4 ♘xd4 9 ♘xd4 ♕xd4 10 ♘c3 a6 11 ♕e2 ♘e7 12 ♖d1 ♘c6 13 ♗xa6 ♕xe5 14 ♕xe5 ♘xe5 15 ♗xb7 ♖b8 N (15... ♖a7 16 ♗xd5= Ulvestad-Rothman, USA 1947) 16 ♗a6 ♖b6= Mortensen-Raivio, Ribe 1978
6...c4
a) 6...a5 7 ♗d3 cxd4 8 cxd4 ♗d7 9 ♗c2 ♘ge7 10 ♘c3 ♘f5? 11 ♗xf5 exf5 12 ♘xd5± Roman-Roos, Bagneux 1978;
b) 6...♗d7 7 b4 cxd4 8 cxd4 ♖c8 N (8...♘ge7 9 ♘c3 ♘f5 10 ♘a4 ♕d8 11 ♗b2 ♘h4 12 ♘xh4 ♕xh4 13 ♗d3 += Unzicker-Gligoric, Stockholm 1952) 9 ♗e2 ♘ge7 10 0-0 ♘f5 11 ♗b2 h5! 12 ♔h1 ♗e7 13 ♘c3 ♘a5! =∓ Formanek-Korchnoi, Beersheva 1978
7 ♘bd2
7 g3 ♗d7 8 ♗h3 ♘a5 9 ♘bd2 f5? 10 exf6 gxf6 11 ♘e5!? N (11 0-0 0-0-0 12 ♖e1 ♗g7 13 ♖b1! ♔b8 14 b4!± Zaitsev-Pokojowczyk, Sochi 1976) 11...fxe5 12 ♕h5+ ♔e7 13 ♕g5+ ♔f7 14 ♘f3 ♗g7 15 ♘xe5+ ♗xe5 16 ♕h5+ ♔e7 17 dxe5∝ Vilmaz-Skembris, Groningen 1978
7...♘a5
7...f6 8 b3 fxe5 9 bxc4 e4 10 ♘h4 ♘f6 11 g3 ♗e7 12 ♖b1 ♕c7 13 ♗e2 0-0 14 0-0 ♘a5∓ Enders-Uhlmann, Eggesin 1978

Diagram

8 g3

31

8 b4 cxb3 9 ♗b2 ♗d7 10 c4 ♘e7!?
(10...dxc4 11 ♘xc4 ♘xc4 12 ♗xc4
♘e7 13 ♗xb3 ♗c6=) 11 c5 ♕c7 12
♗d3 ♗a4 13 ♖c1 g6 14 ♕e2 a6∞
Roos-Bjork, Groningen 1978

**8...♗d7 9 ♗h3 h6 10 0-0 0-0-0 11
♖b1 ♘e7**

11...♔b8 12 ♘e1 ♘e7 13 ♘g2 ♕c7
14 ♕f3 ♗e8 15 ♘f4 ♗a4 16 ♗g4
♗c2 =+ Nicevski-Vilela, Decin 1978

**12 ♘e1 f5 13 exf6 gxf6 14 b4 cxb3
15 ♘d3 ♘g6 16 ♗xb3 ♘xb3 17 ♖xb3**
+= Sax-Marovic, Osijek 1978

1 e4 e6 2 d4

2 ♘f3 d5 3 ♘c3 ♘f6 4 e5 ♘e4 5 ♘e2
♗c5 6 d4 ♗e7 7 ♘g3 c5 8 ♗d3 ♘g5
9 ♘xg5 ♗xg5 10 ♕g4 ♗xc1! =+ Hort-
Romanishin, Leningrad 1977

2...d5 3 ♘c3

3 exd5 exd5 4 ♗d3 c5 5 ♘f3 ♘c6 6
♕e2+ ♗e7 7 dxc5 ♘f6 8 h3 0-0 9 0-0
♗xc5 10 c3 ♖e8 11 ♕c2 ♕d6 12
♘bd2 ♕g3! 13 ♗f5 ♖e2 14 ♘d4 ♘xd4
0-1 Tatai-Korchnoi, Beersheva 1978

3...♗b4 4 e5

a) 4 ♗d3 dxe4 5 ♗xe4 ♘f6 6 ♗g5
♘bd7 7 ♕d3 h6 8 ♗xf6 ♕xf6 9 ♘e2
0-0 10 0-0 c6 11 f4 ♖d8 12 ♕f3 +=
Lutikov-Sahovic, Jurmala 1978;

b) 4 ♘e2 dxe4 5 a3 ♗e7 6 ♘xe4
♘f6 7 ♘2g3 0-0 (7...♘c6 8 c3 0-0 9
♗c4 b6 10 0-0 ♗b7 11 ♘xf6+ ♗xf6

12 ♘h5 e5 13 d5 ♘a5 14 ♗a2 ♗a6
15 ♖e1 += Rajna-Helmers, Roskilde
1978) 8 ♗e2 ♘bd7 9 0-0 b6 10 ♗f3
♖b8 11 c4 ♘xe4 12 ♗xe4 ♘f6 13 ♗f3
♗b7= Bronstein-Petrosian, USSR 1978

4...c5

4...b6 5 ♕g4 ♗f8 6 a4 ♗a6 (6...♘c6
7 h4 ♕d7 8 h5 f5 9 ♕d1 ♗b7 10
♘b1 ♘h6 11 c3 ♘a5 12 b4 ♘c4 13
♗xh6!? ∞/+= Kurajica-Nikolac,
Jugoslavia 1978) 7 ♘b5 ♕d7 8 ♗d3
f5 9 ♕h5+ g6 10 ♕e2 c6 11 ♘d6+
♗xd6 12 exd6 ♗xd3 13 ♕e5 ♘f6
14 ♕xf6 +- Kurajica-Smederevac,
Osijek 1978

5 a3 ♗xc3+ 6 bxc3 ♘e7 7 ♘f3

7 ♕g4 ♕c7 8 ♕xg7 ♖g8 9 ♕xh7 cxd4
10 ♘e2 ♘bc6 11 f4 ♗d7 12 ♕d3 dxc3
13 ♖b1!? ♘f5 14 ♖g1 0-0-0 15 ♕xc3
♘cd4 16 ♕xc7+ ♔xc7 17 ♘xd4 ♘xd4
18 ♔f2± Liberzon-Bank, Israel Final
1978

7...♗d7

7...b6 8 ♗b5+ ♗d7 9 ♗d3 h6 10 a4
♘c6 11 0-0 ♕c7 12 ♖e1 0-0 13 ♗a3
+= Gligoric-Marovic, Osijek 1978

8 ♗d3 ♗a4 9 ♘g5 N
a) 9 dxc5!;

b) 9 0-0 c4 10 ♗e2 ♘bc6 11 ♖e1 h6
12 ♗f1 ♕a5 13 ♕d2 0-0-0 14 g3 g5
15 ♗g5 ♖dg8 16 h3 ♘f5 17 ♖b1
♖g7∓ Gutierrez-Farago, Kikinda

32

1978
9...h6 10 ♕h5 g6 11 ♕h4 ♘f5 12 ♗xf5 gxf5 13 ♕h5 ♕e7 14 ♘h3 ♘d7 15 ♗g5 ♕f8 16 ♗h4 ♕g7 17 ♘f4±
Westerinen-Webb, Roskilde 1978

1 e4 e6 2 d4 d5 3 ♘c3 dxe4 4 ♘xe4 ♘d7

a) 4...♘d7 5 ♘f3 ♘gf6 6 ♘xf6+ ♘xf6 7 ♗g5 ♗e7 8 ♗d3 0-0 9 ♕e2 c5 10 dxc5 ♕a5+ 11 c3 ♕xc5 12 ♖d1 ♘d5 13 ♗xe7 ♘xe7 14 0-0 += Pytel-Sioris, Kallithea 1977;

b) 4...♘f6 5 ♗g5 ♗e7 6 ♗xf6 gxf6 7 ♘f3 b6 8 ♗d3 ♗b7 9 ♕e2 ♕d5!! (9...♘d7 10 0-0-0 c6 11 ♔b1 ♕c7 12 ♖he1 0-0-0 13 ♗a6 ♗xa6 14 ♕xa6+ ♔b7 15 ♕e2± Klovan-Petrosian, Erevan 1975) 10 c4 ♕a5+ 11 ♘c3 ♘d7 12 0-0 0-0-0 13 ♗e4 ♕a6 14 ♗d3 ♕a5= Klovan-Bronstein, Jurmala 1978

5 ♘f3 ♗c6 6 ♗d3

6 ♘eg5 ♗e7 7 ♗d3 ♘d7 8 ♕e2 h6 9 ♘e4 ♘gf6 10 ♘xf6+ ♗xf6 11 c3 0-0 12 ♗f4 ♖e8 13 0-0-0 ♗d5 14 h4 c5 =+ Westerinen-Nogueiras, Jurmala 1978

6...♘d7 7 ♕e2

7 c4 N ♘gf6 8 ♘c3 ♗e7 (8...b6 9 0-0 ♗e7 10 ♗f4 0-0 11 ♖e1 ♖e8 12 ♕e2 ♘f8 13 ♖ad1 ♕c8 14 ♘e5 +=

Polihroniade-Macek, Sinaia 1978) 9 0-0 ♗xf3 10 ♕xf3 c6 11 ♗f4 0-0 12 ♖ad1 ♕a5 13 ♖fe1 ♖fe8 14 g4!?∝ Klovan-Nogueiras, Jurmala 1978
7...♘gf6
7...♗e7 8 0-0 ♘gf6 9 ♘g3 ♗xf3 10 ♕xf3 c6 11 c4 0-0 12 b3 ♖e8 13 ♗b2 += Evans-Segal, Sao Paulo 1978
8 ♗g5 N 8 ♘eg5 ♗xf3 9 ♘xf3 += Sahovic-Ciric, Vranjacka Banja 1976
8...♗e7 9 ♗xf6 ♘xf6 10 0-0-0 ♘xe4 11 ♗xe4 ♗xe4 12 ♕xe4 ♕d5 13 ♕xd5 exd5 14 ♖he1 f6= Martinovic Despotvic, S. Palanka 1978

1 e4 e6 2 d4 d5 3 ♘d2 c5

3...♘c6 4 ♘gf3 ♘f6 5 e5 ♘d7 6 ♗d3 ♘b4 7 ♗e2 c5 8 c3 ♘c6 9 0-0 cxd4 10 cxd4 f6 11 exf6 N ♕xf6 12 ♘b3 ♗d6 13 ♗g5 ♕f7 14 ♗h4 ♘f6= Gavrikov-Muratov, Beltsi 1978
4 exd5 exd5 5 ♘gf3
5 ♗b5+ ♗d7 6 ♕e2+ ♗e7 7 dxc5 ♘f6 8 ♘b3 0-0 9 ♗e3 ♖e8 10 ♘f3 (10 0-0-0!) ♗xc5 11 ♘xc5 ♕a5+ 12 ♕d2 ♕xb5 13 0-0-0 ♗g4 14 h3 ♗h5∝ Tseshkovsky-Vaganian, Lvov 1978
5...♘c6 6 ♗b5 ♗d6 7 dxc5
7 0-0 cxd4 8 ♘b3 ♘e7 9 ♘bxd4 0-0 10 c3 ♗g4 11 ♕a4 ♕d7! 12 ♗e3 ♖fe8 13 ♖fe1 ♗h5 14 ♗e2 ♖ad8= Ivanovic-Portisch, Niksic 1978
7...♗xc5 8 ♘b3 ♗d6 9 0-0 ♘e7 10 ♖e1
10 c3 0-0 11 ♘bd4 ♗g4 12 ♕a4 ♗h5 13 ♗g5 ♕c7 14 h3 a6 15 ♗d3 h6= Raitza-Uhlmann, Eggesin 1978

Diagram

10...0-0 11 h3
11 c3 ♗g4 12 ♗g5 h6 13 ♗h4 ♕c7 14 ♗g3 ♗xg3 15 hxg3 ♖ad8 16 ♕d3 ♗xf3 17 ♕xf3 ♕b6 18 ♗xc6 ♘xc6

33

19 ⮾ad1 ⮺a6! 20 ⮹c5 ⮺c4 21 ⮺e3
½-½ Geller-Vaganian, Lvov 1978
**11...a6 12 ⮗f1 ⮗f5 13 ⮹bd4 ⮗g6
14 c3 ⮾e8 15 ⮗g5 ⮺b6 16 ⮺b3 ⮺c7
17 ⮗xe7 ⮹xe7 18 ⮾ad1 ⮗c5 19
⮗d3** += Velimiroviz-Uhlmann, Niksic
1978

**1 e4 e6 2 d4 d5 3 ⮹d2 ⮹f6 4 e5
⮹fd7 5 f4**

5 ⮗d3 c5 6 c3 b6 (6...⮹c6 7 ⮹e2
[7 ⮺g4?! f5! 8 exf6? ⮹xf6 9 ⮺h4
e5!∓ Tomic-Farago, Dortmund 1978]
7...cxd4 8 cxd4 ⮺b6 9 ⮹f3 f6 10 exf6
⮹xf6 11 0-0 ⮗d6 12 ⮹g3!? 0-0 13
b3 ⮗d7 14 ⮗e3 ⮾ae8 15 ⮾c1 ⮺d8=
Pedersen-Hollsberg, Ribe 1978) 7
⮹h3 ⮗a6 8 ⮗xa6 ⮹xa6 9 0-0 ⮹c7
10 ⮾e1 N (10 ⮺g4 c4 11 ⮹f3 ⮹b8=
Pachman) 10...h6 11 ⮹f4 ⮺c8 12
c4! += Ivanovic-Andersson, Niksic
1978

5...c5 6 c3

6 ⮹df3 cxd4 7 ⮹xd4 ⮹c6 8 ⮹gf3
⮗e7 9 ⮗e3 0-0 10 ⮗d3 ⮹c5 11 0-0
⮹xd3 12 cxd3 ⮗c5 13 ⮺d2 ⮺b6 14
⮺f2 += Pavlov-Durao, Malaga 1978

Diagram

6...⮹c6 7 ⮹df3 ⮺a5

7...f5! 8 ⮗d3 ⮗e7 9 ⮹e2 ⮹f8 N (9...
0-0 10 h3 c4 11 ⮗c2 b5 12 ⮹g5 ⮹b6

13 g4 a5 14 ⮹g3 ⮾a7 15 h4±
Korchnoi-Larsen 1964) 10 h3 ⮗d7
11 ⮘f1 h5 12 g3 ⮺b6 13 ⮘g2 0-0-0∝
Lanka-Vitolins, Jurmala 1978

8 ⮺f2

8 ⮗e3 N cxd4 9 ⮹xd4 ⮹xd4 10
⮗xd4 ⮹b8 11 ⮹f3 ⮗d7 12 ⮗d3 ⮹c6
13 ⮗e3 g6 14 ⮺e2 ⮾c8 15 ⮺f2 ⮗e7
16 h4 += Martinovic-Roos, Bagneux
1978

8...⮗e7 9 g3!

9 ⮗d3 ⮺b6 10 ⮹e2 f6 11 exf6 ⮗xf6
12 ⮘g3 cxd4 13 cxd4 0-0 14 ⮾e1
e5!∓ Reshevsky-Vaganian, Skopje
1976

**9...b5 10 ⮗e3 b4 11 ⮹e2 ⮹b6 12
cxb4 ⮺xb4 13 b3 ⮗d7 14 ⮾c1 ⮗a6
15 ⮹c3 ⮗xf1 16 ⮾xf1 ⮾c8 17 ⮹a4
cxd4 18 ⮹xd4 ⮹db8 19 ⮘g2 0-0 20
⮹f3 ⮾fd8 21 ⮾f2 △ ⮾fc2**± Kagan-
Pasman, Israel Final 1978

King's Gambit

1 e4 e5 2 f4 exf4

a) 2...⮗c5 3 ⮹f3 d6 4 fxe5 (4 c3 ⮹f6
5 d4 exd4 6 cxd4 ⮗b6 7 ⮹c3 0-0 8
e5 dxe5 9 fxe5 ⮹d5 10 ⮗g5 ⮹xc3
N 11 bxc3 ⮺d5 12 ⮗d3 ⮹c6 13 0-0!?
⮹xe5 14 ⮹xe5 ⮺xe5∓ Arnason-
Pedersen, Groningen 1978; 10...f6
11 ⮗c4! c6 12 exf6 gxf6 13 ⮗h6 ⮾e8+
14 ⮘f2 += Suttles-Addison, USA

1965/6) 4...dxe5 5 c3 ♕e7?! N (5...
♗g4 6 ♕a4+! ♗d7 7 ♕c2 ♘c6 8 b4
♗d6 9 ♗c4 ♘f6 10 d3 ♕e7 11 0-0
0-0-0 12 a4 a5 13 b5 ♘b8 14 ♘bd2
♗g4 15 ♘b3± Bronstein-Panov,
Moscow 1947; 5...♘f6) 6 d4! exd4
7 cxd4 ♗b6 (7...♕xe4+ 8 ♔f2 ♗e7
9 ♘c3±) 8 ♘c3 ♗g4 9 ♕a4+ ♘d7
10 ♗g5! f6 11 ♗f4 ♘h6 12 0-0-0 ♘f7
13 ♘d5± Lutikov-Lanka, Jurmala
1978;
b) 2...d5 3 ♘c3 d4 4 ♘ce2 exf4 N
(4...♗g4 5 d3 ♗d6 6 fxe5 ♗xe5 7
♕d2! ♘c6 8 ♘f3 ♗xf3 9 gxf3 ♕h4+
10 ♔d1 f5 11 ♕g5!= Milner-Barry-
Keres, Margate 1937) 5 ♘f3 ♗c5 6
♘xf4 ♘f6 7 d3 0-0 8 ♗e2 ♘c6 9 ♘d2
♘e5 10 h3 a5 11 0-0 a4 =+ Reschke-
Walther, Eggesin 1978;
c) 2...d5 3 exd5 c6 4 ♘c3 exf4 5 ♘f3
cxd5 N (5...♘f6 6 d4 ♗d6 7 ♕e2+
♕e7 8 ♕xe7+ ♔xe7 9 ♘e5! +=
Tetenbaum-Estrin, Moscow 1959) 6
d4 ♘f6 7 ♗b5+ ♘c6 8 ♕e2+ ♗e7 9
♘e5 ♗d7 10 ♘xd7 ♕xd7 11 ♗xf4
0-0 =+ Durran-Sanz, Malaga 1978;
d) 2...d5 3 exd5 e4 4 d3 ♘f6 5 ♘c3?
(5 ♘d2!; 5 dxe4!) 5...♗b4 6 ♗d2 e3
7 ♗xe3 0-0 8 ♕f3 N (8 ♗e2 ♗xc3+
9 bxc3 ♘xd5 10 ♗d2 ♕f6 11 ♕c1
♖e8∓ Gruzman-Kimelfeld, Moscow
1966) 8...♖e8 9 ♗e2 ♗g4 10 ♕g3
♗xe2 11 ♘xe2 ♕e7 12 ♔f2 ♕xe3+
−+ Rohde-Brasket, New York 1977

3 ♘f3
3 ♘c3 ♗e7 N 4 ♗c4 d5 5 ♗xd5 c6 6
♗b3 ♗h4+ 7 ♔f1 ♘e7 8 ♘f3 ♘g6 9
♘xh4 ♕xh4 10 ♕e1 f3 11 ♕xh4
fxg2+ 12 ♔xg2 ♘xh4+ 13 ♔g3 ♘g6
14 ♖f1 += Barclay-O'Hare, Hallsberg
1977/78

3...d5
a) 3...♗e7 4 ♗c4 ♘f6 5 e5 ♘g4 6 d4?
(6 ♘c3) 6...d5 7 exd6 N (7 ♗d3 ♗h4+

8 ♔e2 ♘f2 9 ♕e1 ♘xd3 10 ♕xh4
♘xc1+ 11 ♖xc1 ♕xh4 12 ♘xh4 ♘c6
13 c3 0-0 14 ♔f2 f6 =+ Lutikov-
Estrin, USSR 1951) 7...♗xd6 8 ♕e2+
♕e7 9 ♕xe7+ ♔xe7 10 h3 ♘e3 11
♗xe3 fxe3 12 ♘c3 ♗g3+ 13 ♔e2 ♖e8∓
Durran-Durao, Malaga 1978;
b) 3...♗e7 4 ♘c3 ♗h4+ 5 ♔e2 d6 6
d4 ♗g4 7 ♗xf4 ♘c6 8 ♕d3 ♘ge7 N
9 ♔d2 ♗xf3 10 gxf3 ♕d7 11 ♖d1
0-0-0= Planinc-Ivkov, Jugoslavia Final
1978;
c) 3...♗e7 4 ♘c3 ♘f6 5 d4 d5 6 ♗d3
dxe4 7 ♘xe4 ♘xe4 8 ♗xe4 ♘d7 N
(8...♗d6 9 0-0 ♘d7 10 ♕d3 h6 11 c4
c5 12 b4 += Spassky-Najdorf, Varna
1962) 9 ♗xf4 ♘f6 10 ♗d3 ♗g4 11 c3
0-0= D.Riemsdyk-Ivkov, Sao Paulo
1978

4 exd5 ♘f6 5 ♗b5+ c6 6 dxc6 ♘xc6
6...bxc6 7 ♗c4 ♘d5 8 0-0 (8 ♘c3!
♗e7 9 0-0 0-0 10 d4 ♘b6 11 ♗d3
g5 12 ♘e2 ♗e6 13 b3± Korchnoi)
8...♗e7 N (8...♗d6 9 ♘c3 ♗e6 10
♘e4 ♗c7!=) 9 d4 0-0 10 ♗xd5 ♕xd5
11 ♗xf4 ♗g4 12 ♘bd2= Walther-
Kube, Eggesin 1978

**7 d4 ♗d6 8 0-0 0-0 9 ♘bd2 ♗g4
10 ♘c4**
10 c3 ♗c7 11 ♘c4 ♘e7 12 ♗a4 b5!?
13 ♗xb5 ♕d5 14 ♘a3 ♕h5 15 ♗d3
♘ed5∞ Kinlay-Nunn, England 1977

10...♗c7 11 ♗xc6
11 c3 ♘d5 12 ♕d3 Δ ♗xc6, ♘fe5 Korchnoi
11...bxc6 12 ♕d3 ♗xf3
12...♖e8
13 ♖xf3 ♘d5 14 ♗d2 g5? 15 ♖h3± Schubert-Panczyk, Groningen 1978

1 e4 e5 2 f4 exf4 3 ♗c4 ♘f6
3...f5 4 exf5 ♘f6 5 ♘c3 ♕e7+ 6 ♕e2 ♘c6 7 ♘f3 ♘b4 8 ♗b3 c6 9 d3 d5= Murei-Tatai, Beersheva 1978
4 ♘c3 c6
4...d5 5 exd5 ♗d6 6 ♕e2+ ♗e7 7 d4 0-0 8 ♘f3 c6 9 ♗xf4 cxd5 10 ♗b3 ♘c6 11 0-0 ♗g4 12 ♖ae1! += Bronstein-Klovan, Odessa 1974
5 d4
5 ♕f3 d5 6 exd5 ♗d6 7 h3?! 0-0 8 ♘ge2 g5! 9 0-0 b5! 10 ♗b3 b4∓ Szilagyi-I.Szabo, Hungary 1974
5...♗b4
5...d5 N 6 exd5 cxd5 7 ♗b5+ ♘c6 8 ♗xf4 ♗d6 9 ♘ge2 0-0 10 0-0 ♗g4 11 ♗g5 ♗e7 12 ♗a4 += Bronstein-Nogueiras, Jurmala 1978
6 ♗d3 N
6 e5 ♘e4! 7 ♕f3 d5 8 exd6 0-0 9 ♘e2 ♕h4+!∓ Korchnoi
6...d5 7 e5 ♗g4 8 ♘f3 ♘e4 9 0-0!? ♘xc3 10 bxc3 ♗xc3 11 ♖b1 ♗xd4+ 12 ♔h1 ♘d7 13 ♗xf4∞ Lutikov-Ermenkov, Jurmala 1978

Pirc

1 e4 g6 2 d4 d6
2...♗g7 3 ♘c3 c6 4 f4 d5 5 e5 h5 6 ♗e3 ♘h6 7 ♗e2 ♗g4 8 ♕d2 N ♗xe2 9 ♘cxe2 ♘a6 10 ♘f3 ♘c7 11 h3 ♕d7 12 g3 0-0-0 13 0-0-0 += Lederman-Keene, Beersheva 1978
3 ♘c3 ♗g7
3...♘f6 4 ♗g5 h6 5 ♗e3 c6 6 ♗e2 N

(6 f3 ♗g7 7 ♕d2 ♕a5 8 ♘ge2 b5 9 g3 ♘bd7 10 ♗g2 ♗b7 11 0-0 += Liberzon-Etruk, USSR 1968) 6...♗g7 7 ♘f3 ♕b6 8 0-0 ♕xb2?! 9 ♕d2 ♕a3 10 h3 ♕a5 11 a4 ♘bd7 12 ♗c4 0-0 13 ♗xh6 ±/+− Pribyl-Swic, Lodz 1978)
b) 3...♘f6 4 ♗g5 c6 5 ♕d2 b5 6 ♗d3 ♘bd7 7 f4 ♗g7 8 ♘f3 0-0 9 0-0 ♘b6 10 e5 ♘fd5 N (10...b4 11 ♘e2 ♘fd5 12 f5 c5 13 ♗h6± Soltis-Botterill, Graz, 1972) 11 ♘xd5 ♘xd5 12 f5! dxe5 13 fxg6 hxg6 14 ♘xe5 ♕d6 15 ♖ae1 ♗d7 16 c3 ♖ad8 17 ♗h6± Luczak-Pribyl, Lodz 1978
4 f4
a) 4 ♗e2 ♘f6 5 e5!? ♘fd7 6 exd6 cxd6 7 ♘f3 0-0 8 0-0 ♘f6 9 h3 d5 10 ♗d3 ♘c6 11 a3 ♗f5 12 ♖e1 += Murei-Keene, Beersheva 1978;
b) 4 ♘f3 ♘f6 5 ♗e2 0-0 6 0-0 ♗g4 7 ♗e3 ♘c6 8 ♕d2 e5 9 d5 ♘e7 10 ♖ad1 ♘d7 11 ♘e1 (11 ♘g5∓ Spassky-Parma, Havana 1966) 11...♗xe2 12 ♕xe2 f5 13 f4 exf4 14 ♗xf4 ♗xc3 15 bxc3 fxe4 16 ♕xe4 ♘c5 =+ Geller-Kuzmin, Lvov 1978
4...♘f6
a) 4...c6 5 ♗e3 ♕b6 6 ♕d2? ♕xb2 7 ♖b1 ♕a3 8 ♘f3 ♕a5 9 h3 e6 10 ♗d3 ♘e7 11 g4 b6 12 ♖g1 ♗a6∓ Schramm-Smejkal, Kiel 1978;
b) 4...♘c6 5 ♗e3 ♘f6 6 ♘f3 0-0 7 ♗d3 ♘g4 8 ♗g1 e5 9 dxe5 dxe5 10 h3 N ♘f6 11 fxe5 ♘d7 12 e6 fxe6 13 ♗e3 ♘de5 =+ Mortensen-Smejkal, Kiel 1978

Diagram

5 ♘f3 0-0
a) 5...c5 6 ♗b5+ ♘fd7?! 7 dxc5 N (7 ♗e3 0-0 8 ♕d2 a6 9 ♗xd7 ♘xd7 10 h4± Pupel-Kampenus, Riga 1958)

7...dxc5 8 e5 0-0 9 0-0 a6 10 &d3
b6 11 &e3 &b7 12 e6± Adorjan-
Pocuca, Osijek 1978;

b) 5...c5 6 dxc5 ♛a5 7 &d3 ♛xc5 8
♛e2 0-0 9 &e3 ♛a5 (9...♛c7 10 0-0
♘bd7 11 ♘b5 N ♛b8 12 c4 b6 13 ♘c3
&b7 14 ♖ae1 += Byrne-Christiansen,
USA Final 1978) 10 0-0 &g4 11 a3
♘c6 12 ♚h1 ♘d7 13 ♛e1 ♘c5 14 b4
♘xd3 15 cxd3 ♛d8= Ljubojevic-
Timman, Niksic 1978

6 &d3

a) 6 e5 dxe5 7 dxe5 ♛xd1+ 8 ♚xd1
♘h5 9 &c4! ♘c6 10 &e3!? (10 ♖f1! △
♚e1) 10...&g4 11 ♚e2 N &h6 (11...
g5!?; 11...♘a5! 12 &d3 f6!∓) 12 g3
g5 ∞/= Roos-Greenfeld, Herzlia 1978;
b) 6 &e2 ♘a6 7 0-0 (7 e5) 7...c5 8
♚h1 b6 9 e5 N (9 &d3 &b7 10 d5 ♘c7
=+ Pedersen-Hort, Athens 1969) 9...
♘e8 10 &e3 &b7 11 ♛d2 cxd4 12
&xd4 dxe5 13 fxe5 ♘ec7 △ ♘e6∓
L.Roos-Vadasz, Bagneux 1978

6...♘c6

6...♘a6 7 0-0 c5 8 d5 ♘b4! 9 &c4 e6
10 a3 (10 dxe6 &xe6 11 &xe6 fxe6 =+

Boleslavsky) 10...exd5 11 axb4 dxc4
12 bxc5 dxc5 13 e5 ♘d7 14 ♛d5 a6
15 ♘g5 ♛e7 16 ♘xf7? ♖xf7 17 e6 ♖f5
−+ Barclay-Wengholm, Hallsberg 1977/
78

7 0-0

7 e5 dxe5 8 fxe5 ♘g4 9 &e4 f6 10 h3
♘h6 11 &d5+ ♚h8 12 0-0 ♘f5 13 ♖e1
♘fxd4 14 ♘xd4 ♘xd4 15 ♛xd4 c6
N (15...e6 16 exf6 &xf6 17 ♛c5 exd5
18 &h6± Gligoric-Quinteros, Vinkovci
1970) 16 &f4 cxd5 17 e6 (+=
Quinteros) 17...♛a5 18 ♘xd5 ♖d8
19 c4 b5 20 ♛c5 &b7 21 ♘c7 +−
Hofmann-Muller, Eggesin 1978

7...&g4 8 &e3

8 e5 dxe5 9 dxe5 ♘d5 10 h3!? ♘xc3
11 bxc3 &f5 12 &e3 ♛d7 13 ♛e2 ♖ad8
14 ♖fd1 N ♛c8! 15 ♖ab1 b6 16 ♘d4
½-½ Weinstein-Benko, USA Final 1978

8...e5 9 dxe5 dxe5 10 h3 exf4 N
10...&xf3 11 ♛xf3 ♘d4 12 ♛f2±
Minev-Anagnastopoulos, Sofia 1967
**11 &xf4 &xf3 12 ♛xf3 ♘d7 13 ♖ad1
♘ce5 14 ♛g3 c6 15 ♚h1 ♛e7 =+**
D.Roos-Vadasz, Bagneux 1978

Kikinda 3-19.v.78

				1	2	3	4	5	6	7	8	9	0	1	2	3	4	5	6	
1	Spassov	GM	2450	x	½	½	1	½	½	½	1	½	1	1	1	1	1	1	1	12
2	Nemet	IM	2425	½	x	½	1	½	½	½	½	1	½	1	1	1	1	1	1	11½
3	Kirov	GM	2465	½	½	x	½	1	½	½	½	1	½	½	1	1	½	1	½	10
4	Lim Seang Hoo		2430	0	0	½	x	½	1	½	1	1	½	1	1	½	1	½	1	10
5	Popovic		2400	½	½	0	½	x	½	½	½	1	½	1	1	½	1	1	1	10
6	Farago	GM	2510	½	½	½	0	½	x	1	0	1	1	1	0	½	1	1	½	9
7	Bjelajac		2415	½	½	½	½	½	0	x	½	½	½	0	1	1	1	1	½	8½
8	A.Zapata		2355	0	½	½	0	½	1	½	x	0	½	½	½	1	½	1	1	8
9	S.Bouaziz	IM	2365	½	0	0	0	0	0	½	1	x	½	½	1	1	1	1	1	8
10	S.Popov		2335	0	½	½	½	½	0	½	½	½	x	1	½	½	½	½	1	7½
11	J.A.Gutierrez	IM	2380	0	0	½	0	0	0	1	½	½	0	x	½	1	1	½	1	6½
12	S.Knezevic		2300	0	0	0	0	0	1	0	½	0	½	½	x	½	1	½	1	5½
13	Telecki			0	0	0	½	½	½	0	0	0	½	0	½	x	½	1	½	4½
14	Ilicin			0	0	½	0	0	0	0	½	0	½	0	0	½	x	½	1	3½
15	Blazic			0	0	0	½	0	0	0	0	0	½	½	½	0	½	x	1	3½
16	V.Savic		2330	0	0	½	0	0	½	½	0	0	0	0	0	½	0	0	x	2

Category 5 (2360) GM = 11½ IM = 10

CSSR Final 7-26.v.78

		1	2	3	4	5	6	7	8	9	0	1	2	3	4	5	6	7	
1	Prandstetter	x	½	1	0	½	1	½	1	1	1	½	½	1	1	½	½	1	11½
2	Smejkal	½	x	0	½	½	1	½	½	0	1	½	1	½	1	1	1	1	10½
3	Sikora	0	1	x	0	½	0	1	1	1	1	½	½	1	ǀ0	1	½	1	10
4	Vokac	1	½	1	x	0	0	1	½	½	1	1	½	0	1	0	½	1	9½
5	Ambroz	½	½	½	1	x	½	0	½	0	1	½	½	1	½	1	½	½	9
6	Hausner	0	0	1	1	½	x	½	½	0	½	½	½	1	½	1	1	½	9
7	Ftacnik	½	½	0	0	1	½	x	½	1	0	½	½	½	1	½	1	1	9
8	Plachetka	0	½	0	½	½	½	½	x	½	½	1	1	1	½	½	½	1	9
9	Meduna	0	1	0	½	1	1	0	½	x	0	½	0	0	½	1	1	1	8
10	Neckar	0	0	0	0	0	½	1	½	1	x	½	½	1	½	1	1	½	8
11	Banas	½	½	½	0	½	½	½	0	½	½	x	½	½	½	0	1	1	7½
12	Augustin	½	0	½	½	½	½	½	0	1	½	½	x	0	½	½	½	½	7
13	Tichy	0	½	0	1	0	0	½	0	1	0	½	1	x	1	1	0	½	7
14	Lechtynsky	0	0	1	0	½	½	0	½	½	½	½	½	0	x	1	1	½	7
15	Gross	½	0	0	1	0	0	½	½	0	0	1	½	0	0	x	½	1	5½
16	I.Novak	½	0	½	½	½	0	0	½	0	0	0	½	1	0	½	x	1	5½
17	Jankovec	0	0	0	0	½	½	0	0	0	½	0	½	½	½	0	0	x	3
18	Jansa	½										½	0				½		

Swinoujscie 2-14.v.78

				1	2	3	4	5	6	7	8	9	0	1	2	
1	Vladimirov		2445	x	½	1	1	½	1	1	1	1	½	1	½	9
2	Rigo		2360	½	x	½	0	½	1	1	½	½	½	½	1	6½
3	Lipski		2310	0	½	x	1	½	½	0	1	½	½	1	1	6½
4	Maciejewski		2335	0	1	0	x	½	½	½	½	1	1	0	1	6
5	Iljic		2320	½	½	½	½	x	½	½	½	0	1	1	½	6
6	Pinkas		2360	0	0	½	½	½	x	1	0	½	½	1	1	5½
7	Witkowski	IM	2365	0	0	1	½	½	0	x	½	½	½	½	1	5
8	G.Szilagyi	IM	2365	0	½	0	½	½	1	½	x	½	½	½	½	5
9	A.Schneider		2345	0	½	½	0	1	½	½	½	x	½	½	½	5
10	Bernard		2360	½	½	½	0	0	½	½	½	½	x	½	0	4
11	Schinzel		2400	0	½	0	1	0	0	½	½	½	½	x	½	4
12	Goljak		2325	½	0	0	0	½	0	0	½	½	1	½	x	3½

Cauto 1978

				1	2	3	4	5	6	7	8	9	0	1	2	
1	Vilela	IM	2435	x	½	½	½	½	½	1	½	1	1	1	1	8
2	J.C.Diaz	IM	2340	½	x	1	1	½	0	1	1	1	0	½	1	7½
3	J.J.Hernandez		2350	½	0	x	½	½	1	½	1	½	1	1	½	7
4	A.Palacios		2370	½	0	½	x	1	½	½	½	½	½	½	½	5½
5	Remon		2365	½	½	½	0	x	1	1	0	0	1	½	½	5½
6	Sisniega		2455	½	1	0	½	0	x	0	½	1	0	½	1	5
7	L.Garcia		2325	0	0	½	½	0	1	x	½	1	½	½	½	5
8	L.Bueno		2350	½	0	0	½	1	½	½	x	0	1	1	0	5
9	Agudelo		2305	0	0	½	½	1	0	0	1	x	1	½	½	5
10	Frometa		2235	0	1	0	½	0	1	½	0	0	x	½	1	4½
11	C.Fernandez	IM	2345	0	½	0	½	½	½	½	0	½	½	x	½	4
12	Estevez	IM	2355	0	0	½	½	½	0	½	1	½	0	½	x	4

Category 5   IM = 7½

Russe 20.vi.-4.vii . 78

			1	2	3	4	5	6	7	8	9	0	1	2	3	
1	Grigorov	2335	x	½	1	½	½	1	½	1	½	0	1	½	1	8
2	P.Atanasov	2305	½	x	½	½	½	½	½	½	1	½	1	1	1	8
3	Merdinian	2315	0	½	x	1	½	½	½	½	½	1	1	1	1	8
4	Spiridonov	IM 2405	½	½	0	x	½	½	½	1	½	½	1	1	1	7½
5	Stanciu	2350	½	½	½	½	x	½	½	½	1	½	½	½	1	7
6	Szekely	2435	0	½	½	½	½	x	1	½	½	½	1	½	1	7
7	Kolarov	IM 2435	½	½	½	½	½	0	x	½	½	½	1	½	1	6½
8	Lukacs	IM 2460	0	½	½	0	½	½	½	x	½	1	½	1	1	6½
9	Ilievsky	2420	½	0	½	½	0	½	½	½	x	½	½	1	1	6
10	Mihaljcisin	IM 2385	1	½	0	½	½	½	½	0	½	x	½	½	½	5½
11	Gunev	2380	0	0	0	0	½	0	0	½	½	½	x	1	1	4
12	Filchev		½	0	0	0	½	½	½	0	0	½	0	x	½	3
13	Donev		0	0	0	0	0	0	0	0	0	½	0	½	x	1

Category 5 (2355)   IM = 8

Athens 16-31.v.78

			1	2	3	4	5	6	7	8	9	0	1	2	3	4	
1	Soos	IM 2425	x	½	½	½	½	½	1	½	½	1	½	1	1	1	9
2	Navarovszky	IM 2400	½	x	½	1	1	1	½	0	½	½	½	1	½	½	8
3	Geszosz	2385	½	½	x	½	½	½	1	½	1	1	½	½	0	1	8
4	Skalkotas	2285	½	0	½	x	½	½	1	½	½	1	1	0	1	1	8
5	Ugrinovic	2365	½	0	½	½	x	½	1	½	1	½	½	1	½	1	8
6	Minev	IM 2390	½	0	½	½	½	x	0	0	1	1	½	1	1	1	7½
7	Kokkinos		0	½	0	0	0	1	x	1	0	1	1	1	1	1	7½
8	Makropoulos	2345	½	1	½	½	½	1	0	x	1	0	0	0	1	1	7
9	Grigoriu	IM 2215	½	½	0	½	0	0	1	0	x	½	½	1	½	1	6
10	Skempris	2300	0	½	0	0	½	0	0	1	½	x	½	1	½	1	5½
11	Trikaliotis	2245	½	½	½	0	½	½	0	1	½	½	x	0	½	0	5
12	Balaskas	2235	0	0	½	1	0	0	0	1	0	0	1	x	½	0	4
13	Liverios	2230	0	½	1	0	½	0	0	0	½	½	½	½	x	0	4
14	Paoli	IM 2280	0	½	0	0	0	0	0	0	0	0	1	1	1	x	3½

Category 3 (2307)   IM = 9½

London 16-26.vii.78

				1	2	3	4	5	6	7	8	9	0	
1	Speelman		2410	x	½	½	1	½	½	1	1	1	1	7
2	Botterill		2400	½	x	½	½	1	½	1	½	½	1	6
3	Kraidman	GM	2455	½	½	x	0	1	1	0	1	0	1	5
4	Wade	IM	2335	0	½	1	x	1	½	½	1	0	½	5
5	Goodman		2320	½	0	0	0	x	0	1	1	1	1	4½
6	de Silva	IM	2350	½	½	0	½	1	x	0	0	1	½	4
7	Plaskett		2410	0	0	1	½	0	1	x	1	0	½	4
8	Hodgson		2265	0	½	0	0	0	1	0	x	1	1	3½
9	P.Littlewood		2345	0	½	1	1	0	0	1	0	x	0	3½
10	Durao	IM	2315	0	0	0	½	0	½	½	0	1	x	2½

Category 5 (2360)   IM = 6

Wroclaw 8-24.v.78

				1	2	3	4	5	6	7	8	9	0	1	2	3	
1	Cvetkovic		2390	x	½	½	1	½	½	½	½	½	1	1	1	1	8½
2	Deze	IM	2395	½	x	½	0	½	1	½	1	1	1	1	0	1	8
3	Gonsior		2375	½	½	x	½	1	½	½	0	1	1	0	1	1	7½
4	Grabczewski	IM	2375	0	1	½	x	½	0	½	1	½	½	1	1	1	7½
5	Gliksman	IM	2340	½	½	0	½	x	½	½	1	½	½	1	1	1	7½
6	Bukal	IM	2410	½	0	½	1	½	x	½	1	0	0	½	½	1	6
7	Mititelu		2395	½	½	½	½	½	½	x	0	½	½	½	½	1	6
8	Kubien		2300	½	0	1	0	0	0	1	x	1	½	½	1	0	5½
9	Onat	IM	2335	½	0	0	½	½	1	½	0	x	1	½	1	0	5½
10	Akvist		2335	0	0	0	½	½	1	½	½	0	x	1	0	½	4½
11	F.Bujupi		2260	0	0	1	0	0	½	½	½	½	0	x	1	½	4½
12	Jasnikowski		2335	0	1	0	0	0	½	½	0	0	1	0	x	½	3½
13	Hansson		2345	0	0	0	0	0	0	0	1	1	½	½	½	x	3½

Bagneux vii.78

				1	2	3	4	5	6	7	8	9	0	1	2	3	4	
1	Vadasz	GM	2505	x	½	0	½	1	½	1	1	1	½	1	1	½	1	9½
2	Ghitescu	IM	2450	½	x	1	½	0	½	1	1	½	1	½	½	½	½	8
3	Haik	IM	2425	1	0	x	0	0	½	1	1	1	½	1	½	1	½	8
4	Ostojic	GM	2420	½	½	1	x	1	0	0	½	½	½	½	1	1	1	8
5	Peters		2430	0	1	1	0	x	1	½	½	0	1	1	1	0	0	7
6	Pytel	IM	2390	½	½	½	1	0	x	0	½	1	½	½	½	½	1	7
7	Preissmann		2320	0	0	0	1	½	1	x	½	1	½	½	½	½	1	7
8	Martinovic	IM	2460	0	0	0	½	½	½	½	x	1	½	½	1	1	1	7
9	Seret		2350	0	½	0	½	1	0	0	0	x	½	1	1	½	1	6
10	Schmidt	GM	2505	½	0	½	½	0	½	½	½	½	x	½	0	1	½	5½
11	D.Roos			0	½	0	½	0	½	½	½	0	½	x	½	1	1	5½
12	L.Roos			0	½	½	0	0	½	½	0	0	1	½	x	1	0	4½
13	Giffard		2365	½	½	0	0	1	½	½	0	½	0	0	0	x	½	4
14	Santo-Roman			0	½	½	0	1	0	0	0	0	0	½	0	1	½	x	4

Category 5   GM = 10   IM = 8½

Subotica 27.v.11.vi.78

				1	2	3	4	5	6	7	8	9	0	1	2	3	4	
1	Vadasz	GM	2505	x	½	1	½	½	½	½	½	1	1	1	1	1	½	9½
2	Spassov	GM	2450	½	x	0	1	½	1	½	½	½	1	1	½	1	0	8
3	Todorcevic	IM	2435	0	1	x	½	½	0	1	0	½	1	½	1	1	½	7½
4	Masic	IM	2375	½	0	½	x	½	1	½	½	½	1	½	½	½	½	7
5	Szegi		2240	½	½	½	½	x	0	½	½	½	1	½	1	½	½	7
6	Honfi	IM	2420	½	0	1	0	1	x	1	1	1	0	0	½	0	½	6½
7	Marjanovic	IM	2450	½	½	0	½	½	0	x	½	½	½	½	½	1	1	6½
8	Piasetski	IM	2440	½	½	1	½	½	0	½	x	0	½	1	½	0	1	6½
9	Sines			0	½	½	½	½	0	½	1	x	0	1	1	0	1	6½
10	Rajcevic	GM	2450	0	0	0	0	0	1	½	½	1	x	½	½	1	1	6
11	Karadzic		2340	0	0	½	½	½	1	½	0	0	½	x	½	1	½	5½
12	Bjelajac		2445	0	½	0	½	0	½	½	½	0	½	½	x	1	½	5
13	T.Horvath		2410	0	0	0	½	½	1	0	1	1	0	0	0	x	1	5
14	Galic			½	1	½	½	½	½	0	0	0	0	½	½	0	x	4½

Category 6 (2381)   GM = 9½   IM = 8

Decin 1 9-27.vi.78

			1	2	3	4	5	6	7	8	9	0	1	2	3	4	5	6	
1	Barczay	GM	2465	x	1	½	½	½	½	½	½	½	½	1	½	1	1	1	½	10
2	Vilela	IM	2435	0	x	½	1	½	½	½	½	1	½	½	1	½	1	1	1	10
3	Meduna		2425	½	½	x	½	1	½	½	½	0	1	½	½	1	½	1	1	9½
4	Timoshenko	IM	2530	½	0	½	x	0	1	1	1	½	½	1	½	1	½	1	½	9½
5	Lanc		2375	½	½	0	1	x	½	½	½	1	½	½	½	1	0	½	½	8
6	Skrobek		2460	½	½	½	0	½	x	½	½	½	½	½	1	0	1	½	1	8
7	Pritchett	IM	2405	½	½	½	0	½	½	x	0	1	½	½	1	½	½	½	½	7½
8	Peev	IM	2440	½	½	½	0	½	½	1	x	0	½	0	½	1	1	½	½	7½
9	L.Kovacs	IM	2400	½	0	1	½	0	½	0	1	x	½	0	1	0	½	1	1	7½
10	Augustin	IM	2430	½	½	0	½	½	½	½	½	½	x	½	½	½	½	½	½	7
11	Trapl	IM	2390	0	½	½	0	½	½	½	1	1	½	x	½	0	½	½	½	7
12	Nicevski	IM	2425	½	0	½	½	½	0	0	½	0	½	½	x	½	1	1	1	7
13	Lechtynsky	IM	2420	0	½	0	0	0	1	½	0	1	½	1	½	x	0	½	½	6
14	Pribyl	IM	2455	0	0	½	½	1	0	½	0	½	½	½	0	1	x	½	½	6
15	Grigorian		2500	0	0	0	0	½	½	½	½	0	½	½	0	½	½	x	1	5
16	Prandstetter		2405	½	0	0	½	½	0	½	½	0	½	½	0	½	½	0	x	4½

Category 8 (2430)   IM = 8

Decin 2 9-27.vi.78

			1	2	3	4	5	6	7	8	9	0	1	2	3	4	5	
1	Hausner		2365	x	½	½	0	½	0	½	1	1	1	1	1	½	1	1	9½
2	Gross		2345	½	x	1	1	½	0	1	½	½	½	1	0	½	1	1	9
3	Casper		2315	½	0	x	0	½	½	1	1	1	1	½	1	½	½	1	9
4	Mokry		2310	1	0	1	x	½	1	0	0	½	½	½	1	1	1	1	9
5	Liebert	IM	2420	½	½	½	½	x	1	½	1	½	0	0	½	1	1	1	8½
6	Lukov		2330	1	1	½	0	0	x	1	0	0	1	½	½	1	1	1	8½
7	Drvota		2405	½	0	0	1	½	0	x	1	0	1	1	½	1	1	1	8½
8	Perenyi		2295	0	½	0	1	0	1	0	x	0	½	1	1	1	1	1	8
9	A.Adamski		2365	0	½	0	½	½	1	1	1	x	½	0	½	0	1	½	7
10	Tabor		2370	0	½	0	½	1	0	0	½	½	x	1	0	1	1	1	7
11	Szymczak	IM	2390	0	0	½	½	1	½	0	0	1	0	x	1	1	½	½	6½
12	Jankovec		2370	0	1	0	0	½	½	½	0	½	1	0	x	1	0	½	5½
13	Sejkora		2205	½	½	½	0	0	0	0	0	1	0	0	0	x	½	½	3½
14	Sorm			0	0	½	0	0	0	0	0	0	0	½	1	½	x	1	3½
15	Blatny		2325	0	0	0	0	0	0	0	0	½	0	½	½	½	0	x	2

43

Pernik vii.78

			1	2	3	4	5	6	7	8	9	0	1	2	3	4	5	6	
1 Suba	IM	2430	x	0	½	½	½	½	½	½	1	1	1	½	1	1	1	1	10½
2 Govedarica		2405	1	x	1	½	½	0	½	½	½	½	½	½	½	1	1	1	9½
3 Pinter	IM	2430	½	0	x	½	0	½	½	½	½	½	1	1	1	1	1	1	9½
4 Peev	IM	2420	½	½	½	x	½	½	1	0	½	1	½	½	½	1	½	1	9
5 Radulov	GM	2490	½	½	1	½	x	½	½	½	½	½	½	½	½	½	1	1	9
6 Tseitlin		2510	½	1	½	½	½	x	0	1	½	0	½	1	½	1	1	½	9
7 Ghinda		2445	½	½	½	0	½	1	x	½	½	½	0	1	½	1	1	1	9
8 Spassov	GM	2450	½	½	½	1	½	0	½	x	½	1	½	½	½	½	½	1	8½
9 L.Popov	IM	2435	0	½	½	½	½	½	½	½	x	½	½	½	½	1	1	1	8½
10 Inkiov	IM	2450	0	½	½	0	½	1	½	0	½	x	1	½	½	1	1	½	8
11 Bjelajac		2415	0	½	0	½	½	½	1	½	½	0	x	½	½	1	½	1	7½
12 Minev	IM	2370	½*	½	0	½	½	0	0	½	½	½	½	x	½	½	½	1	6½
13 Kirov	GM	2465	0	½	0	½	½	½	½	½	½	½	½	½	x	½	½	0	6
14 Pernishki		2245	0	0	0	0	½	0	0	½	0	0	0	½	½	x	1	1	4
15 V.Antonov		2345	0	0	0	½	0	0	0	½	0	0	½	½	½	0	x	1	3½
16 Biljap		2230	0	0	0	0	0	½	0	0	0	½	0	0	1	0	0	x	2

Category 7 (2410) GM = 10½ IM = 9

Penang 5-22.vi.78

			1	2	3	4	5	6	7	8	9	0	1	2	3	4	5	6	
1 Shirazi		2285	x	½	½	½	½	½	½	1	1	1	1	1	1	1	1	0	11
2 Torre	GM	2490	½	x	½	½	½	1	½	1	1	1	½	0	1	1	1	1	11
3 Mascarinas		2355	½	½	x	½	½	½	1	½	1	1	½	½	1	1	1	1	11
4 Sharif	IM	2380	½	½	½	x	½	½	½	½	1	1	1	1	½	1	1	1	11
5 Chandler	IM	2390	½	½	½	½	x	½	½	½	½	1	1	1	1	0	1	1	10
6 Ardijansjah	IM	2330	½	0	½	½	½	x	½	½	½	0	1	1	1	1	1	1	9½
7 O'Kelly	GM	2460	½	½	0	½	½	½	x	½	1	½	0	1	0	1	1	1	8½
8 Bachtiar		2335	0	0	½	½	½	½	½	x	1	1	1	½	½	½	½	1	8½
9 Aaron	IM	2295	0	0	0	0	0	½	½	0	0	x	1	½	½	1	1	1	7
10 Chiong		2400	0	0	0	0	0	1	½	0	0	x	0	1	1	1	1	1	6½
11 Rafiq Khan			0	½	½	0	0	0	1	0	½	1	x	0	0	½	1	1	6
12 Wotulo	IM	2245	0	1	½	0	0	0	0	½	½	0	1	x	1	0	½	½	5½
13 Laird			0	0	0	½	0	0	1	½	0	0	1	0	x	1	0	1	5
14 Liew			0	0	0	0	1	0	0	½	0	0	½	1	0	x	½	½	4
15 Hon			0	0	0	0	0	0	0	½	0	0	0	½	1	½	x	½	3
16 B.H. Tan			1	0	0	0	0	0	0	0	0	0	0	½	0	½	½	x	2½

Category 3 IM = 10½

44

Titovo Uzice 25.vi.-10.vii.78

				1	2	3	4	5	6	7	8	9	0	1	2	3	4	
1	Ljubojevic	GM	2605	x	½	0	1	½	½	1	1	½	1	1	1	1	1	10
2	Smejkal	GM	2555	½	x	1	½	½	½	½	½	½	1	½	1	1	1	9
3	Rajkovic	GM	2490	1	0	x	½	½	½	½	½	½	½	½	1	1	1	8
4	Ermenkov	GM	2520	0	½	½	x	0	½	½	1	½	½	1	1	1	½	7½
5	Andersson	GM	2545	½	½	½	1	x	½	½	0	0	½	½	1	1	½	7
6	Bagirov	IM	2505	½	½	½	½	½	x	0	1	1	½	1	0	½	½	7
7	Kurajica	GM	2530	0	½	½	½	½	1	x	½	½	½	½	1	½	½	7
8	Kovacevic	GM	2505	0	½	½	0	1	0	½	x	½	½	½	1	1	½	6½
9	Matulovic	GM	2525	½	½	½	½	1	0	½	½	x	½	½	½	½	½	6½
10	Tringov	GM	2480	0	0	½	½	½	½	½	½	½	x	½	1	½	1	6½
11	Jansa	GM	2505	0	½	½	0	½	0	½	½	½	½	x	1	½	½	5½
12	Jovcic		2330	0	0	0	0	0	1	0	0	0	½	0	0	x	1	1	3½
13	Radoicic			0	0	0	0	0	½	½	0	½	½	½	0	x	1	3½
14	Todorcevic	IM	2425	0	0	0	½	½	½	½	½	½	0	½	0	0	x	3½

Category 10 (2480) GM = 8 IM = 6½

Esbjerg vi.-vii.78

				1	2	3	4	5	6	7	8	9	0	1	2	3	4	
1	Larsen	GM	2620	x	½	1	0	½	1	1	1	1	1	1	1	1	1	11
2	Sigurjonsson	GM	2500	½	x	½	0	1	½	1	½	1	1	½	1	1	½	9
3	Westerinen	GM	2450	0	½	x	½	1	1	½	½	1	0	½	½	1	1	8
4	Mestel	IM	2450	1	1	½	x	½	0	0	1	½	½	1	0	½	1	7½
5	Forintos	GM	2435	½	0	0	½	x	½	1	1	0	1	1	½	1	0	7
6	Sloth		2390	0	½	0	1	½	x	½	½	½	1	½	½	1	½	7
7	Brinck-Claussen		2385	0	0	½	1	0	½	x	½	1	½	½	1	½	½	6½
8	Rath		2405	0	½	½	0	0	½	½	x	½	0	1	1	½	1	6
9	Ogaard	IM	2435	0	0	0	½	1	½	0	½	x	½	½	½	1	1	6
10	L.A.Schneider	IM	2430	0	0	1	½	0	0	½	1	½	x	0	1	0	1	5½
11	Rodgaard		2320	0	½	½	0	0	½	½	0	½	1	x	½	½	½	5
12	J.O.Fries Nielsen		2300	0	0	½	1	½	½	0	0	½	0	½	x	½	1	5
13	Hoi		2340	0	0	0	½	0	0	½	½	0	1	½	½	x	½	4
14	J.Kristiansen		2395	0	½	0	0	1	½	½	0	0	0	½	0	½	x	3½

Category (2381) GM = 9½ IM = 8

IBM 1 12-29.vii.78   1 2 3 4 5 6 7 8 9 0 1 2 3 4

				1	2	3	4	5	6	7	8	9	0	1	2	3	4	
1	Timman	GM	2585	x	1	½	½	1	½	1	0	1	1	½	½	1	1	9½
2	Ribli	GM	2585	0	x	1	1	½	½	1	1	1	½	0	½	1	½	8½
3	Djindjihashvili	GM	2550	½	0	x	½	½	½	1	1	½	½	½	½	1	½	7½
4	Hort	GM	2620	½	0	½	x	½	½	0	½	½	½	1	1	1	1	7½
5	Pfleger	GM	2530	0	½	½	½	x	½	1	½	1	½	½	½	1	½	7½
6	Andersson	GM	2545	½	½	½	½	½	x	½	½	½	1	½	½	0	1	7
7	Romanishin	GM	2610	0	0	0	1	0	½	x	1	½	1	½	½	1	1	7
8	Ljubojevic	GM	2605	1	0	0	½	½	½	0	x	1	1	½	1	0	½	6½
9	Langeweg	IM	2450	0	0	½	½	0	½	½	0	x	1	½	½	1	1	6
10	Adorjan	GM	2515	0	½	½	½	½	0	0	0	0	x	1	½	1	1	5½
11	Miles	GM	2565	½	1	½	0	½	½	½	½	½	0	x	½	0	½	5½
12	Ree	IM	2500	½	½	½	0	½	½	½	0	½	½	½	x	½	0	5
13	Nikolac	IM	2495	0	0	0	0	0	1	0	1	0	0	1	½	x	1	4½
14	Browne	GM	2550	0	½	½	0	½	0	0	½	0	0	½	1	0	x	3½

Cateogry 12 (2550)   GM = 7

IBM 2 12-29.vii.78   1 2 3 4 5 6 7 8 9 0 1 2 3 4

				1	2	3	4	5	6	7	8	9	0	1	2	3	4	
1	Yusupov	IM	2450	x	½	½	½	½	0	½	1	1	1	1	1	1	1	9½
2	L.Christiansen	GM	2490	½	x	½	0	1	½	0	1	0	1	1	1	1	1	8½
3	Ligterink	IM	2440	½	½	x	½	½	1	½	1	1	1	1	0	½	0	8
4	van Wijgerden		2435	½	1	½	x	1	½	½	½	½	0	½	1	½	1	8
5	Kirov	GM	2465	½	0	½	0	x	½	1	½	0	1	½	½	1	1	7
6	Hartoch	IM	2405	1	½	0	½	½	x	0	½	1	½	½	1	0	½	6½
7	Bohm	IM	2410	½	1	½	½	0	1	x	0	1	0	½	½	0	1	6½
8	Borm		2260	0	0	0	½	½	½	1	x	0	½	½	1	1	1	6½
9	Balshan		2415	0	1	0	½	1	0	0	1	x	0	½	½	1	½	6
10	v.d.Sterren		2400	0	0	0	1	0	½	1	½	1	x	1	0	½	½	6
11	A.Rodriguez	GM	2495	0	0	0	½	½	½	½	½	½	0	x	1	1	½	5½
12	Janosevic	GM	2455	0	0	1	0	½	0	½	0	½	1	0	x	1	½	5
13	Taulbut	IM	2405	0	0	½	½	0	1	1	0	0	½	0	0	x	1	4½
14	de Roode			0	0	1	0	0	½	0	0	½	½	½	½	0	x	3½

Category 7 (2409)   GM = 9½   IM = 7½

Lublin 14-30.vii.78

			1	2	3	4	5	6	7	8	9	0	1	2	3	4	5	6	
1	A.Sakharov	IM	2460	x	½	½	½	½	1	½	½	1	½	½	1	0	1	1	1	10
2	Knezevic	GM	2505	½	x	½	½	½	½	½	1	½	½	½	1	1	1	½	1	10
3	Adamski	IM	2470	½	½	x	½	½	½	½	½	1	½	½	½	½	1	1	1	9½
4	Szekely	IM	2440	½	½	½	x	½	½	½	½	½	½	½	½	1	½	1	1	9
5	Commons	IM	2485	½	½	½	½	x	0	½	½	0	1	1	½	1	½	1	1	9
6	Razuvaev	GM	2460	0	½	½	½	1	x	½	½	½	0	½	1	½	1	1	1	9
7	Estrin	IM	2430	½	½	½	½	½	½	x	0	½	1	1	1	½	½	½	½	8½
8	Sikora		2415	½	0	½	½	½	½	1	x	0	1	½	½	½	½	1	½	8
9	Doda	IM	2405	0	½	0	½	1	½	½	1	x	0	1	½	½	½	½	1	8
10	Arapovic		2415	½	½	½	½	0	1	0	0	1	x	0	0	1	1	1	½	7½
11	Nunn	IM	2440	½	½	½	½	0	½	0	½	0	1	x	½	½	½	1	1	7½
12	Skrobek		2460	0	0	½	½	½	0	0	½	½	1	½	x	1	1	½	1	7½
13	Jamroz		2260	1	0	½	0	0	½	½	½	½	0	½	0	x	½	½	1	6
14	Mrdja		2385	0	0	0	½	½	0	½	½	½	0	½	0	½	x	0	1	4½
15	Lipski		2310	0	½	0	0	0	0	½	0	½	0	0	½	½	1	x	½	4
16	Paoli	IM	2280	0	0	0	0	0	0	½	½	0	½	0	0	0	0	½	x	2

Category 8 (2414)   IM = 9

Budapest 12-29.viii.78

			1	2	3	4	5	6	7	8	9	0	1	2	3	4	5	6	
1	Nunn	IM	2440	x	½	½	½	1	1	½	1	0	1	1	½	1	½	0	1	10
2	Csom	GM	2510	½	x	½	1	½	1	½	½	1	½	½	½	½	½	1	½	9½
3	Adorjan	GM	2515	½	½	x	0	½	1	1	½	1	½	½	½	½	½	½	1	9
4	Kuzmin	GM	2560	½	0	1	x	½	1	½	½	½	½	0	½	1	½	1	1	9
5	Vadasz	GM	2505	0	½	½	½	x	0	1	½	½	½	½	1	½	½	1	1	8½
6	Mednis	IM	2460	0	0	0	0	1	x	1	½	½	1	½	½	½	1	1	1	8½
7	Jansa	GM	2505	½	½	0	½	0	0	x	½	½	½	½	½	1	1	1	1	8
8	Malich	GM	2535	0	½	½	½	½	½	½	x	½	½	½	1	½	1	½	½	8
9	Barczay	GM	2465	1	0	0	½	½	½	½	½	x	½	1	½	½	0	1	½	7½
10	Groszpeter		2230	0	½	½	½	½	0	½	½	½	x	1	½	0	1	½	1	7½
11	Lukacs	IM	2460	0	½	½	1	½	½	½	½	0	0	x	½	½	½	½	1	7
12	Ree	IM	2500	½	½	½	½	0	½	½	0	½	½	½	x	½	½	1	½	7
13	F.Portisch	IM	2450	0	½	½	0	½	½	0	½	½	1	½	½	x	1	0	½	6½
14	Regan		2430	½	½	½	½	½	0	0	0	1	0	½	½	0	x	1	0	5½
15	J.Fernandez	IM	2370	1	0	½	0	0	0	0	½	0	½	½	0	1	0	x	1	5
16	Hardicsay		2355	0	½	0	0	0	0	0	½	½	0	0	½	½	1	0	x	3½

Category 9 (2455)   GM = 10   IM = 7½

Cuenca Zonal 24.vii.-9.viii.78

				1	2	3	4	5	6	7	8	9	0	1	2	3	
1	Guil.Garcia	GM	2535	x	½	1	0	1	1	1	½	1	1	1	1	1	10
2	A.Fernandez		2285	½	x	½	½	0	1	1	1	½	½	1	1	1	8½
3	Palacios		2370	0	½	x	½	½	1	0	1	1	1	½	1	1	8
4	Escondrillas		2265	1	½	½	x	½	½	½	1	½	½	½	0	1	7
5	Abreu			0	1	½	½	x	0	½	1	½	½	1	½	1	7
6	Pazos		2240	0	0	0	½	1	x	1	½	½	1	1	1	½	7
7	J.Gutierrez	IM	2380	0	0	1	½	½	0	x	1	1	½	½	1	0	6
8	Veliz		2330	½	0	0	0	0	½	0	x	½	1	1	1	1	5½
9	Nieves		2210	0	½	0	½	½	½	0	½	x	0	1	½	1	5
10	Freile		2260	0	½	0	½	½	0	½	0	1	x	½	0	1	4½
11	Vintimilla		2220	0	0	½	½	0	0	½	0	0	½	x	1	1	4
12	Batres			0	0	0	1	½	0	0	0	½	1	0	x	½	3½
13	Wong			0	0	0	0	0	½	1	0	0	0	0	½	x	2

Ibarra Zonal 24.vii.-9.viii.78

				1	2	3	4	5	6	7	8	9	0	1	2	3	
1	R.Hernandez	IM	2465	x	½	½	½	0	½	½	1	1	1	1	1	1	8½
2	Remon		2365	½	x	1	1	½	½	½	1	½	0	1	1	½	8
3	Ostos		2275	½	0	x	½	0	1	1	½	1	½	1	1	1	8
4	Sisniega		2455	½	0	½	x	0	½	½	1	1	1	1	1	1	8
5	Vantilbury			1	½	1	1	x	½	0	0	1	½	½	½	½	7
6	E.Gonzalez		2205	½	½	0	½	½	x	1	½	½	0	0	1	1	6
7	Guild.Garcia		2365	½	½	0	½	1	0	x	0	½	1	1	0	1	6
8	A.Velasquez			0	0	½	0	1	½	1	x	0	1	½	½	1	6
9	M.Rodriguez		2230	0	½	0	0	0	½	½	1	x	1	1	½	1	6
10	Broomes			0	1	½	0	½	1	0	0	0	x	0	½	1	4½
11	Galarza		2260	0	0	0	0	½	1	0	½	0	1	x	½	1	4½
12	Freyre			0	0	0	0	½	0	1	½	½	½	½	x	½	4
13	L.Smith			0	½	0	0	½	0	0	0	0	0	0	½	x	1½

Polanica Zdroj 5-24.viii.78

			1	2	3	4	5	6	7	8	9	0	1	2	3	4	5	
1	M.Tseitlin		2480	x	0	½	½	½	½	½	½	1	½	1	1	1	1	1	9½
2	Andersson	GM	2545	1	x	½	½	½	½	1	½	½	1	½	0	1	½	1	9
3	Dorfman	IM	2550	½	½	x	½	½	½	1	½	1	1	½	½	½	½	1	9
4	Diesen	IM	2440	½	½	½	x	½	½	½	1	½	½	½	1	1	½	1	9
5	Farago	GM	2510	½	½	½	½	x	½	0	½	½	1	1	1	1	0	1	8½
6	Ghinda	IM	2445	½	½	½	½	½	x	½	½	½	1	½	½	½	1	½	8
7	S.Garcia	GM	2435	½	0	0	½	1	½	x	½	½	0	1	1	1	1	½	8
8	Knezevic	GM	2505	½	½	½	0	½	½	½	x	½	½	½	½	1	½	½	7
9	Schmidt	GM	2505	0	½	0	½	½	½	½	½	x	½	½	½	½	½	½	6
10	Swic		2430	½	0	0	½	0	0	1	½	½	x	½	½	0	1	1	6
11	Bielczyk		2380	0	½	½	½	0	½	0	½	½	½	x	1	½	0	½	5½
12	Kuligowski		2310	0	1	½	0	0	½	0	½	½	½	0	x	½	1	½	5½
13	Sznapik	IM	2430	0	0	½	0	0	½	0	0	½	1	½	½	x	1	1	5½
14	Bonsch	IM	2490	0	½	½	½	1	0	0	½	½	0	1	0	0	x	0	4½
15	Bednarski	IM	2365	0	0	0	0	0	½	½	½	½	0	½	½	0	1	x	4

Category 9 (2452) GM = 9 IM = 7

Vilnius 11.vii.-2.viii.78

			1	2	3	4	5	6	7	8	9	0	1	2	3	4	5	6	
1	Tukmakov	GM	2570	x	½	½	1	½	½	½	½	1	½	½	½	1	1	1	1	10½
2	Petrosian	GM	2620	½	x	1	0	½	½	½	1	½	½	1	1	1	½	½	1	10
3	Gulko	GM	2565	½	0	x	1	0	1	½	½	1	1	1	1	½	½	0	1	9½
4	Beljavsky	GM	2530	0	1	0	x	½	½	½	1	0	½	½	½	1	1	1	1	9
5	Lechtynsky	IM	2420	½	½	1	½	x	½	½	½	½	½	½	1	0	1	½	1	9
6	Dorfman	IM	2550	½	½	0	½	½	x	½	½	½	½	1	½	½	½	1	½	8
7	Csom	GM	2510	½	½	½	½	½	½	x	0	½	½	0	1	½	½	1	1	8
8	L.Espig	IM	2470	½	0	½	0	½	½	1	x	½	½	½	½	1	½	1	½	8
9	Reshevsky	GM	2490	0	½	0	1	½	½	½	½	x	½	1	1	0	½	½	½	7½
10	Dvoretsky	IM	2525	½	½	0	½	½	½	½	½	½	x	1	0	0	½	1	½	7
11	Lebredo	IM	2385	½	0	0	½	½	0	1	½	0	0	x	1	1	0	1	½	6½
12	Kaiszauri	IM	2410	½	0	0	½	0	½	0	½	0	1	0	x	1	1	1	0	6
13	Peshina		2340	0	0	½	0	1	½	½	0	1	1	0	0	x	½	0	1	6
14	Mikenas	IM	2410	0	½	½	0	0	½	½	½	½	½	1	0	½	x	0	½	5½
15	Damjanovic	GM	2455	0	½	1	0	½	0	0	0	½	0	0	0	1	1	x	½	5
16	Chiburdanidze		2340	0	0	0	0	0	½	0	½	½	½	½	1	0	½	½	x	4½

Category 9 (2474) GM = 10 IM = 7½

Bajmok 22.vii.-8.viii.78   1 2 3 4 5 6 7 8 9 0 1 2 3 4 5 6

			1	2	3	4	5	6	7	8	9	0	1	2	3	4	5	6	
1	Matulovic	GM	2525	x	0	1	1	½	1	1	0	½	½	½	1	½	1	1	½	10
2	Barczay	GM	2465	1	x	0	½	½	1	½	½	½	½	½	½	1	1	1	1	10
3	Vukic	GM	2480	0	1	x	½	½	0	½	½	½	1	1	½	½	1	1	1	9½
4	Tringov	GM	2480	0	½	½	x	½	½	½	½	½	½	½	1	1	½	1	1	9
5	Padevsky	GM	2455	½	½	½	½	x	½	½	½	0	1	½	½	½	1	1	1	9
6	Honfi	IM	2420	0	0	1	½	½	x	½	1	1	½	1	1	1	0	0	1	9
7	Deze	IM	2395	0	½	½	½	½	½	x	½	½	0	1	½	1	1	1	1	9
8	Diesen	IM	2440	1	½	½	½	½	0	½	x	1	½	½	0	½	½	1	1	8½
9	Raicevic	GM	2450	½	½	½	½	1	0	½	0	x	½	½	½	½	0	1	1	7½
10	Kovacs	IM	2400	½	½	0	½	0	½	1	½	½	x	1	0	0	1	1	½	7½
11	Joksic		2405	½	½	0	½	½	0	0	½	½	0	x	½	1	1	1	1	7½
12	Dantar			0	½	½	0	½	0	½	1	½	1	½	x	½	½	1	½	7½
13	Karadzic		2340	½	0	½	0	½	0	0	½	½	1	0	½	x	½	1	½	6
14	S.Kovacevic			0	0	0	½	0	1	0	½	1	0	0	½	½	x	0	½	4½
15	Cvorovic			0	0	0	0	0	1	0	0	0	0	0	0	0	1	x	1	3
16	Trabattoni		2435	½	0	0	0	0	0	0	0	0	½	0	½	½	½	0	x	2½

Category 6 (2393)   GM = 11   IM = 9

Primorsko 13-28.ix.78   1 2 3 4 5 6 7 8 9 0 1 2 3 4 5 6

			1	2	3	4	5	6	7	8	9	0	1	2	3	4	5	6	
1	Georgiev	IM	2415	x	1	½	½	1	½	½	½	½	½	½	½	1	1	½	1	10
2	Onat	IM	2335	0	x	0	1	½	½	0	½	1	1	1	1	1	½	1	1	10
3	Lukov		2330	½	1	x	0	½	½	1	½	1	1	1	0	0	½	1	1	9½
4	Pribyl	IM	2445	½	0	1	x	½	½	½	½	½	½	½	½	1	1	1	1	9½
5	Mishuchkov		2410	0	½	½	½	x	½	½	1	½	½	0	1	1	1	1	1	9½
6	Mihaljcisin	IM	2385	½	½	½	½	½	x	½	½	1	½	½	1	0	½	½	1	8½
7	Donchev		2350	½	1	0	½	½	½	x	½	0	1	1	0	1	½	½	1	8½
8	Spiridonov	IM	2405	½	½	½	½	0	½	½	x	½	½	½	1	½	½	1	½	8
9	Sellos		2320	½	0	0	½	½	0	1	½	x	0	1	1	1	0	½	1	7½
10	P.Popov		2375	½	0	0	½	½	½	0	½	1	x	1	½	½	0	½	1	7
11	Swic		2430	½	0	0	½	1	½	0	½	0	0	x	1	½	1	0	1	6½
12	Stankov		2310	½	0	1	½	0	0	1	0	0	½	0	x	½	1	½	½	6
13	Slavov		2210	0	0	1	0	0	1	0	½	0	½	½	½	x	1	½	½	6
14	Biriescu		2390	0	½	½	0	0	½	½	½	1	1	0	0	0	x	½	1	6
15	Mandrov		2290	½	0	0	0	0	½	½	0	½	½	1	½	½	½	x	½	5½
16	Karadimov			0	0	0	0	0	0	0	½	0	0	0	½	½	0	½	x	2

Category 4 (2350)   IM = 10

Kirovakan 4-26.viii.78

				1	2	3	4	5	6	7	8	9	0	1	2	3	4	5	6	
1	Vaganian	GM	2555	x	½	1	½	½	½	½	½	1	1	½	½	1	1	1	1	11
2	Kupreichik	IM	2530	½	x	1	½	½	0	1	1	½	½	1	½	1	1	1	1	11
3	Marjanovic	IM	2450	0	0	x	½	1	½	½	1	1	½	1	1	½	1	1	1	10½
4	Bagirov	IM	2505	½	½	½	x	½	½	1	½	½	½	½	1	1	½	1	1	10
5	Dementiev		2490	½	½	0	½	x	1	½	½	½	½	½	½	½	1	½	½	8
6	Mnatsakanian		2415	½	1	½	½	0	x	0	½	½	½	½	½	0	1	1	1	8
7	Zaichik		2470	½	0	½	0	½	1	x	0	½	½	½	1	1	1	1	0	8
8	A.Petrosian		2415	½	0	0	½	½	½	1	x	½	½	½	½	½	½	1	1	8
9	Bronstein	GM	2570	0	½	0	½	½	½	½	½	x	1	½	½	½	½	1	1	8
10	Szymczak	IM	2390	0	½	½	½	½	½	½	½	0	x	½	½	½	½	1	½	7
11	Stoica	IM	2420	½	0	0	½	½	½	½	½	½	½	x	½	½	½	½	1	7
12	Forintos	GM	2435	½	½	0	0	½	½	0	½	½	½	½	x	½	1	½	½	6½
13	Ornstein	IM	2425	0	0	½	0	½	1	0	½	½	½	½	½	x	½	0	½	5½
14	Plachetka	IM	2470	0	0	0	½	0	0	0	½	½	½	½	0	½	x	½	1	4½
15	Kalashian			0	0	0	0	½	0	0	0	0	0	½	½	1	½	x	1	4
16	Eolian			0	0	0	0	½	0	1	0	0	½	0	½	½	0	0	x	3

Category 8 (2434) GM = 10 IM = 8

Plovdiv 9-26.viii.78

				1	2	3	4	5	6	7	8	9	0	1	2	3	4	
1	Ermenkov	GM	2520	x	½	1	½	½	½	1	½	1	1	1	0	1	1	9½
2	Suradiradja	IM	2330	½	x	0	½	½	1	1	1	½	1	1	1	1	½	9½
3	Palatnik	IM	2490	0	1	x	1	½	½	½	1	½	½	½	1	1	1	9
4	Pinter	IM	2430	½	½	0	x	½	½	½	½	½	1	1	1	½	1	8
5	L.Popov	IM	2435	½	½	½	½	x	½	½	½	½	½	1	1	1	½	8
6	Tringov	GM	2480	½	0	½	½	½	x	½	½	½	½	½	1	1	½	7
7	Peev	IM	2420	0	0	½	½	½	½	x	+	1	½	½	0	½	1	6½
8	Ivanovic	IM	2460	½	0	0	½	½	½	–	x	1	½	0	1	½	1	6
9	Lehmann	IM	2405	0	½	½	½	½	½	0	0	x	½	½	½	½	1	5½
10	Minic	IM	2425	0	0	½	0	½	½	½	½	½	x	½	½	½	1	5½
11	Bohosian		2425	0	0	½	0	0	½	½	1	½	½	x	½	½	½	5
12	Ayanski		2355	1	0	0	0	0	0	1	0	½	½	½	x	½	0	4
13	Merdinian		2315	0	0	0	½	0	0	½	½	½	½	½	½	x	½	4
14	Barreras		2345	0	½	0	0	½	½	0	0	0	0	½	1	½	x	3½

Category 7 (2417) IM = 7½

Eksjo 25.viii.-2.ix.78   1 2 3 4 5 6 7 8 9 0

				1	2	3	4	5	6	7	8	9	0	
1	Schussler		2365	x	½	½	½	½	1	1	½	1	1	6½
2	Wedberg		2370	½	x	0	1	1	1	0	1	½	½	5½
3	Pribyl	IM	2455	½	1	x	½	½	0	½	½	1	1	5½
4	Schneider	IM	2430	½	0	½	x	½	1	½	½	1	1	5½
5	Krnic	IM	2420	½	0	½	½	x	1	0	1	0	1	4½
6	Borkowski		2400	0	0	1	0	0	x	1	1	½	1	4½
7	Akvist		2335	0	1	½	½	1	0	x	½	0	½	4
8	Wagman		2330	½	0	½	½	0	0	½	x	1	½	3½
9	Wademark			0	½	0	0	1	½	1	0	x	0	3
10	Paoli	IM	2280	0	½	0	0	0	0	½	½	1	x	2½

Category 4 (2348)   IM = 6½

Montilla 15-25.viii.78   1 2 3 4 5 6 7 8 9 0

				1	2	3	4	5	6	7	8	9	0	
1	Spassky	GM	2630	x	1	0	½	1	½	1	1	½	1	6½
2	Bellon	IM	2350	0	x	½	1	½	1	½	½	1	1	6
3	Miles	GM	2565	1	½	x	0	½	½	1	½	1	1	6
4	Hort	GM	2620	½	0	1	x	½	½	½	1	1	1	6
5	Gligoric	GM	2565	0	½	½	½	x	½	1	1	1	1	6
6	Ciocaltea	IM	2455	½	0	½	½	½	x	½	½	½	1	4½
7	Sanz		2330	0	½	0	½	0	½	x	½	½	1	3½
8	Visier		2360	0	½	½	0	0	½	½	x	½	1	3½
9	Rivas			½	0	0	0	0	½	½	½	x	1	3
10	Haritver		2245	0	0	0	0	0	0	0	0	0	x	0

Category 8 (2432)   GM = 6½   IM = 5

Albena 1-15.ix.78

				1	2	3	4	5	6	7	8	9	0	1	2	3	
1	Renman		2400	x	1	½	0	1	½	½	1	½	½	1	1	1	8½
2	Spassov	GM	2450	0	x	½	½	½	1	½	1	1	1	½	1	1	8½
3	Velikov	IM	2430	½	½	x	½	½	½	1	1	½	½	½	1	1	8
4	L.Popov	IM	2435	1	½	½	x	½	½	½	½	½	½	½	1	1	7½
5	Spiridonov	IM	2405	0	½	½	½	x	½	1	1	½	0	1	0	1	6½
6	Padevsky	GM	2455	½	0	½	½	½	x	½	½	½	1	½	1	½	6½
7	Ermenkov	GM	2520	½	½	0	½	0	½	x	0	½	1	1	1	1	6½
8	Onat	IM	2335	0	0	0	½	0	½	1	x	1	1	1	0	1	6
9	Inkiov	IM	2450	½	0	½	½	½	½	½	0	x	½	½	1	½	5½
10	Arhipkin			½	0	½	½	1	0	0	0	½	x	½	1	½	5
11	Skalkotas		2285	0	½	½	½	0	½	0	0	½	½	x	0	1	4
12	Prodanov		2335	0	0	0	0	1	0	0	1	0	0	1	x	0	3
13	Liverios		2230	0	0	0	0	0	½	0	0	½	½	0	1	x	2½

Category 6 (2379)   GM = 9   IM = 7½

Teheran Zonal 3-22.viii.78

				1	2	3	4	5	6	7	8	9	0	1	2	3	4	
1	Harandi	IM	2390	x	1	½	1	1	0	½	½	1	½	1	1	1	1	10
2	Shirazi		2285	0	x	0	0	1	1	½	1	½	1	1	1	1	1	9
3	Uitumen	IM	2385	½	1	x	½	½	1	1	0	1	1	½	½	0	1	8½
4	Kouatly	IM	2345	0	1	½	x	0	1	½	½	1	0	1	½	1	1	8
5	Lhagva		2325	0	0	½	1	x	0	1	½	½	½	1	1	1	1	8
6	Ravikumar			1	0	0	0	1	x	0	1	½	0	1	1	1	1	7½
7	Safarzadeh			½	½	0	½	0	1	x	1	0	1	0	1	1	1	7½
8	Hakki			½	0	1	½	½	0	0	x	½	½	½	½	1	1	6½
9	Parameswaran			0	½	0	0	½	½	1	½	x	½	0	1	1	1	6½
10	Catalan			½	0	0	1	½	1	0	½	½	x	0	0	1	1	6
11	Karamian			0	0	½	0	0	0	1	½	1	1	x	0	1	1	6
12	Sursock		2230	0	0	½	½	0	0	0	½	0	1	1	x	0	1	4½
13	Zundui			0	0	1	0	0	0	0	0	0	0	0	1	x	1	3
14	Alkaitoob			0	0	0	0	0	0	0	0	0	0	0	0	0	x	0

Marina Romea 18-29.viii.78

				1	2	3	4	5	6	7	8	9	0	1	
1	Joksic		2410	x	1	½	½	½	½	½	1	½	½	1	6½
2	Karaklaic	IM	2460	0	x	½	1	½	½	½	½	1	1	1	6½
3	Grabczewski	IM	2375	½	½	x	½	½	½	½	½	½	1	1	6
4	Taruffi		2340	½	0	½	x	½	1	½	½	½	1	1	6
5	Padevsky	GM	2455	½	½	½	½	x	½	½	½	½	½	½	5
6	Gliksman	IM	2340	½	½	½	0	½	x	1	½	½	½	½	5
7	Ziembinski		2270	½	½	½	½	½	0	x	½	½	1	½	5
8	Belkadi	IM	2350	0	½	½	½	½	½	½	x	½	0	1	4½
9	Witkowski	IM	2365	½	0	½	½	½	½	½	½	x	½	½	4½
10	Rosino		2295	½	0	0	0	½	½	0	1	½	x	½	3½
11	Magalotti			0	0	0	0	½	½	½	0	½	½	x	2½

Category 5 (2351) IM = 6½

Jelenia Gora 2-12.ix.78

			1	2	3	4	5	6	7	8	9	0	1	2	
1	Maciejewski	2335	x	½	1	½	½	½	½	1	½	1	1	1	8
2	Perenyi	2295	½	x	1	0	½	½	1	½	1	0	1	1	7
3	Jasnikowski	2315	0	0	x	1	1	½	1	½	1	½	0	1	6½
4	Orlov	2375	½	1	0	x	½	1	½	½	½	½	½	½	6
5	Perecz	2290	½	½	0	½	x	1	½	0	½	1	1	0	5½
6	Warwaszynski		½	½	½	0	0	x	½	½	½	1	½	1	5½
7	Begovac	2355	½	0	0	½	½	½	x	1	½	½	½	1	5½
8	Dzieniszewski	2220	0	½	½	½	1	½	0	x	0	1	½	½	5
9	Zatulowskaya	2225	½	0	0	½	½	½	½	1	x	1	0	0	4½
10	Krantz	2315	0	1	½	½	0	0	½	0	0	x	1	1	4½
11	Zoltek	2350	0	0	1	½	0	½	½	½	1	0	x	½	4½
12	Czajka	2240	0	0	0	½	1	0	0	½	1	0	½	x	3½

54

Krosno 2-15.ix.78

				1	2	3	4	5	6	7	8	9	0	1	2	
1	Kojder			x	½	½	0	1	0	1	1	1	1	1	1	8
2	Schinzel		2400	½	x	½	1	½	1	½	½	1	½	½	1	7½
3	Klaric		2340	½	½	x	½	½	1	1	½	0	1	1	1	7½
4	Vaisman	IM	2400	1	0	½	x	½	½	0	1	1	1	½	1	7
5	Sapi		2380	0	½	½	½	x	½	½	½	1	½	1	1	6½
6	G.Szilagyi	IM	2365	1	0	0	½	½	x	½	½	½	½	1	1	6
7	Dobrzynski		2315	0	½	0	1	½	½	x	0	1	½	½	½	5
8	Szymczak	IM	2390	0	½	½	0	½	½	1	x	0	½	½	1	5
9	Gromek		2370	0	0	1	0	0	½	0	1	x	½	½	1	4½
10	Skrobek	IM	2460	0	½	0	0	½	½	½	½	½	x	½	1	4½
11	Borcz			0	½	0	½	0	0	½	½	½	½	x	1	4
12	Galewicz			0	0	0	0	0	0	½	0	0	0	0	x	½

Category 4 (2335)   IM = 7½

Slupsk 28.viii.-8.ix.78

				1	2	3	4	5	6	7	8	9	0	1	2	
1	Mark Tseitlin		2480	x	½	½	1	1	1	1	½	0	½	1	1	8
2	Dobosz		2365	½	x	½	0	½	1	½	1	1	½	1	½	7
3	Bielczyk		2380	½	½	x	½	½	½	½	1	1	½	½	1	7
4	Pokojowczyk		2385	0	1	½	x	1	0	1	0	1	½	1	1	7
5	Bednarski	IM	2365	0	½	½	0	x	½	1	½	1	1	1	1	7
6	W.Schmidt	GM	2505	0	0	½	1	½	x	½	1	½	½	1	1	6½
7	Adamski	IM	2470	0	½	½	0	0	½	x	½	1	½	1	1	5½
8	Bohosjan		2425	½	0	0	1	½	0	½	x	½	1	½	1	5½
9	Peev	IM	2420	1	0	0	0	0	½	0	½	x	1	1	1	5
10	Witkowski	IM	2365	½	½	½	½	0	½	½	0	0	x	0	1	4
11	Grahn			0	0	½	0	0	0	0	½	0	1	x	1	3
12	Bachman		2220	0	½	0	0	0	0	0	0	0	0	0	x	½

Category 6 (2382)   IM = 7

Middlesborough 3-12.ix.78

		1	2	3	4	5	6	7	8	
1	BRD	x	3½	3	2	3	3	3	3½	21
2	Great Britain	½	x	2	1½	3½	3	3	4	17½
3	Italy	1	2	x	3	2	2½	3	3½	17
4	Netherlands	2	2½	1	x	3	2½	2	3	16
5	Denmark	1	½	2	1	x	3½	2	3	13
6	Eire	1	1	1½	1½	½	x	2½	4	12
7	Belgium	1	1	1	2	2	1½	x	2½	11
8	Luxembourg	½	0	½	1	1	0	1½	x	4½

Mexico City 19.viii-7.ix.78
Final A

		1	2	3	4	5	6	7	8	9	0	
1	England	x	3	2½	2½	2½	2½	3½	3	3½	3½	26½
2	USSR	1	x	3	2	3	2½	4	3	3½	3½	25½
3	Cuba	1½	1	x	2	3	4	2½	3½	3	4	24½
4	USA	1½	2	2	x	2½	2½	2½	2½	3	4	22½
5	Brasil	1½	1	1	1½	x	2	2	2	3	3½	17½
6	Canada	1½	1½	0	1½	2	x	1	3	3	2	15½
7	Colombia	½	0	1½	1½	2	3	x	2½	1½	2½	15
8	Mexico	1	1	½	1½	2	1	1½	x	1½	3	13
9	Australia	½	½	1	1	1	1	2½	2½	x	2	12
10	Scotland	½	½	0	0	½	2	1½	1	2	x	8

Tilburg 31.viii.-15.ix.78

				1	2	3	4	5	6	7	8	9	0	1	2	
1	Portisch	GM	2630	x	½	½	1	1	1	½	½	½	0	1	½	7
2	Timman	GM	2585	½	x	½	½	½	½	½	½	1	1	½	½	6½
3	Djindjihashvili	GM	2550	½	½	x	1	0	½	½	½	½	½	½	1	6
4	Hubner	GM	2595	0	½	0	x	½	½	½	1	1	1	½	½	6
5	Miles	GM	2565	0	½	1	½	x	0	0	½	1	½	1	1	6
6	Browne	GM	2550	0	½	½	½	1	x	1	½	½	1	0	0	5½
7	Hort	GM	2620	½	½	½	½	1	0	x	½	0	½	½	1	5½
8	Spassky	GM	2630	½	½	½	0	½	½	½	x	0	1	1	½	5½
9	Larsen	GM	2620	½	0	½	0	0	½	1	1	x	½	½	½	5
10	Ljubojevic	GM	2605	1	0	½	0	½	0	½	0	½	x	½	1	4½
11	Sosonko	GM	2575	0	½	½	½	0	1	½	0	½	½	x	½	4½
12	Ribli	GM	2585	½	½	0	½	0	1	0	½	½	0	½	x	4

Category 14 (2592)

Rzeszow 17-28.ix.78

				1	2	3	4	5	6	7	8	9	0	1	2	
1	Dobosz		2375	x	½	½	0	1	1	1	0	1	1	1	1	8
2	Pokojowczyk		2385	½	x	1	½	½	½	1	1	1	0	½	1	7½
3	Vaisman	IM	2400	½	0	x	½	½	1	½	1	1	½	1	1	7½
4	Fichtl	IM	2310	1	½	½	x	½	0	1	½	½	½	1	1	7
5	I.Nowak		2325	0	½	½	½	x	½	0	1	½	1	½	1	6
6	Szymczak	IM	2390	0	½	0	1	½	x	½	½	½	½	1	1	6
7	Klaric		2340	0	0	½	0	1	½	x	0	1	1	1	1	6
8	Szumilo		2290	1	0	0	½	0	½	1	x	0	1	½	½	5
9	Maciejewski		2335	0	0	0	½	½	½	0	1	x	½	1	1	5
10	Szajna			0	1	½	½	0	½	0	0	½	x	½	1	4½
11	Luczynowicz		2285	0	½	0	0	½	0	0	½	0	½	x	1	3
12	Cojocaru			0	0	0	0	0	0	0	½	0	0	0	x	½

Category 3 (2319)   IM = 8

57

1 c4 c5

1 Ornstein-Prodanov
Albena 78

1 c4 ♘f6 2 ♘c3 e6 3 ♘f3 b6 4 e4 ♗b7
5 ♗d3 d6 6 ♗c2 c5 7 d4 cxd4 8 ♘xd4
♘bd7 8...a6 9 b3 ♗e7 10 0-0 0-0 11
♗b2 ♘c6 12 ♔h1 ♕d7 += Mecking-
Polugaevsky (12) 77 9 0-0 ♗e7 10
b3 a6 11 ♗b2 0-0 12 ♕f3 △ ♖ae1,
♕g3, f4 ♕c7 13 ♖ae1 13 ♕g3 ♕c5?!
14 ♖ad1 ♕c5 14 ♕d3 ♖ac8 15 ♔h1 +=
♕h5?! 15...♖fe8 △ ♗f8, d5, g6 16
f4 ♖fd8 17 ♖f3!? ♘e5?! 18 fxe5
dxe5 19 ♘d5! 19 ♘a4 ♗c5≈ exd5 20
exd5 e4 20...♘c5? 21 ♖h3 +− 21
♖xe4 ♘xe4 22 ♕xe4 ♖e8 23 g4!
♕g6 24 ♕f4 ♕f6 25 ♘f5!! ♕xb2 26
♘h6+ ♔h8 27 ♘xf7+ ♔g8 28 ♗xh7+
♔f8 29 ♘h8+ ♗f6 30 ♕d6+ ♖e7 31
♘g6+ ♔e8 32 ♘xe7 ♕c1+ 33 ♔g2
♕d2+ 34 ♖f2 ♕g5 35 ♔g6+ ♔f8 1-0
Webb

2 Valvo-Gheorghiu USA 78

1 c4 c5 2 ♘c3 b6!? 2...♘c6; 2...g6!
3 g3 ♗g7=; 2...♘f6 3 ♘f3 ♘f6 4 g3
♗b7 5 ♗g2 e6 6 d4 cxd4 7 ♕xd4 ♗e7
8 0-0 d6 9 b3 0-0!∞ 9...a6 10 ♗a3!
+= 10 ♗b2 a6 11 ♖fe1!? ♘bd7 12
e4 ♕c7 13 ♕d2 ♖fe8! △ ♗f8= 14
♘d4 ♗f8 15 ♖ad1 ♖ad8 16 ♗c2 ♕b8!
△ ♗a8, b5 17 ♕f4 ♗a8 18 g4?! ♘e5!∓
19 g5 ♘g6! 20 ♕e3 20 ♕f3 ♘h4! △
♘xg2 −+ ♘h5! 21 ♘e2 d5!! 22 e5
♘h4! 23 ♗f3 23 ♘h1 dxc4! −+ ♗xf3+
24 ♕xf3 g6 25 cxd5 ♗xd5 26 ♕g4
♗a8! △ ♕b7 27 ♘e3 △ ♘c4-d6∓
b5 28 h4 ♖xd1 29 ♖xd1 ♖d8 30
♘d4 30 ♖xd8 ♕xd8 △ ♕d2∓ ♕b7!
31 ♔g2 ♕f3! 32 ♖d2 32 ♕xf3 ♗xf3
33 ♔f1 ♘f4! −+ ♕xe2! −+ 0-1 33
♖xe2 ♗xg2 34 ♔xg2 ♖xd4; 33 ♕xa8
♕e1+! **Gheorghiu**

3 Ogaard-Larsen Esbjerg 78

1 ♘f3 e6 2 c4 c5 3 g3 b6 4 ♗g2 ♗b7
5 0-0 ♗e7 6 ♘c3 ♘f6 7 d4 ♘e4!? 8
♘xe4 ♗xe4 9 ♗e3 0-0 10 ♕a4 ♕c7
11 ♖fd1 d6= 12 ♖ac1 a5!? 13 ♘e1
♗xg2 14 ♔xg2 ♕c6+ 15 ♕xc6 ♘xc6
16 a4 ♖fd8 17 ♘f3 ♘f6 18 b3 h6!?
19 ♖d2? 19 d5 e5!=+ 20 dxe5 20
d5 ♘d4 21 ♘xd4 cxd4 dxe5 21 ♖cd1
♖xd2 22 ♘xd2 22 ♖xd2 ♘d4 ♖d8
23 ♖c1 ♗g5! 24 ♘e4!? 24 ♗xg5
hxg5 25 ♘e4 g4 26 h3 gxh3+ 27 ♔xh3
f5 28 ♘c3 ♖d2 ♗xe3 25 fxe3 f5 26
♘c3 ♖d2 27 ♔f3 ♔f7 27...g5 28 g4!
28 ♖d1 e4+ 29 ♔f2 29 ♔f4 ♖xd1 30
♘xd1 ♔f6 31 g4∓ ♖b2 30 ♖d6 30
♖d7+ ♔e6 31 ♖xg7 ♘e5∓ ♘e5 31
♖xb6 ♘g4+ 32 ♔e1 ♘xe3 33 ♖b5
♘c2+ 34 ♔f2 e3+ 35 ♔f1 g5! 36 h3?
36 ♖xc5 ♖xb3 37 ♘d5 ♖b1+ 38 ♔g2
g4? 39 h3 ♘e1+ 40 ♔h2 ♘f3+ 41
exf3 e2 42 ♖c7+ ♔f8 43 ♖c8+ +=;
38...♖e1∓ ♔e6 −+ 37 ♖xc5 ♖xb3
38 ♘b5 ♖b1+ 39 ♔g2 ♖e1 40 ♘c3
♖c1 41 ♘b5 41 ♘d5 ♘e1+ 42 ♔h2
♖c2 43 ♔g1 ♘f3+! 44 ♔f1 ♘h2+
f4! 42 gxf4 gxf4 43 ♖d5 43 ♖c6+
♔e5 44 ♖c5+ ♔e4 45 ♖d5 ♘e1+ 46
♔h2 ♘f3+! 47 exf3 ♔xf3 48 ♘d4+
♔e4! 49 ♖d8 ♖xc4 ♘e1+ 44 ♔h2
♖xc4 45 ♖d1 ♘c2 46 ♖c1 ♔e5 47 ♔g2
f3+! 48 ♔xf3 ♘d4+ 49 ♘xd4 ♖xc1
50 ♘b3 ♖c7 51 ♘xa5 ♔d4 52 ♘b3+
♔c3 53 ♘c1 ♔c2 54 ♘d3 ♔d2 55
♘e5 ♖c5 56 ♘g4 ♖c6 56...h5! 57
♔f4 ♖c4+ 58 ♔f3 h5 59 ♘h2

Diagram

59...♖c1! 60 a5 ♖h1 61 ♔g2 ♔xe2!!
0-1 62 ♔xh1 ♔f2 **Larsen**

4 Miles-Timman IBM 78

1 ♘f3 ♘f6 2 c4 c5 3 g3 b6 4 ♗g2

♗b7 5 b3 g6 6 ♗b2 ♗g7 7 ♘c3 0-0 8 0-0 ♘a6!? 8...♘c6 9 d4 += **9 d4 d5 10 dxc5** N 10 cxd5 ♘xd5 11 ♘xd5 ♕xd5 12 e3?! Timman-Larsen, Bugojno 78; 12 ♘h4!? ♕d7 13 dxc5!?; 10...cxd4; 10 ♘xd5 **♗xc5** 10...♘e4? 11 c6! ♗xc6 12 ♘d4±; 10...dxc4 11 cxb6 ♘e4?! 12 ♕c1 +=; 11...♕xb6 12 ♘a4 +=; 11...cxb3 12 bxa7 += **11 ♗xd5 ♘xd5 12 ♗xg7 ♔xg7 13 cxd5 ♕xd5 14 ♕xd5 =** 14 ♔c2!?≈ ½-½ **Miles**

5 Magerramov-Sturua USSR 77

1 c4 ♘f6 2 ♘c3 c5 3 ♘f3 d5 4 cxd5 ♘xd5 5 g3 5 e4 ♘b4 6 ♗c4 ♘d3+ 7 ♔e2 +=; 5 e3!? **♘c6 6 ♗g2 g6** 6...♘c7 **7 0-0 ♗g7 8 ♕a4 0-0 9 ♕c4 ♘xc3 10 dxc3 ♕b6!** N 10...b6?! **11 ♖d1?!** 11 ♕h4!? ♗f5 12 ♘h6 ♗xh6 13 ♕xh6 f6!= **♗f5 12 ♘g5?! ♘e5 13 ♕b3** 13 ♕h4?! h6!∓ **h6 14 ♘e4** 14 ♕xb6 axb6∓ **♕a6 15 ♖e1 c4 16 ♕c2** 16 ♕b4?! ♘c6 17 ♕c5 ♖ac8∓ g5! **17 ♗e3 ♕g6 18 ♖ad1 b6 19 h3 g4!∓ 20 h4 ♖ad8 21 ♖d4 ♖d6 22 b3 ♖e6 23 ♖ed1** 23 bxc4 ♘c6 −+ **cxb3? 23...** h5! 24 ♕c1 ♘c6 −+ **24 axb3 ♘c6 25 ♖c4 b5**

Diagram

26 h5! ♕xh5 27 ♖c5! ♕g6 28 ♖dd5 ♗xe4 29 ♗xe4 ♖xe4 30 ♖xc6! ♕xc6

31 ♕xe4 e6 32 ♖d4! 32 ♖e5 ♕xc3 −+ **♕xe4** 32...♕xc3 33 ♕xg4 **33 ♖xe4 ♖c8 34 c4 =+** ½-½ **Gufeld**

6 Ribli-Miles IBM 78

1 ♘f3 ♘f6 2 c4 c5 3 ♘c3 d5 4 cxd5 ♘xd5 5 g3 g6 6 ♗g2 ♗g7 7 0-0 0-0 8 ♘xd5 ♕xd5 9 d3 ♘c6 10 a3 b6!? 11 ♖b1 ♗b7 12 b4?! ♕a2! 13 ♗e3 ♘d4! =+ 14 ♗xd4 cxd4 15 ♖a1 ♕d5 16 ♕a4 ♗c6 17 ♕c2 ♖ac8 18 ♖fc1 ♗d7 19 ♕b2 ♗a4 20 ♘e1 ♕d7 21 ♕a2 ♖c3 22 ♖xc3 dxc3∓ 23 ♖c1 e6 24 e3 ♖c8 25 d4 e5 26 d5 f5 27 ♗f1 27 e4 ♘h6 △ c2 −+ **e4 28 ♘c2 ♖d8** 28...b5!? −+ **29 ♘d4** 29 ♖d1 b5 −+ **♗xd4 30 exd4 c2 31 ♗c4 ♕f8?** 31... f4! −+ **32 ♗b3 ♗xb3 33 ♕xb3 ♕xd5 34 ♕xd5 ♖xd5 35 ♖xc2 ♔e7!∓ 36 ♖c4** 36 ♖c7+ ♖d7; 36 ♖d2 ♖d7 −+ **♖d7 37 h4** 37 ♔f1 ♔e6 38 ♔e2 ♕d5 39 ♖c1 ♖f7 40 ♔e3 g5! △ f4+ −+ **♔e6 38 b5!** ♕d5 39 ♖a4 h6 40 ♔f1 g5 41 hxg5 hxg5 42 ♔e2 f4 43 gxf4 gxf4 44 ♔d2 ♖c7 44...♔e6 45 ♔c2 ♔f5 46 d5! ♔e5 48 d6! **45 ♔d1 e3 46 fxe3 f3 47 ♔e1?** 47 ♔d2!! ♖c2+ 48 ♔e1! ♔e4 49 ♖xa7=; 47...♔e4 48 d5+ △ ♖f4=; 47...♖c1 48 e4+! ♔xe4 49 d5+ ♔e5 50 ♔e3 ♔e4 −+ **48 ♖b4 ♖c1+ 49 ♔f2 ♖c2+ 50 ♔e1 ♔xe3 51 ♖b3+ ♔f4 52 d5 ♖e2+ 0-1 Miles**

7 Rind-Gheorghiu USA 78
1 ♘f3 c5 2 c4 ♘f6 3 ♘c3 d5 4 cxd5
♘xd5 5 g3 5 e4!? += ♘c6 6 ♗g2 g6
7 0-0 ♗g7 8 ♘xd5 ♕xd5 9 d3 0-0 10
♗e3! ♗d7! 10...♗xb2 11 ♖b1 ♗f6 12
♘d4 ♕d6 13 ♘xc6 bxc6 14 ♕c2 +=
**11 ♘d4 ♕d6 12 ♘xc6 ♗xc6 13 ♗xc6
♕xc6 14 ♖c1 ♕e6!** 14...b6? 15 b4!±
15 b3 b6 16 ♕d2 ♖fd8 17 ♖c4 ♖d5!
Δ ♖h5∞ **18 b4 cxb4 19 ♕xb4 b5!
20 ♖c7 ♖d7 21 ♖fc1 ♖xc7 22 ♖xc7
a6!** 22...♕xa2 23 ♕xb5 ♕xe2 24 ♕b7±
23 a4 23 a3 =+ **bxa4 24 ♕xa4 h5 25
♖b7 a5 26 ♖b5 ♕g4!∓ 27 ♕xg4 hxg4
28 ♗c5 a4! 29 ♗xe7** 29 ♗a3 e6 Δ
♗f8∓ **a3 30 ♗xa3 ♖xa3 31 ♖g5 ♖a4
32 ♖c5 ♖a2 33 e3 ♖d2 34 d4 f5 35
♖c6 ♔f7 36 ♖c7+ ♔f6 37 ♖c6+ ♔g5
38 ♔g2 ♗f8 39 ♖c8 ♗b4 40 ♖c6
♖b2 41 ♔f1 ♔h6 42 ♖c7 ♖b1+ 43
♔g2 ♗e1! 44 ♖c2 ♖d1! 45 ♖e2 ♔g5
46 h3**

**46...♗d2!!∓ 47 ♔h2 ♔f6 48 ♔g2 ♔e6
49 f3 ♔d5 50 e4+** 50 hxg4 fxg4 51
fxg4 ♔e4 −+ **fxe4! 51 fxe4+** 51 ♖xe4
gxf3+ 52 ♔xf3 ♖f1+ −+ **♔xd4 52
e5 ♗g5 53 e6 ♗e7 54 ♖a2 gxh3+
55 ♔xh3 ♔e5 56 ♖e2+ ♔f6 57 ♖e4
♖d6 58 ♔g4 ♖xe6 59 ♖a4 ♖b6 60
♖a7 ♖b4+ 61 ♔h3 ♗d6 62 ♖a3 ♖h4+!
63 gxh4 ♗xa3 64 ♔g4 ♗c1 65 ♔f3
♔f5 66 ♔g3 ♗f4+ 0-1 Gheorghiu**

8 A.Petrosian-Kapengut Daugavpils 78
1 ♘f3 c5 2 c4 ♘f6 3 g3 d5 4 cxd5
♘xd5 5 ♗g2 ♘c7 6 ♘c3 ♘c6 7 ♕a4
♗d7 8 ♕e4 g6 9 ♘e5 ♗g7 10 ♘xd7
♕xd7 11 0-0 ♖c8 12 a3 12 ♕a4 ♘e6
13 d3 0-0 14 ♗e3 b6 15 ♖fc1 ♖fc8
16 ♖ab1 ♘ed4 17 a3 ♘a5 =+ Schmidt-
Alburt, Decin 76 **♘e6 13 b4 b6
14 ♖b1 0-0 15 ♕d5!?** N 15 ♗h3;
15 ♘d5 f5? 16 ♕c4 ♘e5 17 ♕a2 c4?
(17...♔h8) 18 ♗b2± Romanishin-
Pinter, Malgrat de Mar 77; 15...♘e5
16 ♗b2 f5 17 ♕e3 ♘d4 18 ♗xd4 cxd4
19 ♕b3 ♔h8 20 ♖bc1 b5 21 ♘f4
♘c4 22 ♖c2 e5 23 ♘d3 ♗h6 24 ♕a2
♕e7 25 ♘c5 ♘b6 26 ♖fc1 e4=+ Bukic-
Schmidt, Vrsac 77; 15...♘cd4! 16
♗b2 f5 17 ♕e3 c4 18 d3 f4!? 19
gxf4 c3 20 ♗xc3 ♘f5 21 ♕d2 ♗xc3
22 ♘xc3 Kasparov-Kapengut, Minsk
78; 22...♘fd4!; 16...♖fe8 17 ♖fc1
♘g5 18 ♕e3 ♕g4= **♖fd8 16 ♕a2
♘e5! 17 ♗h3** 17 ♘d5 c4 **f5 18 bxc5
♖xc5 19 a4** 19 ♘e4 ♕d5! **♔h8 20
♗g2 ♘d4! ½-½ Kapengut**

9 Zilberstein-Gusev Daugavpils 78
1 ♘f3 ♘f6 2 c4 c5 3 d4 cxd4 4 ♘xd4
e5?! 5 ♘bd5 d5 6 cxd5 ♗c5!? 6...♗b4+
7 e3 0-0 8 ♘5c3 e4!? 9 a3 ♕e7 10
♘d2 ♗f5 11 b4 ♗d6 12 ♘c4 += ♘bd7
13 ♗b2 a6 14 ♕d4 ♖fe8 15 ♗e2 ♖ad8

16 g4!? ♗xg4 17 ♘xe4 ♕xe4 18 ♕xe4 ♗xb4+! 19 axb4 ♖xe4 20 ♘d6 ♖xb4 21 ♗a3 ♖a4!= 22 f3 ♘e5 23 ♘xb7 ♖b8 24 fxg4 ♖xb7 25 0-0 ♘xd5 26 ♖fd1 ♖d7 27 ♗b2 ♖xa1 28 ♖xa1 f6 ½-½ Suetin

10 Rashkovsky-Alburt
Daugavpils 78

1 c4 c5 2 ♘f3 ♘f6 3 d4 cxd4 4 ♘xd4 e6 5 g3 d5 6 ♗g2 e5 7 ♘f3 d4 8 0-0 ♘c6 9 e3 ♗c5!? N 9...♗e7 10 exd4 exd4 11 ♗f4 0-0 12 ♘e5 ♘xe5 13 ♗xe5 ♗c5 14 ♘d2 ♖e8 15 ♖e1 ♘g4 16 ♗f4 += Alburt-Furman, USSR Final 75 10 exd4 exd4 11 b4!? 11 ♖e1+; 11 ♘bd2 △ ♘b3 += ♘xb4 12 ♘bd2 d3 13 ♘b3 ♗e7 14 ♘fd4 ♗g4 15 ♕d2 0-0 16 ♗b2 ♕d7 17 ♖fe1 ♖ac8∝ 18 a3 ♘a6 19 ♕xd3 ♘c5 20 ♘xc5 ♗xc5 21 ♕c3 ♖fd8 22 ♘b3 ♗f8 23 ♖ac1 b6 24 ♕e3 ♖e8 25 ♕f4 ♖xe1+ 26 ♖xe1 ♕f5 27 ♕xf5 ♗xf5 28 ♘d4 ♗d7 29 ♖c1 ♗a4 30 ♘b5 a6 31 ♗b7 ♖d8 32 ♗xa6 ♘e4 33 ♘c3 ♘xc3 34 ♗xc3 ♗xa3= 35 ♖a1 ♗c6 36 ♗b5 ♗f3 37 ♖e1 ♗f8 38 ♖e8 ♖d1+ 39 ♖e1 ♖d3 40 ♖e3 ♖xe3 41 fxe3 ½-½ Suetin

11 Mihalchishin-Pfleger Rome 77

1 ♘f3 ♘f6 2 c4 c5 3 ♘c3 g6 4 d4 cxd4 5 ♘xd4 ♗g7 6 g3 0-0 7 ♗g2 d6!? 8 0-0 ♘bd7 8...♘c6 9 ♘c2!± Portisch-Sax, Budapest 71 9 b3 a6 10 ♗b2 ♖b8 11 ♖c1 ♘c5 12 ♕d2 ♗d7 13 ♖fd1 ♖e8 13...♕a5? 14 ♘d5 14 ♘d5 ♘fe4? 14...♘xd5 15 cxd5 a5 += 15 ♕c2 f5 16 b4 ♘a4 17 ♗a1 ♘g5 18 c5 ♖c8 19 c6! bxc6 20 ♕xa4 cxd5 21 ♖xd5+ e6 22 ♗c6 ♗xc6 23 ♘xc6 ♕d7 24 ♗xg7 ♕xg7 25 ♖xd6 ♘e4 26 ♖d3 ♕b7 27 ♖c4! ♕g7 28 ♕c2 ♖c7? 29 ♘a5 ♖xc4 30 ♕b2+

1-0 Pytel

12 Csom-Smejkal Kiel 78

1 c4 c5 2 ♘c3 g6 3 ♘f3 ♗g7 4 g3?! 4 e3 ♘c6 5 ♗g2 e6! 6 a3 ♘ge7 7 0-0 0-0 8 d3 d5 9 cxd5 exd5 10 ♖b1 b6 11 ♗f4 h6 12 ♕c1 d4 13 ♘a4 g5 14 ♗d2 ♗e6 =+ 15 b4 cxb4 16 axb4 ♖c8 17 ♕b2 ♗f5 18 ♖fc1 ♕d7 19 ♕a1 ♘ce7 20 ♘b2 ♘d5 21 ♘d1 ♖xc1 22 ♖xc1 ♖c8 23 ♘e1 23 ♖xc8+ ♕xc8 24 ♕xa7? ♕c2 25 ♕a1 g4 -+ ♘c3? 23...♖xc1 24 ♕xc1 ♕a4? 25 ♗xd5; 24...♗f8∓ 24 ♘xc3! 24 ♗xc3 dxc3 25 ♘c2 ♗b3∓ dxc3 25 ♖xc3 25 ♗xc3? ♖xc3 26 ♖xc3 ♕d4 ♘d4? 25...♗xc3 26 ♗xc3 ♕c7 27 ♗b2 △ e4∓ 26 ♖xc8+ ♕xc8 27 ♕xa7 +- ♘b3 28 ♗e3 ♕c3 29 ♘f3 ♕c2 30 h3 ♕xe4 31 ♕a8+ ♗f8 32 ♕e4 b5 33 ♔h2 ♕b2 34 ♘d4! ♘xd4 35 ♗xd4 ♕xb4 36 ♕e5 ♔h7 37 ♗e4+ f5 38 ♗xf5+ 1-0 Webb

13 Seirawan-Gheorghiu USA 78

1 c4 c5 2 ♘c3 g6 3 g3 ♗g7 4 ♗g2 ♘c6 5 a3 5 ♘f3; 5 e3 a6 6 ♖b1 ♖b8 7 ♕a4! 7 b4 axb4 8 axb4 b5= ♘h6 8 b4 cxb4 9 axb4 b5 10 cxb5 axb5 11 ♘xb5 ♕b6 12 ♘a3! ♘xb4 13 ♘h3 ♘f5 14 ♘f4 14 0-0± ♕c5 15 0-0 ♘a6 16 ♖xb8 ♘xb8 17 ♕a8! ♕e5! 17...♘a6? 18 ♗b7 0-0 19 ♗xa6! +- 18 d3?! 0-0 19 ♗d2 ♘c6!∝ 20 ♖b1 ♘d6!! △ ♗b7, ♖a8 21 ♗xc6 dxc6 22 ♕xc6 g5 23 ♘d5 23 ♘h5 ♕xe2 24 ♘xg7 ♕xd2∓ ♕xe2 24 ♗xg5 ♘f5!!∓ △ ♘d4 25 ♕c2 ♕f3 25...♕e5!? 26 ♖b5∝ 26 ♖b8 ♕xd5! 27 ♖xc8 ♘d4 28 ♖xf8+ ♗xf8 29 ♕c4 ♕xg5 29...♘f3+ 30 ♕xd4 ♕c1+ 31 ♔g2 ♕xa3 32 ♕g4+ ♗g7 33 ♕c8+ ♗f8 34 ♕g4+ ♔h8 35 ♕d4+ ♔g8 36 ♕g4+ ♔h8 37 ♕d4+ f6 38 ♕d8 ♔g7 39 h4 ♕c5

**40 g4 h5! 41 ♕e8 hxg4 42 h5 ♕d5+!
0-1** 43 ♔g3 ♕f3+ 44 ♔h4 ♕h3 mate;
42 ♔g1 ♕f7 45 h6+ ♔g6 **Gheorghiu**

14 Miles-H.Olafsson Lone Pine 78
**1 g3 c5 2 ♗g2 ♘c6 3 c4 g6 4 ♘c3 ♗g7
5 a3 e6 6 ♖b1 a5 7 e4 ♘ge7 8 ♘ge2
d6 9 0-0 0-0 10 d3 ♘d4 11 b4 axb4
12 axb4 ♘ec6 13 ♘xd4 ♘xd4 14
bxc5** 14 ♗e3? ♘c6! **dxc5 15 f4! f5?**
15...e5!?; 15...♘f3+ 16 ♗xf3 ♗xc3 +=
**16 e5± ♖a7 17 ♔h1 ♖f7 18 ♗e3 ♗f8
19 ♗xd4 cxd4 20 ♘b5 ♖a6 21 ♖f2
b6? 22 ♖a1 ♕d7 23 ♖fa2 ♖xa2 24
♖xa2 ♗b7 25 ♕g1 ♗c5 26 ♗xb7!**
26 ♖a7 ♕xb5!? **27 cxb5 ♗xg2+ 28
♕xg2 ♖xa7 += ♕xb7+ 27 ♕g2 ♕xg2+
28 ♔xg2 +− ♕g7 29 ♔f3 h6 30 h4 g5
31 h5 ♖d7 32 ♖a8 ♔f7 33 ♕e2 gxf4
34 gxf4 ♕g7 35 ♖e8 ♔f7 36 ♖c8 ♕g7
37 ♔d1 ♔h7** 37...♔f7 **38 ♔c2 ♕g7
39 ♖c6!** ♔f7 **40 ♘c7 ♖e7 41 ♔c2!**
Zugswang +− **38 ♘c7 ♖g7 39 ♘xe6
1-0 Miles**

15 Hort-Gulko Niksic 78
**1 c4 c5 2 ♘c3 g6 3 g3 ♗g7 4 ♗g2 ♘c6
5 b3 e6** 5...e5!? **6 ♗b2 ♘ge7 7 e3**
d6 8 ♘ge2 0-0 9 0-0 a6 10 d3 ♖b8
11 ♕d2 b5 12 ♖fd1 ♕a5 13 ♖ac1 ♗e6
14 ♘e4 ♕xd2 15 ♖xd2α Polugaevsky-
Bobotsov 66; 7 ♘d5 d6 8 ♘xe7 ♕xe7
9 e3 0-0α Bronstein-Velimirovic,
Reykjavik 77 **6 ♗b2 ♘ge7 7 ♕c1** 7
e3? d5 **d6 8 f4 0-0 9 ♘e4 e5! 10 fxe5
♘xe5 11 ♘f3 f5! 12 ♘f2 ♘7c6 13
♘xe5** 13 0-0 f4∓ **dxe5 14 ♗d5+?**
14 h4!? f4 15 h5 fxg3 16 ♗d5+ ♔h8
17 hxg6 fxg2+ 18 ♔f1 h6 19 d3 ♖f4
20 ♕xf4 exf4 21 ♖xh6 mate; 15...g5
16 h6 ♗f6 17 ♗d5+ ♔h8 18 ♗xc6
bxc6 19 ♘e4± **♔h8 15 ♗xc6** 15 h4
♘e7 16 ♗g2 h6∓ **bxc6 16 ♘d3 ♕e7 17
♕c3?** a5∓ **18 a4 ♗f6 19 ♕c2** 19

♘xe5? ♗b7 20 e3 ♖ae8 21 d4 cxd4
22 exd4 c5 −+; 20 ♕e3 ♖ae8 21 ♘d3
♕g7 −+

**19...f4! 20 gxf4 exf4 21 ♗xf6+ ♕xf6
22 ♕c3 ♕xc3 23 dxc3 ♗g4 24 ♖g1**
24 ♘xc5 ♖f5 −+ **♗h5 25 ♔d2 ♖ad8!
26 ♖ae1 f3 27 exf3 ♖xf3 28 ♖e3
♖f2+ −+ 29 ♔e1 ♖c2 30 ♖g5 ♖xc3
31 ♔d2 ♖xb3 32 ♔c2 ♖a3 33 ♖ge5**
35 ♖xc5 ♗g4 −+ ♖xa4 **34 ♖xc5 ♖a3
35 ♖xc6 ♗g4 36 c5 ♖a4 37 ♘e5 ♗f5+
38 ♔c1 ♖a1+ 39 ♔b2 ♖dd1 40 ♘f7+
♔g7 41 ♖c7 ♖db1+ 42 ♔c3 0-1
Velimirovic**

1 c4 e5

16 Christiansen-Mednis USA Final 78
1 c4 ♘f6 2 ♘c3 c6 3 e4 e5!? 4 ♘f3
4 d4?! ♗b4 5 dxe5 ♘xe4 6 ♕g4
♘xc3 7 a3 ♗f8! =+ **♗b4 5 ♘xe5
0-0 6 ♗e2** N 6 ♘d3 ♗xc3 7 dxc3 ♘xe4
8 ♗e2 d5 9 cxd5 ♕xd5 10 ♗e3 ♘d7
11 ♕b3 ♘df6 12 0-0 ♖e8 13 ♖fe1
♕f5 14 ♗f1 b6= Korchnoi-Tukmakov,
USSR Final 73 **♖e8 7 ♘d3** 7 ♘f3
♘xe4 8 ♘xe4 ♖xe4 9 0-0 d5 10
d4 ♖e8 11 ♗d3 ♗e7!= **♗xc3 8 dxc3
♘xe4 9 0-0 d5! 10 cxd5 ♕xd5 11
♗e3 ♘d7 12 ♗f3 ♘df6 13 ♗d4 ♕d6**
13...♕d8!= **14 ♗e5! ♕d8** 14...♖xe5??

15 ♘xe5 ♕xe5 16 ♕d8+ +– **15 ♗xe4**
♘xe4 16 ♖e1 ♘g5 16...♗f5? 17 ♕f3±
17 ♗c7 ♖xe1+ 18 ♕xe1 ♕f8 19 ♕e3
♗f5 20 ♕xg5 ♗xd3 21 ♖d1 ♕e8!=
22 h4 f6 23 ♕g3 ♗g6 24 b3 ♖c8 25
♕d6 ♗c2! 26 ♖d4 26 ♖d2 ♖xc7!∓
♕e1+ 27 ♔h2 ♖e8 28 ♕g3 ♗f5 29
♕f4?! 29 ♗f4= ♕xc3! 30 h5 h6 31 ♖a4
♕c5! 32 ♖a5 b5 33 ♕c4+! ♕xc4?!
33...bxc4! 34 ♖xc5 cxb3! =+ **34**
bxc4 ♖e2 35 cxb5 cxb5 36 ♔g3
♗e6 36...♗d7! **37 ♖xa7 ♗e8** =+ **37**
a3 ♗f7 38 ♖xb5= ½-½ **Mednis**

17 Uhlmann-Timman Niksic 78

1 c4 g6 2 e4 e5 3 g3 ♗g7 4 ♗g2 ♘c6
5 d3 d6 6 ♘c3 ♘ge7 7 ♘ge2 0-0 8
0-0 f5 9 ♘d5! ♗e6 10 ♗e3 ♕d7 11 ♕d2
♖f7 12 ♖ac1 12 b4 f4 13 gxf4 exf4
14 ♘xf4 ♗xa1∓ **♖af8 13 b4 ♘c8 14**
b5 14 c5 dxc5 15 ♗xc5 ♖d8 Δ ♗xd5;
14...♗xd5 15 exd5 ♘e7 16 c6 bxc6
17 dxc6 ♕e6 Δ d5= **♘d8 15 d4!? c6**
16 dxe5 dxe5 17 exf5 17 ♗c5? ♖e8
Δ f4 **gxf5 18 f4 e4 19 ♖fd1 ♕e8!**
19...♗xd5 20 cxd5 cxb5 21 d6 ♘c6
22 ♕d5± **20 b6!** 20 bxc6 bxc6 21
♘b4 ♖d7 22 ♕c2 ♘b6 **axb6** 20...
cxd5? 21 bxa7! ♘xa7 22 cxd5± **21**
♘xb6 ♘xb6 22 ♗xb6 ♖d7 23 ♕a5?!
23 ♕b4 Δ ♘d4 += **♖xd1+ 24 ♖xd1**
♕h5!= 25 ♖d2 ♗xc4 26 ♘c3! ♗f7
26...♗xc3?! 27 ♕xc3± **27 ♘xe4 ♖e8**
28 ♗f2 b6! 29 ♗xb6 ♗b5! 30 ♘c3
♖e1+ 31 ♔f2 ♗xc3 32 ♕xc3 ♖e2+
33 ♔g1 ♖e1+ ½-½ **Uhlmann**

18 Sahovic-Vitolins Jurmala 78

1 c4 e5 2 ♘c3 ♘f6 3 ♘f3 ♘c6 4 g3
♗b4 5 ♗g2 0-0 6 0-0 e4 7 ♘e1 ♗xc3
8 dxc3 h6 9 ♘c2 b6?! 9...d6 **10**
♘e3 ♘e5 11 f4! exf3 11...♘g6 12 h3
Δ g4, ♕e1, ♕g3 **12 exf3 ♗b7 13 f4!**
♘c6 13...♗xg2 14 fxe5 ♗xf1 15 exf6

♗h3 16 ♕h5 +– **14 ♘d5 ♘a5 15 ♕d4**
♘xd5 16 cxd5± c5 17 ♕d3 ♕c8 18
c4 f5 19 b3 ♖f7 20 ♗b2 ♕f8 21
♖ae1 d6 22 g4! +– ♗c8 22...fxg4
23 ♕g6 ♘c8 24 ♖e6! +– **23 g5 hxg5**
24 fxg5 g6 25 ♕c3 ♖h7 26 ♖e3 ♗d7
27 ♖h3 f4 28 ♖xh7 ♔xh7 29 ♖xf4!
1-0 Sahovic

1 c4 ♘f6

19 Browne-Petursson Reykjavik 78

1 c4 ♘f6 2 ♘c3 e6 3 e4 d5 3...c5
4 e5 ♘g8 5 ♘f3 ♘c6 6 d4 cxd4 7 ♘xd4
♘xe5 8 ♘db5 a6 9 ♘d6+ ♗xd6 10
♕xd6 f6 11 ♗e3!? ♘e7 12 ♗b6 ♘f5
13 ♗xd8 ♘xd6 14 ♗c7 ♔e7 15 c5
♘e8 16 ♗b6 d5 17 cxd6+ ♗xd6
18 0-0-0 ♘ef7 19 g3 ♗d7 20 ♗h3
♖hc8 21 ♖he1 e5 22 ♗g2 ♘c6 23
♗h3 ½-½ Miles-Polugaevsky, Reykjavik
78 **4 e5 ♘e4** 4...d4 5 exf6 dxc3 6
bxc3 ♕xf6 7 d4 c5 8 ♘f3; 4...♘fd7
5 cxd5 exd5 6 d4 c5 7 ♘f3 ♘c6 8
♗b5 a6 9 ♗xc6 += Smyslov-Farago,
Hastings 76/7 **5 ♘f3!?** 5 ♘xe4 dxe4
6 ♕g4 ♘c6 7 ♕xe4 ♕d4 8 ♕xd4
♘xd4 9 ♗d3!? ♗c5 10 ♘e2 += **♘c6**
5...c5 6 cxd5 exd5? 7 ♘xe4 dxe4
8 ♕a4+ +–; 6...♘xc3 7 dxc3 exd5
8 ♗d3 += **6 d4 ♗e7?!** 6...♗b4 7 ♕c2
f5 8 exf6 ♕xf6; 7 ♗d2!? **7 ♗d3 ♘xc3**
8 bxc3 += dxc4 9 ♗xc4 b6 10 ♕e2
10 ♗b5 ♗b7 11 ♕a4 ♕d5! **♗b7 11**
0-0 0-0 12 ♖d1 ♘a5 13 ♗d3 ♕c8?
13...♕e8! **14 ♘g5!± g6** 14...h6 15
♘h7! ♖d8 16 ♕g4 ♔h8 17 ♕h5 ♖g8
18 ♗xh6! gxh6 19 ♕xh6 ♖g2+ 20
♔f1 +–

Diagram

15 h4! 15 ♘xh7? ♔xh7 16 ♕h5+
♔g8 17 ♗xg6 fxg6 18 ♕xg6+ ♔h8

19 ♖d3 ♗f3! =+ **h5 16 g4! ♔g7?**
16...c5 17 ♔h2! ♕c6 18 ♖g1 ♗xg5
19 ♗xg5 ♕f3 20 gxh5 gxh5 21 ♗f6+
+−; 19...hxg4 20 ♖xg4 ♕f3 21 ♖ag1
h5 +− **17 gxh5 ♖h8 18 ♕g4! ♗xg5**
18...♖xh5 19 ♘xf7! +− **19 ♕xg5 ♕d8**
19...♖xh5 20 ♕f6+ ♔g8 21 ♗xg6 +−
20 ♕xd8 ♖hxd8 21 ♗g5 ♖d7 22
♗f6+ ♔h6 23 hxg6 fxg6 24 ♔h2 ♗f3
25 ♖g1 ♗h5 26 ♖g5! +− ♖g8 27
♖ag1 ♖f7 28 f4 ♘c6 29 ♖xh5+ 1-0
29...♔xh5 30 ♗g5 +− **Browne**

20 Benko-Mednis
USA Final 78
1 c4 ♘f6 2 ♘c3 e6 3 ♘f3 d5 4 e3!?
4 d4 c6 5 b3 ♗d6 6 ♗b2 0-0 7 ♗e2
♘bd7 8 ♕c2 ♖e8 8...dxc4!= **9 0-0**
dxc4 10 ♗xc4! 10 bxc4 e5 11 d3
♘c5= △ ♗f5 **♘b6!** 10...e5?! 11 ♘g5!±;
10...♘e5 11 ♘xe5 ♗xe5 12 d4 +=
11 d4 ♘xc4 12 bxc4 c5! 13 dxc5
13 d5 exd5! 14 cxd5 a6 15 a4 ♕e7=
♗xc5 14 ♖fd1 ♕e7 15 ♘e5 15 ♘g5
h6! 16 ♘ge4 ♘xe4 17 ♘xe4 b6 18
♕a4 ♖d8 19 ♖xd8+ ♕xd8 20 ♖d1
♕e7= 21 h3 ♗b7 22 ♖d7 ♕e8 23
♘xc5 bxc5= **♘d7! 16 ♘e4** 16 ♘b5
♘xe5 17 ♗xe5 f6 18 ♗d6; 18 ♘c7?
fxe5 19 ♘xa8 b6 −+ **♘xe5 17 ♗xe5**
f6 18 ♗d6 18 ♘xc5 ♕xc5= **♗xd6 19**
♘xd6 ♖d8 20 c5 b6!= ½-½ 21 ♘e4
♗b7; 21 ♕e4 ♗a6 **Mednis**

1 d4 ♘c6

21 Miles-Mestrovic Lone Pine 78
1 d4 ♘c6!? 2 d5 ♘e5 3 e4 3 f4 ♘g6
4 e4 e6∞ **e6 4 dxe6** 4 f4 ♘c5!?; 4...
♘g6 **dxe6** 4...fxe6 5 ♘c3! += ♗c5??
6 ♕h5+ +−; 5...♗b4?! 6 ♕d4! **5**
♕xd8+ ♔xd8 6 f4 ♘c6 7 ♘f3 ♘f6
8 ♗d3 ♗c5 9 c3 a5 10 ♔e2 e5!?
10...♔e7 11 ♘bd2 △ e5, ♘e4 **11**
fxe5 ♘g4 12 ♗g5+ ♔e8 13 ♗f4 ♗f2 14
♖f1 ♘xd3 15 ♔xd3 ♗e6 16 ♘bd2
h6 17 ♗e3 ♗xe3? 17...♗e7; 17...
♖d8+ 18 ♔e2 ♗e7 **18 ♔xe3 +=** △
♘b3-d4 **a4 19 b4!** △ b5, ♘d4 **axb3**
19...b5 20 ♘d4± **20 axb3 ♕e7 21**
b4 b6 22 b5 ♘a5 23 ♘d4± ♖hd8 24
♖a4 ♖ac8 25 ♖fa1 c5 25...♔e8 26
♘c6 +− **26 ♘f5+** 26 bxc6 ♘xc6∞
♗xf5 27 exf5 c4 27...♖d5 28 ♖xa5
bxa5 29 ♘c4! +− **28 ♘e4 ♖d5 29**
♔f4 g5+ 29...♖xb5? 30 ♘d6 +−
30 fxg6 fxg6

31 ♖xa5! bxa5 32 ♖xa5 g5+ 33 ♔f5
♖f8+ 34 ♘f6! ♖xf6+ 35 ♔e4! 1-0
Miles

Queen's Pawn

22 O.Rodriguez-Beljavsky Alicante 78
1 d4 ♘f6 2 ♘c3 d5 3 ♗g5 g6 4 ♗xf6
exf6 5 e3 c6 6 ♗d3 ♗h6!? 7 ♕f3 f5

8 h3 ♘d7! 8...♕b6 9 0-0-0 f4 10 e4!
9 g4?! 9 ♘ge2 ♘f6 10 ♘f4= ♕b6 **10
♖b1** 10 0-0-0 ♕xd4 11 ♗xf5 ♕b4∓;
11 gxf4 ♘e5∓; 10 ♘ge2!? **f4∓ 11
♘ge2 fxe3 12 fxe3 ♗g7 13 ♕d2?!**
13 0-0 **0-0 14 h4 ♕d8 15 ♖bg1 ♖e8
16 g5 ♘f8 17 h5 b6! 18 ♘f4 a5 19
♖h4 ♗a6 20 ♕h3 ♗xd3 21 cxd3 ♖a7
22 ♖g3 ♕d6 23 ♕h2 ♖ae7 24 ♕g1
♕b4 25 ♔c2 a4** △ a3, ♖xe3! **26
hxg6 fxg6 27 ♘fxd5?! cxd5 28 ♗xd5
♕b5 29 ♗xe7+ ♖xe7** −+ **30 ♕d1 a3
31 b3 ♕c6+! 32 ♔b1** 32 ♔d2 ♖c7 33
♔e2 ♕c2+ 34 ♕d2 ♕b1 −+; 34 ♕xc2
♖xc2+ 35 ♔f3 ♖xa2 −+ **♕c3 33
♖h2 ♗xd4 0-1 Webb**

23 O.Rodriguez-Miles Las Palmas 78
**1 d4 d5 2 ♘f3 ♘f6 3 e3 ♗g4 4 h3
♗h5 5 g4 ♗g6 6 ♘e5 ♘fd7 7 ♘xg6
hxg6 8 c4 dxc4 9 ♗xc4 e6 10 ♘c3
♗e7 11 ♕f3 ♘c6 12 ♗d2 ♗h4 13 ♘e4
0-0 14 g5!? ♗xg5 15 h4 ♗h6** 15...
♗xh4? **16 ♕h3 g5 17 0-0-0± 16
0-0-0 a5 17 ♕g2 ♘b6 18 ♗f1 ♕d5
19 ♘c3 ♕xg2 20 ♗xg2≈ ♘b4 21 ♔b1
♘4d5 22 ♘e4 ♘d7 23 ♖c1 c6 24
f4 ♖fb8 25 a3 ♔f8 26 ♘f2 ♔e7 27
♘d3 ♖c8 28 ♖c2 ♘c7 29 e4?! ♘b5
30 ♗e3 ♘f6 31 a4 ♘c7 32 ♖hc1 ♖d8
33 ♗f3 ♘a6 34 ♖c4 ♘d7 35 b3 ♘b6
36 ♖4c2 ♘c8 37 d5!? exd5 38 exd5
cxd5 39 ♘c5 ♘b4 40 ♖e2 ♘d6??**
40...♖b8 −+ **41 ♘xb7! ♘xb7 42 ♗c5+
♔f6** 42...♘d7 43 ♖e7+ ♔c6 44 ♗xb4+
+− **43 ♗d4+ ♔f5 44 ♖e5+ ♔xf4
44**...♔f6 45 ♗g4 △ ♖e6 mate **45 ♖f1!
♖e8 46 ♗xd5+** 46 ♗e2+?! ♔g3 47
♖g1+ ♔h2 48 ♗f2 ♘d3! **♕g4 47 ♗f3+
♔g3 48 ♗xb7 ♖ad8 49 ♗f2+! ♔g4
50 ♖g1+ ♔f4 51 ♗g3+ ♔g4 52 ♗e1+!
♔f4?** 52...♔h3! 53 ♗f3 ♖d1+!; 53
♖xe8 ♖xe8 54 ♗f3 ♗f4 55 ♖h1+
♗h2 **53 ♖xe8 ♖xe8 54 ♖f1+! +−**

♕e5 55 ♗xb4 ♖b8 56 ♗c3+ ♔e6 57
♖e1+ **1-0 Miles**

24 Lerner-Peresipkin Kiev 78
1 d4 ♘f6 2 c4 d6 3 ♘c3 ♘c6!? 3...
♘bd7; 3...g6 **4 ♗g5** 4 ♘f3!? △ d5
h6 **5 ♗h4** 5 ♗xf6!? += g5 **6 ♗g3
♘h5 7 e3 ♘xg3 8 hxg3 ♗g7 9 ♗d3**
+= **♕d7!? 10 ♗c2** 10 ♕h5 ♕g4 **0-0
11 ♘f3 f5 12 d5** 12 ♘d2!? **♘e5 13
♘xe5 dxe5 14 g4! fxg4 15 ♘e4≈
♕f5** △ g3! **16 ♕d2 ♕g6!? 17 ♘g3
e4! 18 ♗xe4 ♕f6 19 ♖b1** 19 ♖d1
♗d7 20 ♗c2 ♖f7 =+ **21 0-0**

**21...h5!? 22 ♘xh5 ♕h6 23 ♘xg7
♔xg7 24 ♕d4+ ♖f6 25 ♕e5! ♖h8
26 f4!= ♕h2+ 27 ♔f2 gxf4! 28 ♕xe7+
♖f7 29 ♕g5+ ♔f8 30 exf4 ♖h3** △
♖f3+ **31 ♖be1 ♖f3+ 32 ♔e2 ♕xg2+
33 ♔d1 ♖xf1 34 ♕h6+ ♔g8 35 ♕g5+
♔f8 ½-½ Gufeld**

25 Platonov-Alburt Kiev 78
1 d4 ♘f6 2 ♘f3 c5 3 c3 3 c4!?; 3 d5
+= **♕c7** 3...d5 **4 dxc5!? 4 ♗g5!?** 4
g3!? **♘e4 5 ♗h4 d5= 6 e3 cxd4 7 exd4
♘c6 8 ♕b3?!** 8 ♗d3!? **♕f4! =+ 9 ♘a3**
9 ♕c2 ♗f5 10 ♗d3 ♖c8∓ **e6 10 ♗d3?**
10 ♗g3 ♘xg3 11 hxg3 ♕e4+ 12 ♗e2
=+ **♘d2 11 ♘xd2 ♕xh4 12 0-0 ♗d6
13 g3** 13 ♘f3 ♕h5 14 ♘b5 ♗f4! △
g5, g4∓ **♕d8** △ h5, h4 **14 ♖fe1** △

♕xd5 ♗e7 14...0-0 **15 ♘ab1 h5 16 ♘f3 h4 17 ♘bd2 ♗d7 18 ♖ac1 ♖b8 19 ♕d1 hxg3 20 hxg3 ♗d6** △ ♕f6, ♕h6∓ **21 ♔g2! ♕f6 22 ♕e2 ♔e7 23 b4! ♖h5?** 23...♖bg8 **24 ♖h1 ♖bh8 25 ♖xh5 ♖xh5 26 ♖h1 ♖xh1 27 ♔xh1** ♔d8∝ **28 ♔g2 a6?!** 28...e5!? **29 b5! axb5 30 ♗xb5 ♕h6 31 ♘b3 ♔e7 32 a4 f6 33 a5!±** ♕h7 33...♗e8 34 a6 bxa6 35 ♗xc6 ♖xc6 36 ♕xa6 ♗e8 37 ♕b7+ △ ♘c5± **34 ♕a2!? ♕h8 35 ♘h4** ♕a8 **36 ♕e2!** △ ♘f5+ ♔d8 37 ♗xc6 bxc6 **38 ♘g6 ♕b7 39 ♘c5 ♗xc5 40 dxc5 ♕a7 41 ♕b2!** +– ♗e8 41...♕xc5 42 ♕b8+ △ a6 +–; 41...♕xa5 42 ♕b8+ ♗c8 43 ♕d6+ ♗d7 44 ♘f8 +– **42 ♘f8! ♕xa5** 42...♔e7 43 ♕b6! +– **43 ♕b7! 1-0 Gufeld**

---

26 Platonov-Adamski Kiev 78

1 d4 ♘f6 2 ♘f3 e6 3 ♗g5 c5 4 e3 b6 4...♕b6?! **5 ♘bd2 ♕xb2 6 ♗d3** += **5 ♗d3** 5 ♘bd2 ♗b7 6 ♘bd2 ♗e7 6...d5 7 c3 cxd4 8 exd4 ♗e7 **7 0-0 ♘c6 8 c3 0-0 9 a3!?** 9 ♕e2; 9 dxc5!? △ e4 += **d5 10 ♕e2 ♖c8 11 ♖ad1** += ♕c7 **12 ♗f4 ♗d6 13 ♗xd6 ♕xd6 14 e4 dxe4 15 ♘xe4 ♕e7 16 dxc5** 16 ♗b1!? **bxc5 17 ♘xf6+ ♕xf6 18 ♗e4** ♕e7 18...♖c7?! **19 ♖d2 h6 20 ♖fd1** ♖fd8 21 h3 21 ♕b5 ♘d4! ♖xd2 22 ♖xd2 ♖d8 23 ♕b5 23 ♕d1 += ♘d4 **24 ♘xd4 ♗xe4 25 ♘c6 ♗xc6 26 ♖xd8+ ♕xd8 27 ♕xc6 ♕g5!** += **28 g3 ♕c1+ 29 ♔g2 ♕xb2 30 ♕xc5 ♕b7+ 31 ♔g1 f5! 32 c4 ♔f7 33 a4 a6 34 a5 g5 35 ♕d4** 35 ♕b6 ♔e4 **♕c7= 36 c5!? ♕xa5 37 ♕d7+ ♔f6 38 c6 ♕c5!** 38...♕e1+ 39 ♔g2 ♕e4+ 40 ♔h2 ♕f3 41 ♔g1 **39 ♔g2 ♕c4 40 c7 ♕e4+ 41 ♔h2 ♕c2 42 ♕d4+ ♔e7 43 ♕d8+ ♔f7 ½-½ Gufeld**

27 Kirpichnikov-Vitolins
Jurmala 78

1 ♘f3 ♘f6 2 d4 e6 3 ♗g5 c5 3...b6 **4 ♘bd2 ♗b7 5 e4 h6 6 ♗xf6 ♕xf6 7 ♗d3 d6 8 c3 g5?!** 9 ♕a4+ ♔d8 10 0-0-0± Hort-Planinc, Moscow 75 **4 e3 ♕b6?!** 4...♗e7; 4...cxd4 **5 ♘bd2! ♕xb2 6 ♗d3 ♘c6** 6...d5 7 c4! +=; 6...♕b6 **7 0-0 ♕b6 8 ♖b1** 8 ♗xf6! gxf6 9 ♘e4 ♗e7 10 ♖b1 △ ♘xc5≈ **♕c7?!** 8...♕d8 9 e4 cxd4 10 e5 += **9 ♗xf6 gxf6 10 ♘e4** += **b6?** 10...f5 **11 ♘xc5 b6** 12 ♘b3 +=; 10...c4? **11 ♗xc4 d5 12 ♗xd5 exd5 13 ♘f6+** ♔d8 **14 ♘xd5** +–; 10...♗e7!? **11 ♘xf6+ ♔e7 12 ♘h5!±** 12 ♕g5? ♔xf6? 13 ♕f3+ ♔xg5 14 h4+ +–; 12...♔d8! += **♗b7 13 c3 ♗h6 14 ♕a4** △ dxc5, ♕h4+ **cxd4 15 cxd4 ♖ag8?** 15...d5!? **16 d5! exd5 17 ♕h4+ ♔f8 18 ♘f6 ♖g6 19 ♗xg6 hxg6 20 ♘xd5 ♕d6 21 ♕f6 ♕xf6 22 ♘xf6 ♗g7?** 22...♔e7! **23 ♘xd7+ ♔e7 24 ♘c5 ♗a8 25 ♘b3** +– **♘e5 26 ♘xe5 ♗xe5 27 g3 ♗e4 28 ♖bc1 a5 29 ♘d4 ♗xd4 30 exd4 ♔d6 31 ♖fe1 f5 32 ♖e3 ♖b8 33 ♖b3 ♗d5 34 ♖b2 a4 35 ♖b4 ♗xa2 36 ♖xa4 ♗b3 37 ♖b4 ♗d5 38 ♖cb1 ♔c6 39 h4 ♖b7 40 ♖c1+ ♔d6 41 ♔f1 ♖b8 42 ♖c3 ♔d7 43 f3! ♔d6 44 ♔f2 f4?! 45 gxf4 ♗c6 46 ♔g3 ♗d7 47 ♖e3 b5 48 ♖e5 ♖f8 49 ♖bxb5 ♗xb5 50 ♖xb5 ♔e6 51 f5+! gxf5 52 ♔f4 ♖h8 53 ♖e5+ ♔d6 54 ♔g5 1-0 Gufeld**

28 Palatnik-Adamski Kiev 78

1 d4 ♘f6 2 ♗g5 ♘e4 2...g6 **3 ♗h4** 3 ♗f4 d5 4 f3 ♘f6 5 e4!? dxe4 6 ♘c3 exf3 7 ♘xf3≈ Jansa-Sosonko, IBM 75; 3...c5 4 f3 ♕a5+! 5 c3 ♘f6 6 d5 d6 7 e4 g6∝ Alburt-Dorfman, USSR 77 **c5 4 f3 g5 5 fxe4 gxh4 6 e3 e6?** 6...♗h6! 7 ♔f2 cxd4 8 exd4 ♕b6 9 ♘c3 e6 10 ♘f3 ♘c6 =+ **7 ♘d2**

66

♘c6 8 c3 += ♗h6 9 ♘c4! d5

10 ♕h5!± ♗g7? 10...♕g5 11 ♕xg5 ♗xg5 12 ♘f3 ♗e7 13 exd5 △ ♘ce5 **11 ♘d2 cxd4 12 exd4 dxe4 13 ♘xe4 0-0 14 ♘f3 e5?! 15 ♗c4! h6 16 0-0 ♘a5 17 ♗xf7+!** +− **♖xf7 18 ♘xe5 ♖xf1+ 19 ♖xf1 ♘c6 20 ♘f6+ ♕xf6 21 ♖xf6 ♘xe5 22 dxe5 ♗d7 23 ♕f7+ 1-0 Gufeld**

1 d4 d5 2 c4 dxc4

29 Alburt-Romanishin Kiev 78

1 d4 d5 2 c4 dxc4 3 e4!? e5 3...c5!? 4 d5 ♘f6 5 ♘c3 b5!≈ **4 ♘f3 ♗b4+** 4...exd4 5 ♗xc4 ♘c6 6 0-0 ♗g4? 7 ♕b3 ♕d7 8 ♗xf7+!± Pytel-Castro, Dortmund 77; 5...♗b4+ 6 ♘bd2 ♘c6 7 a3!? ♗xd2+ 8 ♕xd2 += Grigorian-Dorfman, USSR 75 **5 ♘c3** 5 ♘bd2 c3 6 bxc3 ♗xc3 7 ♖b1 ♘e7! =+; 5 ♗d2 ♗xd2+ 6 ♘bxd2 exd4 7 ♗xc4 ♘h6 8 ♘b3 0-0∞ **exd4 6 ♘xd4!?** 6 ♕xd4 ♕xd4 7 ♘xd4 ♘f6 8 f3 a6 9 ♗xc4 0-0 10 ♗f4 b5= Tukmakov-Romanishin, USSR 70 **♕e7?! 7 ♗xc4! ♕xe4+ 8 ♕f1 ♗xc3 9 bxc3 ♗e6** 9... ♘f6 10 ♗a3 **10 ♕b3! ♗xc4+ 11 ♕xc4 ♘c6** 11...♘f6 12 ♗h6! +− **12 ♗g5!±♕g6 13 ♖e1+ ♕f8 14 ♘xc6 ♕xc6 15 ♕b4+ ♕d6 16 ♕xb7 ♖d8** 16...♖e8 17 ♖xe8+ △ ♕c8+ +− **17 ♗xd8 ♕xd8**

---

18 ♕xa7 +− **♘f6 19 f3 h5 20 ♕d4 ♕a8 21 ♖d1 ♘e8 22 a4 ♖h6 23 ♕b4+ ♕g8 24 ♕f2 ♖b6 25 ♕d4** 25 ♕e7 ♕xa4 26 ♖d8 ♖e6 **♖d6 26 ♕e4 ♖c6 27 ♖d4 ♗d6 28 ♕d5 ♕b7 29 ♖b4 ♕a7+ 30 ♕d4 ♕a5 31 ♖e1 ♕f5 32 ♖e5 ♕c2+ 33 ♖e2 ♕g6 34 c4 ♕h7 35 ♕d5 ♗f5 36 c5 ♕f6 37 ♖f4 g6 38 g4! hxg4 39 fxg4 ♕h4+ 40 ♕g1 ♖f6 41 ♕d8! 1-0 Gufeld**

30 Peev-Inkiov Pernik 78

1 d4 d5 2 c4 dxc4 3 ♘f3 ♘f6 4 ♘c3 a6 5 e4 b5 6 e5 ♘d5 7 a4 ♘xc3 8 bxc3 ♗b7 8...♕d5 9 g3 ♗e6 10 ♗g2 ♕b7 11 0-0 ♗d5 12 e5!?≈ Balashov-Miles, Bugojno 78 **9 e6!? f6?** 9...fxe6 10 ♗e2 ♕d5 11 ♘g5≈ **10 ♗e2 ♕d5 11 0-0 ♕xe6 12 ♖e1 ♕d7?!** 12...♘d7? 13 ♘g5 ♕g8 14 ♗f3; 12...♕f7!? **13 ♘h4 g6 14 ♗g4 f5 15 ♗f3 c6?** 15...♗xf3 16 ♘xf3 ♗g7±; 16 ♕xf3 ♖a7± **16 g4! +− ♖g8 17 ♖a2 e6 18 ♖ae2 ♕f7 19 ♖xe6 ♕xe6 20 ♖xe6 ♕xe6 21 gxf5+ gxf5+ 22 ♕f1 ♗d6 23 ♕c2 ♖f8 24 ♗xf5 ♗d7 25 ♕e4+ 1-0 Webb**

31 Browne-Portisch
Lone Pine 78

1 d4 d5 2 c4 dxc4 3 ♘f3 3 e4 e5 4 ♘f3!? **♘f6 4 e3 e6** 4...♗g4 5 ♗xc4 e6 6 h3 ♗h5 7 ♘c3 ♘bd7 8 0-0 ♗d6 9 e4 e5 += **5 ♗xc4 c5 6 0-0 a6 7 a4! 7 ♕e2?! ♘c6 8 ♕e2 cxd4 9 ♖d1 ♗e7 10 exd4 0-0 11 ♘c3 ♘d5 12 ♗d3 12 ♕e4!? ♘cb4 13 ♗b1 b6 13...♗d7?! 14 a5! bxa5 14...b5!? 15 ♘e5 15 ♘e4 ♗d7 16 ♘e5 ♗b5 Gligoric-Portisch, Bugojno 78 ♗b7 16 ♘e4 16 ♖a3 ♖c8 17 ♖a3! += f5 18 ♘c5! ♗xc5 19 dxc5 ♖xc5 20 ♖g3 ♖c7 21 h4! ♕c8 22 ♗g5 ♘f6 22...♘c6!? 23 h5 ♘e4 24 ♗xe4 ♗xe4 25 h6! ♘d5**

26 hxg7 26 f3! ♗c2? 27 hxg7 ♖xg7 28 ♖c1 ♘b4 29 ♕f2! +−; 26...f4! 27 fxe4 ♖c2! 28 ♕e1 fxg3 29 exd5 ♖ff2∓; 27 hxg7 ♖xg7 28 ♗xf4 ♖xf4! 29 ♖xg7+ ♔xg7 30 fxe4 ♕c5+ 31 ♔h2 ♘f6 =+; 27 ♗xf4! ♖xf4 28 fxe4 ♘f6 29 ♕d2! +− **♖xg7 27 ♖c1 ♕b7 28 ♗h6 ♖xg3 29 fxg3 ♖c8 30 ♖xc8+ ♕xc8 31 ♕h5 ♕c5+ 32 ♔h2 ♕e7 33 ♘c6 ♕d7 34 ♕g5+** 34 ♘e5 ♔h8 35 ♗f8?! ♕f7! 36 ♗h6? 36 ♘d6 h6! =+ **♕f6 37 ♕h5 ♕g6 38 ♕h4 ♘f6 39 ♔g1??** −+ 39 ♘e5∓ **♗xc6 40 ♕f4 e5 41 ♕d2 ♘e4 42 ♕d8+ ♗e8 43 ♗f8 h6 0-1 Browne**

32 Lerner-Beljavsky Kiev 78

1 d4 ♘f6 2 ♘f3 d5 3 c4 dxc4 4 e3 ♗g4 5 ♗xc4 e6 6 ♘c3 6 h3 ♗h5 7 ♘c3 ♘bd7 8 0-0 ♗d6 9 e4 e5= Hort-Matulovic, Novi Sad 76 **a6** 6...♘bd7!? 7 0-0 ♗d6 8 e4 e5= **7 h3 ♗h5 8 ♗e2** 8 g4!?; 8 0-0 ♘c6 9 ♖e1 ♗d6 10 e4 ♗xf3 11 gxf3∝ **♘c6 9 0-0 ♗d6 10 b3** 10 ♔h1; 10 a3!? **0-0 11 ♗b2 ♕e8!** 11...♕e7 12 ♖c1 ♖fd8 13 ♘d2 += **12 ♘e5?!** 12 ♖c1 ♖d8 13 ♘d2 ♗xe2 14 ♕xe2 ♕e7≈; 12 ♘d2! ♗g6 13 ♘c4 += **♗xe2 13 ♘xe2 ♖d8 14 ♘xc6 ♕xc6 15 ♖c1 ♕b5! 16 ♘c3 ♕g5 17 ♕f3 c6 18 ♖fd1** 18 ♘a4= **♕g6∝ 19 ♕e2?** 19 a3!? **♘d5 20 ♘e4∝ ♗d5 20 e4 ♘xc3 21 ♗xc3 f5! =+ 22 ♗a5**

♖d7 23 e5? 23 ♖e1 ♗e7 24 ♗b6 ♖d5 25 ♕c4 ♕e8 26 ♖d3 ♗f7 27 a4 ♗d8 28 ♗xd8 ♕xd8 29 b4 ♖fd7 30 a5? **♕h4!∓ 31 ♖cd1 ♔f7!** 31...♖xe5 32 g3 ♕e4 33 ♖e3! **32 ♕c3 ♖b5 33 ♖e1 ♖d8 34 ♖e2 ♖bd5 35 ♖ed2 g5! 36 ♖d1 h5 37 ♕d2 ♕f4! 38 ♕e2** 38 ♕xf4 gxf4 39 ♔f1 ♖b5 40 ♖b1 c5! −+ **g4 39 g3 ♕h6 −+ 40 ♔g2 gxh3+ 41 ♔xh3 ♖g8 42 ♔g2 ♖g4 43 ♕d2 ♕xd2 44 ♖3xd2 f4 45 ♔f3 fxg3 46 fxg3 ♔g6 47 ♖d3 ♔g5 48 ♖1d2 ♖d7 49 ♔f2 ♔f5 50 ♖f3+ ♔e4 51 ♖e3+ ♔d5 52 ♖c2 ♖f7+ 53 ♔e2 ♖e4 54 ♔d3 ♖xd4+ 55 ♔e2 ♖xb4 0-1 Gufeld**

33 Lukacs-Mihalchishin USSR 78

1 d4 d5 2 c4 dxc4 3 ♘f3 ♘f6 4 e3 ♗g4 5 ♗xc4 e6 6 h3 ♗h5 7 ♘c3 ♘bd7 8 0-0 ♗d6 9 ♗e2 0-0 10 e4 e5 11 dxe5 ♘xe5 12 ♘d4 ♗g6 12...♗xe2 13 ♕xe2 ♘g6 14 ♘f5 ♗e5 15 f4 ♗xc3 16 bxc3 ♖e8 17 e5 ♘d5 18 ♕f3 += Lukacs-Marszalek, Budapest 76 **13 ♗g5 ♗e7** 13...♖e8? 14 ♘db5± Portisch-Spassky (8) 77 **14 ♘f5! += ♗xf5 15 exf5 c6 16 ♕c2 h6 17 ♖ad1 ♘ed7 18 ♗h4 ♖e8 19 ♗c4 ♕c7?** 19...♕b6 20 ♖fe1 += **20 ♘b5! ♕b8 21 ♗g3 ♘e5 22 ♖fe1 ♗f8** 22...cxb5 23 ♖xe5

23 ♗e6! +− fxe6 24 ♗xe5 ♕c8 25

♘c7 ♘d5 26 ♘xa8 ♕xa8 27 f6 gxf6
28 ♗d4 ♗g7 29 ♕g6 ♘c8 30 ♗e3 ♘e7
31 ♕h5 ♘f5 32 ♗xa7 e5 33 ♗c5 ♘e7
34 ♗xe7 ♖xe7 35 ♕g6 1-0 Webb

1 d4 d5 2 c4 c6

34 Ogaard-Mestel Esbjerg 78
1 d4 e6 2 ♘f3 d5 3 c4 c6 4 ♘c3 dxc4
5 a4 ♗b4 6 e3 b5 7 ♗d2 a5! 8 axb5
♗xc3 9 ♗xc3 cxb5 10 b3 ♗b7 11 bxc4
b4 12 ♗b2 ♘f6 13 ♗d3 ♗e4! 14 ♗xe4
♘xe4 15 ♕c2 f5 16 0-0 16 d5 0-0 17
♘d4! ♘c5! 0-0 17 ♖fd1 ♘d7 18 d5
♘dc5 19 ♘d4 ♕b6 20 dxe6 b3 20...a4
21 f3 21 ♕b1 ♘xe6 22 ♗xf5! ♘6g5!
23 ♖d7 ♖a7 24 ♘e7+ ♔h8 25 ♘d5
♘f3+ 25...♕g6? 26 ♗xg7+ ♔g8 27
♘e7+ +− 26 ♔f1 26 ♔h1?? ♘xf2
mate; 26 gxf3?? ♕g6+ 27 ♔f1 ♘d2+
−+ ♖xd7 26...♘fd2+ 27 ♔g1 ♘df3+ =;
27 ♔e1 ♖xd7 28 ♘xb6 ♖df7 −+ 27
♘xb6 ♘fd2+ 28 ♔g1 ♘xb1 28...
♖df7? 29 ♕e1 +− 29 ♘xd7 ♖d8 30
♖xa5 h6 31 ♖d5?! 31 ♖a7! ♘c5?
32 ♗xg7+ ♔h7 33 ♘f6+ ♔g6 34 ♘d5!;
31...♘f6 32 ♗xf6 gxf6 33 h4! △
♘xf6, ♖h7 mate ♘bc3 32 ♖d3 ♘a4 33
♘c5! ♖xd3 34 ♘xd3 ♘ec5 35 ♘xc5
♘xc5 36 ♔f1 ♘a4 37 ♗d4 ♔g8 38
♔e2 b2 39 ♗xb2 ♘xb2 40 c5 ♔f7
41 e4 ♘a4 42 c6 ♔e6 43 ♔e3 ♘b6
44 h4 ♘c8 45 ♔f4 ♘e7 46 c7 ♔d6
47 h5 ♔xc7 48 ♔e5 ♔d7 49 g4 ♘c6+
50 ♔f5 ♘e7+ 51 ♔e5 ♘c6+ 52 ♔f5
♔e7 53 e5 ♔f7 54 f4 ♘d4+ 55 ♔e4
♘e6 56 ♔e3 ♘d8 57 ♔e4 ♔e7 58
♔f5 ♘e6 59 ♔g6 ♔f8 60 f5 ♘f4+ ½-½

35 Sturua-Haritonov USSR 77
1 ♘f3 d5 2 c4 c6 3 d4 3 g3 ♘f6 4
♘c3 dxc4 5 a4 ♗f5 6 e3 e6 7 ♗xc4
♗b4 8 0-0 0-0 9 ♘h4!? 9 ♕e2 ♗g6
9...♗g4 10 f3 ♗h5 11 g4 ♗g6 12 ♘xg6

hxg6 13 g5 ♘d5∞; 11...♘d5!? 10
♘xg6 hxg6 11 ♕e2 ♘bd7 12 ♖d1
♕e7 13 e4 += e5 14 d5 ♘b6 15 ♗b3
cxd5 16 exd5?! 16 ♘xd5 += ♘c8!
17 ♗g5 ♘d6 =+ 18 ♘b5 18 ♖d4?!
♗c5 19 ♖e4 ♘dxe4 20 ♘xe4∞; 18...
♘f5!∓ a6 19 ♘xd6 ♗xd6 20 ♖d3
e4! 21 ♖h3 ♕e5 22 ♗xf6 gxf6∓
23 ♕d2 f5 24 ♕h6 ♖fc8 25 ♕h7+
♔f8 26 ♕h8+ ♕xh8 27 ♖xh8+ ♔e7
28 ♖xc8 ♖xc8 29 ♔f1 ♗e5 30 ♖b1?!
30 d6+!∓ ♔d6 31 h3 f4 32 ♔e2 f5
33 f3 ♗d4 −+ 34 ♔d1 exf3 35 gxf3
♖h8 36 ♔c2 ♖xh3 37 ♖e1 ♗e3 38
♖f1 g5 39 ♔d3 g4 40 fxg4 fxg4
0-1 Gufeld

36 Andersson-Damjanovic
Torremolinos 78
1 ♘f3 d5 2 d4 ♘f6 3 c4 c6 4 cxd5
cxd5 5 ♘c3 ♘c6 6 ♗f4 e6 7 e3 ♗d6
7...♗e7; 7...♘h5 8 ♗d3!? 8 ♗g3 0-0
9 ♗d3 a6 10 ♖c1 ♕e7= 0-0 8...♗xf4
9 exf4 ♕b6 10 ♕d2≈ 9 0-0 h6 10
♕d2 ♕e7 11 ♖ac1 ♗d7 12 h3 ♖fc8
13 ♘e5 ♗e8 14 ♗h2 ♗b4 15 a3 ♗xc3
16 ♖xc3 ♘xe5 17 ♗xe5 ♘e4= 18
♗xe4 dxe4 19 ♖fc1 ♖xc3 20 ♕xc3
△ d5 f6 21 ♗g3 ♗c6 22 ♕a5 a6 23
b4 ♖d8? 23...♕d8!? 24 ♕b6 △ a4
♕e8 25 a4 ♖d5 25...♗xa4 26 ♕xb7±

26 b5! axb5 27 a5 ♕a8 28 a6 +−

Rd8 29 a7 Rc8 30 Bb8 Kh7 31 Rc5
Rg8 32 Kf1 Bd5 33 Qxb5 Rd8 34
Kg1 f5 35 Qb6 Rxb8 36 axb8Q
Qxb8 37 Qc7 Qxc7 38 Rxc7 b5 39
Rc8 b4 40 Rb8 b3 41 Kf1 g5 42 Ke1
Kg6 43 g3 h5 44 Kd2 h4 45 gxh4
gxh4 46 Kc3 Kf6 47 Rf8+ Kg7 48
Rd8 △ Rxd5 Bc6 49 Rb8 Bd5 50 Rb5
Kf6 51 Rxd5 1-0 Webb

37 Rashkovsky-Kosikov
Daugavpils 78
1 Nf3 Nf6 2 c4 c6 3 d4 d5 4 cxd5
cxd5 5 Nc3 Nc6 6 Bf4 Bf5 7 e3 e6
8 Bb5 Nd7 9 Qa4 Qb6 10 Nh4 Be4!?
10...Bg6 11 Nxg6 hxg6 12 e4 +=;
10...Bg4!? 11 Rc1 Rc8 12 0-0 a6 13
Bxc6 Rxc6 14 Nxe4 dxe4

15 d5!± exd5 16 Nf5 g6 17 Nd4
Rxc1 18 Rxc1 Qxb2?! 19 Rc8+ Ke7
20 Nb3! g5 21 Bxg5+ f6 22 Qb4+!
+- Kf7 23 Qxb7 Be7 24 Qxd5+ Kg7
25 Qxd7 Rxc8 26 Qxe7+ 1-0 Suetin

38 Commons-Mednis
USA Final 78
1 c4 Nf6 2 Nc3 e6 3 Nf3 d5 4 d4 c6
5 Qb3 Be7 6 Bg5 0-0 7 e3 Nbd7 8
Bd3 dxc4 9 Bxc4 c5!? N 10 Rd1
10 0-0!+= cxd4 11 Nxd4 11 Rxd4!?
+= Qa5= 12 Qb5 12 Nh4 Qc7! 13
a4?! 13 Nxe6 fxe6 14 Bxe6+ Kh8

15 Bxd7 a6! 16 Qa4 Bxd7 17 Rxd7
Nxd7 18 Bxe7 Rfe8 =+; 13 Qb3=
Nc5! 14 Be2 Nd7 15 Qc4 Rac8?!
15...Rfc8!=+ 16 0-0!= Qb8 16...
Nxa4?! 17 Qxc7 Rxc7 18 Nxa4
Bxa4 19 Ra1 △ Rxa7 += 17 Qa2
Rfd8 18 Bb5 a6 18...Be8!? 19 Bxd7
Ncxd7 20 Nb3?! 20 Nxe6!? fxe6 21
Qxe6+ Kf8 22 Rxd7 Rxd7 23 Bxf6
Qd6 24 Bxe7+ Qxe7 25 Qh3!? Rc6
26 Qxh7 Rd2∞; 20 Nf3= Bd6! 21
h3 h6 22 Bxf6 Nxf6 23 Nd4 Bb4! =+
24 Qb3? 24 Nce2 =+ Bxc3 25 bxc3
Qc7∓ 26 Rb1 Rd7 27 Rfc1 Ne4
28 Qa3 28 Nxe6? Qd6! -+ Qc5!
29 Qxc5 Rxc5 30 c4 Rdc7 31 Nb3
Rxc4 32 Rxc4 Rxc4 33 Na5 Rxa4
34 Nxb7 Ra2 35 f3 Nc3 36 Rb3 Nd5
37 Nd6 37 e4 Nf4 -+; 37 g3 a5! 38
e4 a4 -+ a5 38 h4 a4 39 Rb8+ Kh7
40 Nxf7 40 e4? Ne3 -+ Nxe3 41
g4 a3! 42 h5?! 42 Ra8! Rg2+ 43 Kh1
a2 44 h5 g5 45 hxg6+ Kxg6 46 Ne5+
Kg5 47 Nc4 Re2 48 Nxe3 Re1+ 49
Kg2 a1Q 50 Rxa1 Rxa1 ∓/-+ g5
-+ 43 Rb3 43 Rb7 Rb2 Nc2! 44
Rd3 Rb2 45 Rd7 a2 46 Nxg5+ Kg8
47 Rd8+ Kg7 48 Rd7+ Kf6 48...
Kf8?? 49 Nh7+ = 0-1 Mednis

39 Browne-Polugaevsky
Reykjavik 78
1 d4 Nf6 2 c4 e6 3 Nf3 d5 4 Nc3
c6 5 e3 Nbd7 6 Bd3 dxc4 7 Bxc4
b5 8 Bb3?! 8 Bd3 a6 9 e4 c5 10
d5 e5 11 0-0 c4 12 Bc2 Bc5=; 10
e5 +=; 8...Bb7 9 e4 b4 10 Na4 c5
11 e5 Nd5 12 0-0 cxd4 13 Re1 g6
14 Bg5 b4 9 Ne2 Bb7 9...c5 10 0-0
Bb7 11 Nf4 cxd4? 12 exd4 Nb6 13
Ng5 += 10 0-0 10 Nf4 Bd6 11 Ng5
Bxf4 12 exf4 h6 13 Nf3= Bd6 11
Nf4 0-0 12 Re1 c5! 12...e5? 13
dxe5 Nxe5 14 Nxe5 Bxe5 15 Nd3

♗d6 16 e4 += **13 d5** 13 ♗xe6? ♗xf4
14 ♗xd7 ♕xd7 15 exf4 ♗xf3 16 ♕xf3
cxd4 =+ **exd5** 13...♗xf4 14 dxe6
♗xf3! 15 gxf3 ♗xh2+ 16 ♔xh2 c4!
=+; 13...e5? 14 ♘e6! **14 ♘xd5 ♖c8!**
14...♘xd5?! 15 ♗xd5 ♗xd5 16 ♕xd5
♘f6 17 ♕c4 +=; 16...♘b6 17 ♕h5 +=
**15 e4 c4 =+ 16 ♘xf6+ ♕xf6 17 ♗g5
♕g6 18 ♗c2 ♖fe8?!** 18...♘e5 19 ♘xe5
♗xe5 20 ♗e7!∞ **19 ♗f4!?** 19 ♗a4!
♗c6? 20 ♗xc6 ♖xc6 21 e5! +−; 19...
♖c7 20 e5!! ♗xf3 21 exd6!! ♖xe1+
22 ♕xe1 ♕xg5 23 ♕e8+ ♘f8 24
g3 ♕f5! 25 ♖e1 g6; 23 g3! ♖c5 24
♗xd7 ♖e5 25 ♕xb4 +− **♗xf4 20 ♕xd7
♕b6 21 ♕f5 ♗h6** 21...♕f6!? =+ **22 e5
g6** 22...♕g6?? 23 ♕xc8!± **23 ♕h3
♗g7 24 e6! ♖xe6?!** 24...♗xf3 25
exf7+ ♔xf7 26 ♕xf3+ ♔g8 27 ♕d5+
♔h8 28 ♖xe8+ ♖xe8= **25 ♘g5 ♖xe1+
26 ♖xe1 h6?** 26...♕f6! 27 ♕xh7+
♔f8 28 ♕h4 ♕d4! =+; 27 ♘xh7!
♕xb2 28 ♗xg6! fxg6 29 ♘g5 ♕f6?
30 ♕h7+ ♔f8 31 ♘e6+ ♔f7 32 ♘xg7
+−; 29...♕c3!∞; 26...b3! 27 axb3
♕a5 28 ♕e3 ♗d4! 29 ♕e7 ♕c7! =+
27 ♘xf7! ♔xf7?? 27...♖f8! 28 ♖e6
♗c8 29 ♖xb6 ♗xh3 30 ♘xh6+! ♔h7
31 ♖xg6 +−; 30...♗xh6 31 ♖xg6+
♗g7 32 gxh3 ♖c8 33 ♖g4± **28 ♕d7+
♔g8 29 ♖e7 ♕d4? 30 ♕e6+! ♔h8
31 ♕xg6 ♗e4 32 ♖xe4 ♕d7 1-0
Browne**

40 Beljavsky-Platonov Kiev 78
**1 d4 d5 2 c4 c6 3 ♘f3 ♘f6 4 ♘c3
e6 5 e3 ♘bd7 6 ♗d3 dxc4** 6...♗b4 7
0-0 0-0 8 ♕c2 dxc4!? **7 ♗xc4 b5 8
♗d3** 8 ♗b3 b4 9 ♘e2 c5 10 0-0 ♗b7
11 ♘f4 += Geller-Whiteley, Moscow
77 **♗b7 9 a3** 9 e4 **♗d6** 9...a6 10
b4 ♗d6 11 0-0 0-0 12 ♘e4 +=; 9...
b4 10 axb4 ♗xb4 11 0-0 ♗e7 △ c5;
9...a5!? **10 0-0** 10 ♕c2!? += **0-0 11**

22...f6?! 22...♕f8= **23 ♗e3 ♖c8 24
♗c4 ♘e5?** 24...♔h8= **25 ♘xe5 ♗xe5
26 ♕b3 ♔f8 27 f3 ♖c6 28 ♖d1±
♗xb2? 29 ♗b5! +− ♖c3 30 ♕xb2
♖xe3 31 ♕d4 1-0 Gufeld**

41 Tukmakov-Sveshnikov Lvov 78
**1 d4 d5 2 c4 e6 3 ♘c3 c6 4 e3 ♘f6 5
♘f3 ♘bd7 6 ♗d3 dxc4 7 ♗xc4 b5 8
♗d3** 8 ♗b3 b4 9 ♘e2 ♗b7 10 ♘f4
♗d6 11 0-0 ♕e7!? += Grigorian-
Dorfman, USSR 76; 9...c5 10 0-0
♗b7 11 ♘f4 ♗d6! 12 ♘g5 ♗xf4 13
exf4 h6 14 ♘f3 0-0=; 9...♗e7! **♗b7**
8...b4 9 ♘e4 ♗b7 10 0-0 c5 11 ♘xc5
♘xc5 12 dxc5 ♗xc5 13 ♕a4+ ♔e7
=+ Sakharov-Sveshnikov, USSR 77
**9 e4 b4 10 ♘a4 c5 11 e5 ♘d5 12
0-0** 12 ♘xc5 ♘xc5 13 dxc5 ♗xc5
14 0-0 h6 15 ♘d2 ♘c3 16 ♕c2 ♕d5
17 ♘f3 ♖d8 18 ♘e1! += Polugaevsky-
Mecking, Manila 75 **cxd4 13 ♖e1 g6**
13...♗e7 14 ♘xd4 ♕a5 15 ♗d2 0-0
16 a3 ♖fd8 17 ♖c1 += Eising-Mednis,

Mannheim 75; 13...♕a5!? **14 &g5
♕a5!** 14...&e7?! 15 &h6! a6 16 ♖c1
&f8 17 &g5 ♕a5 18 ♘d2!± **15 ♘d2!?**
15 ♘xd4 &g7? 16 &b5!± Marjanovic-
Karaklaic, Jugoslavia 77; 15...a6!=
&a6! 16 &xa6 16 ♘c4?! &xc4 17
&xc4 &g7 18 ♕xd4!? ♕xa4 19 &xd5
exd5 20 ♕xd5 ♘b6 21 ♕c5 &f8∓
Gligoric-Ljubojevic, Jugoslavia 76
♕xa6 17 ♘e4 &g7! 18 ♘ac5 18 ♘d6+
♔f8 19 ♕f3 ♘xe5∓ **♘xc5 19 ♘xc5
♕b5 20 ♕xd4 0-0 21 ♘e4 ♕b6!** =+
22 ♕xb6 axb6! 23 ♘f6+? 23 ♘d6!
=+ **&xf6! 24 &xf6 ♖fc8 25 ♖ec1
♕f8∓ 26 g3 ♖xc1+ 27 ♖xc1 ♔e8 28
♖a1 b5 29 &g5 b3 30 a3 ♖c8!** 30...
b4?! **31 ♖c1 ♖c4** −+ **32 ♔f1 ♔d7
33 &h6 ♔c6 34 ♔e2 ♘b6 35 ♔d3
♔d5 36 ♖c3 ♘a4 0-1 Gufeld**

42 Lerner-Platonov Kiev 78
1 d4 d5 2 c4 c6 3 ♘f3 ♘f6 4 e3
4 ♘c3 &f5 4...e6 5 ♘bd2!? &d6 6
b3 0-0 7 &d3 ♘bd7 8 &b2 += **5 ♕b3
♕b6 6 cxd5 cxd5** 6...♕xb3 7 axb3
cxd5 8 ♘c3 += **7 ♘c3 e6 8 &b5+!**
+= **♘c6 9 ♘e5 ♖c8 10 &d2** 10 0-0
&d6 11 &d2 &xe5!? 12 dxe5 ♘e4
**&d6 11 ♖c1 0-0 12 ♘a4! ♕d8 13
&xc6 bxc6 14 ♘c5± △ ♘b7 +− &xe5
15 dxe5 ♘g4** 15...♘d7?! **16 e4! dxe4
17 &f4** △ h3 g5 17...e3 18 &xe3
♘xe3 19 ♕xe3± **18 &g3 ♕d4!? 19
♖c4! ♕d5 20 0-0** △ ♖d1 e3 21 fxe3!
21 ♖d1 exf2+ 22 ♔h1 f1♕+! **♘xe3
22 ♕xe3 ♕xc4 23 b3! ♕b4** 23...
♕g4?! 24 ♘d7 +− **24 &e1! ♕b6 25
♕xg5+ &g6 26 &f2 +− ♕d8 27 ♕f4!
♕d5 28 &e3 ♖b8 29 h4 ♖b5 30 ♖c1
a5 31 h5! &xh5 32 ♘e4 f5 33 ♘f6+
33 exf6? ♕f5 **♖xf6 34 exf6 &g6
34...♔e5 35 ♔h6 ♔c7 36 ♖xc6! +−
35 ♔c7 1-0 Gufeld**

43 Browne-Formanek
Lone Pine 78
1 d4 d5 2 c4 c6 3 e3 ♘f6 4 &d3!?
4 ♘c3 g6 5 ♘f3 &g7 5...&f5 6 ♘c3
0-0 7 0-0 &f5 7...&g4 8 h3 &xf3
9 ♕xf3 += **8 ♖e1 ♘bd7 9 e4** 9 &f1!?
♘e4; 9 b3!? **dxe4 10 ♘xe4 ♘xe4
11 &xe4 &xe4 12 ♖xe4 e5?!** 12...e6=
13 &g5! f6 13...♕c7?! 14 &e7! ♖fe8
15 d5! cxd5 16 cxd5 ♖xe7 17 d6
♕c6 18 dxe7 ♕xe4 19 ♕xd7 ♕c6
20 ♕xc6 bxc6 21 ♖d1 &f6 22 ♘xe5!
+−; 13...♕a5 14 b4! ♕xb4 15 dxe5
+= **14 &h4** 14 dxe5? ♘xe5! 15 ♘xe5
fxg5! 16 ♘d7 ♖f7 =+; 14...fxg5
15 ♖d4! **g5** 14...♕c7!? 15 dxe5 f5!
16 ♖d4 ♘xe5 17 ♘xe5 &xe5?! 18
♖d7 &xh2+ 19 ♔h1 ♕f4 20 g3!;
17...♕xe5 18 ♖d7 ♖ab8? 19 &e7!

15 dxe5! gxh4! 15...♘xe5? 16 ♘xe5
**16 ♖d4 fxe5 17 ♖xd7 ♕f6 18 ♕d3
♖ad8 19 ♖xd8 ♖xd8 20 ♕e4** +=
♕f4! 21 ♖e1 21 ♕xf4? exf4 22 ♔f1
b5! 23 cxb5 cxb5 24 ♖b1 ♖c8! **♕xe4
22 ♖xe4 ♖d1+ 23 ♖e1!** 23 ♘e1?
♖a1! 24 a3 ♖b1 25 ♖e2 ♖c1= **♖xe1+
24 ♘xe1 e4! += 25 b3 ♔f7?** 25...h3!
+= **26 h3! ♔e6 27 ♔f1 ♔e5 28 ♘c2
&f6 29 ♔e2 a5 30 ♔e3 &g5+ 31 ♔e2
&d8 32 ♘e3 ♔d4 33 f4! exf3+ 34
gxf3 ♔c3? 34...&g5! 35 ♘d1+ 35
f4!? ♔c2? 35...♔d4 36 f4 b5 37**

cxb5 cxb5 38 f5 b4 38...a4!? **39
♗e3+ ♚b2 40 ♛d3 ♚xa2 41 ♛c4 ♚a3**
41...a4 42 bxa4 b3 43 ♘d1 b2 44
♘xb2 ♚xb2 45 ♛b5 ♚c3 46 a5 +−
42 ♘c2+ ♚b2 43 ♘d4 ♗f6? 43...♚a3!
44 ♘c6 +− a4 45 bxa4 b3 46 ♘a5
1-0 Browne

44 Evans-Dorfman Sao Paulo 78
1 c4 ♘f6 2 g3 c6!= 3 ♗g2 d5 4 cxd5
4 b3 dxc4 5 bxc4 ♕d4!? 6 ♘c3≈
cxd5 5 ♘f3 ♘c6 6 d4 ♗f5!? 7 ♘c3
e6 8 0-0 ♗e7 9 ♘h4 ♗e4 10 f3 10
♘xe4 ♘xe4 11 ♘f3= ♗g6 **11 e3 ♖c8
12 ♘xg6 hxg6 13 b3 0-0 14 ♗b2 a6
15 ♖f2 ♕a5 16 a3 ♘a7 17 b4 ♕d8
18 ♗f1 ♘e8 19 e4 dxe4 20 ♘xe4**
20 fxe4!? **♘f6 21 ♘c5 ♕b6 =+ 22 ♖c1
♘c6 23 ♕a4** △ b5 ♘b8! 24 ♖fc2 ♖cd8
**25 ♕b3 ♘d5 26 ♚h1 ♗f6 27 ♗g2
♘e7 28 f4 ♘bc6 29 ♘xb7** 29 ♘xe6?!
fxe6 30 ♕xe6+ ♚h8=; 30...♖f7 31
d5 ♗xb2 32 ♖xb2 ♕d4!∓ **♕xb7 30
♗xc6 ♘xc6 31 ♖xc6 ♗xd4 32 ♗xd4
♖xd4∓ 33 ♕f3 ♖fd8 34 ♖6c3 ♕b5
35 ♖c8?** 35 ♖c5 ♕a4 △ ♖d3/♖d1+;
35 ♕f1 ♕a4 △ ♖d1 ♖xc8 **36 ♖xc8+
♚h7 37 ♖c5** 37 ♖c3 ♕d7 △ ♕d1+
♕d7 **38 ♖c2 ♖d3 39 ♕c6 ♖d1+
40 ♚g2 ♕d3 −+ 41 ♚h3** 41 ♖f2 ♕b1
♖g1 42 ♚c5 **♕f1+ 43 ♚h4 ♖g2!**
△ ♕h1 **0-1** 44 ♖xg2 ♕xg2 45 h3 ♕f3
46 ♕g5 ♕xa3 −+ **Webb**

1 d4 d5 2 c4 ♘c6

45 Smyslov-Castro Sao Paulo 78
**1 ♘f3 d5 2 d4 ♘c6 3 c4 ♗g4 4 cxd5
♗xf3 5 gxf3 ♕xd5 6 e3 e6 7 ♘c3
♕d7?!** 7...♗b4 **8 f4 ♘ge7 9 ♗d2
♘f5 10 ♕a4 ♗e7 11 0-0-0± 0-0** 11...
0-0-0?! 12 ♗g2±; 11...♘b4!?

12 ♗e1! △ ♗h3, d5 **♕c8 13 d5 ♘b4**
13...exd5 14 ♘xd5 ♗d6 15 ♗h3;
14...♘d6 15 ♕xc6 **14 e4 ♘h4 15
♗h3 f5 16 a3 ♘a6 17 ♕c4 ♘c5 18
f3!** +− a6 18...♘xf3 19 exf5 **19
♗xh4 b5 20 ♗xe7! bxc4 21 ♗xc5
♖f7 22 dxe6 ♕xe6 23 ♗xf5 ♖xf5
24 exf5 ♕xf5 25 ♗e3 ♖e8 26 ♘d2
♕h3 27 ♖df1 ♖d8 28 ♘e4 1-0 Webb**

1 d4 d5 2 c4 e6

46 Gheorghiu-Herbert USA 78
1 d4 ♘f6 2 c4 e6 3 ♘f3 c5 3...d5;
3...♗b4+; 3...b6 **4 e3 d5 5 ♘c3 ♘c6
6 cxd5** 6 a3 += exd5 6...♘xd5 +=
**7 ♗e2 ♗d6 8 dxc5 ♗xc5 9 0-0 0-0
10 b3!** a6 10...♗f5 11 ♗b2 ♖c8 12
♖c1 h6 13 ♘b5±; 10...d4? 11 ♘a4±
**11 ♗b2 ♗e6 12 ♖c1 ♕e7 13 ♘a4!
♗a7**

14 ♗xa6!!± ♗xe3 14...bxa6 15 ♖xc6± **15 ♗xb7!** 15 ♗xf6 ♕xf6 16 ♗xb7± **♖xa4! 16 ♗xc6 ♗xc1! 17 ♗xf6 ♕xf6 18 ♗xa4 ♗b2 19 ♗b5!** △ ♗d3± **d4 20 ♗d3 ♗c3 21 ♘d2!** △ ♘e4± **♕f4** 21... ♗d5 22 ♕h5! **22 ♘e4 ♗b4 23 ♕c1! ♕f5** 23...♕xc1 24 ♖xc1 ♖a8 25 ♖c2!± **24 ♖d1 h6** 24...♖c8 25 ♕g5!± **25 a3! +− ♖c8 26 ♕b1!! ♗xa3** 26...♗f8 27 b4 **27 ♘d6 ♕c5 28 ♘xc8 ♗xc8 29 ♗c4 ♗f5 30 ♕a1! ♗g4 31 ♖xd4 1-0 Gheorghiu**

47 Miles-Petursson
Lone Pine 78
1 c4 ♘f6 2 ♘c3 c5 3 ♘f3 e6 4 e3 ♘c6 5 d4 d5 6 cxd5 exd5 7 ♗e2 ♗e7 8 0-0 0-0 9 b3 ♘e4 10 ♗b2 ♗f6 11 ♘a4 ♗g4!? 12 h3?! △ 12...♗xf3 13 gxf3 **♗xf3 13 ♗xf3** 13 gxf3 ♘g5 14 ♘xc5 ♗xd4! 15 ♗xd4 ♘xh3+ 16 ♔g2 ♕g5+ = cxd4 **14 exd4 b5?!** 14...♘g5 △ ♘e6 =/=+ **15 ♖c1** 15 ♘c5!? ♘xc5 16 ♖c1 **♘xd4 16 ♗xd4 bxa4 17 bxa4** += **♖e8 18 ♖e1 ♗xd4?!** 18...h6 **19 ♕xd4 ♕b6?!** 20 ♖ed1 ♘f6 21 ♕xb6 axb6 22 ♖d4 ♖ac8 23 ♖xc8 ♖xc8 **24 ♖b4± ♖c1+ 25 ♔h2 h5** 25...h6; 25...♖c6? 26 a5 +− **26 ♖xb6 ♖c2 27 a3 ♖c3 28 a5 ♖xa3 29 a6 ♔h7** 29...d4 30 ♗e2 d3 31 ♗xd3 +− **30 ♗e2 h4 31 ♖b7 ♔g6 32 a7 ♘e4 33 ♖b6+ 1-0 Miles**

48 Knaak-Nogueiras Jurmala 78
1 d4 d5 2 c4 e6 3 ♘c3 c5 4 cxd5 exd5 5 e4!? dxe4 6 d5 f5! 6...♘f6 7 ♗f4!? ♗d6 8 ♗b5+ ♔f8 9 ♘ge2≈ **7 ♗f4** 7 ♗b5+ ♗d7 8 ♗xd7+ ♕xd7 9 ♘h3 ♗d6 10 ♘g5 ♘a6 =+ **♗d6 8 ♗b5+** 8 ♘h3 a6! **♕f7 9 ♘h3 ♘f6 10 ♗c4** 10 ♘g5+?! ♔g6 11 ♕d2 ♗xf4 12 ♕xf4 ♘h5 13 ♕e5 ♕xg5∓ **a6 11 a4 ♖e8 12 ♕d2 ♕e7 13 0-0!?**

N 13 0-0-0 ♔g8 14 ♘g5 ♘bd7 15 ♘e6 b5! 16 axb5 ♘b6 =+; 13 a5 ♘bd7 14 ♘g5+ ♔g8! 15 ♘e6 ♘f8 =+ **♘bd7?** 13...♔g8! 14 ♘g5 h6 15 ♘e6 ♔h7 α/=+ **14 ♘g5+ ♔g8 15 ♘e6± ♘f8?** 15...♘b6

16 ♗xd6 ♕xd6 17 ♘c7! ♗g4 17... ♕xc7? 18 d6+ +− **18 f4! ♗d7 19 ♘xa8 ♖xa8 20 h3 ♘f6 21 a5! +− ♔h8 22 ♖a3 ♘e6 23 ♖b3 b5 24 axb6 ♘d4 25 b7 ♖b8 26 ♖a3 ♗b5** 26...♖xb7 27 ♖xa6 +− **27 ♗xb5 axb5 28 ♖a8 b4 29 ♘e2 ♘b5 30 ♕c2 ♘d7 31 ♕a4 ♕b6 32 ♖xb8+ ♘xb8 33 ♕a8 ♕d8 34 ♖a1 1-0 Gufeld**

49 Sturua-Vladimirov USSR 77
1 d4 d5 2 ♘f3 c5 3 c4 3 dxc5 += e6 4 cxd5 exd5 5 ♘c3 ♘c6 6 g3 ♘f6 7 ♗g2 ♗e7 8 0-0 0-0 9 ♗g5** 9 dxc5 c4 N 9...cxd4 10 ♘xd4 h6 11 ♗e3 ♖e8= **10 ♘e5 ♗e6 11 ♘xc4?** 11 f4 += dxc4 **12 ♗xf6 ♗xf6 13 d5 ♕b6!** =+ **14 ♘a4 ♕b4! 15 a3 ♕b5 16 dxe6 fxe6 17 ♗xc6!? ♕xc6 18 ♘c3 ♗xc3?!** 18...b5 19 ♕c2 ♖b8 20 ♘e4 b4 21 axb4 ♖xb4 =+ **19 bxc3 ♖f5 20 ♕d4 ♖d5 21 ♕e3 ♕d6 22 a4 ♕e5 23 ♕xe5 ♖xe5 24 e3 ♖d8 25 ♖fd1 ♖xd1+** 25...♖ed5 26 ♖xd5 ♖xd5 27 ♖a2 **26 ♖xd1 ♖d5 27 ♖b1 b6 28 ♖b4 ♖c5 29 ♔g2 ♔f7 ½-½ Gufeld**

50 Timman-Gligoric Niksic 78

1 d4 d5 2 c4 e6 3 ♘c3 c5 4 cxd5 exd5 5 ♘f3 ♘c6 6 g3 ♘f6 7 ♗g2 ♗e7 8 0-0 0-0 9 ♗g5 9 dxc5 ♗xc5 10 ♗g5 d4 11 ♗xf6 ♕xf6 12 ♘d5 ♕d8 13 ♘d2 ♖e8!? 14 ♖c1 ♗f8 15 ♘b3 ♗g4 16 ♖e1 ♖e5 17 ♘f4 ♗b4 18 ♘d2 d3 19 ♘xd3 ♗xe2 20 ♖xe2 ♕d3 21 ♗e4!± Timman-Gligoric, Bugojno 78 **cxd4 10 ♘xd4 h6 11 ♗e3 ♖e8 12 ♖c1 ♗f8 13 ♘xc6 bxc6 14 ♘a4 ♘g4!?** 14...♗d7? 15 ♗c5 ♗xc5 16 ♘xc5 ♗g4 17 ♖e1 ♕b6 18 ♕c2 ♖ad8 19 h3 ♗c8 20 b3 ♕b8 21 e3 ♖e7 22 ♖ed1 ♖de8 23 ♖d4± Ljubojevic-Gligoric, Bugojno 78 **15 ♗c5** 15 ♘d4 ♗xc5 **16 ♘xc5 ♕f6 17 h3 ♘e5 18 e4 ♖b8 += 19 b3 ♖b5 20 exd5 cxd5 21 ♖e1!** △ f4 g5 **22 ♕xd5 ♗b7** 22...♗xh3? 23 ♘e4 **23 ♘e4** 23 ♘d7 ♘a6!! 24 ♘c5 ♕f6= **♘f3+! 24 ♔h1!** 24 ♗xf3? ♖xe4 25 ♕xb5 ♕xf3 **♖xe4 25 ♕xb5 ♘xe1 26 ♕xb7 ♖e2?!** 26...♖e7!= **27 ♕xa7± ♘c2** 27...♘d3? 28 ♖f1 **28 ♔g1 ♘d4 29 ♖f1 ♖b2 30 a4 ♖xb3** 30...♘xb3 **31 a5 ♔g7 32 ♖d1 ♖b4 33 a6?** 33 ♕c5! ♘e2+ **34 ♔h2 ♖b6!= 35 ♖d7 ♖xa6 36 ♕e3** 36 ♖xf7+ ♔xf7 37 ♕xa6 ♕xf2 **♖e6 38 ♕f3 ½-½ Gligoric/Maric**

51 Uhlmann-Ribli Niksic 78

1 c4 ♘f6 2 ♘c3 e6 3 ♘f3 d5 4 d4 c5 5 cxd5 ♘xd5 6 e3 ♘c6 7 ♗d3 7 ♗c4 **♗e7 8 0-0 0-0 9 a3 cxd4 10 exd4 ♘f6 11 ♖e1 g6** 11...♘xd4?! 12 ♘xd4 ♗xd4 13 ♗xh7+ ♔xh7 14 ♕xd4 += **12 ♗h6 ♖e8 13 ♘xd5 ♕xd5 14 ♗e4 ♕d6 15 ♗e3** 15 d5! exd5 16 ♕xd5 ♕xd5 17 ♗xd5 ♗d7 18 ♘g5 += **♖d8 16 ♖c1! ♗d7?** 16...♘xd4 17 ♘xd4 ♗xd4 18 ♗xd4 ♕xd4 19 ♕xd4 ♖xd4 20 ♖c7 ♖b8 21 b4∝ **17 ♕d2 ♖ac8 18 b4 b6 19 ♗f4 ♕f8?** 19...e5! 20 ♗xc6 exf4 21 ♗xd7 ♖xc1 22 ♖xc1

♖xd7= **20 d5! exd5 21 ♗xd5± ♘e7** 21...♗g4 22 ♗h6 ♕d6 23 ♖e8+!! ♖xe8 24 ♗xf7+ ♔xf7 25 ♕xd6 +-; 22...♗g7 23 ♗xg7 ♕xg7 24 ♖xc6 ♖xc6 25 ♗xf7+!! +-; 21...♗e6 22 ♖xe6! fxe6 23 ♗xe6+ ♔h8 24 ♕e3 ♖e8 25 b5 ♘d4 26 ♖xc8 +- **22 ♗h6 ♗g7** 22...♕e8?! 23 ♖xc8 ♗xc8 24 ♘g5 +- **23 ♗xg7 ♔xg7 24 ♗b3 f6 25 ♖xc8 ♗xc8 26 ♕c3 ♗g8** 26...♘f5 **27 h3 ♕d6 28 ♘g5! ♕d2?!** 28...♘h6 29 ♘e6+ ♗xe6 30 ♖xe6 ♕f4 31 g3± **29 ♕xd2! ♖xd2 30 ♖e8! 1-0** 30... ♘h6 31 ♖e7+ ♔f8 32 ♖xh7 fxg5 33 ♖h8+ ♔g7 34 ♖xc8 ♖d3 35 ♖c7+ ♔f6 36 ♖c6+ △ ♗c2 +- **Uhlmann**

52 Gheorghiu-Arnason USA 78

1 d4 ♘f6 2 c4 e6 3 ♘f3 c5 4 e3 d5 5 ♘c3 ♘c6 6 cxd5 ♘xd5 7 ♗d3 cxd4 8 exd4 ♗e7 9 0-0 0-0 10 ♖e1! += 10 a3!?; 10 ♗g5= ♗f6!? 10...♘f6 11 a3 b6 12 ♗c2 ♗b7 13 ♕d3! g6! 14 ♗h6 ♖e8 15 ♖ad1 += **11 ♗e4 ♘ce7 12 ♘e5! g6** 12...♗xe5 13 dxe5 ♘xc3 14 bxc3 ♕c7 15 ♕d6!± **13 ♗h6 ♗g7 14 ♗xg7 ♔xg7 15 ♕b3! ♘f6! 16 ♖ad1** 16 ♗f3 ♘f5! =+ **♘xe4 17 ♘xe4** 17 ♖xe4 b6!∝ **b6 18 h4! ♗b7 19 h5 ♘f5! 20 ♕h3 ♕h4! 21 ♕xh4 ♘xh4 22 f3!!± ♖ad8 23 ♘g5!± h6!?** 23...♗d5 24 h6+! ♔g8 25 ♘e4!±

24 ♘exf7! hxg5 24...♖xf7 25 ♘xe6+
**25 ♘xd8 ♖xd8 26 ♖xe6 ♖d7 27
♖de1! ♔h6** 27...♗d5 28 ♖e7+ ♖xe7
29 ♖xe7+ ♔f6 30 h6!! +− **28 ♖e7
♖xe7 29 ♖xe7 ♗d5 30 ♖xa7 gxh5 31
♖a6! ♔g7 32 b3 g4 33 fxg4 hxg4
34 g3! ♗f3+ 35 ♔f2 ♘xd4 36 ♖xb6
♗f3 37 a4 ♔f7 38 a5 ♔e7 39 a6
♔d7 40 a7 ♘e6** 40...♔c7? 41 ♖b8
41 b4 ♘c7 42 b5 ♘a8 43 ♖f6! ♗d5
43...♔c7 44 ♖xf3! gxf3 45 g4 ♔b7
46 g5 ♘c7 47 g6 ♘e6 48 b6! +− **44
♔e3 +− 1-0 Gheorghiu**

53 Tukmakov-Savon Lvov 78

**1 d4 ♘f6 2 c4 e6 3 ♘f3 d5 4 ♘c3
♗e7** 4...♘bd7 5 ♗f4 dxc4 6 e3 ♘d5
7 ♗xc4 ♘xf4 8 exf4 ♗e7 9 d5!? ♘b6
10 ♗b5+ ♔f8! =+ Portisch-Byrne,
Biel 76; 9 ♕c2! △ 0-0-0 += **5 ♗f4
c5** 5...0-0 6 e3 ♘bd7 7 ♕c2 c6 8 cxd5
♘xd5 9 ♘xd5 exd5 10 ♗d3 ♗b4+
11 ♔e2 += Petrosian-Byrne, Moscow
75; 6...b6 7 ♗d3 ♗b7 8 0-0 c5 9 dxc5
bxc5 10 ♕e2 ♘bd7 11 ♖fd1 ♘h5 12
♕c2± Juferov-Klovan, USSR 77; 5...
dxc4!? **6 dxc5 ♘a6** 6...♘c6 7 e3 ♗xc5
8 cxd5 exd5 9 ♗e2 0-0 10 a3 h6 11
0-0 ♗e6 12 ♖c1 ♖c8 13 ♘e5 ♘e7
14 ♕a4 += Quinteros-Bolbochan,
Gallega 76 **7 ♗d6!? 0-0** 7...♗xd6 8
cxd6 ♕xd6 9 e4!? **8 cxd5 exd5 9 e3
♗xd6 10 cxd6 ♕xd6 11 ♗e2 +=
♕b6 12 ♕b3!** 12 ♕c2 ♘e4 13 ♘xd5
♕a5+ **♕xb3 13 axb3 ♘b4 14 0-0 ♗d7
15 ♖fd1 ♖fc8 16 ♘e1! ♔f8 17 ♗f3
♗e6 18 ♘d3 a5 19 h3** 19 ♘xb4?!
axb4 20 ♖xa8 ♖xa8 21 ♘xd5 ♘xd5
22 ♗xd5 ♗xd5 23 ♖xd5 ♖a1+ **♖a6
20 g4! g5** 20...h6 **21 ♘xb4 axb4 22
♖xa6 bxa6 23 ♘xd5 ♘xd5 24 ♗xd5
♖d8 25 ♗f3 ♖xd1+ 26 ♗xd1 ♔e7
27 f4± f6 28 ♔f2 ♔d6 29 ♔f3 h6
30 ♔g3! △ h4 a5 31 h4 ♗g8 32 hxg5**

hxg5 33 ♔f3 ♗h7 34 e4! +− ♗g8
34...gxf4 35 ♔xf4 ♔e6 +− **35 ♔e3
gxf4+ 36 ♔xf4 ♗h7 37 ♗c2 ♗g6**
37...♔e6 38 g5 +− **38 g5 fxg5+ 39
♔xg5 ♗f7 40 ♔f6 ♗g8 41 e5+ ♔d5
42 ♗f5! 1-0 Gufeld**

54 Ribli-Ljubojevic Niksic 78

**1 ♘f3 c5 2 g3 d5 3 ♗g2 ♘c6 4 d4
e6 5 0-0 ♕b6!?** 5...♘f6 6 c4 ♗e7 7
cxd5 exd5 8 ♘c3 += **6 dxc5 ♗xc5
7 c4! ♘f6** 7...dxc4 8 ♕a4! **8 cxd5
♘xd5** 8...exd5 9 ♘c3 += **9 e4 ♘f6
10 ♘c3 ♗g4!? 11 ♕e2 ♗d7! 12 ♗f4!?**
12 ♘a4? ♘d4! e5 13 ♗g5! h6? 13...f6
14 ♗d2 += **14 ♘d5!± ♕a5** 14...♗xf2+
15 ♖xf2! ♕xf2+ 16 ♕xf2 ♘xf2 17
♘c7+ ♔f8 18 ♘xa8 +− **15 ♗d2 ♕d8
16 ♘c3 0-0 17 ♖ad1 ♗e6 18 b4! ♗d4**
18...♗d6 19 h3 ♘f6 20 ♘xf6+ gxf6
21 ♕d2!± **19 ♗xd4 ♗xd4 20 ♘xd4
exd4 21 ♖xd4 +− ♖c8? 22 e5 h5
23 h3 1-0 Ribli**

55 Ilic-Pinkas Poland 78

**1 ♘f3 ♘f6 2 c4 e6 3 g3 d5 4 ♗g2
c5 5 0-0 ♘c6 6 d4 dxc4 7 ♕a4 cxd4
8 ♘xd4 ♕xd4 9 ♗xc6+ ♗d7 10 ♖d1
♕xd1+ 11 ♕xd1 ♗xc6 12 ♘d2!?**
N 12 ♕c2 Zilberstein-Rashkovsky
76; 12 ♗g5 h5!∝ **13 h4 ♘g4 14 ♘xc4
♗c5** 14...♖d8? 15 ♕b3 ♗c5 16
♗e3± **15 e3** 15 ♗e3 ♘xe3 16 ♘xe3
♗xe3 17 fxe3= **g5!?** 15...♖d8 16
♕e2 △ f3, ♔g2, e4 +=

Diagram

16 b4!! 16 hxg5? ♖d8 17 ♕e2 h4!
18 ♕xg4 hxg3 19 fxg3 ♖d1+! 20
♕xd1 (20 ♔f2 ♖h2 mate) ♖h1+
21 ♔f2 ♖xd1 −+; 16 f3? gxh4 17
fxg4 ♖d8 18 ♕e2 hxg4 −+ **♖d8 17
♕e2 ♗xb4 18 hxg5** 18 ♘b2 h4 19

♕xg4 19 ♗b2! h3 20 f3 h2+ 21 ♔h1
♖h3 22 e4 +- **hxg3 20 e4 gxf2+
21 ♔xf2 ♗c3** 21...♖h2+ 22 ♔g1 ♖c2∞
22 ♖b1? 22 ♗b2! ♗xb2 23 ♘xb2
♖h2+ 24 ♔g1 ♖xb2 25 g6! +- **♖d4!∞
23 g6 ♖xc4 24 g7 ♖g8 25 ♗h6 ♖xe4
26 ♕g3 ♗e5** Zeitnot **27 ♕g5 ♗f4
28 ♕f6** Zeitnot **♗e5 29 ♕g5 ♗d4+
30 ♔f1 ♖e5 31 ♕g3 ♖f5+ 32 ♔e2
♗e5** 32...♖f2+ 33 ♔e1! △ ♕b8+ **33
♕g1 ♔e7 34 ♖b3** 34 ♕xa7 ♗xg7 -+
**♖h5 35 ♕c5+ ♔f6 36 ♕f8 ♖h2+ 37
♔d3 ♖h3+ 38 ♔d2 ♖h2+ 39 ♔e3
♖h3+ 40 ♔d2 ♖h2+ ½-½ Ilic**

56 Sturna-Petkevich USSR 77

**1 d4 d5 2 ♘f3 c6 3 c4 e6 4 ♘c3
♘f6 5 ♗g5 ♘bd7** 5...dxc4 6 e3 ♗e7
6...♕a5!? **7 cxd5 exd5 8 ♕c2 0-0
9 ♗d3 ♖e8 10 0-0 h6** 10...♘f8 **11
♗h4 ♘e4 12 ♗xe7 ♕xe7 13 ♗xe4
13** ♖b1 **dxe4 14 ♘d2 f5** 14...♘f6
15 b4! += **15 ♖ae1 ♘f6 16 f3 exf3
17 ♘xf3 ♗e6?!** N 17...♗d7 **18 e4?!**
18 ♘h4 ♘g4 19 ♘xf5 ♗xf5 20 ♕xf5
♘xe3 21 ♕f3 ♕g5 22 h4 **fxe4 19
♘xe4 ♗d5?** 19...♘xe4 20 ♖xe4 ♕c7≈
20 ♘c5! += **♕c7 21 ♘e5 ♖f8** 21...
b6 22 ♘cd3 △ ♘f4 += **22 ♖e3! ♘h7?!**
22...b6 += **23 ♖fe1 b6 24 ♘cd7!
♖fd8 25 ♕g6 ♔h8 26 ♕f5 +- ♕d6
27 ♘g6+ ♔g8 28 ♖e7 1-0 Gufeld**

57 F.Portisch-Ree Tungsram 78

**1 d4 ♘f6 2 c4 e6 3 ♘c3 d5 4 ♘f3
♗e7 5 ♗g5 0-0 6 e3 ♘bd7 7 ♕c2 h6**
7...c5 **8 h4!? c5 9 0-0-0 cxd4 9...
♕a5 10 ♘xd4 dxc4 11 g4** N 11 ♗xc4±
**♘xg4! 12 ♗xc4 ♗xg5 13 hxg5 ♕xg5
14 ♖dg1 ♘df6 15 ♕e2 b5?!** 15...e5∓
**16 ♗xb5 ♗b7 17 ♗c6 ♖ab8 18 f4
♕c5 19 ♗xb7 ♖xb7 20 ♖xg4 ♘xg4
21 ♕xg4 ♖fb8 22 ♕e2**

**22...♖xb2! 23 ♕xb2 ♖xb2 24 ♔xb2
e5! 25 fxe5 ♕xe5 26 ♖h3 h5 27 ♘ce2
g6 28 ♘f4 ♕b8+ 29 ♔a3! ♕c8 30
♔b3 a5 31 a3 ♕g4 32 ♖f3 ♕g1 33
♕a4 ♕e1 34 ♘h3 ♔g7 35 ♘g5 f5 36
♘de6+ ♔f6 37 e4 h4 38 exf5 gxf5
39 ♕b5 ♕e5 40 ♕a4 ♔f6 ½-½ Haag**

58 Portisch-Ljubojevic Niksic 78

**1 d4 ♘f6 2 c4 e6 3 ♘c3 d5 4 ♗g5
♘bd7 5 cxd5 exd5 6 e3 c6 7 ♗d3 ♗d6
8 ♘f3** 8 ♘ge2!? 0-0 9 ♕c2 h6 10 ♗h4
♖e8 11 h3 ♕a5 12 0-0-0±; 8...♘f8
9 ♕c2 h6 10 ♗h4 ♕e7 11 a3 (11
0-0-0!?) ♗d7 12 e4! g5 13 ♗g3 dxe4
14 ♘xe4 ♘xe4 15 ♗xe4±; 9...♘g6
10 ♘g3 0-0 11 ♘h5 ♗e7 12 ♘xf6+
♗xf6 13 ♗xf6 ♕xf6 14 h4 ♖e8 15
h5 ♘f8 16 0-0-0 += **♘f8 9 ♘e5** 9
♗h4 ♘g6 10 ♗g3 0-0 11 ♖b1 ♖e8=
Petrosian-Ljubojevic, Milan 75 **♕e7
10 f4** 10 0-0!? ♗xe5 11 dxe5 ♕xe5

12 f4∞ h6 11 ♗h4 g5! 12 fxg5 12
♗g3 gxf4 13 exf4 (13 ♗xf4 ♘g4)
♗g4 14 ♗e2 (14 ♕d2 ♘h5) ♗xe2 15
♕xe2 ♗xe5 16 dxe5 ♘6d7 17 f5
(17 0-0 f5) 0-0-0∞ hxg5 13 ♗xg5
13 ♗g3? ♘8d7 ♖g8 14 ♗h4 14 h4
♘e6 ♗xe5 15 dxe5 ♕xe5 16 ♕f3 ♘g4
17 0-0-0 ♗e6 18 ♖de1 18 e4 ♘xh2
19 ♕f4 ♘g4 20 ♕b4 ♕c7 21 e4 ♘e5
22 ♗b1 d4! 23 ♕xd4 ♖h8 24 ♕c5
♘d3+ 25 ♗xd3 ♕f4+ 26 ♔b1 ♖xh4
27 ♘d5 cxd5 28 ♖hf1 ♘d7!= 28 ♖xf4
♘xc5 30 ♗b5+ ♔e7 31 ♖xh4 ♘xe4
32 ♗d3 ♖g8 33 ♖e2 ♔d6 34 ♔c1
♗f5 35 ♖f4 ♘e5 36 ♖f1 ♖g3 37 ♖f3
♖g7 38 ♖c2 f6 39 ♖f1 ♖g3 40 ♖f3
♖g7 41 a4 ♗e6 42 a5 a6 ½-½
Velimirovic

Catalan

59 Smejkal-Browne
Reykjavik 78
1 d4 ♘f6 2 c4 e6 3 g3 d5 3...♗b4+!?
4 ♗g2 dxc4 5 ♘f3 5 ♕a4+ ♗d7 6 ♕xc4
♗c6 c5 5...♗e7 6 0-0 0-0 7 ♘e5 ♘c6∞
6 ♕a4+ ♘bd7 7 0-0 a6 8 ♘c3 8 ♕xc4
b5 9 ♕c2 ♗b7 10 dxc5 ♗xc5 11 ♖d1
♕b6 =+ ♗e7 8...♘d5!? 9 dxc5! ♗xc5
9...0-0 10 c6 10 ♕xc4 += b5 11 ♕h4
♗b7 12 ♗g5 12 b4?! ♕b6?! 12...0-0
13 ♖ad1 ♕c7 13 ♖ad1! ♗c6 13...0-0?
14 b4! ♗e7?? 15 ♖xd7 +- 14 e4!
0-0 15 e5 ♘d5 16 ♘e4 ♖fe8 16...f5?!±
17 ♖c1 17 ♘xc5 ♘xc5 18 ♗c1 ♘e7!
19 ♘g5 h6 =+ ♗f8 18 ♖fd1 ♖ac8 19
♗d2 ♗b7?! 19...♘c5! 20 ♘d6 ♗xd6
21 exd6 ♘d3 22 ♗e3 ♘xe3 23 ♖xd3
♘xg2 -+ 20 ♕h5! h6 21 ♕g4 g6 22
♕h4?! 22 ♖xc8 ♖xc8 23 ♕h4 ♘e7?
24 ♗e3; 23...♘c5! 24 ♘xc5 ♗xc5
25 ♕xh6 ♗xf2+ 26 ♔h1 ♘e3!; 24
♘f6+!? ♗xf6 25 exf6 ♘e4 26 ♗e3
♗c5 27 ♘d4! += ♖xc1 23 ♖xc1 23

♗xc1 ♘c5!! 24 ♗e3 ♘xe3! 25 ♘f6+
♔h8 26 ♘xe8 ♘xd1 -+; 24 ♖xd5?
♘xe4! ♘e7! 24 ♘d6 ♘f5 25 ♘xf5
exf5 26 ♗xh6 26 ♗e3!? ♗xh6 27
♕xh6 ♗xf3 28 ♗xf3 ♘xe5 29 ♗d5
29 ♗g2 ♕d4! 30 b3 ♘d3 31 ♖f1 ♖e2
-+; 31 ♕d2?? ♘xc1 -+; 31 ♖c2 f4!
-+ ♕d4!∓ 0-1 time 30 ♗b3!∓
Browne

60 Alburt-Velikov
Kiev 78
1 d4 ♘f6 2 c4 e6 3 g3 d5 4 ♗g2 ♗e7
5 ♘f3 0-0 6 0-0 b6 7 ♘c3 7 ♘e5
♗b7 8 ♕a4 ♕e8!= Alburt-Holmov,
Suhumi 77 ♗b7 8 cxd5 exd5 9 ♕c2
♘a6!? 9...c5 10 ♖d1 c6 10...c5 11
dxc5 ♘xc5 12 ♘d4 ♖c8 13 ♗h3! +=
Palatnik-Velikov, Kiev 78 11 ♘e5
♖e8 12 e4! += ♘c7 13 ♕a4! ♗f8 14
♗g5 14 ♘xc6 ♕d7! 15 exd5 ♘cxd5
16 ♘e5 ♕f5≈ h6 15 ♗xf6 ♕xf6 16
♖ac1 ♕d6 17 ♖d2 ♘e6 18 exd5 cxd5
19 a3!

19...♖ec8? 19...♖ed8 20 ♖e1!± a6?
20...♖cd8± 21 ♕d7! +- ♕xd7 22
♗xd7 ♖d8 23 ♗xb6 ♖ab8 24 ♘bxd5
♖d6 25 ♖ed1 ♖bd8 26 ♘b4 ♖xd4
27 ♗xb7 a5!? 28 ♘c6! ♗f3+ 29
♔g2 ♗xd2 30 ♘xd8 ♖xd8 31 ♗d5!
1-0 Gufeld

78

61 Lysenko-A.Popov USSR 78

**1 c4 ♞f6 2 g3 e6 3 ♗g2 d5 4 ♘f3 ♗e7
5 0-0 0-0 6 d4 b6 7 ♘c3 ♗b7 8 cxd5
exd5 9 ♗f4 c5 10 ♖c1 ♘a6 11 ♕c2**
11 ♘e5 ♘e4 12 ♗e3 ♕d6 13 ♘c4
♕e6 14 ♘xe4 dxe4 15 dxc5 ♘xc5
16 ♕c2 ♖ac8 =+ Browne-Karpov,
Las Palmas 77 **♘c7** 11...♘e4 **12
dxc5 bxc5 13 ♖fd1 += ♘e6 14 ♗e5
♕a5 15 ♗h3! d4 16 ♗xe6 fxe6 17
♘g5 g6 18 ♘xe6 dxc3** 18...♕g4? 19
♘xf8 △ ♕b3+ **19 ♘xf8 ♕xf8 20
♕xc3** 20 ♗xf6? ♗xf6 21 ♖d7 cxb2
−+ **♕xc3 21 ♖xc3 ♘d5 22 ♖cd3
♘b4 23 ♖e3** 23 ♖d7? ♗c8! 24 ♖c7?
♘a6! 25 ♖c6 ♗b7 26 ♖e6 ♔f7 −+
♘d5 23...♘xa2? 24 ♗g7+! +− **24 ♖b3
♗c6 25 ♖b8+ ♖xb8 26 ♗xb8 a6 27
♖c1 ♗b5 28 ♗a7 c4 29 a4 ♗xa4 30
♖xc4 ♗b5 31 ♖c8+ ♔f7 32 e4 ♘f6
33 f3 ♘e8 34 ♗d4 ♔e6 35 ♔f2 h5
36 ♖c1 ♘d6 37 ♖c2** Zeitnot 37 b3
♗a4 38 ♖c1 ♗b5 38...g5≈ **39 b3 +=
♗b7 40 ♗b6 ♘d8 41 ♔e3 ♘c6 42
f4 ♘b4 43 ♗d4 ♘c6 44 ♗c5 ♘d8 45
h3 ♘a5 46 ♖b1 ♘b7 47 ♗d4 ♗e7
48 g4 hxg4 49 hxg4 ♘d6 50 ♖c1
♗d7 51 ♗c5 ♔f7 52 ♔f3! ♘b5 53
♗xe7 ♔xe7 54 b4 ♘d4+ 55 ♔e3
♘c6 56 ♖c4 a5?** 56...♔d6 57 e5+ +=
**57 b5 +− ♘b8 58 b6 ♗xg4 59 b7
♗d7** 59...♔d8 60 f5 +− **60 ♖c8 1-0
Lysenko**

62 Sosonko-Najdorf Sao Paulo 78

**1 d4 ♞f6 2 c4 e6 3 g3 d5 4 ♗g2 ♗e7
5 ♘f3 0-0 6 0-0 dxc4 7 ♕c2 a6 8
a4 ♘c6 9 ♕xc4 ♕d5 10 ♕d3!?** 10
♕xd5 ♘xd5 11 ♗d2 +=: 10 ♘bd2
♖d8 11 e3 += **♖d8** 10...♘b4 11 ♕d1
c5 12 ♘c3 ♕d8 += **11 ♘c3 ♕h5 12
♕c4± ♘d5 13 a5 ♗d7 14 e4 ♗xc3
15 bxc3 ♖ac8 16 e5 ♗a7 17 ♕b3
♗c6 18 c4 ♖b8?!** 18...♖d7 19 ♖d1

**♖cd8 20 ♗b2± 19 ♖d1 ♗e4 20 ♕e3
♘f5 21 d5 ♘c6?** 21...♖c8 22 ♗a3±
22 ♗a3! +− exd5 22...♗xa3 23 dxc6
**23 cxd5 ♗xa3 24 dxc6 ♗b2 25 ♖xd8+
♖xd8 26 ♖a2 ♖d1+ 27 ♘e1 ♗d4 28
cxb7 ♗a7 29 ♖d2 h6 30 ♖xd1 ♔xd1
31 ♗f3 ♕b1 32 ♕xa7 ♕xe1+ 33 ♔g2
1-0 Webb**

63 Palatnik-Kuzmin Kiev 78

**1 d4 ♞f6 2 c4 e6 3 g3 d5 4 ♗g2 ♗e7
5 ♘f3 0-0 6 0-0 dxc4 7 ♘e5** 7 ♕c2
a6 8 a4 c5 9 dxc5 ♘c6 10 ♕xc4
e5!≈ Mihalchishin-Kuzmin, USSR 77
♕d6!? N 7...♘c6 8 ♗xc6 bxc6 9
♘xc6 ♕e8 10 ♘xe7+ ♕xe7 11 ♕a4
e5= Kirov-Geller, Sochi 76; 9 ♘c3
c5 10 dxc5 ♗xc5 11 ♕a4 ♘d5! 12
♘e4∝ Korchnoi-Petrosian (1) 77 **8
♗a3?!** 8 ♘xc4 ♕a6 9 ♕c2 ♖d8 10
♖d1 += **♖d8 9 ♘b5 ♕b6 10 a4 c6
11 ♘xc4 ♕a6 12 ♘ba3** 12 ♘c7 ♕xc4
13 ♘xa8 ♖xd4 14 ♗d2∝ **♗xa3 13
♗xa3 e5! 14 e3** 14 ♗e3 ♗e6 △ ♘bd7
**♗e6 15 b4 ♕b6 16 ♖b1 ♘bd7 17 b5
e4!∓ 18 ♕c2 c5 19 ♗b2** Zeitnot
19 ♗xe4 ♖ac8! 20 ♗g2 cxd4∓; 19
♘c4!? **♖ac8 20 ♘c4 ♕c7 21 ♘e5 c4
22 ♖fc1** 22 ♗xe4 c3! 23 ♗c1 ♘xe5
24 dxe5 ♘xe4 25 ♕xe4 c2 −+ **♗d5
23 ♗f1! ♗xe5 24 dxe5 ♘d7 25 ♕d2!
♗e6** 25...♘xe5? 26 ♗xe5 ♕xe5 27
♗xc4! ♗xc4 28 ♖xc4!∝ **26 ♕d4
♘b6 27 ♕xe4 ♗xa4 28 ♗a3 ♕d7 29
♗xc4? 29** ♕h4! =+ **♗xc4 30 ♖xc4
♘c3! −+ 31 ♖xc3 ♖xc3 32 ♗d6
h6 33 h4 ♖dc8 34 ♕g2 ♖c2 35 ♖b4
♖d2 36 ♕b1 ♕e6 37 ♖f4 ♖c4! 0-1
Gufeld**

64 Beljavsky-Farago Kiev 78

**1 d4 e6 2 c4 ♞f6 3 ♘f3 d5 4 g3 ♗e7
4...c5!? 5 ♗g2 0-0 6 0-0 ♘bd7 6...
dxc4 7 ♕d3!?** 7 ♕c2 c6 8 b3 b6 9

79

Rd1 Bb7 10 Nc3 Ba6!?; 7 b3 **b6!**
7...c6 8 Nc3 b6 9 e3 Ba6 10 b3 Rc8
11 Rd1! += Romanishin- Ciric,
Dortmund 76 **8 cxd5** 8 Nc3?! Ba6 =+
exd5 9 Nc3 Bb7 10 Ng5!? c6!? N 10...
h6 11 Nh3 Re8 12 Nf4 Nf8 13 Qb5
c6 14 Qb3 Bd6= Romanishin-Farago,
Cienfuegos 77 **11 Rd1 h6?!** 11...Re8
12 Nh3 Re8 13 Qc2! += **Nf8 14 Nf4
Bd6 15 Rb1 Qe7 16 a3 Ne6** 16...
Bxf4!? **17 Nxe6 Qxe6
18 b4 Ba6?! 19 Re1 Bc4 20 Na4
Qg4?** 20...b5 += **21 e4!± Qg6 22
f3 b5 23 Nb2 Re7 24 Nxc4 bxc4
25 Rb2 Bc7 26 e5 Bb6 27 Nc3 Ne8 28
Be3 Bc7 29 a4 a5 30 b5 cxb5 31
axb5 Qe6 32 f4 Qd7 33 Na3** Δ Qd6
**Ree8 34 Qa4 Ne6 35 Rd1 g6 36 g4
Ng7 37 h3 Rac8 38 Rc2 Red8 39 Rc3
Qa7 40 Qc2 Qd7 41 Kh1 Qe6?!**

**42 f5! gxf5 43 Rf1 fxg4 44 Rf6
gxh3!? 45 Bxh6!** +- **Qg4 46 Bxh3
Qxd4 47 Rg3 Qa1+ 48 Kh2 Qxe5
49 Rf5 1-0** Gufeld

Dutch

65 Olafsson-Miles Las Palmas 78
1 c4 b6 2 Nc3 e6 3 d4 Bb4!? 3...
Bb7 **4 e3 Bb7 5 Ne2 f5!?** 5...Nf6
6 a3 Bd6!? 7 d5 7 Nb5!?; 7 b4 **Nf6
8 Nd4** 8 g3 **0-0! 9 dxe6 Ne4!≈** 10

Qc2?! 10 Nxe4 fxe4≈; 10 Nd5!?
Nc6≈ **Nxc3 11 Qxc3 Qf6 12 exd7
Bxd7** =+/∓ **13 Bd2** Δ 0-0-0 **Bc5
14 Nf3** 14 0-0-0? Ne4 **Qg6 15 h4
Ne4 16 h5** 16 Qc2 Bg3! -+ **Qg4!
17 Be5** 17 Qc2 Bg3! -+ **Rxe5!** 17...
Nxc3 18 Bxg4 Na4 19 c5!∝ **18
Qxe5 Rae8! 19 Qh2** 19 Qxc7 f4! -+
Qxb7 fxe3 Δ Nxf2 -+ **Bxd2 20
Qxd2 f4** ∓/-+ **21 exf4 Rxf4 22
Qg3!** 22 f3 Qd7+ 23 Kc2 Rd4 -+
Rd4+ 22...Qf5 23 f3 Rd4+ 24 Kc1
Red8 25 Qe1; 22...Qxg3 23 fxg3
Rf2+ 24 Kc3 Re3+ 25 Bd3! Be4 26
Kd4 ∝/∓ **23 Nc3 Qxg3 24 fxg3 c5! 25
Kb3 Re3+ 26 Ka2 Bc8! 27 Rh4
Bg4 28 Rc1 g5 29 hxg6 hxg6** 29...h5
**30 Rc3 Rxc3 31 bxc3 Rd2+ 32
Ka1** 32 Kb3? Bd1 mate **Bd7 33 Bf4
Qg7 34 Rf3 Bc6 35 Rd3 Rf2 36
Rd1 Ba4 37 Re1 Kf6** 37...Bc2 **38
Bd3 Rxg2 39 Rf1+ Kg5 40 Rf3
Bc2!** -+ **41 Bxc2** 41 Bf1 Rh2 -+
Rxc2 42 Rf7 42 Kb1 Rd2 Δ Rd6,
Kg4, Kh3 **Rg4 43 Rxa7 g5 44 Rb7
Kxg3 45 Rxb6 g4 46 a4 Kh4 47 a5
g3 48 a6 g2 49 Rb1 Rf2 50 a7 Rf8
51 Kb2 Ra8 52 Kc2 0-1** Miles

66 Palatnik-Lerner Kiev 78
**1 d4 d6 2 c4 f5 3 Nf3 Nf6 4 g3 g6
5 Bg2 Bg7 6 Nc3** 6 0-0 0-0 7 Nc3
c6 8 d5 +=; 7...Nc6 8 d5 Na5 9 Nd2
c5 10 Qc2 a6 11 b3 += **0-0 7 d5!?**
7 0-0 c6 8 Nd4∝ Qb6 8...c5 9 Ne6 +=
9 0-0 e5!? 10 dxe6 Re8 11 Rb1 +=
**Bxe6 12 Nxe6 Rxe6 13 b4 Nbd7
14 Qb3** Δ c5 **Qc7 15 Ba3** 15 Bd2
**Kh8 16 Rfc1 Re5 17 b5 Nc5 18 Bxc5
Rxc5 19 e3 Nd7!= 20 Na4 Re5 21
bxc6 bxc6 22 Qb7 Rc8 23 c5! d5
24 Qxc7** 24 Bf1!? **Rxc7 25 Nb2 Re8
26 Nd3 Rb8 27 Rxb8+ Nxb8 28
Rb1 Nd7** 28...Rc8?! **29 Rb7** 29 Nf4

♖c8 30 ♘e6 ♖b8 30...♖e8 31 ♖b7
♖xe6 32 ♖xd7 += **31 ♖xb8 ♘xb8
32 ♗f3 ♞g8 33 ♗d1 ♚f7 34 ♘xg7**
34 ♘f4∞ ♚xg7 35 ♚f1 ♞f6 35...♘d7
36 ♗a4 **36 ♚e2 ♞a6 37 ♗a4 ♞xc5
38 ♗xc6 ♚e5 39 f3 ♚d6 40 ♗b5 a6=
½-½ Gufeld**

67 Gheorghiu-Radovici
Rumania 78

**1 c4 e6 2 ♘f3 f5 3 g3 ♘f6 4 ♗g2 ♗e7
5 0-0 0-0 6 d4 d6 7 ♘c3 a5 8 b3 ♞e4
9 ♗b2 ♗f6 10 ♕c2!** += **♞xc3 11
♗xc3 ♞c6 12 e4!** ♕e8!? 12...♘b4
13 ♕e2 fxe4 14 ♕xe4 d5 15 ♕e2
c5 16 ♖ad1 += **13 exf5** 13 e5 dxe5
14 dxe5 ♗e7 15 ♘d4! ♘xd4 16 ♗xd4± **exf5 14 d5**

14...♞e5!? 14...♗xc3! 15 ♕xc3 ♘e5
16 ♘xe5 ♕xe5 17 ♕xe5 dxe5 18
♖ae1± **15 ♞xe5 ♗xe5 16 ♖ae1±** △
f4 +- **f4 17 ♗xe5 dxe5 18 ♕c3!±
♖f5 19 gxf4** 19 ♖e4 △ ♖fe1± ♕g6
20 ♖xe5 ♖xf4 21 ♕e3! ♖f8 21...
♖g4? 22 ♖e8+ +- **22 ♕g3 ♖a6 23
♖fe1 ♕c2 24 ♖g5! g6 25 ♖ge5!±**
25 h4? ♗f5! 26 h5? h6!∓ **♕d2 26
♖5e2 ♕d4 27 ♕xc7 +- ♗g4 28 ♕e5!
♕c5** 28...♕xe5 29 ♖xe5 +- **29 ♖d2
♖af6 30 ♕d4 b6?!** 30...♕b4 31 a3
♕xa3 32 ♕xg4 +- **31 ♕xg4! ♖xf2
32 ♕e6+ 1-0** 32...♚h8 33 ♖xf2 ♕xf2+

♚h1 +- **Gheorghiu**

68 Gheorghiu-Pavlovich USA 78

**1 d4 f5 2 g3 ♘f6 3 ♗g2 e6 4 ♘f3
♗e7 5 0-0 0-0 6 c4 d6 7 ♘c3 a5
7...♘c6; 7...♕e8 8 b3 ♕e8 9 ♗a3!
♞a6 10 ♖e1** △ e4± **♞e4 11 ♕c2 ♕g6
12 ♞e5!±** 12 ♘xe4 fxe4 13 ♘e5 dxe5
14 ♗xe7 e3!! -+ **dxe5 13 ♗xe7 ♖e8
14 ♗a3!±** **♞xc3 15 ♕xc3 exd4** 15...e4
16 ♕xa5 **16 ♕xd4 e5 17 ♕d5+ ♗e6
18 ♕xe5** 18 ♕xa5 e4 19 ♕c3± ♗xc4
19 ♕c3! ♗f7 19...♗xe2 20 ♗xb7 +-
**20 ♗xb7 ♖a7 21 ♗c6 ♖e6 22 ♗f3 h5
23 ♖ad1 ♞b4 24 ♕c5 ♖aa6 25 ♖d8+
♖e8 26 ♕xc7 ♞xa2 27 ♖xe8+ ♗xe8
28 ♖a1 f4 29 ♕xf4 1-0 Gheorghiu**

69 Spassov-Tseitlin Pernik 78

**1 ♘f3 f5 2 d4 ♘f6 3 g3 g6 4 ♗g2 ♗g7
5 0-0 0-0 6 b3 d6 7 ♗b2 ♞e4!? 8 ♘bd2
♞c6 9 e3** 9 ♘c4?! e6 10 d5? ♗xb2
11 ♘xb2 ♘c3; 9 c4 ♞xd2 10 ♕xd2
e5= **11 d5 ♞b8** 11...♘e7 12 ♘g5!?
12 c4 g5 13 ♞e1 ♞d7 13...f4!? **14
f4 ♕e7 15 ♞d3?!** 15 ♘c2 exf4? 16
♗xg7; 15...♕c5= e4 **16 ♞f2 gxf4 17
gxf4 a5 =+ 18 ♚h1 ♗xb2 19 ♕xb2
♕f6 20 ♕c2** 20 ♕xf6 ♖xf6 =+ **♞c5
21 ♖ab1 ♗d7 22 ♖g1 ♚h8 23 a3 ♗e8
24 b4?** 24 ♕e2 **axb4 25 axb4 ♞d7
26 ♕e2 ♗g6 27 ♞h3 h6 28 ♖gc1 b6∓
29 ♞f2 ♖a3 30 ♗h3** △ ♘xe4 ♖e8 **31
♖g1 ♞f8 32 c5 ♖ea8 33 cxb6 cxb6**
△ ♖a2, ♗h5 **34 ♞d1 ♖a2 35 ♖b2
♖a1 36 ♖c2 ♖b1 37 ♞c3** 37 ♖b2
♖aa1 **♖xb4 38 ♞b5 ♖a1 39 ♞d4
♖bb1 40 ♖xb1 ♖xb1+ 41 ♚g2 ♗h7
42 ♕f2 ♖d1! 43 ♖c8** 43 ♖c4 b5
**44 ♖b4 ♕g7+ 45 ♕g3 ♕a7 -+ ♖xd4
44 exd4 ♗g8 45 ♕e3 ♕g6 46 ♚f1 ♞e7
47 ♖b8 ♞xd5 48 ♕g1 ♞e7 49 ♖xb6
♕e6 50 d5?** 50 ♖b4 ♕a2 △ ♗c4+/
♕a3; 50 ♕f2!?∓ **♕xd5 -+ 51 ♕f2**

♕d4+ 52 ♔g2 e3 53 ♖a6 ♗d5+ 0-1
Webb

Benko Gambit

70 Fedder-Webb Roskilde 78
**1 d4 ♘f6 2 c4 c5 3 d5 b5 4 cxb5
a6 5 bxa6 g6 6 ♘c3 ♗xa6 7 e4 ♗xf1
8 ♔xf1 d6 9 ♘ge2?!** 9 ♘f3 ♗g7 10
g3 0-0 11 ♔g2 ♕a5 12 ♖e1 ♘fd7
13 ♖e2 ♘a6 14 ♗f4! += Tarjan-
Webb, Hastings 77/8; 12...♘bd7 Δ
♖fb8, ♘e8-c7 **♗g7 10 h3 0-0 11 ♕g1
♘bd7 12 ♖b1 ♕a5 13 ♗e3?!** 13
♗d2 Δ b3, a4, ♘b5 **♖fb8 14 ♕c2
♘e8 15 ♔h2 ♘c7 16 b3 ♘b5 17 ♘xb5
♖xb5=** 17...♕xb5!? 18 ♘c3 ♕a6 19
a4 ♗e5+ 20 g3 ♗xc3 21 ♕xc3 ♖b4
=+ **18 a4 ♖b6 19 ♗d2 ♕a6 20 ♘c3
♗e5+** 20...c4? 21 b4!; 20...♖ab8 21
♘b5 **21 g3 ♗xc3 22 ♗xc3 c4 23 b4!**
23 bxc4 ♕xc4 =+ ♕xa4 **24 ♕xa4**
24 ♕d2? ♕b5 ♖xa4 **25 ♖a1 ♖xa1**
25...♖ba6 26 ♖xa4 ♖xa4 27 ♖a1 Δ
♗d4 **26 ♖xa1 f5! 27 exf5** 27 ♖a7
♘f6= ♔f7!? 27...gxf5 28 ♖a7 ♘f6=;
27...♘f6 28 ♗xf6= **28 fxg6+ hxg6
29 f3 ♘f6 30 ♖a5 ♘e8 31 b5?** 31
♔g2! ♘c7 32 ♔f2 ♖b5 33 ♔e3!±;
32...♘b5∝ **♘c7 32 ♖a4 ♘xd5 33 ♖xc4
♖xb5 34 ♗d4 e5 35 ♗f2 ♔e6 36
♖c2 ♖b3 37 ♔g2 ♘b4 38 ♖d2 d5
39 h4 d4** 39...♘d3!?

40 ♗xd4!= exd4 41 ♖xd4 ♘d3 42
♖e4+ ♔d5 42...♔f6 43 f4 **43 ♖e8**
½-½ 43...♖b2+ 44 ♔h3; 43...♘e5 44
f4 ♘g4 45 ♖g8 ♔e4 46 ♖xg6 ♘e3+
47 ♔h3 ♖b1 48 ♖e6+ ♔f3 49 ♖xe3+
=; 44 h5!=

71 Beljavsky-Palatnik Kiev 78
**1 d4 ♘f6 2 c4 c5 3 d5 b5 4 cxb5
a6 5 bxa6 g6 6 ♘c3 ♗xa6 7 ♘f3** 7
f4!? **d6 8 g3 ♘bd7 9 ♗h3!? ♘b6?!**
9...♗g7 **10 0-0 ♗g7** 10...♗c4 11 ♘d2
♗xd5 12 ♘xd5 ♘fxd5 13 e4 ♘b4
14 e5!+= Polugaevsky-Szabo, Budapest
75; 11 b3! ♗xd5 12 ♘xd5 ♘bxd5
13 e4± Timman-Stean, Teesside 75
11 ♖e1 0-0 12 e4!? 12 ♗f4 ♘c4 13
♕c1 ♕a5 14 ♖b1 ♖ab8 15 ♘d2 +=
Kraidman-Bellon, Haifa 76 **♘fd7 13
♕c2 ♘c4 14 ♗xd7! ♕xd7 15 b3 ♘e5
16 ♘xe5 ♗xe5 17 ♗b2+= ♖fd8 18 ♘d1
♗xb2 19 ♘xb2 ♕b7! 20 ♖e3! ♗b5
21 ♘d1 ♗d7 22 ♖c3 ♖a3 23 ♘e3 ♗b5
24 ♕b2** 24 ♘c4 += ♖da8 **25 ♘c2
♖3a7 26 ♘e3 ♖a3 27 e5!± dxe5 28
♖xc5 f6 29 ♘c2 ♖a5 30 ♘b4 ♗e8
31 ♖xa5 ♖xa5 32 ♕c3 ♖b5 33 a3
♗f7 34 ♖d1 ♔g7** 34...♗xd5 35 ♘xd5
♖xd5 36 ♖xd5 ♕xd5 27 ♕c4 **35 ♕c4
g5 36 h4! h6 37 hxg5 hxg5 38 ♖d3
f5 39 ♖e3 e4 40 ♕d4+ ♔g6 41 g4!
♗xd5 42 gxf5+ ♔xf5 43 ♖g3 Δ ♕g7
+- e5 44 ♕d1 +- ♔f6 45 ♕d2 e3
46 ♕xe3 ♕g7 47 ♘xd5 ♖xd5 48
♕b6+ ♔f5 49 ♖f3+ ♔g4 50 ♔g2 ♕e7
51 ♕h6 1-0 Gufeld**

Benoni

72 Sofrevski-Sahovic
Jugoslavia 78
1 d4 ♘f6 2 c4 b6 3 ♘f3 ♗b7 4 e3
4 d5 e6 5 a3; 4 ♘c3 c5 5 ♘c3 g6 6
d5 ♗g7 7 e4 0-0 8 ♗d3 d6 9 0-0

♘bd7 10 h3 e5! 11 dxe6?! 11 a3 △
b4 fxe6 12 ♘g5? ♕e7 13 f4 h6 14 ♘f3
♘h5∓ 15 ♘e2 e5 16 fxe5 ♘xe5 17
♘c3 ♗xf3+ 18 ♖xf3 ♗d4+ 19 ♔h1
19 ♗e3 ♖xf3 20 ♕xf3 ♖f8 21 ♕e2
♘f4 22 ♕d2 ♕g5 −+ ♖xf3 20 ♕xf3
♕e5 21 g3 ♖f8 22 ♗f4 ♘xf4 23
gxf4 ♖xf4 24 ♕g2 g5 0-1 Sahovic

73 Tseitlin-Antonov USSR 78
1 d4 ♘f6 2 c4 e6 3 ♘f3 c5 4 d5
exd5 5 cxd5 d6 6 ♘c3 g6 7 e4 ♗g7
8 ♗g5 h6 9 ♗h4 0-0 9...g5! 10 ♗g3
♘h5 10 ♘d2 ♖e8 11 ♗e2 ♘bd7 12
0-0 g5! 13 ♗g3 ♘e5 14 ♕c2 ♘h7 15
f4! gxf4 16 ♖xf4! ♘f8 17 ♖af1
♘fg6

18 ♖f5! a6 18...♗xf5 19 exf5 ♘f8
20 ♗b5 ♘fd7 21 ♘de4± 19 ♗h5!
♖f8?! 19...♖e7! 20 a4 ♖b8 △ b5;
19...♗xf5? 20 exf5 ♕g5 21 ♗xg6 fxg6
22 f6 ♗f8 23 ♘de4± 20 ♗xg6 fxg6
20...♗xg6? 21 ♘c4 ♗xf5 22 exf5
♗d4+ 23 ♔h1 ♘e5 24 ♘e4 ♘xc4 25
♕xc4+ 21 ♖xf8+ ♗xf8 22 ♗xe5 dxe5
23 ♘c4 ♗g7 24 ♕f2!? 24 a4 b5 25
♕f7+ ♔h7 25...♔h8 26 ♕xg6 bxc4
27 ♖f7 ♕g8 28 d6 ♕h7 29 ♕xh7+
♔xh7 30 d7 ♗b7 31 d8♕ ♖xd8 32
♖xb7±; 27...♕g5? 28 ♖xg7! 26
♘xe5 ♕g5 27 ♘f3! ♕e3+ 28 ♔h1 c4!
28...♗g4? 29 ♖e1! ♕d3 30 ♘e5 ♕d2

31 ♕xg6+ ♔g8 32 ♖f1±; 29...♕f2??
30 ♘g5+ 29 ♖e1 ♕b6 30 e5! ♗f5
31 d6 ♖f8 32 ♘d5! ♕f2 32...♖xf7?
33 ♘xb6± 33 ♘f6+ ♔h8 34 ♕e7 ♗h3?!
35 gxh3 ♕xf3+ 36 ♔g1 ♕d3 37 d7
♕d2 38 ♖f1 ♕d4+ 39 ♖f2 h5 40 ♕e8!
△ ♕xg6! 1-0 Tseitlin

74 Perkins-Gheorghiu USA 78
1 d4 ♘f6 2 c4 c5 3 d5 g6 4 ♘c3 ♗g7
5 e4 d6 6 ♗e2 0-0 7 ♘f3 e6 8 0-0
♖e8 8...exd5 9 cxd5α 9 dxe6!?
9 ♘d2; 9 ♖e1; 9 ♔h1 ♗xe6 10 ♗f4
♕b6!= 11 ♕b3! N ♘c6?! 11...♘c6!α
12 ♘g5 ♘bd7 13 ♖ad1 ♗f8 14 ♖d2
a6 15 ♖fd1 ♘e5 16 ♘xe6 16 ♗xe5!=
♖xe6 17 f3 ♕c7 18 ♗g5! △ ♗xf6,
♘d5 ♘ed7 19 ♗f4 ♖ae8 20 ♗f1 h6!
21 g3 ♘e5!? 21...g5 22 ♗e3 ♘e5! =∓
22 ♗g2 g5 23 ♗xe5! 23 ♗e3 g4! 24
f4 ♘f3+ 25 ♗xf3 gxf3∓ ♖xe5 24 ♗h3
b5 25 cxb5? Zeitnot c4!∓ 26 ♕c2
axb4 27 ♗f5 b4 28 ♘d5 ♘xd5 29
♖xd5 ♖xd5 30 ♖xd5 ♕a7+!∓ 31 ♔g2
♕xa2 32 e5∓ 0-1 time Gheorghiu

Nimzo-Indian

75 Blokh-Lysenko USSR 78
1 d4 ♘f6 2 c4 e6 3 ♘c3 ♗b4 4 ♕b3
c5 5 dxc5 ♘a6 6 a3 ♗xc3+?! 6...
♗xc5 7 ♕xc3 ♘xc5 8 b4 8 f3!? ♘a6?!
8...♘ce4 9 ♕d4 d5 10 c5 h6 11 f3
♘g5 12 ♗b2 += Forintos-Kolarov,
Gyula 65 9 ♗b2 0-0 10 e4± b6 11
♘f3 11 ♗d2 △ ♘e2 ♗b7 12 ♗d3
♖c8 13 e5? 13 ♕d4 ♘h5!α 14 ♗c2
♕c7 14...♘f4 15 g3 ♘h3 16 ♕d3 g6
17 ♖f1α 15 ♖c1 g6 15...♘f4 16 ♖g1
♔h8 17 ♕e3 ♘g6 α/+=; 17...♖xc4?
18 ♗b1! +− 16 ♕e3 16 ♗b3 ♘f4 17
♖g1 ♕c6!∓; 17 g3 ♘h3 18 ♖f1 ♕c6
19 ♘d2 ♕g2!∓; 19 ♔e2!α ♕xc4!

16 ♕a2 dxc4 17 ♗f4 17 ♗xc4 ♕a8!∓

17 ♕h6? 17 ♗xg6 ♕g4∞; 17...fxg6!?
18 ♖xc4 ♖xc4 19 0-0 ♖g4∓; 19 ♘d2
♖c2 20 ♕b3 ♖fc8 21 b5 ♗d5! −+; 19
♕h6!? ♗xf3 20 gxf3 ♖xf3 21 0-0
♖g4+ 22 ♔h1 ♘f4 (22...♖h3? 23 ♔c1!)
23 ♖g1 ♖h3 24 ♖xg4 ♖xh6 25 ♖xf4
∞/=+; 23 ♖c1 ♘c5! 24 bxc5 ♖h3!
♗xf3 −+ 18 ♗xg6 18 gxf3 ♕a2 −+
♕e2 mate 0-1 Lysenko

76 Nogueiras-Vitolins, Jurmala 78
1 d4 ♘f6 2 c4 e6 3 ♘c3 ♗b4 4 ♕c2!?
0-0 4...♘c6 5 ♘f3 d5 6 a3 ♗xc3+
7 ♕xc3 ♘e4 8 ♕c2 +=; 5...d6 6 a3
♗xc3+ 7 ♕xc3 a5 8 b3 ♕e7 9 ♗b2
0-0 10 e3 ♖e8=; 4...c5 5 dxc5 ♘a6?!
6 a3 +=; 5...0-0∞ **5 a3** 5 ♘f3 b5!? 6
cxb5 a6 7 e3 ♗b7 8 bxa6 ♗xa6 9
♗e2 c5∞ Mihalchishin-Vitolins, USSR
75; 5...d6 6 ♗g5 h6 7 ♗h4 ♘bd7
8 0-0 ♗xc3+ 9 ♕xc3 ♕e8!?=
Doroshkevich-Holmov, USSR 76
♗xc3+ 6 ♕xc3 b6 6...d6 7 g3 a5!?
7 ♗g5 ♗b7 8 ♘f3 8 e3 d6 9 f3! ♘bd7
10 ♗d3 c5 11 ♘e2 cxd4 12 ♕xd4 +=
d6 9 e3 ♘bd7 10 ♕c2! 10 ♗d3 e5!;
10 ♗e2 ♘e4 **♗xf3?! 11 gxf3 c5 12**
♖d1 ♖c8 13 ♗e2?! 13 d5! △ ♗g2
+= **d5! 14 dxc5?** 14 cxd5! cxd4 15
♕a4 dxe3 16 dxe6 ♘c5 17 ♖xd5
exf2+ 18 ♔xf2 ♘xa4 19 ♖xc8 ♖xc8
20 ♗xf6 △ e7! **♖xc5 15 b4 ♖c7!**

17...b5! =+ **18 ♗xc7 ♕xc7 19 ♕b2**
♘d5 20 ♕d4 ♘7b6 21 f4 a5! 22
♖g1 g6 23 bxa5 ♘a4 24 ♔f1 ♕xa5
25 f5 ♘ac3 26 fxg6 fxg6 27 ♗g4
♖f6 28 ♖a1 ♕c7 29 ♔g2 e5!∓ 30
♕d2 ♕c6 31 f3 h5! 32 ♗xh5 32
♗h3 ♖xf3 △ ♘f4+ −+ gxh5 33 ♔h1+
♔f7 34 e4 ♖xf3! −+ 35 exd5 ♘xd5
36 ♖ad1 ♘f4 37 ♕d7+ ♕xd7 38
♖xd7+ ♔e6 39 ♖b7 ♖b3 40 ♖d1
♘d3 41 ♔g2 e4 42 ♖a1 c3 43 ♖c7
♕d6 44 ♖c8 ♕d7 45 ♖f8 c2 46 ♖ff1
♕d6 47 ♖fc1 ♘xc1 48 ♖xc1 ♖b2 49
♔f2 ♕d5 50 ♔e3 ♔c4 51 ♔d2 e3+
0-1 Gufeld

77 Portisch-Hort Niksic 78
1 d4 ♘f6 2 c4 e6 3 ♘c3 ♗b4 4 e3
0-0 5 ♗d3 d5 6 ♘f3 c5 7 0-0 ♘c6
8 a3 ♗xc3 9 bxc3 ♕c7 10 cxd5 exd5
11 ♘h4 ♖e8 11...♘e7! 12 ♗b2 ♖e8
13 a4 ♗e6 14 ♖c1 c4 15 ♗c2 ♕d7
=+ Petrosian-Averbakh 74; 12 a4
♖e8 13 ♗a3 c4 14 ♗c2 ♘g6= Panno-
Korchnoi, Palma 69 **12 f3 b6** 12...
♘e7 13 g4!± ; 12...♘a5 13 ♖a2 cxd4
14 cxd4 ♘c4 15 ♖e2 b5 16 e4 dxe4
17 fxe4 ♗g4 18 ♘f3 ♕b6 19 ♔h1
+= Donner-Trioanescu, Havana 71;
12...♗d7 13 ♖a2 ♕a5 14 ♗d2 ♕b6

15 ♕b1 Donner-Korchnoi, IBM 72;
15...♕xb1=; 12...♕a5!? 13 ♗d2 ♕d8
14 g3 ♗h3 **13 ♖a2 a5?** 13...♗b7!?
14 ♖e2 ♕d8 15 g3 ♘a5 **14 ♖e2 ♗b7**
14...♗a6 15 ♗xa6 ♖xa6 16 e4!± **15
♗b2 ♖ad8 16 ♕e1 g6 17 g4± ♕c8
18 ♕f2 ♖e7 19 h3 ♗a6 20 ♗xa6
♕xa6 21 e4 dxe4?** 21...♕c4!? 22 e5
♘e8± **22 fxe4 +−** ♕c4 22...♘e8
23 d5 ♘e5 24 c4 ♘xc4 25 ♘f5 +−;
25 ♗a1 +− **23 ♕xf6 ♕xe2 24 ♗c1
♕xf1+ 25 ♕xf1 ♖xe4 26 ♗h6 1-0
Velimirovic**

78 Ogaard-Browne
Reykjavik 78
**1 d4 ♘f6 2 c4 e6 3 ♘c3 ♗b4 4 e3
0-0 5 ♗d3 c5 6 ♘f3 d5 7 0-0 cxd4**
7...dxc4 8 ♗xc4 ♘bd7 **8 exd4 dxc4
9 ♗xc4 b6 10 ♗g5** 10 ♖e1 ♗b7 11
♗d3 ♘c6 12 ♗c2 ♗e7 13 a3 ♖c8 14
♕d3 g6 15 ♗h6 ♖e8 16 ♖ad1 +=
♗b7 11 ♖c1 ♗e7 11...♗xc3 12 ♖xc3
♘bd7!? **12 a3 ♘c6** 12...♘bd7!? **13
♗a2 ♖c8 14 ♕d3 ♖c7! 15 ♖fd1
♖d7 =+ 16 d5?!** ♗xd5! **17 ♘xd5 exd5
18 ♕f5 h6?** 18...g6∓ **19 ♗xh6! ♖d6!
20 ♗g5 d4!=+ 21 ♗b1 g6 22 ♕f4 d3!
23 ♕h4 d2!? 24 ♖c4** 24 ♖xd2? ♖xd2
25 ♗xe7 ♘xe7 −+ **♖e8 25 ♖e4 ♘e5!
26 ♖xe5** 26 ♘xe5 ♗xg5−+ **♗xf3 27
♖xe7 ♗xd1 28 h3 ♗b3 0-1 Browne**

79 Bagirov-Kuzmin USSR 77
**1 d4 ♘f6 2 c4 e6 3 ♘c3 ♗b4 4 ♗g5
c5 5 d5** 5 e3 ♕a5! **h6** 5...♕a5? 6 ♗xf6
6 ♗h4 ♗xc3+ 6...d6; 6...b5; 6...♘xd5?!
7 ♗xd8 ♘xc3 8 ♕b3! ♘e4+ 9 ♔d1
♘xf2+ 10 ♔c1± **7 bxc3 d6 8 e3 e5
9 ♗d3** 9 ♕c2!?; 9 f3; 9 f4!? e4 10
♗e2 △ g4 e4! **10 ♗c2 ♘bd7 11 ♘e2
♕e7 12 ♗a4!** N 12 0-0; 12 ♕b1 0-0
△ g5, ♘h5 **0-0 13 ♗xd7 ♗xd7 14
a4 b6 15 ♕c2** △ a5, ♗xf6 **♗c8! =+**

15...g5?! 16 ♗g3 △ h4 += **16 0-0?**
16 a5 ♗a6; 16 ♗xf6 ♕xf6 17 ♕xe4
♗f5 α/=+ g5! **17 ♗g3 ♗a6 18 ♕a2
♗h5 19 ♘c1 f5!∓ 20 ♕e2 ♕f7 21 f4**
exf3 22 ♖xf3 ♕g6 23 a5

**23...f4! −+ 24 exf4 gxf4 25 ♗f2
♖ae8 26 ♕f1 ♖e4 27 axb6 ♗xc4
28 ♕d1 axb6 29 ♖a4 b5 30 ♖a6 ♖e5
31 ♗xc5 ♖fe8 32 ♔f2 ♖e1! 33 ♖xd6
♕c2+! 34 ♕xc2 ♖f1 mate 0-1 Gufeld**

Queen's Indian

80 Gheorghiu-Benjamin USA 78
**1 d4 ♘f6 2 c4 e6 3 ♘f3 b6 4 a3
♗b7 5 ♘c3 ♘e4!?** 5...d5 6 cxd5 ♘xd5
7 e3±; 6...exd5 **6 ♘xe4 ♗xe4 7 e3
♗e7 8 ♗d3! ♗xd3 9 ♕xd3 0-0 10
d5!± a5 11 0-0 ♘a6 12 e4 ♘c5 13
♕c2 d6** 13...a4 14 e5± **14 ♗e3 a4
15 ♘d4! △** ♘c6± **♗f6 16 ♘c6 ♕d7
17 ♖ad1 ♖ae8 18 ♗xc5! bxc5 19
♕xa4 exd5 20 cxd5** 20 exd5 ♗xb2
21 ♕b3 ♗e5 22 a4± ; 20...♗e2!α
**♗xb2 21 ♕b3 ♗e5 22 f4 △ f5α ♗d4+!
23 ♘xd4 cxd4 24 ♖xd4 f5 25 e5!?**
dxe5 **26 d6+ ♔h8** 26...♖f7!α **27
fxe5 ♖xe5 28 ♕b7! ♖c8 29 ♖c4!
♖b5 30 ♕c6± ♕xc6 31 ♖xc6 ♕g8
32 a4 ♖a5 33 dxc7 ♕f7 34 ♖f4 ♕e7
35 ♖fc4 ♕d7 36 ♖6c5! ♖xc5 37
♖xc5 ♖xc7 38 ♖xc7+ ♕xc7 39 ♔f2**

g5 40 ♔e3 h5?! 41 h4! +– gxh4 42 ♔f4 ♔b6 43 ♔xf5 ♔a5 44 ♔g5 1-0 **Gheorghiu**

81 Kuzmin-Ree Kiev 78
1 d4 ♘f6 2 c4 e6 3 ♘c3 ♗b4 4 e3 b6 5 ♘e2 5 ♘f3 ♗b7 6 ♗d3 ♘e4 7 0-0 f5∝ ♗a6 5...♗b7 6 a3 ♗e7 7 d5 0-0 8 ♘g3 b5 9 dxe6 fxe6 10 ♘xb5 += Grigorian-Kupreichik, USSR 76; 5... 0-0 6 a3 ♗xc3+ 7 ♘xc3 d5 8 ♗e2 ♗a6 9 b3 c5 10 dxc5! bxc5 11 0-0 += Hort-Kaplan, Hastings 75/6 **6 a3** 6 ♘g3 ♗xc3+ 7 bxc3 d5 8 ♗a3 ♗xc4 9 ♗xc4 dxc4 10 ♕a4+!=: 8...h5!? **♗xc3+** 6...♗e7?! 7 ♘f4 d5 8 cxd5 ♗xf1 9 ♔xf1 exd5 10 g4! += **7 ♘xc3 d5 8 b3!?** 8 cxd5 ♗xf1 9 ♔xf1 exd5 10 ♕f3 0-0= Wilder-Weinstein, USA 77 **0-0 9 ♗e2 ♘c6 10 a4 dxc4?** 10... ♕d7 += **11 ♗a3 ♖e8 12 bxc4!** 12 b4!? ♘e7 13 b5 ♗b7 14 0-0 ∝/+= **♘a5 13 ♗b5± c6?** 13...♗b7 14 0-0 a6 15 ♘c3 c5± **14 ♘d6 ♖e7 15 e4! ♖d7 16 e5 ♘e8 17 ♕c2 ♗b7**

18 ♘e4!! ♖xd4 19 ♗b2 ♖d7 20 ♖a3! ♘c5 21 ♖h3 ♗xe4 22 ♕xe4 g6 22... h6 23 ♗d3 ♔f8 24 0-0 c5 25 f4 Δ ♕h7 +– **23 ♕f4 c5** 23...h5!? 24 g4 hxg4 25 ♗xg4 ♕e7 26 ♕h6 **24 ♕h6 f5 25 exf6 ♘xf6 26 0-0!** +– **♗b7 27 ♕f4 ♘e8** 27...♖f7 28 ♕e5 ♕b8 29 ♕c3

+– **28 ♗g4 ♕e7 29 ♖e1 ♘g7 30 ♗xg7 ♕xg7 31 ♕e5+ 1-0 Gufeld**

82 Knaak-Ligterink Jurmala 78
1 d4 ♘f6 2 c4 e6 3 ♘c3 ♗b4 4 e3 b6 **5 ♘e2 ♗a6** 5...♘e4!? **6 ♘g3** 6 a3 ♗xc3+ 7 ♘xc3 d5 8 b3! 0-0 9 ♗e2 ♘c6 10 a4 += Kuzmin-Toth, Reggio Emila 76/7 **0-0** 6...♗xc3+ 7 bxc3 d5 8 ♗a3 ♗xc4 9 ♗xc4 dxc4= Knaak-Partos, Bucharest 75; 8 ♕f3! 0-0 cxd5 exd5 10 ♗xa6 ♘xa6 11 ♕e2 += **7 e4?!** 7 a3; 7 ♗d3 ♘c6! **8 ♗d3 e5∝ 9 d5 ♗xc3+ 10 bxc3 ♘e7 11 ♗g5 ♘e8 12 c5 ♗xd3 13 d6?!** cxd6 **14 cxd6 ♘xd6 15 ♕xd3 ♘b7 16 ♖d1** 16 ♘f5 f6 **d6** 16...f6 17 ♕xd7 **17 ♗xe7 ♕xe7 18 h4?! ♖ad8 19 ♘f5 ♕f6 20 g4!? ♘c5 21 ♕e2 d5** 21...g6 22 g5 ♕e6 =+ **22 exd5 e4 23 c4 ♖fe8** 23...♘d3+ 24 ♔f1 ♖fe8 **24 ♕e3 ♘d3+ 25 ♔f1 g6** 25...b5!? **26 ♘g3 ♕e5 27 h5 ♖d6∝ ½-½ Gufeld**

83 Gheorghiu-De Firmian USA 78
1 d4 ♘f6 2 c4 e6 3 ♘f3 b6 4 ♘c3 ♗b4 5 e3 ♗b7 6 ♗d3 0-0 7 0-0 c5 8 **♘a4!** += **cxd4 9 exd4 ♗e7** 9...d5 10 c5!± **10 ♖e1 d6 11 b4 ♘bd7 12 ♖b1?!** 12 a3!± a5!= **13 bxa5** 13 b5 d5! **♖xa5 14 ♘c3 ♗xf3 15 ♕xf3 d5 16 cxd5!** += **♘xd5 17 ♘xd5 ♖xd5 18 ♗e3 ♘f6 19 ♗c4 ♖d7 20 ♖b5 ♘d5 21 ♗xd5 ♖xd5 22 ♖xd5 exd5!** 22...♕xd5 23 ♕xd5 exd5 24 ♖b1 ♖b8 25 ♖b5!±; 24...♖a8 25 ♖xb6 ♖xa2 26 ♖b8+! ♗f8 27 g3!± **23 ♖b1 ♕d6 24 ♖b5 ♖d8 25 g3 ♕c6! 26 a4 ♗f6 27 h4 h6 28 ♔g2 ♕e6 29 h5 ♖d7 30 g4! ♖a7?! 31 ♖xd5 ♖xa4 32 ♖f5!± ♕c4!** 32...♗xd4 33 ♖f4 ♕d6 34 ♕e4 ♗xe3 35 ♕e8+ Δ ♖xa4 +–; 33...♕d7 34 ♕e4 ♗xe3 35 ♕xa4 +– **33 ♕e4 ♕e6 34 ♕f3 ♕c4 35 ♕e4**

♕e6 36 ♕f3! ♖b4?! Zeitnot 36...
♕b3!∝ 37 ♖d5 ♖a4 38 ♖b5!±

38...♗d8?? 39 ♖e5! +− ♕f6+ 40 ♔g2
g5 41 hxg6 ♖a5 41...fxg6 42 ♖e6 +−
42 ♖e8+ ♔g7 43 d5! △ ♗d4 ♕h4 44
♖g8+! 1-0 44...♔xg8 45 ♕e8+ +−

84 Smejkal-Ogaard Kiel 78

1 c4 ♘f6 2 ♘f3 b6 3 d4 ♗b7 4 e3 e6
5 ♗d3 c5 6 0-0 ♗e7 7 b3 0-0 8 ♗b2
cxd4 9 exd4 d5 10 ♕e2 ♘c6 11 ♘bd2
♖e8 12 ♖ac1 ♗f8 13 ♖fd1 ♖c8 14 ♕e3
g6 15 h3 ♗g7 16 ♘e5 += ♕e7 17 f4
dxc4 18 bxc4 ♕b4! 19 ♗a1! 19 ♘c3
♕a3 △ ♘b4 ♕a4 20 ♘df3 ♘b4 20...
♕xa2 21 ♘c2!≈ 21 ♗e2 21 ♗b1!?
♘xa2 22 ♗c2 ♕a5 23 ♖b1 ♘d5?! 24
♕b3±; 22...♕b4 23 ♖b1 ♕e7 24 ♕d2±

21...♘h5 21...♕xa2? 22 ♗c3? ♘fd5!;
22 ♖d2 ♕a4 23 ♗d1 ♕a5 24 ♗c3 +−;

21...♘xa2? 22 ♖b1 ♘b4 23 ♗c3?
♘bd5; 23 ♗b2±; 21...♘c2!? 22 ♕b3
♕xb3 23 axb3 ♘xa1 24 ♖xa1 a5=
22 ♘e1 ♗f6 23 ♖c3?! 23 a3 += ♗fd5!
24 cxd5 ♗xd5 25 ♕d2 ♘xc3 26 ♗xc3
♖e7 27 ♖b1 ♖ec7 28 ♗b5 28 ♗b4!?
♕a3 29 ♗b4 ♕g3 30 ♖b3 ♕h4 31
♔h2 ♗h6 32 ♘g4 32 g3? ♕d8 △ ♕d5
♗g7 33 ♘e5 ♗h6 34 ♘g4 ½-½ Webb

85 Ree-Miles IBM 78

1 c4 b6 2 d4 e6 3 e4 ♗b7 4 ♘c3 ♗b4
5 f3 ♕h4+!? 6 g3 ♕h5 7 ♗d2 f5 8 exf5
♕xf5 9 ♗b5 ♗xd2+ 10 ♕xd2 ♘a6 11
0-0-0 ♘e7 12 ♗d3 ♕f6 13 ♘h3 ♕xf3
14 ♘g5 ♕h5 14...♕xh1?!± 15 ♖hf1
h6! 16 ♘f7!? 16 ♘e4 0-0-0≈ 0-0 17
g4 ♕h4 17...♕xg4?? 18 ♘xh6+ +−
18 ♕c2? 18 ♕f4! ♘f5 19 ♘e5! ♘e7
20 ♘f7!=; 19...♘d6?? 20 ♕xf8+ +−;
19 exf5? ♕xf4+ 20 ♖xf4 ♖xf7∓
19 ♗xf5 exf5 20 ♕xf5 ♕e7 −+ ♘f5!
19 gxf5 ♘b4! 20 ♕d2 ♘xd3+ 21 ♕xd3
♖xf7 22 fxe6 ♖xf1 23 ♖xf1 dxe6∓
24 ♕g6 24 ♘xc7 ♖c8 25 ♘xe6 ♗d5!
−+ ♗e4! 25 ♕f7+ 25 ♕xe6+ ♔h7 26
♘xc7 ♖f8! −+ ♔h7 26 ♘xc7 26 ♖g1
♖g8 △ ♕xh2 −+ ♕xh2 27 ♖f2 ♕g1+
28 ♕d2 ♗g6 29 ♕f4 ♖c8 30 ♖e2 30
♘xe6 ♖xc4 −+ ♕b1 31 ♘xe6 ♕xb2+
31...♖xc4? 32 ♘g5+! 32 ♔e1 ♕b1+
32...♕b4+ 33 ♔f2 ♕xc4 34 ♘f8+
♖xf8 35 ♕xf8 ♕xd4+ −+ 33 ♔f2
♕f5 34 ♔g3 ♕xf4+?? Zeitnot 34...
♖xc4 −+ 35 ♔xf4∝ ♗d3 35...♗f7
36 d5 36 ♖g2 g5+ 37 ♔e5 ♗xc4 38
d5 ♕g6 39 ♖f2 ♔h5 40 d6 ♖e8 41
♖f6 ♗b5 42 ♖f7 ♗c4 43 ♖f6 ♗xe6 44
♖xe6 ♖d8= 45 ♖e7 g4 46 d7 g3 47
♔e6 ♔g4 48 ♖e8 ♖xd7 49 ♔xd7 h5 50
♖g8+ ♔f4 51 ♖f8+ ♔e3 52 ♖e8+ ♔f3
53 ♖f8+ ♔g4 54 ♖g8+ ♔h3 55 ♔e6
g2 56 ♔f5 ♔h2 56...h4 57 ♖g4! 57
♖h8! g1♕ 58 ♖xh5+ ♔g3 59 ♖g5+

♔f2 60 ♖xg1 ♛xg1 61 ♔e5 ♕f2 62
♔d5 ½-½ **Miles**

86 Miles-Andersson IBM 78

**1 d4 e6 2 c4 ♘f6 3 ♘f3 b6 4 ♗f4!?
♗b7 5 e3 ♗e7 6 ♘c3?!** 6 h3! **♘h5!=
7 ♗g3 d6 8 ♗d3 ♘d7 9 ♕c2 g6 10
♗e4 ♗xe4 11 ♕xe4 0-0 12 ♕c6 a6 13
a4 ♖a7 14 a5 ♘b8 15 ♕e4 c5≈ 16
axb6 ♖xb6 17 ♖b1 cxd4 18 exd4
♕b4 19 ♘d2! ♖d7! 20 0-0 d5 21
cxd5 ♘f6 22 ♕d3 ♘xd5 =+ 23 ♘f3
♕b7 24 ♘e4 ♘f6 25 ♖fe1 ♘c6 26
♘eg5 ♖fd8 27 ♘e5 ♘xe5 28 ♗xe5
♘h5** 28...♘g4!? **29 ♕g3 29 ♘f3 ♗g7
30 ♖a1 a5?? 31 ♖xa5 += ♘f5** 31...
♗b4 32 ♖b5 ♕a6 33 ♖d1 **32 ♖aa1
♕d5 33 ♕e2 ♖b7 34 ♖ec1 h5 35
h3 h4 36 ♖c2 ♖e8 37 ♖ac1 ♖d8 38
♖c7 ♖xc7 39 ♖xc7 ♗d6 40 ♖xd6
♕xd6 41 ♖c4 ♕b6 42 ♕c2** 42 ♕d2 e5
43 ♘xe5 ♕xd4∞ **♗xd4 43 ♘xd4 ♖xd4
44 ♖xd4 ♕xd4 45 ♕c8+ ♔h7** 45...
♔g7? 41 ♕c3 +- **46 ♕c7 ♔g8?!**
46...♕xb2 += **47 ♕b8+ ♔g7 48 b4
+=/± e5 49 b5 ♕c5 50 ♔h2 f6 51
b6 ♕xf2 52 ♕c7+ ♔h8** 52...♔h6 53
♕c1+ +- **53 ♕c8+ ♔g7 54 ♕c7+
♔h8 55 ♕d8+ ♔g7 56 ♕c7+?? Zeitnot
½-½ 56 ♕e7+! ♔h6 57 ♕b4 e4 58
b7 +- ♕f4+ 59 ♔g1 ♕c1+ 60 ♔f2
♕c2+ 61 ♔e3 ♕d3+ 62 ♔f4 g5+ 63
♔f5 e3+ 64 ♔e6! +-**

87 Miles-Browne IBM 78

**1 d4 ♘f6 2 ♘f3 e6 3 c4 b6 4 ♗f4!?
♗b7 5 e3 ♗e7 6 h3! N 0-0 7 ♘c3 d5
8 cxd5 ♘xd5** 8...exd5 += **9 ♘xd5
♗xd5 10 ♗d3 += ♗b4+ 11 ♔e2 ♗d6
12 ♗xd6 cxd6** 12...♕xd6!? **13 ♕c2
f5!?** 13...h6 14 ♖hc1 △ e4, ♕c7± **
14 ♗c4** 14 e4!? ♗b7! **15 exf5 ♘c6!∞
♗xf3+** 14...♗xc4+ 15 ♕xc4 d5 16
♕c2±; 14...♕c7 15 ♖hc1 +=/± **15**

---

gxf3 ♕f6 16 ♖ac1 ♔h8 17 ♗b3!± f4
17...♘d7 18 ♕c7 +-; 17...♘a6 18
♕c4 +- **18 ♕e4?!** 18 e4!± ♕xd6
19 ♕c3!; 18...♘d7 19 ♕c7 ♖ad8 20
♕xd6!? ♘c5 21 dxc5 ♖xd6 22 cxd6!±
d5 18...fxe3!? 19 ♕xa8 d5 20 ♗xd5
♕xd4∞; 20 fxe3 ♕xf3+ = **19 ♕xf4
♕xf4 20 exf4 += ♘d7 21 ♖c7 ♘f6
22 f5! ♘h5!** 22...exf5 23 ♔d2± **23
fxe6 ♘f4+ 24 ♔e3 ♗xe6 25 ♖e7 ♘f4
26 ♖g1 ♘g6 27 ♖e6 ♘f4 28 ♖e5 ♘g6
29 ♗xd5** 29 ♖xg6!? **♘xe5** 29...♖ad8
30 ♖eg5 ♘f4 31 ♗e4 ♘xh3 32 ♖xg7
+=; 30 ♖xg6!? += **30 ♗xa8 ♘c4+
31 ♔d3 ♘xb2+ 32 ♔c3 ♘a4+ 33
♔b4 ♖xa8 34 ♔xa4 ♖d8 35 ♖g4 +=
♖d5 36 ♔b4 ♔g8 37 ♖e4 ♔f7 38
♔c4 ♖a5 39 ♖e2 a6 40 d5 40 ♖b2!?
♖a4+ 41 ♔d3 ♖a3+?** 41...♖h4=
41...♖f4= **42 ♔d4 ♖a4+ 43 ♔e5 ♔e7
44 ♖b2?** 44 ♖c2 ♔d7 45 f4 += b5
45 ♖c2 ♔d7 46 f4 46 d6 ♖c4!=
**b4! 47 f3 ♖a3 48 ♖g2 g6 49 f5 ♖xf3
50 fxg6 hxg6 51 ♖xg6 ♖e3+ 52 ♔d4
♖xh3 53 ♔c5** 53 ♖xa6 ♖a3!= **♖c3+
54 ♔xb4 ♖d3 55 ♔c4 ♖a3 56 ♖g2
♔d6 57 ♔b4 ♖d3 58 ♖g6+ ♔xd5
59 a4 ♖d4+ 60 ♔a5 ♔c5 61 ♖xa6
♖d8 62 ♖a7 ♖c8 ½-½ Miles**

88 Timman-Gulko Niksic 78

**1 d4 e6 2 ♘f3 ♘f6 3 c4 b6 4 g3 ♗a6
5 ♕a4 c6 6 ♘c3 b5?! 7 cxb5 cxb5
8 ♘xb5 ♕b6 9 e3** 9 ♘c3! ♗b4 10
♗g2 ♘c6 11 0-0 ♗xc3 12 bxc3 ♗xe2
13 ♖e1 ♕a6 14 ♕xa6 ♗xa6 15 ♘e5
+=; 10...0-0 11 ♕d1! ♘e4 17 ♗d2±
**♗b7 10 ♗e2 ♗c6 11 ♕c4 ♕b7 12 0-0
♗xf3** 12...a6!? 13 ♘c3 ♗xf3 14 ♗xf3
♕xf3 15 ♕c8+ ♔e7 16 d5∞; 16 b3?
♘e4! **13 ♗xf3 ♕xf3 14 ♕c8+ ♔e7
15 ♕c5+** 15 b3!? ♘e4 16 ♗a3+ ♔f6
17 ♗xf8 ♔f5?! 18 h3!±; 17...♔g6!?
18 ♕b7 ♘c6!∞ **♔d8 16 ♕c8+ ♔e7**

17 ♕c5+ ½-½ Velimirovic

89 Beljavsky Gulko Lvov 78
**1 d4 ♘f6 2 c4 e6 3 ♘f3 b6 4 g3 ♗a6!?
5 ♕a4** 5 b3 ♗b4+ 6 ♗d2 ♗e7!? 7 ♘c3
d5 8 cxd5 exd5 9 ♗g2 0-0 10 0-0
♘bd7 11 ♘e5! += Petrosian-Korchnoi
(8) 77; 5 ♕c2 c5 6 ♗g2 ♘c6 7 0-0
cxd4 8 ♖d1 ♖c8 9 ♕a4 ♘a5 10 ♘a3∝
Sveshnikov-Kupreichik, USSR 76; 9...
♗b7!? **♗e7** 5...c5 6 ♗g2 ♗b7 7 0-0 ♕c8
8 ♗f4 cxd4 9 ♘xd4 ♗xg2 10 ♔xg2
♗c5 11 ♖d1 +=Balashov-Polugaevsky,
USSR 76; 5...♕e7!? 6 a3 ♕d6 7 ♘bd2
c5 8 e4 ♘c6 9 ♕xc6 ♘xc6 10 d5 +=
Olafsson-Timman, Wijk aan Zee 77
6...c6!? 6 ♘c3 b5 7 cxb5 cxb5 8
♘xb5 ♕b6≈ Tukmakov-Gulko, USSR
77 **6 ♘c3** 6 ♘bd2!? **♗b7 7 ♗g2 ♘e4
8 ♕c2!?** 8 ♘xe4 △ 0-0 += **♘xc3 9
♕xc3 0-0 10 0-0 ♗e4** 10...c5 11 ♖d1
d6 12 b3 ♘d7 13 ♗b2= **11 ♘e1!?**
11 ♗f4 ♘c6 12 ♖fd1 d5 13 ♘e5=
♗xg2 12 ♘xg2 c6 12...c5 13 d5 +=
**13 ♗f4! += d6 14 d5! exd5 15 cxd5
c5 16 e4 ♘d7 17 ♕c2 b5! 18 h4!?
♘f6 19 ♖ad1** 19 ♘e3?! ♘h5 ♖e8 20
♖fe1 c4 21 e5 dxe5 22 ♗xe5 ♗b4 23
♖e2 ♘g4 24 ♗c3! ♗xc3 25 ♖xe8+
♕xe8 26 ♕xc3 26 bxc3 += ♕e2!
27 ♖d2 ♕e4 28 ♕d4 ♕xd4 29 ♖xd4
♘e5 30 ♔f1 ♔f8 31 ♘e3 ♖d8 32 d6
f6!= 33 ♖d5 a6 34 a4 ♘f7 35 axb5
axb5 36 d7 ♘e5 36...♔e7?! 37 ♘f5+
37 ♖xb5 ♖xd7 38 f4**

Diagram

**38...♖d3! 39 ♖b8+ ♔f7 40 ♖b7+
♔f8** 40...♔g6? 41 ♔e2 ♘c6 42 f5+!
+− **41 ♖b8+ ½-½ Gufeld**

90 Savon-Romanishin Lvov 78
1 d4 ♘f6 2 c4 e6 3 ♘f3 b6 4 g3 ♗b4+

5 ♗d2 5 ♘bd2 **a5** 5...♗xd2+ 6 ♕xd2
♗a6?! 7 ♕c2 c5 8 ♗g2 ♘c6 9 ♕a4!
♕c8 10 0-0 0-0 11 ♖d1 cxd4 12
♘xd4± Keller-Duckstein, Zurich 75;
10 ♘e5?! ♘xd4! 11 ♗xa8 ♕xa8
12 f3 ♗b7! 13 ♘c3 0-0 14 ♗b5 d6 15
♘xd4 dxe5 16 ♘c2 ♗xf3!∓ Minev-
Szabo, Marianske Lazne 59; 7 b3!?
♗b7 8 ♗g2 0-0 9 0-0 d6 10 ♘c3 ♘e4
11 ♘xe4 ♗xe4 12 ♕e3 ♗b7 += Miles-
Larsen, Bugojno 78; 5...♕e7 6 ♗g2
♗b7 7 0-0 ♗xd2 8 ♕xd2 0-0 9 ♘c3
♘e4 10 ♘xe4 ♗xe4 11 ♕f4!± Hubner-
Larsen, Las Palmas 76 **6 ♗g2 0-0 7
0-0 ♗a6!? 8 ♕c2** 8 a3 ♗e7 9 ♘e5 ♖a8
10 ♕c2 d6 11 ♘d3 d5 12 cxd5 exd5
13 ♘c3 += Estevez-Romanishin,
Cienfuegos 77; 8 ♘e5 c6 9 ♗xb4
axb4 10 ♕b3 d5 11 ♖d1 ♕e7 12 ♘d2
♗b7 13 e4 ♖d8∝ Tukmakov-
Romanishin, USSR Final 77; 8 ♘e5
♖a7 9 ♗xb4 axb4 10 a3!± Ivkov-
Romanishin, Novi Sad 75 **d5 9 ♗xb4
axb4 10 ♘bd2 ♗b7 11 ♖fc1** 11 ♘e5!?
**♘c6 12 e3 ♖a7 13 cxd5 exd5 14
♗f1!** △ ♗b5 **♖a8** 14...♕a8!? 15 ♗b5
♘a5 16 ♕xc7?! ♖c8 17 ♕xb6 ♘c4!
18 ♘xc4 dxc4 △ ♗xf3/♘d5∓
Friedgood **15 a3 += ♕d6 16 ♗b5
bxa3 17 ♗xc6 axb2 18 ♖xa7 bxc1!+
19 ♕xc1 ♗xc6** 19...♕xc6 20 ♕xc6 △

♘e5 +− 20 ♘e5± ♗d7 21 ♕xc7 ♕xc7 22 ♖xc7 ♗h3 23 f3 h5 24 ♔f2 ♖c8 25 ♖b7 ♖c1! △ ♖h1 26 ♘xf7 ♖h1 27 ♘g5 ♖xh2+ 28 ♔g1± ♖g2+ 29 ♔h1 ♘e8 30 ♖b8 ♔f8 31 ♘f1! 31 ♘xh3 ♖xd2 32 ♘f4± ♖f2 32 ♘xh3 ♖xf1+ 33 ♔g2 ♖e1 34 ♔f2 ♖b1 35 ♘f4 +− ♖b2+ 36 ♔e1! ♖b5 37 ♘xh5 △ ♘xg7 Friedgood ♔f7 38 ♖b7+ ♔g6 39 ♘f4+ ♔f6 40 ♖d7 g5 41 ♘xd5+! 41 ♖xd5?? ♖b1+ −+ Freidgood ♔e6 42 ♖d8! ♖b1+ 1-0 Gufeld

91 Sahovic-Ivkov Jugoslavia 78
1 d4 ♘f6 2 c4 e6 3 ♘f3 b6 4 g3 ♗b7 5 ♗g2 ♗b4+ 5...♗e7 6 0-0 0-0 7 ♘c3 ♘e4 8 ♗d2 += 6 ♗d2 6 ♘bd2 0-0 7 0-0 c5= ♗xd2+ 7 ♕xd2 d6 8 0-0 ♘bd7 9 ♘c3 ♘e4 10 ♘xe4 ♗xe4 11 d5 11 ♘e1!? ♗xg2 12 ♘xg2 0-0 13 e4 e5 14 d5 ♘c5 15 f3 △ b4 ♗xf3!= 12 ♗xf3 12 dxe6 ♗xg2 13 exd7+ ♕xd7 14 ♔xg2 0-0= e5 13 b4 a5! 14 a3 0-0 15 e4 ♕e7 16 ♗g2 ♖a7 17 ♖ac1 axb4 18 axb4 ♖fa8 19 ♖c2 ♕e8 20 f3 ♖a1 21 ♖fc1 ♖xc1+ 22 ♕xc1 ♖a4 23 ♔b2 h5 24 h4 ♕a8 25 ♗h3 ♘f6 26 c5 bxc5 27 bxc5 ♕a7 28 ♔h2 ♖a1 29 ♗g2 ♘d7 30 ♕b5! ♘f6 30...♘xc5 31 ♕e8+± 31 ♕b4 ♖a4 32 ♕c3 32 cxd6?? ♖xb4 33 dxc7 ♖b8! −+ ½-½ Sahovic

92 Sahovic-Gipslis Jurmala 78
1 d4 ♘f6 2 ♘f3 e6 3 g3 b6 4 ♗g2 ♗b7 5 0-0 c5 6 c4 cxd4 7 ♕xd4 7 ♘xd4 += d6 8 ♘c3 a6 9 ♗e3!? ♘bd7 10 ♘g5 ♗xg2 11 ♔xg2 ♗e7?! 11...♕c7 12 ♘ge4 ♘c5 13 ♖fd1 ♗fxe4 14 ♘xe4 ♘xe4 15 ♕xe4 ♖b8 16 ♗f4 += 0-0 17 ♖ac1 ♕d7 18 b4 ♕a4? 18...♖bc8 19 ♖xd6! ♕xb4 20 ♖b1 ♕a5

21 ♖xe6! fxe6 22 ♕xe6+ ♔h8 23 ♗xb8 ♗c5 24 ♗f4 +− ♕xa2 25 ♖d1 ♕c2 26 ♖d7 a5 27 h4 Zeitnot 27 ♖xg7! +− a4 28 h5 ♕f5 29 ♕xf5 ♖xf5 30 e4 ♖f8 31 h6 ♖e8 32 hxg7+ ♔g8 33 ♖a7 a3 34 ♗h6 ♖c8 35 ♖a4 ♕f7 36 ♗c1 ♔xg7 37 ♗xa3 ♗xa3 38 ♖xa3 ♖xc4 39 ♖a7+ ♔g6 40 ♔f3 ♖c2 41 ♖b7 ♖b2 42 ♔e3 h5 43 f3 ♔g5 44 ♖g7+ ♔f6 45 ♖d7 b5 46 ♔f4 ♖b3 47 ♖b7 ♔g6 48 ♖b8 b4 49 e5 ♔h7 50 ♔e4 ♔g7 51 ♔f4! ♔h7 52 g4 h4 53 ♖b7+ ♔g6 54 e6 ♖b1 55 e7 ♔f7 56 g5 ♖g1 57 ♔f5 h3 58 g6+ ♔e8 59 ♔f6 1-0 Sahovic

93 Browne-H.Olafsson
Lone Pine 78
1 d4 ♘f6 2 c4 e6 3 ♘f3 b6 4 g3 ♗b7 5 ♗g2 d5 5...♗e7 6 0-0 0-0 7 ♘c3 ♘e4 6 cxd5 exd5 7 0-0 ♗d6?! 7...♗e7 8 ♘c3 8 ♘h4!? g6 9 ♗h6 ♘g4 10 ♕c1; 8...♕d7 9 ♕c2 0-0 9 ♗g5 += h6 9...♘bd7 10 ♘b5 ♗e7 11 ♗f4! c6 12 ♘d6± 10 ♗xf6 ♕xf6 11 ♖c1 ♘d7 12 ♕b3 ♕e6! 12...c6? 13 e4!± 13 ♘b5 c6 14 ♘xd6 ♕xd6 15 ♖fd1 f5?! 16 e3! ♖ae8 17 a4!± ♔h8 18 a5 ♗a6 19 ♕c2 ♗b5 19...c5? 20 dxc5 bxc5 21 ♘h4 +.− 20 axb6 axb6 21 ♖a1 g6 22 ♖a3?! 22 ♖a7! ♖a8 23 ♖da1 ♖xa3 24 ♖xa3 ♖c8 24...c5? 25 ♕c3! c4 26 ♘e5± 25 h4!

♕e6 25...♘f6? 26 ♘e5 +− **26 ♗h3!**
♖f8 27 ♖a7 ♕e4 27...c5 28 dxc5!
bxc5 29 b4! ♕e4 30 ♕b2+ ♔g8 31
♗g2! ♕xb4 32 ♕xb4 cxb4 33 ♘d4
+−; 29...cxb4 30 ♕b2+ ♔g8 31 ♕xb4
♗c6 32 ♘d4 ♕f6 33 h5! +− **28 ♕d1!**
c5 28...♘f6 29 ♘e5 +−; 28...♖d8 29
♖xd7 +−

29 ♖xd7! +− ♗xd7 30 ♘e5 f4?!
30...♗e8 31 ♗g2 +− **31 ♘xd7! fxe3**
32 ♘xf8 e2 33 ♕e1 cxd4 34 ♘xg6+
1-0 34...♔g7 35 ♘f4 d3 36 ♘xd3
♕xd3 37 ♗g4 +− **Browne**

94 Beljavsky-Savon Lvov 78
1 d4 ♘f6 2 c4 e6 3 ♘f3 b6 4 g3 ♗b7
5 ♗g2 ♗e7 6 ♘c3 ♘e4 7 ♕c2 ♘xc3
8 ♕xc3 0-0 9 0-0 ♗e4 10 ♘e1 10
♗f4 ♘c6 11 ♖fd1 d5 12 ♘e5 ♘xe5
13 ♗xe5 ♗xg2 14 ♔xg2 c6 15 ♖ac1
½-½ Petrosian-Korchnoi (10) 77; 10
♖d1 ♗f6 11 ♗f4 ♘c6 12 ♘e5 ♗xg2 13
♔xg2 ♕e7 14 ♖d2! △ ♖ad1 +=
Tukmakov-Gulko, USSR 78 **♗xg2 11**
♘xg2 c5 11...c6 12 ♗f4 += **12 d5!?**
12 dxc5!? △ ♗f4, ♖ad1 += **exd5 13**
cxd5 d6 14 ♘e3 14 ♗f4 ♗f6 15 ♕c2
+= Friedgood **♗f6** 14...♘d7 **15 ♕c2**
♘a6!? 15...♘d7 16 ♘f5 ♘e5 17 f4!
+= **16 ♗d2 ♘c7 17 ♗c3 ♘b5 18 a4!**

+= **♘d4** 18...♘xc3 += **19 ♕d3 ♕d7**
20 ♖a2! ♖ae8 21 b4 g6 22 ♘c4 △
bxc5 Friedgood **♗g7 23 bxc5 bxc5?!**
23...dxc5! += **24 ♗xd4! cxd4** 24...
♗xd4 25 e3 ♗g7 26 ♖b1± **25 ♖b1±**
♖c8 26 ♖ab2? 26 ♖b5± **♕xa4! 27**
♘xd6 ♖cd8 27...♖c3 28 ♕b5 +=
Friedgood **28 ♕b5 ♕xb5 29 ♘xb5**
a6! 29...♖xd5 30 ♘xa7 d3! += **30**
♘c7 d3 31 ♖d2 dxe2 32 ♖xe2 a5
32...♖d7 **33 ♖d1 ♖d7 34 d6 ♖fd8**
35 ♘b5 ♗f8= 36 ♖a2 ♖a8 36...♗xd6??
37 ♖d2 +− Friedgood **37 ♖da1 ♖a6**
38 ♖xa5 ♖xa5 39 ♖xa5 ♗xd6 ½-½
Gufeld

95 Palatnik-Velikov Kiev 78
1 d4 ♘f6 2 c4 e6 3 ♘f3 b6 4 g3 ♗b7
5 ♗g2 ♗e7 6 ♘c3 0-0 7 0-0 d5 7...
♘e4 **8 cxd5!?** 8 ♘e5 ♘a6!? 9 cxd5
exd5 10 ♗g5 ♘e4!∞; 9 ♗f4 c5 10
♖c1 ♘e4 11 cxd5 exd5 12 ♗e3 ♕d6
13 ♘c4 ♕e6 =+ Browne-Karpov,
Las Palmas 77; 9 ♗e3 c5 10 ♖c1
♘e4= Browne-Tal, Las Palmas 77
exd5 9 ♕c2! += **♘a6** 9...♘bd7
10 ♖d1 c5 11 dxc5 ♘xc5 11...
bxc5?! 12 e4 **12 ♘d4 ♖c8 13 ♗h3!**
♖a8 14 ♗e3 ♖e8 15 ♘f5 ♘e6 15...
♗f8 16 ♗g5± **16 ♘xe7+ ♕xe7 17**
♗d4! ♘xd4 18 ♖xd4 ♕c5 19 e3
♘e4 20 ♖c1 ♘g5 21 ♗g2 ♖ac8 22
♕d1! ♘e4 22...♖ed8 **23 ♗h3 ♖c7**
24 ♘e2 ♕e7 25 ♖c2! ♖xc2 26 ♕xc2
♕e5 27 ♘f4 ♘g5 28 ♗g2 ♘e6 29
♘xe6 fxe6 29...♖xe6 30 ♗xd5! ♗xd5
31 ♖xd5 **30 ♕a4± ♕b8 31 ♖d1!**
a6 32 ♕d4 ♕c7 33 h4 h6 34 ♖d3
♕d6 35 ♖b3! b5 36 ♖c3 ♖c8?! 37
♖xc8+ ♗xc8 38 b4 ♗b7 39 ♕a7
♕c7 40 ♗f3 ♔f8 41 ♔h2 ♕c6 42
♕b8+ ♗c8 43 ♗h5! △ ♕f4+ ♕d7 **44**
♗g6 ♕g8 45 a3 ♔f8 46 ♔g1 ♕b7

47 ♕f4+ ♔g8 48 ♕f1 ♕e7 49 ♕b8! ♕d7 50 ♕e1 ♕d8 51 h5 ♕f8 52 ♕c7 ♔h8 53 f4! +− ♔g8 54 ♔d2 ♔h8 55 ♕d3 ♔g8 56 ♕d4 ♔h8 57 ♕f7 1-0 Gufeld

96 Sturua-Ivanov
USSR 77
1 d4 ♘f6 2 c4 e6 3 ♘f3 b6 4 g3 4 ♘c3 ♗b7 5 ♗g5!? ♗b7 5 ♗g2 ♗e7 5...♗b4+ 6 0-0 0-0 7 ♘c3 ♘e4 7... d5?! 8 ♘e5 += 8 ♕c2 8 ♗d2!? ♘f6 9 ♖c1 += ♘xc3 9 ♕xc3 c5 9...♘f6?! 10 ♕c2 += 10 ♖d1 d6 11 ♗f4 ♘d7 12 dxc5 12 d5!? ♘xc5 13 b4 ♘e4 14 ♕d3 f5 14...d5 15 cxd5 ♕xd5 16 ♘d2?! ♕xd3 17 cxd3 g5!= Tal-Gulko, Moscow 77 15 ♘d2!± d5 16 cxd5 ♕xd5 17 ♘xe4 ♕xd3 18 exd3 fxe4 19 a3 ♗f6 20 ♖ac1 ♖ad8 21 ♖c7 ♖f7 22 ♖dc1 ♖dd7 23 ♗xe4 ♗xe4 24 ♖c8+! ♖f8 25 dxe4 ♗b2 26 ♖xf8+ ♔xf8 27 ♖c8+ ♔f7 28 a4 +− ♖d4 29 ♖c7+ ♔g6 30 ♖xa7 ♖xb4 31 ♗e3 ♗d4 32 ♗xd4 ♖xd4 33 f3 ♔f6

34 e5+! ♔xe5 35 ♖xg7 ♖xa4 36 ♖xh7 ♖a2 37 ♖h5+! ♔d4 38 ♖b5 ♖a6 39 h4 ♔c4 40 ♖b1 b5 41 g4 b4 42 ♔g2 b3 43 h5 1-0 Gufeld

Grunfeld

97 Gligoric-Gulko Niksic 78
1 d4 ♘f6 2 c4 g6 3 ♘c3 d5 4 cxd5 ♘xd5 5 e4 ♘xc3 6 bxc3 ♗g7 7 ♗c4 0-0 8 ♘e2 ♕d7 9 0-0 9 h4?! ♗g4!∓ b6 10 ♗e3 10 ♕d3!? ♗b7 11 e5 ♘c6 12 ♘f4 e6 13 ♕h3 ♘a5 14 ♗e2 c5 15 ♗e3 16 cxd4 += Gligoric-Vaganian, Jugoslavia-USSR 75 ♖a6!? 11 ♗d5? 11 ♗xa6! ♘xa6 12 e5∝; 12 ♕d3 ♘b8 13 e5∝ ♘c6 12 ♕a4 ♗b7 13 ♘f4 ♖ad8 14 ♕c2 e6 15 ♗b3 ♘a5 16 d5? 16 ♖ad1 exd5 17 ♘xd5 c6 18 ♘f4 ♕e7 19 ♖fe1 ♕e5 20 ♖ac1 ♖d7 21 f3 ♖fd8 22 ♘e2 ♘xb3 22...c5!? 23 ♘a4 ♘c6 24 ♗xc6 ♗xc6∓ 23 axb3 c5 =+ 24 ♕c2 ♖cd1 a5 25 ♖xd7 ♖xd7 26 ♖d1 ♕e7 27 c4? 27 ♔f2 =+ ♖xd1+ 28 ♕xd1 e5 29 ♗xe5 30 ♕d2 ♕d6 31 ♕xd6 ♗xd6 32 ♗g5 ♗c7 33 ♘c3 ♗c6 34 ♔f2 ♔f7 35 h4 35 h3! ♗e5 36 ♗d2 ♔e6 36... ♗f6! 37 ♔e2 ♗f6 38 ♗e1 ♔d6 39 ♔d3 ♗d7 39...♔c7! △ ♔b7-a6, b5 40 ♘d5 ♗d8 41 ♗g3+ ♔c6 42 ♘c3 f4? 42...♔b7!? △ ♔a6, b5 43 ♗xf4 ♗xh4 44 ♕d2? 44 ♘h6! =+ h5 45 ♗e5 ♗g5+ 46 f4 ♗h4 47 ♘e4 b5 48 g3 ♗e7 49 cxb5+ ♔xb5 50 ♘f6 ♗f5 52 ♔c4 ♗d8 53 ♘c3 a4 −+ 54 bxa4 ♗a5+ 55 ♔c4 ♗e1 56 a5 ♗xg3 57 a6 ♔b6 58 ♘d5+ ♔xa6 59 ♔xc5 h4 60 ♘e3 ♗d3 61 ♘d5 0-1
Velimirovic

98 Alburt-Kuzmin Kiev 78
1 d4 ♘f6 2 c4 g6 3 ♘c3 d5 4 ♘f3 ♗g7 5 cxd5 ♘xd5 6 e4 6 e3 0-0 7 ♗c4 ♘xc3 8 bxc3 c5 9 0-0 ♕c7 10 ♕e2 b6 11 ♗b2 ♘c6 12 ♖ac1 ♗b7= Kuzmin-Kochiev, USSR 76 ♘xc3 6...♘b6!? 7 ♗e3 0-0 8 ♗e2 ♗g4≈ 7 bxc3 0-0 7...c5! 8 ♗e2 0-0 9 0-0 b6 10 ♗e3 ♗b7= 8 ♗e2 b6 9 0-0 ♗b7 9...c5 10 ♕d3 10 e5?! ♕d7!? 10...♘d7

11 Bg5!? += 11 Bf4 Qc6!? 12 d5
12 Nd2 f5!? Qa4 13 Qe3 c6!= 14
Bd1! Qa5 15 Bb3 cxd5 15...Qxc3
16 Qxc3 Bxc3 17 Rac1 Bg7 18 Bxb8
Δ dxc6∞ 16 exd5 Bxd5 17 Bxd5
Qxd5 18 Qxe7 Nc6! 18...Bxc3 19
Rad1≈ 19 Qa3 Qc4 20 Be3∞ Rfd8
21 Nd4 Bxd4 21...Nxd4 22 cxd4
Bxd4 23 Rac1≈ 22 cxd4 Nxd4 23
Rad1 Rd5! =+ 24 Qe7!? Nf5 25
Qb7 Rad8 26 Rxd5 Qxd5 27 Qxa7
b5 28 Bg5 Ra8 29 Qc7 Qxa2∓ 30
Re1 Qb2 31 Qc6 Δ Re8+ = Rf8 32
Bf6 Qd2 33 Rb1≈ b4 34 h3 Nd4 35
Qb6 Ne2+ 36 Kh2 Nc3 37 Be5!
Nd5 37...Re8 38 Rxb4 Nd5 39 Qb5
38 Qd6 Re8 39 Rb3! Qe1 40 Bb2
Qe4 41 Rf3 ½-½ Gufeld

99 Adamski-Lehmann

1 c4 Nf6 2 Nf3 g6 3 Nc3 d5 4 cxd5
Nxd5 5 d4 5 e4!? Bg7 6 e4 Nxc3
6...Nb6!? 7 bxc3 0-0 7...c5 8 Be2
c5 9 0-0 9 Be3 Qa5!? 10 Qd2 Rd8=
b6 9...cxd4 10 cxd4 Nc6 11 Be3
Bg4 12 d5! += 10 Bg5!? N 10 Be3
Ba6?! 10...Bb7 11 Bxa6 Nxa6 12
Qe2 += Nc7 13 Rfd1 cxd4 14 cxd4
Qd7 14...Rc8 15 Rac1 Rfc8 16
Qd3 Ne6 17 Be3 Rxc1 18 Rxc1
Rc8 19 Rxc8+ Qxc8 20 d5± Nc5
21 Qc2

21...Qb7?! 21...Qa6 22 g3 f5? 23
Bxc5 bxc5 24 Ng5 +- Bd4 25 Qa4
Qb8 26 d6! exd6 27 Qd7 Bg7 28
Qe6+ Kh8 29 Nf7+ 1-0 Gufeld

100 Portisch-Uhlmann
Niksic 78

1 d4 Nf6 2 c4 g6 3 Nc3 d5 4 Nf3
Bg7 5 Qb3 dxc4 6 Qxc4 0-0 7 e4
Na6!?∞ 8 Be2 c5 9 d5 9 dxc5 Qa5
e6 10 Bg5 Qb6! 11 0-0 11 Bxf6?!
Bxf6 12 e5 Bg7 13 d6 Nd7 exd5 12
exd5 h6! 13 Bf4 Re8 14 Be5! Bf5
14...Qxb2? 15 Rab1 Qa3 16 Nb5
Qa5 17 Nd6± 15 b3 Qb4! 16 a3
16 Rad1 Rad8 Δ Qb8-d7 Qxc4 17
Bxc4 17 bxc4 Nb8 Δ Nbd7 Nb8!
18 Nb5! Nbd7 19 Nc7 19 Bd6?
a6! 20 Nc7 b5 21 Nxa8 bxc4 22
Nc7 Rc8 Δ cxb3∓; 19 Bxf6!? Bxf6
20 Rad1 Red8! 21 Nd6 Rab8 22
Nxf5 gxf5 23 a4 Ne5= Bxe5 20 Nxe5

20...Nxd5!!= 21 Nxe8 21 Bxd5 Bxe5
22 Nxa8 Bxa1 23 Nc7 Rc8; 21 Nxa8
Bxe5 22 Rae1 Nf6 23 Bb5 Re7 24
Nc7 Be4 25 f3 Bc2∓ Bxe5 22 Rae1
22 Rad1? Nc3∓ Rxe8 23 Bxd5 Bd3
24 Bxb7 24 f4 Bd4+ 25 Kh1 Rd8
26 Rf3 Ba6 27 Nc4 b5 28 Bf1 Bb7
29 Rh3 Bc8= 30 Rxh6? Kg7 31
Rh4 Bf2 -+ Bxf1 25 Kxf1 ½-½
Uhlmann

101 Sahovic-Lanka Jurmala 78

1 d4 ♘f6 2 ♘f3 g6 3 c4 ♗g7 4 ♘c3
d5 5 ♗f4 0-0 6 e3 6 ♖c1 Sahovic
c5! 7 dxc5 ♕a5! 7...♘e4?! 8 ♖c1
8 ♕a4 ♕xc5 9 ♕b5 ♕xb5 10 ♘xb5
♘a6 11 ♖d1 ♗e6=; 8 ♕b3!? dxc4
9 ♗xc4 ♕xc5= Sahovic; 9...♘c6
10 0-0 ♗g4 11 h3 ♖ad8 12 ♕e2
∝/+= 10 ♗b3 10 ♘b5 ♕b4+ 11 ♘d2
♘d5!? ♘c6 11 0-0 ♕a5 11...♕h5
12 h3 ♖d8 13 ♘d2! += 12 h3 12 ♕e2
♗f5 13 ♕e2 13 ♘d4 ♗d7 14 ♕e2 e5=
Gulko-Tseshkovsky, Sochi 75 ♘e4!
13...e5?! 14 ♗xe4 ♗xe4= 15 ♘g5
N 15 ♘d2= ♗d5 16 ♗c7?! 16 ♗xd5
♕xc7 17 ♗xd5 ♕e5! =+ 18 ♕b5!?
♘d8! 19 ♖c5 a6 20 ♕c4 ♕xb2∓ 21
♖c7 e6 22 ♗f3 h6 23 ♘e4 ♘c6 24
♕b3 ♕e5! 25 ♕xb7?! Zeitnot 25
♕b6 Sahovic ♖a7 26 ♕xa7? 26 ♕xc6∓
♗xa7 27 ♖xa7 ♕a5?! 27...f5! △ ♖f7
−+ 28 ♖d1 ♕xa2 28...f5! 29 g3 a5
30 ♖d6 ♖c8? 30...♗e5 31 ♖dd7
♕a1+ 32 ♔g2 ♖f8 33 ♘d6 += a4
34 ♘xf7 ♕f6 35 ♗e2! △ ♗c4 a3?
35...♖xf7 36 ♖xf7 ♕xf7= 36 ♗c4
Zeitnot ♕f5 37 ♖dc7 g5? 37...♕xf7?
38 ♗xe6! +− 38 g4!± ♕e4+ 38...
♕f6 Sahovic 39 ♔g1 ♖b8? Zeitnot
39...♕b1+ Sahovic 40 ♘xg5! ♖b1+
41 ♗f1 ♖xf1+ 41...♕e5 42 ♖c8+ ♗f8
43 ♘h7 ♖b8 44 ♖xb8 ♕xb8 45 ♘f6+
♔h8 46 ♖h7 mate; 41...♕g6 42 ♖c8+
♗f8 43 ♖aa8 ♕xg5 44 ♖xf8+ ♔h7
45 ♖h8+ ♔g7 46 ♖g8+ +− Sahovic
42 ♕xf1 ♕b1+ 43 ♔g2 ♗f8 43...hxg5
44 ♖xg7+ ♔f8 45 ♖gb7 +− 44 ♘h7!
+− ♕e4+ 45 f3 ♕e5 46 ♖c8 ♕b2+
47 ♔g3 ♕e5+ 48 ♔h4 1-0 Gufeld

102 Farago-Ftacnik Kiev 78

1 d4 ♘f6 2 c4 g6 3 ♘c3 d5 4 ♘f3
♗g7 5 ♗f4 0-0 5...c5!? 6 dxc5 ♕a5
7 cxd5 ♘xd5 8 ♕xd5 ♗xc3+ 9 ♗d2

♗e6! += Grigorian-Tseshkovsky, USSR
77 6 e3 c5 6...c6 7 ♗e2 dxc4 8 ♗xc4
♕a5 9 ♕d2 c5!= Farago-Korchnoi,
IBM 76; 9 ♖c1 += 7 dxc5 ♘e4?!
7...♕a5! 8 ♖c1 ♖d8! 9 ♕b3 ♘e4!
10 cxd5 ♘d7 11 ♘d4!= Farago-
Rajna, Hungary 74; 8...♗e6!? 8 ♖c1!
+= 8 ♗e5 ♘xc3 9 bxc3 ♗xe5 10
♘xe5 ♕c7∝ ♘xc3 9 bxc3 ♕a5 10
cxd5 ♗xc3+ 11 ♘d2 ♗f5 11...♘d7 +=

12 e4!!± ♗xe4 13 ♕b3! ♗d4 14
♕c4 14 ♕xb7!? ♗xc5 15 ♗c4! ♗b2
15 ♖d1 ♗f5 16 ♗e2 ♘a6 17 c6 ♘c5
18 g4! +− ♗e4 18...♘c8 19 ♖b1 +−
19 0-0 ♗xd5 20 ♕xd5 ♖ad8 21 ♘c4!
bxc6 22 ♕xd8! 1-0 Gufeld

103 Miles-Mariotti
Las Palmas 78

1 d4 ♘f6 2 ♘f3 g6 3 c4 ♗g7 4 ♘c3
d5 5 ♗g5 ♘e4 6 cxd5 ♘xg5 7 ♘xg5
e6 8 ♘f3 exd5 9 e3 0-0 10 b4 c6
11 ♗e2 ♕d6 12 ♕b3 ♗e6 13 0-0
♘d7 14 ♖ac1 ♖fc8 15 ♖fd1 ♗f8
16 b5 16 ♖b1 += ♕a3 17 bxc6 bxc6
18 ♘a4 ♖ab8 19 ♕xa3 ♗xa3 20 ♖c3
♗e7 20...♗b4 21 ♖b3 += 21 ♖dc1
♖b4 22 ♗d1 ♘b6? 22...♖c4 △ c5
23 ♘c5 +=/± ♗xc5 24 ♖xc5 ♘d7!
25 ♖5c3 25 ♖a5 c5! 26 ♖xa7 c4∝
c5! 26 dxc5 ♖c4 27 ♗b3 ♖xc3 28
♖xc3 ♖xc5 29 ♖xc5 ♘xc5 30 ♘d4

+= ♔f8 31 ♔f1 a5 32 ♔e2 ♔e8 33 ♗c2!
♔d7 34 h4 ♔d6 34...h6 35 f3 ♗c8?
35...h6 36 h5 ♗a6+ 37 ♔d2 ♗f1 38
g4 ♘e6 39 ♘xe6 ♔xe6 40 h6± ♗b5
41 f4 41 ♔c3? ♗e2 ♗d7 42 ♔c3
♔d6 43 g5 ♔c5 44 a3 ♗c8? 44...
♗c6? 45 f5 ♗e8 46 f6! Zugswang
♔d6 (46...♗d7? 47 ♗xg6) 47 ♔d4
♗d7 48 ♗b3 ♗e6 (48...♗c6 49 e4!)
49 ♗a4 ♗f5 50 ♗e8 ♗e6 51 a4 ♔c7
52 ♔c5 △ ♗c6 +−; 44...d4+!? 45
exd4+ ♔d5 46 ♗b3+ ♔e4 47 ♗xf7
♔xf4 48 ♗xg6 ♔xg5 49 ♗xh7 ♔xh6
50 ♗d3 +−; 44...♗f5! 45 ♗a4 d4+!
46 exd4+ ♔d5∞; 45 ♗xf5 gxf5 46
♔d3 ♔d6!= 45 ♗a4 ♗f5 46 ♗e8 d4+
46...♗e6 47 f5! gxf5 48 g6 +−; 47
a4 +− 47 exd4+ ♔d5 48 ♗xf7+ ♔e4
49 d5! ♔xf4 50 ♗xg6! 1-0 Miles

104 Beljavsky-Tukmakov Lvov 78
1 d4 ♘f6 2 c4 g6 3 ♘c3 d5 4 ♗f4
♗g7 5 e3 c5 5...0-0 6 a3 c6 7 ♘f3
♗g4 8 h3 ♗xf3 9 ♕xf3 e6 B.Balogh-
Hardiscay, Budapest 77 6 dxc5 ♕a5 7
♖c1 dxc4 8 ♗xc4 0-0 9 ♘f3 ♘c6
10 0-0 ♕xc5 11 ♘b5 ♕h5 12 ♘c7
♖b8 13 h3 ♘e4 14 b4 a6 14...♗xb4?
15 ♘d5! ♘xd5 16 ♗xd5 △ ♗xb8/
♗xe4 15 ♗e2 ♖d8 16 ♕e1 ♕f5 17
♘xa6 bxa6 18 ♖xc6 ♗b7 19 ♖b6
e5

95

20 ♘xe5 ♗d2 20...♗xe5 21 g4! △ ♗xe5
21 ♘c6 ♗xc6 22 ♖xb8 ♖xb8 23
♕xd2! 1-0 Friedgood

105 Beljavsky-Ftacnik Kiev 78
1 d4 ♘f6 2 c4 g6 3 ♘c3 d5 4 ♗f4
♗g7 5 e3 0-0 5...c5 6 ♕b3! += c6
7 ♘f3 ♕a5 7...dxc4 8 ♘d2 ♘bd7 9
♗e2 ♘h5! 9...dxc4 10 ♗xc4 e5=;
10 ♘xc4 △ ♘e5± 10 ♗xh5 10 ♗g3
♘xg3 11 hxg3 ♘f6 dxc4 11 ♗xc4
♕xh5 12 0-0 b6 △ ♗a6 13 ♖fd1 ♗a6
14 a4! += e5! 15 ♘xe5 ♘xe5 16
dxe5 ♗xe5 17 ♗xe5 ♕xe5 18 a5!
bxa5 18...b5?! 19 ♖d2 △ ♖ad1±
19 ♕a3 ♖ab8 20 ♖d2 ♗b7 21 ♕xa5
c5! 22 ♖ad1 a6 23 ♕a4 ♖fe8 24
♕c4 △ ♖d7 ♖e7 25 h3 ♔g7 26 b3
♖ee8 27 ♖d7 ♖e7 28 ♖xe7 ♕xe7
29 ♘a4 ♘c8 30 ♖c1 ♕g5! 31 ♕g4
♕e5 32 h4 h6! 32...h5?! += 33 ♕c4
♗d5!? 34 ♕xa6 ♕e4 35 ♕f1 ♕xh4
36 ♘xc5 36 ♖xc5 ♖xc5 37 ♘xc5
♕b4= ♖e8 37 ♖d1 ♖e5 38 ♖d4
♕e7 39 b4 ♖g5 40 e4 ♗c6≈ 41 ♕d3
h5 42 ♖d6 ♗b5 43 ♕d4+ ♔h7 44
♖d5 44 ♖b6!? += ♖g4 45 ♘d7 ♗xd7
46 ♖xd7 ♖xe4 47 ♖xe7 ♖xd4 48
♖xf7+ ♔h6 49 ♖b7 ♖d1+ 50 ♔h2
♖d2 51 f3 51 ♔g3 h4+ ♖b2 52 f4
♖b3 53 g3 ♖b2+ 54 ♔h3 ♖f2!= 55
♖c7 ♖b2 56 ♖b7 ♖f2 57 ♖c7 ♖b2
58 ♖c4 ♖b3 59 ♔h4 ♔g7 60 g4 hxg4
61 ♔xg4 ♔f6 62 ♖e4 ♖b1 63 ♔f3
g5 64 fxg5+ ♔xg5 65 ♔e3 ♔f5 ½-½
Gufeld

106 Romanishin-Kuzmin Kiev 78
1 ♘f3 ♘f6 2 c4 g6 3 g3 ♗g7 4 ♗g2
0-0 5 d4 c6 5...d5 6 cxd5 ♘xd5 7
♘c3 ♘b6 6 ♘c3! 6 d5?!; 6 0-0 d5
7 cxd5 cxd5 8 ♘e5 ♘g4! 9 ♗xg4
♗xg4 10 ♘c3 ♘c6 11 h3 ♗d7! 12
♘xd5 ♘xd4 13 ♗g5 ♖e8 14 ♖ac1

♘c6 15 e4 h6= Vladimirov-Ohotnik,
USSR 77 **d5 7 cxd5 cxd5 8 ♘e5
♘bd7?!** 8...♗f5; 8...e6 △ ♘fd7 **9 0-0
♘xe5 10 dxe5 ♘g4 11 ♕xd5!** +=
11 ♘xd5 ♘xe5 12 ♕b3 ♘c6 13 ♖d1
e6 14 ♘c3 += **♘xe5 12 ♕c5! ♕d6!
13 ♕xd6 exd6 14 ♗g5 ♘c4 15 ♖ac1
♗e6** 15...♘xb2 16 ♗e7 ♖e8 17 ♘d5
♗e6 18 ♘f6+ ♗xf6 19 ♗xf6 △ ♗xb7±
16 ♘d5 ♘xb2 17 ♘c7 ♖ac8 17...
♖ab8 18 ♗e7 ♖fc8 19 ♗xd6 **18 ♗xb7
♖b8 19 ♗a6 ♖b6?** 19...♗xa2 20 ♗e7
d5 21 ♗xf8 ♔xf8 += **20 ♗e3 ♖xa6
21 ♘xa6 ♗xa2 22 ♘b4 ♗c4 23 ♘d3!**
♗xd3 23...♘xd3 24 ♖xc4! +− **24
exd3 ♘xd3 25 ♖c6!**± 25 ♖cd1 ♘e5 26
♖xd6 ♘c4 27 ♖a6 ♘xe3 △ ♗h6 +=
**d5 26 ♖d6 ♘b4 27 ♗xa7 ♖c8 28
♖d1 ♗e5 29 ♖d7 ♖c4 30 ♖e1 ♗f6
31 ♖e8+ ♔g7 32 ♖b8 ♘c6 33 ♖bb7**
Zeitnot **♘d8 34 ♖b6 ♘c6 35 ♖bb7
♘d8 36 ♖bc7 ♖xc7 37 ♖xc7 ♘e6 38
♖d7 d4 39 f4 h5 40 ♔g2 ♔f8?** 40...
h4!± **41 ♔f3!** +− **1-0 Gufeld**

107 Sturua-Zaid USSR 77

**1 d4 ♘f6 2 c4 g6 3 ♘f3 ♗g7 4 g3
0-0 5 ♗g2 d5 6 cxd5 ♘xd5 7 0-0
♘b6 8 ♘c3 ♘c6 9 e3** 9 ♗f4!? e5 10
d5 **♘a5 11 e4 ♗g4** 11...c6 12 ♗g5
♕d7 += **12 h3 ♗xf3 13 ♕xf3 c6 14
♖d1** += cxd5 **15 ♘xd5** 15 exd5
♘ac4!? **♘c6 16 ♗e3 ♘d4 17 ♗xd4!**
exd4 **18 ♘f4 ♖c8 19 ♕b3 ♕c7 20
♘d3 ♕d7 21 ♖ac1±** ♘a4 **22 e5 b5**
22...b6!? **23 ♕d5! ♕xd5 24 ♗xd5
♘b6 25 ♗b7 ♖c4 26 ♗a6! ♖a4 27
♗xb5 ♖xa2 28 ♖a1 ♖xa1 29 ♖xa1
♖a8 30 b4! ♗f8 31 ♗c6 ♖c8 32
b5 ♖c7 33 f4 h5 34 ♔g2 ♘d7 35
♔f3 ♘c5 36 ♘b4 ♘b3 37 ♖a4 ♗xb4
38 ♖xb4 ♘a5** 38...♘c5 39 ♖xd4 +−
39 ♗d5 +− **♖c3+ 40 ♔e4 d3 41
♔e3 ♖a3 42 b6! axb6 43 ♖xb6** △

♖xg6+ **♖c3? 44 ♖xg6+ ♔f8 45 ♖f6
♘c4+ 46 ♗xc4 1-0 Gufeld**

108 Hoi-Swic Poland 78

**1 d4 ♘f6 2 c4 g6 3 ♘c3 d5 4 ♗g5
♘e4 5 ♗h4 ♘xc3 6 bxc3 dxc4** 6...
♗g7 7 e3 c5 **7 e3 ♗e6 8 ♖b1 b6
9 ♘f3 ♕d5?!** 9...♗g7 10 ♗e2 0-0 11
0-0 ♗d5 12 ♘d2 c5= **10 ♗e2 ♕a5
11 0-0 f6 12 ♕c2 c6 13 ♘d2 b5 14
a4!**±

**14...a6 15 ♖a1 ♕d8 16 ♗f3 ♗d5 17
e4 ♗e6 18 axb5 cxb5 19 d5 ♗f7 20
e5! +− ♗xd5 21 exf6 ♗xf3 22 ♘xf3
♕d3 23 f7+! 1-0** 23...♔xf7 24 ♘e5+;
23...♔d8 24 ♖fd1 **Konikowski**

King's Indian

109 Ghitescu-Helmers Roskilde 78

**1 c4 g6 2 e4 c5 3 ♘f3 ♗g7 4 d4 ♕a5+
5 ♘c3 ♘c6 6 d5 ♘d4** 6...♗xc3+!?
**7 bxc3 ♘e5 7 ♗d2 ♘xf3+ 8 ♕xf3
d6 9 ♗d3 ♘f6 10 h3 0-0 11 0-0 e6?**
11...♘d7?! 12 ♕e2 ♘e5 13 ♗c2 ♕b4
14 ♗b3 △ ♘b5±; 11...a6! **12 ♗g5!
♘d7 13 ♕e2 f6** 13...♗xc3? 14 bxc3
exd5 15 exd5± **14 ♗d2 ♘e5 15
♗c2 ♘f7 16 dxe6 ♗xe6 17 ♘d5 ♕d8
18 f4 ♕d7 19 ♘e3 ♘d8 20 ♗c3 ♘c6
21 f5 ♗f7 22 fxg6 ♗xg6 23 ♘f5 ♗xf5
24 exf5 ♘d4! 25 ♗xd4 cxd4 26**

♕d2 ♖fe8 27 ♕xd4 ♕c6 28 ♖fe1
♕c5 29 ♕xc5 dxc5 30 ♗e4! ♕f8
31 ♗xb7 ♖xe1+ 32 ♖xe1 ♖b8 33
♗c6 ♖xb2 34 ♖e8+ ♔f7 35 ♖c8 ♗h6
35...♖xa2? 36 ♘d5+ ♔e7 37 ♖c7+
♔f8 38 ♖f7+ +− **36 ♖c7+ ♔f8 37
♖xa7 ♗f4!** 38 g4!? 38 a4? ♗g3! ♗b8
39 ♖xh7 ♗h2+ 40 ♔f1 ♖xa2 41
♗d5 ♗e5 42 g5! ♖a1+ 43 ♔e2 ♖a6
44 g6 ♖a2+ 45 ♔d1 **1-0**

110 Sahovic-Ligterink Jurmala 78

**1 d4 ♘f6 2 ♘f3 g6 3 c4 ♗g7 4 ♘c3
0-0 5 e4 d6 6 ♗e2 e5 7 0-0 ♘c6 8
d5 ♘e7 9 b4** 9 ♘e1 ♘d7 10 ♘d3
f5 11 exf5 ♘xf5 12 f3 ♘f6 13 ♘f2
♘d4 14 ♗e3 ♘h5= Djindjihashvili-
Geller, USSR 75; 11 ♗d2 ♘f6 12
f3 f4 13 ♖c1 g5 14 c5 ♘g6 15 cxd6
cxd6 16 ♘b5∞ **♘d7** 9...♘h5 10 c5
♘f4 11 ♗xf4 exf4 12 ♖c1 h6 13 h3
g5 14 a4! += Diesen-Day, Lone Pine
77; 10 ♘d2!? ♘f4 11 ♗f3 f5 12 a4
g5 13 exf5 ♘xf5 14 g3 ♘h3+!? 15
♔g2 ♕d7!∞ Keene-Kavalek, Teesside
75; 10 g3 f5 11 ♘d2 ♘f6 12 c5 f4
13 ♘c4 g5 14 ♗a3 ♘h3 15 ♖e1 ♖f7∞
Sosonko-Uhlmann, IBM 75 **10 c5!?**
N 10 ♗e3 f5 11 ♘g5 ♘f6 12 f3 f4
13 ♗f2 +=; 10 ♘d2 **dxc5 11 bxc5
♘xc5 12 ♗a3≈ b6 13 ♗xc5 bxc5 14
♘a4 f5!** 14...♕d6 15 ♖c1 ♗h6 16
♖c2 **15 ♘xc5 ♕d6∞** 15...fxe4 16
♘g5± Sahovic **16 ♖c1 ♕h8 17 ♕a4
c6! 18 dxc6 ♘xc6 19 ♖fd1 ♘d4 20
♘xd4 exd4 21 ♗f3** += fxe4 22 ♘xe4
22 ♗xe4 ♖b8 23 ♕xa7 ♖b2≈ **♕f4
23 ♘g3 ♗g4 24 ♘e2! ♕g5**

Diagram

25 h4!± ♕xh4 26 ♖xd4 h5 26...♗xd4
27 ♕xd4+ ♔g8 28 ♗xg4 +− Sahovic
27 g3 ♕g5 28 ♗xg4 ♖ae8?! 29 ♖e4

**29 ♖f4± ♖xe4 30 ♕xe4 ♕xg4 31
♕xg4?** Zeitnot 31 ♘f4± ♔h7 32 ♖c7
+− Sahovic **hxg4 32 ♖c4 ♖d8!≈
33 ♖xg4 ♖d2 34 ♘f4 ♖xa2 35 ♘xg6+
♔g8 36 ♘h4 ♔f7 37 ♘f5 ♗f8 38
♖c4 a5 39 g4 a4 40 ♖c7+ ♔g6 41
♖c8 ½-½ Gufeld**

111 Spassov-Zapata
Kikinda 78

**1 ♘f3 ♘f6 2 c4 g6 3 ♘c3 ♗g7 4 e4
d6 5 d4 0-0 6 ♗e2 e5 7 0-0 ♘c6
8 d5 ♘e7 9 b4 ♘e8?!** 9...♘h5 10
**♘d2 f5 11 f3 f4 12 c5 h5 13 ♘c4
♖f7 14 a4 ♔h7?** 14...♗f8! Δ ♖g7,
g5 **15 ♗a3 ♗f8 16 b5 g5 16...b6!?
17 c6 Δ a5± 17 b6!± cxb6?** 17...
axb6!? 18 cxb6 cxb6 19 ♖b1 ♖a6
20 ♕b3 += **18 ♘xd6 ♘xd6 19 cxd6
♘g6 20 ♘b5 ♕f6 21 ♘c7 ♖b8 22
♖c1 ♖d7 23 ♕b3 ♖d8** 23...♗xd6?
24 ♘e8 +− **24 ♖fd1 ♗xd6 25 ♗xd6
♕xd6 26 ♘b5 ♕f6 27 ♘xa7 ♗d7 28
♗b5!** Δ ♖c7 +− **♔h6 29 ♖c7 ♗xb5
30 ♘xb5 g4 31 d6! gxf3 32 gxf3
♘h4 33 ♔h1 ♖g8 34 d7 ♖g6 35 ♘d6!**
35 ♖c8? ♕g5 36 ♕c2 ♘xf3 Δ ♕g1+
♖g7 35...♖f8 36 ♘f7+! ♖xf7 37
♕xf7! ♕xf7 38 d8♕ +− **36 ♘e8 +−
♕g5 37 ♖c2 ♖g6 38 ♘d6 +− ♔g7
39 ♘f7 ♕e7 40 d8♕ ♖xd8 41 ♘xd8
1-0 Maric**

112 Ligterink-Westerinen
Jurmala 78
**1 d4 ♘f6 2 c4 g6 3 ♘c3 ♗g7 4 e4
d6 5 ♗e2 0-0 6 ♘f3 e5 7 0-0 ♘c6
8 d5 ♘e7 9 ♘e1 ♘d7 10 ♘d3 f5 11
♗d2** 11 exf5 ♘xf5 12 f3 ♘f6 13 ♘f2
♘d4 14 ♗e3 ♘h5 **fxe4?!** 11...♘f6
12 f3 f4 13 c5 g5 14 cxd6 cxd6 15
♘f2 += Sosonko-Kavalek, Wijk aan
Zee 77; 13 ♖c1 c5!?; 11...c5!? 12
f4 a6 13 a4 exf4 14 ♗xf4 ♗xc3 15
bxc3 fxe4∝ Beljavsky-Vogt, Cienfuegos 76 **12 ♘xe4 ♘f5 13 f3!** +=
♘d4 14 ♗df2 ♘f6 15 ♖c1?! 15 ♘xf6+!
Δ ♘e4 **♗f5 16 ♗d3 ♘h5!∝ 17 c5!?**
dxc5 18 ♗g5 ♕e8 19 ♖xc5 ♕d7 20
♕d2 b6 21 ♖c3 ♗f4 22 ♗xf4 exf4
23 ♖fc1 ♗e5!= 24 ♗c4 b5! 25 ♗f1
♖ad8 26 d6!? cxd6 27 ♖c7 ♕e8
28 ♖xa7 d5 29 ♘c5 ♖a8! 30 ♖xa8
♕xa8 31 ♘fd3 ♗g7 32 ♘xf4 ♕xa2
33 ♔h1 ♖d8 34 ♗d3 ♗xd3 35 ♘fxd3
♘b3! 36 ♕g5! ♖d6 37 ♘xb3 ♕xb3
38 ♘c5 ♗f6 39 ♘xb3 ♗xg5 ½-½ 40
♖c8+ = **Gufeld**

113 Shamkovich-Knaak Jurmala 78
**1 d4 ♘f6 2 ♘f3 g6 3 c4 d6 4 ♘c3
♘bd7 5 e4 e5 6 ♗e2 ♗g7 7 0-0 0-0
8 ♗e3 ♘g4 8...h6!? 9 ♗g5 f6 10 ♗d2
c6!?** 10...♘h6 11 ♕c2 exd4 12 ♘xd4
♘e5 13 ♖ad1 f5 14 ♕c1! += Spassov-
Shamkovich, Vrnjacka Banja 76; 11
b4! ♘f7 12 ♕c2 ♖e8 13 ♖ad1 c6
14 ♖fe1 += Bukic-Sigurjonsson,
Ljubljana 77 **11 b4** 11 ♕c2!? ♕e7
12 ♖ad1 ♘h6 13 ♗c1 f5 14 exf5 gxf5
15 ♖fe1 += Ree-Knaak, Budapest 77
f5 12 dxe5 12 d5 f4! 13 ♗c1 c5!
14 ♘b5 ♘df6 15 ♘g5 a6 =+ **♘dxe5
13 exf5 gxf5 14 ♘xe5 dxe5 15 ♖c1
♗e6** =+ 16 h3 ♘h6 17 ♗e3 ♕c7 18 f4
**♖ad8 19 ♕a4 exf4! 20 ♗xf4 ♗d4+
21 ♔h1 ♕g7 22 ♘b1**

22...♘g4! 23 ♕b3 Δ ♕g3 **♘f2+ 24
♔h2 ♘e4 25 ♕f3 ♕h8?! 25...♖d7!**
Δ ♖df7∓ **26 ♘d2 ♗e5 27 ♘xe4 fxe4
28 ♕e3** 28 ♕xe4?? ♖xf4 Δ ♖d4 -+
**♖xf4 29 ♖xf4 ♗xh3! 30 gxh3 ♖f8
31 ♖f1 ♕g5 32 ♔h1 ♖xf4 33 ♖xf4
♕xf4 34 ♕xf4 ♗xf4 35 ♗g4 =+** ♗d2
36 b5 ♗g7 37 ♔g2 ♔f6 38 ♗c8 cxb5
39 cxb5 b6 40 ♔f2 ♔e5 41 ♔e2 ♗g5
42 ♗b7= ♔d4 43 ♗c6 e3 44 ♗d7 ♔c5
45 ♗e8 ½-½ **Gufeld**

114 Taimanov-Kirpichnikov
Jurmala 78
**1 c4 g6 2 ♘c3 ♘f6 3 e4 d6 4 d4 ♗g7
5 ♘f3 0-0 6 ♗e2 e5 7 0-0 exd4 7...**
♘c6! **8 ♘xd4 ♖e8 8...**♘bd7 **9 f3
♘c6?!** N 9...c6 10 ♘c2! ♘a6 11
♔h1 += 10 ♗e3 += ♘e5 11 ♕d2 c6
12 ♖ad1 a6!? 13 a4 ♕a5 14 ♖b1
♗e6 14...♕b4!? += 15 ♘xe6 ♖xe6
16 b4 ♕c7 17 a5± ♕e7!? 18 ♖fc1
♘ed7 19 ♗f1 h5 20 ♗g5 ♕f8 21 ♘e2
♘h7 22 ♗e3 ♕d8 23 ♖b3 ♘hf8 24
♖a3 ♕e7 25 ♘d4 ♖e5 26 ♗f4 c5! 27
♘c2?! 27 ♘xe5 += ♖e6 28 b5?!
♗b2 29 ♖b3 ♗xc1 30 ♕xc1 ♕d8 31
b6 ♘e5 32 ♗d2 ♘c6 33 ♖d3 ♘d7
34 ♗c3 ♘de5 35 ♖d1 ♘h4 36 ♗e2
♖f8 37 g3 ♕d8 =+ ½-½ **Gufeld**

115 Taimanov-Lanka Jurmala 78
1 c4 ♘f6 2 ♘c3 g6 3 e4 d6 4 d4 ♗g7

5 ♗e2 0-0 6 ♗g5 6...h6 **7 d5** 7 dxc5 **♕a5 8 ♕d2 ♕xc5 9 ♘f3 ♗g4!** 10 0-0 ♗xf3 11 ♗xf3 ♘c6 12 ♗e2 ♘d7!= Fuller-Evans, Haifa 76 **h6** 7...♕a5!? 8 ♗d2 e6 9 ♘f3 exd5 10 exd5 ♗g4 11 0-0 ♘bd7 12 h3 ♗xf3 13 ♗xf3 a6 14 a4 += Farago-Andersson, Cienfuegos 77 **8 ♗d2!?** 8 ♗f4 e6 9 dxe6 ♗xe6 10 ♗xd6 ♖e8 11 ♘f3 ♘c6 12 0-0 ♘d4!≈; 8 ♗e3 e6 9 ♕d2 exd5 10 exd5 ♔h7 11 h3 ♖e8 12 ♗d3 b5!∞ **e6 9 ♘f3** 9 h3!? exd5 10 exd5 ♖e8 △ ♘e4 **exd5 10 exd5 ♗f5** 10...♖e8 △ ♘e4= **11 0-0 ♕a6?!** 11...♘e4 **12 a3 ♘c7 13 b4 b5 14 ♖c1!** += bxc4 15 ♗xc4 **♘d7 16 bxc5! ♘xc5 17 ♗e3 ♗g4 18 h3 ♗xf3 19 ♕xf3 ♘d7 20 ♕e2 ♔h7 21 ♗b5!?** ♗xb5 **22 ♗xb5 f5!? 23 ♕d2 a6 24** ♗xd7! ♕xd7 25 ♖c6 ♖f7 26 ♖b1 f4!? 27 ♗xf4 ♕f5 28 ♖b4! a5 29 ♖bc4 ♖b8 30 ♗g3 ♖b2 31 ♖c2 ♖b3 32 ♖c7 ♖b5 33 ♖xf7 ♕xf7 34 ♗xd6 ♖xd5 35 ♕f4± ♕e6 36 ♗b8 ♖d4 37 ♕c7 ♕e1+ 38 ♔h2 ♖d1 39 ♗a7 h5!? 40 ♖c4 g5 41 ♕f7 ♕g1+ 42 ♔g3 ♖d3+ 43 ♗e3 ♖xe3+!? 44 fxe3 ♕xe3+ 45 ♔h2 ♕e5+ 46 ♔g1 ♕a1+ 47 ♔f2 ♕b2+ 48 ♔e3! ♕b3+ 48...♕xa3+ 49 ♔e4 +− **49 ♔e4 ♕b1+ 50 ♔d5 ♕b5+ 51 ♔d6 ♕b6+ 52 ♔d7 ♕b7+ 53 ♖c7 ♕b5+ 54 ♔c8! +− ♕a6+ 55 ♖b7 ♕c6+ 56 ♔b8 ♕d6+ 57 ♔a7 1-0 Gufeld**

116 Hort-Gligoric Niksic 78
1 d4 ♘f6 2 c4 g6 3 ♘c3 ♗g7 4 e4 d6 5 f3 0-0 6 ♗e3 e5 7 d5 c5 8 ♗d3 ♘h5 9 ♘ge2 f5 10 exf5 gxf5 11 ♕d2 a6 12 a4 ♘d7 13 ♗g5 ♕e8 13...♗f6!? **14 0-0 ♘df6** △ e4 **15 ♗c2 ♗d7 16 ♖ab1 ♕c8?** 16...♕d8! **17 a5 ♕c7 18 ♘a4 e4?** 18...♗xa4! += **19 ♘b6± ♖ae8 20 ♖be1 ♔h8**

21 ♔h1! ♖g8 22 ♘f4! ♗xf4 23 ♕xf4 ♖ef8 23...exf3 24 gxf3!± **24 ♕h4 ♗e8** 24...♘c8!?± **25 fxe4 ♘xe4 26 ♗d8! +− ♕b8 27 ♗e7 ♖f7 28 ♗xe4 fxe4 29 ♕xe4** 29 ♖xf7!? ♗xf7 30 ♘d7 ♕e8 31 ♘f6! +− ♗xb2 **30 ♖xf7 ♗xf7 31 ♕f4! ♗g6 32 ♘d7 ♕c7 33 ♗f6+ 1-0 Hort**

117 Knaak-Gufeld Jurmala 78
1 d4 ♘f6 2 c4 g6 3 ♘c3 ♗g7 4 e4 d6 5 f3 0-0 6 ♗e3 ♘c6 7 ♘ge2 a6 8 ♕d2 ♖b8 9 0-0-0 b5 10 h4 e5 10...h5!? **11 d5 ♘a5** 11...♘e7?! 12 c5± **12 ♘g3 b4** 12...♘xc4 13 ♗xc4 bxc4 14 h5 += **13 ♘b1 c6** 13...h5 14 b3 += **14 dxc6 b3!? 15 a3 ♗e6?!** 15...♘xc6 16 ♕xd6 ♕xd6 17 ♖xd6 ♘d4 18 ♘c3 ♘e8 19 ♖d5 ♗e6 20 ♖a5± **16 ♕xd6 ♕c8?** 16...♕xd6 17 ♖xd6 ♗xc4 18 c7 ♖bc8 19 ♗b6 ♗xf1 20 ♗xa5 ♗xg2 21 ♖g1 ♗xf3 22 ♘d2± **17 c7 ♖a8** 17...♖b7 18 c5 ♘c4 19 ♗xc4 ♗xc4 20 ♘d2! ♗e6 21 ♕xa6 ♕xc7± 18 ♕xa6? ♘xc4; 18 ♗b6!?± **18 ♕c5! ♗b7 19 ♕b6 ♘d7?** 19...♖e8!?±; 19...♘e8 20 ♘c3 ♘xc7 21 ♕xb3 +− **20 ♖xd7! +− ♗xd7 21 ♘c3 ♖e8 22 ♘d5 ♗c6 23 c5 f5 24 ♘e2 f4 25 ♗f2 ♗xd5 26 exd5 e4 27 fxe4 ♖xe4 28 ♘c3 ♖d4!? 29 d6 ♘a5!? 30 ♗xd4** 30 ♕xa5?? ♕f5 ♗xd4 31 ♗d3 ♗xc3 **32 c6!** 32 bxc3 ♕e6 33 ♖d1 ♕e3+

34 ♔b1 ♕f2 35 ♗c4+ ♘xc4 36 ♕xb3
+− ♗e5 33 ♕xa5 ♕e6 34 ♖e1 ♕xd6
35 ♗c4+ 0-1 Gufeld

118 Gheorghiu-Pohl USA 78

1 c4 ♘f6 2 ♘c3 g6 3 e4 d6 4 d4 ♗g7
5 f3 e5 6 d5 6 ♘ge2!? += c6 7 ♗e3
0-0 8 ♗d3 ♘a6 9 ♘ge2 ♘c5 10 ♗c2
cxd5 11 cxd5 a5 11...a6?! 12 b4
12 0-0 ♗d7 13 a3 ♕c7! 13...a4? 14
♗xc5 dxc5 15 ♗xa4± 14 ♔h1 ♖fc8
15 ♖c1 15 b4 axb4 16 axb4 ♖xa1
17 ♕xa1 ♘a6∞ ♕d8 16 b4 axb4 17
axb4 ♘a6 18 ♖b1 ♕e8 19 ♗d3 ♘h5
△ ♘f4 =+ 20 b5 ♘c5 21 ♗xc5!±
dxc5 22 ♗c4! ♘f4 23 d6! △ ♘d5

23...♗e6 23...♘e6 24 ♘d5± 24 ♘xf4
exf4 24...♗xc4 25 d7 +− 25 ♘d5
♗xd5 26 ♕xd5 ♕d7 27 e5 ♖e8 28
♖fe1 b6 29 e6! +− fxe6 30 ♕xa8!
♖xa8 32 ♗xe6+ ♕xe6 33 ♖xe6 +−
△ ♖e7/d7 1-0 Gheorghiu

119 Gheorghiu-Whitehead USA 78

1 d4 ♘f6 2 c4 g6 3 ♘c3 ♗g7 4 e4
0-0 5 ♗e3 d6 6 f3 e5 7 d5 c6 8 ♗d3
cxd5 9 cxd5 ♘h5 10 ♘ge2 f5 11
♕d2 11 exf5 gxf5 12 0-0± ♗d7 12
0-0-0 a6 13 exf5! gxf5 14 ♘g3!!
♗xg3 14...f4 15 ♘xh5 fxe3 16 ♕xe3±
15 hxg3 b5 16 ♗h6 ♕e7 17 ♗xg7
♔xg7 17...♕xg7 18 ♖h5!± 18 ♖h5!
♘c5 19 ♖dh1 ♔h8 20 g4!± b4 21

♗e2 e4! 22 ♘c2! 22 fxe4? ♘xe4
♖a7 23 ♘f4!! +− ♕g7 23...♕f6 24
g5 +− 24 ♖xh7+ ♕xh7 25 ♘g6+ ♔g8
26 ♖xh7 ♖xh7 27 ♘xf8 27 ♕g5!
+− ♖h1+ 28 ♗d1 ♕xf8 29 ♕g5! ♗d7
30 ♕d2 fxg4 31 ♕f6+ ♕e8 32 ♕xd6!
+− exf3 33 gxf3 ♘d3 34 ♗e2 34
♕g6+! +− ♗c1 35 ♕xb4 ♗xa2 36
♕e4+ ♔d8 37 fxg4 1-0 Gheorghiu

120 Beljavsky-Ermenkov
Alicante 78

1 d4 ♘f6 2 c4 g6 3 ♘c3 ♗g7 4 e4 d6
5 f3 0-0 6 ♗g5 ♘bd7 6...c5; 6...h6
7 ♕d2!? 7 ♘ge2 c5 8 d5 ♘e5 9 ♘g3
h6 10 ♗d2 h5= Petrosian-Reshevsky
63 c5 8 d5 a6 9 ♘ge2 ♖b8 10 ♘c1
♖e8 10...♕a5!? 11 a4 ♘e5 11 ♗e2
♘b6?! △ ♘a8-c7, ♗d7, b5; 11...e6!?
12 0-0 e6 13 a4 exd5 14 cxd5 ♘a8
15 ♗d3 ♘c7 15...b5? 16 axb5 axb5
17 ♘xb5; 15...c4 16 ♘f2± 16 b4!
cxb4 17 ♘xb4 a5 18 ♘c2± ♘a6 19
♔h1 ♘c5 20 ♘d4 ♗d7 21 ♖a2 ♖c8
22 ♘cb5 ♗xb5 23 ♗xb5 ♖e5 △ ♘fxe4
24 ♗f4 ♖e7 25 ♖c2?! ♖ec7 26 ♖a2
♘h5 27 ♗g5 ♗f6 28 ♗e3 ♗e5?! 28...
♗g7 29 g4 ♘f6 30 ♕g2 ♕e7 31 ♖e2
♘fd7 32 f4 ♗g7 33 ♗g1 ♘f8? 33...
♔h8±

34 e5! +− dxe5 35 fxe5 ♗xe5 36
♘f5 gxf5 37 gxf5+ ♘g6 37...♔h8 38

f6 **38 fxg6 hxg6 39 ♖fe1 f6 40 ♕xg6+**
♕g7 41 ♕h5 ♕h7 42 ♖g2+ ♔h8
42...♖g7 43 ♖xg7+ ♕xg7 44 ♗xc5
43 ♖xe5 fxe5 44 ♕xe5+ ♖g7 45
♗d4 ♘e6 46 dxe6 ♖c1+ 47 ♔g1 b6
1-0 Webb

121 Tarjan-Taulbut
Lone Pine 78

1 d4 g6 2 e4 d6 3 c4 ♗g7 4 ♘c3
♘f6 5 f4 0-0 6 ♘f3 c5 7 d5 e6 8
dxe6!? fxe6 8...♗xe6?! += **9 ♗e2**
9 g4 Mariotti-Gligoric, Praia da Rocha
69; 9 ♗d3 Soos-Taulbut, Berne 77
♘c6 10 0-0 a6 11 ♗e3?! 11 ♔h1 +=
♘g4 12 ♗d2 d4 Δ ♘xf3+, ♗d4+
13 g3 13 ♔h1 ♘xf3 14 ♗xf3 ♘xh2 −+
b5!? 14 ♘xd4 ♗xd4+ 15 ♔g2 ♘f6
16 cxb5 axb5 17 ♘xb5 17 ♗xb5
♗b7 =+ **♗xb2 18 ♖b1 ♗d4 19 ♘xd4**
cxd4 =+ 20 ♕c2 d5!? 20...♗a6! 21
♗xa6 ♖xa6 22 ♕xc4 ♕c8 23 ♕xd4
♕c6 =+ **21 e5 ♘e4 22 ♗b4 ♖e8** 22...
♖f7!? **23 a3 ♗a6 24 ♗xa6 ♖xa6**
25 ♖fc1 ♕d7 26 ♕d3 ♖c6 27 ♗d2
27 ♕xd4 ♖ec8 28 ♖xe6 ♕xc6∝
♖ec8 28 ♖xc6 ♕xc6 29 ♖c1 ♕b7
30 ♖xc8+ ♕xc8 31 ♗b4 h5?? 31...
g5! 32 fxg5 ♕c1 33 ♕b5 ♕c2+ 34
♔g1 ♕f2+ 35 ♔h1 ♕f7 36 ♔g2 d3
37 ♕xd3 ♕f2+ 38 ♔h1 ♘g5 −+ **32**
a4 g5 33 fxg5 ♕c1 34 ♕b5 ♕c2+
35 ♔h1?? 35 ♔g1 ♕f2+ 36 ♔h1
♕f7 37 ♔g2 d3∝ **♘f2+ 36 ♔g1 ♘h3+**
37 ♔h1 ♕e4 mate 0-1 Taulbut

122 Larsen-Mestel Esbjerg 78
1 ♘f3 g6 2 e4 d6 3 c4 ♗g7 4 d4 ♘f6
5 ♘c3 0-0 6 ♗e3 c6 7 h3 a6 8 e5 ♘e8
9 ♕c1 ♘d7 9...c5!? 10 dxc5 dxe5∝
10 exd6 ♘xd6 11 ♗h6 c5 12 ♗xg7
♔xg7 13 ♕f4 f6 13...b6 14 0-0-0
♗b7 15 d5 b5 **14 0-0-0 ♕a5 15 ♗d3**
15 h4! cxd4 16 ♕xd4 ♕c5 17 ♘d5±

cxd4 **16 ♕xd4 ♘c5 17 ♖he1 ♖f7**
17...♗e6 **18 g4 ♗d7** 18...♗e6 19 ♘e5!
♖f8 20 ♘d7!! **19 g5?** 19 h4 Δ ♘g5;
19 ♗c2 ♖c8 Δ ♘e6 **♘f5 20 ♗xf5**
20 ♕f4 ♖c8 Δ b5 =+ **♗xf5 21 ♘h4??**
21 ♖xe7?? ♘b3+ 22 axb3 ♕a1+
23 ♔d2 ♕xb2+ 24 ♔e1 ♖xe7+; 21
♖e3 ♖c8 22 ♘h4 ♘e6∓ **♘d3+ 22**
♖xd3 ♗xd3 23 ♘f3 ♖d8 24 ♕h4
24 ♘d5 ♗xc4 25 ♖xe7 ♕xd5 −+
♕c5 25 ♖d1 ♖ff8 26 gxf6+ exf6 27
♘d2 ♕g5 28 ♕g3 ♕xg3 29 fxg3 ♖fe8
30 a4 ♖c8 31 ♘b3 ♖e3 32 ♘a5 ♖xg3
33 ♘xb7 ♖xc4 0-1

123 Vadasz-Adorjan Hungary 78
1 ♘f3 g6 2 e4 ♗g7 3 d4 d6 4 c4
♗g4!? 5 ♗e2 ♘c6 6 ♘bd2 6 ♗e3
e5 7 d5 ♗xf3 8 ♗xf3 ♘d4= **e5 7**
d5 ♘ce7 7...♗xf3 8 ♘xf3 ♘d4 9
♘xd4 exd4 10 0-0 ♘e7 11 ♖b1!±
8 ♕b3 b6!? 8...♗c8 9 c5! **9 ♘xe5!**
♗xe2 10 ♕a4+ b5! 10...♕f8? 11
♘d7+ ♔e8 12 ♘xb6+ Δ ♘xa8 +−
11 ♕xb5+ ♔f8 12 ♘d7+ ♔e8 13
♘f6+ 13 ♘b6+? c6! −+ ♔f8 14 ♘xg8!?
14 ♘d7+ ♔e8 15 ♘f6+ =

14...♘f5!! 15 exf5 ♖b8! 16 ♕xb8?
16 ♕a4 ♗d3 17 f6! ♔xg8! 18 fxg7
♕e7+ 19 ♘e4 ♕xe4+ 20 ♗e3 ♔xg7

21 0-0-0 (1) 21...♛xc4+ 22 ♔xc4 ♗xc4 23 b3 ♗a6 24 ♗xa7 ♖b5 25 ♗d4+ f6 26 ♖he1 ♖f8! △ ♗b7 +=/=; (2) 21...a5? 22 ♖he1 ♖b4 23 ♘h6+ ♔xh6 24 ♖xe4 ♖xa4 25 ♖xd3 ♖xa2 26 ♖e7±; (3) 21...♖xb2!? 22 ♔xb2 ♛e5+ 23 ♔a3 ♖b8 24 ♛b3 ♖xb3+ 25 axb3 ♛c3 26 ♖he1 c5! 27 ♗d2 (27 dxc6 ♛a5+ 28 ♔b2 ♛e5+ =) 27...♛c2 28 ♗a5! ♗xc4 29 bxc4 ♛xc4≈ ♛xb8 17 ♘xe2 ♖xg8 18 ♖e1 ♕e7!? 19 fxg6 hxg6 20 ♔f1+ ♔d7 21 ♘e4 ♖e8 22 c5!? ♛b5+ 23 ♔g1 dxc5 23...f5? 24 c6+! 24 ♗h6!? ♗d4! 25 ♖ad1 ♛xb2 25...f5? 26 ♖xd4! ♖xe4 27 ♖dxe4 fxe4 28 ♘g7!= 26 ♘c1 26 ♖d2? ♖xe4! ♛b6 27 d6! ♖e6! 27...cxd6? 28 ♖xd4! +-; 27...f5? 28 ♘f6+!! ♗xf6 29 dxc7+ ♗d4 30 ♖xe8 +- 28 dxc7 ♔xc7 29 ♗f4+ ♔c6 30 h4 ♛b2 31 ♗g3 ♖xa2!? 32 ♔h2 a5 33 f3 a4 34 ♖d2 ♛b3 35 ♖c1 ♗e3 36 ♘xc5 ♗xc5 0-1 time **Adorjan**

124 Gulko-Velimirovic Niksic 78

1 c4 g6 2 ♘c3 ♗g7 3 g3 ♘f6 4 ♗g2 0-0 5 d4 d6 6 e3 c5 7 ♘ge2 ♘c6 8 0-0 ♗g4!? 9 h3 cxd4 10 exd4 ♗xe2 11 ♘xe2 d5 12 cxd5 ♘xd5 13 ♘c3 13 ♛b3 e6 14 ♛xb7 ♛d6∝ ♘xc3 13...♘b6!? 14 d5 ♘d4 15 g4?! ♘c4 16 b3 ♛a5 17 ♗g5 ♘b2 18 ♛d2 ♛xc3 19 ♛xc3 ♘e2+ 20 ♔h1 ♗xc3 21 ♗xe7 ♖fe8 22 d6 ♖xe7 23 dxe7 ♖e8∓ Smederevac-Velimirovic, Pula 75 **14 bxc3 ♖c8 15 ♖e1 ♖e8 16 ♗f4 ♘a5 17 ♛a4 ♖c4 18 ♛a3 ♗f8 19 ♛b2 ♛c8 20 ♖ad1 a6** 20...♖xc3 21 ♖c1± **21 ♗f1 ♖a4 22 h4! ♘c4 23 ♛c2 b5 24 h5 ♛f5?** 24...♘b6!? **25 hxg6 hxg6 25 ♛xf5 gxf5 26 ♗h3 ♖xa2 27 ♗xf5 e6 28 ♗d3 ♘b6 29**

♖a1 ♖xa1 30 ♖xa1 ♘a4 30...♖a8!? **31 c4 ♘b2 32 ♗e4 ♘xc4?** 32...bxc4= **33 ♖xa6 ♖d8 34 ♗c6 b4 35 ♗b5 ♘d6 36 ♗d3± ♘e8 37 ♖b6 h6** 37... ♖xd4? 38 ♖b8 +- **38 ♗e5 ♗g7 39 ♗e2 ♗f8 40 ♔g2 ♗d6 41 ♗xd6?** 41 ♔f3± ♘xd6= **42 ♗d3 ♘e8 43 ♖xb4 e5 44 ♗b5 exd4 45 ♗xe8 ♖xe8 46 ♖xd4 ♖e5 47 g4 ♖a5 48 ♖d6 ♔g7 49 ♔g3 ♖b5 50 f4 ♖b3+ 51 ♔f2 ♖b2+ 52 ♔f3 ♖b3+ 53 ♔e4 ♖h3 54 f5 ♖g3 55 f6+ ♔h7 56 ♔f4 ♖g1 57 ♖d7 ♔g8 ½-½** 58 ♖d8+ ♔h7 59 ♖f8 ♖xg4+ 60 ♔f3 ♖f4+ **Velimirovic**

125 Smyslov-Gulko Lvov 78

1 d4 ♘f6 2 ♘f3 g6 3 c4 ♗g7 4 g3 0-0 5 ♗g2 d6 6 0-0 ♘c6 7 ♘c3 ♗f5 7...a6 8 h3 ♖b8 9 e4 b5!? 10 cxb5 (10 e5!? ♘e8? 11 cxb5 axb5 12 ♗f4±; 10...♘d7 11 cxb5 axb5 12 ♘g5 dxe5! 13 ♗xc6 exd4∝ Szekely-Weinstein, Budapest 76) axb5 11 ♖e1 b4 12 ♘e2!? Tukmakov-Juferov, USSR 77 **8 d5 ♘a5 9 ♘d4 ♗d7** 9... ♘xc4 10 ♘xf5 gxf5 11 ♛d3 △ ♛xf5 **10 b3 c5 11 dxc6 bxc6 12 ♗d2 ♖b8** △ c5, ♘c6-b4 **13 ♖c1 c5 14 ♘c2 ♘c6 15 ♘e3 ♘b4 16 a3 ♘c6 17 ♘cd5 a5 18 ♗c3 ♘xd5 19 ♘xd5 ♗e6 20 ♘f6+! ♗xf6 21 ♗xf6 exf6 22 ♗xc6± ♛b6 23 ♗a4 ♖fd8 24 e4 ♛b7 25 ♖e1 f5 26 exf5 ♗xf5 27 ♖c3 d5 ½-½ Friedgood**

126 Spassov-Peev Pernik 78

1 ♘f3 g6 2 c4 ♗g7 3 d4 d6 4 ♘c3 ♘d7 5 g3 e5 6 ♗g2 ♘h6?! 7 0-0 0-0 8 e4 c6 9 ♖b1! 9 h3 ♛b6 f6? 9...a5 10 a3 △ b4±; 9...exd4 10 ♘xd4 ♛b6 11 ♘de2 ♛b4 +=; 9...♛b6 10 d5 c5 += **10 b4!± ♘f7 11 ♛b3 ♖e8 12 ♗e3 ♛c7 13 ♖bd1 ♘f8 14 d5** △ c5 **b6 15 dxc6 ♛xc6 16 ♘d5 ♗e6**

102

17 ♖c1 ♘d7 18 ♘d2 ♖ac8 19 ♘b1
♕b7 19...♘b8 20 ♘bc3 ♘b8 21 f4
exf4 21...♕d7!? △ f5 22 gxf4 ♕d7
23 ♗d4 ♕d8 24 ♘b5 ♘c6 25 ♗b2
a6 26 f5! +− gxf5 26...♗xd5 27
exd5 +− 27 exf5 ♗d7 28 ♘d4 ♘xd4
29 ♗xd4 ♖b8 30 ♘f4 ♗h6 31 ♗d5
♕e7 32 ♘h5 ♗g5 33 ♕g3 ♔h8 34
h4 ♖g8 35 hxg5 1-0 Webb

1...b6

127 Maric-Sahovic Jugoslavia 78
1 e4 b6 2 d4 ♗b7 3 ♘d2 3 ♗d3 d5
3...c5; 3...e6 4 e5 ♕d7 5 ♘gf3 5 f4
e6 6 ♗d3 ♗a6 7 ♗xa6 ♘xa6 8 c3
♕b5!= 9 ♕e2 ♕xe2+ 10 ♔xe2 c5
11 ♘b3 ♘e7 12 ♗e3 ♘f5?! 12...♘c6
13 g4 ♘xe3 14 fxe3 += ♗e7 15 ♘bd2
♖c8 15...h5 16 g5 h6 17 h4 ♘b8
18 ♖ag1 cxd4 19 exd4 h5 20 ♘e1
20 g6 f6 21 exf6 gxf6! 22 g7 ♖g8
g6 21 ♘d3 ♘c6 22 ♖c1 0-0 23 ♔e3
♖fd8 24 ♖hf1 ♗f8 △ ♘e7-f5 ½-½
Sahovic

128 Ermenkov-Sahovic Jurmala 78
1 e4 b6?! 2 d4 2 ♘f3 ♗b7 3 ♘c3 e6
4 d4 ♗b4 5 ♗d3 ♘f6 6 ♕e2 d5 7
exd5 ♘xd5= Kagan-Sahovic, Biel 76
♗b7 3 ♗d3 3 f3!? d5 4 e5 ♕d7 5
♗e3 e6 6 f4 c5 7 c3 ♘c6 8 ♘f3 +=
Barle-Sahovic, Jugoslavia 77 e6 4
♘e2! 4 ♘f3 c5 5 c3 ♘f6!?; 5 0-0 cxd4
6 ♘xd4 ♘c6 7 ♘xc6 ♗xc6 8 ♘c3 +=
Westerinen-Larsen, Geneva 77 c5 4...
♘c6!? Sahovic 5 c3 ♘f6 6 ♘d2 cxd4?
6...d6 Sahovic 7 cxd4 ♘c6 8 a3!
Sahovic ♗e7 9 0-0 0-0 10 b4! +=
d6 11 ♗b2 ♖c8 12 ♘g3 ♘d7? 12...
♘e8! += 13 f4 g6 14 ♕g4!± ♘f6
15 ♕h3 ♘e8?! 16 d5! exd5 17 exd5
♘b8 18 f5! ♗f6 19 fxg6 hxg6 19...
fxg6 20 ♕e6+ ♔g7 21 ♖xf6 +− Sahovic

20 ♖xf6! ♘xf6 21 ♖f1 ♘bd7 22 ♘de4
♘h7 23 ♘xd6 +− 23 ♕h6!? ♘e5
24 ♘h5! gxh5 25 ♘f6+ ♘xf6+ 26
♖xf6 ♘xd3 27 ♖g6+ +− ♘df6 24
♘xc8 ♗xc8 25 ♕h6 ♕xd5 26 ♗xg6!
fxg6 27 ♕xg6+ ♔h8 28 ♘h5 1-0
Gufeld

129 L.A.Schneider-Sahovic
Jurmala 78
1 e4 b6 2 d4 ♗b7 3 ♗d3 e6 4 ♘e2
d5 4...c5; 4...♘c6 5 ♘d2 5 e5 c5;
5 exd5 ♕xd5! dxe4 6 ♗xe4 ♘c6
7 0-0 ♘f6 8 ♗f3 ♕d7 9 ♘c4 0-0-0∝
10 ♗f4 ♘d5 11 ♗g3 g5 12 ♘e3 f5
13 ♘xd5 exd5 14 ♘c3 g7 15 ♘b5
a6 16 ♗xc7!? axb5 17 ♗xb6! ♖de8
18 ♗e2? 18 ♕d3 ♘d8 19 ♕d3 ♘e6
20 ♖fe1 ♕c6 21 ♗a7 ♖hf8 22 ♗h5
♖e7 Zeitnot 23 ♕a3 ♖c7 24 ♖e3
♕a6! 25 ♕xa6 ♗xa6 26 ♖xe6 ♖xa7
27 c3 b4 28 cxb5 ♗xd4 29 ♖c1+
♔b8 0-1 Sahovic

Sicilian 2 c3

130 Hulak-Adorjan Osijek 78
1 e4 c5 2 ♘f3 ♘c6 3 c3 d5 4 exd5
♕xd5 5 d4 e6 6 ♗d3 ♘f6 7 0-0 ♗e7
8 dxc5 0-0! 9 ♕c2 9 b4?! ♖d8 10
♗c2 ♕xd1 11 ♖xd1 ♖xd1+ 12 ♗xd1
a5∓; 9 ♗e3 ♖d8 10 ♗c2 ♕xd1 11
♖xd1 ♖xd1+ 12 ♗xd1 ♘g4 =+ ♖d8

**10 ♖d1 ♕xc5 11 ♗g5 h6 12 ♗xf6?!
♗xf6 13 ♘bd2 ♗e7** 13...♗d7 14
♘e4=; 13...♕b6; 13...♕f8!? **14 ♗h7+
♔h8 15 ♗e4 ♗d7 16 ♘b3 ♕b6 17
♕e2** 17 ♖xd7!? ♖xd7 18 ♗xc6 ♕xc6!
19 ♘e5 ♕d5! 20 ♘xd7 ♕xd7 =+;
20 ♘xf7+ ♔g8 21 ♕g6 ♕d1+ **♔c7
18 ♕e3 ♗f6 19 g3?!** 19 ♗c2 ♘e5!;
19 ♖d2 **♔g8 20 ♖d2 ♗e8 21 ♖ad1
♖xd2 22 ♖xd2 ♖d8 23 ♔g2?! b6 24
♖xd8 ♕xd8 25 ♘bd4 ♗e7! 26 c4?!
♕c7? 26...g6! Δ ♘f5 27 b3 ♕c5 28
a4 a6 29 ♗b7 g5!? 30 ♘c2?** 30 h3!
♕c7! 31 ♗xa6 31 ♗e4 ♗c6 32 ♘b4
♗b7!∓ **♘f5 32 ♕d3 ♗c6 33 ♔g1
♗a8! 34 g4?** Zeitnot 34 ♘d2 ♕c6
35 f3 g4 ∞/∓

**34...♕f4! 35 gxf5 ♗xf3 36 ♘e1 ♗e4
37 ♕e3 ♕g4+ 38 ♔f1 ♗d4! 39 ♕g3
♕xf5 40 c5 ♗xc5 41 ♗d3 ♔g7!** 41...
♗xf2? **42 ♖xe4 ♗xe1+ 43 ♗xf5 ♗xg3
44 hxg3 exf5 45 b4 +− 42 h4? ♗xf2!
43 ♗xe4 ♗xe1+! 0-1 Adorjan**

131 Holmov-Korsunsky USSR 78
1 e4 c5 2 ♘f3 e6 3 c3 d5 4 exd5 exd5
4...♕xd5± **5 ♗b5+!?** 5 d4 ♗d7 6
♗xd7+ ♕xd7 6...♘xd7!?= **7 0-0
♘f6?!** 7...♗d6! Δ ♘e7= **8 d4 ♗e7
9 ♘e5 ♕c8 10 ♕a4+ ♘c6 11 ♖e1** +=
cxd4 **12 cxd4 ♘d7 13 ♘c3?!** 13♘xc6
♕xc6 14 ♕a3 ♘e5!; 14 ♕b4 ♘e5?

**15 ♖xe5 ♕xc1+ 16 ♖e1 0-0 17 ♕xe7
♕xb2 18 ♘a3 +−; 14 ♕d1! += ♘dxe5
14 dxe5 ♗b4! 15 ♖d1 ♗xc3 16 bxc3
0-0 17 ♗a3** 17 ♖xd5 ♘xe5 18 ♖xe5?
♕xc3 −+ **♖fe8 18 f4 ♕g4 19 h3 ♕h4
20 ♗c5**

20...♘xe5?! 20...d4 21 cxd4 ♕xf4
22 ♕b3! Δ ♖f1; 20...g5?! **21 ♗f2±
♘f3+ 22 gxf3 ♕xh3 23 ♖xd5?!** 23
♖e1 ♖e6 24 ♖xe6 fxe6 25 ♕d7 ♖f8
26 ♖e1 h6! **24 ♕d4 ♕xf3 25 ♖e1
♕g4+ 26 ♔h2 ♖xe1 27 ♗xe1 ♕e2+
28 ♗f2 ♕xa2∞ 29 ♖d7 ♖c8** 29...b6
30 ♖xb7 ♕c2 31 ♕xa7 ♖c6 31...♖xc3
32 ♖xf7 ♕g6 33 ♖xg7+! +− **32
♖xf7 ♖g6 33 ♖e7! +−♕xc3 34 ♖e8+
♔h7 35 ♕a8 ♖f6 36 ♕e4+ ♖g6 37
♖e6 1-0 Gufeld**

2 ♘c3/2 d3

132 Romanishin-Savon Kiev 78
1 e4 c5 2 ♘f3 d6 3 ♘c3 ♘f6 4 g3
4 e5 dxe5 5 ♘xe5 e6 Δ ♘bd7; 5...a6!
6 a4 e6 7 b3 ♕c7 8 ♗c4 ♘c6= Tisdall-
Kastner, New York 76 **♘c6 5 ♗g2
e5!?** 5...♗g4 6 h3 ♗xf3 7 ♗xf3 g6
8 d3 ♗g7= **6 0-0 ♗e7 7 d3 0-0 8 h3=**
8 ♗g5 ♘d4 9 ♗xf6 ♗xf3+! 10 ♕xf3
♗xf6= **♖b8 9 ♘h2!?** 9 a4 a6 Δ b5≈
b5 10 ♘g4 10 f4 exf4 11 gxf4 b4 12
♘e2 d5! ♗xg4! **11 hxg4 b4 12 ♘d5**

&xd5 13 exd5 &d4 14 c3 14 &e3
&b5 15 &d2 &g5!∝ 16 &e1 16 cxb4
&xd2 17 ♕xd2 cxb4 18 ♕xb4 &d4≈;
16 f4!? exf4 17 gxf4 bxc3 18 bxc3
&f6 19 ♖c1∝ bxc3 17 bxc3 ♕c8!
18 ♕a4 ♖b6 19 ♖b1 ♕b7?! 19...♖a6!
20 ♖b3! g6 21 f4 exf4 22 gxf4 &f6
23 &d2 ♖fb8 24 ♕e4? 25 g5 &g7
25 f5∝ ♕d7! 25 g5 &g7 =+ 26 ♖e1?
26 f5!? =+ &c7 27 ♕e7 ♕xe7 28
♖xe7 ♖xb3 29 axb3 &b5 30 d4?
Zeitnot 30 ♖d7!∓ cxd4 31 c4 &c3
32 ♖xa7 d3! −+ 33 ♖a2?? &xa2 0-1
Gufeld

21 &b4= 21 ♔xg2? ♕xc3∓ &xf1
22 ♖xf1 ♖fc8 23 ♖fd1 h6 24 ♖d2
♖d8 25 ♖c2 ♕d7 26 ♖ac1 ♖ac8
27 &c5 &xc5 ½-½ **Gufeld**

3 &b5

133 Kirpichnikov-Ligterink
Jurmala 78

1 e4 c5 2 &f3 e6 3 d3 3 b3!? ♕f6
4 e5 &d5 5 &b2 &e7 6 g3∝ &c6
3...d5 4 &bd2 &c6 5 g3 &f6 6 &g2
&e7 7 0-0 a5!? 8 a4 b6 9 ♖e1 &b7
10 c3 += Geller-Larsen, Biel 76;
5...g6 6 &g2 &g7 7 0-0 &ge7 8 ♖e1
0-0 9 e5 ♕c7 10 ♕e2 += 4 g3 d5
4...g6 5 &g2 &g7 6 0-0 &ge7 7 c3
e5!=; 4...d6 5 &g2 g6 6 0-0 &g7 7
c3 e5 8 a3 &f6 9 b4 0-0 10 b5 &e7
11 a4 a6 12 &a3 += Geller-Spassky,
Moscow 75 5 &bd2 &d6 6 &g2 &ge7
7 0-0 0-0 8 ♖e1 8 &h4 ♕c7 9 f4 f6
10 c3 &d7 11 ♕h5 &e8 12 ♕e2 &f7
13 &df3 += Rigo-Sax, Hungary 76;
8 &h4 b6 9 f4 f6 10 ♖e1 &c7 11 c3
a5= Sax-Ligterink, IBM 76; 8...&c7!?
9 f4 dxe4 10 dxe4 b6 11 e5 &a6 12
♖e1 ♕d7 13 ♕h5!? ∝/+= &c7!? 8...
♕c7 9 b3 &d7 10 &b2 d4 11 &c4
e5= 9 c3 a5 10 &f1 10 a4!? a4 11
exd5 &xd5= 12 d4 cxd4 13 &xd4
&xd4 14 ♕xd4 &b6 15 ♕d1 a3! 16 ♕f3
♕c7 16...axb2 17 &xb2 Δ c4 += 17
bxa3 &d7 17...&xc3 18 &f4 Δ ♖ac1
18 &b2 &c6∝ 19 ♕e2 &xc3 20 &xc3
&xg2

134 Rath-Larsen Esbjerg 78

1 e4 c5 2 &f3 &c6 3 &b5 ♕b6 4
&c3 e6 5 0-0 &ge7 6 ♖e1 &d4 7
&f1?! 7 &c4 &ec6 8 d3 &e7 9 &xd4
cxd4 10 &e2 0-0 11 c4?! 11 c3 &b4
12 &d2 e5 12...d6!? 13 f4 d6 14
f5 a5!? 15 f6? 15 g4? ♕d8! (Δ g6∓)
16 g5 f6 16 h4 fxg5 17 hxg5 g6∓;
15 ♖b1 =+ gxf6 16 &h6 ♕d8 17 &g3
&xe1 18 ♕xe1 &h8 19 &xf8 ♕xf8
20 ♕f2 ♕h6 21 &e2 &b4! 22 a3 22
♖f1 &xa2 &c2 22...&a6!? 23 ♖f1
&e6 24 ♕xf6+ ♕xf6 25 ♖xf6 ♖a6!
26 ♖f2 26 &d1? &e1! &e3 27 &h5
♕g7 28 ♖d2 ♖b6 29 ♕f2 &g4! 29...
♖b3 30 &f1 =+ b5?! 31 &xe3 dxe3+
32 ♔xe3 bxc4 33 &d1 ♖xd3+ 34
♖xd3 cxd3 35 ♔xd3 f5 36 b4= 30
&xg4 &xg4+ 31 ♔g1 31 ♔e2!? &xh2
32 &f5+ ♔f6 33 ♖c2 a4∓ &e3 32 &e2
32 &f1 ♖b3 33 ♔f2 ♖xb2 h5 33 &c1
♖c6 34 a4?! f5 35 exf5 d5 −+ 36
b3 dxc4 37 dxc4 37 bxc4 ♖b6 ♔f6
38 &e2 &xf5 39 ♔f2 ♖b6 40 ♖d3
h4?! 40...e4 41 ♔f3 &d6 42 ♔g4
&e4 43 ♔xh4 &c5 44 ♖f3+ ♔e6 −+

45 ♕g5 d3 46 ♘g3 e4 47 ♖f6+ ♔d7
48 ♖f5 ♖d6 49 ♖xc5 e3! 49...d2?
50 ♘xe4 =+ 50 ♘f5 e2 51 ♘xd6 d2
52 ♖d5 d1♕ 53 ♘e4+ ♕xd5+ 54
cxd5 e1♕ 55 ♘f6+ ♔d8 56 ♘h5 ♕e3+
57 ♘f4 ♕xb3 58 g4 ♕xa4 59 h4
♕e4 60 ♘e6+ ♔e7 0-1 Larsen

135 Gufeld-Vaiser USSR 78

1 e4 c5 2 ♘f3 ♘c6 3 ♗b5 e6 4 0-0
♘ge7 5 ♖e1 a6?! 6 ♗xc6 ♘xc6 7 d4 cx
d4 8 ♘xd4 d6 9 ♘xc6 9 ♘c3 += ♗e7
10 ♘xc6! △ ♕g4± Christiansen-Bellon,
Torremolinos 76 bxc6 10 ♕g4!? ♕f6?!
11 e5! ♕g6? 11...dxe5 12 ♘c3 ∝/+=
12 ♕c4± ♗d7 13 exd6 ♗xd6 14 ♘c3
♕h5 14...♕xc2 15 ♘e4 +– 15 ♗f4 15
h3 0-0 16 ♖d1 ♕e5 17 g3± ♗xf4 16
♕xf4 0-0 17 ♖ad1 ♗e8 17...♖fd8 18
♕c7 ♖ac8 19 ♖xd7 +– 18 ♖e5 ♕g6 19
♖d3 +– f6 19...h6 20 ♖g3 ♕xc2 21
♕xh6 +– 20 ♖xe6 ♕g5 21 ♕xg5 fxg5
22 f3 c5 23 ♖dd6 a5 24 ♖e5 g4 25 fx
g4 ♗g6 26 ♖d2 ♖ae8 27 ♖xe8 ♖xe8
28 ♔f2 ♖b8 29 b3 c4 30 ♔e3 cxb3 31
cxb3 ♖e8+ 32 ♔d4 ♖d8+ 33 ♔e3 ♖e8+
34 ♔f4 ♖f8+ 35 ♔g3 ♗f7 36 ♖d4 ♖c8
37 ♘e4 ♗g6 38 ♘d6 ♖c3+ 39 ♔f4
♗b1 40 ♖c4 1-0 Gufeld

136 Lutikov-Kirpichnikov
Jurmala 78

1 e4 c5 2 ♘f3 ♘c6 3 ♗b5 e6 3...♘f6!
4 0-0 4 ♗xc6 bxc6 5 0-0 ♘e7 6 b3
♘g6 7 ♗b2 f6 8 d4 cxd4 9 ♘xd4 ♗c5?!
10 c4 0-0 11 ♘c3 += Timman-Vizier,
Las Palmas 77; 8 e5 ♗e7 9 exf6
♗xf6 10 ♗xf6 ♕xf6 11 ♘c3 0-0 12
♘e4 ♕e7 13 ♘fg5! ∝/+= Uusi-Gulko,
USSR 77 ♘ge7 4...a6?! 5 ♗xc6 dxc6
6 d3 ♕c7 7 e5 f5! 8 a4 a5 9 ♘a3
♗e7 10 ♘c4 += Hort-Kurajicz,
Vinkovci 76 5 ♖e1 5 b3!? ♘d4! 6
♘xd4 cxd4 7 ♖e1 a6 8 ♗f1 ♘c6=;

5 c3 d5 6 exd5 ♘xd5 7 d4 cxd4 8
cxd4 ♗e7 9 ♘c3 0-0 10 ♖e1 ♗d7
11 ♘xd5 += Vasjukov-Timoshenko,
USSR 75 ♘g6!? 6 c3 a6 7 ♗f1 d6 8
d4 ♗e7 9 ♘a3 0-0 10 ♘c2 += e5 11
dxc5 dxc5 12 ♘e3 ♘h4? 12...♕a5!?
13 ♘xh4 ♗xh4 14 ♘c4! ♕xd1 15
♖xd1 ♖d8 16 ♘d5± ♗e6 17 ♗e3
♖ac8 18 g3 ♘a5? 18...♗f6!

19 gxh4! ♘xc4 20 ♘e7+ ♔f8 21
♘xc8 ♖xc8 22 ♗c1 ♗g4 23 ♖d5 f6
24 b3 ♘b6 25 ♖d3 +– c4 26 ♖g3
♗e2 27 ♗a3+ ♔f7 28 ♖e1 ♗h5 29
♗c1 cxb3 30 axb3 ♘d7 31 ♗a3 ♘c5
32 ♗xc5 ♖xc5 33 h3 ♖c7 34 ♖d3
♔e7 35 ♔g2 a5 36 ♖a1 ♗f7 37 ♖g3
♔f8 38 b4! axb4 39 ♖a8+ ♗e8 40
cxb4 ♖c4 41 b5 ♖c5 42 ♖b3 ♔e7
43 ♖b8 ♖xb5?? 43...♗xb5 44 ♖xb7+
♗d7 45 ♖d3 +– 44 ♖xe8+ 1-0 Gufeld

137 Margutev-Korsunsky USSR 78

1 e4 c5 2 ♘f3 ♘c6 3 ♗b5 g6 4 0-0
♗g7 5 ♖e1! ♘f6 6 c3 0-0 7 d4 cxd4
8 cxd4 d5 9 e5 ♘e4 9...♘e8 += 10
♗xc6 10 ♘c3 ♘xc3 11 bxc3 ♕a5
12 ♗g5 ♗f5= Matanovic-Gufeld,
Vrnjacka Banja 76 bxc6 11 ♘bd2
♕b6?! N 11...c5 12 dxc5 ♘xc5 13
♘b3 ♘xb3 14 ♕xb3∝; 11...♘xd2
△ f6 12 ♘xe4 dxe4 13 ♖xe4 ♖d8
14 ♕e1 ♗e6 15 ♗d2 a5 15...♕xb2?

16 ♗b4 △ ♖e2 16 ♗c3 += ♘d5 17
♖e3 ♗h6 18 ♖d3 ♕a6 19 ♖dd1 f5!
20 ♘d2 a4 21 ♘f1 ♖f8 22 f3 ♖f7
23 ♗d2 f4 24 ♗b4 ♖b8 25 ♗a3 g5!
26 h3 ♗f8≈ 27 e6?! 27 ♘d2 h5 28
♘e4 ♖g7 29 ♘c3 g4 30 ♘xd5 cxd5∞
♖g7 28 ♖d2 h5 29 ♗c5 ♕c8 30 ♕e5
♕e8 31 ♖e1 ♖g6 32 ♕f5 ♖b7 33
a3 Zeitnot ♗g7 Zeitnot 33 ♖f2 ♗h6
34 ♖e5 ♖f6 35 ♕c2 ♗b3 36 ♕e2 ♖g6
37 ♘d2 ♗g7 38 ♘xb3 ♗xe5 39 ♘a5
♖b5 40 ♕xe5 ♖xa5 41 h4! += 41
♖c2 ♖g7 42 d5 ♕g6 43 ♗d4 ♖xd5
44 ♕b8+ ♔h7 45 ♗xg7 ♖d1+ 46 ♔h2
♔xg7 gxh4 42 ♕xh5 ♖a8 43 ♖e2
43 ♕xh4 ♖xe6 44 ♕xf4 ♕g6= ♖g7
44 ♕xh4 ♕g6 45 ♗xe7 ♕b1+ 45...
♕d3 46 ♗f6!= 46 ♔f2 ♕d1 47 ♗f6
♖xg2+ 48 ♔xg2 ♕xe2+ 49 ♔g1 ♕xe6
50 ♕h8+ ♔f7 51 ♕xa8 51 ♕g7+=
♕e1+ 52 ♔g2 ♕g3+ 53 ♔f1 ♕xf3+
54 ♔e1 ♕xf6 55 ♕h8+?? Zeitnot
33 ♔xa4= ♕g5 56 ♕g7+ ♔h4 57 ♕f6+
♔h3 58 ♕d2 ♕e3+ 59 ♔c2 f3 60
♕f5+ ♔g3 61 ♕g6+ ♔f2 62 ♕xc6
♔e1! −+ 63 ♕c5 ♕d2+ 64 ♔b1 f2 65
♕e5+ ♔d1 66 ♕f5 ♕c1+ 0-1 Gufeld

138 Kuksov-Semeniuk USSR 78
1 e4 c5 2 ♘f3 ♘c6 3 ♗b5 g6 4 0-0
♗g7 5 ♖e1 ♘f6 5...e5 6 b4!? += 6 e5
6 c3 +=; 6 ♘c3 0-0 7 e5 ♘e8 8 ♗xc6
dxc6 9 h3 ♘c7 10 b3 ♘e6 11 ♗b2
♘d4 12 ♘e4 b6 13 d3 += Panno-
Szmetan, Bogota 77 ♘d5 7 ♘c3 ♘c7
7...♘xc3 8 dxc3 0-0 9 ♕d5! += 8 ♗xc6
dxc6 9 h3 9 ♘e4 ♘e6 10 d3 0-0 11
a4 b6= 0-0 10 d3 ♘e6 11 ♘e4!?∞ f5
12 exf6 exf6 13 ♗e3 b6 14 c3 14
♕e2?! h6 14...♗a6!? 15 ♕b3! +=
♔h7 16 ♘g3 f5 17 ♗d2 ♕xd3? 17...
♕d6! += 18 ♖ad1 ♕b5 19 ♕c2≈ c4
20 h4! a5 20...♘c5 21 ♘d4± 21 h5±
g5 22 ♗e3 a4 23 ♗xb6!! ♕xb6 24

♘xf5 ♔h8 25 ♘xg7 ♔xg7 26 ♕g6
+− ♖a7 27 ♕xh6+ ♔g8 28 ♕xg5
♕xb2 29 ♖d8! 29 h6?! ♕xc3 a3
29...♖xd8 30 ♕xd8+ ♔h7 31 ♘g5+
♔h6 32 ♕f6+ 30 ♖ee8 ♖f7 31 ♖xf8+
♖xf8 32 h6 ♕xc3 33 h7+ ♔xh7 34
♖xf8 ♗e6 35 ♘e5 ♕e1+ 36 ♔h2
♕e4 37 f4! 1-0 Gufeld

2...♘c6, 5...e5

139 Trossman-Salov USSR 78
1 e4 c5 2 ♘f3 ♘c6 3 d4 cxd4 4 ♘xd4
♘f6 5 ♘c3 e5 6 ♘db5 d6 7 ♘d5 ♘xd5
8 exd5 ♘e7!? 8...♘b8 9 c4 ♗e7 10 ♗d3
0-0 11 0-0 ♘d7 12 ♗e3 a6 14 ♘c3
f5 15 f3! += Lein-Bilek, Rome 76
9 c3 9 c4 a6? 10 ♕a4!; 9...♘f5!∞
♘f5!? 9...♘g6 10 a4 ♗e7 11 g3?!
0-0 12 ♗g2 f5 13 0-0 f4 =+ Kuzmin-
Sveshnikov, USSR 76; 11 ♗e2 △ 0-0=
10 ♕a4? 10 ♗e2= ♗d7 11 ♗d3 a6
12 ♗xf5 ♗xb5 13 ♕g4 g6 14 ♗c2
♕c7! =+ 15 ♗a4!? ♕a5! 16 ♗c2?
16 ♗xb5+! ♗g7 17 a4 ♗d7 18 ♕f3
0-0 19 0-0 f5! 20 ♖d1 ♖ae8 21 h4?!
21 ♕e2 =+ e4 22 ♕g3 ♗e5! 23 ♗f4
♕c5∓ 24 h5 ♗xf4 25 ♕xf4 e3 26
♕d4 e2! 27 ♖e1 ♕xd4 28 cxd4 f4!
29 hxg6

29...f3!! 30 gxh7+ ♔h8 31 ♗g6 ♖e7
32 ♗h5 ♖g7 33 g3 ♖xg3+! 34 fxg3

f2+ 35 ♔g2 f1♕+ 36 ♖xf1 ♖xf1 37 ♖xf1 ♘h3+! 0-1 Gufeld

140 Verner-Kim USSR 78
1 e4 c5 2 ♘f3 ♘c6 3 d4 cxd4 4 ♘xd4 ♘f6 5 ♘c3 e5 6 ♘db5 d6 7 ♗g5 a6 8 ♘a3 b5 9 ♘d5 9 ♗xf6 ♗e7 10 ♘xe7 ♘xe7 10...♕xe7 11 ♗d3 += 11 ♗xf6 11 ♕f3?! ♗g4! 12 ♕e3 d5! =+ Planinc-Govedarica, Jugoslavia 77 gxf6 11 ♕d3?! N 12 c4 ♗b7! 13 cxb5 ♗xe4 14 ♕a4 d5 15 bxa6+ ♔f8; 12 ♕d2 ♗b7 13 0-0-0 d5 14 exd5 ♗xd5! =+; 14...♕d5!? ♗b7 13 0-0-0 d5 14 exd5 ♗xd5 =+ 15 c4 15 ♔b1 ♖c8 16 ♔b1?? 16 ♗e2 ♗e4! -+ 0-1 Gufeld

141 Gufeld-Gavrikov USSR 78
1 e4 c5 2 ♘f3 e6 3 d4 cxd4 4 ♘xd4 ♘f6 5 ♘c3 ♘c6 6 ♘db5 d6 7 ♗f4 e5 8 ♗g5 a6 9 ♘a3 b5 10 ♘d5 ♗e7 11 ♗xf6 ♗xf6 12 c3 ♗g5 13 ♘c2 0-0 14 a4 bxa4 15 ♖xa4 a5 16 ♗b5 ♘a7 N 16...♘e7 17 ♗c4 ♗d7 18 ♖a2 ♘c8 19 0-0 ♘b6 20 ♘xb6 ♕xb6 21 ♗d5 ♖ac8 23 ♘a3! += ♕a6 23 ♕f3! ♔h8 24 b3! 24 ♔h5 f6 f5 25 ♘c4± a4

26 exf5! ♖c5 26...♖xf5 27 ♖xa4! 27 ♖d1! 27 ♗b7 ♕a7 28 ♘xd6 e4!∞ ♖xf5 28 ♕g4! +- 28 ♖xa4?? ♕xa4 29 bxa4 ♖xf3 30 gxf3 ♗xa4 -+; 29 ♕xf5 ♗xf5 30 bxa4 ♗c2 -+ e4

28...h5 29 ♕xh5+ ♗h6 30 ♕g6 +-; 28...g6 29 ♗e4 +- 29 ♕xe4 ♕b5?! 30 ♖xa4 h5 31 ♖a8+ 1-0 Gufeld

142 Semeniuk-Timoshenko USSR 78
1 e4 c5 2 ♘f3 ♘c6 3 d4 cxd4 4 ♘xd4 ♘f6 5 ♘c3 e5 6 ♘db5 d6 7 ♗g5 a6 8 ♘a3 b5 9 ♘d5 9 ♗xf6 ♗e7 10 ♗xf6 ♗xf6 11 c3 0-0 12 ♘c2 ♗g5 12... ♖b8!? 13 ♕f3!? ♗g5 14 h4 ♗h6 15 g4 f6 16 ♖d1 ♗e6 17 ♕g2 ♖b7 18 ♗e2 g6 19 ♖h3 ♘e7 20 ♘cb4! ♘xd5 21 exd5 ♗c8 22 ♘xa6 f5 23 g5 ♗g7 24 ♘b4 f4! 25 ♗g4 e4∞ Sveshnikov 13 a4 bxa4 14 ♖xa4 a5 15 ♗c4 ♘ce3 ♖b8 16 ♕c2 ♗e6 17 ♗c4 ♗xe3 18 ♘xe3 ♗xc4 19 ♖xc4 ♘e7 20 0-0 ♕b6 21 ♖b1 ♖fd8 22 b4 d5= Klovan-Kalinichev, USSR 75 ♖b8 15...♗d7 16 b3 16 ♕a1 ♗e6 17 0-0 Δ ♖b1, b4 Ghinda-Dumitracu, Rumania 75 ♔h8 16...♗e6 17 ♕a1 g6 18 0-0 ♕d7 19 ♖d1 f5 20 exf5 gxf5 21 b4 += Karpov-Sveshnikov, USSR Final 73 17 0-0 f5 18 exf5 ♗xf5 19 ♘ce3 ♗e6 20 ♕d3 ♕d7 21 ♖d1 ♕f7 22 f3 ♖fd8 23 ♔h1 h6≈ 24 ♘f1 ♘d4?! 25 cxd4 ♗xd5 26 ♖xa5 ♗xc4 27 bxc4 d5 27...exd4 28 cxd5 ♖xd5 29 ♕c4 ♖bd8 30 h4! ♗f4 30...♗xh4? 31 dxe5! +- 31 ♖xd5 ♖xd5 32 g3 ♗xg3 33 ♘xg3 ♕xf3+ 34 ♔h2 ♕xd1 35 ♕xd5 exd4 +=/= 36 ♕a8+ ♔h7 37 ♕e4+ ♔h8 38 ♕e8+ ♔h7 39 ♕e4+ ♔h8 40 ♘f5 ♕d2+ 41 ♔g3 ♕c3+ 42 ♔g4 d3 43 ♘e7 ♕b3 44 ♘g6+ ♔g8 45 h5 ♕b8 46 ♕d5+ ♔h7 47 ♕xd3 ♕c8+ 48 ♕f5 ♕c4+ 49 ♘f4+ ♔h8 50 ♕e6 ♕a4 51 ♕d6 ♕a1 52 ♔f5 ♕b1+ 53 ♔e6 ♕e4+ 54 ♔f7 ♕f5+ 55 ♔e8 ♕b5+ 56 ♔e7 ♕g5+ 57 ♔d7 ♕b5+ 58 ♔c8 ♕c4+ 59 ♔d8 ♕e4 60 ♘e6 ♔h7 61 ♘f8+ ♔h8 62 ♕g6 Zeitnot ♕a8+ 63 ♔e7 ♕xf8+! ½-½ Lysenko

143 Honfi-Piasetski Subotica 78
1 e4 c5 2 ♘f3 ♘c6 3 d4 cxd4 4 ♘xd4
♘f6 5 ♘c3 e5 6 ♘db5 d6 7 ♗g5 a6
8 ♘a3 b5 9 ♗xf6 gxf6 10 ♘d5 f5 11
♗xb5!? axb5 12 ♘xb5 ♖a4!? 12...♖a7
13 ♘xa7 ♘xa7 14 exf5!? ♗xf5 15
♕f3 ∝/+=; 12...♕g5!? N Honfi-
Horvath, Subotica 78 **13 ♘bc7+
♔d7 14 0-0 ♖xe4** 14...♘e7? 15 c4
♖xc4 16 ♕b3 ♖c5 17 ♕a4+ ♘c6 18
b4 +− V.Petronic-Porubsky, Budapest
78 **15 ♕h5 ♘e7 16 ♕xf7≈ ♔c6 17
c4! ♖g8** 17...♘xd5? 18 cxd5+ ♔b6
19 ♖fc1 +− Horvath-Joksic,
Jugoslavia 78 **18 ♖fc1 ♖g7?** 18...
♖eg4! 19 g3 ♖4g6 20 c5 ♔b7!? Δ
♖8g7 **19 ♘e6!! ♗xe6 20 ♕xe6 ♖eg4
21 g3 ♖4g5 22 ♘b4+ ♔b7 23 c5!±
♖5g6 24 c6+! ♔a8 25 ♕b3 25 ♕d7
+− ♕b6 26 c7 +− ♔b7 27 ♕d5+!
1-0 Maric**

144 Kayumov-Semeniuk USSR 78
1 e4 c5 2 ♘f3 ♘c6 3 d4 cxd4 4 ♘xd4
♘f6 5 ♘c3 e5 6 ♘db5 d6 7 ♗g5 a6
8 ♘a3 b5 9 ♗xf6 gxf6 10 ♘d5 f5 11
♗d3 ♗e6 12 ♕h5 ♗g7 13 0-0 f4 13...
h6? 14 c3 0-0 15 ♘c2 fxe4 16 ♗xe4
f5 17 ♘f4 +− Spassky-Sveshnikov,
USSR Final 73 **14 c3 0-0 15 ♘c2
f5!?** 15...♔h8 16 a4 bxa4 17 ♖xa4
a5∝ **16 ♘cb4** 16 a4? ♗xd5! 17 exd5
♘e7∓ **♗xb4 17 ♘xb4 a5 18 ♘c6?**
18 exf5 ♗f7 19 ♕h3 ♕d7 20 ♘c2
d5 21 ♖ad1 ♖a6 22 ♕g4 ♖h6∓; 22
f6!? ∝/=+ ♕c7 **19 exf5**

Diagram

19...♗c4! −+ N 19...♗d5? 20 ♘d4!!
♕b7 21 ♘e6 ♖f6 22 f3 ♔h8 23 ♗e4!
♗c6 24 ♘g5 h6 25 ♗xc6 ♕xc6 26
♘e4± Petrushin-Karasev, USSR 77;
21...♗xg2 22 f6 ♗xf6 23 ♗xh7+! +−;

**20 f6 ♗xf6 21 ♗e4 d5! 22 ♗f5 ♗xf1
23 ♖xf1 ♖a6 0-1 Lysenko**

**145 Beljavsky-Sveshnikov
Lvov 78**
1 e4 c5 2 ♘f3 e6 3 d4 cxd4 4 ♘xd4
♘c6 5 ♘c3 ♘f6 6 ♘db5 d6 7 ♗f4
e5 8 ♗g5 a6 9 ♘a3 b5 10 ♗xf6 10
♘d5 gxf6 11 ♘d5 f5 12 ♗d3 12 ♕d3
fxe4! 13 ♕xe4 ♗d7 14 f4 f5 15 ♕f3
♗g7∝; 12 exf5 ♗xf5 13 ♗d3 ♗e6
14 ♗e4 ♗g7 15 ♕h5 ♖e8; 13 c3 ♗e6
14 ♘c2 ♗g7 15 ♘e3 ♗e7!? 16 g3
♘xd5 17 ♘xd5 0-0-0= Gufeld-
Timoshenko, USSR 76 **♗e6 13 ♕h5**
13 c4!? ♕a5+! 14 ♔f1 ♗xd5=; 13
0-0; 13 c3 **♗g7 14 c3** 14 0-0-0? ♖c8!
15 ♔b1 ♗xd5! 16 exd5 ♘e7 17 f3
0-0 18 ♖he1 ♖c8 =+ Semeniuk-
Timoshenko, USSR 76 **0-0 15 exf5
♗xd5 16 f6 e4 17 fxg7 ♖e8 18 ♗e2
♖e5 19 ♕h6 b4!?** 19...♖g5; 19...♕g5!?
20 ♘c2 20 ♘c4 ♗xc4 21 ♗xc4 bxc3
22 bxc3 d5 23 ♕xc6 ♖c8 24 ♕xa6
♖xc4 25 0-0 ♖xc3 =+; 22 ♗b3 Δ
0-0∝ **bxc3 21 bxc3 ♗e6** 21...♕a5
22 0-0 ♕xc3 22 ♘e3 ♘d4 23 ♗g4≈
**22 0-0 ♕g5 23 ♕xg5 ♖xg5 24 ♖fd1
♖c5!=** 25 ♖xd6 ♖xc3 26 ♘e3 Δ
♗c4! += **♖c5! 27 ♗g4 ♖d8 28 ♖xd8+
♘xd8 29 ♖d1 ♗xg4 30 ♘xg4** 30
♖xd8+?! ♔xg7 =+ ½-½ **Gufeld**

146 Byrne-Timman Bugojno 78

1 e4 c5 2 ♘f3 ♘c6 3 d4 cxd4 4 ♘xd4
♘f6 5 ♘c3 e5 6 ♘db5 d6 7 ♗g5 a6
8 ♘a3 b5 9 ♗xf6 gxf6 10 ♘d5 f5
11 ♗d3 ♗e6 12 ♕h5 ♗g7 13 0-0 f4
14 c3 0-0 15 ♖ad1 N 15 ♖fd1 ♖b8
△ ♕d7/b4 16 ♘c2 ♕d7 △ ♗g4 17
♕e2 ♔h8! 17...f5 18 ♘cb4 ♘xb4
19 ♘xb4 a5 20 ♘a6 ♖b6 21 ♘c5
♕e8 22 ♘xe6± ; 21...dxc5 22 exf5
△ f6± 18 ♖fe1 f5 19 ♘cb4 ♘xb4
20 ♘xb4 a5 21 exf5 ♗g8 21...♗xf5
22 ♘d5 f3 23 ♕xf3 ♗g4 24 ♕e4 +−;
22...♗e6 23 ♗e4/♕h5 += 22 ♘c2
♗xa2 23 ♖a1 ♗d5 24 ♖xa5 f3! 25
gxf3 ♗h6 △ ♖g8+, ♕g7∓ 26 ♘e3
♗c6 27 ♖a6 △ ♖xc6 ♔b7 27...♗f4!?
△ 28 ♖xc6 ♕xc6 29 ♗e4 ♕d7 30
♘d5 ♕g7+ 31 ♔h1 ♕h6 28 ♖xc6
♕xc6 29 ♗e4 ♕c7 30 ♔h1 ♗f4 31
♘d5 ♕g7 32 ♗xf4 exf4≈ 33 ♖g1
♕e5 34 ♕d2 ♖g8 35 ♖d1 b4 35...
♕g7 36 ♕d4; 35...♖b6 38 ♗d5 △ ♗e6
36 ♕xd6 ♕xd6 37 ♖xd6 bxc3 38
bxc3 ♖bd8 38...♖bc8 39 ♗d5 ♖gf8
40 ♗e6 ♖xc3 41 ♖d4=; 38...♖fc8
39 ♖d7 △ f6 39 ♖xd8 ♖xd8= 40
c4 ♖c8 41 ♗d5 ♔g7 42 ♔g2 ♔f6 43
♗e6 ♖c5 44 ♔f1 ♖a5 45 ♔g2 h6 46
♔f1 ♖a3 47 ♔g2 ♖c3 48 h4 ♔e5 49
♔g1 ♖xf3 50 ♔g2 ♖c3 51 ♔h2 ½-½
Bellin/Wicker

147 Volovik-Rundquist USSR 78

1 e4 c5 2 ♘f3 ♘c6 3 d4 cxd4 4 ♘xd4
♘f6 5 ♘c3 e5 6 ♘db5 d6 7 ♗g5 a6
8 ♘a3 b5 9 ♗xf6 gxf6 10 ♘d5 f5 11
exf5 ♗xf5 12 c3 12 ♗d3 ♗e6 13 ♗e4
♗g7 14 ♕h5 ♖c8= ♗g7 12...♗e6 13
♘c2 ♗xd5 14 ♕xd5 ♘e7 15 ♕b3
♗g7≈ Mecking-Ljubojevic, Manila 76
13 ♘c2 0-0 14 ♘ce3 14 a4? bxa4
15 ♘ce3 ♗d7 16 ♕h5 f5 17 ♗d3 e4
18 ♗c4+ ♔h8 19 ♘f4 ♘e5 =+

Korsunsky-Sveshnikov, USSR 76

♗g6?! 14...♗e6 15 g4! ♕h4 16 ♗g2
♖a7 17 ♗e4 f5 18 ♗xf5 ♗xf5 19 gxf5
♕e4 20 ♖g1 ♖xf5 21 ♕g4 ♕xg4 22
♖xg4 ♖f8 23 a4 += Torre-Ljubojevic,
Manila 76 15 h4 h6 16 g4 e4 17
♗e2 ♖c8 18 ♘f5 ♗xf5 19 gxf5 ♘e5
20 ♖g1! +− N 20 ♕d2? ♖c5 21
f6 ♗xf6 22 0-0-0 ♗xh4 23 ♖dg1+
♗g5 24 ♖xh6 ♘f3 25 ♗xf3 ♖xd5∓
Quinteros-Ljubojevic, Manila 76 ♔h7
20...♕xh4? 21 f6!; 20...♔h8? 21 ♕d2!;
20...f6 21 ♘f4 21 ♕d2 ♕xh4 21...
♖c5 22 0-0-0 ♘d3+ 23 ♗xd3 ♖xd5
24 ♗xe4! ♖xd2 25 f6+ +− 22 0-0-0
f6 22...♖c5 23 ♖h1 ♕xf2 24 ♘f6+!
+−; 22...♕xf2 23 f6 +− 23 ♘f4 ♕xf2
24 ♘e6 ♖f7

25 ♖xg7+! ♖xg7 26 ♕xh6+!! 1-0
Lysenko

148 Velimirovic-Kurajica
Jugoslavia Final 78

1 e4 c5 2 ♘f3 ♘c6 3 d4 cxd4 4 ♘xd4
♘f6 5 ♘c3 e6 6 ♘db5 d6 7 ♗f4 e5
8 ♗g5 a6 9 ♗xf6 gxf6 10 ♘a3 b5
11 ♘d5 f5 12 g4!? N fxg4 12...fxe4?!
13 ♗g2 13 c3 ♗h6 13...h5 14 h3 α/±
♗g7 15 ♘c2 △ a4, ♘ce3± 14 ♘c2
♘e7!? 15 ♘cb4 15 ♘f6+ ♔f8 16
♘xg4 ♗xg4 17 ♕xg4 ♖g8 18 ♕h5
♖g6 =+; 16...♗f4 =+ ♔f8 15...♗e6

110

16 ♘xe7 ♛xe7 17 ♘xa6 **16 ♗xe7**
♛xe7 17 ♞d5 ♛b7 18 h3 18 ♗e2
♗e6 19 ♗xg4 ♗xd5=; 18 a4 bxa4
19 ♖xa4 ♛xb2 20 ♖b4 ♛a3 21 ♖b3
♛c5 22 ♘b6 ♖a7 23 ♘xc8 ♛xc8
24 ♛xd6+ ♔g7 28 ♛xe5+ f6≈ **♗e6!**
18...gxh3 19 ♛h5! ♗f4 20 ♗xh3 ♗e6?
21 ♗xe6 fxe6 22 ♘xf4 exf4 23 ♛h6+
♔g7 24 ♛xf4+ ♔e7 25 0-0-0± 20...
h6≈ **19 hxg4 ♗g5= 20 ♗e2 ♗xd5**
21 ♛xd5 ♛xd5 22 exd5 ♔g7 23 a4
♖hb8 24 b4 e4! 25 ♔d1 ♖c8 26 axb5
axb5 27 ♔c2 ½-½ 27...♖xa1 28 ♖xa1
♖xc3+ 29 ♔xc3 ♗f6+ = **Bellin/Wicker**

149 Gufeld-Chekhov
USSR 78
1 e4 c5 2 ♘f3 e6 3 d4 cxd4 4 ♘xd4
♘f6 5 ♘c3 ♘c6 6 ♘db5 d6 7 ♗f4
e5 8 ♗g5 a6 9 ♘a3 ♗e6 9...b5 10
♘c4 ♖c8 11 ♗d3?! 11 ♗xf6! +=
♗e7= 12 0-0?! 12 ♗xf6 ♗xf6 13
♘e3 b5! **13 ♗xf6** 13 ♘e3? ♘xe4!∓
bxc4 14 ♗xe7 ♘xe7 15 ♗e2 0-0
15...d5 **16 ♛d2** 16 ♗f3 =+ ♛b6 16...
d5= **17 ♖fd1 ♛xb2?!** 17...♖fd8=
18 a3! △ ♖db1 **♛b6 19 ♛xd6** 19
♖ab1?! ♛a5? 20 ♘d5 +=; 19...♛a7!
20 ♛xd6 ♘c6∓ **♘c6 20 ♘d5!** 20
♖ab1? ♛a7∓ **♗xd5?!** 20...♛a7! 21
♘b4 ♘d4 22 ♗f1 a5 23 ♛xe5 axb4
24 ♛xd4 ♛xd4 25 ♖xd4 b3≈ **21**
♖ab1!± ♛a7 22 exd5 ♘d4 22...♖fd8
23 ♛xc6 ♖xc6 24 dxc6 +- **23 ♛xe5**
♘b5 23...♖fe8 24 ♛xd4 ♛xd4 25
♖xd4 ♖xe2 26 d6 ♖xc2 27 d7 ♖d8 28
♖e4! ♔f8 29 ♖be1 +- **24 ♛b2 ♛e7**
25 a4 25 ♗f1!? ♛xa3 26 ♛b4!±
♛xe2 26 axb5 c3 27 ♛b3 axb5 28
d6 b4 29 h3?! 29 d7 ♖b8 30 ♖e1
△ ♖e7, g3, h4± **♖b8 30 ♖d4?!** Zeitnot
30 ♖e1±; 30 ♖d3± **g6 31 ♖bd1?!**
♖b7 32 g3?! ♖b5 ½-½ **Gufeld**

150 Marcinkiewicz-Kocur
Corr. 77
1 e4 c5 2 ♘f3 ♘c6 3 d4 cxd4 4 ♘xd4
♘f6 5 ♘c3 e5 6 ♘db5 d6 7 ♗g5 a6
8 ♗xf6 gxf6 9 ♘a3 f5 10 ♛h5 d5 10...
b5?! 11 exf5! b4 12 ♗c4 +- **11**
0-0-0 11 ♘xd5? ♗xa3 12 bxa3 ♛a5+
13 c3 ♗e6 14 ♖c1 0-0-0 15 ♗c4 ♛c5
16 ♗b3 fxe4 17 ♘e3 ♘d4∓ Schwarz-
Virkulov, USSR 72; 14 0-0-0 fxe4
15 ♘f6+ ♔e7 16 ♘xe4 ♛xa3+ 17
♔d2 ♖ad8+ -+ Kuzmin-Kupreichik,
USSR 72 **♗xa3 12 ♘xd5!** 12 bxa3
♘d4 13 exf5 ♛a5 14 ♖xd4! exd4
15 ♗b5+ axb5 16 ♖e1+ ♔d8!∞ **♗f8**
12...♗e6 13 ♗c4 ♘d4 14 ♖he1 ♖c8
15 ♖xd4! exd4 16 exf5 ♛a5 17
♖xe6+ ♔d8 18 ♛h4+ ♔d7 19 ♘f6+
♔c7 20 ♛f4+ 1-0 Pripis-Malinin,
USSR 75; 12...♗d6? 13 ♛h6 △ ♘f6+;
12...♗c5!? **13 ♗c4** △ ♘b6 **♖b8 14 exf5**
♗g7 14...b5? 15 ♘b4! +- **15 ♖d3!**
h6 16 f4 ♔f8 16...0-0? 17 f6 +-
17 ♖hd1 ♗f6

18 ♘c7! 18 ♘b6?! ♛e8 19 ♘xc8
♖xc8 20 ♖d7 ♖h7 ♛e7 18...♛xc7
19 ♖d7 +- **19 ♖d8+! ♔g7** 19...
♘xd8 20 ♖xd8+ ♔g7 21 ♖xh8 +-
20 ♖xh8 ♗g5 20...♔xh8 21 ♛xh6+
♔g8 22 ♘d5 +- **21 f6+!** 1-0
Konikowski

2...♘c6, 4...g6

151 Parma-Velimirovic
Jugoslavia Final 78

1 e4 c5 2 ♘f3 ♘c6 3 d4 cxd4 4 ♘xd4
g6 5 ♘c3 ♗g7 6 ♘b3 ♘f6 7 ♗e2 0-0
8 0-0 d6 9 ♔h1 a6?! 9...a5!? 10 f4
♗d7 11 ♗f3 ♖c8 12 ♗e3 ♕c7 13
♘d5 ♘xd5 14 exd5 ♘b8?± 14...♘a5
15 ♘xa5 ♕xa5 16 c3 += **15 c3 a5
16 a4 ♘a6 17 ♗e2 ♘c5 18 ♘d4 e5
19 dxe6 fxe6 20 ♘b5 ♗xb5 21 ♗xb5
♔h8 22 ♕e2 e5?** 22...♘e4 23 ♗g1
d5± **23 fxe5 dxe5 24 ♖xf8+ ♖xf8**
24...♗xf8 25 ♖f1 ±/+− **25 ♕c4 ♖c8
26 ♖d1 h5** 26...b6 27 b4 +−; 26...
♗f8 27 ♖f1 +− **27 ♗xc5 ♕xc5 28
♕e6 ♔h7 29 ♖d6 1-0 Bellin**

152 Uhlmann-Ljubojevic
Niksic 78

1 c4 c5 2 ♘f3 g6 3 d4 ♗g7 4 e4 cxd4
5 ♘xd4 ♘c6 6 ♗e3 d6 7 ♘c3 a6
7...♘f6 Δ 0-0 **8 ♗e2 e6?** 8...♘f6 **9
♕d2!± ♘e5 10 ♖d1 ♕c7?** 10...f5 Δ
♘f7±

11 ♘db5! axb5 12 ♘xb5 ♕c6 12...
♕d7 13 ♘xd6+ ♔f8 14 ♗c5 ♘e7 15
♕f4 ♕c6 16 ♘xf7! +− **13 ♘xd6+
♕e7** 13...♔f8 14 ♕b4! ♘e7 15 ♘f5!!
+−; 14...♖a4 15 ♘xc8+ ♖xb4 16

♖d8+ ♕e8 17 ♘c5+ +− **14 ♕b4 +−
♕f6 15 f4 g5 16 fxe5+ ♕g6 17 ♘xf7!
1-0** 17...♔xf7 18 ♗h5 mate **Maric**

153 Haag-Szlovak Hungary 78

1 e4 c5 2 ♘f3 g6 3 d4 cxd4 4 ♘xd4
♗g7 5 c4 ♘c6 6 ♗e3 ♘f6 7 ♘c3 ♘g4
8 ♕xg4 ♘xd4 9 ♕d1 ♘e6 10 ♖c1
♕a5 11 ♕d2 b6 12 ♕d5!? 12 ♗d3 +=
♕xd5 13 exd5+ N ♘d4! 14 ♗d3 d6
14...♔d8± **15 ♗xd4 ♗xd4 16 ♘b5
♗xb2 17 ♖b1 ♗f6 18 ♘c7+ ♕d7?**
18...♔d8± **19 ♘xa8 ♗d4 20 ♗c2 ♗a6
21 ♗a4+ ♕c8 22 ♕d2 ♕b8 23 ♔d3
♗c5 24 ♖he1 1-0 Haag**

3 ♗b5+

154 Gufeld-Platonov
Vladivostok 78

1 e4 c5 2 ♘f3 d6 3 ♗b5+ ♘c6 4 0-0
♗d7 5 c3 a6 6 ♗xc6 ♗xc6 7 ♖e1 ♘f6
8 d4 ♗xe4 9 ♗g5 ♗c6! 9...♗xb1?!
10 ♖xb1 e6 11 ♗xf6 gxf6 += **10
♗xf6 gxf6 11 d5 ♗d7** 11 ♘h4 cxd4 12
cxd4 d5!? **♗d7 12 ♘h4 ♖g8** 12...h5!?
**13 ♕h5 ♕c7 14 ♕xh7 ♗g7 15 ♕d3
e6! =+ 16 c4** 16 ♕f3 0-0-0 17 dxe6
♗xe6 18 ♕xf6 ♖g4!∓ Δ ♗g7 **0-0-0
17 ♘c3 f5 18 ♖ad1** 18 a3; 18 ♖ab1
Δ b4-b5 **♖g4 19 dxe6** 19 ♘f3 e5!?
**fxe6 20 ♘f3 ♗e7 21 ♘d5?! exd5
22 ♖xe7 ♖e4?!** 22...dxc4 23 ♕xd6
♕xd6 24 ♖xd6 ♗c6 25 ♖xd8+ ♔xd8
26 ♖e3∓ **23 ♗g7 d4? 24 ♘g5 ♖ee8**
24...♖e5 25 ♕g3 ♖de8 26 f3 Δ h4 +=
**25 h4! += ♕a5?! 26 ♘f7 ♖e1+ 27
♔h2± ♖xd1 28 ♕xd1 ♖f8 29 ♘xd6+
♕c7 30 ♕f3 ♕b6 31 ♘xf5 +−** 31
♕xb7+?!±; 31 ♘xb7 ♕c6± **♕d8
32 g4 ♗xf5 33 gxf5 ♕c6 34 ♕f4
♕c8 35 h5 ♖h8 36 f6 ♖xh5+ 37 ♔g3
♖h1** 37...♖h8 38 f7 ♕e6 39 f8♕+ +−
38 ♖g8+ ♕d7 39 ♕f5+ 1-0 Gufeld

155 Tarjan-Byrne
USA Final 78

1 e4 c5 2 ♘f3 d6 3 ♗b5+ ♘d7 4 d4
cxd4 5 ♕xd4 ♘gf6 6 ♗g5 e6 7 ♘c3
♗e7 8 ♗xf6 8 0-0-0!? gxf6 9 ♕d2
a6 10 ♗xd7+ ♗xd7 11 ♘d4 0-0 11...
♕c7!? △ 0-0-0 12 f4 ♔h8 13 0-0 b5
14 ♔h1 ♕b6 15 ♖ae1 △ f5 b4 16
♘ce2 ♕b7 17 ♘g3 += d5 18 f5 e5
19 ♘f3 △ ♕h6, ♘h5 ♗b5 20 ♖g1
♖ad8 21 exd5 ♕xd5 22 ♕h6 ♖g8
23 ♘e4 ♖g7 24 ♖e3 24 ♘xf6? ♕c6
♗c6 24...♕xa2? ♘xe5! 25 fxe5 f6±;
25...♕xb2!?∝ 25 b3 ♗b7 26 h3!
△ ♘xf6 ♕c6 27 ♖e2 ♖gg8?! 27...
♖dg8!? 28 ♖ge1 ♖d5 29 ♘h2! ♖d4
30 ♘g4 △ ♘gxf6 ♖xe4 31 ♖xe4
♕xc2 32 ♖4e2 ♕xf5 33 ♖f2 ♕g6 34
♕h4!± ♕g5 34...♗d8 35 ♖d1! 35
♕xg5 ♖xg5 36 ♖c1!± h5 37 ♖c7
hxg4 38 ♖xb7 ♗c5 39 ♖xf6 gxh3
40 gxh3 e4 41 ♔fxf7 ♔g8 42 ♖fc7
e3 43 ♖c8+ ♗f8 44 ♖bb8 ♖f5 45
♔g2 △ ♖xf8+ 1-0 Shamkovich

156 Kuzmin-Browne
Reykjavik 78

1 e4 c5 2 ♘f3 d6 3 ♗b5+ ♗d7 4 a4?!
♘c6 5 0-0 ♘f6 6 ♕e2 a6?! 6...g6;
6...♖c8!? 7 ♗xc6 ♗xc6 8 ♘c3 8 e5!?
dxe5 9 ♘xe5 ♖c8 10 ♘xc6 ♖xc6
11 a5 e6 12 ♘a3 += e6 9 d4 cxd4
10 ♘xd4 ♗e7 11 ♖d1 ♕c7 11...♗d7
12 a5! 12 ♗f4! e5 12...0-0 13 e5!
dxe5 14 ♗xe5 ♕a5 15 ♘b3 ♕b6 16
a5; 13...♘d5?! 13 ♘xc6 bxc6 14 ♗g5
a5! 14...0-0? 15 ♗xf6 ♗xf6 16 a5!
△ ♘a4-b6± 15 ♕c4! ♖c8 16 ♗xf6
♗xf6 17 b4! 0-0! 17...axb4? 18
♕xb4 ♗e7 19 a5± 18 bxa5 18 b5?
cxb5 19 ♕xc7 ♖xc7 20 ♘xb5 ♖xc2=
♗e7! 19 ♖ab1 19 a6?! ♕a5! △ d5,
♖fd8 ♕xa5 20 ♖b7 d5! 21 ♕b3
21 exd5 cxd5 22 ♕xd5 ♕xc3= ♗c5!

21...d4? 22 ♖xe7 dxc3 23 ♖dd7
♖b8 24 ♖xf7! +- 22 exd5 ♗d4!
23 ♘e2 ♕xd5! 24 ♔f1?! 24 ♕xd5
cxd5 25 ♘xd4 exd4 26 ♖xd4 ♖xc2
27 g3 += ♕c5 25 ♘g3 25 ♘xd4 exd4
26 ♖d7 ♕e5= ♕a5 26 ♘f5 ♖a8 27
♖b4 c5 28 ♖c4 ♕a6! 29 ♕d3 ♕e6
29...♖fd8 30 ♖e1 ♖fe8 =+ 31 c3?!
e4! 31...♗xf2 32 ♘xg7! =+

32 ♘xd4 cxd4 33 ♕xd4 ♕a6 33...
♖ad8 34 ♖xe4! 34 ♖e2 34 ♔g1??
♖ad8 35 ♖xe4 ♖f8 -+ h6 34...h5!?
35 ♕d5 ♖ac8 36 ♖xc8 ♖xc8 37 ♕b5
37 ♕xe4 ♖xc3= ♕a7 38 ♕b4 ♕a6 39
♕b5 ♕e6= 40 ♖e3 f5 41 g3 g5 42
♕b7 ♖e8 43 ♕c7 ♖c8 44 ♕b7 ♖e8
45 ♕c7 ♖c8 46 ♕b7 ½-½ Browne

157 Haag-Molnar Hungary 78

1 e4 c5 2 ♘f3 d6 3 ♗b5+ ♗d7 4
c4 ♘c6 4...e5! 5 0-0 5 d4!; 5 ♘c3!
e5 6 ♘c3 g6 7 d3 ♗g7 8 ♘d5 f6?!
8...h6 += △ a3, b4 9 a3 ♘ge7 10
b4! 0-0 10...cxb4 11 axb4!? (11 ♘xe7)
♘xd5 12 cxd5 ♘xb4 13 ♗xd7+ ♕xd7
14 ♗a3 ≈/± 11 ♖b1 ♗g4 12 bxc5
♘d4

Diagram

13 ♘xd4!? 13 ♘xe7+ ♕xe7 14 cxd6
♕xd6 15 c5!± ♗xd1 14 ♘e6 ♕a5?

14...♘xd5 15 exd5 ♕e7 16 cxd6 ♕xd6 17 c5±; 14...♕b8!? 15 ♖xd1! ♘xd5 16 cxd5 dxc5 17 ♘xc5≈ **15 ♖xd1 ♘c6 16 a4! ♘d4 17 ♘xd4!?** 17 ♗d2 exd4 18 cxd6 a6 19 ♗d7 ♕c5! 20 ♗f4 ♚h8 21 h4 ♖ad8 22 ♖xb7 ♖f7? 22...♕a3! 23 ♖e1! ♕xd3 24 ♗g4!± **23 ♖c7 ♕a3 24 ♗e6 ♖ff8 25 c5 ♕xa4 26 ♖b1 ♖fe8 27 ♖xg7 ♖xe6 28 ♖bb7 ♕d1+ 29 ♚h2 ♕h5 30 ♗g3** 30 ♖xh7+ ♚g5 31 f3 gxh4 32 ♗f4 h3 33 g4 ♕h4 34 ♗g3 ♕h6 35 ♘f4 ♖e5 36 ♖gc7 ♖ee8 37 ♘h5 f5 38 ♗f4 ♕g6 39 exf5 ♖e2+ 40 ♚xh3 ♕g3 41 ♘f6 1-0 Haag

158 Kim-Rashkovsky USSR 78
1 e4 c5 2 ♘f3 d6 3 ♗b5+ ♗d7 4 ♗xd7+ ♘xd7!? 4...♕xd7 **5 0-0!** 5 d4 cxd4 6 ♕xd4 ♘gf6 7 0-0 ♕b6!=; 5 c4 ♘gf6 6 ♘c3 e6 7 0-0 ♗e7 8 d4 cxd4 9 ♘xd4 a6 10 b3 0-0 11 ♗b2 ♕c7 12 ♕e2 ♖fe8 Δ ♗f8∝ Sharif-Andersson, Haifa 76; 5...g6 6 0-0 ♗g7 7 ♘c3 ♘gf6!?≈ **♘gf6 6 ♖e1** 6 ♕e2 e6 7 c3 ♗e7 8 d4 0-0 9 e5 ♘e8=; 7 b3!? ♗e7 8 ♗b2 0-0 9 c4 += **e6 7 c3** 7 c4 ♗e7 8 ♘c3 0-0 9 d4 cxd4 10 ♘xd4 ♖c8 11 b3 a6 12 ♗b2 ♕a5=; 7 d3 ♗e7 8 d4 cxd4 9 cxd4 d5 10 e5 ♘e4 =+ **11 ♘bd2 ♘xd2 12 ♗xd2 0-0 13 ♕b3 ♕b6 14 ♖ec1 ♖ac8** 14... ♗d8? 15 ♕a4! +− **15 ♖xc8 ♖xc8**

16 ♕xb6 ♘xb6 17 ♖c1 ♖c6 18 b3 f6 19 ♘e1 19 exf6 gxf6 20 ♚f1 ♗a3 21 ♖xc6 bxc6 22 ♚e2 ♗d6 Δ e5 =+ **fxe5 20 dxe5 ♘d7 21 ♘d3 ♕f7 22 ♚f1 ♗c5! 23 ♚e2 h5∓ 24 f3?** 24 ♘xc5 ♗xc5 25 ♚d3 ♘xd3 25 ♕xd3 ♖xc1 26 ♗xc1 ♚g6 −+ **27 ♗e3 b6** 27...a6 28 ♚d4∓ **28 g3 ♚f5 29 h3 g5 30 ♗d4 h4 31 gxh4 gxh4 32 ♗f2 ♚xe5 33 ♗e1 ♚f4 34 ♚e2 e5 35 a4 d4 0-1 Gufeld**

159 Mednis-Byrne USA Final 78
1 e4 c5 2 ♘f3 d6 3 ♗b5+ ♗d7 4 ♗xd7+ ♕xd7 5 c4 ♘c6 6 ♘c3 g6 6...♘f6 7 0-0 g6 8 d4 cxd4 9 ♘xd4 ♗g7 10 ♖e1!? N 0-0 11 ♗g5?! ♖ac8 12 ♘de2 ♘e5! 13 ♗xf6 ♗xf6= Tarjan-Zuckerman, USA Final 78 **7 d4 cxd4 8 ♘xd4 ♗g7 9 ♗e3 ♘f6 10 f3 0-0 11 0-0 ♖fc8 12 b3 ♘e8** 12... ♕c7!? Δ ♕a5 **13 ♕d2** 13 ♖c1 ♘c7?! 14 ♘de2 ♕e8 15 ♕d2 += Kapengut-Muhin, USSR Final 72; 13...b6 **b6 14 ♖ad1!? N ♖ab8 15 f4 += e6 16 h3 a6 17 ♖f2** 17 a4!? **b5 18 cxb5 ♘xd4 19 ♗xd4 ♗xd4 20 ♕xd4 ♕c5 21 ♘e2 axb5 22 f5!**

22...e5! 23 ♕d3 23 ♕e3 ♕b6!= **b4! 24 ♖df1 ♕a7 25 ♚h2 ♖b7 26 ♕d2 ♖cc7 27 ♘g3** 27 ♕h6 ♖c2 **♖c3 28 ♖e2** 28 fxg6 hxg6 29 ♕g5 ♕e3 30

♕g4 ♘g7∝ ♕a6≈ ½-½ **Mednis**

160 Dolmatov-Azmajparashvili
USSR 78

**1 e4 c5 2 ♘f3 d6 3 ♗b5+ ♗d7 4 ♗xd7+
♕xd7 5 0-0 ♘f6** 5...e6 6 c4 ♗e7 7
d4 cxd4 8 ♘xd4 ♘f6 9 ♘c3 0-0 10
b3 a6 11 ♗b2 ♖c8 12 ♕e2 += Barle-
Andersson, Pula 75; 5...♘c6 **6 ♕e2**
6 ♘c3 ♘c6 7 d4 cxd4 8 ♘xd4 g6=;
6 e5!? += **♘c6 7 c3 e6 8 d4 cxd4
9 cxd4 d5 10 e5 ♘e4 11 ♗e3** 11
♖d1 ♗e7 12 ♘e1 h6 13 f3 ♘g5∝;
12 ♘d2 ♘xd2 Δ ♗e7= **f6!** 11...♗e7?
♘e1 Δ f3 +- **12 ♘bd2** 12 exf6?!
gxf6 =+ **♗e7?** 12...♘xd2 13 ♕xd2
fxe5 Δ ♗e7∝ **13 exf6 gxf6 14 ♘xe4
dxe4 15 ♘d2 ♕d5 16 ♕g4 0-0-0** 16...
f5?! 17 ♕h5+ ♔d7 18 ♖d1± **17
♕xe4 ♕xe4** 17...♘xd4? 18 ♖ac1+
♔b8 19 ♗xd4 ♕xe4 20 ♗xa7+ +-;
18...♘c6 19 ♗xa7! ♕xd2 20 ♖xc6!
+- **18 ♘xe4 ♘xd4 19 ♖ac1+ ♔b8
20 ♖c4 ♘f5!** 20...♘c6 21 ♘c5 ♗xc5
22 ♖xc5 += **21 ♗c5 ♗xc5 22 ♖xc5
b6! 23 ♖c3 ♘d4 24 ♖e3 ♖hf8 25
f4! ♖f7 26 g3 ♘f5 27 ♖c3 ♖d4!
28 ♖e1 ♘d6! 29 ♘xd6+ ♖xd6 30
♖e2 ♖c7?!** 30...♖e7 31 f5 e5 +=
31 ♖ce3 ♖cc6?! 32 ♔g2 32 g4! Δ
♖h3± ♔c7 33 g4 ♖c4! 34 ♖xe6
♖xf4 35 ♔g3 ♖f1= 36 ♖e7+ ♖d7
37 ♔h4 f5! 38 g5 f4 39 ♔h5 f3 40
♖c2+ ♔d8 41 ♖xd7+ ♔xd7 42 ♔h6
♖g1! ½-½ **Gufeld**

161 Taulbut-Georgiev
Groningen 77/78

**1 e4 c5 2 ♘f3 d6 3 ♗b5+ ♗d7 4
♗xd7+ ♕xd7 5 0-0 ♘f6** 5...♘c6 6 c3
♘f6 7 d4 cxd4 8 cxd4 d5 9 e5 ♘g8
10 a3 e6 11 b4 += Dolmatov-
Georgiev, Groningen 77/78; 7...♘xe4
8 d5 ♘e5 9 ♖e1 ♘xf3+ 10 ♕xf3

♘f6 11 ♘a3∝ Taulbut-A.Rodriguez,
IBM II 78 **6 e5! dxe5 7 ♘xe5 ♕c7?!**
7...♕c8 8 ♕f3 e6 9 ♘c3 ♗e7 10 d3
0-0 11 ♗f4 ♘a6 12 ♖fe1 ♘b4 13
♖ac1 ♘fd5= Bellin-Ubilava, Tbilisi 77
8 d4 ♘c6 8...e6 9 ♗f4 ♗d6 10 ♘a3!±
Δ ♘b5/♘ac4; 8...cxd4 9 ♗f4 ♕b6
10 ♘d2± **9 ♗f4 0-0-0 10 c3!** 10
♘g6? e5∓ **♘xe5** 10...cxd4 11 ♘xc6
♕xc6 12 cxd4± **11 ♗xe5 ♕c6 12
♘d2 e6 13 b4! ♗d5** 13...c4 14 ♕e2
b5 15 a4 **14 ♕f3 f6 15 ♗g3 h5 16
h3 g5 17 c4** 17 bxc5?! g4∝ **♗f4
18 d5 exd5 19 ♗xf4 gxf4 20 b5 ♕d7
21 ♖fd1 ♕f5?** 21...d4 22 ♘e4 ♗e7
23 ♘c3 Δ ♘d5± **22 cxd5 ♖xd5
23 ♘c4 ♖xd1+ 24 ♖xd1 ♖h7 25
♕a3 ♖d7** 25...b6 26 ♘xb6+ +- **26
♖e1 ♕d5 27 ♕xa7 ♕xc4 28 ♕a8+
♔c7 29 ♕a5+ ♔d6** 29...b6 30 ♕a7+
30 ♕b6+ ♔d5 31 ♕e6+ 1-0 Taulbut

Najdorf

162 Parma-Hamann Kiel 78

**1 e4 c5 2 ♘f3 d6 3 d4 cxd4 4 ♘xd4
♘f6 5 ♘c3 a6 6 a4!? e6** 6...e5!?
7 ♗e2 ♘c6 8 ♗e3 ♗d7?! 8...d5! (Δ
♗b4) 9 ♘xc6 bxc6 10 e5 ♘d7 11
f4 c5∝ **9 f4 ♗e7 10 0-0 0-0 11 ♔h1
♕c7 12 ♕e1 ♘xd4 13 ♗xd4 ♗c6**
13...e5 14 fxe5 dxe5 15 ♕g3 ♗d6
16 ♗e3 Δ ♘g5± **14 ♕g3± g6 15 f5!**
e5 15...♗xe4? 16 ♘xe4 ♗xe4 17
f6 Δ ♕h4-h6 **16 ♗e3 b5 17 ♗h6
♖fc8** 17...♖fe8 Δ ♔h8, ♘g8 **18 ♗d3
b4?** 18...♔h8 Δ ♘g8

Diagram

19 ♗c4!! ♔h8 19...bxc3 20 fxg6 hxg6
21 ♕xg6+ +-; 19...♘h5 20 ♕g4
♘f6 21 fxg6!! ♘xg4 22 ♗xf7+ ♔h8
23 g7 mate **20 ♗xf7! bxc3 21 fxg6**

hxg6 22 &g7+! ♛xg7 23 ♛xg6+ ♛f8
24 &e6 △ ♛f7 mate/♛g8 mate &xe4
25 ♛f7 mate 1-0 Maric

163 Dorfman-Tukmakov Lvov 78
1 e4 c5 2 ♘f3 d6 3 d4 cxd4 4 ♘xd4
♘f6 5 ♘c3 a6 6 &c4 e6 7 &b3 b5
8 0-0 &e7 8...♘b7 9 ♖e1 ♘bd7 10
&g5 ♘c5 11 &d5! b4 12 &xb7 ♘xb7
13 ♘d5!± Akopian-Agzamov, USSR
76 9 a4!? 9 ♛f3 ♛b6 10 &e3 ♛b7
11 ♛g3 g6 12 &h6!± Ermenkov-
Ostojic, Kecskemet 77; 9...♛c7 10
♛g3 ♘c6!=; 9 f4 0-0 10 e5 dxe5 11
fxe5 &c5 12 &e3 ♘fd7 13 ♛h5 &xd4
14 &xd4 ♘c6 15 ♖ad1 += Bravo-
Quinteros, Fortaleza 75; 11...♘fd7
12 ♛h5 ♘c6 13 ♘xc6 ♛b6+ 14 ♛h1!
♛xc6 15 ♖f3 &b7 16 &f4! +=
Bednarski-Dueball, Vratsa 75 b4 10
♘a2 0-0 10...♛b6!? 11 c3 bxc3 12
♘xc3 0-0 13 a5 ♛b7 14 f4 ♘c6 15
♘xc6 ♛xc6 =+ 11 ♘xb4 ♛b6 12
c3 a5!? N 12...♘xe4 13 &c3 ♛c7
14 f4 += 13 ♘d3 ♘xe4 14 ♘f4!?
14 &e3 ♘a6 15 &c2 ♘f6 15...d5?!
16 &e3 ♛b7!? 17 ♘h5! ♘xh5 18
♛xh5 g6 19 ♛h6 &f6 20 ♘f3 &g7
21 ♛h4 ♛xb2 22 ♖fc1 ♛b8 23 ♘g5
h6 24 ♘h3 e5! 25 g4≈ ♘c5! 26
♖xh6 ♘e6 27 &e4 ♖a7 28 ♖ab1 ♛c7
29 &d5 △ &xe6, ♘g5 +- ♛e7 30
&g5 ♛d7 31 &e3 ♛e7 32 ♛xe7 32

&g5 ♛d7 ♖xe7 33 f3 ♘c7 34 &b3
&e6 35 ♖d1 e4= 36 &xe6 ♘xe6
36...♖xe6?! 37 ♘g5 37 ♖xd6 exf3
38 ♛f2 &xc3 39 ♛xf3 &b4 40 ♖d3
½-½ Gufeld

164 Matanovic-Hulak
Jugoslavia Final 78
1 e4 c5 2 ♘f3 d6 3 d4 cxd4 4 ♘xd4
♘f6 5 ♘c3 a6 6 &e2 e5 7 ♘b3 &e7
8 a4!? &e6 9 f4 ♛c7 10 f5 &c4 11
&xc4 ♛xc4 12 ♛e2 ♛c7 13 0-0±
♘bd7 14 a5 b5 15 axb6 ♛xb6+ 16
♛h1 0-0 17 &e3 ♛b7 18 ♛d3 &d8?!
19 ♖fd1 &c7 20 h3 ♖fc8 21 ♖a4
h6 22 &g1 &b8?! 22...♘b6? 23 ♘a5
+-; 22...♘b8!? 23 ♖da1 ♘c5 24
♘xc5 dxc5 25 ♛c4! ♖c6 25...♛xb2?
26 ♖b1 ♛xc2 27 ♖a2 +- 26 b3
&c7 27 ♖d1 ♖d8 28 ♘d5 ♘xd5 29
♖xd5 ♖cd6 29...&d6 30 ♖a1 △ ♖ad1
+- 30 ♖xd6 ♖xd6 31 ♖a1 +- 1-0
31...♖c6 32 ♖d1 △ ♖d5/♖d7 Bellin

165 Mestel-Browne
Lone Pine 78
1 e4 c5 2 ♘f3 d6 3 d4 cxd4 4 ♘xd4
♘f6 5 ♘c3 a6 6 &e2 e5 7 ♘b3 &e7
8 &e3 &e6 9 0-0 ♘bd7 10 a4 0-0
11 a5 ♖c8! 11...♛c7?! 12 ♘d5!
♘xd5 13 exd5 &f5 14 c4± 12 ♛d2
12 f4 ♛c7 13 ♖fc1?! 13 ♖fd1 ♖fd8
14 f3= ♛c6! 14 &f3 &c4! =+ 15
♛d1 ♖fd8 16 ♘d5?! 16 ♘d2 ♘xd5
17 exd5 ♛b5! 18 &e4 g6! 18...♘f6?
19 &f5! ♖a8 20 &b6! ♖f8 21 ♘d2!
♘xd5? 22 ♘xc4 ♛xc4 23 b3 ♛c6
24 &e4 ♘c3 25 &xc6 ♘xd1 26 &xb7
♖ab8 27 &xa6 +- 19 ♘d2 &xd5 -+
20 c4 &xc4 21 ♖xc4 ♖xc4 22 ♘xc4
♛xc4 23 &xb7 ♛b5! 24 ♛f3 ♛g7?!
24...♖b8! 25 ♘c6 ♛xb2 -+ 25 b3
&f6 26 &c6 ♛b4 26...♛xb3 27 ♘h6+
+- 27 &xd7 e4? 27...♖xd7∓

28 ♗h6+ ♔xh6 29 ♕xf6 ♖xd7 30 h4 d5?! 30...♕xb3 **31 ♕f4+ ♔g7 32 ♕xe4 ♕c3! 31 ♕xa6 ♕c3! 32 ♖f1 d4 33 ♕b5 ♕c7 34 ♕b4 e3! 35 fxe3 dxe3 36 ♖e1 ♕e5** 36...♕g3? **37 ♕f8+ ♔h5 38 ♕c5+ 37 ♕g4 ♖d3 38 b4 ♖a3 39 ♕f3 f5?** 39...♕d4! **40 g3 ♖b3 41 a6 ♕d4 42 ♕f4+ ♔xf4 43 gxf4 ♖xb4 44 ♖a1 ♖b8?** 44...e2! **45 a7?** ♖a4!; **45 ♔f2 45 ♔g2 ♖a8 46 ♔f3 ♔h5 47 ♔xe3 ♔xh4?? 47...♔g4= 48 ♔f3 1-0 Browne**

166 Tseshkovsky-Tukmakov
Lvov 78
1 e4 c5 2 ♘f3 d6 3 d4 cxd4 4 ♘xd4 ♘f6 5 ♘c3 a6 6 f4 ♕c7 7 ♗e2 7 ♗d3 g6 8 0-0 ♗g7 9 ♔h1 ♘bd7 10 ♕e1 b5 11 ♘f3 e5 12 fxe5 dxe5 13 ♗g5 ♗b7 14 a4! Tseshkovsky-Savon, Sochi 75 **e5 8 ♘b3 b5 9 ♗f3 ♗b7 10 0-0 ♘bd7 11 a3 exf4** 11...♗e7 **12 ♗xf4 ♘e5 13 ♘d4 g6 14 ♔h1! ♖d8** 14... ♗g7 **15 ♘dxb5! axb5 16 ♘xb5 ♕e7 17 ♘xd6+ ♔f8 18 ♘xb7 ♘xf3 19 ♗d6 15 ♗g5 ♗e7** 15...♗g7 **16 ♗e2± 16 ♗h6 ♕c5 17 ♘b3 ♕c8 18 ♘a5 ♖a8 19 ♗g7 ♖g8 20 ♗xf6 ♗xf6 21 a4! b4 22 ♘d5 ♗xd5 23 ♕xd5 ♕e7** 23...♕xc2 **24 ♗d1 24 ♗e2 ♕c5 25 ♖ae1? 25** ♗xa6 **♖d7 26 ♖f4 ♖c7 27 ♖ef1 ♕xd5 28 exd5 ♖xc2 29 ♗xa6 ♗g5? 29...♖a8 30 ♘c6+ ♖xc6 31**

dxc6 ♗xf4 32 c7! ♗e3 33 c8♕ ♖xc8 34 ♗xc8 ♘d3 35 g3 d5 36 a5 ♔d8 37 ♗b7 f5 38 ♗xd5 ♘xb2 39 ♖b1 ♗d4 40 a6 ♘d3 41 ♖b3 1-0

167 Kavalek-Byrne
USA Final 78
1 e4 c5 2 ♘f3 d6 3 d4 cxd4 4 ♘xd4 ♘f6 5 ♘c3 a6 6 f4 g6 6...e5; 6...e6; 6...♕c7 **7 ♘f3 ♗g7 8 e5 ♘h5!?** N 8... ♘g4 **9 h3 ♘h6 10 ♗c4 0-0 11 g4±** 9 ♗c4 0-0 10 ♘g5! △ g4

10...e6?! 10...♕c7!? **11 ♗xf7+ ♖xf7 12 ♘xf7 ♔xf7 13 g4 dxe5 14 gxh5 exf4∞;** 11 ♗b3!? dxe5 12 ♘d5 ♕d8 13 ♘xf7!; 12...♕d6 13 f5∞ **11 g4 ♘xf4 12 ♗xf4 dxe5 13 ♕xd8 ♖xd8 14 ♗e3± h6 15 ♘ge4 b5 16 ♗b3 f5 17 gxf5 gxf5 18 ♗b6! ♖f8 19 ♘d6** △ ♘xc8 **♗d7 20 0-0-0 +− ♔h7 21 ♖hg1 e4 22 ♘e2** △ ♘f4 **♗e5 23 h4 a5 24 a3 ♖a6 25 ♗c7 ♖a7 26 ♗b6 ♖a6 27 ♗c5!** △ ♘xe4 **♖f6 28 ♗a2 ♖g6 29 ♘f7! ♖xg1 30 ♖xg1 ♗f6 31 ♗d4 ♗xd4 32 ♘xd4 b4 33 ♘e5 ♗c8 34 ♘xf5! 1-0** 34...exf5 35 ♗g8+ ♔h8 36 ♘f7 mate **Shamkovich**

168 Rusakov-Moiseev USSR 78
1 e4 c5 2 ♘f3 d6 3 d4 cxd4 4 ♘xd4 ♘f6 5 ♘c3 a6 6 g3!? e5 6...♗g4 **7 ♘de2 7 ♘b3 ♗e7 8 ♗g2 ♗e6 9 0-0**

117

0-0 10 f4 ♘bd7 11 f5 ♗c4 12 ♖e1
b5= Kurajica-Vujacic, Stockholm 75/
76 **♘bd7** 7...♗e6 8 ♗g2 ♘bd7 9 a4
♗e7 10 0-0 ♖c8 11 h3 ♕c7 12 ♗e3
0-0 13 g4 += Holmov-Petkevich,
USSR 76 **8 a4 ♗e7 9 ♗g2 0-0 10 0-0
♖b8** 10...b6 11 ♘d5?! ♘xd5 12
exd5 a5! =+ Mestel-Ghitescu, Moscow
77 **11 a5** 11 h3 b5 12 axb5 axb5
13 ♖a7?! b4 14 ♘d5 ♗b7 15 ♗d2!∝
Mestel-Balashov, Moscow 77; 13 b4!?
b5 12 axb6 **♘xb6** 12...♕xb6!? **13
b3** += **♗b7 14 ♕d3! ♕c7** 14...d5?!
15 exd5 ♘bxd5 16 ♘xd5 ♘xd5
17 ♖d1± **15 h3 ♖bc8 16 ♗e3 ♘bd7
17 ♕d1** △ ♘d5; 17 ♖a2!± **♖fd8
18 ♖a2 ♘c5 19 ♘d5 ♘xd5 20 exd5
f5 21 f4!** += **g6 22 c4 ♖b8 23 ♕c2
♗c8 24 ♖b1 ♗f6 25 ♔h2 ♖e8 26 b4
♘e4! 27 ♖b3! h5!? 28 fxe5** 28 ♗xe4?!
fxe4 29 ♕xe4 ♗f5 **♗xe5 29 ♗f4
♕g7! 30 ♗xe5 ♕xe5 31 ♕b2! ♕e7?**
31...♕xb2 +=; 31...h4!? 32 ♕xe5
♖xe5 33 gxh4 a5!∝ **32 ♘f4 ♘h7 33
h4!± ♘f6 34 ♗f3 ♘g4+ 35 ♔g2 ♘e3+
36 ♖xe3! ♕xe3 37 ♕f6 1-0 Gufeld**

169 Holmov-Vitolins USSR 78

**1 e4 c5 2 ♘f3 d6 3 d4 cxd4 4 ♘xd4
♘f6 5 ♘c3 a6 6 g3 g6?!** 6...b5 7 ♗g2
♗b7 8 0-0 e6 9 ♖e1 △ a4±; 6...e5
7 ♘de2 ♗e7 8 ♗g2 ♘bd7!= **7 ♗g2
♗g7 8 0-0 0-0 9 h3** += **♕c7** 9...♘bd7
10 ♗g5 h6 11 ♗e3 += **10 ♗g5 ♘bd7
11 ♕d2 ♘b6 12 b3 e5!? 13 ♘de2
♗e6 14 ♖fd1 ♖fd8 15 ♖ac1 ♘c8!?**
△ b5, ♘b6 **16 ♘d5! ♗xd5 17 exd5
♘e7 18 c4 ♘e8 19 g4!±** **f6 20 ♗e3
f5 21 ♕b4?** 21 f4!± ♕d7 22 ♗b6
fxg4! 22...♖dc8 23 c5!± **23 ♗xd8
♖xd8 24 ♕c3?!** 24 hxg4 ♕xg4 25
♕xb7 ♘f5 += **♘f6≈ 25 hxg4 ♘xg4
26 ♗h3 h5 27 ♘g3** 27 f3 e4 **♘f5
28 ♕d3 ♘h4 29 f3 ♖f8 30 fxg4 hxg4?**

30...♖f3! 31 ♕e4 hxg4 32 ♖d3 ♖f4∝;
31 ♕e2 hxg4 32 ♖d3 ♖xd3 △ gxh3∝
**31 ♗g2 ♘f3+ 32 ♗xf3 ♖xf3 33 ♕xg6
+- ♖xg3+ 34 ♔h2 ♖h3+ 35 ♔g2
♖h6 36 ♕g5 e4 37 ♖h1 ♖f6 38 ♖cf1
♖f3 39 ♕g6! 1-0 Gufeld**

170 Vakhrushev-Soloviev
USSR 78

**1 e4 c5 2 ♘f3 d6 3 d4 cxd4 4 ♘xd4
♘f6 5 ♘c3 a6 6 ♗g5 ♘bd7 7 f4 ♕b6
8 ♘b3 h6** 8...♕e3+ 9 ♕e2 ♕xe2+
10 ♗xe2 += Polugaevsky **9 ♗xf6**
9 ♗h4 ♕e3+ 10 ♗e2 ♕xf4 11 ♗g3
♕e3 12 ♘d5 ♘xd5 13 exd5 ♘f6
14 ♗f2 ♕e5 15 c4 g6∝ Boleslavsky
♘xf6 10 ♗e2 10 e5 dxe5 11 fxe5
♘g4 12 ♕e2 ♘e3= Polugaevsky;
11...♕e3+?! 12 ♕e2 ♕xe2+ 13 ♗xe2
♘g4 14 ♘d5± e6? 10...♕e3!≈ **11
♕d3!± ♕c7 12 ♗f3 ♗e7 13 0-0-0 ♘d7**
13...♗d7 △ 0-0-0 **14 ♔b1 b5?! 15
e5 d5 16 ♗xd5! exd5 17 ♘xd5 ♕d8
18 ♕g3 ♔f8** 18...0-0 19 ♘d4! +−
**19 ♘d4 ♘b8 20 ♘xe7 ♕xe7 21 f5
♕c7 22 f6 gxf6**

23 ♘f5!! +− **♗xf5** 23...♖g8 24 ♕c3
♘c6 25 ♕c5+! +−; 23...♖h7 24 exf6!
+− **24 exf6 ♕xc2+** 24...♕xg3? 25
♖d8 mate **25 ♔a1 ♕e8 26 ♕g7 ♖f8**
26...♘d7 27 ♖he1+ ♗e4 28 ♕xh8+
♘f8 29 ♖d4 +− **27 ♕xf8+! 1-0 Lysenko**

171 Berlinsky-Dvoris
USSR 78
1 e4 c5 2 ♘f3 d6 3 d4 cxd4 4 ♘xd4
♘f6 5 ♘c3 a6 6 ♗g5 e6 7 f4 b5 8 e5
dxe5 9 fxe5 ♕c7 10 ♕e2 10 exf6
♘fd7 11 0-0-0 ♗b7 12 ♕g4 12 ♕h5
g6 13 ♕h4 ♗g7 14 ♗e7 ♕xe5 15 ♗xb5
♕h5!∓ Quinteros-Polugaevsky, Manila
76 ♕b6!? 12...♕xe5 13 ♗e2 h6 13...
♘xe5? 14 ♕h5 ♘bd7 15 ♖he1 ♘f6
16 ♗xf6 gxf6 17 ♘xe6! ♕xe6 18
♗g4 f5 19 ♔b1 ♗d6 20 ♗xf5± Minic
14 ♕h3 14 ♗f4!? ♘xe5 15 ♖he1
♘bd7 16 ♗h4 g5! 16...g6?! 17 ♗g4!
h5 18 ♗xe6!± Kavalek-Polugaevsky,
Las Palmas 74 17 ♗xg5 ♖g8 17...
hxg5!? Balashov 18 ♘xe6∞ hxg5
19 ♗g4?! N 19 ♗h5 ♗d6 20 ♕f5
♖h8 21 ♗xf7+ ♔e7 22 ♘xg5 +=
Kavalek-Polugaevsky, Manila 75 fxe6
20 ♗xe6 0-0-0 21 ♖xe5 21 ♗xg8
g4! g4 22 ♕h7?! 22 ♗xg4 =/=+ ♖g7
23 ♕f5 ♔b8? 23...♗d6! 24 ♘d5
♕a7! 25 ♘f6? (25 ♖e3! ∞/=+) ♗xe5
26 ♗xd7+ ♖gxd7 27 ♘xd7 ♕e3+
28 ♔b1 ♔c7! −+; 24...♕c6 25 ♖e3
24 ♗xd7 ♖gxd7 24...♖g5?! 25 ♕f4!
25 ♖xd7 ♕g1+ 26 ♔d2 ♕xg2+ 27
♔d3 ♖c8 28 ♖e6 b4? 28...♕h3+
29 ♖b6!± ♕h3+ 30 ♔d4 ♕h8+ 30...
♗c5+ 31 ♕xc5 ♖xc5 32 ♖bxb7+ ♔c8
33 ♔xc5 bxc3 34 ♖dc7+! ♔d8 35
♖h7 31 ♕e5+ ♕xe5+ 32 ♔xe5 ♖c7
33 ♖xc7 ♔xc7 34 ♘a4 +− ♗c6 35
♖xa6 ♗d6+ 36 ♔f5 ♗d7+ 37 ♔g5
♗e7+ 38 ♔h5 ♔b7 39 ♖h6 ♗f5 40
b3 ♔c7 41 c3 1-0 Lysenko

172 Saharov-Feldman
Corr. 77
1 e4 c5 2 ♘f3 d6 3 d4 cxd4 4 ♘xd4
♘f6 5 ♘c3 a6 6 ♗g5 e6 7 f4 b5?!
8 e5 dxe5 9 fxe5 ♕c7 10 ♕e2 ♘fd7
11 0-0-0 ♗b7 12 ♕g4 12 ♘xe6!?

fxe6 13 ♕g4 Winslow-Browne, Canada
76 ♕xe5 12...♕b6 13 ♗e2 ♘xe5
14 ♕h3±; 13 ♗xb5!? 13 ♗e2 13
♗xb5 axb5 14 ♖he1 h5 15 ♕h4
♕c5 16 ♕g3 ♘f6!?∞; 14 ♘cxb5
f5!? 15 ♘xf5?! exf5 16 ♕c4 ♘a6?
17 ♖he1 ♗e4 18 ♖d5± 16...♗e7!
♘f6? 13...h6? 14 ♗f4 ♕c5 15 ♖he1
+−; 13...♗c5!? 14 ♗xf6 ♕xf6 14...
gxf6 15 ♖he1 ♕g5+ 16 ♕xg5 fxg5
17 ♗h5 +− 15 ♘cxb5! axb5 16 ♗xb5+
♔e7 17 ♕g3! 1-0 17...e5 18 ♖he1
+− Kasparov

173 Knox-Curtin
Middlesborough 78
1 e4 c5 2 ♘f3 d6 3 d4 cxd4 4 ♘xd4
♘f6 5 ♘c3 a6 6 ♗g5 e6 7 f4 b5 8 e5
dxe5 9 fxe5 ♕c7 10 ♕e2 ♘fd7 11
0-0-0 ♗b7 12 ♕h5?! 12 ♕g4± g6
13 ♕h4 ♗g7 14 ♗xb5! ♗xe5? 14...
axb5 15 ♘cxb5 ♕b6 16 ♗d8! +−;
14...0-0!∞

15 ♘xe6! N fxe6 15...♕b6 16 ♘g7+
♗xg7 17 ♖he1+ +− 16 ♕b4! ♗d6
17 ♗xd7+ ♘xd7 17...♔xd7 18 ♖xd6+
+− 18 ♕xd6! 18 ♖xd6?! 0-0! ♕xd6
19 ♖xd6 ♘f8 20 ♖g1 h6 21 ♖b6 hxg5
22 ♖xb7 ♖xh2 23 ♘e4! +− ♘d7
24 ♖d1 ♘e5 25 ♘f6+ ♔f8 26 ♖f1
1-0 26...♘f7 27 ♘g4 ♖h7 28 ♘e5
+− Knox

174 Timman-Ribli Niksic 78
1 e4 c5 2 &f3 d6 3 d4 cxd4 4 &xd4
&f6 5 &c3 a6 6 &g5 e6 7 f4 &b6 8
&d2 &xb2 9 &b1 9 &b3 &a3 10
&xf6 gxf6 11 &e2 &c6! 12 0-0 &d7
13 &h1 &c8 14 f5?! &e5 15 fxe6
fxe6 16 &h5+ &d8 17 &e2 &c7 18
&f4 &b8∓ Ligterink-Geller, Wijk aan
Zee 77 &a3 10 f5 &c6 11 fxe6 fxe6
12 &xc6 bxc6 13 e5 dxe5 13...&d5?!
14 &xf6 gxf6 15 &e4 &e7 16 &e2
h5 17 &b3 &a4

18 &xf6+! 18 c4 f5 19 0-0 fxe4 20
&e3 &xa2∞ Kavalek-Fischer, Sousse
67 &xf6 19 c4 &h4+ 20 g3 &e7 21
0-0 &d7 21...&a7 22 &b8 &c7 23
&d3 &c5+ 24 &h1 &e7 25 &g6 &d6
26 &f6 &e8 27 &xh5 &ce7 28 &d1+
&d4 29 &xd4+ exd4 30 &xd4+ &c7
31 &b6+ &d7 32 &d4+ = Vitolins-
Gavrikov, USSR; 23 &d3 &g8 24
&h7 &g7 25 &h6± 22 &b7 &d8?
22...c5! 23 &d1 &c6 24 &f3 &d6;
23 &d3!? 23 &d3 &c5+ 23...&g8 24
&f2 +− 24 &h1 &g8 25 &e2! &e7
25...&h8 26 &g5 &c2 27 &xe5 +−
26 &xh5 &g7 26...&d4 27 c5 &df8
28 &xf8 &xf8 29 &g5+ +− 27 &h6
&xc4 27...&dg8 28 &f6+ &d6 29
&d1+ &xd1 30 &xd1 +− 28 &xg7+
&d6 29 &f6 &d4!? 30 &fb1 &d3
30...&c2!? (Δ &f5) 31 &g6± 31

&7b3 +− &f5 32 &xd8 &xh5 33
&b8+?! 33 &f8+ &d5 34 &e7 &d5
34 &c7 &h7 35 &e1 &f7 36 &d3
&c4 37 &d2 37 &b8! &xd3 38 &b3+
&c3 39 &d1+ &e4 40 &c2+ +−; 37...
&d5 38 &xe5+; 37...&c5 38 &xe5+
+− &c3 38 &xd7 &f3+ 39 &g1 1-0
Timman

175 Saharov-Banstatis
Corr. 77
1 e4 c5 2 &f3 d6 3 d4 cxd4 4 &xd4
&f6 5 &c3 a6 6 &g5 e6 7 f4 &b6 8
&d2 &xb2 9 &b3 &a3 10 &xf6 gxf6
11 &e2 &c6 12 0-0 &d7 13 &f3!?
N 13 f5 &e5! 14 fxe6 fxe6≈ &a5
14 &h1 &xb3 15 cxb3 b5 16 &d4
16 f5!? &c5! 16...&e7? 17 b4± 17
&xf6 &g8 18 &g3 &xg3 18...&g6?!
19 &xg6 hxg6 20 b4! &xb4 21 f5
gxf5 22 &h5 &e7 23 &xf7+ &d8
24 &h8+ &c7 25 &d5+ exd5 26
&c1+ &b6 27 &xa8± 21...exf5 22
exf5 &xf5 23 &d5 &c5 24 &f3±;
21...&c8 22 fxg6 fxg6 23 &f1±
19 hxg3 &c8 20 &d5 exd5 21 &h5
&e7 22 &h8+ &f8 23 &f6 23 &g8?
&c3! 24 &xf7+ &d8∓ ½-½ Kasparov

176 Fernandez-Nunn
Budapest 78
1 e4 c5 2 &f3 d6 3 d4 cxd4 4 &xd4
&f6 5 &c3 a6 6 &g5 e6 7 f4 &b6 8
&d2 &xb2 9 &b3 &c6 10 &xf6!
gxf6 11 &a4 &a3 12 &b6 &b8 13
&c4 &a4 14 &f2!? e5 15 &d3 exf4
15...b5!? 16 &xf4 &e5 17 &b6 &c6
18 &d5 &g4+ 19 &e2 &h6 20 &f1
&g7 21 &d4 &c5 22 &b3 &a3 22...
&c6 23 &c1 &a4? 23...&xc1 26
&f4 &e5 27 &xf6+ &f8 28 &hf1
&e6 27 &c5! dxc5 28 &xe5 &g4+
29 &e1 &a5+ 30 c3 &d8 31 &c4
&h5 32 &b1 b6 33 &c1!

33...♛a3 34 ♛xh5! ♛xc1+ 35 ♔f2
♛f4+ 36 ♔g1 ♛c7 37 ♞xh7+ ♖xh7
38 ♖xf7+ ♔e8 39 ♛xh7 1-0 Haag

177 Taborov-Zhidkov USSR 78

1 e4 c5 2 ♞f3 d6 3 d4 cxd4 4 ♞xd4
♞f6 5 ♞c3 a6 6 ♗g5 e6 7 f4 ♗e7 8
♛f3 ♛c7 9 0-0-0 ♞bd7 10 ♗d3 h6
10...b5 11 ♖he1 ♗b7 12 ♛g3! +=
11 ♗h4 11 h4!? ♞c5 12 f5∝; 11 ♔h3
♞b6 12 ♖hf1 += g5 12 e5 12 fxg5
♞c5 13 ♛e2 ♞fg4 14 ♞f3 ♞xf3 15
gxf3 hxg5 16 ♗g3 ♞e5 17 h4 gxh4
18 f4 ♞xd3+≈ Ljubojevic-Browne,
Wijk aan Zee 76 gxh4 12...dxe5?
13 ♞xe6! 13 exf6 ♗xf6!? 13...♞xf6
14 f5 e5 15 ♞de2 ♗d7 16 ♗e4 ♞c6
17 ♞d5 ♗xd5 18 ♗xd5 ♞xd5 19
♖xd5 ♗g5+ = Stean-S.Garcia, Lublin
75; 16 ♞e4! ♗c6 17 ♞xf6+ △ ♗c4
+= 14 ♛e4? 14 ♛e3! ♛c5 15 ♗g6±;
14...♛b6 15 ♗c4±; 14...♞b6! 15
♞e4 ♗e7 16 f5 e5 17 f6 ♗f8∝ ♞b6!
=+ 15 ♖hf1 d5 16 ♛e3 ♛c5 17 ♞ce2
♗d7 18 ♔b1 0-0-0 19 c3 ♔b8 20 ♞g1!?
△ ♞f3-e5 ♞a4! 21 ♞gf3 ♛b6 22 ♛d2
♖c8 23 ♔a1 ♖c7 24 ♞e5 ♖hc8 25
♖de1 25 ♞xf7?! ♗e8 26 ♛f2 ♛c5
△ ♞xc3 27 ♖e3 ♗b5 28 ♛d2 28
♗xb5 ♛xd4!∓ ♗xd3 29 ♛xd3 ♛b6
30 ♞b3 ♔a8 31 ♖ee1 ♛d6? 31...a5∓
32 ♛h7 ♛e7 33 ♛d3 ♞b6 34 ♞d4
♛d6 Zeitnot 35 ♛h7 ♖h8 36 ♛d3

♞c4 37 ♞df3 ♞b6 38 ♖e2 ♖hc8 39
♛h7 ♛e7 40 ♛d3 ♞a4 41 ♞d2? 41
♖c1 ♞xb2 42 ♔xb2 ♖xc3 43 ♛xc3
♖xc3 44 ♔xc3 ♛a3+∓ 45 ♔c2 ♛xa2+
46 ♔d3 ♛a3+ 47 ♔c2 ♛a4+ 48 ♔d3
♗e7! 49 ♖b1 ♗b4! 50 ♞b3 ♗d6 51
g3 h5! 52 ♞d2 ♗b4 53 ♖ee1 53
♞b3 a5∓ a5 54 ♖ec1 hxg3 55 hxg3
h4 56 gxh4 ♗xd2 57 ♖c8+ ♔a7 58
♞c6+ bxc6 59 ♔xd2 ♛xf4+ 60 ♔c2
d4! 61 h5? 61 ♖cb8 ♛f2+ 62 ♔d1
♛f3+ 63 ♔d2 c5 64 ♖8b7+ ♔xb7 65
♖xb7+ ♔xb7 66 h5 a4 67 h6 a3
68 ♔c1 a2 69 ♔b2 d3 −+ d3+ 62
♔c3 ♛e5+ 0-1 Gufeld

Sozin

178 Brummer-Gheorghiu USA 78

1 e4 c5 2 ♞e2 ♞c6 3 d4 cxd4 4 ♞xd4
♞f6 5 ♞c3 d6 6 ♗c4 6 ♗g5; 6 ♗e2;
6 f4!? ♛b6!? 6...e6 7 ♞xc6 bxc6 8
0-0 g6!∝ 9 ♗b3 ♗g7 10 ♗e3 ♛c7 11
f3!? 11 f4 △ ♛f3 0-0 12 ♖f2 △ ♖d2
e6 △ d5 =+ 13 ♞a4 d5 14 exd5 cxd5
15 c4!? dxc4 16 ♖c1 ♗a6! 17 ♗xc4
♗xc4 18 ♖fc2 ♞d5! 19 ♗d4 19 ♖xc4
♞xe3 20 ♖xc7 ♞xd1 21 ♖xd1 =;
19...♛xc4!! 20 ♖xc4 ♞xe3 21 ♛e2
♞xc4 22 ♛xc4 ♖ac8 △ ♖fd8∓ ♗e2!!
20 ♛d2 20 ♛xe2 ♗xd4+ ♗xd4+ 21
♛xd4

21...♛f4!! −+ 22 ♛xf4 ♝xf4 23 g3 ♞d3! 0-1 24 ♖xe2 ♘xc1; 24 ♖a1 ♝xf3 −+ **Gheorghiu**

179 Ligterink-L.A.Schneider
Jurmala 78
1 e4 c5 2 ♘f3 ♞c6 3 d4 cxd4 4 ♞xd4 ♞f6 5 ♞c3 d6 6 ♝c4 e6 7 ♝b3 ♝e7 8 ♝e3 a6 9 ♛e2 ♛c7 10 0-0-0 ♞a5 10...0-0 11 g4 ♘xd4 12 ♖xd4 b5 13 g5 ♘d7 14 ♖g1 ♖d8!? += **11 g4 b5** 11...♘xb3+ 12 axb3 b5 **12 g5 ♞xb3+ 13 axb3 ♞d7 14 b4?!** 14 ♘f5!? exf5 15 ♘d5 ♛d8 16 exf5 ♝b7 16 f6! gxf6 17 ♖he1 ♝xd5 18 ♖xd5 ♖g8∝; 14 h4 b4 15 ♘a4 ♘c5 16 h5 ♝d7! 17 ♔b1! +=; 15 ♘a2 ♝b7 16 h5 ♛a5 17 ♔b1 ♝xe4 18 f3 ♝f5 19 ♘xb4!? += Ljubojevic-Hamann, IBM 75 **0-0** 14...a5! 15 ♘dxb5 ♛b8≈ **15 ♖hg1 a5?!** 15... ♞b6!? △ d5 **16 ♞cxb5 ♛b7 17 ♞b3!** += axb4 18 ♞xd6 ♝xd6 19 ♖xd6 ♛xe4 **20 ♖g4! ♛e5 21 ♛d3 ♖a2 22 ♖gd4± ♛xh2?!** 22...♘b8 23 ♖d8!; 22...♖d8!? **23 ♖xd7 ♝xd7 24 ♖xd7 ♖aa8 25 ♛d1! +− ♛e5 26 ♛d4 ♛b5 27 ♛d3 ♛c6 28 ♝c5 ♖fc8 29 f3 ♛a4 30 ♖d4 ♖ab8 31 ♖h4 g6 32 ♖d4 ♛b5?! 33 ♛xb5 ♖xb5 34 ♝e7 ♖f5** 34...♖e5 **35 ♖d3 ♖e8 36 ♝f6 e5 37 ♞c5 h6 38 ♞e4 hxg5 39 ♞d6 e4 40 ♞xe4 40** fxe4 ♖f1+ 41 ♖d1 ♖xd1+ 42 ♔xd1 ♖e6 43 e5 +− **♛f8 41 ♝xg5 ♖a8 42 ♝f6 ♖h5 43 ♝d2! ♖h2+ 44 ♛e3 ♖xc2 45 ♖d7** △ ♘d6 +− ♖ac8 **46 ♖b7 ♖e8 47 ♛f4 ♖c6 48 ♞g5 ♖a6 49 ♛h6!** △ ♝g7+, ♘f6+ +− ♖ea8 **50 ♛h7! ♖e6 57 ♝g7+ ♛e8 52 ♞f6+ ♛d8 53 ♖xf7 ♖a2 54 ♞e4 ♖a5 55 ♝f6+ ♛e8 56 ♛xg6 ♖a1 57 ♖b7 ♖f1 58 ♞g5 1-0 Gufeld**

180 Velimirovic-Ivanovic
Niksic 78
1 e4 c5 2 ♘f3 ♞c6 3 d4 cxd4 4 ♞xd4 ♞f6 5 ♞c3 d6 6 ♝c4 e6 7 ♝e3 ♝e7 8 ♛e2 a6 9 0-0-0 ♛c7 10 ♝b3 0-0 11 ♖g1 ♞a5 12 g4 b5 13 g5 ♞xb3+ 14 axb3 ♞d7 15 f4 b4 16 ♞f5! 16 ♘a4 ♝b7 17 f5 e5 18 f6 exd4 19 fxe7 ♖fe8 20 ♖xd4 ♖xe7∝ Velimirovic-Ivanovic, Belgrade; 16... ♘c5! **exf5 16...♘c5 17 e5!? 17 ♞d5 ♛d8 18 exf5 ♖e8 19 g6 fxg6 20 fxg6 h6 21 ♛c4 ♛h8 22 ♝d4 ♝f8 22...** ♝b7 23 ♝xg7+ ♛xg7 24 ♘f6! d5 25 ♘h5+ ♛h8 26 ♖xd5 ♝xd5 27 g7+ ♛h7 28 ♛d3+ ♛g8 29 ♛xd5+ ♛h7 30 ♛f7 ♖g8 31 ♛g6 mate; 22...♘f6 23 ♖de1 ♝f5 24 ♖xe7! ♖c8 25 ♝xf6 ♖xc4 26 ♖xg7 ♖xc2+ 27 ♛d1 +−; 22...♝f6 23 ♘c7≈ **23 ♞c7 ♞c5 23...** d5! 24 ♛c6 ♝b7 25 ♛xb7 ♖b8 26 ♛a7±; 24...♖b8 25 ♘xe8 ♛xe8 26 ♖ge1 ♛d8 27 ♛xd5±; 26...♝b7 27 ♛xb7 **24 ♞xa8 ♝e6 25 ♛e2!!** 25 ♛f1 ♘xb3+ 26 cxb3 ♛xa8∝ ♛xa8 25...♝f5 26 ♛h5! ♘xb3+ 27 cxb3 ♛c8+ 28 ♘c7! ♛xc7+ 29 ♝c3 bxc3 30 ♛xf5±; 25...♘xb3+ 26 cxb3 ♛c8+ 27 ♛c2 ♛xa8 28 ♛b1± ; 26... ♝xb3 27 ♛h5 ♛c8+ 28 ♛b1 ♛g8 29 ♘b6 +−; 25...♛a5 26 f5 +− **26 ♛h5 ♛g8 27 ♝xc5 dxc5 28 f5 +− ♝d5 29 f6** 29 ♖xd5 ♛xd5 30 f6 ♖e5! 31 f7+ ♛h8∝ **♖d8 30 f7+ ♛h8 31 ♛h4 a5 32 ♖ge1 a4**

Diagram

33 ♛xd8! ♛xd8 34 ♖e8 ♛g5+ 35 ♛b1 ♛xg6 35...♝xf7 36 ♖xf8+ ♝g8 37 ♖dd8 +− **36 ♖xf8+ ♛h7 37 ♖h8+ ♛xh8 38 f8♛+ ♝g8 39 ♖d8 ♛e6 1-0** 40 ♛xg8+ ♛xg8 41 ♖xg8+ ♛xg8 42 bxa4 +− **Velimirovic**

181 Yurtaev-Ubilava USSR 77

1 e4 c5 2 ♘f3 d6 3 d4 cxd4 4 ♘xd4 ♘f6 5 ♘c3 ♘c6 6 ♗c4 e6 7 ♗e3 ♗e7 8 ♕e2 a6 9 0-0-0 ♕c7 10 ♗b3 10 ♖g1 0-0 11 g4 ♘xe4 12 ♘xe4 d5 13 ♗d3 dxe4 14 ♗xe4 e5 15 ♘f5 ♗e6∝ **0-0 11 ♖g1 ♘d7 12 g4** 12 ♔b1 ♘c5 13 ♕h5 △ g4, ♖g3-h3 **♘c5 13 g5 b5?!** 13...♗d7 14 ♕h5 ♖fc8 15 ♖g3 g6 16 ♕h6 ♗f8 17 ♕h4 ♗e7= **14 ♕h5?!** 14 ♗d5! ♗d7 15 ♘xc6 ♗xc6 16 ♗xc5 dxc5 17 ♗xc6 ♕xc6 18 e5 △ ♘e4 += **b4 15 ♖g3** 15 ♘a4 ♗d7 16 ♘xc5 ♘xd4 17 ♘xd7 ♘xb3+ 18 axb3 ♖fc8 19 ♖d2 ♕d7= **bxc3 16 ♖h3 ♘xb3+ 17 axb3 cxb2+ 18 ♔b1 h6 19 ♘xc6** 19 ♖g1 ♘xd4 20 ♗xd4 e5 21 gxh6 g6 22 ♖xg6+ ♔h8 −+ **♕xc6 20 ♖g1 ♕xe4 −+ 21 g6** 21 gxh6 g6 −+ **e5 22 ♖hg3 ♗f5 0-1 Gufeld**

182 Donchev-Semkov Varna 78

1 e4 c5 2 ♘f3 ♘c6 3 d4 cxd4 4 ♘xd4 ♘f6 5 ♘c3 d6 6 ♗c4 e6 7 ♗e3 a6 8 ♗b3 ♗e7 9 ♕e2 ♕c7 10 ♖g1 0-0 11 g4 ♘d7 12 g5 ♘c5 13 0-0-0 ♗d7 14 ♖g3 ♖fc8 15 ♕h5 g6 16 ♕h6 ♗f8 17 ♕h4 ♘xb3+?! 17...♗e7! △ h5 **18 axb3 b5?!** 18...♗e7 **19 ♖h3 ♗g7 20 ♕xh7+ ♔f8 21 f4 ♘e7 22 ♘f3!** N 22 ♖d2 += **b4 23 ♗d4! e5** 23...

♗xd4 24 ♘xd4 bxc3 25 ♕h6+ ♔e8 26 ♕h8+ ♘g8 27 ♕xg8+ ♔e7 28 ♕g7 cxb2+ 29 ♔xb2± **24 fxe5 dxe5** 24...♗xh3 25 exd6 **25 ♗xe5! ♗xe5**

26 ♖xd7 ♗f4+ 27 ♔b1 ♖xd7 28 ♕h6+ ♔e8 29 ♕h8+ ♘g8 30 ♕xg8+ ≈ **♔e7 31 ♕g7** △ ♕f6+, ♖h8 mate **♕xh3 32 ♘d5+ ♔d6 33 ♕f6+ ♔e6 34 ♕xf4+ ♔c5** 34...♔d7 35 ♘d4 ♕d6 36 ♕xf7+ +− **35 ♕e3+ ♔d6 36 ♕b6+ ♔d7** 36...♖c6 37 ♕xb4+ ♔d7 38 ♕b7+ +− **37 ♕b7+ ♔e8 38 ♘d4! ♖ab8 39 ♕a7 ♖a8?** 39...♕d6!? 40 ♘f6+ ♔d8 41 e5 ♕c7 42 ♕xa6 ♖b6 43 ♕d3! +−; 40...♔f8 41 ♘d7+ ♔g7 42 e5! +−; 41...♕e7 42 ♕xb8!! +− **40 ♕xa8! +− ♖xa8 41 ♘xe6 fxe6 42 ♘c7+ ♔d7 43 ♘xa8 ♔c6 44 h4 ♔b7 45 h5 1-0 Maric**

Richter Rauzer

183 Gufeld-Zaichik USSR 78

1 e4 c5 2 ♘f3 d6 3 d4 cxd4 4 ♘xd4 ♘f6 5 ♘c3 ♘c6 6 ♗g5 ♕b6 7 ♘b3 e6 8 ♗d3 ♗e7 9 0-0 0-0 10 ♔h1 a6 10...♗d7; 10...h6?! 11 ♗e3 ♕c7 12 f4 a6 13 ♕f3 b5 14 ♖ae1 b4 15 ♘d1 ♗b7 16 ♘f2 e5 17 f5 ♘a5 18 ♘d2 d5 19 ♘g4± Gligoric-Littlewood, Hastings 64/65 **11 f4?!** 11 a4 +=; 11 ♕e2 += **h6 12 ♗xf6** 12 ♗h4 ♘xe4

123

13 ♘xe4 ♗xh4 14 ♘xd6 =+ ♗xf6 =+
13 ♕h5! ♕c7 14 g4! b5 14...♘b4?!
15 e5 15 g5? hxg5 16 fxg5 g6∓
dxe5 15...♘xe5!? 16 fxe5 ♗xe5≈
16 g5= 16 ♘e4 ♗b7!? 17 ♘xf6+
gxf6α∓; 17 g5 ♗e7∓ g6! 16...♗e7
17 gxh6 g6 18 ♖g1 ∓/+=

17 gxf6! gxh5 18 ♖g1+ ♔h8 19
♖g7 ♕b6! 21 ♖h7+ 21 ♘e4?! ♖g8?
22 ♖h7+ ♔xh7 23 ♘g5+ ♔h8 24
♘xf7 mate; 21...♕e3 ♔g8 22 ♖g7+
½-½ Gufeld

184 Gufeld-I.Ivanov
Vladivostok 78

1 e4 c5 2 ♘f3 ♘c6 3 d4 cxd4 4 ♘xd4
♘f6 5 ♘c3 d6 6 ♗g5 e6 7 ♕d2 a6 8
0-0-0 ♕b6 N 9 ♘b3 ♕c7 10 ♗e2
10 ♗d3!? += b5 11 ♗xf6 gxf6 12
♗h5 ♗b7 13 f4 13 ♕f4?! ♕e7 14
♖xd6? ♕xd6 15 ♕xf6 ♕e7 16 ♕xh8
♕g5+ –+ 0-0-0 14 ♕f2 14 a3 ♔b8
15 ♔b1 ♖c8 16 a3 ♖g8= 17 ♖d3?!
b4 17...f5!? 18 exf5 ♘e7!α 18 axb4
♗xb4 19 ♖g3 ♖xg3 20 hxg3 f5! 21
exf5 ♗g7 22 ♗f3! ♗xc3 23 bxc3
23 ♗xb7 ♕xb7 24 bxc3 ♘d5 25
♖xh7 ♘xc3+ 26 ♔c1 exf5α ♘d5!?
23...♕xc3 24 ♗xb7 ♔xb7 25 ♖xh7
+= 24 ♗xd5 24 ♖xh7 ♘xc3+α ♗xd5
25 ♖xh7 exf5 26 ♕d4 ♗xb3! 27 cxb3
♕xc3 28 ♕b6+ ♔a8 29 ♕xa6+ ♔b8

30 ♕xd6+ ♖c7! 31 ♕b6+ ♖b7 32
♕d6+ ♔a7 33 ♕a3+ ♔b8 34 ♕f8+
½-½ Gufeld

185 Kasparov-Panchenko USSR 78

1 e4 c5 2 ♘f3 ♘c6 3 d4 cxd4 4 ♘xd4
♘f6 5 ♘c3 d6 6 ♗g5 e6 7 ♕d2 a6
8 0-0-0 ♗d7 8...h6 9 f4 b5 10 ♘xc6
10 ♕e1 ♘xd4 11 ♖xd4 ♕b6 12 ♖d2
♗e7 13 ♗d3 b4 14 ♘d1 ♗b5!=
Karpov-Torre, Manila 2 76; 10 a3;
10 ♗xf6!? Δ f5 ♗xc6 11 ♗d3 ♗e7
11...♕a5!? 12 e5 12 ♖he1 0-0 13
e5 dxe5 14 ♕f2!? h6!α Karpov-
Tal, USSR 76 dxe5 13 fxe5 ♘d7
13...♘d5!? 14 ♘e4 0-0 15 ♗xe7 ♕xe7
16 ♖hf1 f6= Tseshkovsky-Gheorghiu,
Manila 76 14 ♗xe7 ♕xe7 15 ♗e4
15 ♕f4 ♘c5 16 ♘e4 ♗xe4 17 ♗xe4
♖c8!≈ Mecking-Polugaevsky (8) 77
♗xe4 15...♖c8!? 16 ♗xc6 ♖xc6
17 ♘e4α G.Garcia-Ostojic, Bogota
77 16 ♗xe4 ♗xe5 17 ♕d4! += f6
18 ♘d6+ ♔f8 19 ♖hf1 Δ ♕xe5 ♔g8
20 g4! h6 21 h4 ♘f7 22 ♕e4! ♖f8
23 ♘f5± ♕e8 24 ♘d4 e5 24...♘d8
25 g5! 25 ♘f5 h5?! 25...♕e6± 26
♖g1!± ♖h7 27 ♕b7! 27 g5 fxg5 28
hxg5 g6 ♔h8 28 gxh5 ♕e6 29 ♘xg7!!
+- ♕xa2 29...♖xg7 30 ♖xg7 ♔xg7
31 ♖g1+ +- 30 ♕e7 ♖g8 30...♕a1+
31 ♔d2 ♖d8+ 32 ♔e3 +- 31 ♕xf6
♕a1+ 32 ♔d2 ♕a5+ 32...♖d8+ 33
♕xd8+ +- 33 ♔e2 ♖gxg7 34 ♖xg7
♖xg7 35 ♖g1 1-0 Gufeld

186 Klovan-Mochalov USSR 78

1 e4 c5 2 ♘f3 ♘c6 3 d4 cxd4 4 ♘xd4
♘f6 5 ♘c3 d6 6 ♗g5 e6 7 ♕d2 a6 8
0-0-0 ♗d7 9 f4 9 f3!?; 9 ♗e2 b5 9...
♗e7 10 ♘f3 b5 11 ♗xf6 gxf6 12
♔b1 ♕b6 13 f5 0-0-0 14 g3 ♔b8
15 fxe6 fxe6 16 ♗h3 ♗c8 17 ♕e1!±
Karpov-Liberzon, Bad Lauterberg 77

10 ♘xc6 10 ♗xf6 gxf6 11 ♔b1 ♕b6
12 ♘ce2 ♖c8 13 g3 ♘a5 14 b3 ♗b7
15 ♗g2 += **♗xc6 11 ♕e3 ♗e7** 11...
♕c7 12 ♘d5!± **12 ♗xf6 gxf6** 12...
♗xf6 13 ♘d5!? ♗xd5 14 exd5 e5
15 ♕e4 ♕e7 16 f5 ♕a7 Gufeld-
Ermenkov, Jurmala 78 **13 f5** 13 ♔b1;
13 ♗d3!? **♕a5** 13...b4 14 ♘e2 e5
15 ♘g3 ♕a5 16 ♗c4 += R.Byrne-
Radulov, Montilla 75 **14 ♔b1 b4
15 ♘e2 ♕e5!?** N 15...e5 16 ♘g3 d5
17 ♗e2∝ **16 ♘d4!** 16 ♘g3?! h5! =+
♗xe4 **17 ♕h3!?** 17 fxe6 fxe6 18
♔b3 ♔f7 19 ♘xe6 d5 20 ♘d4 ♖hc8
=+ **♕d5** 17...♗f5?! **18 fxe6 fxe6 19
♕xe6 ♕xe6 20 ♘xe6 += ♖c8 21
♖d2 ♕d7 22 ♘f4 ♖c5 23 ♗xa6 b3!?
24 ♗d3!** 24 axb3? ♖a5 25 ♖e1 f5∓
bxa2+ 25 ♔a1 f5 **26 ♗xe4 fxe4 27
♖e1 ♗f6 28 ♖xe4± ♖a8** Δ ♗xb2+
**29 ♘d3 ♖b5 30 c4 ♖f5 31 ♖f4 ♖xf4
32 ♘xf4 ♗g5 33 g3** 33 ♖f2!? ♔c6
34 ♖c2?! 34 ♖f2 ♗xf4 35 ♖xf4
♔c5 36 g4 ♔b4 37 ♖d4 ♔b3 38 ♖d3+
Δ ♖xd6± **♗xf4 35 gxf4. ♔c5 36
♖d2 ♖a6??** 36...♖f8 **37 b3** +− ♔b4
**38 ♖xa2 ♖c6 39 ♔b2 ♔c5 40 ♔c3
♖c8 41 ♖a6 1-0 Gufeld**

187 Westerinen-Ermenkov
Jurmala 78

1 e4 c5 2 ♘f3 d6 3 d4 cxd4 4 ♘xd4
♘f6 5 ♘c3 ♘c6 6 ♗g5 e6 7 ♕d2 a6
8 0-0-0 ♗d7 9 f4 b5 10 ♗xf6 gxf6
11 ♘xc6?! 11 f5!? += ♗xc6 **12 ♕e3
♕e7!=** 12...♗e7 13 ♗d3 ♕c7 14 ♔b1
♔b7 15 ♖he1 Δ f5± **13 a3?!** 13
♗d3 ♕a7 14 ♕h3 b4 15 ♘e2 ♕c5
16 f5 e5 17 ♘g3 a5= Ljubojevic-
Gheorghiu, Manila 1 76 **h5! 14 ♗d3
♕a7 15 ♕h3 ♗h6 16 ♖hf1 ♕c5** Δ a5,
b4 **17 ♔b1 a5** =+ **18 e5 b4 19 ♘e4
♗xe4 20 ♗xe4 d5 21 ♗g6!? f5!∓
22 ♗xh5 bxa3 23 ♕xa3 ♕xa3 24**

bxa3 ♖b8+ **25 ♔a2 ♖c8! 26 ♖d2
♗xf4 27 ♖xf4 ♖xh5 28 g3 ♔e7 29
♔b3 ♖c5! 36 ♖df2 f6! 31 exf6+**
31 ♖e2 fxe5 32 ♖xe5 ♖xh2 33 ♖fxf5
♔d6 Δ ♖hxc2 −+ **♔xf6 32 g4 ♖h4
33 gxf5 ♖xf4 34 ♖xf4 e5! 35 ♖f1
d4 36 ♔b2 e4 37 ♖d1 e3! −+ 38 ♔c1**
38 ♖xd4 e2 39 ♖e4 ♖e5 −+ **♖xf5
39 ♖e1** Δ c3 **♖f2 40 c3 ♔e5 41 h4
♖h2 42 ♔d1 ♔e4 43 cxd4 ♔d3! 44
♔c1 ♔xd4 45 ♖g1 ♖xh4 46 ♔c2
♖h2+ 47 ♔b3 e2 48 ♔a4 ♖h5 0-1
Gufeld**

188 Klovan-Podgaets USSR 77

1 e4 c5 2 ♘f3 ♘c6 3 d4 cxd4 4 ♘xd4
♘f6 5 ♘c3 d6 6 ♗g5 e6 7 ♕d2 a6
8 0-0-0 ♗d7 9 f4 b5 10 ♗xf6 gxf6
10...♕xf6?! **11 e5 dxe5 12 ♘dxb5±
11 ♘f3 h5 12 ♔b1 b4 13 ♘e2 ♕b6
14 ♘ed4 ♘xd4 15 ♘xd4 a5?!** 15...
♖c8!? **16 ♗c4 += ♕c5 17 ♕d3 ♖b8
18 f5 e5 19 ♘b3 ♕c7 20 ♖he1** Δ
♕d5 **♗c6 21 ♘d2 ♖g8 22 ♕f3 h4
23 ♘f1?!** 23 ♖e2!± ♗h6 24 ♕h5 ♗g5
25 ♘f3 ♗b5 26 ♗xb5 ♖xb5 27 ♕h7
♖f8 28 ♘xg5 fxg5 29 ♖ed2 +− ♗h6
24 ♕h5?! 24 ♘e3 ♗xe3 25 ♖xe3 +=
♗g5 25 ♖xd6 ♕xd6 26 ♕xf7+ ♔d8
27 ♕xg8+ ♔c7 28 ♕f7+ ♔b6 29
♗d5 29 ♘d3!? **♖d8≈ 30 ♘e3** 30
♖d1 ♕c5= ♗xe3 31 ♖xe3 ♗xd5 32
exd5 ♕xd5 33 ♕xd5 ♖xd5 34 ♖d3
♔c5 35 ♔c1 e4 36 ♖xd5+ ♔xd5 37
♔d2 ♕e5 38 ♔e3? Zeitnot 38 c4 bxc3+
39 ♔xc3 ♔xf5 40 ♔d2= ♔xf5 39
c4? 39 g4+ hxg3 40 hxg3 ♔e5 41
g4 ♔d5 42 c3=; 39...♔xg4 40 ♔xe4
♔h3 41 ♔f3 ♔xh2 42 ♔f2 bxc3
40 bxc3 ♔e5∓

Diagram

41 c4 f5 42 g3 h3? 42...hxg3 43 hxg3

a4 44 a3 ♔d6 45 ♔d4 ♚c6 46 c5
♔b5 47 ♔d5 e3 48 c6 ♚b6! 49 ♔d6
e2 50 c7 e1♕ 51 c8♕ ♕xg3+∓ 43
a4 ♚e6 44 ♚e2 ♚d6 45 ♚d2 ♚c5 46
♚c3 e3 47 ♚d3 e2 48 ♚xe2 ♚xc4
49 ♚e3 ♚b4 50 ♚f4 ♚xa4 51 ♚xf5
♚b4 52 g4 a4 53 g5 a3 54 g6 a2
55 g7 a1♕ 56 g8♕ ♕f1+ 57 ♚e5
♕e2+ 58 ♚f6 ♕b2+ 58...♕xh2 59
♕g4+ ♚c3 60 ♕f3+ ♚d2 61 ♕d5+?
♚e1 62 ♕e4+ ♚f1 63 ♕c4+ ♚e2
64 ♕c1+ ♚f2 65 ♕c5+ ♚e3 66 ♕c2+
♚f3 67 ♕c6+ ♚g3! −+ 59 ♚e7 ♕xh2
60 ♕g4+ ♚c3 61 ♕f3+ ♚d2 62 ♕d7!=
62 ♕d5+ ♚e1 63 ♕a5+ ♚d2 64 ♕a1+
♚e2 65 ♕a6+ ♚d3 66 ♕a2+ ♚e3 67
♕a7+ ♚f3 −+ ♕g2 63 ♕f4+ ♚d3 64
♕d6+ ♚c2 65 ♕c5+ ♚d1 66 ♕h5+
♚d2 67 ♕a5+ ♚e3 68 ♕c3+ ♚e4
69 ♕c4+ ♚e5 70 ♕e6+ ♚d4 71 ♕b6+
♚c4 72 ♕a6+ ½-½ Gufeld

Scheveningen

189 Horvath-Spassov Subotica 78
1 e4 c5 2 ♘f3 d6 3 d4 cxd4 4 ♘xd4
♘f6 5 ♘c3 ♘c6 6 ♗e2 e5 7 ♘b3 ♗e7
8 0-0 0-0 9 ♔h1 a5 9...♗e6 10 f4
exf4 11 ♗xf4 d5 12 e5 ♘e4 13 ♗d3 +=
Karpov-Timman, Bad Lauterberg 77
10 a4 ♗e6 11 f4 ♘b4 12 f5!? 12
♗e3 ♗d7 13 ♗g5 ♗c6 13...♘xe4?!
14 ♘xe4 ♗xg5 15 f6± 14 ♗xf6 ♗xf6

15 ♘d5 15 ♗c4!? △ ♘d5 += ♘xd5!
15...♗xd5 16 exd5 △ c3± 16 exd5
♗d7 17 ♘d2 e4! 18 ♘xe4 += ♗xb2
19 ♖b1 ♗e5 △ ♕h4 20 f6!? gxf6
20...g6 21 ♕d2±; 20...♗xf6 21 ♘xf6+
gxf6 22 ♗d3± 21 ♗b5 f5 22 ♗xd7?!
22 ♘d2! △ ♘f3/♘c4 += ♕xd7 23
♘g5 ♗g7!= 24 ♖f4?! 24 ♖b5! △
♕d3 ♖ac8 25 c4 ♖fe8 26 ♕d3 h6
=+ 27 ♘f3 ♖e4! 28 ♖xe4 fxe4 29
♕xe4 ♕xa4∓ 30 ♘d2 ♕d7 31 ♕d3
a4 32 ♘e4 ♖a8! −+ 33 ♕f3 △ ♘f6+
♕e7 34 c5 a3 34...dxc5? 35 d6 ♕d7
36 ♖xb7 35 cxd6 a2! 36 ♖f1 ♕xe4
0-1 Maric

190 Bronstein-Lanka Jurmala 78
1 e4 c5 2 ♘f3 ♘c6 3 d4 cxd4 4 ♘xd4
♘f6 5 ♘c3 d6 6 ♗e2 e5 7 ♘f3 h6
8 0-0 ♗e6 8...♗e7 9 b3 0-0 10
♗b2 a6 11 ♘d2! ♘d4 12 ♗d3
b5 13 ♖c1 ♗b7 14 ♘e2 ♘e6 15
♘g3 g6 16 c4± 9 b3 9 ♖e1 ♗e7
10 ♗f1 0-0 11 b3 ♖c8 12 ♗b2
♗g4!∝ ♗e7 10 ♗b2 0-0 11 ♘d2!?
N 11 ♕d2 a6 12 h3 ♕a5 13 ♖ad1
♖ac8 14 a3 ♖fd8= ♘d4? 11...d5!?
12 exd5 ♘xd5 13 ♘xd5 ♗xd5 14
♘c4 += 12 ♗d3 ♖c8 13 ♘e2 ♗xe2+
14 ♕xe2 ♘d7 15 c4± a6 16 ♘b1
♘c5 17 ♘c3 ♗b5 18 ♖ad1 ♕a5
18...♕c7 19 ♗b1! ♖fd8 20 g3! +−
♕b6 21 ♔h1 ♗e7 22 f4 f6 23 ♘d5
♗xd5 24 exd5 ♕c7 25 fxe5 dxe5
26 ♕g4 e4 27 b4 1-0 Gufeld

191 Kapengut-Mishuchkov
USSR 78
1 e4 c5 2 ♘f3 e6 3 d4 cxd4 4 ♘xd4
♘f6 5 ♘c3 d6 6 ♗e2 ♘c6 7 0-0 ♗e7
8 ♗e3 0-0 9 f4 a6 10 a4 10 ♕e1
♘xd4 11 ♗xd4 b5 12 ♖d1 ♕c7 13
e5 dxe5 14 fxe5 ♘d7 15 ♘e4 ♗b7
16 ♘f6+ ♔h8!∝ ♕c7 11 ♕e1 ♘xd4

126

11...♗d7 12 ♕g3 ♖ac8 13 ♘xc6 ♗xc6
14 ♗d4 g6 15 f5 +=; 12 ♘b3!? **12
♗xd4 e5 13 ♗e3** 13 fxe5 dxe5 14
♕g3 ♖e8 15 ♔h1 ♗d8= exf4 **14 ♖xf4
♗e6 15 ♖d1!?** N 15 ♕g3 ♘d7 16 ♗d4
♘e5 17 ♗d3 ♕a5= ♖fe8 **16 ♕g3 ♘d7
17 ♗d4 ♘e5 18 ♖df1 ♕a5 19 ♘d5!
♕xa4** 19...♗xd5 20 exd5 ♕xd5 21
♗c4 **20 c4!± ♗xd5 21 exd5 ♗f8
22 ♗g4 ♕c2** 22...♘xc4 **23 ♗f5
♕a4 24 ♕c3** 24 ♗xh7+?? ♔xh7
25 ♖h4+ ♔g8 26 ♕h3 ♘g6 −+ ♖ed8
25 ♗xe5 dxe5

**26 ♗xh7+ ♔xh7 27 ♕h3+ ♔g8 28
♖h4 +− ♗c5+ 29 ♔h1 ♔f8 30 ♕e6
♗f2 31 ♖h8 mate 1-0 Gufeld**

192 Helmers-Jakobsen Roskilde 78
1 e4 c5 2 ♘f3 e6 3 d4 cxd4 4 ♘xd4
♘f6 5 ♘c3 d6 6 ♗e2 ♘c6 7 ♗e3 ♗e7
8 0-0 0-0 9 f4 a6 10 ♕e1 ♘xd4!
10...♕c7?! 11 ♕g3 += **11 ♗xd4 b5
12 ♖d1! ♗b7 13 ♗f3 ♕c7 14 e5
♘e8!** 14...dxe5 15 fxe5 ♘d7 16
♗xb7 ♕xb7 17 ♘e4 **15 ♗xb7 ♕xb7
16 ♘e4 d5 17 ♘g5!** 17 ♘c5?! ♕c6
18 b4 a5 △ ♘c7-a6 ♖c8 **18 c3 b4
19 cxb4 h6 20 ♘f3 ♗xb4 21 ♕e2
♘c7 22 ♖c1 ♘b5 23 ♗e3 ♖fd8 24
♖xc8 ♖xc8 25 a4! ♘a7 26 f5!** exf5
**27 ♘d4 g6 28 g4! ♖e8 29 gxf5 ♖xe5
30 fxg6 fxg6 31 ♕g4 ♕h7** 31...♖xe3

32 ♕xg6+ ♕g7 33 ♕xg7+ +− **32
♕h3 h5** 32...♕g7 33 ♗xh6! ♖h5
34 ♕xh5 ♕xd4+ 35 ♗e3+ +− **33
♗f3 ♖e7 34 ♘g5+ ♔g8 35 ♖f6 ♔g7
36 ♘e6+ ♔xf6 37 ♗d4+ ♔f7 38
♗d8+ ♔e8 39 ♘xb7 ♖xb7 40 ♕e6+
1-0**

193 Lanka-Ligterink
Jurmala 78
**1 e4 c5 2 ♘f3 e6 3 d4 cxd4 4 ♘xd4
♘c6 5 ♘c3 d6 6 ♗e3 ♘f6 7 ♗e2 ♗e7
8 0-0-0-0 9 f4 a6** 9...♗d7 10 ♘b3
♕c7 11 ♗f3 ♖fd8 12 ♘b5!? ♕b8
13 c4 +=; 9...♘xd4 10 ♕xd4! b6 11
♗f3 ♗b7 12 ♖fd1 += **10 ♕e1** 10 a4!?
♕c7 11 ♔h1 ♖e8 12 ♗f3 ♘xd4 13
♗xd4 e5= Torre-Kaplan, USA 75
♗d7 10...♘d7!? 11 ♖d1 ♖e8 12 ♘c4!?
♘f8 13 a3 ♗d7 14 ♕f2 △ f5 +=
Beljavsky-Andersson, Cienfuegos 76;
10...♘xd4! 11 ♗xd4 b5 △ ♗b7=
**11 ♕g3 b5 12 a3 ♘xd4 13 ♗xd4 ♗c6
14 ♔h1 +=** ♕d7 △ a5 **15 ♗d3 a5
16 ♖ae1 b4 17 axb4 axb4 18 ♘d1**
g6 **19 ♘f2 ♖fe8 20 ♗xf6 ♗xf6 21
♘g4 ♗g7 22 h4?!** 22 e5! += f5! 23
exf5 exf5 24 ♘e3 d5 =+ 25 h5 ♔f7!
**26 ♕h3 ♕d6 27 ♖d1 ♕f6 28 ♖fe1
♖e6 29 ♘f1 ♖ae8 30 ♖xe6 ♕xe6 31
♘d2 ♕e3! 32 ♕h2 ♖xb2 33 ♘f3
♔g7 34 ♕g3 ♗c1?** Zeitnot 34...♗f6!∓
35 ♕g5! +− d4 35...♕xf4 36 h6+
△ ♖xc1 +− **36 h6+ ♔f7 37 ♗c4+
1-0 Gufeld**

194 Sigurjonsson-Ogaard
Esbjerg 78
**1 e4 c5 2 ♘f3 e6 3 d4 cxd4 4 ♘xd4
♘c6 5 ♘c3 a6 6 ♗e2 ♕c7 7 0-0 ♘f6
8 ♔h1 ♗e7** 8...♗b4!? **9 f4 d6 10 ♗e3
0-0 11 ♕e1 ♗d7** 11...♘xd4 12 ♗xd4
b5 **12 ♕g3 ♔h8 13 a3!?** △ ♗d3; 13
♖ad1 b5? 14 e5! Larsen-Hort 78!?;

13...Rac8 **b5 14 Bd3 Rab8** 14... Rad8!? **15 Nxc6! Bxc6 16 Bd4 e5** 16...b4 17 e5! bxc3 18 exf6 Bxf6 19 Qh3 +-; 16...Rbd8 17 Rae1± **17 fxe5 Nh5 18 Qh3 dxe5 19 Rf5 exd4** 19...Nf4 20 Bxe5 **20 Rxh5 h6 21 Nd5** 21 e5 Bg5 22 Rxg5 dxc3 23 Rh5 Kg8 **Bxd5** 21...Qb7? 22 e5! **22 exd5± Δ Rxh6+ +- Qf4** 22... Qd6 23 Rf1± **23 Rf1 Qe3 24 Qg4 Rb6?!** 24...Kg8 25 Qf5 g6 26 Qg4+; 24...Kg8 25 Rhf5 Δ R5f4± **25 Rhf5 Kg8** 25...Rg6 26 Rxf7 Rxf7 Qc8+ Rf8 28 Rxf8+ Bxf8 29 Qxf8+ Kh7 30 g3 +- **26 R5f4! Bd6? 27 Rf6 Bc5**

28 d6!! Δ Qf5 Rxd6 28...Bxd6 29 Qf5 g6 30 Rxg6+; 28...Qg5 29 Rxf7 Rxf7 (29...Bxd6 30 Qe6! +-) 30 Qc8+ +- **29 Qf5 Qxd3** 31...g6 30 Qxg6+! fxg6 31 Rxf8+ Kg7 32 R1f7 mate **30 Qxd3 Rxf6 31 Rxf6 gxf6 32 Qg3+ Kh8 33 Qc7 1-0 Sigurjonsson**

195 Soloviev-Lysenko USSR 78
1 e4 c5 2 Nf3 Nc6 3 d4 cxd4 4 Nxd4 Nf6 5 Nc3 d6 6 Be3 e6 6...Ng4 7 Bb5 Nxe3 8 fxe3 Bd7 9 0-0 e6! 10 Bxc6 bxc6 11 e5!? Be7! 12 Qh5 0-0 13 exd6 Bxd6 14 Ne4 Be7 15 Rad1 Qb6! 16 Rf3! Be8! 17 Rh3 h6 18 Rg3 Kh7 19 Rf1 Qd8! 20 c4 a5 21

Qe5 Rg8≈ Gipslis-Tukmakov, USSR 77; 7 Ng5?! Qb6 8 Bb5 e5 9 Nd5 Qxd4 10 Nc7+ Kd7 11 Qxd4 exd4 12 Nxa8 b6 13 a4! Bb7 14 a5∞ 7 f4 Qa5?! 8 Qf3 Nxd4 9 Bxd4 e5 10 fxe5 dxe5 11 Bb5+! +- Bd7

12 Bxe5! Qxb5 13 Bxf6 Bc4 13... gxf6 14 Qxf6 Rg8 15 Qe5+ +- **14 Bd4 Rd8 15 0-0-0 Bxa2 16 Qf5! Qa6 17 Nf6?** 17 Nxa2!? Qxa2 18 Qb5+ Rd7 19 Qe5+±; 17 Nd5!? Bxd5 18 exd5 Qa1+ 19 Kd2 Bb4+ 20 Ke3!± **Qxf6 18 Rxd8+ Qxd8 19 Rd1 Bd6** 19...Qc7?! 20 Nb5 Qc6 21 Nxa7 Qc7! 22 Nb5∞; 21...Be6?? 22 Nxc6 Bxf5 23 Rd8 mate **20 e5** 20 Nxa2 0-0 21 e5 Qa5= **Be6 21 Qf4 Qf6!!=** 21...0-0 22 exd6 += **22 Qa4+** 22 Qxf6 gxf6 23 exd6 Rg8≈ **Bd7 23 exf6** 23 Qxa7 Qxe5!; 23 Qxd7+ Kxd7 24 exf6 Ke6!= **Bxa4 24 Rxd6 Bc6 ½-½ Lysenko**

196 Kochiev-Beljavsky Lvov 78
1 e4 c5 2 Nf3 Nc6 3 d4 cxd4 4 Nxd4 Nf6 5 Nc3 d6 6 f4 6 Bg5; 6 Bc4; 6 Be3; 6 Bg5 e6 7 Qd2 a6 8 0-0-0 Bd7 9 f4 b5 10 Bxf6 gxf6 R.Byrne-Radulov, Montilla 75 Qb6 7 Nb3 e6 8 Qe2 Be7 9 Be3 Qc7 10 g4 a6 11 g5 Nd7 12 a4 b6 13 h4 Nc5 14 h5 Nb4 15 Bg2 Bb7 16 0-0 0-0-0

17 f5 e5 18 ♖ad1 ♕b8 19 ♖d2 f6 20 gxf6 gxf6 21 ♕c4 a5 22 ♘b5 ♕c6 23 ♘xc5 bxc5 24 ♕e6 ♖d7 25 ♖fd1 ♘a6 26 ♔h2 26 ♘xd6? ♘c7 −+ **♘c7 27 ♘xc7 ♖xc7 28 b3 ♗c8 ½-½ Friedgood**

197 Mihalchishin-Taborov USSR 78

1 e4 c5 2 ♘f3 d6 3 d4 cxd4 5 ♘xd4 ♘f6 5 ♘c3 e6 6 f4 ♗e7 6...♘c6 7 ♗e3 a6?! 8 ♕f3 ♕c7 9 0-0-0 ♗e7 10 g4! += Mihalchishin-Beljavsky, USSR 77; 7...♗d7 8 ♕f3 ♘xd4 9 ♗xd4 ♗c6 10 0-0-0 ♕a5 11 ♗c4! +=; 7...♗e7 **7 ♕f3** 7 ♗e3 **♘c6 8 ♗e3 ♕c7** 8...e5?! 9 ♘xc6 bxc6 10 f5! ♕a5 11 ♗c4 ♖b8 12 0-0-0! += Timman-Liberzon, Haifa 76; 8...0-0 9 0-0-0 ♗d7 10 ♖g1!± **9 ♗d3** 9 0-0-0!? **a6 10 0-0 0-0 11 ♖ae1 ♗d7 12 ♔h1 b5 13 g4 ♘xd4 14 ♗xd4 ♗c6** 14...e5 15 fxe5 dxe5 16 ♕g3 ♘xg4 17 ♘d5 ♕d8 18 ♗d6≈ **15 g5 ♘d7 16 ♘d5! ♕d8** 16...exd5?!± **17 ♕h5?! exd5 18 ♖f3** 18 exd5 ♗xd5+ 19 ♔g1 g6 20 ♕h6 f6 21 ♗xg6 ♖f7; 18 e5!?≈ **♘e5!** 18...dxe4 19 ♖h3 exd3+ 20 ♔g1 h6 21 ♗xg7 +− **19 fxe5** 19 ♖h3 h6 20 gxh6 g6 **g6!** 19...♗xg5? 20 e6! △ exd5 +−

20 ♕xh7+!! ♔xh7 21 ♖h3+ ♔g8 22 exd6 f6 23 e5!! ♗xd6 24 exf6! △ f7+ +− **♗f7 25 ♖h6!** 25 ♗xg6?

♗e8 26 ♖e7 ♕c8 ♗c5 25...♗f8!? 26 ♖xg6+ ♔h8 27 ♖e7! ♗e8 28 ♗f5! ♕xe7 29 fxe7 ♘g7 30 ♖h6+ ♔g8 31 ♗h7+ = 26 ♖xg6+ ♔h8 27 ♖h6+ ♔g8 28 ♖g6+ ♔h8 29 ♖h6+ ♔g8 30 ♖g6+ ½-½ Gufeld

Dragon

198 Ljubojevic-Miles IBM 78

1 e4 c5 2 ♘f3 d6 3 d4 cxd4 4 ♘xd4 ♘f6 5 ♘c3 g6 6 ♗c4 ♗g7 7 h3 0-0 8 ♗b3 a6!? 8...♘c6 **9 0-0 b5!? 10 a4!?** 10 ♖e1 **♗b7 11 ♗g5 b4 11... ♘bd7!?** 12 axb5 axb5 13 ♘dxb5 += ♖xa1 14 ♕xa1 ♘xe4 15 ♘xe4 ♗xe4 16 ♘xd6± 14...♗xe4 15 ♘xd6! ±; 13...♘c5!?; 12 ♖e1; 11...♘xe4? 12 ♘xe4 ♗xe4 13 ♖e1± **12 ♘d5 ♘bd7 13 a5** 13 ♘xb4? ♕b6∓ ♖c8 **14 ♖e1 ♘c5! 15 ♗xf6 exf6 16 ♘xb4** 16 ♗a2 ♖e8 17 ♘xb4 f5α **♘xb3! 17 cxb3** 17 ♘xb3 f5∓ ♖e8 17...f5 18 exf5α **18 ♕d2! f5 19 exf5 ♖xe1+ 20 ♖xe1 ♕xa5 =+ 21 ♖e7 ♗a8 22 ♔h2 ♗f6 23 ♖e2 ♗c5 24 ♘bc2 ♕d5 25 f4! ♕g7 26 fxg6 hxg6 27 ♕e3 ♖c7 28 ♖d2α ½-½ Miles**

199 Panchenko-Gufeld USSR 78

1 e4 c5 2 ♘f3 d6 3 d4 cxd4 4 ♘xd4 ♘f6 5 ♘c3 g6 6 ♗e2 ♗g7 7 0-0 0-0 8 ♗e3 ♘c6 9 ♕d2 9 ♘b3; 9 f4?! ♕b6! **d5 10 exd5** 10 ♘xc6 bxc6 11 e5α **♘xd5** 10...♘b4 11 d6!? **11 ♘xd5 ♗xd4= 12 c4** 12 ♗c4= **e5 13 f4 ♗e6 14 fxe5 ♘xe2+ 15 ♕xe2 ♗xd5 16 ♖ad1 ♗xc4 17 ♕xc4 ♕c8 18 ♕xc8 ♖axc8 19 ♖d7 ♗xe5 20 ♖xb7 a5! 21 b3 ♖c2 22 ♖h6 ♔g7? 23 ♔h1 ♗g7 24 ♗xg7 ♔xg7 25 a4 ♔h6! 26 ♔g1!** 26 ♖a7 ♖e8! **f5 27 ♖f2 ♖c1+ 28 ♖f1 ♖c2 29 ♖f2 ½-½ Gufeld**

200 Balashov-Geller Lvov 78
1 e4 c5 2 ♞f3 d6 3 d4 cxd4 4 ♞xd4
♞f6 5 ♞c3 g6 6 ♝e2 ♝g7 7 0-0 0-0
8 ♝g5 8 ♝e3 ♞c6 9 ♞b3 ♝e6 10 f4
b5?! 11 f5 b4?± Spassky-Miles,
Bugojno 78 ♞c6 9 ♞b3 ♝e6 9...a5
10 a4 ♞b4 11 ♖e1 ♝e6 12 ♞d4 ♖c8
13 ♞xe6 fxe6 14 ♖a3!? Vasyukov-
Gufeld, USSR 75; 14 ♛d2? ♖xc3!
10 ♚h1 a5 11 a4 ♖c8 12 f4 ♞b4
13 ♞d4 ♝c4 14 ♞db5 d5 15 ♝xc4
♖xc4 16 ♝xf6 ♝xf6 17 exd5 ♛b8
18 ♛e2 ♖xf4

19 d6! ♖xf1+ 20 ♖xf1 ♛d8 21 ♖d1!
exd6 22 ♖xd6 ♛e7 23 ♛xe7 ♝xe7
24 ♖d7 ♝f6 25 ♞e4 ♝xb2 26 c3
♞c6 27 ♖xb7 ♖d8 28 g3 ♞e5 29 ♚g2
f5? 30 ♞f6+ ♚f8 31 ♞xh7+ ♚g8 32
♞d4! △ ♞xf6+, ♞e6 mate ♖d6 33
♖xb2 ♚xh7 34 ♖b5 ♞c4 35 ♚f2 ♖d7
36 ♚e2\ ♖e7+ 37 ♚d3 ♞e5+ 38 ♚c2
♞g4 39 ♖xa5 ♞xh2 40 ♖b5 ♞f1 41
a5 ♖a7 42 ♞c6 ♖c7 43 ♞b4 ♞e3+
44 ♚d3 ♞c4 45 a6 1-0 Friedgood

201 Larsen-Miles Las Palmas 78
1 e4 c5 2 ♞f3 d6 3 d4 cxd4 4 ♞xd4
♞f6 5 ♞c3 g6 6 ♝e2 ♝g7 7 0-0 0-0
8 ♚h1 ♞c6 9 ♞b3 ♝e6 10 f4 ♞a5
11 f5 ♝c4 12 ♝g5 ♖c8 13 ♝d3 b5
14 ♛d2?! b4! 15 ♞e2 15 ♞d1/b1
♞xe4 -+; 15 ♞a4 =+ d5! 16 e5 16

♛xb4 dxe4∓ ♞e4 17 ♝xe4 dxe4 =+
18 ♖fd1 18 ♛xd8 ♖fxd8 19 ♞xa5
♝xe2∓ ♞c6! 19 ♛e3 19 ♛e1 ♛c7
=+/∓ ♛b6! 20 ♛xe4 20 ♛xb6 axb6
21 f6 ♝xe2 =+ ♞xe5 21 ♞g3 21
♝xe7? gxf5 -+ ♝a6! △ ♝b7 22 ♝xe7
♖c4! 22...♝b7 23 ♛xb4 ♖xc2 24
♖d2α 23 ♞d4 23 ♝xf8!? ♖xe4 24
♝c5 ♛c7! 25 ♞xe4 ♞g4/♝g7∓; 23
♖d4 ♖fc8 =+/∓ ♖e8 24 ♝g5 24 f6
♝xf6 25 ♝xf6 ♛xf6 26 a3 ♖c7! 27
axb4 ♝b7 28 ♛e2 ♖ce7! -+ 29 ♖xa7
♞g4! ♝b7 25 ♛h4 25 ♛f4 h6 -+;
25 ♛e3 h6 ∓/-+ ♞f3! -+ 26 ♞xf3
26 gxf3 ♖xd4 27 ♖xd4 ♝xf3+ -+
♖xh4 27 ♞xh4 ♝f6! 28 ♝xf6 ♛xf6
0-1 Miles

202 Tseshkovsky-Gufeld
USSR 78
1 e4 c5 2 ♞f3 d6 3 d4 cxd4 4 ♞xd4
♞f6 5 ♞c3 g6 6 ♝e3 ♝g7 7 f3 ♞c6
8 ♝c4 0-0 8...♞c6 9 ♛d2 ♝d7 10
0-0-0 ♖c8 11 ♝b3 ♞e5 12 h4 h5 13
♚b1 13 g4!? hxg4! 14 h5 ♞xh5 15
♝h6 e6α ♞c4 14 ♝xc4 ♖xc4 15
♞ce2?! N 15 ♞b3 ♛c7 16 ♝d4 ♝e6
17 g4! += Tukmakov-Sosonko, IBM
74 b5! 16 c3 16 ♝h6 e5! 17 ♝xg7
♚xg7 18 ♞b3 d5! 19 exd5 ♝f5∓
♛b8 17 ♞b3 ♖fc8 =+ 17...b4?! 18
cxb4 ♖xb4 19 ♝xa7! 18 ♞ec1 ♛c7
19 ♞d3 19 ♛f2? b4 a5 20 ♛f2 ♖c6!
21 ♞d4 ♖a6 22 ♝g5 e5?! 22...♛b7∓
23 ♝xf6! ♝xf6 24 ♞c2 ♝e6 25 ♞e3
b4 25...♛a7?! 26 f4! 26 ♖c1 26
cxb4 ♝xa2+? 27 ♚xa2 axb4+ 28 ♚b3!
+-; 26...axb4 27 ♞xb4 ♛a5 α/=+
♛a7! 27 c4 ♝d8! 28 ♛e2 ♖ac6?
28...b3! 29 a3 ♖ac6!; 29 axb3 a4
α/=+ 29 g3 ♝b6 30 ♞d5 ♝d4≈ 31 g4
Zeitnot b3! Zeitnot 32 gxh5 32
axb3?! a4 33 b4 a3 34 b3?? a2 35
♛xa2 ♖a6 -+ bxa2+ 33 ♚xa2

33 ⬧ 1 a4 34 hxg6 a3 35 gxf7+
♔xf7 ♖xc4 34 ♖xc4 ♖xc4 35 hxg6
35 ♘ e5?? ♖a4+ 36 ♔b3 ♖b4+ −+
♕b7 6 gxf7+ ♔xf7 37 ♕b1 ♗xd5
38 e ♖5 ♕xd5 39 ♖c1! ♖xc1+ 40
♕xc1 a4 41 h5 ♕c4+ 42 ♔b1 ½-½
Gufel

203 ♔ ovan-Gufeld USSR 78
1 e4 ♘5 2 ♘f3 d6 3 d4 cxd4 4 ♘xd4
♘f6 ! ♘c3 g6 6 ♗e3 ♗g7 7 f3 ♘c6
8 ♕d 0-0 9 ♗c4 ♗d7 10 h4 ♖c8 11
♗b3 ♘5 12 0-0-0 ♘e5 13 ♗g5 ♖c5
14 f♘ N ♘c4 14...♘c6 15 ♕d3 15
♗xc4 ♖xc4 =+ b5 16 e5 dxe5? 16...
♘g4∝ 17 ♗xf6! 17 ♘dxb5? ♕c8!
18 ♘xf6 ♗f5!∓ ♗xf6 18 ♘dxb5
♘xb2 !

19 ♖ g6+ 19 ♔xb2 e4 20 ♕xd7 ♕a5
21 ♖ ♖4! +− ♗g7 20 ♕xb2? 20 ♘e4
♖c6 1 ♘bd6! +−; 20...♘c4 21 ♕xh5
+− ♖c8! += 20...a6? 21 ♕xa6 +−
21 ♖ ♖d7! ♕xd7 22 ♕xh5 22 ♖d1?!
♕c8 ♖xb5 23 ♘xb5 Zeitnot 33
♖d1 exf4+ −+ ♕xb5 24 fxe5 e6
25 ♖ ♖1 ♖c8 26 ♖e3 ♖c5 27 ♕g5!
♔h7 27...♖xe5 28 ♖xe5 ♕xe5+
29 ♔ ♘e5 ♗xe5+ 30 ♔a3 ♗g3 31 h5
♔g7 32 ♘c4± 28 ♕h5+ 28 a4!?
♖xe5 ? 29 ♕xg7+ ♔xg7 30 ♖g3+ +−;
28... ♖b8! 29 ♔a2 ♖xe5 30 ♖xe5 ♗x
e5 ∝ −= ♔g8 29 ♕g5 ♔h7 ½-½ Gufeld

204 Sigurjonsson-Mestel Esbjerg 78
1 e4 c5 2 ♘f3 d6 3 d4 cxd4 4 ♘xd4
♘f6 5 ♘c3 g6 6 ♗e3 ♗g7 7 f3 ♗d7
8 ♕d2 ♘c6 9 0-0-0 ♖c8 10 g4 ♘e5
11 h4 h5 12 g5 ♘h7 13 f4 ♘g4 14
♗g1 14 f5 △ ♗h3 0-0 15 ♖h3!? 15
♔b1 e5=; 15 f5!? ♗xd4!? 16 ♗xd4
gxf5 17 exf5 ♗xf5 18 ♗d3 ♗g6∝
e5! 16 ♘db5 exf4 17 ♖d3? 17 ♘xd6
♘e3! 18 ♗xe3 ♖xc3 19 bxc3 (19
♘xb7 ♕c8) ♗xh3∝; 18 ♘xb7 ♗xc3
19 bxc3 ♕c7!; 18 ♘xc8 ♗xc3 19
bxc3 (19 ♕xd7 ♗xb2+) ♘xd1 ♕a5∓
18 ♘xd6 ♖xc3 19 ♖xc3 19 bxc3?
♕a3+ 20 ♔b1 ♗e6; 19 ♔b1 ♖xd3
♕xa2 20 ♕xf4 ♕a1+ 21 ♔d2 ♕xb2
22 ♖b3 ♕a2 △ ♘e5/♗a4 23 ♘c4
♗a4 24 ♖db1 ♖d8+ 25 ♗d3 ♗xb3
26 ♖xb3 ♘f8 27 ♕c7 ♖d7 28 ♕b8
b6 29 ♕e2 ♕a1 30 ♗e3 ♕h1 31 ♕g3
♘e6 32 ♖b5 ♘xe3 33 ♔xe3 a6 34
♖d5 ♖xd5 35 exd5 ♕xd5 36 ♕b8+
♔h7 37 ♘xb6 ♗d4+ 38 ♔e2 ♕g2+
39 ♔d1 ♕g1+ 0-1

2...e6, 4...a6

205 Kuzmin-Velikov Kiev 78
1 e4 c5 2 ♘f3 e6 3 d4 cxd4 4 ♘xd4
a6 5 ♗d3 5 c4!? ♗c5 6 ♘b3 6 c3!?
+= ♗a7 6...♗b6 7 ♘c3 ♘c6 8 ♕e2
♘ge7 9 ♗e3 0-0 10 0-0-0 += 7 0-0
7 ♕e2! ♘c6 8 ♗e3 ♗xe3 9 ♕xe3 ♘f6
10 ♘c3 d6 11 0-0-0 b5 12 ♖d2! +=
Byrne-Larsen, Biel 76 ♘c6 8 ♕e2
8 c4 ♘ge7 9 ♘c3 0-0 10 ♕e2 e5=
d6 8...♘ge7!? 9 ♗e3 ♗xe3 10 ♕xe3
♘f6 11 c4 11 ♘c3 0-0 12 ♖ad1 ♕c7
△ b5= 0-0 12 ♘c3 12 ♖d1!? ♕c7 13
♘c3 += ♘e5 12...e5 13 ♖fd1 ♗e6
14 ♗e2 += 13 ♗e2 ♕c7 14 ♖fd1 b6!
N 14...♘xc4?! 15 ♗xc4 ♕xc4 16
♖xd6 +− 15 ♖ac1 ♗b7 16 ♘d2 16
♘d4 ♖fd8 17 ♘f3 ♘g6!= 17...♘eg4

131

18 ♕f4?! e5; 18 ♕d3 += **18 h3 ♖ac8
19 ♗f1 ♗a8 20 a3 ♕b8 21 ♕d4 ♘c6**
△ ♕b7 **22 a4** 22 b4 **♕b7 23 ♖e1 h6
24 ♖cd1 ♕e7 25 ♖c1?!** 25 b4!? **♕b7
26 b4 ♕b8 27 ♖b1 ♕c7 28 ♖ec1
♗a8 29 ♕e3** 29 ♘e1!? **♕b8**

30 c5?! dxc5 **31 ♗xa6** cxb4! **32
♗xc8** bxc3≈ **33 ♖xc3 ♖xe4 34 ♖xb6
♖d1+ 35 ♘e1 ♖xe1+ 36 ♕xe1 ♕xb6
37 ♖c4** 37 ♕e3 **♗d5 38 ♕b4 ♕a7!∓ 39
♖c2 ♘e5 40 a5?! ♘c6 41 ♕b6 ♕xa5**
−+ **0-1 Gufeld**

206 Rohde-Miles Lone Pine 78

**1 e4 c5 2 ♘f3 e6 3 d4 cxd4 4 ♘xd4
a6 5 ♗d3 ♘c6 6 ♘xc6 dxc6 7 0-0 e5
8 ♘d2 ♗d6 9 ♘c4 ♗c7 10 b3 N ♘e7
11 ♕h5 ♘g6 12 ♗a3 b5 13 ♘e3 ♗f4
14 ♕f3 ♗d6 15 ♗xd6 ♕xd6= 16 ♖fd1
♕c5** 16...♕a3!? **17 a4 ♖b8 18 axb5
axb5 19 ♖ab1 0-0 20 b4 ♕e7 21
♗f1 g6** =+ **22 c3 h5 23 ♖d2 ♗e6
24 ♖bd1 ♖a8 25 ♖d6 ♖fc8** 25...
♗d5!? **26 h4?** 26 g3! **♘h3+ 27 ♗xh3
♗xh3 28 g4!** =+ **♗b3! 27 ♖1d2 ♕xh4
28 g3 ♕g5 29 ♔h2 ♘e6 30 ♖b2
♕e7 31 ♖dd2 ♘g5 32 ♕h1 ♖a3** −+
33 ♗g2 ♖ca8 34 f4 Zeitnot **exf4
35 gxf4 ♘e6 36 ♕g3 ♕f6 37 f5 ♕xc3
38 ♕e1 ♕e5+ 39 ♕f2 ♘f4 40 ♗f3
♕xb2 41 ♖xb2 ♘d3+ 42 ♔e2 ♘xe1
43 ♔xe1 ♗c4 44 ♔f2 ♖a2 45 ♖xa2**

♖xa2+ 46 ♔g3 0-1 Miles

207 Panchenko-Miles
Las Palmas 78

**1 e4 c5 2 ♘f3 e6 3 d4 cxd4 4 ♘xd4
a6 5 ♘c3 ♕c7 6 ♗e2 b5 7 0-0 ♗b7
8 ♗f3 ♘c6 9 ♖e1** 9 ♘xc6= **♗d6 9...
♘e5!? 10 g3** 10 ♘dxb5?? axb5 11
♘xb5 ♗xh2+ 12 ♔h1 ♕b6 −+; 10
♘xc6 **♗xd4 11 ♕xd4 ♘e5** =/=+ **12
♕d3 ♘e7 13 ♗g2** 13 ♗d2 0-0 **14 f4?**
14 ♗d2 **♗xc3 15 ♕xc3** 15 bxc3 ♖fc8
=+ **♕xc3 16 bxc3 ♖fc8** =+ **17 ♗a3**
17 ♖d1 ♖c7 =+ ♔f8 **18 ♖e3 ♖c4?**
=+/∓ **19 g4!? ♔e8 20 g5 ♖ac8 21
♗b4 d5! 22 ♗xe7 d4! 23 ♖h3** 23
cxd4 ♔xe7∓ **♕xe7 24 ♖xh7 ♖xc3
25 ♖xg7 ♖xc2!** △ 26...♔f8 27 ♖h7
♖xg2+ **26 g6** Zeitnot 26 ♗f3 ♔f8
△ ♖8c3 −+; 26 ♘h1 ♖c1+ **♖xg2+
27 ♕xg2 ♗xe4+ 28 ♔g3 ♗xg6** −+
**29 ♖d1 ♖d8 30 f5 exf5 31 ♖c1 ♕f6
32 ♖xg6+ fxg6 33 ♖c6+ ♔e5 0-1
Miles**

208 Rohde-Gheorghiu USA 78

**1 e4 c5 2 ♘f3 e6 3 d4 cxd4 4 ♘xd4
a6 5 ♗d3 ♘c3 ♘f6 6 0-0 d6 7 f4!?**
7 ♔h1; 7 ♕e2; 7 b3; 7 c4 **♘bd7!**
△ ♘c5= **8 ♕h1! g6** 8...♘c5 9 e5!± **
9 f5!? ♘e5 10 fxe6 ♗xe6! 11 ♗g5
♗g7 12 ♘c3 0-0 13 ♘de2** 13 ♕d2
♕b6!∓ **h6 14 ♗h4 ♖c8 15 ♕e1** 15
♘f4? ♗g4∓ **g5 16 ♗f2 ♘fg4 17 ♗g1
♘xd3 18 cxd3 d5!∓**

Diagram

**19 ♘d4! ♗xd4 20 ♗xd4 dxe4 21
♕xe4** 21 ♘xe4?? ♕xd4 −+ **♕d6!
22 ♗g1** 22 g3?? ♖xc3 −+ **f5 23 ♕f3
b5 24 a3! ♘e5 25 ♕h3! ♕g7 26
d4!∝ ♘g6 27 d5 ♗d7 28 ♖ae1 ♖ce8
29 ♕d3 ♘e5 30 ♗d4 ♕g6! 31 ♕c2**

♞g4 32 ♗g1 a5! △ b4∓ 33 ♖xe8 ♖xe8 34 ♞xb5! ♕xd5! 34...♗xb5?? 35 ♕xf5+ ♔h5? 36 ♖f3 +−; 35... ♔g7 36 ♗d4+ ♞e5 37 ♖e1 +− 35 ♞c7 ♕e4! 36 ♕d2! 36 ♕xe4 ♖xe4∓ ♖e7 37 ♞d5 ♖e5 38 ♞c3 ♕b4 39 ♖c1 ♗c6! 40 h3 ♞f6 41 ♗d4 ♖e6 42 ♔g1 ♞h5! 43 ♗e3 ♞g3 44 ♕d4 ♕b3! −+ 45 ♗f2 ♕xb2 46 ♖b1 Zeitnot ♕xc3! 47 ♕xc3 ♞e2+ 48 ♔h2 ♞xc3 49 ♖c1 ♞e4 50 ♗d4 f4 0-1 Gheorghiu

209 Weinstein-Christiansen
USA Final 78
1 e4 c5 2 ♞f3 e6 3 d4 cxd4 4 ♞xd4 a6 5 ♗d3 g6!? 6 c4 6 ♞d2; 6 f4 ♗g7 7 ♗e3 ♞e7 8 ♞c3 0-0 9 0-0 d5? 9... ♞bc6!= 10 exd5 exd5 11 ♖c1! dxc4 11...♞bc6 12 ♞xc6 bxc6 13 ♗c5± 12 ♗xc4 ♞d7? 12...♞bc6!? 13 ♞f3!± b5?! 14 ♗d5! ♞xd5 15 ♕xd5 ♖b8 16 ♖fd1 ♖e8 17 ♗f4 ♖b6 18 ♗g5 ♗f6 19 ♞e4! +− ♗xg5 20 ♞exg5 ♖f6 20...♕e7 21 ♖e1; 20...♖f8 21 ♖xc8 21 ♞e5! ♕b6 22 ♞g4 ♖f4 22...♖f5 23 ♞h6+ 23 ♞xf7 ♔g7 24 ♞d6 ♖e5 25 ♞xe5 ♕xf2+ 26 ♔h1 1-0 Shamkovich

2...e6, 4...♞c6

210 Spassky-Karpov Bugojno 78
1 e4 c5 2 ♞f3 e6 3 d4 cxd4 4 ♞xd4 ♞c6 5 ♞b5 d6 6 c4 ♞f6 7 ♞1c3 a6 8 ♞a3 ♗e7 9 ♗e2 0-0 10 0-0 b6 11 ♗e3 ♗b7 12 ♕b3 ♞d7 13 ♖ad1 13 ♖fd1 ♞c5 14 ♕c2 ♞f6 15 ♖ab1 ♞b4!? 16 ♕d2 ♗xc3 17 bxc3 ♞xe4 18 ♕b2 ♞xa2!= Averbakh-Polugaevsky, Palma de Mallorca 72 ♞c5 14 ♕c2 14 ♗xc5 bxc5 15 ♕xb7?? ♞a5 −+ ♕c7 14...♗f6 15 ♞ab1 ♕c7 16 a3 ♖fd8 17 b4 ♞d7 18 ♕b3 ♖ac8≈ Gaprindashvili-Kushnir (12) 69 15 f4 ♖fd8 16 ♗f3 ♖ac8 += 17 ♕e2 ♕b8 18 ♕f2 18 ♖d2!? ♗a8 19 ♖d2 ♗f6! 20 ♞ab1 ♗e7! 21 ♞a3 ♗f6 22 ♞ab1 ♗e7 ½-½ Bellin

211 Westerinen-Taimanov
Jurmala 78
1 e4 c5 2 ♞f3 ♞c6 3 d4 cxd4 4 ♞xd4 e6 5 ♞c3 a6 6 ♗e2 6 g3 ♞ge7 7 f4!? ♞xd4 8 ♕xd4 b5 9 ♗g2 ♗b7 10 0-0 ♖c8 11 ♕f2 f5 12 ♗e3 ♖c4 13 ♖ad1 += Radev-Ogaard, Pernik 76; 6 ♗f4!? ♞ge7 7 ♗f4! += 7 f4 ♞xd4 8 ♕xd4 b5 9 0-0 ♗b7? 10 f5!± Gufeld-Taimanov, Vilnius 75; 9...♕c7!? ♞g6 7...d6!? 8 ♞b3 ♞g6 9 ♗g3 ♗e7 10 0-0 0-0 11 ♕d2 e5≈ 8 ♗g3 8 ♞xc6 bxc6 9 ♗d6 ♗xd6 10 ♕xd6 ♕e7=; 8 ♗e3 ♕c7 9 0-0 b5! 10 ♞xc6 ♕xc6 11 ♕d4 b4 12 e5 ♗b7 13 ♗f3 ♕c7= Tal-Taimanov, USSR 76 ♗e7 8... d6?! 9 ♕d2! ♗e7 10 ♖d1± 9 ♞b3 9 ♕d2 0-0? 10 h4! b5 11 0-0-0± Kupreichik-Taimanov, USSR 76; 9... ♗g5!∞; 9 0-0!? 0-0 10 ♕d2 d6 11 ♖ad1 ♞xd4 12 ♕xd4 e5 13 ♕d3 ♗e6 14 ♞d5 += Urzica-Barczay, Zurich 76 b5? 9...d6! 10 ♕d2 0-0 11 ♖ad1 ♞ge5= 10 ♕d2 0-0 11 ♖d1 += △ ♗d6 ♕b6 12 ♗d6 ♗xd6 13 ♕xd6 ♖b8 14 0-0 ♞ce5 15 ♕xb6 ♖xb6 16 f4!±

♞c6 17 ♖d6 ♖b7 18 g3 ♖c7 19 ♖fd1 ♞b8

20 ♖b6?! 20 ♗d3! △ a4± ♗b7 21 ♞a5 ♗a8 22 a4 bxa4 23 ♖a1 ♞e7! 24 ♖xa4 f5= 25 exf5 ♞xf5 26 ♖ab4 ♖cc8 27 ♗d3 ♞e3 28 h3 h6 29 ♔f2 ♞f5 30 ♞e4 g5! 31 ♞d6 ♞xd6 32 ♖xd6 gxf4 33 gxf4 ♔f7 34 ♖db6 ♔e7 35 c3 ♖g8 36 ♗e4 ♖xe4 37 ♖xe4 ♖c5 38 ♖eb4 ♖xa5 39 ♖xb8 ♖g6 ½-½ Gufeld

212 Haag-Szabolcsi Hungary 78
1 e4 c5 2 ♞f3 e6 3 d4 cxd4 4 ♞xd4 ♞c6 5 ♞c3 ♕c7 6 ♗e3 a6 7 ♗e2 ♞f6 8 0-0 ♗b4 9 ♞xc6 bxc6 10 ♞a4 0-0 11 ♞b6 ♖b8 12 ♞xc8 ♖fxc8 13 ♗xa6 ♖d8 14 ♗d3 ♗d6 15 f4?! 15 ♔h1= e5 16 f5 ♖xb2 17 g4 h6 17... ♕a5 △ ♗c5= Karpov 18 ♔h1?! N 18 h4?! ♗f8 19 g5 ♞d5! =/=+ ♗f8? 18...♗e7! 19 h4 ♖b4! △ ♖xe4∓ 19 g5 hxg5 20 ♕xg5 ♗e7 ·21 ♕c1 ♕b7 22 ♖g1 ♔h7 22...c5! 23 ♕e3 c4? 24 ♗h6! 23 ♕e3 ♖h8 24 ♕g3 ♔g8 25 ♗c1 ♗f8 26 ♕xe5 ♖b1 26... ♕b8 27 ♗xb2 ♗d6 28 ♖xg7+ 27 ♖xb1 ♕xb1 28 ♗b2 d6 1-0 Haag

213 L.A.Schneider-Taimanov
Jurmala 78
1 e4 c5 2 ♞f3 e6 3 d4 cxd4 4 ♞xd4

♞c6 5 ♞c3 a6 6 ♗f4?! d6! 7 ♞f3?! 7 ♗g3 ♞f6 8 ♗e2 ♗d7 9 ♞b3 ♕c7 10 f4α b5 8 ♕d2 ♖a7! 9 0-0-0 ♖d7 =+ 10 g4 ♕a5! 11 ♔b1 ♞f6 12 g5 b4! 12...♞h5?! 13 ♗e2!? 13 gxf6 =+ ♗xe4 14 ♕e3 d5 15 ♞fd4 ♞xd4 16 ♞xd4 ♗d6!∓ 17 ♗xd6 ♞xd6 18 ♞xe6!? fxe6 19 ♕xe6+ ♔d8 20 ♖xd5 ♕xd5!! 21 ♕xd5 ♞b5! 22 ♕f3 ♗b7 −+ 23 ♕g4 ♖xh1 24 ♗h3 ♗c6 25 a4 bxa3 26 ♕f4 ♖b7 27 bxa3 ♞c3+ 0-1 Gufeld

214 L.A.Schneider-Jakobsen
Roskilde 78
1 e4 c5 2 ♞f3 e6 3 d4 cxd4 4 ♞xd4 ♞c6 5 ♞c3 a6 6 ♗f4 d6 7 ♞f3 ♗e7 8 ♕d2 ♕c7 9 0-0-0 ♞e5 10 ♕d4 f6 11 ♕a4+! 11 ♞d2 ♕f7 11...♗d7? 12 ♗b5! △ ♞d4± 12 ♞d4 h5?! 12... ♖b8!? 13 ♔b3 ♖b8!? 13...b5? 14 ♞d5! 14 h4 b5 15 ♗g3 ♞c6 16 ♞ce2?! 16 ♞xc6 △ ♔b4 ♞a5 17 ♕d3 ♞h6 18 f3 e5!?

19 ♞b3 ♞xb3+ 20 axb3 b4 21 f4 ♗b7 22 ♗e1 a5? 22...♞g4! 23 ♞g3 exf4 24 ♞xh5 d5 25 exd5 ♗d6 △ g6 26 g3! △ ♗h3 ♖bd8 27 ♗h3 g6?? 28 ♗e6+ 1-0

215 Korsunsky-Suetin USSR 78
1 e4 c5 2 ♞f3 ♞c6 3 d4 cxd4 4 ♞xd4

♕c7 5 ♘c3 e6 6 g3 a6 7 ♗g2 d6 8
0-0 ♗d7 8...♗e7; 8...♘f6 9 ♖e1 ♗e7
10 ♘xc6 bxc6 10...♗xc6 11 ♕g4 h5
12 ♕e2 b3 +=; 11 ♗f4!? **11 b3!?**
11 ♕g4?! h5 12 ♕e2 h4≈; 11 ♘a4
♖b8 12 c4 c5 13 ♘c3 ♗f6 17 c4±
♘f6 12 e5! dxe5 13 ♗b2 0-0 14 ♕e2
♗c5 N 14...♘d5 15 ♘xd5 cxd5 16
♗xe5 ♗d6 17 c4± **15 ♘a4 ♗d4 16**
♖ad1 += ♗xb2 16...♖ad8 17 ♘a3!?
♖fe8 18 c3 ♘a7 19 ♗d6± **17 ♘xb2**
e4 18 ♘c4 18 ♗xe4 ♘xe4 19 ♕xe4
c5 20 ♕e5! += c5 18...e5!? **19 ♘d6**
♗c6 20 ♘xe4 ♗xe4 21 ♖xe4 ♘xe4
22 ♕xe4 ♖fd8?! 22...♖ad8 += **23**
♖d3 g6 23...♖xd3 24 ♕xa8+ ♖d8
25 ♕xa6 ♖d2 += **24 ♖ed1 ♖ab8 25**
♕f4!? e5? 25...♖xd3 26 ♕xc7 ♖xd1+
27 ♔g2 ♖dd8! 28 ♕xc5 ♖bc8! 29
♕a5 ♖d5; 29 ♕g5 ♖d5! 30 ♔c1?
♖c3 **26 ♕f6+ ♖d4** 26...♖xd3!? Δ a5
27 ♕xa6 e4 28 ♖3d2 ♖bd8 29 ♕e2
♕a5 29...♕e5 30 c3± **30 ♖xd4 cxd4**
31 ♕xe4 ♕xa2 32 ♔g2 ♕b2 33 ♕h4
♖d6 34 ♕f4 ♖d7? 34...♖d5! **35**
♕e4 ♖d8 36 ♕e7 ♖d5? 37 c4! +-;
36...♖c8 α/± **35 ♕b8+ +- ♔g7 36**
♕e5+ f6 37 ♕c5 g5 38 h4! gxh4
39 ♕f5 ♖c7 40 ♕g4+ ♔f7 41 ♖xd4
♕xc2 42 ♕h5+ ♕g6 43 ♕d5+ ♔g7
44 ♖xh4 ♖f7 45 b4 f5 46 b5 ♖f6
47 ♕e5 ♕f7 48 ♖d4 ♕b7+ 49 ♔g1
♔f7 50 ♖h4 h6 51 ♖c4 ♔g6 1-0
Gufeld

216 Ivanovic-Kurajica
Jugoslavia Final 78
1 e4 c5 2 ♘f3 ♘c6 3 d4 cxd4 4 ♘xd4
♕c7 5 ♘c3 e6 6 ♗e2 a6 7 0-0 ♘f6
8 ♔h1 ♗b4 9 ♗g5 9 ♕d3; 9 ♘xc6
bxc6 10 ♕d4?! c5 Kaplan-Karpov,
Madrid 73; 10 f4!? d5 11 e5 ♘d7
12 ♕e1 0-0?! 13 ♘xd5! += Planinc-
Kirov, Maribor 77; 12 ♘a4 ♘b6 13

♘xb6 ♕xb6 14 ♗d3 g6= Matanovic-
Kurajica, Jugoslavia Final 78 **♗xc3**
10 ♗xf6 gxf6 11 bxc3 ♘e7!? N 11...d6
12 f4 ♗d7 13 ♖b1 ♕e7 14 ♕e1 h5 15
♕h4 ♖h6 16 ♗f3 ♘a5 17 e5! +-
Zichichi-Giustolisi, Italy Final 76
12 ♕d2 d5 13 ♕h6 13 exd5!? ♘xd5
14 c4α dxe4 **14 ♕xf6 ♘g6 15 f3**
15 f4 ♕xc3 16 ♖ab1±; 15...♕e7
16 ♕g7 f5 =+ e5 15...e3? 16 ♗d3
Δ ♗xg6/♖fe1± **16 ♘f5 ♗xf5 17**
♕xf5 e3 18 ♖ad1 0-0 19 ♖d3 19
♖d7 ♕xc3 α/∓ ♖ac8 20 ♖xe3 ♕b6≈
21 ♖e4!? 21 ♖d3 ♕b2 ♖xc3 22 ♗c4
22 h4! f6 23 ♖g4 ♔h8 24 ♗d3 ♖c7
♔g7 23 ♗b3 ♖c7 24 ♖d1 24 h4 ♕f6
25 ♕g5 h6 26 ♕g3 ♔h7 =+; 25 ♕xf6+
♔xf6 ≈/=+ **♕f6 25 ♕g4** 25 ♕xf6+
h6 26 ♖b4?! h5 27 ♕e4 ♖d8 28 ♖xd8
♕xd8 29 h4 ♕f6 30 g3 b5 31 ♗d5
31 a4 ♖d7 32 ♗d5 ♕d8; 31 c4 ♕d6
♘e7 32 c4 ♖d7 33 ♖b3 bxc4 34 ♗xc4
♘f5 35 ♕e1 35 f4 ♖d4 Δ ♕c6+ -+;
35 ♔g2 ♖d2+ 36 ♔h3 ♘d6 37 ♕c6
♕f5+ 38 g4 ♕f4 -+; 36 ♗e2 ♖xa2 -+
♘d4 36 ♖d3 ♘xf3 37 ♕d1 ♖xd3 38
♕xd3 a5 39 ♗d5 ♘d4 40 ♔g2 ♕d6
41 ♕c4 ♘f5 42 ♔f3 42 ♔f2 ♕b6+
-+ **♕a3+ 0-1 Bellin/Wicker**

217 Velimirovic-Rajkovic
Jugoslavia Final 78
1 e4 c5 2 ♘f3 e6 3 d4 cxd4 4 ♘xd4
♘c6 5 ♘c3 ♘f6 6 ♗f4!? d6 6...♗b4
7 ♘b5 7 ♘f3?! 7 ♗g3 ♘xd4!? 8 ♕xd4
♘h5!? 9 ♗b5+ ♗d7 10 0-0 ♘xg3 11
hxg3 a6 12 ♗xd7+ ♕xd7 13 ♖ad1
♕c6=; 7 ♘db5 e5 8 ♗g5 ♗e7 **8 ♕d2**
0-0 9 0-0-0 ♕a5 10 ♗c4 ♘e5 11
♗b3 b5! 12 ♕e1 12 ♘xe5 dxe5 13
♗xe5 b4 14 ♗xf6 ♗xf6∓ **b4 13 ♘b1**
♗b7 14 ♘bd2 ♖fc8∓ 15 ♔b1 ♕b5
16 ♘d4 ♕e8 17 ♗g3 17 ♘xe6 fxe6 18

♗xe6+ ♔h8 19 ♗xc8 ♖xc8∓ a5 18
f4 a4! 19 ♘d5 19 ♗xe6 fxe6 20
fxe5 dxe5 21 ♗xe5∓; 19 fxe5 axb3
20 exf6 bxc2+ 21 ♘xc2 ♕a4 22 ♘xb4
♗xf6! −+ 23 e5 ♕xb4 24 exf6 ♖xa2!!;
23 ♘b3 ♖c4!; 19...dxe5∓ ♘c6 20
♘xe6 20 ♘xc6 ♗xc6 21 ♗xc6 ♕xc6
22 ♖c1 a3 −+ fxe6 21 ♗xe6+ ♔h8
22 e5 ♘d4! −+ 23 ♘c4 23 ♗xc8
♕xc8 24 exf6 ♕xc2+ 25 ♔a1 ♘b3+
26 ♘xb3 axb3 27 a3 ♖xa3+!; 23
exf6 ♗xf6 24 ♗xc8 ♕xc8 25 ♖c1
a3 −+ ♘xe6 24 exf6 ♗xf6 25 ♘xd6
♕c6 26 ♘xc8 ♖xc8 27 ♕xb4 ♕xc2+
28 ♔a1 ♘d4 △ ♘b3+ 29 ♖b1 ♕xb1+!
0-1 Bellin

4♘

218 Jakobsen-Rosenlund Roskilde 78
1 e4 c5 2 ♘f3 e6 3 d4 cxd4 4 ♘xd4
♘c6 5 ♘c3 ♘f6 6 ♘xc6 bxc6 7 e5
♘d5 8 ♘e4 ♕c7!? 8...f5!? 9 ♗g5?
♕c7 9 f4 c5! 9...♗e7 10 c4 △ c5±
10 c4 ♘b4 11 g3 11 ♗e2!? ♗b7 12
♗g2 ♖d8!? 13 0-0 d5 14 exd6 ♗xd6
15 ♕e2 0-0 16 ♗e3 ♗e7 17 a3 ♘c6!

18 ♕f2 18 ♘xc5/♗xc5 ♘d4! ♘d4
19 ♖ad1! 19 b4? ♗xe4 20 ♗xe4
cxb4∓ ♗a6 ½-½ 20 ♘xc5 ♗xc5 21
♗xd4 ♖xd4 22 ♖xd4 e5 23 fxe5 ♕xe5
24 ♖fd1 ♗xc4!=

219 Peshina-Shlekis USSR 78
1 e4 c5 2 ♘f3 ♘c6 3 d4 cxd4 4 ♘xd4
♘f6 5 ♘c3 e6 6 ♘xc6!? bxc6 7 e5
7 ♗d3 d5 8 0-0 ♗b4 9 ♕e2= ♘d5
8 ♘e4 8 ♘xd5!? △ ♗d3, ♕e2, 0-0
f5 8...♕c7 9 f4 f5 10 exf6 ♗xf6
11 ♘xf6+ gxf6 12 ♕h5+ ♔d8 13 ♗d2
d5 14 0-0-0± Kurajica-Rossolimo,
Montilla 72; 8...♕a5+!? 9 exf6 ♗xf6
10 ♘d6+ ♗xd6 11 ♕xd6 ♗a6 11...
♕b6! 12 ♗d3 c5 13 ♗f4 ♗b7 14
0-0 ♖c8= 12 c4! += 12 ♗xa6 ♕a5+
♕b6 △ ♕xf2+, ♘e4+ 13 ♗d3 c5
14 ♗f4!± ♕b4+ 15 ♗d2 ♕xb2 16
0-0 ♕d4 16...♕xd2? 17 ♗g6+ +−
17 ♕xa6 ♕xd3 ·18 ♖ad1 ♕f5 19
♘c3 0-0 20 ♗xf6 ♖xf6 21 ♖xd7 ♖b8
22 ♖xg7+! 1-0 Gufeld

2...e6, 4...♘f6

220 Vitolins-Knaak Jurmala 78
1 e4 c5 2 ♘f3 e6 3 d4 cxd4 4 ♘xd4
♘f6 5 ♘c3 d6 6 ♗b5+!? N ♗d7 7
♕e2 ♘c6 7...♗xb5 8 ♕xb5+ ♕d7 9
♗g5 8 ♗e3 a6 9 ♗xc6 bxc6= 10 0-0-0
♕c7 11 g4 c5! 12 ♘b3 ♗c6 13 ♗g5?!
13 f3!? △ g5, h4-h5∞ ♗e7 =+ 14
♗xf6 ♗xf6 15 ♘d5 ♗xd5 16 exd5
0-0 16...e5 17 ♘d2 ♗g5 18 ♔b1=
17 dxe6 a5! 18 exf7+ ♕xf7 19 ♖xd6
♖fe8! 19...a4? 20 ♘xc5 ♕xa2 21
♕e6+ 20 ♕d1 ♗e7! 21 ♖d5 ♖ed8?
21...♕xf2!? =+; 21...a4!? 22 ♘xc5
a3! 23 ♔b1 axb2 24 ♘b3 ∞/=+ 22
♖xd8+ ♖xd8 23 ♕e2 a4 24 ♘a5 ♕xa2
25 ♕c4+ ♕xc4 26 ♘xc4 ♖d4 27 ♘e3
♗g5∞ 28 h3 ♖f4 29 h4 ♗f6 30 g5
♗e5 31 ♘d1 ♕f7 32 c3 ♗c7 33 ♔b1
♔g6= 34 ♔a2 ♗b8 35 ♔a3 ♔h5 36
♖e1! ♖xh4 37 ♖e7 ♖h1 38 ♖d7
♔xg5 39 ♔xa4 39 ♖xg7+?! ♔f6∞
♗e5 40 ♘e3 h5 41 ♖d5 ♔f4! 42 ♖xc5
g5 43 ♘c4 ♖e1! 44 ♘xe5 ♖xe5 45

b4!? h4! 46 ♖c8 ♕f3 47 ♖h8 ♖e4
48 ♕b5 ♕g2! 48...♔xf2 49 ♖h5 ♖g4
50 c4 ♔g2 51 c5 h3 52 c6 **49 c4 h3
50 c5 h2 51 c6 ♖h4** 51...h1♕ 52
♖xh1 ♔xh1 53 c7 ♖e8 54 ♔c6 ♔g2
55 b5 g4 56 b6 ♔xf2 57 b7 g3 58
c8♕ +− **52 ♖xh4 gxh4 53 c7 h1♕
54 c8♕ ♕f1+ 55 ♕a4 ♕d1+ 56 ♕a5
♕a1+ 57 ♕b5 ♕e5+ 58 ♕a4 ♕e4!?
59 f3!= ♕xf3 60 b5 h3 61 b6 h2
62 ♕c2+ ♕h3 63 ♕h7+ ½-½ Gufeld**

221 Taulbut-Vilela Mexico 78
1 e4 c5 2 ♘f3 e6 3 d4 cxd4 4 ♘xd4
♘f6 5 ♘c3 d6 6 g3 ♗e7 7 ♗g2 0-0
8 0-0 a6 9 ♘ce2!? Δ c4, ♘c3, b3, ♗b2
♗d7 9...♕c7! 10 b3? e5∓; 10 a4=
10 c4 ♕c8!? 10...♘c6 11 b3 ♖b8
12 ♗b2 ♘xd4 13 ♘xd4 b5= **11 b3 e5
12 ♘c2** 12 ♘f5 ♗xf5 13 exf5 ♘c6∓
♗e6 12...♗h3 13 ♘c3 b5 14 ♘e3 +=
**13 ♘e3 += ♘bd7 14 ♗a3 ♕b8 15
♘f5?!** 15 ♕d2! Δ ♖fd1 ♗xf5 16 exf5
♖a7! **17 ♘c3 b5 18 cxb5 axb5 19
♗b4 ♘c5 20 ♘d5 ♘xd5 21 ♕xd5
♖d8 22 a3?!** 22 ♖fd1 ♘d7 23 ♖fc1
♘f6 24 ♕d2 d5 25 ♗xe7 ♖xe7 26
♕b4 ♖ee8 =+ 27 a4! 27 ♖c5 e4 28
♕d4 ♕a7 e4 28 ♕d4! bxa4 29 bxa4
♕e5 30 ♕xe5 ♖xe5 31 a5 ♖e7 32
a6 ♖a7 33 ♖cb1 ♕f8 34 ♖b7 ♖xb7?
34...♖da8 35 ♗f1 += **35 axb7 ♕e7
36 ♖a8 ♘d7 37 f6+ gxf6** 37...♘xf6
38 b8♕ **38 ♗h3 ♘b8 39 ♗c8 ♘c6
40 ♖a6 ♘b8 41 ♖a8 ♘c6 42 b8♕
♘xb8 43 ♖xb8 ♕d6 44 ♖a8 ♕c7 45
♗b7 ♖xa8** 45...♖d7/♖d6 46 ♗a6 +−
**46 ♗xa8 ♕d6 47 ♗b7! ♕e5 48 f4+!
exf3** 48...♔d4 49 ♕f2 ♔c4 (49...f5
50 ♗c8 +−) **50 ♔e2 f5 51 ♗c8 d4
52 ♗xf5 d3+ 53 ♔e3 ♔c3 54 ♗xe4
d2 55 ♗f3 +− 49 ♕f2 ♕e4 50 ♗c6
f5 51 ♗a4 d4** 51...f4 52 ♗c2+ +−
52 ♗c6+ ♕e5 53 ♕xf3 d3 54 ♕e3 d2

55 ♗f3 f6 56 ♗e2 ♕d5 57 ♗d1 ♕e5
58 ♗f3 h6 59 ♗e2 ♕d5 60 ♗d1 1-0
60...♔e5 61 ♗f3 Zugzwang **Taulbut**

222 Shamkovich-Benko
USA Final 78
1 e4 c5 2 ♘f3 e6 3 d4 cxd4 4 ♘xd4
♘f6 5 ♘c3 d6 6 g4 a6 7 g5 ♘fd7 8
♗e3 b5 9 a3 ♘b6 10 ♖g1 ♘8d7 11
f4 ♗b7 12 f5 e5 12...exf5 13 exf5!
♕e7 14 ♕d2 ♘e5 15 f6!

13 ♘e6!? N fxe6 14 ♕h5+ g6? 14...
♔e7 15 fxe6 ♔xe6 16 ♗h3+ ♔e7
17 ♖f1 ♕e8 18 g6! ♘f6 19 ♕xe5+!
dxe5 20 ♗c5+ ♔d8 21 ♗xb6+ ♔e7
22 ♗c5+ =; 18...♕xg6 19 ♕h4+ ♔e8
20 ♗f5; 17...g6 18 ♕f3 ♕e8 19 ♗xb6±
**15 fxg6 ♕e7 16 gxh7 ♗g7 17 0-0-0±
♕e8 18 g6 ♘f6?** 18...♖c8 **19 ♕xe5!**
♕c6 19...dxe5 20 ♗c5 mate **20 ♖xd6!
♕xd6 21 ♗c5 +− ♖ad8 22 ♗h3** Δ
♕xe6+ ♖c8 **23 ♗xd6+ ♖xd6 24 ♕g5**
Δ e5 e5 **25 ♕xe5+ ♗e6 26 ♗xe6
♖xe6 27 ♕c5+ ♕e8 28 ♕f5 ♖e7 29
♖d1 ♘fd7 30 ♘d5! ♗xd5 31 ♕xd5
♗e5 32 ♕c6 ♕d8 33 ♖d5 ♖f8 34
♕a8+ 1-0 Shamkovich**

223 Lutikov-Knaak Jurmala 78
1 e4 c5 2 ♘f3 e6 3 d4 cxd4 4 ♘xd4
♘f6 5 ♘c3 d6 6 g4 h6 7 ♗g2!? 7 g5
hxg5 8 ♗xg5 ♘c6 9 ♕d2 ♕b6 10 ♘b3

a6 11 0-0-0 ♕c7 12 f4 ♗e7 13 h4 +=
Spassky-Ribli, Manila 76; 7 h4!? ♘c6
8 ♘b3 8 h3 ♗d7 9 ♗e3 a6 10 ♕e2
♖c8?! 11 f4 ♕a5 12 ♘b3 ♕c7 13 0-0
♗e7 14 ♕f2 += Matulovic-Sax, Vrbas
77; 8 g5 a5!? 8...♗d7 9 h4 d5 10
exd5 ♘xd5 11 ♘xd5 exd5 12 ♗e3
+= 9 a4 ♗e7?! 9...d5! 10 exd5 ♘b4≈
10 h3 e5 11 ♗e3 ♘b4 12 ♕d2 ♗e6
13 0-0 += ♖c8 14 f4 exf4 15 ♖xf4
♗xb3 16 cxb3 ♘d7 △ ♗g5 17 ♖f5!
♘e5 18 ♖af1 g6 19 ♖5f2 ♗h4 20
♖e2 ♗g5 21 ♖d1± ♖c6 22 ♖f2 0-0
23 ♗f1 ♗xe3 24 ♕xe3 ♕h4 25 ♗b5
♘xg4!? 26 hxg4 ♕xg4+ 27 ♔h2
♕h4+ 28 ♔g2 ♖c5 29 ♖g1! ♖e5 30
♔f1 d5 31 ♕f4 ♕h3+ 32 ♔e1 ♖e6
33 ♖h2! +− ♘d3+ 34 ♗xd3 ♕xd3
35 ♕h6 ♖xe4+ 36 ♘xe4 ♕xe4+
37 ♖e2 ♕b1+ 38 ♔f2 ♕f5+ 39 ♔g3
d4 40 ♖f2 ♕d3+ 41 ♖f3 ♕e2 42 ♖h1
♕e5+ 43 ♔f2 1-0 Gufeld

1 e4 c6

224 Maric-Bozovic
Jugoslavia 78
1 e4 c6 2 d4 d5 3 ♘c3 dxe4 4 ♘xe4
♘d7 5 ♕e2?! ♘df6 6 ♗f4 △ ♘d6+
♘xe4 7 ♕xe4 ♘f6 8 ♕d3 ♗g4 9 ♗e2!
♗xe2 10 ♘xe2 e6 11 ♕b3?! 11 0-0-0
♕b6 12 ♕xb6 axb6 13 0-0 ♘d5 14
♗d2 ♗d6 15 c4 += ♘f6 15...♘b4
16 a3 ♘d3? 17 ♗c3 +− 16 ♘c3 0-0
17 ♖fd1! ♖fd8 18 f3 e5 19 ♗e3 ♘d7
19...exd4 20 ♗xd4 ♘d7! 21 b3 +=;
20...♗c5 21 ♗xc5 bxc5 22 ♘a4±
20 ♘e4 ♗e7 21 d5! c5 21...f5 22
dxc6 bxc6 23 ♘d6± 22 a3 h6 23
g4± ♖a6 24 ♔g2 ♘f8

Diagram

25 b4!! ♖da8 25...cxb4 26 d6 ♗h4

27 axb4 26 bxc5 ♖c8!? 26...♖xa3
27 ♖xa3 ♖xa3 28 c6! +− 27 cxb6
♖xc4 28 ♖dc1! ♖xc1 29 ♖xc1 ♖xa3
30 ♖c7 ♗h4 31 ♗d2! ♖b3 32 ♖xb7
♗d8 33 ♖b8!! ♗xb6 34 d6 +− ♖b1
△ ♖g1+ 35 ♔h3 ♖f1 36 ♖xb6 ♖xf3+
37 ♔g2 ♖d3 38 ♖b8 f6 39 ♗b4 ♔f7
40 ♖xf8+! ♔xf8 41 d7+ ♔f7 42
♘d6+ ♔e7 43 ♘b7+! ♔xd7 44 ♘c5+
1-0 Maric

225 Mestel-Sloth Esbjerg 78
1 e4 c6 2 d4 d5 3 ♘d2 dxe4 4 ♘xe4
♘d7 5 ♘f3 ♘gf6 6 ♘xf6+ ♘xf6 7 g3
♗g4 8 ♗g2 g6 8...♕a5+ 9 c3 ♕a6
Taulbut-Benko, Lone Pine 78 9 c3
♗g7 10 0-0 0-0 11 ♖e1 e6 12 h3
♗xf3 13 ♕xf3 ♘d5 14 h4 h6 15 ♗d2
♕b6 16 b3 a5 17 ♖ad1 ♖fd8 18
♕e2 a4 19 b4 ♕a6 20 ♕f3 ♕c4 20...
b5!? 21 ♖a1 21 ♗f1 ♕xa2 ♘e7 22
♖e4 ♘f5 23 ♗f4 ♘d6 24 ♖ee1 ♘b5 25
♖e3 ♕d5 26 ♕e2 ♕d7 27 ♗e4 h5 28
♗c2? ♗xc3! 29 ♖xc3 ♕xd4 30 ♖c1
♕xc3 31 ♗xg6 ♕xb4 32 ♗xh5 ♖d4
33 ♗e3 ♖d7 34 ♖c5 e5 35 ♖c4 ♕b1+
36 ♔h2 ♕h7 37 ♕f3 f5 38 g4 f4 39
♗c5 ♕d3 40 ♕xd3 ♖xd3 41 g5 ♗f8
0-1

226 Bronstein-Lutikov
1 e4 c6 2 d4 d5 3 ♘c3 dxe4 4 ♘xe4
♗f5 5 ♘c5!? b6 5...♕b6 6 g4!? ♗g6

138

7 f4 e6 8 ♕e2 ♗e7 9 h4 h5 10 f5! +=
Bronstein-Beljavsky, USSR 75 **6 ♘b3
♘f6** 6...e6 7 ♘f3 ♘bd7= **7 ♘f3 ♘bd7
8 g3 a5?!** 8...e6 **9 ♗g2 e6 10 0-0 a4**
10...♗d6?! 11 ♘e5; 10...♖c8 **11 ♘bd2
+= ♗e7 12 ♘e5 c5?**

13 ♘c6! 13 ♗xa8 += ♕c8 **14 ♘c4!±
♖a6 15 dxc5 bxc5** 15...♘xc5 16
♘xe7 ♔xe7 17 ♕d6+ Δ ♗c6+ +-
**16 ♘d6+ ♗xd6 17 ♕xd6 ♖xc6 18
♗xc6 ♗e4 19 ♗xa4 +- ♕a8 20 b3
♕d5 21 ♗xd7+ ♘xd7 22 ♕xd5 exd5
23 ♗f4 0-0 24 ♖ad1 d4 25 ♖d2 ♘f6
26 b4 1-0 Gufeld**

227 Marczell-Saharov Corr 77

**1 e4 c6 2 d4 d5 3 ♘c3 dxe4 4 ♘xe4
♗f5 5 ♘g3 ♗g6 6 h4 h6 7 ♘f3 ♘d7
8 h5 ♗h7 9 ♗d3 ♗xd3 10 ♕xd3 ♕c7
11 ♗d2 ♘gf6 12 0-0-0 e6 13 ♕e2
0-0-0 14 ♘e5 ♘b6 15 ♗a5 ♖d5 16
♗xb6 axb6 17 c4 ♖a5** 17...♖d8 18
♘e4 ♘xe4 19 ♕xe4 ♗d6 20 f4 f5 21
♕e2 ♗xe5 22 ♕xe5 ♕xe5 23 dxe5
g5! 24 hxg6 ♖dg8=; 20 ♘f3 ♗e7 Δ
♗f6= **18 ♔b1 ♗d6 19 f4 ♖d8 20
♖d2 b5 21 c5 ♗xe5 22 fxe5 ♖a4!
N 23 ♕f2!? ♘g4 24 ♕f4 ♘xe5 25
b3 ♕a5!?** 25...♖b4 26 ♖hd1 ♘c4
27 ♕xc7+ ♔xc7 28 ♖f2∝ **26 bxa4
26** ♖hd1 ♘c4! 27 bxa4? ♕c3∓;
27 bxc4 ♕c3 28 ♖b2 ♖b4= **♕b4+**

27 ♕c1 27 ♖b2 ♕xb2+ ♕c3+? 27...
♕c4+ 28 ♔d1 ♘d3∝ **28 ♕d1 ♘c4
29 ♖f1 e5** 29...♘xd2? 30 ♘e2! ♕a1+
31 ♔xd2 ♕xa2+ 32 ♔e3 bxa4 33
♕xf7 +- **30 ♕f5+ ♔b8 31 ♘e4 ♕b4
32 ♕e2?!** ♘xd2 33 ♕xe5+ ♕a7 34
♘xd2 ♖xd4 35 ♕e3 bxa4∝ 36 ♕e1
36 ♖xf7 ♖xd2+ = f5! 37 a3 ♕b2
38 g3 ♖d5 39 ♘f3 39 ♕f4? ♖e5+
40 ♔f2 ♖e4 ♕c2 40 ♘d2 ♖d3 41
♕f4 ♖xa3 42 ♕b4 ♖xg3 ½-½ 43 ♖f4
♕c1+ 44 ♔e2 ♖g2+ 45 ♔d3 ♖g3+ =;
43 ♕b6+ = **Kasparov**

228 Chudinovsky-Gabdrahmanov
USSR 78

**1 e4 c6 2 d4 d5 3 ♘c3 g6 4 ♘f3
♗g7 5 h3 ♘f6** 5...dxe4 6 ♘xe4 ♘d7
7 ♗c4 ♘gf6 8 ♘xf6+ ♘xf6 9 0-0 0-0
10 ♖e1 += Balashov-Petrosian, USSR
76; 5...♘h6 **6 e5** 6 ♗d3!? += ♘e4 6...
♘fd7 7 ♗f4 e6 8 ♕d2 += **7 ♘xe4**
7 ♗d3!? ♘xc3 8 bxc3 c5 9 dxc5 ♕a5
10 0-0 0-0 11 ♗e3 += Gheorghiu-
Cardoso, Torremolinos 74 **dxe4 8
♘g5 c5!** 9 ♗c4 9 e6 ♗xe6 10 ♘xe6
fxe6 11 dxc5=; 9 dxc5!? ♕a5+ 10 ♗d2
♕xc5 11 ♗c3 ♘d7 12 ♗d4 ♕a5+!∝
0-0 10 c3!? 10 e6 f6 11 ♘xe4 b5
12 ♗e2 cxd4 13 ♗f3 ♘c6 14 0-0 ♕b6
15 ♖e1 ♗b7 =+ Spassky-Tseshkovsky,
USSR 74 **cxd4 11 cxd4 b5?** 11...
♘c6! 12 ♗e3 ♕a5≈ Malley-Pytel,
Dortmund 75 **12 ♗b3 ♗b7 13 h4!?**
13 ♗c2!± **♗d5 14 h5! ♗xb3 15 axb3
♕d5 16 hxg6 hxg6 17 ♕g4 ♕xd4
18 ♖h8+! +- 1-0 Gufeld**

229 Velimirovic-Hort Niksic 78

**1 e4 c6 2 d4 d5 3 exd5 cxd5 4 c4
♘f6 5 ♘c3 e6 6 ♘f3 ♗e7 7 cxd5
♘xd5 8 ♗d3 ♘c6 9 0-0 0-0 10 ♖e1
♗f6 11 ♗e4 ♘ce7 12 ♕c2** 12 ♗g5!?
♗xg5 13 ♘xg5 h6 14 ♘f3∝; 12 ♕d3!?

g6 13 ♗h6 ♗g7 14 ♗xg7 ♕xg7 15 ♘e5 b6 16 h4!? 16 ♘xd5 exd5 17 ♗d3 ♗e6 += Kavalek-Hort, Nice 74 ♗b7 17 h5 ♘f5! 18 ♕d2 ♕h4! 19 g4!? 19 ♘xd5 ♗xd5 20 ♗xf5 exf5 21 ♖e3 ♕g5!=; 19 ♖ad1 ♘xc3! 20 ♗xb7 ♘xd1∓; 19 g3!? ♕xh5 20 ♔g2 ♕h6 21 f4 ♔h8 22 ♖h1 ♕g7∝ f6! 19...♘d6? 20 ♗xd5 ♗xd5 21 ♘xd5 exd5 22 ♔g2! ♘e4 23 ♖xe4! dxe4 24 ♖h1 ♕e7 25 hxg6 fxg6 26 ♕h6+ ♔g8 27 ♘xg6 +– 20 gxf5? 20 ♗xd5! ♗xd5 21 ♘xd5 exd5 22 ♕f4 ♘h6 =+; 22 gxf5!= fxe5 21 h6+ 21 dxe5 gxf5! 22 ♗xd5 exd5! Δ d4, ♔h8, ♖g8; 21 fxe6 ♕g4+! 22 ♔h2 (22 ♔f1 ♗a6+ –+) ♕xh5+ 23 ♔g1 ♕g4+ 24 ♔h2 ♖f4! 25 f3 ♕h5+ 26 ♔g1 ♖h4 27 ♕g2 ♘f4 28 ♕g3 ♖h3 29 ♕g4 ♖h1+ 30 ♔f2 ♕h2+ –+; 21... ♘f4 22 ♗xb7 ♘h3+ 23 ♔g2 ♖xf2+ 24 ♕xf2 ♕xf2+ 25 ♔xh3∝ ♕h8 22 fxg6 22 fxe6 ♕g4+ 23 ♔h2 ♖f4! hxg6 23 ♘xd5 ♕g4+! 24 ♕f1 24 ♔h2 ♗xd5 25 ♗xd5 exd5 26 ♖xe5 ♖f3! 27 ♖e3 ♖af8∓ ♗a6+ 25 ♗d3 ♗xd3+ 26 ♕xd3

26...♖xf2+! 27 ♕xf2 ♖f8+ 28 ♔e3 ♖f3+ 29 ♔d2 ♖xd3+ 30 ♕xd3 ♕xd4+ 31 ♔c2 ♕f2+! 32 ♔b3 exd5 33 ♖ac1 d4 34 ♖h1 34 ♖f1! ♕g2! 35 ♖h1 ♕d5+ 36 ♔a3 ♕d6+ 37 ♔b3 ♔h7∓

♕f7+ 35 ♔b4 ♔h7 36 ♖ce1 ♕d5 –+ 37 ♖c1 a5+ 38 ♔a4 ♕d7+ 39 ♔b3 e4 40 ♔c4 d3 0-1 Hort

230 Nicevski-Stanojevic Jugoslavia 78
1 e4 c6 2 d4 d5 3 exd5 cxd5 4 c4 ♘f6 5 ♘c3 g6 6 ♕b3 ♗g7 7 cxd5 0-0 8 ♘ge2 b5!? N 9 ♕xb5 ♗a6 10 ♕b3 ♘bd7 11 ♘f4 11 g3 Δ ♗g2 ♗xf1 12 ♔xf1 ♘b6 13 a4 ♖b8 14 ♕a2 a5 15 h4 ♕d7 16 h5 ♖fd8≈ 17 hxg6 hxg6 18 d6?! e6?! 18... ♕xd6! 19 ♘xg6 ♘g4 20 ♘f4 ♕xd4 21 ♘h3 ♘c4∓ 19 ♘fe2 ♘fd5 20 ♗g5 ♖dc8 21 ♘b5? 21 ♗h4 Δ ♗g3 ♘xa4 22 ♕xa4 ♖xb5 23 ♕a3 f6 24 ♗d2? 24 ♗h6 ♗h8 25 ♗d2 Δ ♕h3∝ ♖c2∓ 25 ♗c1 ♘b4 26 ♕g3 g5 27 ♖a3 ♖d5 28 ♕h2 ♕b5! Δ ♖xc1+/♕xe2+ 0-1 **Maric**

231 L.A.Schneider-Sloth Esbjerg 78
1 e4 c6 2 d4 d5 3 exd5 cxd5 4 ♗d3 ♘c6 5 c3 ♘f6 6 ♗f4 ♗g4 7 ♕b3 ♘a5 8 ♕a4+ ♗d7 9 ♕c2 a6!? 9...e6 10 a4 ♘c4!? 11 b3 ♘d6 12 ♗xd6 exd6 13 ♘e2 g6 14 0-0 ♗h6! 15 ♘d2 0-0 16 ♖fe1 ♖c8 17 ♘f1 ♖e8 18 ♕b2 ♘e4 19 c4 ♕h4 20 ♘eg3 20 ♘fg3 ♘xf2! ♗g7 21 ♘xe4 dxe4 22 g3 ♕g4 23 ♘e3 ♕g5 24 ♗f1 f5 25 ♖ad1 ♗e6 26 ♕a3 f4 27 ♘g2 ♗g4! 28 ♘xf4 28 gxf4 ♕f6 29 ♗e2 ♗f3! ♗xd1 29 ♖xd1 e3! 30 ♕xd6 30 fxe3 ♖xe3 31 ♕xd6 ♖d8 32 ♕b6 ♖e4 33 ♘e6 ♕e3+ 34 ♔g2 ♖d7 ♖cd8 31 ♕b6 exf2+ 32 ♔xf2 ♖e4 33 d5 ♖f8! 34 ♗e2 ♖exf4+ 35 gxf4 ♕xf4+ 36 ♔g1 ♗e5 37 ♕e6+ ♔h8 38 ♕h3 ♕f2+ 39 ♔h1 ♕xe2 0-1

232 Hort-Bellon Montilla 78
1 e4 c6 2 d4 d5 3 exd5 cxd5 4 ♗d3

g6 5 c3 ♗g7 6 ♗f4 ♘h6!? 7 ♘f3 0-0
8 0-0 ♘c6 9 ♖e1 ♔h8! 10 ♘bd2 f6
11 b4 a6 12 a4 e5= 13 ♗xh6 ♗xh6
14 b5 axb5 15 axb5 15 ♗xb5 e4∓
♖xa1 16 ♕xa1 e4! 17 bxc6 exd3 =+
18 cxb7 ♗xb7 19 ♘b3 ♗c8!

20 ♖d1? 20 h3 △ ♖d1 ♗g4! 21 h3
21 ♖xd3? ♗f5 22 ♖d1 ♗c2 ♗xf3
22 gxf3 ♕d7∓ 23 ♖xd3 ♖b8 24
♘d2? 24 ♘c5 ♕xh3 25 ♕f1 ♕h5 △
♗f4 −+ ♕f5! −+ 25 ♕f1 ♗xd2 0-1
26 ♖xd2 ♕g5+ **Maric**

1...♘c6

233 Taulbut-Balinas
Lone Pine 78
1 e4 d6 2 d4 ♘f6 3 ♘c3 ♘c6!? 4 ♘f3
4 d5; 4 h3 ♗g4 5 ♗b5?! a6 6 ♗xc6+
bxc6 7 h3 ♗d7?! 7...♘h5 △ d5, ♗g6
8 0-0 h6 8...e6 9 ♘g5± 9 e5 ♘d5 10
♘e4 ♗f5 11 ♕e2 e6 12 ♖d1 ♘b6 13
b3 ♗xe4?! 13...♗e7 14 c4 0-0 15
♗f4± 14 ♕xe4 d5 15 ♕g4 g6 16
a4 c5 16...♗g7 △ 0-0 17 a5 ♘d7 18
c4 c6 19 dxc5 ♗xc5 19...♘xc5 20
♘d4 ♕d7 21 ♗a3± 20 cxd5 cxd5
21 ♕a4 ♕f8 22 ♗d2 ♕g7 23 ♖ac1
♗a7 24 b4 ♘b8?! 24...♖c8 25 ♖xc8
♕xc8 26 ♖c1 ♕b7 27 ♕c6± 25 ♕c2
♕d7 26 ♕c7 ♖d8 26...♕b5 27 ♕e7 +−
27 h4 ♕xc7 28 ♖xc7 ♘d7 29 ♖b7

♘b8?! 30 ♗e3 ♕g8 30...♘xe5 31
♗d4 ♔f6 32 ♖xb8 +− 31 ♗d4 ♘f8
32 ♖c1 ♘h7 33 ♖c6 △ b5, a6-a7
g5 34 hxg5 ♘xg5 35 ♘xg5 hxg5 36
♖c3 ♕g7 37 ♖f3 ♖f8 38 g4 ♕g8 39
♖f6 Zugzwang ♕h8 40 ♖fxf7 ♖xf7
41 ♖xf7 ♕g8 42 ♖b7 ♔f8 43 ♕g2
♕e8 44 f4 gxf4 45 g5 ♕f8 46 ♕f3
1-0 Taulbut

1...d5

234 Christiansen-Commons
USA Final 78
1 e4 d5 2 exd5 ♘f6 3 d4 ♘xd5 4 ♘f3
♗g4?! 4...g6; 4...c6 5 c4 ♘b6 6 c5!
♘6d7 6...♘d5 7 ♕b3!±; 6...♗xf3
7 ♕xf3 ♘d5 8 ♕b3!± 7 ♗c4 △ ♗xf7+/
♘g5; 7 ♗e2 e6 8 ♗e3 b6± Shamkovich-
Rogoff, USA Final 78 e6 8 ♗e3
8 h3 ♗h5 9 ♗e3 ♘c6!? 10 ♘c3 ♗e7
11 a3 e5?! 12 d5 ♘d4 13 g4! ♘xf3+
14 ♕xf3 ♗g6 15 b4± Byrne-Rogoff,
USA Final 78 b6 9 ♘c3 bxc5 9...
♗e7 10 b4± 10 d5! ♗d6 10...e5 11
d6! △ ♕d5 11 dxe6 fxe6 12 h3 ♗f5
13 g4 ♗g6 14 ♗xe6 +− ♘c6 15 0-0
h6 15...♘e7 16 ♗g5 16 ♕a4 ♘b4 17
♖fe1 ♘d3 17...♕c2 18 ♗xd7+ ♕xd7
19 ♗g5+ +− 18 ♗xd7+ ♕xd7 19
♗g5+ ♗e5 20 ♘xe5 ♕xa4 21 ♘xd3+
♕f8 22 ♗e7+! ♕g8 23 ♘xa4 ♗xd3
24 ♘xc5 **1-0 Shamkovich**

Vienna

235 Wibe-Westerinen Gausdal 78
1 e4 e5 2 ♘c3 ♘f6 3 ♗c4 ♘c6 3...
♘xe4 4 ♕h5 ♘d6 5 ♗b3 ♘c6 6 ♘b5∞
4 d3 ♘a5 5 ♗b3 ♘xb3 6 axb3 d6
6...d5! 7 exd5 ♘xd5 8 ♘f3 ♗g4!=
7 f4 exf4 8 ♗xf4 ♗e7 9 ♘f3 0-0 10
0-0 c6 10...d5! 11 e5 ♘e8 12 d4 c5!;
11 ♘xd5 ♘xd5 12 exd5 ♕xd5 13

♗xc7? ♕c5 **11 h3 d5 12 e5 ♘e8 13 ♕d2 h6?** 13...♘c7! △ ♘e6 **14 ♘e2 ♗f5 15 g4 ♗g6 16 ♘g3 ♕d7 17 ♕h2± ♘c7 18 ♖ae1 ♘e6 19 ♗xh6!** gxh6 **20 ♕xh6 +− ♘g7 21 ♘d4 ♖fe8 22 ♘h5! ♖xh5 23 gxh5 ♗f8 24 ♖g1 f6 25 e6 ♕c7+ 26 ♔h1 ♖e7 27 ♕xf6 ♖ae8 28 h6 ♔h7 29 ♕g6+ ♔g8 30 hxg7 ♗xg7 31 ♘f5 1-0 Pytel**

236 Vorotnikov-Zlotnik USSR 78
1 e4 e5 2 ♘c3 ♘f6 3 g3!? ♗b4 3...♗c5; 3...d5 **4 ♗g2 c6!?** 4...d6 **5 ♘ge2** c6 **6 0-0 ♘bd7 7 d3** += **5 ♘ge2 0-0 6 0-0 d5=** 7 exd5 cxd5 7...♘xd5 += **8 d4 exd4 9 ♘xd4 ♗xc3 10 bxc3 ♕a5** =+ **11 ♕d3 ♘bd7 12 ♗f4 ♘c5 13 ♕e3** 13 ♕d2? ♘fe4 ♖e8 **14 ♕c1! ♗d7** 14...♕xc3 **15 ♘b5 15 ♕b2 ♖ac8**

16 a4!∞ ♘fe4 16...♗xa4 **17 ♕b4 17 ♖a3 ♕a6 18 ♖b1 ♕f6** 18...♗xa4 **19** ♘f5≈ **19 ♗e3 ♘d6 20 ♗xd5 ♘xa4 21 ♕a1 b5 22 ♘xb5 ♘xb5 23 ♖xa4 ♘xc3 24 ♖xa7! ♕f5** 24...♘xb1 **25** ♕xf6 gxf6 **26 ♖xd7≈ 25 ♖bb7 ♕xd5 26 ♖xd7 ♕f3 27 ♕a6!** 27 ♖xf7 ♘e2+ **28** ♔f1 ♕h1+ **29** ♔xe2 ♖xd2+ **30** ♔d3 ♕e4 mate **♖b8 28 ♖ab7 ♖bc8?** 28...♖a8 **29 ♖a7=** 29 ♕d3 ♘e2+ **30 ♔f1 ♘c1 31 ♕d5! +− ♖xe3?** Zeitnot **32 ♖d8+ ♖e8 33 ♖xe8+ ♖xe8 34 ♕xf3 1-0 Gufeld**

237 Vorotnikov-Mihalchishin USSR 78
1 e4 e5 2 ♘c3 ♘f6 3 g3 f4 d5 4 exd5 ♘xd5 **5 ♗g2 ♘xc3** 5...♗e6 **6** ♘f3 ♘c6 **7 0-0 ♗e7 8 ♖e1** += **6 bxc3 ♗d6 7 ♘e2** 7 ♖b1 c6 **8 ♘f3 0-0 9** 0-0 ♘d7 **10 ♖e1 ♕c7∞ 0-0** 7...♘c6 **8 ♖b1 0-0 9 0-0 ♕d7 10 d3** += **8 0-0 c6 9 d3 ♘d7 10 c4!? N 10 f4 ♖e8 11 h3 ♘f6 12 fxe5 ♗xe5 13 d4 ♗d6 14 ♗g5 ♗e7** =+ Matanovic-Mihalchishin, Vrnjacka Banja 78 **♘f6** 10...♘c5! **11 ♘c3 ♗g4 12 ♕e1 ♖e8 13 ♖b1 ♕c7 14 ♗e3 ♘d7 15 f3 ♗e6 16 ♘e4=** ♗e7 **17 ♕f2 f5! 18 ♗h3** 18 ♘c3 b6= **b6 19 f4 ♗xc4 20** dxc4 20 ♗xf5 ♗xa2 **21 ♖be1 ♖f8! 22** ♗xd7 ♕xd7 **23 c4 ♗b3** fxe4 **21 fxe5 ♘xe5 22 ♕f4 ♗d6 23 ♕xe4 ♘g6 24 ♗e6+ ♔h8 25 ♗d4** 25 ♖f7? ♕xf7 **♘f8 26 ♖be1** 26 ♖f6!? ♗c5! −+ **♘xe6 27 ♖e3 ♕d7** −+ **28 ♕g4 ♗c5 29 ♗xc5 ♘xc5 0-1 Gufeld**

2 ♗c4

238 Larsen-Spassky Tilburg 78
1 e4 e5 2 ♗c4 ♘f6 3 d3 ♘c6 4 ♘c3 ♗c5 5 ♗g5 h6 6 ♗h4 d6 7 ♘a4 ♗b6 8 ♘xb6 axb6 **9 f3! ♗e6 10 ♘e2 d5** 10...♕e7!? **11 ♗xf6** gxf6 **12 exd5 ♗xd5 13 ♘c3!** += **♗e6! 14 ♗xe6** fxe6 **15 ♕d2 f5 16 0-0** 16 0-0-0? b5!; 16 a3!? **♕d4+ 17 ♔h1 0-0-0 18 ♖ae1 h5 19 a3** 19 ♕f2 ♕b4 **h4 20 ♕f2 ♖hg8?!** 20...♕d7 **21 ♕xd4** exd4 **22 ♘b1± ♕d7 23 ♘d2 ♔e7 24 ♖f2 ♕f6 25 f4 ♖de8** 25...♘e7 **26 ♖fe2 ♖d6 27 ♘c4 ♖c6 28 b4!;** 25...b5 **26 ♖fe2 ♖d6 27 ♖e5! 26 h3 e5?!**

Diagram

27 ♖fe2 27 fxe5+! ♖xe5 **28 ♖xe5**

♘xe5 29 ♖f4 ♘c6 30 ♘f3!; 29...♖e8 30 ♖xd4 ♘c6 31 ♖c4! ♖e7 28 ♘f3 exf4 29 ♖xe7 ♘xe7 30 ♘xd4 ♘d5 31 ♖e6+ ♔f7 32 ♖h6? 32 ♖e2! ♘e3 33 ♖xh4 ♘xg2? 33...c5! 34 ♖h7+ ♔f6 35 ♖h6+ 35 ♖xc7? ♘e1 36 ♖xb7 f3 ♔g5 36 ♖h7 ♖h7 ♔f6 37 ♔g1!? c5 38 ♘e2 f3 39 ♘c3 ♘h4+?? 39...♘e3+ 40 ♔f2 ♘xc2 41 ♔xf3 ♘e1+! 40 ♔f1 ♔g5 41 ♘d5 +− ♖e8 42 ♖g7+ ♔h6 43 ♖e7 ♖g8 44 ♖e6+! ♔g5 45 ♖xb6 ♖e8 46 ♘c7! ♖g8 47... ♖e2? 48 ♘e6+ 47 ♘e6+ ♔f6 48 ♘xc5+ ♔e5 49 ♖h6 ♔f4!? 49...♘g2 50 ♔f2 50 ♖xh4+ ♔e3 51 ♘e4! fxe4 51...♖g2 52 ♘c3 52 ♖xe4+ ♔d2 53 ♔f2 1-0 Larsen

Spanish

239 Egorvsky-Gusikov USSR 78

1 e4 e5 2 ♘f3 ♘c6 3 ♗b5 a6 4 ♗a4 b5 5 ♗b3 d6 6 c3 6 d4!? ♘xd4 7 ♘xd4 exd4 8 c3 dxc3 9 ♕d5 (9 ♘xc3!?∝) ♗e6 10 ♕c6+ ♗d7 11 ♕d5=; 8...d3 9 a4 ♗d7 10 axb5 ♗xb5 11 ♘a3 ♗d7 12 ♕xd3± Bronstein; 8 a4 ♗b7 9 0-0 ♘f6 10 ♕e2 ♕d7 11 c3 ♗e7= Keres; 8 ♗d5 ♖b8 9 ♘c6+ ♗d7 10 ♗xd7+ ♕xd7 11 ♕xd4 ♘f6 12 ♘c3 ♗e7 13 0-0 0-0=; 6... exd4 7 ♗d5 ♗b7 8 ♘xd4 +=; 6...♗g4? 7 dxe5 ♗xf3 (7...dxe5 8 ♕d5! +−;

7...♘xe5 8 ♘xe5! +−) 8 ♗xf7+ ♔xf7 9 ♕d5+ ♔e7 10 ♗g5+ ♘f6 11 exf6+ gxf6 12 ♕xc6 +− **♗a5 7 ♗c2 c5 8 d4 ♕c7 9 ♘bd2** 9 dxe5 dxe5 10 ♕d5? ♘c4! **♗e7 10 ♘f1** 10 dxe5?! dxe5 11 ♘f1 g6 12 ♗g5 ♗g7 13 ♘e3 (13 ♗xe7) f6 14 ♗h4 ♗e6 15 b3 c4! 16 b4 ♖d8 17 ♕e2 ♘c6 18 ♗g3 0-0 19 0-0 ♔h8 20 ♖ad1 f5! 21 ♘g5 ♗g8 22 exf5 gxf5 23 ♕h5 ♖d6 24 f4 ♖xd1! 25 ♕xd1 e4!∓ Aronin-Gusjkov, USSR 66 **cxd4 11 cxd4 ♗g4 12 dxe5** 12 ♘e3 ♗xf3 13 gxf3 ♖c8 ∝/=+ **dxe5 13 ♘e3 ♖d8 14 ♗d2 ♗xf3 15 ♕xf3** 15 gxf3 ♘ac6 **♘ec6 16 ♗b1?∓** 16 ♖c1! ♗b4 17 ♗xb4 ♘xb4 18 0-0 ♘xa2 19 ♘d5 ♖xd5 20 exd5 ♘xc1 21 ♖xc1∝ **♖xd2! 17 ♕xd2 ♘d4 18 ♕g3 ♘c4+! 19 ♘xc4 bxc4 20 ♕d1** 20 ♖c1!? ♗b4+ 21 ♖c3∓ **♗b4 21 ♕xg7**

21...♕d6!! −+ 22 ♕xh8+ ♔e7 23 ♗d3 23 ♕a8 ♘c6+ 24 ♔e2 ♕d2+ 25 ♔f3 ♕f4+ −+ **♘b3! 0-1 Lysenko**

240 Janssens-Delplancq Corr 76-78

1 e4 e5 2 ♘f3 ♘c6 3 ♗b5 a6 4 ♗a4 d6 5 ♗xc6+ bxc6 6 d4 f6 7 ♗e3 ♘e7 8 h4 h5! 8...♗e6? 9 h5! **9 ♘c3 ♘g6 10 ♕d3 ♗e7 11 0-0-0 ♗e6** 11...♗d7 **12 d5 cxd5 13 ♘xd5 0-0 14 ♕c4 c5?** 14...♖c8! 15 ♕xa6 ♖a8! 16 ♕c6

Rxa2 17 Qxc7 Qa8 18 Nxe7+ Nxe7 19 Qxe7 Re8! 20 Qc7 Rc8∝ **15 g4! Rf7** 15...hxg4 16 h5 **16 gxh5 Nf8 17 Rdg1 Qb8 18 Qd3 Qb5** 18...Bd7 19 c4 **19 Nc7 Qxd3 20 cxd3 Rab8 21 Nxe6 Nxe6 22 h6 f5 23 Ne1 f4 24 Bd2 Qh7 25 hxg7 Nd4 26 Qd1 Rxg7 27 Rxg7+ Qxg7 28 Bc3 Ne6 29 Qe2 Rh8 30 Nf3 Rh5 31 b4! cxb4 32 Bxb4 Qf7 33 Rc1 Rh8** 33...Bxh4? 34 Rh1 **34 Rc6 Rxh4 35 Bxd6 1-0**

241 Povah-Westerinen
London 78
1 e4 e5 2 Nf3 Nc6 3 Bb5 a6 4 Ba4 d6 5 Bxc6+ bxc6 6 d4 f6 7 Be3 g6 7...Ne7 **8 Qd2!?** 8 Nc3 Nh6 9 dxe5 fxe5 10 Qd2 Nf7 11 h4 h6 12 0-0-0 Bg7 13 h5 g5 14 Ng1 Be6 15 Nge2 Qb8 16 g3 g4∓ Short-Westerinen, London 78 **Bg7 9 Nc3 Ne7 10 dxe5 fxe5 11 Bh6 0-0 12 h4!? Bg4 13 Nh2 Qd7** 13...Be6 14 Bxg7 Qxg7 15 h5 Qb8 16 Nf3!± **14 Bxg7 Qxg7 15 f3 Be6 16 h5 Rab8 17 0-0-0 Rb4 18 hxg6 Nxg6 19 Nf1± Rfb8 20 Ng3! Qg8!** 20...Rxb2? 21 Nh5+ Kf7 22 Qh6 Ke7 23 Qg5+ Kf8 24 Nf6 +- Δ Rxh7; 21...Kh8 22 Nf6 Bxa2 23 Qh6 +- **21 b3 Rd4 22 Qe2** 22 Qe3!? Rxd1+ 23 Qxd1 Δ Qh6, Ne3-f5 a5 22...Rb6 23 Qe3!± **23 Qa6 Qd8?** 23...Qc8! 24 Qxc8+ Bxc8∝ **24 Rxd4!** 24 Nh5? Qg5+ 25 Kb1 Rxd1 26 Nxd1 Qxg2∓; 24...Bc4!? 25 bxc4? Qg5+ -+; 25 Qxc6∝ **exd4 25 Nce2** Qg5+ 25...c5 26 f4± **26 Qb1 Qd2 27 Qxc6** 27 Qa7 Rb4!∝ **d3 28 Qc3!** 28 Qxc7!? Rc8 29 Qxh7+ Kf8 30 Qh6+ Kxh6 31 Rxh6 dxe2 32 Nxe2 Qg7∝ **Qxc3** 28...dxc2+ 29 Qxc2 Qb4 30 Qc3 Qa3 31 Nd4 Bf7 32 f4 Nxf4 33 Ndf5 Ne6 34 Ne7+ Kf8 35 Qh8+

+- **29 Nxc3 Bf4?!** 29...dxc2+ **30 Qh5! dxc2+ 31 Qxc2 Ng6** 31...Nxh5 32 Rxh5± **32 f4 Nf8 33 g4 Rb4 34 Qd3 c5 35 f5 Bf7 36 Nf6+ Qg7 37 g5 c4+ 35 bxc4 Bxc4+ 39 Qe3 Bf7 40 Ng4 d5 41 f6+ Qh8 42 Ne5 d4+ 43 Qd3 Be8 44 Nd5 Bb5+ 45 Qd2 Rb2+ 46 Qc1 Rxa2 47 Qb1 Re2 48 Ne7 Be8 49 g6 Nxg6 50 Nxg6+ Bxg6 51 Nxg6+ Qg8 52 Ne5!** 52 Rxh7 Kxh7 53 f7± d3 52...Rxe4 53 Rg1+ Kf8 54 Nd7+ Kf7? 55 Rg7+ Ke8 56 f7+ +-; 54...Ke8 55 Rg8+ Kxd7 56 f7 Rf2 57 f8Q Rxf8 58 Rxf8 +- **53 f7+ Qf8 54 Rxh7 1-0**
Povah

242 Faibisovich-Vorotnikov
Daugavpils 78
1 e4 e5 2 Nf3 Nc6 3 Bb5 a6 4 Ba4 d6 5 0-0 Bg4 6 h3 h5 7 Bxc6+ bxc6 8 d4 Qf6 9 Nbd2 Be6 10 Nb3 10 dxe5 dxe5 11 Nb3 Bd6 12 Qe2 Ne7 13 Na5 Qg6 14 Nh4 ½-½ Hait-Vorotnikov, Vilnius 77 **Qg6 11 Qd3!** N 11 dxe5 Bxh3 12 Nh4 Qxe4 13 gxh3 Qxh4 14 Qf3 d5 15 Na5!± M.Ivanov-Vorotnikov, Yalta 76; 11 Nh4?! Qxe4 12 Nf3 f6 13 Re1 Qd5 14 Bd2 Ne7 15 Rc1 Bf5 16 c4∝ Bangiev-Vorotnikov, Vilnius 77 **Be7** 11...f6!? 12 Nh4 Qf7 13 Qc3 Ne7 14 f4 Bc4 15 Rf2 exd4 16 Nxd4 c5 17 Nf3 g6 18 f5!? Kim-Vorotnikov, Daugavpils 78 **12 dxe5 Bxh3 13 Nh4 Bxh4 14 Qxh3 Be7 15 Bf4 Nh6 16 Rfe1** 16 exd6! cxd6 17 Nd4!? Qxe4 18 Bxd6 Qxd4 19 Rad1 Qxd6!; 17 Na5! 0-0 18 Nxc6 |Rfe8 19 f3 Bg5 20 Qg3 +-; 17... Qxe4 18 Bxd6 +- **Ng4 17 exd6 cxd6 18 Rad1** 18 Nd4! **0-0 19 Nd4 Rfe8!? 20 Nxc6 d5!? 21 Nxe7 Rxe7 22 Rxd5** 22 exd5? Qxc2! -+

♖xe4 23 ♗e3 f5 23...♘xe3? 24
♖xh5 +− **24 ♛f3 f5 25 ♗d2 ♖xe1+
26 ♗xe1 ♖e8 27 ♖d1 ♔h8?** 27...
♛xc2? **28 ♛d5+ ♔f8 29 ♗b4+**; 27...
♛g5 (△ ♛h4) 28 g3 fxg3 29 fxg3
♖e3 ∝/± **28 ♛xf4 ♛xc2 29 ♛d2 ♛c7
30 g3 ♛b7?** 30...♛f7 **31 ♛g5 +− ♖e5
32 ♛d8+ ♔h7 33 ♛d3+ ♔h8 34 ♗c3
♛f7 35 ♖d2 ♖e1+ 36 ♔g2 ♛b7+ 37
♛d5 ♛xd5+ 38 ♖xd5 ♖e2 39 ♖xh5+
♔g8 40 ♔f3 1-0 Kapengut**

243 Verdu-Beliavsky Alicante 78
**1 e4 e5 2 ♘f3 ♘c6 3 ♗b5 a6 4 ♗a4
♘f6 5 d3 d6 6 ♘bd2** 6 c3; 6 c4 g6=
**7 0-0 ♗g7 8 ♖e1 0-0 9 c3 ♖e8 10
a3** △ b4; 10 b4? b5 11 ♗b3 a5 =+
b5 11 ♗c2 ♘b8 11...d5!? **12 b4 a5?!**
12...c5 △ ♗b7, ♘bd7 **13 ♗b2 ♘fd7
14 c4! c6 15 d4** += **♘a6 16 ♗d3 ♖b8
17 ♛e2 axb4 18 cxb5 cxb5 19 a4?**
19 ♗xb5 ♛b6 20 a4 += **bxa4! 20
♖xa4** 20 ♗xa6 a3 21 ♗xa3 bxa3 22
♖xa3 exd4∓; 21 ♗c1 exd4∓

**♘c7∓ 21 ♘c4 ♛e7 22 ♛d2 exd4 23
♖xb4?!** 23 ♘xd4 ♗b7 24 ♘a5≈;
23...♗xd4 24 ♗xd4 ♘c5 25 ♖a7 =+
**♖xb4 24 ♛xb4 ♘e5! −+ 25 ♗e2
♘xf3+ 26 ♗xf3 d5 27 ♘d6 ♖d8 28
♗a3 dxe4 29 ♖xe4 ♗e6 30 ♛b6 ♖a8**

**31 ♗b2 ♘d5 32 ♛c6 ♖b8 33 ♘c4 ♗b4
34 ♛a4 ♘d3 35 ♛c2 ♘xb2 36 ♘xb2
♛a3 37 ♖e2 ♗f5 38 ♛d2 d3 0-1
Webb**

244 Lanka-L.A.Schneider Jurmala 78
**1 e4 e5 2 ♘f3 ♘c6 3 ♗b5 a6 4 ♗a4
♘f6 5 d4 exd4 6 0-0 ♗e7** 6...d6 7
♘xd4 ♗d7 8 ♗xc6 bxc6 9 ♘c3 ♗e7
10 ♗f4 0-0 11 e5!± Gipslis-Kostro,
Dubna 76 **7 ♖e1** 7 e5 ♘e4 8 ♘xd4
0-0 9 ♘f5 d5 10 ♗xc6 bxc6 11 ♘xe7
♛xe7 12 ♖e1 += Mnatsakanian-
Smejkal, Erevan 76 **0-0** 7...b5 8
e5 ♘xe5 9 ♖xe5 d6 10 ♖e1 += **8 e5
♘e8** 8...♘d5 9 ♘xd4 ♘xd4 10 ♛xd4
♘b6 11 ♗b3 += **9 ♗f4 f6** 9...b5 **10
♗xc6 dxc6** 10...bxc6?! 11 ♛xd4 ♖b8
12 ♘bd2 ♛h8 13 b3 +− **11 ♛xd4
♛xd4 12 ♘xd4 f5!** 12...♗c5 13 c3
♗xd4 14 cxd4 fxe5 15 ♗xe5 ♗e6
16 ♘c3 += Gipslis-Dorfman, USSR
75 **13 ♘f3?!** 13 e6!? g5 14 ♗e5 c5
15 ♘b3 ∝/=+; 13 ♘c3 g5 14 ♗d2
♘g7 15 ♖ad1 ♘e6 △ c5= Gipslis-
Ivkov, IBM 76 **g6! 14 ♗g5?!** 14 ♘bd2
♗xg5 15 ♘xg5 h6 16 ♘f3 ♗e6 =+
**17 ♘bd2 ♘g7 18 ♖e3 ♖ad8 19 ♖ae1
♖d7 20 ♘b3 b6 21 a4 ♖fd8 −+ 22 ♘c1
♗d5 23 e6!? ♖e7 24 ♘e5 ♖xe6 25 f3
f4?!** 25...♔h7 26 c4; 25...c5!? **26 ♖3e2
♘f5 27 c4 ♘e3 28 cxd5 ♖xe5 29
♘d3 ♖f5 30 ♘xf4! ♖xf4 31 ♖xe3
cxd5 32 ♖e7 =+ ♖f7 33 ♖7e6! ♔h7
34 a5!= bxa5 35 ♖xa6 ♖b8 36 ♖xa5
♖d7 37 ♖d1 d4 38 ♖d2 ♖b3 39 ♖c5!
♔g7 40 ♔f2 ♔f7 41 ♖c6 h5 ½-½
Gufeld**

245 Maric-Micov Jugoslavia 78
**1 e4 e5 2 ♘f3 ♘c6 3 ♗b5 a6 4 ♗a4
♘f6 5 d4 exd4 6 0-0 ♗e7 7 ♖e1 0-0
8 e5 ♘e8 9 ♗f4 b5?!** 9...d6; 9...d5
10 ♗b3 ♗b7 11 ♗d5 ♖b8 12 ♘xd4

♘xd4 13 ♕xd4 d6 14 ♗xb7 ♖xb7 15 ♘c3 dxe5 16 ♕xe5 ♗f6 17 ♕e4 += ♕c8 17...♗xc3 18 ♕xb7 ♗xe1 19 ♖xe1±

18 ♗e5! ♖b6 19 ♘d5 ♖e6 20 ♕f4! 20 ♕g4 ♕b7! ♗d8 21 ♖ad1 c6 22 ♘e3± ♘f6 22...g6 23 ♘g4± 23 ♘f5 c5 24 ♕g5 g6 25 ♘h6+ ♔g7 26 ♘f5+ ♔h8 26...♔g8 27 ♖e3 (△ ♕h6 +-) ♖xe5 28 ♖xe5 ♘d7 29 ♘e7+ +- 27 ♕h6 ♖g8 28 ♘d6 ♕d7 29 ♘e4?! 29 ♕f4 ♕e7 30 ♗xf6+ +- ♖xe5 29...♕e8 30 ♘g5! ♖xe5 31 ♖xe5 ♕xe5 32 ♘xf7 mate 30 ♖xd7 +- ♘xd7 31 ♕d2 ♘f6 32 ♘xf6 ♖xe1+ 33 ♕xe1 ♗xf6 34 c3 ♖d8 35 g3 ♖d6 36 ♕e3 c4 37 ♕c5 ♖e6? 37... ♖d1+ 38 ♔g2 ♔g7 39 a4 +- **38 ♕f8 mate 1-0 Maric**

246 Vitolins-Mihalchishin
USSR 78
1 e4 e5 2 ♘f3 ♘c6 3 ♗b5 a6 4 ♗a4 ♘f6 5 0-0 b5 6 ♗b3 ♗b7 7 d4 7 d3 ♗e7 8 c4! d6 9 ♘c3 bxc4 10 ♗xc4 ♘a5 11 ♕a4+ c6 12 ♗xf7+!± Matanovic-Mihalchishin, Jugoslavia 76; 7 ♖e1 ♗c5 8 c3 d6 9 d4 ♗b6 10 ♗g5 h6 11 ♗h4 ♕d7 12 a4 += Karpov-Tseshkovsky, USSR 76; 7 c3 ♘xe4 8 d4 exd4 9 ♖e1 d5 10 ♘g5 ♗e7 11 ♖xe4! +=; 8...d5 ♘xd4 8 ♘xd4

8 ♗xf7+?! exd4 9 e5 9 c3 ♘xe4!? 10 ♖e1 ♗e7 11 ♕g4∞ ♘e4 10 c3! dxc3 10...d3! 11 ♕f3! ♕e7 12 ♘d2 ♘c5!∞ 11 ♕f3 d5 11...♕e7 12 ♘xc3 ♘c5 13 ♘d5 ♗xd5 14 ♗xd5 ♖b8 15 ♗e3± 12 exd6 ♕f6!? N 12...♘xd6 13 ♗xf7+± 13 ♖e1 0-0-0 14 dxc7 ♕xc7 15 ♕xf6 ♘xf6 16 ♘xc3 ♗c5 17 ♗g5 ♖d7= 18 ♖ac1 ♔b6 19 a4 ♖e8! 20 ♖xe8 ♘xe8 21 ♘xb5!? 21 ♗xf7 ♗xf2+! h6 22 ♗f4 g5 23 ♗b8! axb5 24 a5+ ♔xa5 24...♔c6 25 ♗a7 25 ♖xc5 ♔b4 26 ♖c3 ♖d2 27 ♗c2 ♗e4! 28 ♖b3+ ♔c4 29 ♖c3+ ♔b4 30 ♖b3+ ♔a5 31 ♖a3+ ♔b6 32 ♗a7+ ♔c7 33 ♖c3+ ♔d7 34 ♗b3 ♖xb2 =+ 35 f3 ♗g6 36 ♗d5! b4 37 ♖c5 ♘c7 38 ♗c4 b3 39 ♗b8 ♘e6 40 ♖b5 ♗c2 41 ♗e5 ♖b1+ 42 ♔f2 ♔c6 ½-½ Gufeld

247 Rantanen-Kaiszauri
Gausdal 77
1 e4 e5 2 ♘f3 ♘c6 3 ♗b5 a6 4 ♗a4 ♘f6 5 0-0 b5 6 ♗b3 ♗b7 7 ♖e1 ♗c5 8 c3 d6 9 d4 ♗b6 10 ♗g5 h6 11 ♗h4 ♕d7!? 11...♕e7; 11...0-0-0 12 a4 0-0-0 13 axb5 axb5 14 ♘a3 g5 15 ♗g3 h5!? 15...exd4 16 ♘xb5 += Karpov-Tseshkovsky, USSR Final 76 16 h4!? ♖dg8 16...gxh4 17 ♗xh4 ♖h6 17 ♘xg5 exd4 18 ♕f3! ♕e7 19 ♘xb5 dxc3 20 ♕xc3 ♘g4 21 ♗xf7 ♖f8 22 ♖e2 ♘ce5 23 ♘xd6+?! 23 ♗d5! c6 24 ♘xd6+ ♔xd6 25 ♗e6+ ♔b8 26 ♗xg4 +- ♕xd6 24 ♗e6+ ♔b8 25 ♗xg4 ♗d4 26 ♕a5 hxg4 27 ♖d2 c5? 27...♕b6 28 ♖xd4 ♕xa5 29 ♖xa5 ♘c6±

Diagram

28 ♖xd4! +- ♕xd4 29 ♘e6 1-0 Iskov

248 Gufeld-Kozlov
Vladivostok 78
**1 e4 e5 2 ♘f3 ♘c6 3 ♗b5 a6 4 ♗a4
♘f6 5 0-0 b5 6 ♗b3 ♗b7 7 ♖e1 ♗c5
8 c3 d6 9 d4 ♗b6 10 ♗g5 h6 11
♗h4 ♕d7 12 a4 0-0-0 13 axb5 axb5
14 ♘a3 g5 15 ♗g3 h5** 15...exd4 16
♘xb5 += Tumakov-Tseshkovsky,
Odessa 74 **16 h4 gxh4!?** N 16...
♖dg8 17 ♘xg5 exd4 18 ♗xf7 ♖xg5
19 hxg5 h4 20 ♗h2 dxc3 21 ♗g6!
♘e7 22 gxf6 ♘xg6 23 bxc3 ∞/+=;
20...♘g4 21 g6 dxc3 22 g7±
Chiburdanidze-Kaiszauri, Vilnius 78
17 ♗xh4 ♖h6 18 dxe5 ♘xe5= 18...
♖g8 19 exf6 ♕g4 20 g3 ♘xe5 21
♔g2± **19 ♘xe5 dxe5 20 ♕xd7+**
20 ♕f3 ♕g4! **♖xd7 21 ♖ad1**
21 ♗c2 ♗c6 22 ♔f1 ♘e8! Δ
♘d6, f6= **♘xe4 22 ♖xd7 ♔xd7 23
♗xb5** 23 ♗xf7 ♘xf2! **f6 24 ♗c2 ⅟₂-⅟₂**
Gufeld

249 Kapengut-Malanjuk
Daugavpils 78
**1 e4 e5 2 ♘f3 ♘c6 3 ♗b5 a6 4 ♗a4
♘f6 5 0-0 b5 6 ♗b3 ♗b7 7 ♖e1 ♗c5
8 c3 d6 9 d4 ♗b6 10 ♘h4!?** 10 ♗g5;
10 ♗e3 **♕d7!?** N 10...exd4 11 ♘f5
0-0 12 cxd4 g6 13 ♘h6+ ♔g7 14
♗e3 ♘xe4? 15 ♘xf7! ♖xf7 16 ♗xf7

♔xf7 17 d5 +−; 10...g6 11 ♘f3±;
10...♘e7 11 ♕f3 h6 12 ♘d2 ♕d7!
13 ♘f1 ♕g4 += Kapengut-Kupreichik,
Minsk 75 **11 ♗g5 0-0-0 12 d5** 12
♘f5?! ♘xe4! 13 ♗xd8 ♕xf5 14 ♕f3
♕xf3 15 gxf3 ♘xf2! 16 ♔xf2 exd4!
17 ♔g3 ♘xd8∓ **♘e7 13 ♗xf6 gxf6
14 ♕f3 ♖hg8!**

15 g3 15 ♕xf6? ♘g6 16 ♘f5 ♘f4
17 ♘e7+ ♔b8 18 ♘xg8 ♖xg8 −+;
16 ♘xg6 ♖xg6 17 ♕f5 ♕xf5 18
exf5 ♖f6∓ **♕h3 16 ♔h1 ♖g4?!** 16...
c6!? 17 ♕xf6? cxd5 18 ♕xe7 dxe4
−+; 17 ♘f5 ♘xf5 18 exf5 ♕g4∓;
17 c4! bxc4 18 ♗xc4 cxd5 19 ♗xd5∞
**17 ♘d2 ♖dg8 18 ♖g1 ♔b8 19 ♕xf6
♘g6?!** 20 **f3!?**± 20 ♗d1! **♗xg1 21
♖xg1 ♗xh4 22 fxg4 ♘g6 23 ♗d1
♗c8 24 g5 h6? 25 ♘f1?!** 25 ♕xf7!
♖f8 26 ♕xg6 ♖f2 27 ♘f1 ♖xf1 28
♕xh6 +− **♖f8 26 ♖g2 ♗g4 27 ♗xg4
♕xg4 28 ♕f5 ♕xg5** 28...♕xf5 29 exf5
♘e7 30 ♘e3 hxg5 31 f6± **29 ♕xg5
hxg5 30 ♘e3 +=♔c8 31 ♖f2 ♔d7
32 ♔g2 f6 33 b3 ♘e7 34 ♔h3 ♔e8
35 ♔g4 ♔f7 36 ♖c2 c6 37 c4 c5 38
b4!? ♖c8! 39 bxc5 ♖xc5 40 cxb5
axb5 41 h4 gxh4 42 ♖xc5!**± 42
gxh4 ♖xc2 43 ♘xc2 f5+ 44 ♔g5 +=
dxc5 43 gxh4 c4?! 43...♖c8 44 ♘f5
c4 45 ♔f3 ♔g6 46 ♔e3 ♔h5?! 47
♔d2 b4 48 d6 ♘b6 49 ♘e7 ♘d7 50

&d5± 44 d6 &c6 45 h5 c3 46 d7!
+– &d8 47 &f5 &e6 48 h6 &d4+
49 &g4 &c6 50 &h5 &d8 51 h7!
&g7 52 h8&+ &xh8 53 &g6 &g8 54
&xf6 &f8 55 &c2 &b7 56 &b4 1-0
Kapengut

250 Savon-Balashov
Lvov 78
1 e4 e5 2 &f3 &c6 3 &b5 a6 4 &a4
&f6 5 0-0 &e7 6 &xc6 dxc6 7 d3
7 &c3 &d7 8 d4 exd4 9 &xd4 0-0
10 &f4 &c5 11 &xd8 &xd8 =/=+
Miles-Hort, Hastings 75/7; 11 &e3
&e6 12 &ad1± Tal-Szabo, Leipzig
60; 7 &e1 &g4 8 h3 &h5?! 9 d3 &d7
10 &bd2 f6 11 &f1! += Savon-
Furman, USSR 75; 7 &e1 &d7 8
&a3?! &xa3 9 bxa3 0-0 10 d3 &e8
11 &c3 &e7 12 &e3 c5∞ Ljubojevic-
Portisch (4) Milan 75 &d7 8 &bd2
8 d4 exd4 9 &xd4 0-0 10 &c3 &e5
11 b3?! &c5 12 &ce2 &h4! 13 f4?!
&g4! =+/∓ Kurajica-Smejkal, Wijk
aan Zee 76 0-0 9 &c4 f6 10 &h4
10 &h1 &c5 11 &h4 g6 12 g3 &h3
13 &g2 &d7 14 &g1 &ad8 15 &h6
&f7 16 &ge3 += Taimanov-Furman,
Leningrad 76 &c5 11 &f5 11 &f3
&e6 12 &f5 &d4 13 &xd4 &xd4 14
&e3 += Hort-Spassky (12) 77 &xf5
12 exf5 &d7 13 &g4 &fe8 14 f3 a5
15 &e3 b5 16 &d2 &b7 17 &e4 &d6
18 &g3 &f8 19 h4 &h8 20 h5 h6
21 &g6 &c8 Δ &e7-d5 22 &g4 &e7
23 &e4 &d5 24 a3 &ed8 25 &f2
a4 26 &e2 &e8 Δ &f4 &xh5 27
g4 &f4 28 &g3 &d5 29 &h2 &eb8
30 &e3 b4 31 axb4 31 &xf4 exf4
32 &xf4 &d6 33 &e4 bxa3∓ &xb4
32 &xd5 cxd5 33 &a2 &ab8 34 &c1
&d6 Δ 35...e4 36 fxe4? &e2 –+
35 &d1 e4 36 &xf4 &xf4 37 dxe4
dxe4 38 fxe4 &xb2 –+ 39 &xb2

&xb2 40 &h3 &xc2 41 &d3 &e5
Δ &c3, a3, a2 0-1 Zugzwang; 42 &f1
&f2 **Friedgood**

251 Kasparov-Litvinov
USSR 78
1 e4 e5 2 &f3 &c6 3 &b5 a6 4 &a4
&f6 5 0-0 &e7 6 &e1 b5 7 &b3 0-0
8 d4 d6 9 c3 &g4 10 &e3 &a5?!
10...exd4 11 cxd4 &a5; 10...d5!?
11 dxe5 &xf3 12 &xf3 dxe5 13 &c2
&c4 14 &c1 c6! N 14...c5 15 &d1±
15 b3 &b6 16 &d2 a5 17 &f1 &fd7
18 &e3 a4?! 13...g6! 19 &f5! 19 &b2?!
g6 axb3 20 &xb3 &f6 20...c5? 21
&g3 g6 22 &h6+ &g7 23 &g4± 21
&e3 &c7 21...c5 22 &ad1 c4? 23
&xb6 22 &ad1 c5 23 &d6! &h8
23...c4 24 &xb6 &xb6 25 &xf6±;
23...g6 24 &ed1! gxf5 25 &xf5 &g7
26 &h6! +–

24 &h3! 24 &xf6?! &xf6 25 &xg7
&xg7? 26 &h6+ +–; 25...&g8!∞
g6 24...c4 25 &xb6 &xb6 26 &xf6±;
25 &d1! &d8 26 &g3 g6 27 &xb6
&xb6 28 &xe5+ f6 29 &xf6! +–
25 &h6 gxf5? 25...&g8! 26 &xf7?
&g7!∓; 26 &ed1 &af8 27 h4 &d8
28 h5 gxf5 29 exf5 f6 30 &e6 &b8
31 &xd8 &xd8 32 &xf6+ &g7 33
&xd8 +– 26 &xf6 f4 27 &f5! 1-0
27...&d8 28 &xc5! +– **Kasparov**

252 Smyslov-Savon USSR 78
1 e4 e5 2 ♘f3 ♘c6 3 ♗b5 a6 4 ♗a4 ♘f6 5 0-0 ♗e7 6 ♖e1 b5 7 ♗b3 d6 8 c3 0-0 9 d4 ♗g4 10 ♗e3 exd4 10... d5?! 11 exd5 exd4 12 ♗xd4! ♘xd4 13 cxd4 ♗b4 14 ♘c3 a5 15 a3± Gulko-Geller, USSR 78 **11 cxd4 d5!?** 11...♘a5 12 ♗c2 ♘c4 13 ♗c1 c5 14 b3 ♘b6 15 ♘bd2 ♘fd7= Klovan-Geller, USSR 75; 14...♘a5 15 ♘bd2 cxd4 16 h3 ♗h5 17 g4 d3!∝ Kurajica-Matanovic, Skopje 76 **12 exd5!?** 12 e5 ♘e4 13 ♘c3 ♘xc3 14 bxc3 ♘a5 15 ♗c2 ♘c4 16 ♗c1 f5= **♘xd5 13 ♘c3! ♘xe3** 13...♘xc3?! 14 bxc3± **14 fxe3 ♘a5∝ 15 ♗c2 c5 16 ♕d3 g6 17 ♘e5 cxd4 18 ♕xd4 ♗e6** =+ 19 ♗e4 ♖c8 20 ♘d5 ♗c5 **21 ♕d1 f6? 22 ♘f4! ♕xd1 23 ♖axd1 ♗xa2** 23...fxe5 24 ♘xe6 ♖fe8 25 ♘xc5 ♖xc5 26 b4 **24 ♘d7 ♗b3!? 25 ♗d5+!± ♗xd5 26 ♘xd5 ♖f7 27 b4! ♖xd7 28 ♘xf6+ ♔f7 29 ♖xd7+ ♔xf6 30 bxa5** +− h5 **31 ♔f2 ♗b4 32 ♖b1 ♗xa5 33 ♖d6+ ♔g7 34 ♖xa6 ♖c2+ 35 ♔f3 ♗c7 36 ♖xb5 1-0** 36... ♗xh2 37 ♖bb6 +− **Gufeld**

253 Gulko-Portisch Niksic 78
1 e4 e5 2 ♘f3 ♘c6 3 ♗b5 a6 4 ♗a4 ♘f6 5 0-0 ♗e7 6 ♖e1 b5 7 ♗b3 d6 8 c3 0-0 9 d4 ♗g4 10 ♗e3 exd4 11 cxd4 ♘a5 11...d5!? **12 e5 ♘e4 13 ♘c3 ♘xc3 14 bxc3 ♘a5 15 ♗c2 ♘c4 16 ♕d3 g6 17 ♗h6 ♖e8 18 ♕e2 c5!** 19 h3 ♗e6 20 a4 b4∓; 16 ♗c1 f5 17 ♕d3 c6∝; 16...♕d7=; 13 ♘bd2!? ♘xd2 14 ♕xd2 ♗xf3 15 gxf3 ♗b4 16 ♕c2 ♗xe1 17 ♕xc6 ♗b4 18 ♗xd5± 15 ♖ec1? ♗b4 16 ♕c2 ♘xd4! 17 ♗xd4 ♕g5 −+ Pietzsch-Holmov, Kecskemet 62 **12 ♗c2 c5** 12...♘c4! 13 ♗c1 c5

13 dxc5! 13 d5? ♘c4 14 ♗c1 ♘e5; 13 h3 ♗xf3 14 ♕xf3 ♘c4 15 b3 ♘xe3 16 ♕xe3 cxd4 17 ♕xd4 ♘d7 =+; 15 ♗c1? cxd4 16 ♕d3 ♕b6 17 f4 d5! 18 exd5 ♗b4 19 ♖d1 ♖fe8∓ N.Littlewood-Tal, Hastings 63/4 **dxc5 14 ♘bd2 ♘c6** 14...♘d7!? 15 h3 ♗h5 16 ♖c1 ♖c8 17 ♗b1 ♖e8 18 b3 Tseshkovsky-Hennings, Kislovodsk 72; 18...c4∝ **15 ♖c1 ♗b4 16 ♗b1 ♖c8 17 h3 ♗e6 18 ♘b3 ♕b6 19 ♘g5 ♖fd8 20 ♕f3!± ♘d7** 20...♘d3 21 ♗xd3 ♖xd3 22 e5?! ♘d5 23 ♕e4 ♗xg5 24 ♕xd3 ♘xe3 25 fxe3 c4 26 ♕d4 ♕c7≈; 22 ♕e2! ♗c4 23 ♘d2 ♖xd2 24 ♕xd2 ♗xa2 25 ♕c2! h6 26 e5 hxg5 27 exf6 ♗xf6 28 ♗xc5±; 22...♖xb3 23 axb3 ♗xb3 24 e5 ♘d5 25 ♘xh7±; 22...♖dd8 23 ♘xc5 ♗xc5 24 ♖xc5 ♖xc5 25 b4± **21 e5 g6 22 ♕g3 ♘f8 23 ♘e4 ♗xb3 24 axb3 ♘e6** 24...♘d3 25 ♗xd3 ♖xd3 26 b4± **25 f4 ♘d4 26 f5!** +− **♘xf5 27 ♘f6+ ♔h8 28 ♗xf5 gxf5 29 ♗g5 ♖g8** 29... ♖d4 30 e6 fxe6 31 ♕e5 ♘c6 32 ♕xe6 +−; 30 ♕f3 +− **30 e6! c4+ 31 ♔h1 f4 32 ♕c3 ♖g7** 32...cxb3 33 exf7 **33 ♘h5 f6 34 ♗xf6 ♗xf6 35 ♕xf6 ♖g8 36 ♘xg7 ♖xg7 1-0 Velimirovic**

254 Gulko-Geller Lvov 78
1 e4 e5 2 ♘f3 ♘c6 3 ♗b5 a6 4 ♗a4

♘f6 5 0-0 ♗e7 6 ♖e1 b5 7 ♗b3 d6
8 c3 0-0 9 d4 ♗g4 10 ♗e3 **10 d5**
d5 10...exd4 11 cxd4 ♘a5 **11 exd5**
11 dxe5 ♘xe5 12 exd5 ♗xf3 13
gxf3 ♕d7 **exd4** 11...♘xd5 12 dxe5
♘xe3 13 ♖xe3 ♗c5 14 ♖e1! **12 ♗xd4**
12 ♗g5 ♘xd5! 13 ♗xd5 ♕xd5 14
♗xe7 ♗xf3 15 ♕xf3 ♕xf3 16 gxf3
♖fe8 17 cxd4 ♘xe7 **♗xd4 13 cxd4**
13 ♕xd4 ♗xf3 14 gxf3 ♘d7! 15 ♕d2
♗c5 **♗b4** 13...♖e8 14 h3 ♗h5 15 g4
♗g6 16 ♘e5 **14 ♘c3 a5** 14...♗xc3
15 bxc3 ♘xd5 16 ♕d3 ♗e6 17 ♖e5
h6 18 ♖ae1; 16...♗xf3 17 ♕xf3 c6
18 ♖e5 **15 a3 ♗xc3 16 bxc3 a4 17**
♗a2 ♕d6 17...♘xd5 18 ♕d3 ♗e6 19
♖e5 **18 h3 ♗xf3?** 18...♗f5 19 ♖e5
♗e4 20 ♘g5 ♗xd5 21 ♘xh7! ♔xh7
22 ♗xd5 ♘xd5 23 ♕h5+; 18...♗h5
19 ♕d3 ♕xa3 20 ♗c4 bxc4; 19 ♖e3
♕xa3 20 ♗c4 ♕d6 21 ♗xb5 ♘xd5
22 ♖e5 ♘xc3 23 ♕d3 ♗xf3! 24 ♕xc3
♗d5 25 ♖xa4; 19...♘xd5 20 ♗xd5
♕xd5 21 ♖e5 ♗xf3 22 ♖xd5 ♗xd1
23 ♖xd1 c6 24 ♖c5 ♖fc8 25 ♖c1 Δ
c4 **19 ♕xf3 ♕xa3** 19...♖ab8 20 ♕g3!
♕xa3 21 ♕xc7 ♖bc8 22 ♕a5 ♕xc3
23 ♕xb5 ♕xd4 24 ♖ad1 ♕a7 25 d6;
21...♖fc8 22 d6! ♖xc7 23 dxc7 ♕d6
24 cxb8♕+ ♕xb8 25 ♖e7; 21...b4
22 cxb4 ♕xb4 23 ♖eb1 ♕xd4 24
♕xb8 **20 ♗c4 ♕d6 21 ♗xb5 ♕xd5**
21...a3 22 ♗c6 Δ c4; 21...♘xd5
22 ♖xa4 **22 ♕xd5 ♘xd5 23 ♗c6 ♖ad8**
24 ♗xd5 ♖xd5 25 ♖xa4 ♖c8 25...c5
26 ♖a5 **26 ♖c4 ♔f8 27 ♔f1 ♖a5 28**
♖c6 ♖a7 29 g4 h6 30 ♖e5 ♖b8 31
♔e2 ♖b2+ 32 ♔e3 g6 33 h4 ♖c2
34 f3 ♖a3 35 ♖ec5 ♖a1 36 ♖xc7
♖e1+ 37 ♔f4 ♖f2 38 ♖e5 ♖ef1 39
♖e3 f6 40 ♖c8+ ♔f7 1-0

255 Vitolins-Klovan USSR 78
1 e4 e5 2 ♘f3 ♘c6 3 ♗b5 a6 4 ♗a4

♘f6 5 0-0 ♗e7 6 ♖e1 b5 7 ♗b3 d6
8 c3 0-0 9 h3 ♘a5 10 ♗c2 c5 11 d4
♘c6!? **12 d5** 12 ♘bd2 cxd4 13 cxd4
♘d7 14 ♘b3 a5 15 ♗e3 a4 16 ♘c1∞
♘a7!? 12...♘a5 13 b3 += **13 ♘bd2**
13 b4 ♘d7 14 a4 cxb4 15 cxb4
bxa4 Δ ♘b6≈; 13 g4!? ♗d7 14 ♘f1
♘c8 15 a4 15 ♘e3 ♕c7 16 b3 ♘b6
17 c4 ♖fb8 18 a4∞ Vitolins-Klovan,
Jurmala 78; 15 b3!? **bxa4** 15...♘b6
16 b3 bxa4 17 bxa4 ♕c7 18 ♘e3
16 ♗xa4 ♗xa4 17 ♕xa4 ♘b6 18 ♕c2
a5 19 c4 a4 20 ♘e3 ♕d7 21 ♘d2?!

21...♘h5= 22 ♘b1?! ♗g5 22...g6!? =+
23 ♘a3 ♖ab8 23...g6 **24 ♗d2 g6 25**
♗a5 f5 26 exf5 gxf5 27 ♗xb6 ♖xb6
28 ♘b5 += ♖a6 29 ♖xa4 ♖xa4 30
♕xa4 ♘f4 31 ♕a6 ♘d3 32 ♖f1 32
♖a1 ♗xe3 Δ f4! ♖d8 **33 ♕c6 ♗xe3**
34 fxe3 ♘xb2 35 ♖a1 ♘xc4 35...
♕e7! Δ ♕g5 **36 ♖a7 += ♕xc6 37**
dxc6 ♖c8 38 c7 ♔f8! 39 ♖b7 ♔e7
40 ♘a7 ♔d7 41 ♘xc8 ♔xc8 42 ♖b8+
♔xc7 43 ♖h8 d5! 44 ♖xh7+ ♔d6
45 h4! ♘xe3 46 h5 c4 47 h6 ♘g4
48 ♖h8 48 ♖d7+?! ♔xd7 49 h7 c3
50 h8♕ c2 51 ♕g7+ ♔c6 =+ **♘xh6**
49 ♖xh6+ ♔c5 50 ♔f2 c3 51 ♔e2 d4=
52 ♔d3 52 ♖f6 c2 53 ♔d2 d3 54
♖xf5 ♔d4 55 ♖f8= e4+ **53 ♔c2**
♔c4 54 ♖c6+ ♔b4 55 ♖b6+ ♔c4
½-½ Gufeld

256 Savon-Dorfman Lvov 78
1 e4 e5 2 ♘f3 ♘c6 3 ♗b5 a6 4 ♗a4
♘f6 5 0-0 ♗e7 6 ♖e1 b5 7 ♗b3 d6
8 c3 0-0 9 h3 ♘a5 10 ♗c2 c5 11 d4
♘d7!? 11...♘c6 12 ♘bd2 cxd4 13
cxd4 ♘d7 14 ♘b3 a5 15 ♗e3 a4 16
♘bd2 ♗f6 17 d5 ♘d4 18 ♖c1 ♗b7
19 ♗b1 += Gufeld-Romanishin, USSR
75; 11...♕c7 12 ♘bd2 ♗d7 13 ♘f1
♖fe8 14 d5 ♘b7 15 ♘3h2!± Karpov-
Unzicker, Milan 75; 12...cxd4 13
cxd4 ♗b7 14 ♘f1 ♖ac8 15 ♗d3 ♘d7
16 d5 f5 17 ♘g3 f4 18 ♘f5 +=
Yudovich-Berta, corr 76 **12 ♘bd2**
12 dxc5 dxc5 13 ♘bd2 f6 14 ♘h4∝
cxd4 12...♗b7 13 ♘f1 cxd4 14 cxd4
♖c8 15 ♖e3 g6 16 ♗d2 += **13 cxd4
♗f6** 13...♘c6 14 ♘b3 a5 15 ♗e3 a4
16 ♘c1 exd4 17 ♘xd4 ♘xd4 18 ♗xd4
♗f6 19 ♘e2 ♗b7= Tal-Larsen, Biel
76; 15 ♗d3 ♗a6 16 d5 ♘b4 17 ♗f1
a4 18 ♘bd4! exd4 19 a3 +=
Shamkovich-Benjamin, USA 76; 13...
exd4!? **14 d5** 14 ♘f1!? exd4 15 ♘xd4
♘e5 16 ♘e3 Δ ♘d5, a4 += **♘b6 15
♘f1** 15 b4=; 15 b3 ♘b7 16 ♘f1 ♗d7
17 ♗d2! ♕c7 18 ♘e3 += **♗d7 16 b3
♘b7 17 ♗e3** 17 g4?!; 17 ♗d2 +=
♘c5!? 18 a4! bxa4 19 b4 ♘b3 19...
♘b7 20 ♗xb6 ♕xb6 21 ♗xa4 +=
20 ♗xb3 axb3 21 ♕xb3 ♕b8 Δ ♖c8
22 ♖ec1 ♖c8 23 ♘1d2 ♖xc8
♘xc8!? **♗d8 24 ♘e1 f5=** 25 exf5
25 f3 f4 26 ♗f2 g5∝ **♗xf5 26 ♘ef3
♗g6 27 ♖xc8 ♘xc8! 28 ♕c4 ♗f7 29
♖xa6 ♖xa6 30 ♕xa6 ♗xd5 31 ♕a4**
Δ ♕e8 **♗f7 32 ♕d7 ♕c7** 32...♗b6?
33 ♘g5 +− **33 ♕g4 ♘b6 34 ♘g5 ♗xg5
35 ♗xg5 h5! 36 ♕g3 ♘d5 37 b5 ♕c2
38 ♕a3 ♕f5=** ½-½ Gufeld

257 Savon-Geller Lvov 78
1 e4 e5 2 ♘f3 ♘c6 3 ♗b5 a6 4 ♗a4
♘f6 5 0-0 ♗e7 6 ♖e1 b5 7 ♗b3 d6

8 c3 0-0 9 h3 h6 10 d4 ♖e8 11 ♘bd2
♗f8 12 ♗c2!? 12 ♘f1 ♗d7 13 ♘g3
♘a5 14 ♗c2 c5 15 b3 cxd4 16 cxd4
♘c6 17 ♗b2 ♖c8 18 ♕d2! += Gufeld-
Savon, USSR 75 **♗d7 13 ♗d3** 13
a3!? g6 14 ♘f1 ♗g7 15 d5 ♘e7 16
c4 c6∝ **♕b8 14 b3 g6 15 ♗b2 ♗g7
16 d5 ♘d8 17 c4 += ♘h5 18 ♗f1
♘f4 19 ♕c2 c6** 19...f5 **20 ♖ec1 cxd5
21 cxd5 ♘b7 22 b4!**

♖c8 22...a5 23 a3± **23 ♕d1!** 23
♕b3?! **♕a7 24 ♖xc8 ♖xc8 25 ♖c1
♖xc1 26 ♕xc1 ♕b6 27 ♘e1!± h5
28 ♕c2 ♘d8 29 ♘b3 h4 30 ♗c1 ♘b7
31 ♗e3 ♕d8 32 ♕d2 g5 33 ♔h2 ♕c8
34 ♘f3 ♗f6 35 ♘g1! Δ g3 ♗g7 36
g3 +− hxg3+ 37 fxg3 f5!? 38 exf5
♗xf5 39 gxf4 gxf4 40 ♗b6 ♕c2 41
♕xc2 ♗xc2 42 ♘e2 ♗f6 43 ♔g1 ♗d8
44 ♗g2 ♗f7 45 ♘c3 ♗f5 46 ♘d2 ♔f8
47 ♘ce4 ♗h4 48 ♗f2 ♗e7 49 ♔h2
♔e8 50 ♗f3 ♕d8 51 ♗g4 ♘h6 52
♗xf5 ♘xf5 53 ♘f3 ♕d7 54 h4 ♗f8
55 ♘fg5 ♗g7 56 ♔h3 ♘e7 57 ♘c3
1-0 Gufeld**

258 Rohde-Beljavsky Alicante 78
1 e4 e5 2 ♘f3 ♘c6 3 ♗b5 a6 4 ♗a4
♘f6 5 0-0 ♗e7 6 ♖e1 b5 7 ♗b3 0-0
8 c3 d5 9 exd5 ♘xd5 10 ♘xe5 ♘xe5
11 ♖xe5 c6 12 d4 ♗d6 13 ♖e1 ♕h4
14 g3 ♕h3 15 ♗e3 ♗g4 16 ♕d3 ♖ae8

17 ♘d2 ♖e6 18 a4 f5 18...bxa4;
18...♕h5 **19 ♕f1 ♕h5 20 f4 bxa4**
20...♖fe8?! 21 axb5 ♖xe3 22 ♖xe3
♖xe3 23 bxc6!± **21 ♖xa4 ♖b8 22
♗f2!** 22 ♗xd5+ cxd5 23 ♕g2 ♕e8
24 ♕xd5 ♔h8≈ 25 ♘c4? ♗xf4!∓
Johannsson-Mortensen, Glucksburg 77
**♖xe1 23 ♕xe1 ♖e8 24 ♕f1 ♖e2
25 ♖xa6!** 25 ♘c4? ♗xf4! **♗h3** 25...
♖xd2? 26 ♖xc6 ♗h3 27 ♗xd5+ ♔f8
28 ♖c8+ ♔e7 29 ♕e1+ ♖e2 30 ♕a1
+− **26 ♕d1** 26 ♕c1? ♖xd2 27 ♕xd2
♕f3 **♗g4 27 ♕f1 ♗h3**

28 ♖xc6!? ♗xf1 29 ♗xd5+ ♔f8 30
♗f3 ♕e8 31 ♘xf1 ♗e7 32 b4 ♖b2
33 d5 ♕a8 34 ♖c7 34 d6? ♗xd6 ♕a6
35 ♗d4 ♕d3 36 d6?? 36 ♘g2≈; 36
♗h1≈ ♕xf3 37 dxe7+ ♔f7 0-1 Webb

259 Kuzmin-Beljavsky USSR 78

**1 e4 e5 2 ♘f3 ♘c6 3 ♗b5 a6 4 ♗a4
♘f6 5 0-0 ♗e7 6 ♖e1 b5 7 ♗b3 0-0
8 c3 d5 9 exd5 ♘xd5** 9...e4!? **10
♘xe5 ♘xe5 11 ♖xe5 c6 12 d4** 12
g3 ♗d6 13 ♖e1 ♕d7! 14 d4 ♕h3≈
**♗d6 13 ♖e1 ♕h4 14 g3 ♕h3 15
♗e3 ♗g4 16 ♕d3 ♖ae8 17 ♘d2 ♖e6
18 ♕f1** 18 a4 f5 19 ♕f1 ♕h5 20
f4 bxa4 21 ♖xa4 g5 22 ♖xa6 gxf4≈
Tal-Geller, USSR 75; 18 c4!? bxc4
19 ♘xc4 ♗f4! 20 ♕f1 ♕h6 21 ♗c1!
♗h3 22 ♖xe6 fxe6 23 ♕d1 ♗xc1

24 ♖xc1 ♕f6 25 f3!± Byrne-Geller,
Las Palmas 76 **♕h5 19 ♕g2** 19 a4!?
bxa4 20 ♖xa4 f5 21 c4 +=; 19 c4
♘xe3 20 ♖xe3 ♖h6 21 ♕g2 c5 22
d5 ♗e5∓ **♖fe8 20 ♘f1** 20 ♗xd5?!
cxd5 21 a4 bxa4! △ ♗f4!∓ **f5** △
f4 −+ **21 ♗d2 ♗f3 22 ♗d1**

22...♖e2! 23 ♖xe2! 23 ♗xe2 ♖xe2
−+ ♗xg2 24 ♖xe8+ ♕xe8 25 ♔xg2
♕e4+ =+ **26 ♔g1** 26 ♗f3 ♕c2∓ **f4
27 a4! g5** 27...h5!? **28 axb5 axb5
29 ♗b3! h5 30 ♖c1 ♕e6** △ ♕h3, f3
**31 c4 bxc4 32 ♖xc4 ♗c7 33 ♗a4
f3 34 ♗d1 ♕f6**∝ ½-½ Gufeld

260 Taulbut-Mihalchishin
Mexico 78

**1 e4 e5 2 ♘f3 ♘c6 3 ♗b5 a6 4 ♗a4
♘f6 5 0-0 ♗e7 6 ♖e1 d6!? 7 ♗xc6+
bxc6 8 d4 exd4 9 ♘xd4 ♗d7 10 ♘c3
0-0 11 ♕f3 ♖b8** 11...♘e8 12 e5 d5
13 ♘b3 g6 14 ♗h6 ♘g7 15 ♗xg7 ♔xg7
16 ♘a4 ♕b8 17 ♘ac5 ♗f5 18 ♕c3
♕b6= Boleslavsky-Shamkovich, USSR
64; 11...♖e8 12 e5 dxe5 13 ♘xc6
♗xc6 14 ♕xc6 ♗b4!∝ Keres-Spassky,
USSR 62 **12 ♖b1! ♖b6 13 h3 g6**
△ c5, ♗c6 **14 ♘b3 ♘h5** 14...c5 15 e5!
15 ♗e3 ♖b8 16 e5! dxe5?! 16...♘g7
17 ♘e4 dxe5 18 ♖bd1±; 16...d5 17
♘a4± **17 ♗h6 ♖e8 18 ♖xe5** △ ♖xh5,
♕g3+ **♘g7** 18...♗f6 19 ♖xe8+ ♗xe8

20 ♘e4± 19 ♖d1 ♝e6 19...♘f5? 20 ♖xf5 +− 20 ♝e4 +− ♖b5 21 ♖xe6 fxe6 22 ♕c3 e5 23 ♕c4+ ♚h8 23... ♖d5 24 ♖xd5 cxd5 25 ♕xd5+ ♔h8 26 ♕xe5+ ♗f6 27 ♕xf6+ +− 24 ♕f7 ♖g8 25 ♘f6 ♗xf6 26 ♖xd7 ♕xd7 27 ♕xd7 1-0 Taulbut

261 Lutikov-Westerinen Jurmala 78
1 e4 e5 2 ♘f3 ♘c6 3 ♗b5 a6 4 ♗xc6 dxc6 5 0-0 ♗d6!? 6 d4 exd4 7 ♕xd4 f6 8 ♘bd2?! 8 e5 fxe5 9 ♘xe5 ♕f6! 10 ♖e1 ♘e7=; 8 ♖e1 ♘e7 9 e5 fxe5 10 ♘xe5 0-0 11 ♗g5 ♗e6 12 ♘c3 ♘f5 =+ Grigorov-Westerinen, Wroclaw 77; 8 ♗e3 ♘e7 9 ♘bd2 ♗e6 10 ♖ad1∝; 8 b3!? ♗e6 9 ♘a3 ♘h6 10 ♗xd6 cxd6 11 c4 0-0 12 ♘c3+ = Kagan-Zwaig, Hastings 76/77 ♗e6 8...♘h6!? 9 ♘c4 ♘f7 10 ♘xd6! cxd6 11 ♗f4= 9 b3 ♝e7 10 ♗b2 10 ♘c4 ♗b4 11 ♘e3 c5 12 ♕xd8+ ♖xd8 13 ♗b2 ♔f7 14 ♖fd1= Schneider-Lutikov, Jurmala 78 0-0 11 ♖ad1 ♕e8!= 12 e5?! 12 ♘c4= fxe5 13 ♘xe5 c5! 14 ♕e4 ♗d5!

15 ♕g4 h5! =+ 16 ♕h3 ♘g6 17 ♘xg6 17 ♖fe1? ♘f4 −+ ♕xg6 18 c4 ♗c6 19 f3 ♖ae8∓ 20 ♘e4 ♗xe4 21 fxe4 ♖xf1+ 22 ♖xf1 ♖xe4 23 ♕f3 ♚h7 24 ♗c1 b5! −+ 25 cxb5 axb5 26 g3 h4 27 ♗g5 c4! 28 ♚g2 c3 29 ♕d3 h3+! 30 ♚h1 30 ♔xh3? ♖h4+ −+

♖e5 31 ♕xg6+ ♚xg6 32 ♗c1 b4 0-1 Gufeld

262 Borkowski-Wedberg Eksjo 78
1 e4 e5 2 ♘f3 ♘c6 3 ♗b5 ♗c5 4 0-0 ♘d4 5 b4!? 5 ♘xd4 ♗xd4 6 c3 ♗b6 7 d4 c6 8 ♗c4 d6 ♗xb4 5...♘xf3+ 6 ♕xf3 ♗xb4 7 ♗b2; 5...♘xb5 6 bxc5 d6 7 a4 6 ♘xd4 exd4 7 ♗b2 ♕f6 8 e5? 8 c3 ♗c5 9 ♕h5 ♗b6 10 cxd4 ♘e7 11 e5 ♕f5 12 ♕e2 0-0 13 ♖e1 Masjejev-Telus, Corr 69; 10...♗xd4 11 e5 ♕b6 12 e6! ♕b6 9 ♗a4 ♘e7 10 ♕g4 ♗c5 11 ♗c1 11 ♗a3 ♗xa3 12 ♘xa3 ♕a6 0-0 12 ♗xd7 ♗xd7 13 ♕xd7 ♖ad8 14 ♕a4 ♘g6 15 ♘a3 15 ♖e1 ♖fe8; 15 f4 d3+ 16 ♔h1 ♖d4 ♘xe5 16 ♖b1 ♕g6 17 ♕b5 ♘f3+ 18 ♔h1 ♘h4 19 ♖g1 ♖fe8! 20 ♕xb7 20 ♕xc5 ♖e1! d3 21 ♕xc7 ♗xf2 22 ♗b2 ♗xg1 23 ♖xg1 dxc2 24 ♕f4 ♖e4 25 ♕c7 ♖ee8 26 ♕f4 ♕e4 27 ♕xe4 ♖xe4 28 ♗c3 ♖a4 29 ♘xc2 ♖xa2 30 ♖c1 ♖a6 31 ♘e3 f6 32 ♚g1 ♘g6 33 ♘f5 ♘f4 34 ♖e1 ♖e6 35 ♖a1 ♘e2+ 36 ♚f1 ♘xc3 37 bxc3 ♖d7 38 ♘d4 ♖e5 39 ♘c6 ♖c5 40 ♘xa7 ♖b7 41 ♖a6 ♖xc3 42 ♖c6 ♖a3 43 ♘c8 ♖b2 44 ♖c1 ♖aa2 45 ♘d6 ♖f2+ 46 ♚e1 h5 0-1

263 Klovan-Kupreichik USSR 78
1 e4 e5 2 ♘f3 ♘c6 3 ♗b5 ♘d4 4 ♘xd4 exd4 5 0-0 ♗c5 5...c6 += 6 d3 6 b4!? ♗xb4 7 ♗b2 ♗c5 8 c3 ♕f6 9 ♕h5 +=; 6...♗b6 7 c4 dxc3 8 ♘xc3 c6 9 ♗a4 ♘e7 10 d4 += Gipslis-Pavlenko, USSR 75; 7...c6∝ c6 6... ♘e7 7 ♕h5 ♗b6 8 f4!? += 7 ♗a4 ♘e7 8 ♘d2 d5 9 c3!? 9 exd5 ♘xd5 10 ♖e1 ♗e6 11 ♘e4 ♗e7 12 ♗b3 0-0 13 ♗d2 ♕d7 14 ♕h5! f6? 15 h3 ♖ae8 16 ♖e2 += Karpov-Kupreichik, USSR 76; 14...f5!= dxe4?! 10 ♘xe4

♗b6 11 ♘b3 0-0 12 ♕h5 12 ♘g5 ♔h8
△ f6 ♘d5 13 ♘g5 += ♕d7 14 c4?! 14
h3 += ♘b4 15 c5 15 ♗d2 ♘xd3 16 ♗c2
f5! ♗c7 16 h3 16 ♖fe1 ♘xd3? 17 ♘f6+!
gxf6 18 ♗xf6 ♕g4 19 ♕xf7+!! +−; 16...
♕g4 =+ ♕f5= 17 ♖ad1 ♗e6 18 ♗xe6 fx
e6 19 ♕g4 ♘xa2 20 ♗d2 a5 21 ♘g5 ♕x
g4 22 hxg4 ♖fe8! 23 ♖a1 h6!? 23...
♘b4∝ 24 ♖xa2 hxg5 25 ♗xg5 ♕f7 26
♗d2 ♖a6 27 f4 ♖d8 28 ♖fa1 ♖d5 29 b4
♕e8 30 ♕f2 Zeitnot ♕d7?! 30...axb4
31 ♖xa6 bxa6 32 ♗xb4= 31 ♕f3 ♕c8?!
32 ♕e4 += ♗d8 33 bxa5 33 g5!? ♖xc5
36 ♖b2? 36 f5 += b6 37 ♖ab1 bxa5∓
38 ♖b8+ ♕d7 39 ♖1b7+ ♗c7 40 ♖g8
♕c6 41 ♖xc7+! ♕xc7 42 f5! ♖d7
43 f6 e5! 44 fxg7 ♖g6 45 ♗xa5+
♕d6 46 ♖a8 ♖dxg7 47 ♗d8 c4 47.:.
♖g8 =+ 48 dxc4 ♖xg5?! 48...♖g8!
49 ♖a6+ ♕c5 50 ♗f6 ♖xg5!= 49
♗xg5 ♖xg5 50 ♖d8+ = ♕c5 51 ♕d3
e4+ 52 ♕xe4 ♖xg4+ 53 ♕d3 ♖g3+=
54 ♕d2 ½-½ Gufeld

264 Gufeld-Lutikov Vladivostok 78
1 e4 e5 2 ♘f3 ♘c6 3 ♗b5 ♘d4 4 ♘xd4
exd4 5 0-0 ♘e7 6 d3 += c6 7 ♗a4
d5 8 ♘d2 dxe4 9 ♘xe4 ♘f5 10 ♗g5
10 ♗f4 +=; 10 ♗b3 += ♗e7 11 ♗xe7
♕xe7 12 ♖e1 0-0 13 ♗b3 a5?! 13...
♗e6 14 ♘d2 += 14 a4 ♗e6 15 ♗xe6!
15 ♘d2 += ♕xe6 16 ♘d2!±

♕g6 17 ♕f3 ♖fe8 18 ♖e4! ♖xe4
19 ♕xe4 ♕f6 20 ♖e1 h5 21 ♕e5 ♕g6
22 ♘f3 ♕f6 23 ♕e7 +− ♕d6 24
♕xb7!? ♖b8 25 ♕a7 25 ♕a6 ♕c5!
♖xb2 26 h4 26 ♘g5 ♕e7!; 26 ♖e8+
♕h7 27 g3 ♕d5 g6 27 ♘g5 ♕d5 28
♕c7! ♖xc2 29 ♖e5 ♕b3 30 ♖e8+
♕g7 31 ♕e5+ 1-0 Gufeld

265 Kasparov-Roizman USSR 78
1 e4 e5 2 ♘f3 ♘c6 3 ♗b5 ♘d4 4 ♘xd4
exd4 5 0-0 ♗c5 6 d3 c6 6...♘e7?
7 ♕h5 ♗b6 8 ♗c4 0-0 9 ♗g5± 7
♗c4 d6 8 f4! N 8 ♕h5 g6 9 ♕f3 ♕e7
10 c3 +=; 8...♕f6? 9 f4 ♕g6 10 ♕f3
♘f6 12 e5±; 8...♕e7 9 ♗g5 ♘f6 10
♕h4 h6 11 f4 ♖g8 12 ♗xf6 ♕xf6
13 ♕xf6 gxf6 14 f5 b5 15 ♗b3 a5∝
Saharov-Listengarten, USSR 78 ♘f6
9 e5 dxe5 9...♘d5 10 ♗xd5 cxd5
11 ♕h5 0-0 12 ♘d2 += 10 ♗xf7+!?
♕xf7 11 fxe5 ♕d5 12 exf6 gxf6
13 ♘d2 ♖g8 14 ♘e4 ♗e7 15 ♗f4 ♖g6
16 ♕e2 ♗g4 17 ♕f2 ♖ag8 18 ♖ae1 h5
18...♕g7 19 ♗g5! ♕d8 19...♖xg5?
20 ♘xf6 +−; 19...♗h3? 20 ♘xf6
♗xf6 21 ♕xf6+! +−; 20...♕xg2+
21 ♕xg2 ♗xg2 22 ♖xe7+! +− 20
♕f4 ♗e6 21 h4 ♗d5? 21...♗g4 22
g4! ♕g7 22...♖h8! 23 ♗xf6 ♖xg4+
24 ♕xg4 hxg4 25 ♗xe7+! ♕xe7
26 ♘c5+ +−; 23...♗xf6 24 g5 ♗xe4
25 ♖xe4 ♕g7 26 ♖e6 ♖f8 27 ♕h2±
23 gxh5 fxg5 24 ♕e5+ ♕h6 25 hxg6
gxh4 26 ♖f5 ♕xg6 27 ♕h2 1-0
Kasparov

266 Romanishin-Lehmann Kiev 78
1 e4 e5 2 ♘f3 ♘c6 3 ♗b5 d6 4 d4 ♗d7
4...exd4 5 ♕xd4!? 5 ♘c3 exd4 5...
♘f6; 5...♘ge7 6 dxe5 dxe5 7 ♗g5 +=
6 ♘xd4 g6 6...♘f6 7 ♗xc6 bxc6 8
♕d3 += 7 0-0 7 ♗e3 ♗g7 8 ♕d2 ♘f6
9 f3 0-0 10 ♗xc6 bxc6 11 ♗h6! +=;

7 h4!? ♗g7 8 ♗xc6 bxc6 9 h5 ♕b8
10 ♕d3 += Gusev-Zheljandinov, USSR
76 ♗g7 8 ♘xc6!? N 8 ♗xc6 bxc6 9
f4 c5 10 ♘de2 f5!= ♗xc6 8...bxc6
9 ♗c4 ♘f6 10 ♗g5 0-0 11 ♕f3 +=
h6 12 ♗h4 g5 13 ♗g3 ♔h8 14 ♗d3!
♘d7!? 15 ♕e2 △ f4 ♘c5 15...♕e7!?
16 f4 ♘xd3+ 17 ♕xd3! +− 17 cxd3
d5!

g4?! 18 f5 △ f6! ♕f6 19 ♖ad1 ♖ae8
20 ♕c4 ♖g8 21 ♘d5! ♗xd5 21...♕xb2?
22 f6 +− 22 exd5 ♕xb2 23 ♕xc7 ♖e2
24 ♖de1! ♖xe1 25 ♗xe1 25 ♖xe1
♕d4+ △ ♕xd5 ♗d4+ 26 ♔h1 ♕b5?!
26...♕b6 27 c4! ♕a6 28 ♗g3 ♕xa2
28...♗c5 29 ♕xf7 +− 29 ♕xd6 ♔h7
30 ♕c7 +− b5 30...♗g7 31 ♕f4 +−
31 f6! ♕xc4 32 ♕xf7+ ♔h8 33 ♕xg8+!
1-0 Gufeld

267 Westerinen-Larsen Esbjerg 78
1 e4 e5 2 ♘f3 ♘c6 3 ♗b5 ♘ge7?!
4 0-0 ♘g6 5 c3 d6?! 5...a6 6 ♗a4 d6
6 d4 ♗d7 7 d5 ♘b3! ♘b8 8 ♕b3!?
8 ♗xd7+ ♘xd7 9 c4 ♗e7 10 ♘c3 +=
♕c8 9 ♘a3 ♗e7 10 ♗xd7+ ♘xd7
11 ♘c4 ♘h4 12 ♘xh4 ♗xh4 13 f4
exf4 14 ♗xf4 0-0 15 e5 dxe5 16
♗xe5!? a5!= 17 ♗d4 a4 18 ♕c2 ♖a6
19 ♘e3 ♕d8! 20 ♖ad1 ♗f6 21 ♗xf6
♘xf6 22 c4 22 ♔h1! ♕e7 23 ♕c3
♕c5 24 ♕d4?! ♕xd4 25 ♖xd4 ♖e8

26 ♖d3 ♘e4 27 ♘d1 ♘c5 =+ 28
♖df3?! f6 29 ♖e3 ♖xe3 30 ♘xe3
♔f7 31 ♖b1 h5 32 ♔f2 f5 33 ♔e2
g6 34 ♘c2 ♖a8 35 ♖e1 h4 36 h3?
♖b8! 37 ♔e3 ♘e4 38 ♔d4 c5+! 39
♔d3 b5 40 b3 b4 41 ♖b1 a3 41...
♘c3!?; 41...♖a8? 42 a3! 42 ♖f1 ♔f6
43 ♘e3 ♘c3!? 43...♔e5 44 ♘d1 ♖h8
44 ♘g4+ ♔g7 45 ♘e5 ♗xa2 46 ♘d7
♖c8 47 ♘b6 ♖e8 48 ♘a4 ♘c3 49
♘xc5 49 ♘xc3 bxc3 50 ♖a1 f4 51
♖xa3 ♖e3+ 52 ♔c2 ♖g3 −+ ♖e2 50
♘a6 ♖xg2 51 ♘xb4 ♘e4 −+ 52 ♔d4
52 ♖a1 ♘c5+ ♔d2 53 ♖d1 ♘xb3+
54 ♔c3 ♘c5 55 ♔d4 ♘b3+ 56 ♔c3
♖g3+ 57 ♔c2 57 ♖d3 ♘c5! ♘c5 58
d6 ♖g2+ 59 ♔c3 ♘e4+!

60 ♔b3 ♖g3+ 61 ♘d3 61 ♔a4 ♘c3+
62 ♔a5 ♘xd1 63 d7 a2; 61 ♔a2 ♘c3+
62 ♔a1 ♘xd1 63 d7 ♘c3; 61 ♔c2
♖c3+ 62 ♔b1 ♘xd6 63 ♖xd6 ♖b3+
♘c5+ 62 ♔xa3 ♔f6 63 ♔b4 ♖xd3 64
♖a1 ♘e6 65 c5 g5 66 ♖a6 ♔e5 0-1
Larsen

268 Kristiansen-Larsen Esbjerg 78
1 e4 e5 2 ♘f3 ♘c6 3 ♗b5 ♘ge7?!
4 0-0 ♘g6 5 d4 5 c3! exd4 6 ♘xd4
♘c5 7 ♗e3 ♗xd4 8 ♗xd4 0-0= 8...
♘xd4? 9 ♕xd4 ♕g5 10 e5!; 10 ♗e2?
♘f4!; 10 ♘c3?? ♘h4! −+! 9 ♘c3 d6
10 ♗xc6?! bxc6 11 f4 f5 12 ♕d2

155

12 ♕h5 fxe4 13 f5 ♕h4! c5 13 ♗e3
♗b7 14 ♖ae1?! 14 exf5 ♖xf5 =+
fxe4 15 f5 ♘e5 16 ♗g5 ♕d7 17 ♕f2?
17 ♕f4? h6!; 17 f6 gxf6? 18 ♗xf6
♖xf6? 19 ♖xf6 ♕g7 20 ♘d5!; 17...
d5!∓ 18 fxg7 ♖xf1+ 19 ♖xf1 d4 20
♖f8+ ♖xf8 21 gxf8+ ♔xf8 22 ♕f4+
♘f7 23 ♗h6+ ♔e8 24 ♘xe4 ♕c6 25
♘f6+ ♔d8 ♗a6! −+ 18 ♘e2 ♖ae8
19 ♕h4 ♖xf5 20 ♖xf5 ♕xf5 21 ♘g3
♕g6 22 ♗f4 ♘d7 23 b3 ♘f6 24 c4
♗b7 25 h3 h6 26 ♗e3 ♘d7 27 ♖f1
♖f8 28 ♖xf8+ ♘xf8 29 ♔h2 ♘e6
30 ♕e7 ♕f7 31 ♕h4 ♗c6 32 ♕g4 ♕f6
33 ♘f5 ♔h7 34 ♕g1 ♘d4 35 ♘g3
♘c2 36 ♗f4 e3 37 ♔h2 a5 38 h4 ♗d7
39 ♕xd7 ♕xf4 40 h5 e2 0-1 Larsen

269 Westerinen-Lanka Jurmala 78
1 e4 e5 2 ♘f3 ♘c6 3 ♗b5 f5 4 ♘c3
4 d3!? += ♘d4!? 5 ♗c4 5 ♗a4!?
♘f6 6 exf5 ♗c5 7 d3 c6 8 0-0 d5 9
♘xe5 0-0 10 ♘e2!± Karpov-Bellon,
Montilla 76 c6 6 d3!? N 6 0-0 d6 7
♖e1 ♘xf3+ 8 ♕xf3 f4 9 g3 +=; 6...♘f6
7 ♘xe5!? fxe4 8 ♘f7 ♕e7 9 ♘xh8
d5 10 ♗e2± Geller-O.Rodriguez, Las
Palmas 76 ♘xf3+ 7 ♕xf3 ♕f6!?∝
8 ♕e2 8 0-0 fxe4 9 ♕xe4 ♘e7 △
d5∝; 8 ♗xg8 ♖xg8 9 exf5 d5 10 ♕h5+
g6≈; 8 exf5 ♘e7!∝ f4! 9 ♗d2 ♘e7
10 0-0-0 d6 11 f3 ♗d7 12 ♕f2 g5
13 h4 g4 14 fxg4 ♗xg4 15 ♖df1 h5
16 d4 ♘g6 17 d5?! 17 dxe5!?

Diagram

17...c5!= 18 ♗b5+ ♔e7 19 g3 ♗h6
20 ♘e2 ♖af8 21 gxf4 22 b4!?∝
♘xf4 22 ♘xf4 ♗xf4 23 ♔b1 ♔d8!
24 ♕e1 ♔c8 25 a3 ♖h7 26 ♗d3 ♖hf7
=+ 27 ♗c3! ♕h6 28 ♔a2 ♗e3 29
♖xf7 ♖xf7 30 ♖f1 ♖xf1 31 ♕xf1
♕f4 32 ♗e1 ♔d8 33 ♕g2 ♔e7 34

♗g3 ♕f6 35 c4 ♗d4 36 ♕f1 ♕h6
37 ♕e1 ♗d7 38 ♔b1 a6 39 ♔c1 ♕g6
40 ♗e1 ♕g2 41 ♗d2 ♔e8 41...b5!?
42 ♗g5 b5 43 ♕d2= ♕xd2 44 ♗xd2
♔d8 ½-½ Gufeld

270 Kristiansen-Wedberg
Gausdal 78
1 e4 e5 2 ♘f3 ♘c6 3 ♗b5 f5 4 ♘c3
♘d4!? 5 ♘xe5 5 exf5; 5 ♗c4; 5 ♗a4;
5 ♘xd4? exd4 6 ♘e2 c6! 7 ♗d3 fxe4
8 ♗xe4 d5 9 ♗f3 d3!∓ ♕f6 6 ♘f3
♘xb5 6...fxe4 7 ♘xd4 ♕xd4 8 0-0±
7 ♘xb5 fxe4 8 ♘xc7+? 8 ♕e2! ♕e7
9 ♘fd4 d6 10 0-0 ♘f6 11 d3 a6 12
♘c3 ♗g4 13 f3 exf3 14 ♕f2 0-0-0=
♔d8∓ 9 ♘xa8 exf3 10 ♕xf3 ♕xf3
11 gxf3 b6 12 ♘xb6 axb6 13 d3 ♗b7
14 ♗e3 ♔c7 15 ♔e2 ♘e7 16 c4? ♘f5
17 d4 ♗a6! 18 ♖hc1 d5 19 b3 ♗a3
20 ♖c2 ♔b7 21 ♔d3 ♘d6 −+ 22 ♗c1
dxc4+ 23 bxc4 ♘xc4! 24 ♔e4 24
♖xc4 ♗xc4+ 25 ♔xc4 ♗xc1 26 ♖xc1
♖c8+ ♖e8+ 25 ♔d5 ♖d8+ 26 ♔e6
♗f8! 27 ♗g5 ♖e8+ 28 ♔d5 b5 △
♘b6 mate 29 ♖xc4 bxc4 30 ♖b1+
♔a7 31 ♗e3 c3 32 ♔c6 ♗a3 33 ♖g1
♗b7+ 34 ♔d7 ♖xe3 35 fxe3 ♗xf3
0-1 Pytel

271 L.A.Schneider-Nogueiras
Jurmala 78
1 e4 e5 2 ♘f3 ♘c6 3 ♗b5 ♘f6 4 0-0

♗c5!? 5 ♘xe5 5 c3 0-0 6 d4 ♗b6 7 ♖e1 exd4 8 ♘g5! h6 9 ♘h4 d6 10 ♗xc6! bxc6 11 ♘xd4 += Cabrillo-Popov, Jugoslavia 76 ♘xe4 6 ♕e2 ♘xe5 7 ♕xe4 ♕e7 8 ♘c3 8 d4 ♘c6! 9 ♕g4 h5! =+ Timoshenko-Gulko, USSR 77 ♘g6 9 ♖e1 0-0 10 ♕xe7 10 d4 ♕xe4 11 ♖xe4 f5 ♗xe7 11 d4 11 d3= ♗f6 12 ♘d5 ♗d8 13 ♘e3 c6 14 ♗f1 d5 15 ♗d2 ♗c7 =+ 16 c4?! 16 g3 dxc4 17 ♗xc4 ♗e6! 18 ♗xe6 fxe6 19 ♘c4 ♖ad8 20 ♗c3 ♘f4 21 ♖ad1 ♖f5!∓ 22 ♖d2 ♖g5 23 g3 ♖g6 24 ♘e5 ♗xe5 25 dxe5 ♘d5 26 ♗b4 ♖d7 27 ♗d6 ♖g5 28 a4!? ♖f7 29 b4 ♖g4 30 b5?! 30 ♖b2∓ ♖xa4 31 bxc6 bxc6 32 ♖c1 ♖a6 33 ♖b2 ♖b6! −+ 34 ♖xb6 axb6 35 ♖xc6 ♖b7 36 f4 ♔f7 37 ♖c8 ♔g6 38 ♖e8 b5 39 ♗c5 39 ♖xe6+ ♔f5 40 ♖e8 b4 −+ ♖c7 40 ♗b6 ♖c6 41 ♗a5 ♖a6 42 ♗e1 ♔f5 43 ♖g8 ♔g4! 44 f5 exf5 45 ♖xg7+ ♔f3 46 ♖g5 ♘e3 0-1 Gufeld

Ponziani

272 L.A.Schneider-Westerinen
Jurmala 78

1 e4 e5 2 ♘f3 ♘c6 3 c3!? f5 3...♘f6 4 d4 ♘xe4 5 d5 ♘b8 6 ♘xe5 ♕e7 7 ♕d4 d6 8 ♕xe4 ♕xe5 9 ♗d3 ♕xe4+ 10 ♗xe4 ♘d7 1.1 ♗e3 += Miles-Gligoric, Bad Lauterberg 77; 4...d6 5 ♗b5 ♗d7 6 ♘bd2 ♗e7 7 dxe5 ♘xe5 8 ♘xe5 dxe5 9 ♕b3 0-0 10 ♗xd7 ♘xd7 11 ♕c2 ♘c5 12 ♘f3! += Miles-Smyslov, Hastings 76/77 4 d4 4 exf5 ♕f6∝ fxe4 4...exd4 5 exf5! d5 6 ♗b5! += 5 ♘xe5 ♘f6!? 5...♕f6 6 ♘g4! ♕g6 7 ♗f4! d6 8 ♘e3 ♘f6 9 ♘a3 += Ljubojevic-Pachman, Manila 76 6 ♗g5 ♗e7 6...♕e7!? 7 ♘g4 d5≈ 7 ♘d2 0-0 8 ♗e2 += ♕e8 △ ♕g6 9 0-0 d6 10 ♘xc6 bxc6 11 f3 ♕g6!? 12 ♘xe4!

♘xe4 13 ♗xe7 ♘h3 14 ♗c4+! d5

15 ♕e2± ♖fe8 16 fxe4 ♖xe7 17 ♗d3 dxe4 18 ♗c4+ ♗e6 19 ♖f4! ♗d5 20 ♖af1 h6 21 ♗b3 △ c4 ♗xb3 22 axb3 a5! 23 ♖f5 ♕h7 24 h4! ♖b8 25 h5 ♕e8 26 ♖1f4 ♖b5! 26...♖xb3?! 27 ♖xa5 +− 27 g4 ♖xf5 28 ♖xf5 ♕g8! += 29 ♕c4! ♕xc4 30 bxc4 a4 31 ♖e5! 31 ♖a5 e3 32 ♔f1 ♖e4 ♖f7 32 ♖xe4 ♖f3 33 c5 a3! 34 bxa3 ♖xc3 35 a4! 35 ♖d7? ♖g3+ = ♖a3 36 ♔f2 ♖xa4 37 ♔e3 += ♖a1 38 ♔f4 ♖f1+ 39 ♔e5 ♖f8 40 d5 ♖e8+ 41 ♔d4 ♖d8 42 ♖e5 g6?! 42...♔g8 43 ♖e7+ ♔g8 44 ♖xc7 ♖xd5+ 45 ♔c4 gxh5 46 ♖xc6± ♖g5 47 gxh5 ♖xh5 48 ♖d6! ♔f7 48...♖h1 49 c6 ♖h1 50 ♔b5 ♔e7 51 ♖d5! h5 52 c7 ♖c1 53 ♔b6 h4 54 ♔b7 +− ♖b1+ 55 ♔c8 h3 56 ♖e5+ ♔f7 57 ♖h5 ♖b3 58 ♔d7 ♖d3+ 59 ♔c6 ♖c3+ 60 ♔b7 ♖b3+ 61 ♔a6 1-0 Gufeld

273 Chekhov-Psahis Vilnius 78
1 e4 e5 2 ♘f3 ♘c6 3 c3 ♘f6 4 d4 ♘xe4 5 d5 ♘b8 6 ♘xe5 6 ♗d3 ♘c5 7 ♘xe5 ♘xd3+ ♘f6?! 6...♕e7 7 ♕d4 d6 8 ♕x e4 ♕xe5 9 ♗d3 ♕xe4 10 ♗xe4; 6... ♘c5 7 ♕g4 0-0 8 ♕xe4 d6 9 ♕c4 b5!? 7 ♗e2 ♗c5 7...♗e7 8 0-0 0-0 9 ♘d3 ♗e7 9...♗b6 10 d6 10 c4 d6 11 ♘c3 ♗f5 12 g4! ♗xd3 12...♗g6 13 f4 13

&xd3 ♘fd7 13...♘bd7 14 g5! ♘e8 15
f4 **14 f4** ♘a6 14...&f6 **15 g5! c6?!**
15...♘ac5 16 &c2 a5 **16 ♖f3** △ &xh7+,
♖h3+, ♛h5; 16 &xh7+ ♔xh7 17 ♛h5+
♔g8 18 ♖f3 f5! 19 ♖h3 ♘f6 20 gxf6
&xf6; 16 &e3 △ &d4 **f5 17 &e3 ♘dc5**
18 &c2 ♘b4 19 &b1 a5 20 a3 ♘ba6
21 &c2 ♛b6? 21...♛d7 22 ♖b1! ♛c7
23 ♖h3 g6 24 b4! axb4 25 axb4 ♘d7
26 dxc6 bxc6 27 c5! 27 b5 ♘xb4
27...dxc5 28 &b3+ ♔h8 29 bxc5 △
&d4+ **28 cxd6! &xd6 29 ♖xb4 &xb4**
30 &b3+ ♖f7 1-0

3 &c4

274 Speelman-Durao London 78
1 e4 e5 2 ♘f3 ♘c6 3 &c4 &c5 4
c3 ♛e7 5 d4 &b6 6 0-0 d6 7 a4 a6
8 h3 ♘f6 9 ♖e1 0-0 10 b4 10 ♘a3
♔h8 11 ♘c2 ♘g8 12 ♘e3 &a7 13
♘d5 ♛d8= Contedinni-Euwe, Leipzig
60; 10 &e3!?; 10 &g5!? **♔h8** 10...♘d8
11 ♖a2 11 &a3 ♘g8 12 ♛d3 f6=
Van Schletinga-Euwe, Maestricht 46
exd4?! 11...♘g8 △ f6 **12 a5 &a7** 12...
&e6! **13 cxd4 ♘xb4 14 ♖ae2 ♘g8!?**
15 d5 △ &a3 c5 16 e5

16...♛d8? 16...&f5 **17 e6! ♛xa5 18**
♘g5 ♘h6 19 exf7 +− &f5 19...♘d7
20 ♖e8 &g6 21 ♛e2 ♛a4 21...♘xf7
22 ♖xa8 ♖xa8 23 ♛e8+!; 21...&xf7

22 ♘xf7+ ♘xf7 **23 ♖xa8 ♖xa8 24**
♛e8+!; 21...♖axe8 22 fxe8♛ &xe8
23 ♛xe8 ♛d8 24 ♛xd8 ♖xd8 25
♖e7 +− **22 ♖xa8 ♖xa8 23 ♛e7 ♛c2**
23...♘xf7 24 ♘xf7+ ♔g8 25 ♘h6+!
24 ♛e8+ ♖xe8 25 ♖xe8+ 1-0
Speelman

275 Miles-Sanz Montilla 78
1 e4 e5 2 ♘f3 ♘c6 3 &c4 &c5 4
c3 ♘f6 5 d3 d6 6 b4 &b6 7 a4 a6
7...a5?! 8 b5 += **8 0-0 h6** 8...0-0
9 ♘bd2 0-0 10 &a2 △ ♘c4 **&a7 11 b5**
11 ♘c4 b5!?; 11...&e6 ♘a5 **12 &a3**
+= **♖e8 13 ♛c2 &e6 14 &xe6 ♖xe6**
15 ♖fb1 d5 15...♘g4?! 16 d4 +=/±;
15...&b6 16 &b4 += **16 &b4! c5?**
16...&b6 17 c4! △ c5±; 16...c6 17
&xa5 ♛xa5 18 b6! **17 &xa5 ♛xa5**
18 b6! +− ♖xb6 18...♘xb6 19 ♘b3
+−; 18...&b8 19 ♘b3 ♛xb6 20 ♘d4
+− **19 ♘b3 ♖xb3 20 ♛xb3 ♖d8**
21 ♛xb7 &b8 22 c4 dxc4 23 dxc4
♛c3 24 ♖d1 ♖e8 25 ♘d2 ♛d4 26 h3
♘h5 27 ♛c6 ♖f8 28 ♘f1 ♛xc4 29
♘e3 ♛e2 30 ♛xc5 ♘f4 31 ♘f5 ♖e8
31...♛xe4? 32 ♛xf8+ +− **32 ♖e1**
♛h5 33 ♛e3 g6 34 ♘g3 ♛g5 35 ♔h2
h5 36 ♛f3 &a7 37 ♘e2 ♘e6 38 ♖ab1
♘c5 39 ♘c3 ♖d8 40 ♘d5 f5 41 exf5
e4 42 ♛e3 ♛xe3 43 ♘xe3 ♘d3 44
♖e2 &xe3 45 fxe3 gxf5 46 ♖b6 ♖e8
47 ♖xa6 f4 48 exf4 ♘xf4 49 ♖e3
1-0 Miles

276 Botterill-Tatai
Middlesborough 78
1 e4 e5 2 ♘f3 ♘c6 3 &c4 ♘f6 4 d3
&e7 5 ♘bd2 0-0 6 0-0 d6 7 a4 &e6
8 ♖e1 ♘d7 9 c3 &f6 10 b4 += a5
11 b5 ♘cb8? 11...♘a7! △ ♘c8-b6
12 d4 ♖e8 13 &xe6 ♖xe6 14 ♘c4
♖e8 **15 ♖a2!±** ♛c8 **16 &a3 ♖e6**
17 ♖d2 17 d5 ♖e8 18 b6 &e7! +=

b6 18 h3 18 g3!? h6 19 ♖d3 △ 20
dxe5 ♘xe5 21 ♘fxe5 ♗xe5 22 f4
**h6 19 dxe5 ♘xe5 20 ♘fxe5 ♗xe5
21 ♘xe5 ♖xe5 22 f4 ♖e8 23 e5 ♘d7
24 exd6 cxd6 25 ♖xe8+ ♕xe8 26
♖e2** 26 ♖xd6 ♕e3+ 27 ♔h1 ♕xc3
28 ♖xd7 ♕xa3= **♕c8 27 ♕xd6 ♕xc3
28 ♕d5 ♖b8 29 ♕xd7** 29 ♖e7 ♖f8;
29 ♗d6 ♘f6 **♕xa3 30 ♖e8+ ♖xe8
31 ♕xe8+ ♕f8 32 ♕c6 ♕d8 33 ♔h2
g6 34 ♕e4 ♕d6 35 h4 h5 ½-½ Botterill**

Scotch

277 Ljubojevic-Gligoric Niksic 78
**1 e4 e5 2 ♘f3 ♘c6 3 d4 exd4 4 ♘xd4
♗c5** 4...♘f6 5 ♘xc6 bxc6 6 e5 ♕e7
7 ♕e2 ♘d5 8 c4 ♗a6= **5 ♘b3** 5 ♗e3
♕f6 6 c3 ♘ge7= **♗e7** 5...♗b6! 6 ♘c3
d6 7 ♘d5 ♕h4! 8 ♕f3 ♘f6! 9 ♘xf6+
♕xf6 10 ♕xf6 gxf6 11 ♗b5 f5 12
exf5 ♗xf5 13 c3 0-0-0∓ Radulov-
Gligoric, Vrbas 77 **6 c4! ♘f6 7 ♘c3
0-0 8 ♗e2 ♖e8 += 9 0-0 a5! 10 a4
d6 11 ♗e3 ♘d7 12 ♘b5! ♗f6 13
♕c2 ♘b4 14 ♕d2 b6** 14...♖xe4 15
♘xa5 **15 ♖ad1 ♗b7** 15...♖xe4? 16 ♗f3
**16 f3 ♘c5 17 ♘xc5 bxc5 18 ♖fe1
♕e7 19 ♗f1 ♖ad8 20 ♘c3?! ♗xc3!
21 ♕xc3** 21 bxc3!? ♘c6 **♖b8 =+
22 ♗f2 ♗a8 23 ♖e2 ♘c6!? 23...f6
24 e5! dxe5 25 ♖d5 f6** 25...♘d4!?
26 ♖exe5 ♕xe5 27 ♖xe5 ♖xe5 28
♕xa5∓ **26 ♖xc5 ♖bd8 27 ♖d2 ♘d4**

Diagram

28 ♕xa5! 28 ♖xa5? c5! **♘b3 29
♖xd8!?** 29 ♖xc7 ♕f8 30 ♕b6 ♖xd2
31 ♕xb3 ♖b8 32 ♗b6 ♔h8≈; 30
♗c5 ♘xa5 31 ♖xd8 ♖xd8 32 ♗xf8
♔xf8≈ **♘xa5 30 ♖xe8+ ♕xe8 31
♖xa5 e4 32 fxe4 ♗xe4 33 ♖b5 ♕d7
34 a5 ♕d1 35 ♖d5! ♕a4!∓ 36 ♖d4!?**

f5 37 ♗e1 37 b4 **♕f7 38 ♗c3 c5∓
39 ♖d2 g5 40 ♗e2 ♕c6 41 ♗h5+
♕e6 42 ♗d1 g4 43 g3 h5 44 ♗e2
♕c7 45 ♗d1?** 45 ♗d3 ♗f3 46 ♗e2
h4 46 gxh4 g3 −+ △ gxh2+, ♕g3+
**47 hxg3 ♕xg3+ 48 ♔f1 ♕h3+ 49
♕e1 ♕h1+ 50 ♔f2 ♕g2+ 51 ♔e1 ♕g1+
52 ♔e2 f4 53 ♖d8 ♔e7 54 ♖d5 ♕g2+
55 ♔e1 ♕g1+ 56 ♔e2 f3+ 57 ♔d2
♗xd5 58 cxd5 f2 59 ♗e2 f1♕ 60
♗xf1 ♕xf1 0-1 Gligoric**

278 Micov-Ivkov Jugoslavia 78
**1 e4 e5 2 ♘f3 ♘c6 3 d4 exd4 4 ♘xd4
♘f6 5 ♘c3 ♗b4 6 ♘xc6 bxc6 7 ♕d4?!**
7 ♗d3 ♕e7 8 ♗d3 ♗c5 9 ♕a4 ♘g4
10 ♘d1 10 0-0 ♕h4 −+ **♖b8 11 a3
f5 12 h3 ♘e5 13 0-0 fxe4 14 ♗xe4**
14 ♕xe4 d5 15 ♕e2 0-0∓ **0-0∓ 15
♗e3 ♗xe3 16 ♘xe3 d5 17 ♗d3 ♖xb2
18 ♕xa7**

18...♗xh3! **19 ♛d4** 19 gxh3 ♘f3+
20 ♔h1 ♛h4 21 ♔g2 ♛g5+ 22 ♔h1
♛f4 −+ ♗xg2!! **20 ♔xg2 ♛g5+ 21
♘g4 ♗xg4** −+ **22 f4 ♘e3+ 23 ♔f3
♗xc2 24 ♗xc2** 24 ♛xb2 ♖xf4+ 25
♔e2 ♛g2+ 26 ♔d1 ♘e3+ −+ ♖xc2
25 ♖g1 ♖xf4+! 26 ♛xf4 ♖c3+ **0-1
Maric**

**279 Dolmatov-Lerner
USSR 78**
1 e4 e5 2 ♘f3 d6 3 d4 3 ♗c4!? exd4
4 ♘xd4 ♘f6 4...g6 **5 ♘c3 ♗e7** 5...
♘c6 6 ♘xc6 bxc6 7 ♗e2 △ 0-0 +=
6 ♗e2 6 ♗f4 +=; 6 g3!? d5 7 e5 ♘g4
8 ♘f3 ∝/+= Palatnik-Holmov, USSR
72 **0-0** 6...a6!? **7 0-0** 7 f4∝ ♖e8
7...♘c6 8 ♘xc6 bxc6 9 b3 ♘d7! △
♗f6= **8 f4 ♗f8 9 ♗f3** += ♘a6!? **10
♖e1 c6** 10...♘c5 **11 e5 11 ♗e3 d5
12 e5±**

12...c5? 12...♘d7 **13 exf6!** ♖xe3
14 ♖xe3 cxd4 15 ♖xd5! +− ♗f5
15...dxe3? **16 ♗xf7+** +− **16 ♖e5!
♗g6 17 fxg7 ♔xg7** 17...♗xg7 **18
♘e4 f6 19 ♛xd4 ♗xe4** 19...fxe5 20
♛xe5+ ♔h6 21 g4 +− **20 ♛xe4 ♘c5
21 ♛f3 fxe5 22 ♛g4+ ♔h6 23 ♖e1
♘d7 24 ♔h1** △ ♖e3 +− ♗c5 **25 ♖d1
♘f8 26 ♗xb7 1-0 Gufeld**

**280 Westerinen-Wahlbom
Gausdal 78**
**1 e4 e5 2 ♘f3 d6 3 d4 exd4 4 ♘xd4
4 ♛xd4 ♘c6 5 ♗b5 ♗d7 6 ♗xc6
♗xc6 7 ♘c3 ♘f6 8 ♗g5 ♗e7 9 0-0-0±
g6** 4...♘f6! **5 c4! ♗g7 6 ♘c3 ♘c6
7 ♗e3 ♘ge7?** 7...♘f6 **8 h4!±** h6 9
♛d2 ♘e5 10 0-0-0 ♘7c6 11 f3 ♗e6!?
**12 ♘xe6 fxe6 13 ♗e2 ♛e7 14 f4
♘f7 15 ♗f3 a6 16 ♛c2 0-0 17 g4
♖ab8 18 g5 h5 19 ♖hf1 ♘h8 20
♔b1 b5 21 cxb5 axb5 22 e5 ♘a5
23 ♘e4 ♘c4 24 ♘f6+ ♗xf6 25 gxf6
♛h7 26 ♗a7 +−** ♖a8 **27 ♗xa8 ♖xa8
28 exd6! cxd6 29 ♗d4 ♛b7 30 ♖g1
♔f7 31 ♖g5 ♛a6 32 a3 ♛c6** △ ♖xa3
33 ♛d3 ♔f8 34 ♖xh5! gxh5 **35 ♛h7
♘f7 36 ♛g7+ ♔e8 37 ♛g8+ ♔d7 38
♛xf7+ ♔c8 39 ♛xe6+ ♔b7 40 f7
♛f3 41 ♛d7+ ♔a6 42 f8♛! ♘xa3+
43 ♔c1 1-0 Pytel**

281 Sturua-Chipashvili USSR 78
1 e4 e5 2 ♘f3 d6 3 d4 3 ♗c4!? ♘d7
3...exd4; 3...♘f6 **4 ♘c3 ♘gf6 5 ♗e2**
5 ♗c4 += g6 5...♗e7 **6 ♗g5 ♗g7?**
6...h6 7 ♗h4 += **7 dxe5 dxe5**

**8 ♘xe5! ♘xe5 9 ♛xd8 ♔xd8+ 10
♘d5 ♘d7 11 0-0-0 +−** ♗h6!? **12
♗xh6 ♘xe4 13 ♗f3!** 13 ♗e3 ♘xf2

14 ♗g5+ f6 15 ♘xf6 ♘xh1 16...♘xd1
17 ♖xd1 +− 16 ♘d5+ ♚e8 17 ♖e1+
♘e5 18 ♖xe5+ ♚d7 19 ♖e7+ ♚c6
20 ♖xc7+ ♚b5 21 ♗e2+ ♚a4 22 b3+
♚a3 23 ♗e7+ ♚xa2 24 ♘c3+ ♚a1
25 ♗a3 1-0 Gufeld

282 Povah-Pedersen
Middlesborough 78

1 e4 e5 2 ♘f3 d6 3 d4 ♘f6 4 ♘c3
♘bd7 5 ♗c4 ♗e7 6 0-0 0-0 7 h3 7
♕e2 c6 8 a4 ♕c7 9 h3 b6 10 ♖d1
♗b7 11 dxe5 dxe5 += c6 8 a4 a5
9 b3 9 ♕e2 h6 10 ♕e2 ♕c7 11 ♗b2
exd4?! 11...♘h5!? △ ♘f4 12 ♘xd4
♖e8 13 f4 ♗f8 13...d5 14 exd5 ♗a3
15 ♕xe8+ ♘xe8 16 ♗xa3± 14 ♕f3
♕b6 15 ♖ad1 ♘c5 15...♘e5!? 16
fxe5 dxe5 17 ♘ce2 exd4 18 ♘xd4
+= ♖xe4? 19 ♗xf7+!± 16 e5!? dxe5
17 fxe5 ♖xe5 18 ♕h1 ♗e6? 18...
♗d7!∝ 19 ♘xe6 ♘xe6 20 ♘e2 ♘g5
21 ♕d3 ♖e3 22 ♕f5 ♘c5! 23 ♕xc5
♗xc5 24 ♗xf6 gxf6 25 ♖xf6 b5!
25...♚g7 26 ♖df1± 26 axb5 cxb5
27 ♗xb5 ♘e4 28 ♖f4! ♖xe2 29 ♖g4+
♚f8 30 ♗xe2 ♘f2+ 31 ♚h2 ♘xd1
32 ♗xd1 ♖d8 33 ♗e2 33 ♖c4?! ♗d6+
34 ♚g1 ♗g3 35 ♗e2 ♖e8 36 ♚f1 h5
△ ♖e5-f5, h4∝ ♖d2 34 ♗d3 ♗d6+
35 ♚g1 ♗c5+ 36 ♚f1 ♗b4 37 ♖c4
♚g7 38 ♗e2 ♖d5 39 ♚f2 ♖e5 40 ♚f3
♚f6 41 ♗d3 ♗c5 42 ♖f4+ ♚g7 43
♗c4 f5! 44 g4 ♖e3+ 45 ♚g2 fxg4
46 ♖xg4+?! 46 hxg4!? ♚f6 47 ♗d3
♖e6! 48 h4 ♚e5 49 h5 ♖f6 50 ♖e4+
♚d5 51 ♖e8 ♗b4 52 ♗g6 ♗d6 53
c3! ♗c7 54 ♖h8 ♗f4 55 ♖a8 ♗c7
56 ♖h8 ♗f4 57 ♖d8+ ♚c5 57...♖d6?
58 ♖a8±; 57...♗d6 58 ♖d7 ♚c6 59
♖h7 ♗f4 60 ♖e7 △ ♖e4-c4, ♗e4-f3,
♚f2-e3 58 ♖d4 ♗e5 59 ♖c4+ 59
♖d3!? ♚d6 60 ♗e4 ♚d7?! 60...♖f4!
61 ♖c6+ ♚d7 62 ♗d5 h4 63 ♖xh6

♗xc3 64 ♗f3∝ 61 ♖c5 ♗c7 62 ♗f5+
♚d6 63 ♖b5 ♖f8 64 c4 64 ♚f3? ♖b8=
♖g8+ 65 ♚f3 ♚e7 66 ♖c5 ♗d6 67
♖xa5 ♖g3+ 68 ♚e4 ♖xb3 69 ♖a7+
♚f6 70 ♖a6 ♚e7 71 ♚d5 ♗f4 72
♖e6+ ♚f7 73 ♗g6+ ♚g7 74 c5?!
74 ♖e7+! ♚f6 75 ♖f7+ ♚g5 76 ♖f5+
♚g4 77 c5 ♖c3 78 c6 ♖c1 79 ♖f6
♖d1+ 80 ♚c5 ♗e3+ 81 ♚b5 ♖c1 82
♚a6 ♗f4 83 ♚b7 ♚g5 84 ♖e6 ♖c3
85 ♗e8 △ ♚c8-d7-e7-f8-g7 ♖e3! 75
♗e4 ♖h3 76 ♗g6 ♖e3 77 ♖a6 ♖e5+
78 ♚d4 ♖e1?! 78...♖e7!∝ 79 ♖a7+
♚f6 80 ♖f7+ ♚g5 81 c6 ♖c1 82 ♖f5+
♚g4 83 ♖f6 ♚g5 84 ♖e6 ♗g3 85
♚d5 ♗f4 86 ♗e8! ♖d1+ 87 ♚c5 ♖c1+
88 ♚b6 ♖b1+ 89 ♚a7 ♖a1+ 89...
♖b2 90 ♖e7 ♖c2 91 ♚b7 △ ♖e6,
♚c8 90 ♚b7 ♖b1+ 91 ♚c8

91...♖d1 91...♖c1 92 ♚d7 ♖d1+ 93
♚e7 ♖c1 94 ♚f8 ♖c3 95 ♚g7 ♚g4
96 ♚g6!±; 95...♚f5?? 96 ♗d7! ♚g5
97 ♖xh6 +− 92 ♖g6+ ♚h4 93 ♖g2
♖d2 94 ♖g1 ♖d3 95 ♗g6 ♖d4 96
♖b1 △ ♖b3-c3, ♚b7, c7 ♖c4 97 ♚d7
♖c5 98 ♖g1 ♖c4 99 ♗e8 ♖c3 100
♖g2! ♚h3 100...♖g3? 101 ♖c2±
101 ♖g6 ♚h4 102 ♚e7 ♗g5+ 103
♚f8 ♗f4 103...♚xh5?? 104 c7! △
♖c6+ +− 104 ♖e6 ♚g5 105 ♚g7 ♖a3!?
105...♚g4! 106 ♚g6 ♖c1 107 ♗d7
♚g3 108 ♚g7 △ ♖g6+, ♖xh6± 106

♖g6+ 106 ♖xh6? ♗e5+ 107 ♔h7
♖a7+ 108 ♗d7 ♖a8 109 ♖g6+ ♔xh5=
♔h4! 106...♔f5?? 107 ♗d7+ ♔e4
108 ♖xh6! ♗xh6 109 ♔xh6 ♖c3 110
♔g5! ♖g3+ 111 ♔h4 +−; 107...♔e5?
108 c7 +− **107 ♔f6!** 107 ♖xh6!?
♗xh6+ 108 ♔xh6 ♖g3?? 109 ♔h7
♔g5 110 ♔g7! ♔f5+ 111 ♗g6+ ♔e6
112 h6 ♔d6 113 h7 ♖h3 114 ♗e8!
♖g3+ 115 ♔h6! +−; 108...♖d3!
109 ♗d7 ♖d6+ 110 ♔g7 ♖xc6!=;
109 ♔g7 ♖d8! 110 ♔f8 ♔g5=; 110
h6 ♖xe8 111 h7 ♖e7+ 112 ♔g6 ♖e8=;
♖e3! 107...♖c3? 108 ♖g1 (Δ ♗d7)
♖g3 109 ♖h1+ ♖h3 110 ♖f1
♔g3 (110...♗g5+ 111 ♔f5!) 111
♖c1! ♗c7 112 ♔g6 +−; 107...♖f3
108 ♖g2 ♗g5+ 109 ♔g6 ♖f6+ 110
♔g7 ♖e6 (110...♖f1 111 ♖c2 +−)
111 ♗d7 ♖e7+ 112 ♔g6 Δ ♖g4 +−;
107...♗g5+? 108 ♖xg5 hxg5 109 h6
+− **108 ♖g8 ♖g3 109 ♖g6 ♖e3 110
♗f7 ♖f3?** 110...♖c3! 111 ♔f5 (111
♗d5 ♔xh5; 111 ♗e8 ♖e3=) ♗g5 112
♖d6 (Δ ♖d4+, ♖c4) 112...♖c5+ 113
♔e4 ♔g4!∝ **111 ♖g2 ♗g5+ 112 ♔g7
♖c3 113 ♗e8 ♗f4** 113...♖e3 114
♗d7! (Δ ♔g6 +−) ♔xh5 115 ♖h2+
♗h4 116 c7 +− **114 ♔f6 ♖c5 115
♖g1** Δ ♗d7 +− **♖c4?** 115...♗e3!±
116 ♗d7 ♗c7? 116...♗e3 (116...♗g5+?
117 ♖xg5 hxg5 118 h6 +−) 117 ♖e1
♗g5+ 118 ♔g6 (Δ ♖g1, ♖g4+/♖xg5)
♔g3 119 ♖g1+ ♔f4 120 ♖xg5 hxg5
121 h6 +−; 118...♗f4 119 ♖g1 ♗e3
120 ♖h1+ ♔g3 121 ♖h3+ ♔f2 122
♖xe3 ♔xe3 123 ♔xh6 +− **117 ♔g6
♗e5 118 ♔xh6 1−0 Povah**

Petroff

283 Geller-Smyslov Lvov 78
1 e4 e5 2 ♘f3 ♘f6 3 d4 exd4 3...
♘xe4 4 ♗d3 (4 dxe5!? d5!?) d5 5

♘xe5 ♗d6 6 0−0 0−0 7 ♘c3 Gufeld-
Makarichev **4 e5 ♘e4 5 ♕xd4 5 ♗b5!?**
♘c6 (5...♗b4 6 c3 dxc3 7 0−0 cxb2
8 ♗xb2∝; 5...c6? 6 ♕xd4 d5 7 exd6
♘xd6 8 ♗d3±; 5...a6 6 ♕xd4 +=)
6 0−0 (6 ♘xd4? ♘xf2!) a6 7 ♕e2!?
♘c5 8 ♗c4 ♗e7 9 ♖d1 d5! 10 exd6
♕xd6 11 ♘c3! ♗e6 12 ♗e3 ♗xc4 13
♕xc4 b5 14 ♕f1! ♘e6 15 ♘e2= ½−½
Shamkovich-Smyslov, USSR Final 71
d5 6 exd6 ♘xd6 7 ♘c3 7 ♗g5 ♕d7
8 ♘c3 ♘c6 9 ♕d2 ♗f5 10 ♘d5 ♘cd4?
11 ♘xd4 ♕xd5 12 ♗b5+! ♗d7 (12...
c6 13 ♘xc6!±) 13 ♗xd7+ ♕xd7
14 ♕e2+ ♘e7 15 0−0−0± Espig-Thal,
DDR Final 72; 7 ♗d3 ♘c6 8 ♕f4
♗e7 9 ♘c3 0−0 10 ♗e3 ♕d7?! 11
0−0−0 ♕g4 12 ♗d5! ♗d8 13 ♘g5!±
Adorjan-Androvitzki, Hungary 71 **♘c6**
7...♗f5 8 ♗g5! f6 9 ♗f4 ♗xc2?! 10
♖c1 ♗g6 11 ♗b5+! c6 12 0−0!±
**8 ♕f4 g6 9 ♗d2 ♕e7+ 10 ♗e2 ♗e6
11 0−0** 11 ♘d4 ♗h6 12 ♘xc6 ½−½
Geller-Smyslov, USSR Final 71 **♗g7
12 ♖ae1 0−0−0 13 ♕a4 ♕b8 14 ♗d3
♘c8 15 ♗g5 f6 16 ♗e3 ♕b4!? 17
♗xa7+!? ♘8xa7 18 ♕xb4** 18 ♖xe6
♕xa4 (18...♕xb2 19 ♘e4 Δ ♘c5
+=) 19 ♘xa4 ♗b4∝ **♘xb4 19 ♖xe6
♗xd3 20 cxd3 ♖xd3 21 ♖e7 ♖g8
22 ♖fe1 ½−½ Friedgood**

284 Sveshnikov-Kochiev Lvov 78
**1 e4 e5 2 ♘f3 ♘f6 3 ♘xe5 d6 4 ♘f3
♘xe4 5 ♘c3!? ♘xc3** 5...♘f6 6 d4
♗e7 7 ♗g5 ♗g4 8 ♕d2 += **6 dxc3!**
6 bxc3 ♗e7 7 d4 0−0 8 ♗d3 ♗g4=
♗e7 7 ♗f4 7 ♗d3 ♗g4 8 ♕e2 ♘c6
9 ♗f4 ♕d7 10 h3 ♗h5 11 g4 ♗g6
12 0−0−0 ♗xd3 Δ 0−0−0= **0−0** 7...
♘c6!? 8 ♕d2 ♗g4 9 ♗e2 0−0 10 0−0−0
♖e8∝ **8 ♕d2 ♘d7 9 0−0−0 ♘c5 10
♘d4!?** N 10 h3 ♖e8 11 ♗c4 ♗e6!
12 ♗xe6 ♘xe6 13 ♗e3 a5 14 h4 a4

15 a3 Qd7= Savon-Kochiev, USSR 78
Re8 11 f3 11 Bd3!? Ne6 12 Be3 Nxd4
13 cxd4 13 Bxd4?! Bg5 =+ Bf6 14
Bd3 Be6 15 h4 c5! =+ 16 Bg5 16
dxc5 dxc5 17 Bxc5 Qc7 Δ Bxa2∓
h6 17 d5!? 17 Bxf6 =+ Bd7 18 Bf4
b5 19 c3 c4 20 Bc2 b4! 21 cxb4 a5!∓
22 b5 Qb6 22...Bxb5! 23 Rde1
Bxb2+?! 24 Kxb2 Qf6+ 25 Ka3!;
23...Qc7!∓ 23 a4 Bxb5 24 axb5 Qxb5
25 Rde1 Qxb2+ 26 Kd1 Qa1+?!
26...a4!?≈ 27 Qc1 Qd4+ 28 Qd2
Qa1+ ½-½ Gufeld

King's Gambit

285 Lutikov-Lanka Jurmala 78
1 e4 e5 2 f4 Bc5 3 Nf3 3 Nc3!? d6
4 fxe5!? N 4 Nc3 Nf6 5 Bc4 Nc6 6
d3 a6 7 fxe5 dxe5 8 Bg5∞ dxe5 5
c3 Qe7?! 5...Nf6 6 d4! exd4 7 cxd4
Bb6 7...Qxe4+? 8 Kf2! +- 8 Nc3
Bg4 9 Qa4+!± Bd7 10 Bg5 f6 11 Bf4
Nh6 12 0-0-0 Nf7 13 Bd5 Qd8 14
Qa3! c6 15 Be3 Be6 16 Nf5 Rg8

17 Bd3 17 Re1! Δ d5 +- Nf8! 18
Rhe1 Bc7 19 Bxc7 Qxc7 20 e5 g6
21 g4!! gxf5 22 gxf5 Bd5 23 exf6+
Qd8 24 Qe7+ Qxe7 24...Kc8 25 Ne5
+- 25 fxe7+ Ke8 26 exf8Q+ Kxf8
27 Ne5 Rg2 28 Nd7+ Kg7 29 Re7
+- h5 30 h4! Nh6 31 Ne5 Rf8 32

Ng6 Rc8 33 Nf4 Rg4 34 Ne6 Nd6
35 f6 Ne4 36 f7 1-0 Gufeld

286 Iskov-Toth
Middlesborough 78
1 e4 e5 2 f4 exf4 3 Bc4 Nf6 4 Nc3
c6 5 d4 5 Bb3 Fischer d5 5...Bb4
6 Qf3?! d5 7 exd5 0-0 8 Nge2 cxd5
9 Bd3 Bg4 Spielmann-Bogoljubow 23;
6 e5 Ne4 7 Qf3∞ 6 exd5 cxd5 7 Bb5+
Bd7 7...Nc6 8 Bxf4 Bd6 9 Nge2
0-0 10 0-0 Bxf4 11 Rxf4 += Bronstein-
Tseshkovsky, USSR 78 8 Bxd7+
8 Qe2+!? Qxd7 9 Bxf4 Bb4 10 Be2
0-0 11 0-0 Nc6 12 Qd3 12 Ng5!?
Rae8 13 Rad1 Bxc3 14 Nxc3 Ne4
15 Nxe4 Rxe4 16 c3 Rfe8 17 Bd2
Ne7 18 Rdf2 Ng6 19 Bg3 f6 20
Qd1 Qb5 21 Qh5 Qd7 22 Rf5 Ne7
23 R5f3 g6 24 Qh6 Nf5!? 25 Rxf5
gxf5 26 Qxf6 Rf8 26...Qe6! 27 Qxf5
Qxf5 28 Rxf5 Re2 29 Be5!? Rxb2
30 Rg5+ Kf8 31 Rh5∞ 27 Qg5+
Qg7 28 Rxf5 Re2 29 Rxf8+± Kxf8
30 Qd8+ Kf7 31 Qxd5+ Kg6 32
h4! Qe7 33 Qg8+ Kf5 34 Qd5+ Kg6
35 h5+ Kh6 36 Bf4+ Qg7 37 Be5+
Kh6 38 Qf3?! Zeitnot 38 Bf4+!
Kg7 39 Be5+ Rxb2 39...Re1+ 40
Kf2 Qh4+ 41 g3 Qe4 42 Qf4+! Kxh5
43 g4+ Kh4 44 Bf6+ Kh3 45 Qg3
mate; 42...Kg6 43 Qf6 mate 39
Qf4+? 39 g4!! +- Δ 40 Qf4+ Kg5
41 Qf8+ Kg7 42 Bf4 mate; 39...Kg5
40 Qf5+ Kh4 41 Bf6+ Kg5! 39...
Kxh5 40 g4+ Kg6 41 Qf5+ Kh6
42 Qh5 mate 40 Bg7+ Kxh5 41
Qf7+ Kg6 42 Qf3+ Kg4 43 Qf7+
Kg6 44 Qf3+ Kg5 45 Qg3+ Kf5 46
Qh3+! Kg5 46...Ke4 47 Qf3 mate
47 Qg3+ Kf5 48 Qh3+ Kg4 49 Qxh7+
Kg6 50 Qh3+ Kg4 51 Qh7+ Kg5
51...Ke6 52 Qg8+ = 52 Qh6+ Kf5
½-½ Iskov

French

287 Groszpeter-Sinkovits
Hungary 78

1 ♘c3 e6 2 d4 d5 3 e4 ♗b4 4 ♗d3
dxe4 5 ♗xe4 c5 6 ♘e2 ♘f6 7 ♗f3
♘c6 8 a3 ♗xc3+ 9 bxc3 e5 10 ♗g5!
cxd4 11 0-0!? N h6? 11...dxc3!
12 ♗xf6 ♕xf6 13 cxd4 0-0 14 d5 ♘d4
15 ♘xd4 exd4 16 ♖b1 ♗f5! 17 ♖xb7
a5 18 ♖c7 ♖ac8 19 ♖c6 ♖xc6 20 dxc6
♕d6 21 h3 ♕c5 22 ♕d2 ♖d8 23 c4!
♗e6 24 ♖d1 ♗xc4 25 ♖c1 d3 26 ♕c3
d2 27 ♖d1 ♖d3 28 ♕c2 ♕e7 29
♕xc4 ♕e1+ 30 ♔h2 ♖xf3

31 ♕c5!! ♖f5? 32 ♕xf5 ♕xd1 33 c7
1-0 Haag

288 Lutikov-Sahovic Jurmala 78
1 e4 e6 2 d4 d5 3 ♘c3 ♗b4 4 ♗d3
4 exd5 exd5 5 ♗d3 ♗e7 6 ♕h5!? ♕d7
7 h3 ♘f5 8 ♘e2 ♘c6 9 ♗e3 +=
Lombardy-Timman, Teesside 75 dxe4
5 ♗xe4 ♘f6 6 ♗g5 6 ♗f3 ♘bd7?!
6...c5! 7 dxc5 ♕xd1+ 8 ♖xd1 ♘bd7=;
7 a3 ♗xc3+ 8 bxc3 ♕a5 9 ♗xf6 ♕xc3+
10 ♔f1 gxf6 11 ♘e2 ♕c4∝ 7 ♕d3!
+= h6 8 ♗xf6 ♕xf6 9 ♘e2 0-0 10
0-0 c6 11 f4!± ♖d8 12 ♕f3 ♕e7
13 a3 ♗d6 13...♗xc3 14 ♔h1 ♘f6
15 ♗d3 b6?! 16 ♘e4 ♗b7 17 ♘2g3
♘xe4 18 ♗xe4 ♖ac8

19 f5! ♗xg3 20 ♕xg3 ♖xd4 21 f6
♕f8 22 ♖f4 ♖cd8 23 h4 g6 24 ♖af1
♔h8 Zeitnot 25 ♔h2 ♖d1 26 ♖1f2
♗c8 26...♖1d2± 27 ♗d3! ♕d6 28
♕f3 e5?! 29 ♖e4 ♖a1 30 ♕e3 +-
♔h7 1-0 31 h5 ♗f5 32 ♖xf5 gxf5
33 ♖xe5 +- Gufeld

289 Lehmann-Farago Kiev 78
1 e4 e6 2 d4 d5 3 ♘c3 ♗b4 4 exd5
exd5 4...♕xd5?! 5 ♘f3 ♘f6 6 ♗d3
+= 5 ♕f3?! 5 ♗d3= ♕e7+! 6 ♗e3
6 ♘e2 ♘c6 7 ♗e3 ♘f6 8 h3 ♗xc3+!
Δ ♘e4 += ♘f6 Δ ♘g4 7 h3 ♘e4?!
7...♘c6 8 ♘ge2 ♘c6 9 0-0-0!= ♗xc3
10 ♗xc3 ♕xc3 11 bxc3 ♗e6 12 ♕g3
0-0-0 13 ♕xg7 ♖dg8?! 13...♗f5!≈
14 ♕h6 ♗f5 15 ♔d2 ♕a3 16 ♕h5?
16 ♗d3= ♗e4 17 f3

17...♗xc2!∓ 18 ♔xc2 ♕xa2+ 19 ♔d3
19 ♔c1 ♖e8! Δ ♕a5 -+ ♖e8 20 f4!?

20 ♖d2 ♕c4+ 21 ♔c2 ♘b4+ −+ ♞a5
21 ♕e2 ♕b3 22 ♖a1 ♞c4 23 ♕g4+
♚b8 24 ♗c1 ♖hg8 25 ♕f3 ♖g3! −+
26 ♗e2 26 ♕xg3 ♕d1+ −+ ♖xe2!
27 ♔xe2 ♕c2+ 28 ♔f1 ♖xf3+ 29
gxf3 ♕xc3 0-1 Gufeld

290 Pytel-Labadie
Val Thorens 78

1 e4 e6 2 d4 d5 3 ♘c3 ♘f6 4 ♗g5
♗b4 5 exd5 exd5 6 ♕f3 ♗e6 7 ♗d3
♘bd7 8 ♘ge2 h6 9 ♗d2 ♗g4 10 ♕e3+
♕e7 11 ♕xe7+ ♕xe7 11...♗xe7 12
♘b5 ♗d8 13 ♗f4 12 f3 ♗e6 13 a3
♗xc3 13...♗d6 14 ♘b5 14 ♗xc3
♖fe8 15 ♔f2 ♘b6 16 b3 ♘c8 17 ♖he1
♔d8 18 ♗b4 ♗d7 19 c4 ♘d6 20 ♘g3
♖xe1 21 ♗xe1! ♗e6 22 c5 ♘c8 23
b4 ♘e7 24 ♗d2 g6 25 b5 ♔d7 26
a4 ♘e8 27 a5 ♘g7 28 ♗f4 ♘f5 29
♘xf5 ♘gxf5 30 g4 ♘g7 31 ♗e5 ♖g8
32 c6+! ♔c8? 32...bxc6 33 bxc6+
♘xc6 34 ♗b5 ♘e6 35 ♖c1 ♘d8 36
♖c5!± 33 ♗f6 1-0 Pytel

291 Filipowicz-Rajna Warsaw 78

1 e4 e6 2 d4 d5 3 ♘c3 ♗b4 4 ♘ge2
dxe4 5 a3 ♗e7! 5...♗xc3+ 6 ♘xc3
f5? 7 f3! exf3 8 ♕xf3 ♕xd4 9 ♕g3!
♘f6 10 ♕xg7 ♕e5+ 11 ♗e2 ♖g8 12
♕h6 ♖g6 13 ♕h4 ♗d7 14 ♗g5 ♗c6
15 0-0-0± Alekhine-Nimzovich, Bled
31; 8...♕h4+ 9 g3 ♕xd4 10 ♘b5±
6 ♘xe4 ♘f6 7 ♘2g3 7 ♘2c3 0-0
8 ♗e3 ♘c6 9 ♕d2 e5 10 d5 ♘xe4
11 ♘xe4 ♘d4 12 ♗c4 ♗f5≈ Moe-Pytel,
Nice 74 0-0 7...♘c6 8 c3! ♘c6 9 f4!
b6 9...♘xe4 10 ♘xe4 ♕d5 11 ♕f3
♗d7 12 ♗d3 += Filipowicz-Webb,
Roskilde 78 10 ♗d3 ♗b7 11 0-0
♕d5 11...♕d7 12 ♘g5 ♖ad8 13 ♔h1
♘a5 14 b4 ♕d5 15 ♘3e4!± Rogers-
Sisniega, Wijk aan Zee 77 12 ♘xf6+
♗xf6 13 ♗e4 ♕d7 14 ♕f3 ♖ab8

15 ♗e3 ♘a5 16 ♖xb7 16 f5! exf5
17 ♗xb7 ♘xb7 18 ♘xf5± ♘xb7 17
f5 ♘d6! 18 fxe6 fxe6 18...♕xe6 19
♘h5± 19 ♕g4 ♘c4 20 ♗h6 ♔h8!
21 ♘h5 ♗xd4+ 22 ♕xd4 22 cxd4 gxh6
23 ♖ae1 ♖g8 24 ♕h4≈; 23...♖f5 24
♖xe6?? 25 ♖xf1+; 25 ♔xf1 ♘e3+ −+
♕xd4+ 23 cxd4 gxh6 24 ♖fc1! 24
♖ac1 ♖xf1+ 25 ♔xf1 ♘e3+ Δ ♘d5 =+
♘e3? 24...b5! 25 b3 ♘a5! 26 ♖xc7 ♘x
b3 += 25 ♖xc7 ♖bd8 26 ♖e1! ♖xd4!
27 h3 ♘d5 28 ♖xa7 ♖g8 28...♖e8 29
♖xe6 ♖xe6 30 ♖a8+ +− 29 ♖xe6 ♖d2
30 g4 ♖c8 31 ♖e1 ♖d8 32 ♖d7! ♖f8

33 ♘f6!! ♗xf6 34 ♖xd2 ♔g7 35
♖e7+ ♔g6 36 ♖d6 h5 37 ♖xb6 hxg4
38 ♖ee6 h5 39 ♖xf6+ ♖xf6 40 ♖xf6
♔xf6 41 hxg4 hxg4 42 ♔g2 1-0
Filipowicz

292 Westerinen-Sahovic Jurmala 78

1 e4 e6 2 d4 d5 3 ♘c3 ♗b4 4 e5 b6
5 h4!? N 5 ♗d2 ♕d7 6 ♘f3 ♗a6
♗xa6 ♘xa6 8 ♘e2 ♗f8 9 ♘f4 c5 10
♕e2 ♘b4 11 ♗e3 += Liberzon-Hubner,
Bad Lauterberg 77; 6 ♘ce2!? ♗f8
7 a4 a5 8 f4 ♗a6 9 ♘f3 h5 10 f5!≈
Shamkovich-Forintos, Mladenovac 75;
5 a3!? ♗f8 6 ♘f3 c5 7 ♗g5 ♗e7 8 h4
a6 9 ♕d2 ♗b7 10 ♘e2 ♘c6 11 ♗f4
♕c7 12 g3 += Kurajica-Korchnoi,
IBM 76 ♕d7 6 h5 h6 7 f4!?∞ ♗e7
8 ♘f3 ♗xc3+ 9 bxc3 ♗a6 10 ♗xa6

♘xa6 11 a4! ♘b8 12 a5 ♘bc6 13 axb6
cxb6 14 ♕d3 += ♘a5 15 g4! ♘c4 16
♘h4 0-0-0 15 f5 f6! 18 ♗f4 ♘c6 19
♘g6 ♖he8

20 0-0! exf5 21 gxf5 fxe5 22 dxe5
♘6xe5 23 ♘xe5 ♘xe5 24 ♕a6+ ♕b7
25 ♕xa7 ♘c6 26 ♕a4 ♖e2?! 26...d4!
+= 27 ♕b5! △ ♖a6 ♖de8 28 ♖a6
♘a7 29 ♖xb6 ♕xb6 30 ♖xb6 ♖8e7
31 ♖a1± ♖b7 32 ♖ba6 1-0 Gufeld

293 Ivanovic-Vaganian Niksic 78
1 e4 e6 2 d4 d5 3 ♘c3 ♗b4 4 e5 c5
5 a3 ♗xc3+ 6 bxc3 ♘e7 7 ♘f3 ♕a5
7...♗d7!? 8 dxc5 ♕c7 9 ♗d3 ♗a4
10 ♖b1! Spassky-Korchnoi (10) 78
8 ♕d2 ♘bc6 9 ♗d3 ♗d3 9 ♗e2 b6!? 10
a4 ♗a6 11 dxc5? ♗xd3! 12 ♕xd3
12 cxd3 =+ bxc5 13 0-0 c4 14 ♕d2
0-0 =+ 15 ♗a3 ♖fe8 16 ♗b4 ♕d8!
17 ♗xe7 17 ♖ae1 ♘g6 △ f6∓ ♕xe7
18 ♖ae1 f5! 19 exf6 19 ♘d4 ♘xd4∓
♕xf6∓ 20 ♘d4 e5 21 ♘xc6 21 ♘b5
♖ad8 22 ♘c7 ♖f8 23 ♘xd5 ♕f7 24
♖d1 ♔h8 −+ ♕xc6 22 f4 ♕c5+ 23
♔h1 e4 23...exf4 24 ♕xf4 ♖xe1 25
♖xe1 ♖f8 26 ♕e5= 24 ♖e3 ♖ad8
25 f5 ♖d6 26 g4?! d4 27 cxd4 ♖xd4
28 ♕f2 ♕d6 29 g5 ♖d2 30 ♕h4?
30 ♕f4 =+ ♖d1! 31 ♕f2 ♖e5 32
♕e2 32 f6 ♖xg5 33 f7+ ♔f8 34 ♖xe4
♕d5?? 35 ♕c5+ +−; 34...♕c6! −+

♖xf1+ 33 ♕xf1 ♕d5 34 f6 ♖xg5 35
fxg7 ♔xg7 36 ♕a1+ ♔g6 37 ♕e1 ♔f6
38 ♕f2+ ♔e6 39 ♕e1 a5 40 h3 ♔d6
41 ♕b1 ♔c7 42 ♕f1 ♖f5 43 ♕g2
♖f3 −+ 44 ♖xf3 exf3 45 ♕g7+ ♔c6
45 ♕f6+ ♔c5 47 ♕e7+ 47 c3 f2+
48 ♔h2 ♕d6+ 49 ♕xd6+ ♔xd6 50
♔g2 ♔e5 51 ♔xf2 ♔e4 52 ♔e2 h6 53
h4 h5 −+ ♕d4 48 ♕f6+ ♕e3 49 ♔h2
♕e4! 50 ♕c3+ ♔e2 51 ♕b2 f2 0-1
52 c3+ ♔f3 −+ Taulbut

294 Carleton-Botterill
British Final 78
1 e4 e6 2 d4 d5 3 ♘c3 ♗b4 4 e5 c5
5 a3 ♗xc3+ 6 bxc3 ♘e7 7 ♕g4 ♕c7
8 ♕xg7 ♖g8 9 ♕xh7 cxd4 10 ♘e2
♘bc6 11 f4 dxc3 11...♗d7 12 ♕d3
dxc3 13 h4!? 12 h4!? 12 ♘xc3 ♘xe5!
13 ♘b5 ♕b8 14 fxe5 ♕xe5+ 15
♔d1 a6! =+ Guimard-Frydman 42
♗d7 13 h5 0-0-0 13...d4 14 h6 ♖f8?
15 ♕d3 0-0-0 16 ♘xd4! +− Carleton-
Orton, England 70 14 ♕d3 ♘f5
15 h6 ♖g6 16 h7 ♖h8 17 ♖h5 17
♖b1 f6 18 exf6 ♗e8 19 ♕xc3 ♖xh7
20 ♖xh7 ♕xh7 21 ♖b3 ½-½ Vasyukov-
Doroshkevich, Moscow 67; 21...d4!
=+ Ivkov f6 18 exf6 ♗e8 19 ♖xf5
exf5 20 ♕xf5+ ♔b8! 20...♕d7 21
♕xd7+ ♗xd7 22 ♘xc3 ∝/+= 21 ♘xc3
♕xh7 22 ♗e3! d4!! 22...♖g3?! 23
♕xh7 ♖xe3+ 24 ♔d2 ♖xh7 25 ♔xe3
d4+ 26 ♔f2 dxc3 27 ♗d3± 23 ♗xd4
♗d7 23...♘xd4 24 ♕e5+ ♔a8 25
♕xd4∝ 24 ♗e5+ ♔a8 25 ♕e4 ♕h4+
26 ♗d2 ♗xe5 27 fxe5 ♖g4 28 ♕e1
♖g3!∓ △ ♕f4+ 29 ♔c1 ♕f4+ 30
♔b2 ♖e3 31 ♕d2 ♕xe5 32 ♗d3 ♗e6
33 ♖f1 ♖d8 34 f7 ♖f8 35 ♔b1 ♖xf7
36 ♖xf7 ♗xf7 37 ♘e4 ♕d4 38 ♕b4
♕xb4 39 axb4 ♗g6 40 ♘c5 ♖g3 41
♗e2?! 41 ♗xg6 ♖xg6∓; 41 ♗f1 ♖g4
42 b5 ♖f4! ♖xg2 42 ♗f3 ♖xc2 43

Bxb7+ Kb8 −+ Δ a5 44 Be4 Rxe4
45 Nxe4 Rc4 46 Nd2 Rxb4+ 47 Ka2
Kc7 48 Ka3 Rh4 49 Kb3 Kb6 50
Nc4+ Kc5 51 Na3 Rf4 52 Nc2 Rg4
53 Na3 Rh4 54 Nc2 Rf4 55 Na3
Rh4 56 Nc2 a6 57 Na3 Rb4+ 58
Ka2 Rg4 59 Kb3 Re4 60 Nc2 Rf4
61 Na3 Rh4 62 Nc2 a5 63 Na3 Rf4
64 Nb1 Rb4+ 65 Ka2 Kc4 66 Na3+
Kc3 67 Nb1+ Kc2 68 Na3+ Kc1 69
Ka1 a4 70 Ka2 Rb2+ 71 Ra1 Rb3
72 Ka2 Kd2 73 Nb1+ Kc2 74 Na3+
Kc3 75 Nb1+ Kb4 76 Nd2 Rh3
0-1 Botterill

295 Casse-Botterill England 78
**1 e4 e6 2 d4 d5 3 Nc3 Bb4 4 e5 c5
5 a3 Bxc3+ 6 bxc3 Ne7 7 Wg4 Wc7
8 Wxg7 Rg8 9 Wxh7 cxd4 10 Ne2
Nbc6 11 f4 Bd7 12 Wd3 dxc3 13
Rb1 0-0-0** 13...Nf5 14 h3!?; 13...d4
14 Nxd4 Nxd4 15 Wxd4 Nf5 16 Wf2
Wc6 17 Rg1 We4+ 18 We2 Wd4 19
Wf2 We4+ = Maric/Moles **14 Nxc3
Na5** 14...a6?? 15 Wxa6 +− **15 Nb5
Bxb5 16 Rxb5** 16 Wxb5 Nc4 17 Bxc4
dxc4 18 0-0 Nf5 =+ **Nf5 17 g3 Rh8!?**
N 17...Nc4 18 Be2 Wc6 19 Rb3 Wc5∞
Sherbakov-Krasnov, USSR 59 **18 Bg2
a6 19 Rb4 Wc5 20 Bd2?** 20 h3 Rdg8
21 g4 Nh4 Δ Nc4 Rxh2!∓ **21 Rxh2
Wg1+ 22 Bf1 Wxh2 23 Wc3+ Kb8** 23...
Nc6 24 Bxa6!? Wg1+ 25 Ke2 Nxg3+
26 Kf3∞; 25...Nfd4+ −+ **24 Wf3 Nxg3
25 Bxa6 Wg1+ 26 Bf1 Nc4 27 Bc1
Rh8 28 Wf2 Rh1 0-1 Botterill**

**296 Gaprindashvili-Borngasser
Dortmund 78**
1 e4 e6 2 d4 d5 3 Nc3 Nc6 4 e5!?
4 Nf3 f6 5 Bb5 a6 5...fxe5? 6 Wh5+
g6 7 Wxe5 +− **6 Bxc6+ bxc6 7 Nf3
c5 8 0-0 cxd4 9 Wxd4 c5 10 Wh4 f5**
10...fxe5? 11 Wh5+ g6 12 Wxe5 Nf6

13 Nxd5! **11 Bg5 Wd7 12 Ne2 Ne7**
12...Bb7 13 Nf4 Wf7 14 Ng6! Wxg6
15 Wa4+± **13 Nf4 Wf7 14 Rad1 Rb8
15 b3 Ng8 16 Wg3 We8** 16...Wc6
**17 c3 a5 18 h4 Wc6 19 h5 Wf7 20
Bh4 Rb7 21 Rfe1 We8 22 Wg5 Rg8
23 Wg3 Rh8** Δ Ng8-f6 **24 h6! gxh6
25 Nh5 Ng6 26 Bf6 Rg8 27 Nd2
Wf7 28 Wf3 Bd7 29 g3 Rb6 30 Kh2
Bc8 31 Nf1 We8 32 Ne3 Bb7 33
Rd2! Wb5 34 Wd1 Wc6 35 Rg1 Rb8
36 g4 fxg4 37 Rxg4 Rb7 38 f4 Rd7
39 f5 exf5 40 Nxf5 We6 41 Rf2
d4 42 cxd4 cxd4 43 Rxd4?!** 43 Bh4
Δ Nf6+ **Nxe5 44 Rxd7 Ng4+ 45
Wxg4 Rxg4 46 Rd8+ Wf7 47 Rxa8?**
47 Ng7!? Kg6!!; 47 Rxf8+! Kxf8
48 Ng7+ Ke8 49 Nf6+ Δ Nxg4 We1
**48 Rxf8+ Kxf8 49 Be7+ Kf7 50
Nxh6+ Kg6 51 Nxg4 Kxh5 52 Nf6+
Wg6 53 Rg2+ Kf7 54 Ng8 We5+ 55
Rg3 Wh5+ 56 Kg2 Wd5+ 57 Kg1 Wd1+**
½-½

**297 Gild.Garcia-Sisniega
Mexico 78**
**1 e4 e6 2 d4 d5 3 Nc3 Nf6 4 Bg5
Bb4 5 e5 h6 6 Bd2** 6 Be3!? **Bxc3
7 bxc3 Ne4 8 Bd3** 8 Wg4 g6 9 Bd3
Nxd2 10 Kxd2; 8...Wf8 9 Bc1 **Nxd2
9 Wxd2 b6** 9...c5 **10 f4** 10 Wf4; 10
h4 **Ba6 11 Nf3 Bxd3 12 Wxd3** 12...
cxd3 c5 13 dxc5!?; 12...Wd7; 12...
Nc6; 12...0-0!? 13 0-0 **c5 13 dxc5!?**
13 f5!? c4 14 We3 exf5 15 e6!? fxe6!?
16 Wxe6+ We7 17 Wxe7+ Kxe7 18 Ne5
Re8! 19 0-0 Nd7=?;15...Nc6!?;15Wf4;
15 0-0!? **bxc5 14 0-0 Nc6 15 Rab1** 15
f5 **0-0 16 g4?!** 16 Rb5?! a6 17 Rxc5?
Wb6 18 We3 =+/∓; 16 f5!? c4?! 17
We3 exf5 18 Nd4!? Nxd4 19 cxd4
Rb8! 20 Rbe1 Wd7 21 Rf2 Rb2∞; 21
Rf3?! Rf4?!; 21 Re2; 19 Wxd4!?; 18
Wf4; 18 Rd1; 16...exf5! 17 Wxf5 We7

f6 =+ **17 ♕e3** 17 ♖be1 **♖c8! 18
♖b5?!** 18 ♖be1 **d4! 19 ♕e4 dxc3
20 exf6?! ♘d4!∓ 21 ♖b7** 21
fxg7? ♖xf4! **♖xf6** △ ♖xf4 **22
♘e5 ♕d5! 23 ♕xd5** 23 ♖e1 ♕xe4
24 ♖xe4 ♘xc2 −+; 23...♖xf4!?
exd5 24 f5 24 ♖f2 ♖xf4! **♘xc2
−+ 25 ♘g6 ♖f7 26 ♘e7+ ♔f8
27 ♘g6+ ♔e8 28 ♖b3 d4 29 ♖c1
♘e3 30 ♖e1 ♖d7 31 ♖xc3 dxc3
32 ♖xe3+ ♔d8 33 ♖xc3 ♖d2 34 h4
♖b8 35 ♖c1 ♖b4 36 ♘e5 ♖e4 37
♘f3 ♖xg4+ 38 ♔h1 ♖d3 39 ♘e5 ♖h3
mate 0-1 Speelman**

298 Kovan-Shereshevsky USSR 78
**1 e4 e6 2 d4 d5 3 ♘c3 ♘f6 4 ♗g5
♗b4 5 e5 h6 6 ♗e3!?** 6 ♗d2 ♘e4 **7
♕g4 g6** 7...♔f8!? **8 a3 ♗xc3+ 9 bxc3
♘xc3** 9...c5 10 ♗d3 ♕a5 11 ♘e2 +=
♗d3 ♘c6 11 h4 ♘e7 11...♕e7?! 12
h5 g5 13 f4 gxf4 14 ♕xf4 ♗d7 15
♘f3 0-0-0 16 ♗f2 += Klovan-
Makarichev, USSR 78; 15 ♘h3!?
0-0-0 16 0-0 ♖dg8 17 ♕f6! ♕xf6 18
♖xf6 ♖g3 19 ♔f2 ♖hg8 20 ♘f4 +=
12 ♘f3!? N 12 f3 ♗d7 13 ♕f4 ♘f5
14 ♗f2 += Kurajica-Dvoretsky, Wijk
aan Zee 76 **♗d7 13 h5** 13 ♕f4?! ♘f5
14 ♗c1 c5 15 dxc5 ♘e4 16 g4 =+
g5 14 ♘xg5!? 14 ♘h2 ♘f5 15 ♕h3
c5 16 dxc5 += hxg5 **15 ♗xg5 ♗c6
16 ♗f6 ♔d7!** 16...♖g8? 17 ♕xg8+ +−
**17 ♕f4 ♕g8 18 g4 ♖e8 19 f3 ♖h7
20 ♔d2?** 20 ♔d2! ♘a4 21 ♖ag1 ♘b2
22 ♗xh7 ♕xh7 23 ♗xe7 ♖xe7 24 g5±

Diagram

20...♘e4 =+ 20...♘a4 21 c3 △ ♕c2,
♔f2, ♖ag1± **21 fxe4** 21 ♕e3!? ♘xf6
22 exf6 ♘c8 23 ♗xh7 ♕xh7 24 0-0-0
♘d6 25 ♖dg1 =+ ♕xg4 **22 exd5
♗xd5∓ 23 ♕f2 ♗xf6 24 ♖g1 ♕xh5**

25 ♕xf6 Zeitnot **♕h4+ 26 ♔f2 ♕xf2+
27 ♔xf2 ♖h2+ 28 ♔e3 ♖eh8 29 ♖g3
♖8h3 30 ♖xh3 ♖xh3+ 31 ♔d2 ♖h1
32 ♖xh1 ♗xh1** =+ **33 ♔c3 ♗f3 34
♔b4 ♔c6 35 c4 ♔d7 36 ♗c2 b6 37
♗a4+ ♔c6 38 ♗c2 a5+ 39 ♔c3 ♗f3
40 ♗h7 ♗g2 41 ♗d3 ♔e7 41 c5! ♗c6
42 cxb6 cxb6 43 ♔c4 ♔f8 44 ♗e2
♔g8** 44...♔g7 **45 ♗h5!= 45 ♗d1
♔h7 46 ♗h5 ♔g7 47 ♔d3 b5 48
♔c3 ♗d7 49 ♔d3 ♗e8 50 ♗f3 ♔g6
51 d5! exd5 52 ♗xd5 ♗d7 53 ♔d4
♗e6 54 ♗e4+ ♔g5 55 ♔c5 ♔f4 56
♗c6 b4 ½-½ Gufeld**

299 Bronstein-Zlotnik USSR 78
**1 e4 e6 2 d4 d5 3 ♘d2 a6 4 ♘gf3
c5 5 dxc5 ♗xc5 6 ♗d3 ♘c6 7 0-0 ♘b4
8 ♗e2** 8 e5 ♘xd3 9 cxd3 ♘e7 10 ♘b3
♗a7 11 ♗e3 ♘e7 9 a3 ♘bc6 10 b4
♗b6 11 ♗b2 0-0 12 c4 ♗c7 13 ♕c2
♘g6 14 ♖fd1 dxc4 15 ♘xc4 ♕e7
16 e5 ♖d8 17 ♖xd8+** 17 ♕e4 ♗d7
18 ♘d6 ♖b8 19 h4 f6 ♗xd8 17...
♕xd8 18 ♖d1; 17...♘xd8 18 ♗d4
♗d7 19 ♗c5 ♕e8 △ ♗c6, ♘f4 **18
♕e4 ♗d7 19 ♖d1 ♖b8 20 h4 ♘f8 21
h5 h6 22 ♘h2 ♕h4 23 ♘g4 ♕h8 24
♘d6 ♕e7** 24...♕xh5 25 ♘f6 ♕g6 26
♕xg6 fxg6 27 ♘f7 mate; 24...♔g8
25 ♕f3 ♕e7 26 ♘f6+ ♔h8 27 ♘xd7
♘xd7 28 ♕xf7 ♘dxe5 29 ♕f4; 28...
♘cxe5; 28 ♘xf7 **25 ♕f3 ♗c7 26 ♘xf7+**

♕g8 27 ♘f6+ gxf6 27...♔xf7 28
♘d5+ +− 28 ♘xh6+ ♔h8 29 exf6
♕h7 30 ♕e3 e5 31 ♗d3 ♗b6 32 ♕c1
♗e6 33 ♗xh7 ♘xh7 34 ♖d6 ♗b3 35
♖xc6 bxc6 36 ♗xe5 ♖e8 37 ♕xc6
1-0

300 Larsen-Sloth Esbjerg 78

**1 e4 e6 2 d4 d5 3 ♘d2 c5 4 exd5
exd5 5 ♘gf3 5 ♗b5+!? c4!? 6 ♗e2
6 b3!? cxb3 7 axb3 ♗b4; 6...b5?
7 a4 ♕e7+ 8 ♕e2 c3 9 ♕xe7+ ♔xe7
10 ♘a3+!; 6...♕e7+? 7 ♗e2 b5 8
0-0 ♘c6 7 0-0 ♗d6 7...a6!? 8 b3 +=
cxb3 9 axb3 ♘ge7 10 ♖e1 0-0 11
♘f1 ♗f5 12 ♘h4!? ♗e6 13 c3 ♕d7
14 ♗d3 ♘g6 15 ♘xg6 hxg6 16 ♗a3!
♖fc8?! 17 ♗xd6 ♕xd6 18 ♕d2 a5
19 ♘g3 ♖ab8 20 h4!± b5 21 h5 ♗d7!
22 hxg6 fxg6 23 ♕g5 ♗e8 24 ♕g4
24 ♖xe8+?! ♖xe8 25 ♗xg6 ♖e6**

**24...♗d7! 25 ♕xg6 ♕xg6 26 ♗xg6
b4 27 ♖ac1?** 27 cxb4! ♖xb4 28
♗f5 ♗xf5 29 ♘xf5 ♖xb3 30 ♖ac1
♔h7 31 g4! **bxc3 28 ♖xc3 ♗xd4 29
♖xc8+** 29 ♖d3 ♖b4! 30 ♖e7 ♖c1+
31 ♔h2 ♘f3+! **♖xc8 30 ♖e7 ♖d8
31 f4?!** 31 ♘h5 ♘e6 32 ♗f7+ ♔f8
33 ♖xd7 ♖xd7 34 ♗xe6 ♖d6 35
♘g4 ♖b6=; 32 f4 d4 33 f5 ♘f8=
♘c6! Zeitnot **32 ♖e1 ♔f8 33 ♔f2
♔e7?!** **34 ♗c2 ♖c8 35 ♗d1 ♖a8 36**

♔h5 ♘c6 36...♔g8!= **37 g4 ♗e8 38
g5 ♘d4 39 ♖e5 ♖d8 40 ♘g3 ♖b8
41 ♘f5!?** 41 ♖xd5 ♘xb3 += ♗xf5
41...♘xb3! 42 ♘xg7 ♔xg7 43 ♗xb3
♖xb3 44 ♖xe8 ♔g6 45 ♖e6+ ♔f5
46 ♖f6+ ♔e4 47 g6 ♖b8 48 ♔g3 ♖b1
49 ♔h4 ♖g1=; 48 g7! ♖g8 49 ♖f7
a4 50 f5 +−; 47...♖b2+! 48 ♔g3 ♖b1=
**42 ♖xf5+ ♔e7 43 ♖xd5 ♖b4 44 ♖e5+
♔f8 45 ♖f5+** 45 ♔e3 a4 46 bxa4
♗xa4 47 ♘h5 += **♔e7 46 ♖e5+** 46
♔g3 a4 47 bxa4 ♗xa4 48 ♗xa4 ♖xa4
49 g6 ♖a1= **♔f8 47 ♖xa5 ♖xf4+ 48
♔e3 ♖b4 49 ♔d3 ♗d7??** 49...♔e7+
**50 ♖e5 +− ♖b6 51 ♗c3 ♗e6 52
b4 ♖c6+ 53 ♔b2 ♖b6 54 ♗b3
b5 ♗c4 55 ♗a4 ♗d7 55 ♔c3 ♖b5 56
♖xb5 ♗xb5 57 ♗c4 ♗d7 58 ♘d4 ♔e7
59 ♔e5 ♗g4 60 ♗b5 ♗e6 61 ♗c6 ♗b3
62 b5 ♔d8 63 ♔d6 ♔c8 64 ♔e7 ♗c2
65 b6 ♔b8 66 ♔f7 g6 67 ♔f6 ♗d3
68 ♔e5 ♗c2 69 ♗e4 ♗a4 70 ♔f6 ♗e8
71 ♗xg6 ♗c6 72 ♔e5 ♔b7 73 ♗e4
1-0 Larsen**

301 Geller-Vaganian Lvov 78

1 e4 e6 2 d4 d5 3 ♘d2 c5 4 ♘gf3 ♘c6
4...cxd4 5 exd5 ♕xd5 6 ♗c4 ♕d6 7
0-0 ♘f6 8 ♘b3 ♘c6 9 ♘bxd4 ♘xd4
10 ♘xd4 a6 11 ♗b3 ♗e7 12 c3 0-0
13 ♕f3 += Jansa-Petrosian, Moscow
77; 10...♗e7 11 b3 0-0 12 ♗b2 ♕f4
13 ♕e2 ♕e4 14 ♕d2! += Geller-
Vaganian, USSR 76; 4...a6 5 exd5
exd5 6 dxc5 ♗xc5 7 ♘b3 ♗a7 8 ♗d3
♘f6 9 0-0 += Shamkovich-McCarthy,
USA 76; 4...♘f6!? 5 exd5 exd5 6
♗b5+ ♗d7 7 ♗xd7+ ♘bxd7 8 0-0
♗e7 9 dxc5 ♘xc5 10 ♘d4 0-0 11
♘f5 += Bronstein-Petrosian, USSR 75
**5 exd5 exd5 6 ♗b5 ♗d6 7 dxc5 ♗xc5
8 ♘b3 ♗d6 9 0-0 ♘e7 10 ♖e1** 10 c3
0-0 11 ♘bd4 ♕c7 12 ♗e2 ♘xd4 13
♕xd4 += Kostro-Holmov, Dubna 76;

0-0 11 c3 **♗g4** 12 **♗g5 h6** 13 **♗h4**
♕c7 14 **♗g3 ♗xg3** 15 **hxg3 ♖ad8=**
16 **♕d3 ♗xf3** 17 **♕xf3 ♕b6** 18
♖xc6 18 ♘d3 a5∞ **♘xc6** 19 **♖ad1**
♕a6! 20 **♘c5!** 20 ♘c1 d4! =+;
20 a3 ♕b6! **♕c4** 21 **♕e3** ½-½
Gufeld

302 Velimirovic-Uhlmann
Niksic 78
1 **e4 e6** 2 **d4 d5** 3 **♘d2 c5** 4 **exd5**
exd5 5 **♘gf3 ♘c6** 6 **♗b5 ♗d6** 7 **dxc5**
♗xc5 8 **♘b3 ♗d6** 9 **0-0 ♘ge7** 10 **♖e1**
0-0 11 **h3** 11 ♗g5 f6 12 ♗h4 ♕b6!
13 ♗e2 ♗e6 14 ♗g3 ♘e5! 15 ♘fd4
♗d7= Gipslis-Korchnoi, IBM 76; 11
♗g5 ♗g4 12 h3 ♗h5 13 ♗xc6 bxc6
14 ♘bd4 ♖c8 15 c4 h6 16 ♗xe7 ♗xe7
17 g4 ♗g6 18 ♘e5 += Peters-Ervin,
Lone Pine 78 **a6 12 ♗f1** 12 ♗d3 ♗f5
♗f5 13 **♘bd4 ♗g6** 14 **c3 ♖e8** 15
♗g5 ♕b6 15...♕c7 **16 ♕b3 ♕c7?!**
16...♕xb3 += **17 ♗xe7 ♘xe7** 18 **♖ad1**
♗c5 19 **♗d3 ♗h5?!** 20 **♖e5! ♗xf3**
20...♗g6 21 ♗xg6 hxg6 22 ♖de1±
21 ♘xf3± h6 22 ♗b1 ♗d6 23 **♖e2**
♖ad8 24 **♕c2 g6** 25 **♖de1 ♖f8** 26
♕d2 ♔g7 26...♔h7 27 h4 △ h5 +-
27 ♕d4+ ♔h7 28 ♕h4 ♖d7 29 **♕g4**
♘g8 30 **♘d4 ♘f6** 31 **♕f3 ♔g7**

32 ♗xg6! ♔xg6 33 ♕d3+ ♔g7 33...

♘e4 34 **f3 f5** 35 **fxe4 fxe4** 36 **♖xe4!**
34 ♘f5+ ♔g8 34...♔h8 35 ♕d4 ♕d8
36 ♘xh6 +- **35 ♗xh6+?!** 35 ♕d4!
+- **♔h8 36 ♕d4 ♗h2+ 37 ♔h1 ♕f4**
38 g3 ♕xh6 39 ♔xh2 ♔g7 40 **♖e5!**
♖h8 41 h4 ♕g6 42 ♔g2 ♖h5 43
♖xh5 ♕xh5 44 ♖e5 ♕h6 45 ♖g5+
♔h7 46 ♖f5 ♖d6 46...♔g7 47 ♔h3
△ g4 **47 ♔h3 ♖e6 48 f3 ♕g6 49 g4**
♘g8 50 ♕d3 ♕h8 50...♘f6 51 h5 +-
51 ♖h5+ ♘h6 52 ♕xg6 +- fxg6
53 ♖xh6+ ♔g7 54 g5 ♖e5 54...♖e2
55 h5 gxh5 56 ♖b6 +- **55 ♔g4 ♖e2**
56 h5 gxh5+ 57 ♔xh5 ♖xb2 58 ♖d6
♖h2+ 59 ♔g4 ♖xa2 60 ♔f5 ♖b2 61
♖xd5 ♖b6 62 f4 ♖c6 63 ♖d7+ ♔g8
64 ♖xb7 ♖xc3 65 ♖b6 a5 66 ♔g6
♖c8 67 ♖a6 1-0 Taulbut

303 Ivanovic-Gulko
Niksic 78
1 **e4 e6** 2 **d4 d5** 3 **♘d2 c5** 4 **♘gf3**
♘c6 5 **exd5 exd5** 6 **♗b5 ♗d6** 7 **dxc5**
♗xc5 8 **0-0 ♘ge7** 9 **♘b3 ♗d6** 10
h3! 0-0 11 **♘bd4 ♗c7!** 12 **♖e1 ♕d6**
13 ♗g5 ♘g6 △ ♘ge5xf3/♗f5-e4xf3
14 c4 ♗d7 14...dxc4 15 ♘xc6 bxc6
16 ♕xd6 ♗xd6 17 ♗xc4 += **15 ♘xc6**
bxc6 16 ♗a4 ♖fe8 += **17 cxd5 cxd5**
18 ♖xe8+ ♖xe8 19 ♗e3 ♗b6 20 ♗xb6
axb6 21 ♗xd7 ♕xd7 22 ♕d4 ♕d6 23
g3 23 ♖d1 ♘f4 h6 24 ♖d1 ♖e2 25
a4 25 ♕xd5? ♕xd5 26 ♖xd5 ♖xb2
27 ♖d6 ♔f8 △ ♘e7-d7 **♕e6 26 ♔g2**
♘e7 27 ♕c3 ♘f5 28 ♖c1 28 ♘d4?
♕e4+ ♕e4 29 ♔g1 ♘e3 29...d4 30 ♕c6
♘xg3 31 fxg3 ♕e3+ 32 ♔h1 ♕f2 33
♕c8+ △ ♕f5+ +- **30 ♘h4 g5 31 ♕f6**
♖c2 32 ♖xc2 ♕xc2 32...♘xc2??
33 ♘f5 ♕e1+ 34 ♔g2 ♕e4+ 35 ♔h2
+- **33 fxe3 gxh4 34 gxh4 ♕xa4 35**
♕xb6 ♕xh4 36 ♕d4 ♕xh3 37 b4 h5
38 b5= ♕g3+ 39 ♔f1 ♕h3+ ½-½
Taulbut

304 Velimirovic-Ljubojevic
Niksic 78

1 e4 c5 2 ♘f3 ♘c6 3 c3 e6 4 d4 d5
5 exd5 exd5 6 ♗b5 ♗d6 7 dxc5 7
♗e3!? cxd4 8 ♗xd4!; 7...c4 8 b3 +=
♗xc5 8 0-0 ♘ge7 9 ♘bd2 0-0 10 ♘b3
♗d6 11 ♗g5 11 h3!? += ♗g4!? 12
♗h4 ♕b6! 13 ♗d3 ♘e5 13...a5? 14
♗xh7+; 13...♘f5?? 14 ♗xf5 +- 14
♗e2 ♘c4 15 ♗xe7 ♗xe7 16 ♕xd5
16 ♕c2 a5 =+ ♘xb2 17 ♖ab1 17 ♕e4
♕e6 18 ♕c2 ♘c4 ♘a4 18 ♕c4 ♗d7∓
19 ♘bd4 ♕d6 20 ♖xb7 ♖fc8 21 ♘f5
21 ♕d3 ♘c5 ♗xf5 22 ♕xa4 ♖xc3
23 ♘d4 ♗e4 24 ♖d7 ♗c6! 25 ♖xd6
25 ♕xc6 ♖xc6 26 ♖xd6 ♖xd6 27
♘f5 ♖d7 −+; 25 ♘xc6 ♕xd7 −+
♗xa4 26 ♖a6 ♖a3 27 ♗b5?? ♗xb5
28 ♖xa3 ♗xf1 0-1 Taulbut

305 Noguieras-Sahovic
Jurmala 78

1 e4 e6 2 d4 d5 3 ♘d2 ♘c6 4 ♘gf3
♘f6 5 e5 ♘d7 6 ♗d3 ♘b4 7 ♗e2 c5
8 c3 ♘c6 9 0-0 b6!? 10 c4?! 10
♖e1 Δ ♘f1 ♗b7 11 cxd5 exd5 12
♘b1 ♗e7 13 ♘c3 cxd4 14 ♘xd5 ♘dxe5
15 ♘xe7 ♕xe7 16 ♘xe5 ♕xe5 17
♗a6 0-0-0!∓ 18 ♖e1 ♕d5 19 ♗d3
♕b8 20 ♗e4 ♕d6 21 ♕h5 f6 22 ♗d2
♘e5 23 f4 ♘c6 23...♘c4? 24 ♗xb7
♘xd2 25 ♗a6 24 ♖ac1 g6 25 ♕b5
♖c8 26 ♖c4 ♖he8 27 ♖cc1 f5 28
♗d3 ♖xe1+ 29 ♖xe1 ♕c5 30 ♕a4
♕d5 31 ♗c4 ♕d6 32 ♗d3 ♕d5 Zeitnot
33 ♗c4 ♕d6 34 ♗d3 ♘d8 35 ♕e8
♕d5 36 ♕e5+ ♕xe5 37 ♖xe5 ♘c6 38
♖e6 ♔c7 39 ♖f6 ♖d8 40 ♖f7+ ♖d7
41 ♖xd7+ ♔xd7 42 ♗b5 ♔d6 43 ♗xc6
♔xc6

Diagram

44 ♗b4+ ♔d5 45 ♔f2 ♔e4 46 ♗d6

♗d5 47 a3 ♗b3 47...♘c4 48 g3?
48 ♔e2 a5!! 49 ♗c7 d3 50 ♔e1 ♔f3
51 ♗xb6 a4 52 ♗a5 ♔g2 53 ♗d2 ♔xh2
54 ♔f2 ♔h3 55 ♗c1 ♔g4 56 ♗d2 h6?
56...h5! 57 ♗c1 g5? 57...h5! 58 ♗d2
g5!! 59 fxg5 f4!! 60 ♗xf4 h4 −+
58 fxg5 hxg5 59 ♗e3 ♔h5 60 ♗d2
♔g6 61 ♗c1 ♗c4 62 ♔e3 ♔f6 63 ♗d2
♗b5 64 ♔d4 ♔g6 65 ♔e3 ♔h5 66
♔f2 ♗c6 67 ♗e3 ♔e4 68 ♗d2 f4 69
gxf4 g4 70 ♗e1 ♔g6 71 ♔e3 ♗f5 72
♗f2 ♔f6 73 ♗e1 ♔e6 74 ♔d4 ♔d6
75 ♗b4+ ♔c6 76 ♗e1 ♔b5 77 ♗d2
g3 78 ♗e3 ♔c6 79 ♔c4 ♔d6 80 b4
axb3 81 ♔xb3 ♔d5 82 ♔c3 ♔e4 83
♔d2 ♗d7 84 ♗b6 ♗b5 85 ♗c7 ♔f5
86 a4 ♗c4 87 a5 ♗a6 88 ♗b8 g2 89
♗a7 ♔xf4 90 ♗g1 ♔e4 91 ♗f2 ♔d5
92 ♗g1 ♔c4 93 ♗f2 ♔b4 94 ♗g1
♔xa5 95 ♗f2 ♔b4 96 ♗g1 ♔c4 97
♗f2 ♔d5 98 ♗g1 ♔e4 99 ♗f2 ♗c8
100 ♗g1 ♗f5 101 ♗f2 ♔f4 102 ♗g1
♔g3 103 ♔e1 ♗e4 104 ♔d2 ½-½
Sahovic

306 Westerinen-Nogueiras
Jurmala 78

1 e4 e6 2 d4 d5 3 ♘c3 dxe4 4 ♘xe4
♗d7!? 5 ♘f3 5 g3!? += ♗c6 6 ♘eg5?!
6 ♗d3 ♘d7 7 ♕e2 ♘gf6 8 ♘g3 ♗d5
9 0-0 c5 10 ♗e3 ♕b6 11 c3 += Parma-
Forintos, Maribor 77; 6...♗xe4 7 ♗xe4
c6 8 ♕e2 ♘f6 9 ♗d3 g6!? 10 0-0 ♗g7

11 ♗d2 0-0 12 c4 += Rajkovic-Ciric, Vrnjacka Banja 76 **♗e7!** 6...h6? 7 ♘xf7; 6...♘f6 7 ♘e5 **7 ♗d3 ♘d7! 8 ♕e2 h6! 9 ♘e4** 9 ♘xe6 fxe6 10 ♗g6+ ♔f8 11 ♕xe6 ♗b4+ Δ ♕e7 −+ **♘gf6 10 ♘xf6+ ♗xf6 11 c3 0-0 =+ 12 ♗f4 ♖e8 13 0-0-0** 13 0-0 e5! 14 dxe5 ♘xe5 15 ♘xe5 ♗xe5 16 ♗xe5 ♕d5! **♗d5 14 h4 c5! 15 g4 g5!∓ 16 hxg5 hxg5 17 ♗e5 cxd4 18 ♗xd4** 18 cxd4 ♗xa2∓ **♗xd4 19 ♗h7+ ♔g7 20 ♖xd4 ♖h8 21 c4 ♗xf3 22 ♕xf3 ♕f6! −+ 23 ♕c3 ♘c5 24 ♖h3 e5?!** 24...♖xh7! 25 ♖f3 ♕e5 26 ♖e3 ♖h1+ 27 ♔d2 ♕h2 −+ **25 ♖d5 ♘e6 26 ♖xe5?!** 26 ♗f5! ♘f4 27 ♖xh8 ♘e2+ 28 ♔d2 ♘xc3 29 ♖h7+ ♔f8 30 ♔xc3∓ **♖xh7 27 ♖f3 ♖h1+ −+ 28 ♔d2 ♖d8+ 29 ♖d5 ♖xc3+ 30 ♔xc3 ♖c1+ 31 ♔b4 ♖xd5 32 cxd5 ♘f4 33 d6 ♖c6 34 ♖a3 a6 35 ♖a5 f6 36 d7 ♖d6 37 ♔c5 ♖xd7 38 ♔b6 ♘d5+ 39 ♔c5 ♔f7 0-1 Gufeld**

307 Mik.Tseitlin-Ospiov Corr. 78

1 e4 e6 2 d4 d5 3 ♘d2 dxe4 4 ♘xe4 ♗e7 5 ♘f3 ♘f6 6 ♗d3 ♘bd7 7 ♘xf6+ ♘xf6 8 ♕e2 0-0 9 ♗g5 c5 10 0-0-0! += 10 dxc5 ♕a5+ 11 c3 ♕xc5 12 0-0= **cxd4 11 h4 ♕a5 12 ♔b1 ♖d8 13 ♘e5** 13 ♗xf6 ♗xf6 14 ♗xh7+? ♔xh7 15 ♘g5+ ♗xg5 16 hxg5+ ♔g8 17 ♕h5 ♔f8∓ **h6** 13...♗d7 14 ♗xf6 ♗xf6 15 ♗xh7+ ♔xh7 16 ♕h5+ ♔g8 17 ♕xf7+ ♔h8 18 ♘xd7 ♕c7 19 ♕h5+ ♔g8 20 ♘xf6+ gxf6 21 ♖d3 +−

Diagram

14 g4! hxg5 15 hxg5 ♗d6 16 f4 ♗xe5 17 gxf6 ♗xf6 18 g5 ♕f8 19 gxf6 gxf6 20 ♖h7 ♗d7 21 ♕e4 f5 22 ♕xd4 ♕e7 23 ♗b5! 1-0 23... ♗xb5 24 ♕c5+ ♔f6 25 ♖h6+ ♔g7 26 ♕g1+!; 23...♕xb5 24 ♕d6+ ♔f6

·25 ♖h6+ ♔g7 26 ♕e7! **M.Tseitlin**

308 Botterill-Goodman
London 78

1 e4 e6 2 d4 d5 3 ♘d2 ♗e7 4 ♘gf3 ♘f6 5 e5 ♘fd7 6 ♗d3 c5 7 c3 b6 8 ♕e2 ♘c6 9 0-0 9 a3!? cxd4 10 cxd4 ♘b4 11 ♗b5 a6 12 ♗a4 b5 13 ♗b3 ♕b6 14 ♖d1 a5 15 ♘f1 a4 16 ♗c2 ♘xc2 17 ♕xc2 h6! 18 ♗f4 ♗a6 18...♕a5! **19 ♘g3 g6** 19...♕a5! **20 ♕d2 += ♗f8 21 ♖ac1 b4 22 b3 a3 23 ♖c2 ♖c8 24 ♖xc8+ ♗xc8 25 ♖c1 ♗a6 26 h4!** Δ h5, ♗e3, ♘h2, f4 **♘b8** Δ ♘c6-a7-b5-c3 **27 h5 g5 28 ♗e3 ♘c6 29 ♘h2 ♗g7 30 ♘g4 ♕d7** 30... 0-0 31 ♘e4!?; 31 ♘xg5! +− **31 ♘e4! ♕b5 32 ♘c5+** 32 ♘d6 ♕e2∝ **♗c7** 32...♔e8 33 ♗xg5? hxg5 34 ♕xg5 ♘xd4! 35 ♕xg7 ♘e2+ −+; 33 f4 +− **33 ♘xa6+ ♕xa6 34 ♖xb4± ♗f8 35 ♕d2 ♔b7 36 f4! gxf4 37 ♗xf4 ♕b6 38 ♗e3 ♖g8 39 ♘f6 ♖g3 40 ♔h2 ♗b4 41 ♕f2 ♖xe3 42 ♕xe3 ♘xe5! 42...♕xd4 43 ♕xd4 ♘xd4 44 ♘g8 +− 43 ♔h3! 43 g3? ♗d2! ♘c6 44 ♖d1 ♗f8 45 ♘d7 ♕d8 46 ♘xf8 ♕xf8 47 ♖f1 +− ♕g7 48 ♖f4 ♔b6 49 ♕c3 f6 50 ♕c5+ ♔b7 51 ♖g4 ♕f7 52 ♖g6 ♘e7 52...e5 53 ♕d6 +− 53 ♖xh6 ♕g7 54 ♕c1 ♘f5 55 ♖g6 ♕h7 56 g4 ♘xd4 57 ♕f4 1-0 Botterill**

309 Ivanovic-Andersson Niksic 78
1 e4 e6 2 d4 d5 3 ♘d2 ♘f6 4 e5 ♘fd7
5 ♗d3 c5 6 c3 b6 7 ♘h3! += ♗a6 8
♗xa6 ♘xa6 9 0-0 ♘c7 10 ♖e1 h6?!
10...♗e7 11 ♘f3! **11 ♘f4 ♕c8?! 12
c4!±** ♕b7 13 dxc5 ♗xc5 14 cxd5
♘xd5 15 ♘e4 0-0-0! 15...♗e7± **16
♕e2 ♔b8 17 ♘xd5 exd5!** 17...♕xd5
18 ♗f4 △ ♖ed1 **18 ♘d6 ♗xd6 19 exd6
♘c5?!** 19...g5!? **20 ♗f4± ♕a8 21
♖ac1** △ b4, ♖c7 **♖d7 22 ♖ed1! g5
23 ♗g3 ♘e4 24 ♕d3! ♘xg3 25 ♕xg3
♖hd8 26 ♖c7!** +- ♕a6 26...♖xc7
27 dxc7 ♖c8 28 ♖c1 △ ♕d6 +-
27 ♖xd7 ♖xd7 28 ♕e5! △ ♕e8+
**♕c8 29 ♕xd5+ ♔b8 30 b4 a6 31 g3
♕c3 32 ♖d4** △ ♖c4!, ♖c8+ ♕c1+
**33 ♔g2 ♕c8 34 ♖c4 ♕b7 35 ♖c6
♕a7 36 a4 g4 37 b5 axb5 38 axb5
♔b8 39 h3 h5 40 ♔h2 1-0** 40...gxh3
41 ♔xh3 △ ♕e5, ♕e8+/♖c1-a1
Taulbut

310 Cvachoucek-Iveges Corr 77/78
1 e4 e6 2 d4 d5 3 ♘d2 ♘f6 4 e5 ♘fd7
5 ♗d3 c5 6 c3 ♘c6 7 ♘e2 cxd4 8
cxd4 f6 9 exf6 ♕xf6 **10 0-0!?** 10
♘f3 ♗b4+ 11 ♗d2 ♗xd2+ 12 ♕xd2
0-0 13 0-0 e5 14 dxe5 ♘dxe5 15
♘xe5 ♘xe5 16 ♘d4 +=; 11 ♔f1?!
0-0 12 ♗g5 ♕f7 13 ♗h4 e5!? α/∓
**♘xd4 11 ♘xd4 ♕xd4 12 ♘f3 ♕f6
13 ♗g5 ♕f7 14 ♕c2!** 14 ♖c1≈
Merdkovic-Bagirov, USSR 58 **g6** 14...
♘f6 15 ♘e5 ♕e7 16 ♘g6+ hxg6 17
♕xg6+ ♔d8 18 ♘f7+ Wenglowski-
Gergel, Corr 72 **15 ♖ac1** △ ♕xc8+
♕g7 15...♘f6; 15...♘c5 **16 ♖fe1 ♕f7
17 ♕e2 ♘c5 18 b4! 1-0** 18...♘xd3
19 ♖xc8 ♘xe1 20 ♖c7+

311 Nunn-Mednis Budapest 78
1 e4 e6 2 d4 d5 3 ♘d2 ♘f6 4 e5 ♘fd7
5 ♘gf3 c5 6 c3 ♘c6 6...b6 7 ♗b5!
♗a6 8 a4 ♘xb5 9 axb5 a5 10 0-0
♗e7 11 c4 0-0 12 cxd5 exd5 13 ♕b3
c4 14 ♕e3 ♖e8 15 b3 cxb3 16 ♕xb3±
Nunn-Sowray, England 78 **7 ♗d3
cxd4 8 cxd4 ♕b6 9 0-0 ♘xd4 10 ♘xd4
♕xd4 11 ♘f3 ♕b6 12 ♕c2 ♘c5** 12...
h6 13 ♗f4 ♘c5 14 ♗e3 ♕a5? 15
b4! ♕xb4 16 ♖ab1 ♕a3 17 ♗b5+
♔d8 18 ♖fc1 b6 19 ♖b3 ♕xc1+
20 ♕xc1 ♘xb3 21 ♕c6 ♖b8 22 ♕e8+
♔c7 23 ♕xf7+ ♔d8 24 ♘g5! ♖b7
25 ♘xe6+ ♗xe6 26 ♕xe6 ♘c5 27
♕e8+ ♔c7 28 e6 1-0 Nunn-Whiteley,
London 78; 14...♕b4; 14...♘d7α **13
♕e2 ♗e7 14 ♗d2** 14 ♗e3 0-0 15
♖ac1 ♕b6 16 ♗b1 f5 16...♕xb2
17 ♖c3 △ ♖b3α **17 exf6 ♘xf6** 17...
♗xf6 **18 h4!?** 18 ♗c3 ♗d7 19 ♖fe1
19 ♗d4 ♗b5! ♗b4 19...♖ac8 20 ♗d4
♕a5 21 ♖xc8 ♖xc8 22 ♘g5 += **20
♗d4 ♕a5?!** 20...♕a6? 21 ♗d3 ♕xa2
22 ♖a1 ♕b3 23 ♘d2 ♗xd2 24 ♕xd2
(△ ♖a3) 24...♘e4 25 ♗xe4 dxe4
26 ♗xg7±; 20...♕d8 21 ♖ed1 ♕e7=
21 ♖ed1 ♖ae8 22 ♕e5 += △ ♘g5,
♗xh7+ **♕a6 23 ♗d3** 23 ♘g5? ♗d6 24
♗xh7+ ♔h8 25 ♕e3 e5 26 ♗d3 exd4
27 ♕xd4 ♕a4! -+ **b5** 23...♕d6 24
♕e2 △ ♗xa7/25 a3 ♗a5 26 ♘c5 **24
♕e2** △ ♘e5, ♗xd7 **♕b7 25 ♘e5 a6
26 g4!? ♖e7 27 g5 ♘e4 28 f3 ♘d6?**
28...♗xg5! 29 ♕g2 h6 30 h4 ♘h7
31 ♕g6? ♘f6 32 ♘g4 e5 33 ♘xh6+
♔h8 -+; 31 ♘g6! += **29 a3 ♗a5 30
♗c5!±** ♘c8 30...♗b6 31 ♘xd7 +-;
30...♖c8 31 ♔g2!± **31 ♕g2 ♗e8 32
♕c2 g6 33 ♗xe7 ♘xe7 34 ♘g4 ♘f5
35 ♗xf5 gxf5 36 ♘e5 ♗d8 37 f4 d4?
38 ♕g3 ♗b6 39 ♕g2 ♕e7 40 ♖c8
♗h5 41 ♖xf8+ ♕xf8 42 ♖c1** △ ♕a8+,
♖c8 **d3 43 ♘xd3** +- **♕d6 44 ♘e5
♕d4 45 ♖c8+ ♗e8 46 ♕f3** △ ♖xe8+,
♕h5+ **♗d8** 46...♕g1+ 47 ♔h3 △
♖xe8+ ♔xe8 ♕c6+ **47 ♔h3 ♕d2 48**

♕c3 ♕d1 49 ♕d3 ♕h5+ 50 ♔g3 ♗e7
51 ♕d7 1-0 51...♗c5 52 g6 ♗f2+ 53
♔g2 **Nunn**

312 Larsen-Brinck-Claussen
Esbjerg 78
1 e4 e6 2 d4 d5 3 ♘d2 ♘f6 4 e5 ♘fd7
5 c3 c5 6 f4 ♘c6 7 ♘df3 cxd4 8
♘xd4?! ♘xd4?! 8...♕b6; 8...♘c5 9
cxd4 ♘b6? 9...♘b8! 10 ♘f3 ♗e7
11 ♗d3 ♗d7 12 0-0 h5 13 b3 g6 14
♗d2± ♔f8 15 a4 ♔g7 16 g3 a5 17 h3
♘c8 18 ♕e1! ♕b6 19 ♖b1 ♗b4 20
♗xb4 axb4 21 ♕d2 ♘e7 22 ♖fc1
♖ac8 23 ♔f2! 23 ♖xc8 ♖xc8 24 ♖c1±
♕a5 △ ♖c3, b5; 23...♖xc1 24 ♖xc1
♖c8±

24 ♖xc8! ♖xc8 25 g4 hxg4 25...♖c3
26 gxh5; 25...♖h8 26 ♖c1 +- 26
hxg4 ♖c3 26...♖h8 27 ♖c1 27 f5
exf5 28 ♖h1 ♘g8 28...f4 29 ♕xf4
♘g8 30 ♖h7+! 29 gxf5 +- ♕b6 30
f6+ ♔f8 31 ♖h8 ♗g4 32 ♖xg8+ 1-0
Larsen

313 Sveshnikov-Balashov Lvov 78
1 e4 c5 2 c3 e6 3 d4 3 ♘f3! += d5
4 e5 4 exd5 exd5 5 ♘f3 a6 6 ♗e3
c4 7 b3 cxb3 8 axb3 ♘f6 9 ♗e2 +=
Dvoretsky-Smejkal, Wijk aan Zee 76;
5...♘c6 6 ♗c2 cxd4 7 cxd4 ♗d6 8
♘c3 ♘ge7 9 ♗g5 f6 10 ♗h4 0-0 11

♗g3 ♗b4= Sveshnikov-Dorfman, USSR
76; 6 ♘b5!? ♗d6 7 ♗e3 cxd4! 8 ♗xd4
♘e7 9 ♗xg7 ♖g8 10 ♗d4 ♖xg2∞
Sveshnikov-Polugaevsky, USSR 76
♘c6 5 ♘f3 ♗d7 5...♕b6! 6 dxc5 6
♗e2 ♘ge7 7 0-0 ♖c8 8 ♖e1 cxd4 9
cxd4 ♘f5∞ Menvielle-Larsen, Las
Palmas 76; 6...f6!?; 6 ♗d3 ♕b6!?
♗xc5 7 ♗d3 ♘ge7 8 b4!? N 8 0-0
♘g6 9 ♖e1 ♕c7 10 ♗xg6? fxg6! 11
♗f4 0-0 12 ♗g3 ♘e7 13 ♘bd2 ♘f5
14 ♘b3 ♗a4 =+ Sveshnikov-
Balashov, USSR 76; 10 ♕e2= ♗b6
9 b5 ♘a5 10 0-0 ♖c8 11 a4 △ ♗a3
♘g6 12 ♗a3 ♗c5! 13 ♗xc5 ♖xc5
14 g3 ♕c7 =+ 15 ♖e1 ♘c4 16 ♕e2
0-0 17 h4! f6 17...a6!? 18 ♗xg6!
hxg6 19 exf6 ♖xf6 19...gxf6 20
♕d3 △ h5 20 ♘d4 ♘d6 20...e5?!
21 ♘b3 ♖c4 22 ♘1d2! ♖xc3 23
♖ac1 ♖f8 23...♖xc1 24 ♖xc1 ♕b6
25 ♘c5∞ 24 ♕e5 ♖xc1 25 ♖xc1 ♕b6
26 ♘c5∞ ½-½ **Gufeld**

314 Sveshnikov-Savon
Lvov 78
1 e4 c5 2 c3 e6 2...d5 3 d4 d5 4 e5
♘c6 5 ♘f3 ♗d7 6 dxc5?! ♗xc5 7
♗d3 f6!? N 7...♘ge7 8 b4 ♗e7 8...
♗b6 9 b5 ♘xe5 10 ♘xe5 fxe5 11
♕h5+ ♔f8 11...g6 12 ♕xe5 ♗f6 13
♕g3∞ 12 ♕xe5 ♗f6 13 ♕d6+ ♘e7
14 0-0 e5 15 ♗a3 ♔f7 16 ♘d2 ♖e8
16...e4 17 ♗e2 ♗xc3 18 ♖ac1 ♗xd2
19 ♖c7 ♔e8 20 ♗g4! +- 17 ♖ad1
♗g4 18 ♕xd8 ♖axd8 19 f3 ♗e6 20
c4= ♘f5 21 cxd5 ♖xd5 22 ♗xf5
♗xf5 23 ♘c4 ♖xd1 24 ♖xd1 ♔g6
25 ♘d6 25 ♘e3 ♗e6 =+ ♖d8 26 ♖c1
△ ♖c7 ♖d7 27 ♘xf5 ♔xf5 28 ♗b4
e4 28...♖d5 29 ♖c5 29 ♔f2 29 fxe4+?!
=+ exf3 30 ♔xf3 ♖d3+ 31 ♔e2 ♖d5
32 ♖c5 ♔e4 33 ♖xd5 ♔xd5 34 ♔d3 g6
35 h3 h5 ½-½ **Gufeld**

315 Dankert-Sahovic Biel 78
**1 e4 e6 2 ♘f3 b6 3 d4 ♗b7 4 ♗d3
c5 5 0-0** 5 d5!? exd5 6 exd5 ♘xd5
7 0-0 **cxd4 6 ♘xd4 d6** 6...♘c5 7
♘b3 ♘e7 **7 ♘c3 ♘f6 8 f4 a6! 9 ♔h1
♘bd7 10 ♕e2 ♘c5 11 ♗d2** 11 b4!?
**♗e7 12 b4 ♘xd3 13 cxd3 0-0 14
♖f3?** 14 ♖ac1 ♖c8 15 ♖c2 ♕d7
16 ♖fc1∞ **♖e8! 15 ♖h3 ♗f8 16 ♖f1
g6 17 f5?!** exf5 18 ♗g5 ♗g7 19 ♕f2
♖c8

**20 ♘xf5 gxf5 21 ♖g3 ♖xc3 22 ♗h6
♗h5** 22...♘g4?? 23 ♖xg4 fxg4 24
♕xf7+ +− **23 ♖xg7+ ♘xg7 24 ♕d4
f6 25 ♕xc3 ♕e7 26 ♖f3 ♕e5 0-1
Sahovic**

Alekhine

316 Peresipkin-Alburt Kiev 78
1 e4 ♘f6 2 ♘c3 d5 2...e5; 2...d6
**3 exd5 ♘xd5 4 ♘xd5 ♕xd5 5 d4
♘c6 6 ♘f3 e5!?** N 6...♗g4 7 ♗e2
0-0-0 8 c3 e5= **7 ♗e3** 7 dxe5 ♕xd1+
8 ♔xd1 ♗g4 9 ♗f4 ♘c5 =+; 7 ♘xe5
♘xd4 ♗g4?! 7...exd4 8 ♘xd4 ♘c5!?∞
**8 dxe5 ♗xf3 9 ♕xf3 ♕xf3 10 gxf3
♘xe5 11 0-0-0!** += ♗d6 11...♘xf3?
12 ♗g2± **12 ♗b5+ ♔f8** 12...♔e7 13
♖he1 △ f4± **13 ♗e2!± f5?!** 13...♘g6
14 ♖d5! ♕e7! 15 ♗d4 15 f4 ♘g6

16 ♖f5 ♖hf8 += **♘c6 16 ♗xg7 ♖g8
17 ♗c3 ♖af8 18 ♗d3 ♖g5 19 ♗d2
♖h5 20 h4 ♕d7 21 ♗g5?!** 21 f4±
♘e5! **22 ♗e2 f4 23 ♖hd1 h6 24 ♖xe5
hxg5 25 hxg5 ♖g8 26 ♖b5?** 26
♖xf5!± **♕c6! 27 ♖g1 ♗e7 28 ♖a5
a6 29 ♖a4 ♖hxg5?** 29...♖gxg5! +=
**30 ♖g4! ♗d6 38 ♖d4 b5 32 ♖d1 ♗e5
33 c3 ♖5g7 34 ♖dg1 ♗f6 35 ♔c2
♖g5 36 ♖e1 ♗e5 37 a4!** 37 ♘xb5+
axb5 38 ♖xe5 ♖xe5 39 ♖xg8 ♖e2+
= **♗d6 38 a5! b4? 39 ♖eg1 ♗e7 40
♘xa6 bxc3 41 ♘c4! ♖xg4 42 fxg4
♖g5 43 ♖e1! +− ♗d6 44 a6 ♗c5 45
f3 cxb2 46 ♖e8! ♗d4 47 ♖d8 ♗b6
48 ♔xb2 ♔c5 49 ♗d3 ♔b4 50 ♖b8
♔a5 51 ♖b7 ♔b4 52 ♗f5** △ ♖xb6,
a7 +− **♖g8 53 ♗e4 ♔a5 54 a7 ♗d4+
55 ♔b3 ♖a8 56 ♔c4! 1-0 Gufeld**

317 Roos-W.Schmidt Bagneux 78
**1 e4 ♘f6 2 e5 ♘d5 3 ♘c3 ♘xc3 4
dxc3 d6 5 ♗f4 ♘c6 6 ♘f3 dxe5 7
♕xd8+ ♘xd8 8 ♘xe5 c6 9 0-0-0 f6
10 ♗g3 e5?!** 10...♗e6 △ g6, ♗h6
11 ♗c4± ♘f7 11...♗e6? 12 ♖xd8+
12 ♖he1 g6? 13 ♗xe5 1-0 13...♘xe5
14 ♘xe5 ♗h6+ 15 ♔b1 fxe5 16 ♖xe5+
♔f8 17 ♖d8+ ♔g7 18 ♖e7+ ♔f6 19
♖f7+ ♔g5 20 ♖xh8; 14...fxe5 15
♖xe5+ ♗e7 16 ♖de1

318 Dobrovolsky-Hardicsay
Prievidza 78
**1 e4 ♘f6 2 e5 ♘d5 3 c4 ♘b6 4 c5
♘d5 5 ♗c4 e6 6 ♘c3 ♗f4!?** 6...♘xc3?
+=; 6...d6= **7 ♕g4? 7 d4!? ♘xg2+
8 ♔f1 ♕h4 9 ♘f3 ♘f5!** △ d6 =+ **♕h4!
−+ 8 h3 ♘xg2+ 9 ♔f1 h5! 10 ♕e2
♘f4 11 ♕e4** 11 ♕d1 ♘g6! 12 d4
♘xe5 −+ **♘g6 12 ♕e2 ♘xe5! 0-1
Hardicsay**

319 Velimirovic-Kovacevic
Jugoslavia 78
1 e4 ♞f6 2 e5 ♞d5 3 c4 ♞b6 4 d4
d6 5 f4 dxe5 6 fxe5 ♞c6 7 ♗e3 ♗f5
8 ♞c3 e6 9 ♞f3 ♗e7 10 d5 exd5 11
cxd5 ♞b4 12 ♞d4 ♗d7 12...♛d7;
12...♞g6 13 ♗b5+!± 13 ♛f3 13 e6
fxe6 14 dxe6 ♗c6 15 ♛g4 ♞h4+
16 g3 ♗xh1 17 0-0-0 ♛f6 18 gxh4
0-0 19 ♗e2±; 19 ♗b5 c5 14 dxc6
bxc6 15 e6!? 15 a3 ♞4d5 16 ♞xd5
♞xd5 17 ♗c4 ♛a5+!= Ljubojevic-
Hartston, Las Palmas 74 fxe6 15...
♗xe6 16 a3 ♞4d5 17 ♞xc6 ♛c7 18
♞xe7 ♛xe7 19 ♗b5± 16 0-0-0 ♞6d5
17 a3 ♞xc3

18 ♞xe6!± ♛a5 19 ♞xg7+ ♛d8 20
♖xd7+! ♛xd7 21 ♛g4+ ♛c7 22 axb4
♞a2+ 23 ♛b1 ♞xb4 24 ♗c4∞ ♛b7
25 ♛d7+ ♛c7 26 ♖d1 △ ♞e6 +− ♖ad8
26...♞d5 27 ♖xd5! +− 27 ♛xc7+
♛xc7 28 ♞e6+ ♛b7 29 ♞xd8+ ♖xd8
30 ♖xd8 ♗xd8 31 g4! ♞d5 32 ♗c1
♗h4 33 ♗d3 ♞f6 34 g5 +− ♞g4 35 h3
♞f2 36 ♗f5 ♛c7 37 ♗f4+ ♛d8 38 ♛c2
♛e7 39 ♛d2 ♛f7 40 ♛e2 ♛g7 41
♗e3 ♞h1 42 ♛f3 ♞g3 43 ♗d3! 1-0
Maric

320 Gufeld-Peresipkin USSR 78
1 e4 ♞f6 2 e5 ♞d5 3 d4 d6 4 ♞f3
♗g4 5 ♗e2 c6 6 ♞g5 ♗xe2 7 ♛xe2

dxe5 8 dxe5 e6 9 0-0 ♗e7 10 ♞e4
+= 0-0 11 c4 ♞b4 12 ♖d1 ♛c7 13
♗g5! ♗xg5 14 ♞xg5 ♞bd7 15 a3
15 ♛e4!?; 15 ♛d2 a5 16 ♛xd7??
♖fd8 −+ h6 16 ♞f3 16 ♞xe6 fxe6
17 axb4 += ♞a6 17 ♞c3 ♖fd8 18
b4 ♞f8 19 ♞e4 19 c5± △ ♖d6 ♖xd1+
20 ♖xd1 ♞ab8 21 ♞d6 a5 22 b5?!
cxb5 23 cxb5 ♞bd7 24 h4 ♛c3 25
♛e4?! ♛xa3 26 ♛xb7 ♛b3! 27 ♖a1?!
27 ♖c1 ♛d5 28 ♖c6! += ♛d5!= 28
♛xd5 28 ♛c7 ♛c5 29 ♛b7= exd5
29 ♞d4 a4 30 f4 ♞e6 31 ♞xe6 fxe6
32 ♛f2? 32 f5! ♞xe5 33 fxe6=; 32
♖a3! ♞b6 33 ♛f2 ♖a7 34 ♛e3 ♖c7
35 ♛d2= a3∓ 33 ♛e3 ♖a4 34 g3 a2
35 ♛d2 ♞c5 36 b6 Zeitnot 36 ♛c3
d4+ 37 ♛b2 d3 −+ ♞b3+ 37 ♛c3
♞xa1 38 b7 ♞b3 39 b8♛+ ♛h7 0-1
Gufeld

321 Byrne-Vukic Bugojno 78
1 e4 ♞f6 2 e5 ♞d5 3 d4 d6 4 ♞f3
♗g4 5 ♗e2 e6 6 h3 6 0-0 ♗e7 7 c4
♞b6 8 ♞c3 0-0 9 ♗e3 d5!? 10 c5
♗xf3 11 gxf3! ♞c8 12 f4! a5 13
f5 ♗g5 14 f4 ♗h6 15 fxe6 fxe6 16
♗g4± Shamkovich-Vukic, New York
76; 12 b4!? f6 13 f4 fxe5 14 fxe5
♛e8 15 ♗d3 ♗d8 16 ♛g4± Matanovic-
Vukic, Jugoslavia 75; 12...a6 13 f4
♛d7 14 ♗d3 ♗d8 15 a4 c6 16 ♞e2
f5 17 ♛h1± Matanovic-Vukic,
Jugoslavia Final 78 ♗h5!? 6...♗xf3
7 ♗xf3 c6 8 c4 ♞b6= 7 0-0 ♗e7 8
c4 ♞b6 9 ♗e3 9 exd6 cxd6 10 ♞bd2
♞c6 11 b3 d5 12 c5 ♞d7 13 ♗b2
0-0 14 ♞c3! b6 15 b4 bxc5 16 bxc5
♛c7 17 ♛a4 ♗g6 18 ♞b3 e5?!±
Kapengut-M.Ivanov, USSR 76; 18...
a6 19 ♞a5 ♞db8 +=; 17...♗xf3 18
♞xf3 e5 19 ♗b5 exd4 20 ♗xc6 ♞xc5
21 ♛xd4± Kapengut 0-0 10 ♞c3 d5
10...♞8d7 11 exd6 cxd6 12 b3 ♖c8

13 Rc1 Nf6 14 g4 Bg6 15 Nh4 d5= Adorjan-Corden, Birmingham 74 **11 c5** 11 cxd5 exd5 12 Bd3 Nc6 13 g4 Bg6 14 Bf5 Qe8 15 Ne2 f6= Gulko-Bagirov, Baku 77 Bxf3 **12 gxf3 Nc8 13 f4 f5!**= 13...g6? 14 Kh2?! Kh8? 15 f5! +− Levitna-Alexandria (4) 75; 14 f5!; 13...Nh4 14 Bd3 g6 15 Qg4 Kh8 Diesen-Vaganian, Hastings 74/75 **14 b4 b6 15 a3 c6 16 Kh2 Rf7 17 Na4 Bf8 18 Rc1** 18 b5!? **Rb7 19 Bd2!** += g6 20 Bd3 Kh8 21 Qf3 b5 22 Nb2 Na6 23 Be2 Rab8 24 Nd3 Rg7 25 Rg1 Be7 26 Ne1 Rb7 27 Qg2 Nc7 28 Nf3 Bh4 29 Nxh4 Qxh4 30 Qg3 Qxg3+ 31 fxg3 Rf7 32 g4 Ne7 33 Rg3 Rb8 34 g5 Rg7 35 h4 Kg8 36 h5 Kf7 37 Rh3 a6 38 Kg2 Rf8 39 Ra1 Ke8 40 a4 Kd7 ½-½

322 Tseshkovsky-Alburt
Daugavpils 78
1 e4 Nf6 2 e5 Nd5 3 d4 d6 4 Nf3 Bg4 5 Be2 e6 6 0-0 Be7 7 c4 Nb6 8 Be3 0-0 9 Nc3 d5 10 c5 Bxf3 11 gxf3!? Nc8 11...Nc4 12 Bxc4 dxc4 13 Qa4± **12 f4 Nc6** 12...Nh4 13 Bd3 g6 14 f5!±; 12...a5 13 f5!± **13 f5?!** 13 Bd3 f5≈ **exf5 14 Bf3 Bg5 15 Nxd5 f4! 16 Nxf4 Bxf4 17 Bxf4 Qxd4≈ 18 Bg3 N8e7 19 Qc2 Qd7 20 Qe4 Qe6 21 b4 Nf5** 21...a6 **22 Rfe1 Rfe8 23 Qf4 Nfd4 14 Bg4! Qg6 25 b5!? Nxe5?** 25...Nxb5 26 Bf5 Qh6 27 Qxh6 gxh6 28 e6 +=

Diagram

26 Bd1! Nec6 27 Rxe8+ Rxe8 28 bxc6 Re1+ 29 Kg2 Qd3 30 Be2!! Rxe2 31 cxb7 Rb2 33 c6 +− Qc4 **34 Qe4! h6 35 Rd1 Qxc6 36 Rxd4 Rxb7? 37 Rd8 mate 1-0 Suetin**

323 Hulak Vukic
Jugoslavia Final 78
1 e4 Nf6 2 e5 Nd5 3 d4 d6 4 Nf3 Bg4 5 Be2 e6 6 0-0 Be7 7 h3 Bh5 8 c4 Nb6 9 exd6 9 Nc3 cxd6 10 Nbd2 0-0 11 b3 Nc6 12 Bb2 Bg6!? N 12...d5 13 a3 a5 14 Nc3?! 14 Re1! Bf6! 15 Re1 e5 16 dxe5 dxe5 17 Bf1 Nd7 18 b4? 18 Ne4 e4!∓ 19 Bxf6 Nxf6 20 b5 exf3 21 bxc6 fxg2 22 Bxg2 bxc6 23 Bxc6 Ra6 24 Bg2 Rd6 25 Ra2 Nh5! 26 c5 Rd3 27 Re3 Rxe3 28 fxe3 Qe7 29 Nc4 Qxc5 30 Qd5 Qc7 31 Rd2 Nf6 32 Qb5 Be4! −+ 33 Rd6 Bxg2 34 Kxg2 Ne4 35 Qc6 Qe7 36 Rd4 f5 37 Qd5+ Kh8 38 Qe5 Qg5+ 39 Kh2 Qh5 40 Qf4 Δ Rxe4 Ng5 41 Ne5 Qxh3+ 42 Kg1 Ne6 0-1 Maric

324 Ree-Palatnik Kiev 78
1 e4 Nf6 2 e5 Nd5 3 d4 d6 4 Nf3 g6 5 Bc4 5 Ng5!? Nb6 5...c6 6 0-0 Bg7 7 exd6 Qxd6 8 Nbd2 += 6 Bb3 a5!? 6...Qg7 7 Qe2 Nc6 8 0-0!? dxe5 9 dxe5 Nd4 10 Nxd4 Qxd4 11 e6 += Geller-Alburt, USSR 75 7 a4 Bg7 7...d5 8 0-0 Bg7 9 Bf4 Δ Nbd2 += 8 exd6 8 0-0 cxd6 9 0-0 0-0 10 Bg5!? N 10 Nc3 Bg4 11 Nb5 Nc6 12 c3 d5= Bg4 11 c3 h6 12 Bh4 Nc6= 13

♘bd2 d5! **14 h3 ♗xf3 15 ♘xf3 ♕d7 16 ♗g3 ♖ac8 17 ♖e1 e6 18 ♕e2** 18 ♕d3!? **♖a8!?**

19 h4?! h5 20 ♗f4 ♖fe8 21 ♘e5 ♘xe5 22 dxe5 22 ♗xe5 ♗xe5 23 ♕xe5 ♖ac8 △ ♘c4 **♕d8!** =+ 23 ♗g5 ♕c7 24 ♗e3?! **♗xe5 25 ♖ad1 ♖ac8 26 ♗g5 ♘d7!∓ 27 g4 hxg4 28 ♕xg4 ♘f6 29 ♗xf6 ♗xf6 30 h5 g5 31 ♖d3 ♕f4! 32 ♕g2 ♗e7 33 ♖ee3 ♕f6 34 ♖g3 ♔h8 35 ♖gf3 ♕g7 36 ♕g3 f5! 37 h6 ♕f6 −+ 38 ♖d4 ♖g8 0-1 Gufeld**

325 Savon-Alburt Kiev 78
1 e4 ♘f6 2 e5 ♘d5 3 d4 d6 4 ♘f3 g6 5 ♘g5!? 5 ♗c4 c6 6 0-0 ♗g7 7 exd6 ♕xd6 8 h3 += **c6!** 5...f6?! 6 c4 ♘b6 7 e6! fxg5 8 d5 ♗xe6!?∝; 6 exf6 exf6 7 ♗c4! fxg5 8 ♗xd5 c6 9 ♗b3 ♕e7+ 10 ♗e3 a5 11 0-0± Mnatsakanian-Alburt, USSR 77 **6 c4!** += 6 ♗c4 ♗g7 7 ♕e2 0-0 8 0-0 dxe5 9 dxe5 h6 △ ♗g4=; 6 h4?! dxe5 7 dxe5 ♕c7 8 ♕e2 h6 9 ♘h3 ♗g7∝ Barczay-Bohm, Wijk aan Zee 77 **♘c7 7 ♕f3 f6 8 exf6 exf6 9 ♘e4 f5?** 9... ♗g7! 10 ♗f4 0-0!≈ **10 ♘ec3 ♘e6?!** 10...♗g7 **11 d5± ♘d4 12 ♕e3+ ♕e7 13 ♘a3 a6** 13...c5 14 ♘cb5 ♕xe3+ 15 ♗xe3 ♘xb5 16 ♘xb5 ♔d7 **14 ♕xe7+ ♗xe7 15 ♗e3 ♗f6** 15...c5 16

♗xd4 cxd4 17 ♘e2 ♗f6 18 0-0-0 +− **16 dxc6 ♘dxc6 17 0-0-0 ♗e6!? 18 ♖xd6 ♕f7 19 c5 ♗e5 20 ♖xe6! ♕xe6 21 ♗c4+ ♕f6 22 ♘d5+ ♕g7 23 f4!** 23 ♘b6 f4! **♗d4 24 ♗xd4+ ♘xd4 25 ♘b6 ♖a7 26 ♖d1 ♖d8 27 ♘c2 ♘bc6 28 ♘xd4 ♖xd4 29 ♖xd4 ♘xd4 30 ♔d2 ♕f6 31 ♔c3 ♘e6?** 31...♘c6 △ ♘e7± **32 ♗xe6 ♔xe6 33 b4! +− a5 34 b5 a4 35 a3 h6 36 h4 ♖a5 37 ♕b4 ♖a7 38 g3 g5** 38...♔e7 39 ♘d5+ ♔d7 40 ♘c7 b6 41 cxb6 ♖b7 42 ♔c5 +− **39 hxg5 hxg5 40 fxg5 ♕f7 41 ♘c8 ♖a8 42 ♘d6+ ♕e6 43 ♘xb7 ♖g8 44 b6 ♖xg5 45 ♘a5! ♖xg3 46 b7 1-0 Gufeld**

326 Vadasz-Haik Bagneux 78
1 ♘f3 g6 2 e4 ♗g7 3 d4 ♘f6 4 e5 ♘d5 5 h4 5 c4 ♘b6 6 c5 ♘d5 7 ♗c4!± h6 6 c4 ♘b6 7 d5 d6 8 e6 fxe6 9 h5 9 ♗d3!? **g5 10 ♗d3 exd5! 11 ♗g6+ ♕f8 12 cxd5 e6∓ 13 dxe6 ♗xe6 14 0-0 ♘c6 15 ♘c3 ♕d7 16 a4 g4 17 ♘d2** 17 ♘h4 ♗f6 **♘d4 18 a5 ♘c4 19 ♘xc4 ♗xc4 20 ♗e3! ♗b3?** 20...c5!∓ **21 ♕d2??** 21 ♕d3 **♘f3+!! 22 gxf3 gxf3 23 ♖a4** 23 ♗f4 ♕h3 24 ♗xd6+ ♔g8 ♗xa4 24 ♗f4 ♗c6 25 ♕h2 ♕g4 0-1 Pytel**

Pirc

327 Bisguier-Taulbut
Lone Pine 78
1 e4 d6 2 d4 ♘f6 3 ♘c3 g6 4 ♘ge2 ♗g7 5 g3 0-0 6 ♗g2 e5 7 0-0 ♘bd7 8 ♖e1 ♖e8 9 h3 exd4?! 9...c6 10 a4 a5 11 ♗e3 += **10 ♘xd4 ♘c5 11 ♗f4 ♘h5?!** 11...♘e6! += **12 ♗e3 ♘f6 13 f3 a5 14 ♕d2 ♘fd7?! 15 ♖ad1 a4 16 ♘db5 +− b6 17 ♗g5 f6** 17...♗f6 18 ♗xf6 ♘xf6 19 e5 +− **18 ♕d5+ ♔h8 19 ♕xa8 fxg5 20**

♘d5

20...♘e5! 21 ♘dxc7 ♖f8 22 ♖xd6
♕e7 23 ♘d5 ♘xf3+! 24 ♗xf3 ♕e5
25 ♔h2 ♗d7 26 ♕xf8+ 26 ♕a7 ♖xf3
27 ♖g1 ♖f2+ 29 ♖g2 ♖xg2+ 30 ♔xg2
♕xe4+ −+ ♗xf8 27 ♖xb6 ♗xb5 28
♖xb5 ♗d6 29 ♖g1 ♕d4?! 29...h5 △
♔g7, g4 30 ♖g2 h5 31 ♖b6 ♕e5
32 ♔h1 a3?? 32...♔g7 △ g4 −+ 33
bxa3 ♔g7 34 ♖b1 g4 35 hxg4 hxg4
36 ♗xg4 ♘xe4 37 ♘f4 ♘xg3+ 38
♖xg3 ♕xf4 39 ♖b7+ ♔h6 40 ♖bb3
♕e4+ 41 ♖g2 ♕e1+ 42 ♖g1 ♕e4+
43 ♖g2 ½-½ Taulbut

328 Katalymov-M.Tseitlin
USSR 78

1 e4 d6 2 d4 ♘f6 3 ♘c3 g6 4 ♗e2
♗g7 5 g4?! 5 h4; 5 ♘f3 += ♘a6!?
5...♘c6α; 5...c5! 6 g5 ♘fd7 7 d5
a6 8 h4 b5 9 h5 ♕a5 =+ 6 g5 ♘d7
7 h4 c5! 8 d5 8 ♗xa6 bxa6 9 ♘ge2α
c4!? 9 h5 ♘ac5 10 h6 ♗xc3+ 11 bxc3
f6! 11...♘xe4? 12 ♕d4 12 ♕d4 ♕a5
13 ♗d2 0-0 14 f4 b5 15 ♘f3 △ e5
♕c7 16 0-0 e5! =+ 17 dxe6 ♘xe6
18 ♕e3 ♗b7 19 f5 ♘xg5 20 ♘xg5
fxg5 21 fxg6 hxg6 22 h7+ ♔h8!∓
23 ♕d4+ ♕xh7 24 ♗xg5 ♖ae8 25
♖xf8 ♗xf8 △ ♘e6 26 ♕xa7?! 26
♔f2∓ ♘e6 27 ♕e3 ♘xg5 28 ♕xg5
♖xe4 −+ 29 ♘f3 ♕b6+ 30 ♔f1 ♕e5

31 ♕h4+ ♔g7 32 ♗xb7 ♕xb7 33
♔f2 ♕f7+ 34 ♔g1 ♕f3 35 ♖f1 ♕e3+
36 ♔f2 ♖g5+ 37 ♔h2 ♕e5+ 38 ♔f4
♕e2+ 39 ♔h3 39 ♖f2 ♕h5+ −+ ♕g2+
0-1 Gufeld

329 Browne-Taulbut
Lone Pine 78

1 e4 g6 2 d4 d6 3 ♘c3 ♗g7 4 ♘f3
♘f6 5 ♗e2 0-0 6 0-0 c6 7 a4 ♕c7
8 h3 e5 9 dxe5 dxe5 10 ♗c4 ♘h5
11 ♖e1 ♘d7 11...♘f4? 12 ♗xf4 exf4
13 e5 ♘d7 14 ♕d4 ±/+− 12 ♗e3
♘f4 13 a5 h6? 13...♖d8 14 ♘g5?!
♘f8 15 ♕c1 ♘4e6!=; 14 ♕c1!? +=
14 ♕c1 b5?! 15 axb6 ♘xb6 16 ♗b3
♗e6? 17 ♗xe6 fxe6 18 ♘d2 ♕e7
19 ♘h2 ♕g5 20 g3!? 20 ♖g1 △ ♕d1,
♕g4 +− ♕h5 21 gxf4 exf4 22 ♗xb6
f3 23 ♘f1 23 ♘c7 ♗e5+ 24 ♗xe5
♕xe5+ 25 ♔h1 ♕h5= ♗e5+ 24 ♘g3
g5 25 ♖h1 25 ♘ce2!? fxe2? 26 f4!;
25...g4 26 ♘g1 axb6 27 ♖xa8 ♖xa8
+=/± axb6 26 ♖xa8 ♖xa8 27 ♘d1
27 ♕d1± ♕h4 28 ♘e3 ♕xe4?? 28...
h5 29 ♘ef1 ♕f4 30 ♕xf4 ♗xf4 31
♔g1 h4 32 ♘h5 ♗e5 −+; 29 ♔g1
♗xg3 30 fxg3 ♕xg3+ = 29 ♘g4 ♗xg3+
30 ♔xg3 ♖a1?? 31 ♘f6+ 1-0 Taulbut

330 Andersson-Uhlmann
Niksic 78

1 ♘f3 g6 2 e4 d6 3 d4 ♘f6 4 ♘c3
♗g7 5 ♗e2 0-0 6 0-0 c6 6...♗g4 7
♗e3 ♘c6 8 ♕d2 e5 9 d5 += 7 ♖e1
♗g4 8 ♗g5?! 8 h3!? ♕a5 9 ♕d2 ♘bd7
10 ♖ad1 e5 11 d5 c5 11...cxd5!?
12 ♗xf6 ♘xf6 13 ♘xd5 ♕xd2 14
♘xf6+ ♗xf6 15 ♘xd2 += 12 a4 a6
13 h3 13 ♖a1 b5 ♗xf3 14 ♗xf3 b5
15 axb5 axb5 16 ♖b1 c4 16...b4
17 ♘d1 c4 18 ♕e2 ♖fc8 19 ♘e3 ♘b6
20 ♕f1= 17 b4 cxb3 18 ♖xb3 ♖ab8
18...b4!? 19 ♖b2 h6?! 20 ♗e3 ♘c5?!

179

21 ♗xc5 dxc5 22 ♖eb1 b4 23 ♘d1
♖fd8?! 23...♖fc8! 24 ♘e3 ♘e8 25
♘c4 ♕a4

26 ♕e1! ♘d6 27 ♘xd6 ♖xd6 28
♖a1?! ♕e8 28...♕b5 29 ♖ba2 c4 30
♗e2± 29 ♖a5 ♕c8 30 ♗e2 ♕c7 31
♖a4 ♖dd8 32 ♗c4± ♖a8 33 ♖ba2
♖xa4 34 ♖xa4 ♗f8 35 ♕a1 ♖b8?!
35...♗d6 36 ♖a7 ♕b6 37 d6! ♗xd6
38 ♖xf7 ♔h8 39 ♕d1 ♖d8 40 ♕f3
1-0 Andersson

331 Ligterink-Lutikov
Jurmala 78
1 e4 ♘c6 2 ♘f3 d6 3 d4 ♘f6 4 ♘c3
g6 5 ♗e2 ♗g7 6 d5 ♘b8 7 0-0 0-0 8
h3 8 ♗g5 c6 9 ♘d2 ♘bd7 10 a4 a5
11 ♘b3 ♘e5∝; 8 ♖e1!? c6 9 a4 9
♗g5 ♗d7 10 a4 a5 11 ♖e1 += a5 9...
♘bd7 10 ♖e1 ♘e5 11 ♗f1 e5 b4!±
10 ♖e1!? 10 ♗e3; 10 ♗g5= ♘a6
11 ♗f1 ♘b4 12 ♗g5 h6 13 ♗f4 ♗d7
14 ♕d2 ♕h7 15 ♗c4 ♖c8= 16 ♗b3
cxd5 17 exd5 ♖c5!? 18 ♗e3 ♖xc3!
19 bxc3 ♘e4 20 ♕c1 ♘xc3 21 ♗d4!
♗xd4 22 ♘xd4 ♘bxd5∝ 23 ♕d2 e6!
24 ♗xd5 ♘xd5 25 ♘b3 ♕c7 26 ♘xa5
♖a8 27 ♘b3 ♖xa4 28 ♖xa4 ♗xa4
29 ♖e4!= ♗xb3 30 cxb3 ♕d8 ½-½
Gufeld

332 Vogt-Ftacnik
CSSR-DDR 78
1 e4 d6 2 d4 ♘f6 3 ♘c3 g6 4 ♘f3
♗g7 5 ♗e2 0-0 6 0-0 ♘c6 7 d5 7 ♗e3
♘e5 7...♘b8; 7...♘b4 8 ♘xe5 dxe5
9 ♗e3 a6 9...e6 10 ♕d2 10 ♕d3
♕d6 11 ♖fd1 ♖d8 12 h3 ♗d7?!
12...e6 13 a4 e6 14 a5 exd5 15 exd5
♕b4 △ ♘c6 16 ♕c1 ♘e8 17 ♖a3
♖ab8 18 ♘a2 18 d6 ♗c6∝ ♕e7 19
c4± f5 20 ♗g5 ♘f6 21 ♗xf6 ♘xf6 22
b4 e4 23 f4! ♗e8 △ c6 24 ♕d2 ♖d7

25 g4! fxg4 26 hxg4 ♗f7 27 ♕d4
♖e8 28 ♖e3 ♕d6 29 g5 ♘h5 30 ♗xh5
gxh5 30...♕xf4 31 ♗e2 ♖e5 32 ♖h3±
31 ♖xe4 ♖xe4 32 ♕xe4 c6 33
c5 ♕g6 34 ♘c3 ♗xd5 35 ♕e5
△ ♘e4 ♕f7 36 ♘xd5 cxd5 37 f5 h4
37...d4? 38 ♖xd4 ♖xd4 39 ♕xd4
♕xf5 40 ♕d8+ ♔f7 41 ♕f6+ ♕xf6
42 gxf6 ♔xf6 43 b5 +- 38 ♖d4 ♕h5
39 ♕e6+ ♖f7 39...♔f8 40 ♕f6+ ♔g8
41 ♔f2± 40 ♕e8+ +- ♔g7 41 ♕e5+
41 f6+ ♔g6 42 ♕g8+ ♔f5 43 ♖xd5+
♔e6 44 ♖d6+ ♔f5 45 ♕c8+ ♔g6
46 ♖d5 +-; 43...♔e4 44 ♖d2! ♕g4+
45 ♖g2 ♕d1+ 46 ♔h2 +- ♔f8 41
♔g8 42 f6 h6 43 ♕f5 ♕h8 44 ♖g4
hxg5 45 ♖xg5 ♕d1+ 46 ♔h2 ♕d2+
47 ♖g2 +-; 43...♕xg5+? 44 ♖g4 +-
42 ♕h8+ ♔e7 43 f6+ ♔d7 44 ♖xd5+
♔e6 44...♔c6 45 ♖d6+ ♔b5 46 ♕e8+

180

+− **45 ♖d6+ ♔f5 46 ♕c8+ ♔f4** 46...
♔g6 47 ♖d5 +− **47 ♖d4+ ♔e5 48
♖g4 ♖f8 49 ♕c7+ ♔f5 50 ♕f4+
♔e6 51 ♕e4+ ♔f7 52 ♕xb7+ ♔g6 53
♕e4+ ♔f7 54 g6+ 1-0 Vogt**

333 Taimanov-Gufeld USSR 78

**1 ♘f3 g6 2 e4 d6 3 d4 ♘f6 4 ♘c3
♗g7 5 ♗e2 0-0 6 0-0 ♗g4 7 ♗e3 ♘c6
8 ♘d2** 8 ♕d2 ♗xe2 8...e5 9 d5 **9
♕xe2 e5 10 d5 ♘e7** 10...♘d4 **11 a4**
11 ♖fd1!? **c6 12 dxc6 bxc6=** 13 ♖fd1
d5?! 13...♕c7 △ ♖fd8, d5= **14 ♗c5
+=** ♕**c7 15 ♗b3 ♖fd8** 15...♖fe8 16
♗xe7 ♖xe7 17 exd5 cxd5 18 ♘xd5
♘xd5 19 ♖xd5 e4 20 c3 ♖b8 21 ♖b5±
16 exd5 ♘exd5 16...cxd5 17 ♘b5
♕b7 18 ♕xe5± **17 ♘e4 ♘xe4 18 ♕xe4
h6** 18...♖ab8!? **19 ♕c4 ♖d7 20 ♖d2
♖ad8 21 ♖ad1 ♘b6 22 ♕a6** 22 ♖xd7
♖xd7 23 ♖xd7 ♕xd7 24 ♗xb6 axb6
25 g3 ♕d5!=; 22 ♕b4!? **♗f8 23 ♗xf8
♔xf8 24 ♕a5?! ♖d5! 25 ♕c3** 25
♕b4+ ♕d6∓ **♕d6! =+ 26 a5!** 26 ♕e3
♘xa4 27 ♕xh6+ ♔g8 =+ **♘a4 27 ♕e3
♘xb2 28 ♖xd5 cxd5 28 ♖b1 ♘c4 30
♕xa7 ♘a3** Zeitnot 30...♖d7 31 ♕c5
♔e7! 32 a6 ♖c7!∓; 31 ♕a8+ ♔g7 32
a6 ♘b5∓ ½-½ **Gufeld**

334 Chernikov-Gufeld USSR 78

**1 ♘f3 g6 2 e4 d6 3 d4 ♘f6 4 ♘c3
♗g7 5 ♗e2 0-0 6 0-0 ♗g4 7 ♗e3 ♘c6
8 ♕d2 e5 9 d5 ♘e7 10 ♖ad1 ♘d7
11 ♘e1?!** 11 ♘g5! ♗xe2 12 ♘xe2
h6 13 ♘h3 ♕h7 14 f4 exf4 15 ♘exf4
♗xb2? 16 c3 ♗a3 17 ♘e6! fxe6 18
♗xh6±; 15...♘e5! △ ♘g8 f6 **♗xe2
12 ♕xe2** 12 ♘xe2 f5 13 exf5 gxf5
14 f4 ♘b6! =+ **f5 13 f4 exf4 14
♗xf4 ♗xc3! 15 bxc3 fxe4 16 ♕xe4
♘c5 =+ 17 ♕c4 ♕d7 18 ♘d3 ♕a4!
19 ♕xa4 ♘xa4 20 c4 ♘f5 21 ♖de1**
21 g4 ♘d4 22 ♗h6 ♖xf1+ 23 ♖xf1

♘xc2 24 ♖f2 ♘d4 25 ♗e3 c5 26 ♖f6
b5! 27 ♖xd6 ♘b6 28 ♗xd4 ♘xc4
29 ♗xc5 ♘xd6 30 ♗xd6 ♖d8 31
♗b4 ♖xd5 =+ Faibisovic-Karasev,
USSR 77 **♖ae8 22 ♗d2?!** 22 c5 ♘c3!
23 cxd6 cxd6 24 ♖xe8 ♖xe8 25 g4
♘d4 26 ♗xd6 ♘xd5 =+ Urtaev-
Karasev, USSR 77 **♘d4∓ 23 ♖xf8+
♔xf8 24 ♗h6+ ♔f7 25 ♖f1+ ♔g8 26
♘f2?! ♘f5 26**...♘xc2?? ♘e4 **27 ♗f4
h5 28 ♘d3 ♖e4 −+ 29 c5 ♘c3 30
cxd6 cxd6 31 ♖e1? ♖xe1+ 0-1
Gufeld**

335 Ostermeyer-Botterill
Middlesborough 78

**1 e4 d6 2 d4 g6 3 ♘c3 ♗g7 4 ♗e2
♘f6 5 ♘f3 0-0 6 0-0 ♗g4 7 ♗e3 ♘c6
8 ♕d2 e5 9 d5 9 dxe5= ♘e7 10 ♖ad1
♗d7! 11 ♘e1 b5!?** 11...♘g4 12 ♗xg4
♗xg4 13 f3 ♗d7 14 f4 ♗g4 15 ♖b1
c6∝ **12 f3 ♕b8 13 ♘b1!? N △ c4;
13 ♘d3 a5 14 ♘f2 ♘h5** Bangiev-
Hait, USSR 77; 13...♖d8! 14 ♘f2
c6 Fridstein **♘h5** 13...♖d8 14 c4 c6
15 dxc6 ♗xc6 16 cxb5 ♗xb5 17
♗xb5 ♕xb5 18 ♘c3 += **14 c4 bxc4
15 ♗xc4 f5 16 ♘d3 △ ♘xe5 ♔h8
17 ♖c1 ♘f6 18 ♘c3 c6!= 19 ♗g5
cxd5 20 exd5 ♕b7 21 ♘f2 ♖fc8 22
b3 ♖c7 △ ♘c8-b6 23 ♕e2 a6 24 a4
♘c8 25 a5 ♗e8** 25...♘a7!? △ ♘b5
26 ♖fd1 ♘a7 27 ♗e3 27 ♗xa6 ♕xb3
=+ **♘b5 28 ♘a4 ♖b8 29 ♘b6 ♖e7∝
30 ♘d3?! e4! 31 ♘f4 exf3 32 ♕xf3
♘g4 =+** Zeitnot **33 ♘e6?? ♗xe3??**
33...♖xe6 34 dxe6 ♕xf3 35 gxf3
♘xe3 −+ **34 ♕xe3 ♗e5 35 ♕h6 ♗f7
36 ♖d3 ♗g8?** 36...♗xe6 37 dxe6 ♘d4+
38 ♔h1 ♗xb6 =+ **37 ♖h3 ♘d4?** 37...
♗xe6 38 dxe6 ♘d4+ 39 ♔h1 ♗xb6
40 axb6 d5 41 ♗xb5 axb5 42 ♕xg6
+= **38 ♘f8! ♖g7 39 ♘xg6+** 39 ♘bd7?!
♖xf8 40 ♘xf8 ♕c8! 41 ♘xg6+ ♖xg6

42 ♕xg6 ♘e2+ 43 ♗xe2 ♕xc1+ 44
♔f2 ♕f4+ −+ ♖xg6 40 ♕xg6 ♕c7 41
♖f1!± ♖f8 42 ♔h1 ♖f7 43 b4 ♕e7
44 ♗xa6 ♖g7 45 ♕h5 ♗f7 46 ♕h4
♕c7 47 ♕f2 f4 48 ♗d3 +− ♕d8 49
♕h4 ♕g8 50 ♖xf4 1-0 time Botterill

336 Groszpeter-Mednis Budapest 78
1 e4 d6 2 d4 ♘f6 3 ♘c3 g6 4 ♘f3
♗g7 5 ♗e2 0-0 6 0-0 ♗g4 7 ♗e3 ♘c6
8 ♕d2 e5 9 d5 ♘e7 10 ♖ad1 ♗d7
11 ♗h6 ♘c8!? N 11...♗xh6 12 ♕xh6
+= Planinc-Ree, WaZ 74; 11...♘e8
12 g3 += Planinc-Donner, WaZ 74;
11...♘h5 12 ♗xg7 ♔xg7 13 g3 +=
Haag-Botterill, Birmingham 75

12 ♗xg7 ♔xg7 13 ♘e1 c5! 13...c6?!
14 f4! += 14 f4 14 dxc6 ♗xc6!= exf4
15 ♕xf4 ♕e7 16 ♘d3 ♘b6!= 16...
b5? 17 e5!± 17 ♖f2 ♖ae8 18 ♖df1
♘g8! 18...♘xe4 19 ♘xe4 ♕xe4 20
♕f6+ ♔g8 21 ♕xd6 ♕xd5 22 ♕xc5
+= 19 ♕g3 a6! 20 h4 ♗c8 21 h5
♘d7 22 ♘f4 ♘df6?! 22...♘e5!= 23
♘h3?? 23 hxg6! fxg6 (23...hxg6?!
24 ♗h5! ♘xe4 25 ♘xe4 ♕xe4 26
♗xg6! fxg6 27 ♘h5+ +−) 24 ♗h5!
♘xh5 25 ♘xh5+± ♗xh3 24 ♕xh3?!
24 gxh3 b5∓ ♘xe4 −+ 25 ♘xe4
♕xe4 26 ♗d3 ♕xd5 27 ♖f4 ♕e6
28 ♕h2 ♕e5 29 ♖1f3 ♘h6 30 ♕h3
♕g5 31 hxg6 hxg6 32 ♖f1 ♖h8 33

♕f3 ♖e7 34 ♗c4 ♘f5 35 ♕c3+ ♖e5
36 ♖1f3 36 ♕b3 ♕h5 ♖h4! 37 ♖xh4
♕xh4 38 ♕b3 ♕d4+ 39 ♔h2 ♖h4+
40 ♔g1 ♖e1+ 41 ♗f1 ♕d4+ 42 ♔h2
b5 43 g3 ♕d2+ 44 ♔h3 c4 45 ♕a3
♘e3 0-1 Mednis

337 Velikov-Ftacnik Kiev 78
1 e4 g6 2 d4 ♗g7 3 ♘f3 d6 4 ♘c3
♘f6 5 h3 0-0 6 ♗e3 b6!? 7 ♗c e4
8 ♗g5 h6 9 ♗h4 ♗b7 10 ♕e2 g! 11
♗g3 d5! 12 ♗d3 c5 13 exd5 cx l4!?
13...exd5 14 0-0-0 ♖e8 15 ♘e5 cxd4
16 ♘b5 ♘e4 17 ♗xe4 dxe4 18 ♘ f7!
♔xf7 19 ♘d6+; 17...♗xe5 18 ♗ 7+
♔xh7 19 ♗xe5 ♔g8 20 ♖he1 f6 21
♕h5; 16...♘fd7 17 ♘xf7!; 15... fd7
16 ♕d3 14 ♘b5! 14 ♘xd4 ♘xd5 15
♕e4 ♖e8! 16 ♕h7+ ♔f8 17 ♘db5
♘f6 exd5 15 0-0 15 ♘d6 ♘e4! ♘e4
16 ♘bxd4 ♖e8 17 ♖fe1 ♘c6 18
c3! ♕d7 18...♘xg3 19 ♕xe8+ ♖xe8
20 ♖xe8+ ♖xe8 21 fxg3 ♖e3 22 ♖d1
19 ♕d1 a6 20 ♘xc6 ♗xc6 21 ♘d4
f5!? 22 ♗h2 f4 23 ♕h5 ♗xd4 24
cxd4 ♕g7 25 ♖ad1 ♗a4 25...♗xf2
26 ♔xf2 ♕xd4+ 27 ♔f1 ♖xe1+ 28
♔xe1 26 b3 ♗b5 27 ♗xb5 axb5 28
h4! ♖f8?! 28...♘f6 29 ♖xe8+ ♖xe8
30 ♕f3 ♕g6 31 ♖c1 29 hxg5 hxg5
29...♕xg5 30 ♕xg5 hxg5 31 ♖a1
30 f3! ♘f6 31 ♕h3 ♖xa2 31...g4 32
fxg4 ♘xg4 33 ♖d2 ♖ae8 34 ♖f1 ♖e3
35 ♕h5; 33...♖f6 34 ♕f3 32 ♕e6+
♔h8 32...♕f7 33 ♕d6! 33 ♖e5 g4?
34 fxg4 ♕h7 35 ♗xf4?! 35 ♖f5! f3
36 ♖xf6 ♖xg2+ 37 ♔f1 ♖f2+ 38 ♔xf2
♕xh2+ 39 ♔xf3 ♕h3+ 40 ♔f4 ♕c4+
36 ♖d2 ♖a1+ 37 ♔h2 37 ♖e1 ♖xe1
38 ♕xe1 ♕xb3 ♕h7+ 38 ♔g3 ♖h1
39 ♖f2 ♘e4+? 39...♕d3+ 40 ♔f3
♕h7 41 ♖f2= 40 ♖xe4 ♕h4+ 41
♔f3 dxe4+ 42 ♔e2!! ♖xf4 42...♖f6?
43 ♕xf6+ ♕xf6 44 ♘e5 43 ♕e5+

Xf6! 44 Wxf6+ Wxf6 45 Xxf6 Xb1
46 e3 Xe1+ 46...Xxb3+ 47 xe4
Xg3 48 f5 Xd3 49 g6 g8 50
Xxb6 f8 51 Xb8+ e7 52 Xxb5
Xxd4 53 g5 47 Wd2 Xb1 48 c2
Xg1 49 Xxb6 49 Xf2 Xxg2+ 50 c3
Xg3+ 51 b4 Xd3 52 Xe6! Xxd4+
53 xb5 g7 54 g5 Xd3 54...f7
55 Xe5 g6 56 b4! h5 57 c5 55
c4 Xe3 56 b4 Xe1 57 d4! 57 b5?
e3! 58 d3 Xb1 59 b6 Xb3+ Xb1
58 c3 Xc1+ 59 b2 Xe1 60 c2
e3 61 Xe4! g6 62 d3 Xd1+ 62...
Xb1 63 xe3 xg5 64 Xc4! 63
xe3 xg5 64 Xd4! Xc1 65 e4 f6
66 d5 Xc8 67 Xc4 Xb8 68 d6
f5 69 Xc5+ e4 70 b5 d4 71
Xh5 c4 72 c6 Xc8+ 73 b7 1-0

338 Van der Wiel-Taulbut
Groningen 77/8
1 e4 g6 2 d4 d6 3 c3 g7 4 f4 f6
5 c4 c5 6 e5 fd7 7 exd6 0-0!
8 e3 8 dxe7 Wxe7+∝ exd6 9 Wd2
c6 10 dxc5 dxc5 11 0-0-0 d4!?
12 f3 b6! 13 e2 d5 14 xd4
cxd4 15 xd4 xc3 16 Wxc3 b6
Δ Xd8 17 We3 f5∓ 18 c3 Xfe8
19 Wf2 Xac8 20 g4 e4 21 Xhg1
Xed8 Δ xd4 0-1 Taulbut

339 Skrobek-Pribyl Decin 78
1 e4 g6 2 d4 g7 3 c3 d6 4 f4 f6
5 f3 c5 6 b5+ d7 7 e5 g4 8 e6
8 h3 xb5 9 xb5 dxe5 10 hxg4
Wa5+ 11 c3 e4 12 g5 Wxb5 13 dxc5
d7 14 xe4 xc5 15 xc5 Wxc5
16 Wa4+ b5 17 We4 Xc8 18 e3
Wc4 19 Wxc4 Xxc4 20 0-0 +=
Pokojowczyk-Bitman, Poland 78 xb5
9 exf7+ d7 10 xb5 Wa5+ 11 c3
cxd4 12 xd4 xd4 13 Wxd4 13
Wxg4+?! Wf5 14 Wf3 c6 15 e2
We6 =+ Tringov-Benko, Sarajevo 67

c6 14 Wc4! Wa6?! 15 b5 Xhf8
16 d2 Xac8 17 We2± f6 18 0-0
Xxf7 18...d4? 19 xd4 Wxe2 20
xe2 Xxc2 21 Xad1 e4 22 g3
xd2 23 Xf2 +- 19 Xfe1 d8 20
c4! e8 21 c3 g8 22 Xad1 Xc6

23 c5! +- 23 Xxd6!? Xxf4 23...dxc5
24 Wd3! 24 cxd6 Wb6+ 25 h1 Xf2
26 We5 Xxc3 27 c7+! f7 28 dxe7
f6 29 exd8+ 1-0 Konikowski

340 Ljubojevic-Timman Niksic 78
1 e4 d6 2 d4 f6 3 c3 g6 4 f4
g7 5 f3 c5 6 dxc5 Wa5 7 d3
Wxc5 8 We2 0-0 9 e3 Wa5 10 0-0
g4 11 a3 11 Xad1 c6 12 c4
h5 13 b3 xc3 14 bxc3 Wxc3 15
f5 f6 16 h3 xf3 17 Wxf3 a5 18
Xd3 Wc7∝ Spassky-Fischer (17) 72
c6 12 h1 d7 13 We1 c5 14 b4
xd3 15 cxd3 Wd8 16 Xc1 xf3
17 Xxf3 e6! 18 e2 18 Xh3 (Δ f5)
f5! a6 19 d4 e7 20 f2 f5 20...
d5 21 e5 f5 22 g4!± 21 c3 Wd7
22 d5 e5! 22...exd5 23 xd5 += 23
exf5 xf5 24 fxe5 xe5 25 e4
Xae8 26 h3 g7 27 We2 Xe5 28
Wd3 Xfe8 29 c3 h6 ½-½ 30 Xd1
e3!? 31 g4!?∝ Taulbut

341 Ljubojevic-Timman Tilburg 78
1 e4 d6 2 d4 f6 3 c3 g6 4 f4 g7

5 ♘f3 c5 6 dxc5 6 ♗b5+!?; 6 e5!?
**♕a5 7 ♗d3 ♕xc5 8 ♕e2 0-0 9 ♗e3
♕a5 10 0-0 ♗g4 11 ♕f2 ♗xf3 12 ♕xf3
♘c6 13 ♘e2?** 13 a3 ♘d7 14 ♗d2=
♘d7

**14 c3?? ♘de5 −+ 15 fxe5 ♘xe5
16 ♕h3 ♘xd3 17 ♕d7 ♕a6 18 ♕xe7
♖ae8 19 ♕h4 d5 20 ♘g3 f5 21 e5
f4 22 ♗xf4 ♕b6+ 23 ♔h1 ♘f2+ 24
♖xf2 ♕xf2 25 ♖f1 ♕xb2 26 ♕g5 0-1**
Miles

342 Kapengut-Zaichik
Daugavpils 78
**1 e4 d6 2 d4 ♘f6 3 ♘c3 g6 4 f4 ♗g7
5 ♘f3 0-0 6 ♗d3 ♘a6 7 e5** 7 0-0 c5
8 d5 ♖b8 9 ♕e2 Tseitlin-Chikovani,
USSR 76; 9 a4 ♘b4! Suetin-Vadasz,
Budapest 2 76 **dxe5** 7...♘e8; 7...♘d7
8 0-0 c5 9 ♗e3 ♘b4 10 ♗c4 cxd4
11 ♗xd4 ♘c6∓ De Greiff-Mouostori,
Corr 66; 8 ♕e2 c5 9 d5 ♘b4=
Pederson-Sirkia, Siegen 70; 8 ♘e2
c5 9 c3± ; 8 ♘e4 ♘b4 9 ♗e2 ♘b6
Mednis-Vadasz, Budapest 2 76; 8...
dxe5 9 ♗xa6 bxa6 10 dxe5 ♘b6
Jansa-Adorjan, Sochi 76 **8 dxe5**
8 fxe5 ♘d5 9 ♘xd5 ♕xd5 10 c4 ♘d5
Bisguier-Benko, New York 64 **♘d5
9 ♘xd5 ♕xd5 10 ♕e2 ♗f5 11 ♗xf5
gxf5 12 ♗e3 c5** 12...♖fd8 13 0-0
♘b4 14 a3 ♘c6 15 ♖fd1 ♕e6 16 ♘g5

♕g6 Parma-Ree, Titovo Uzice 66;
17 ♕b5!± Parma; 12...f6 13 exf6
♗xf6 14 0-0 ♕e4 15 c3 ♘c5 16 ♘d2
♕d3 17 ♕f2 ♘a4 18 ♖ab1 c5 19
♘f3 Ree-Timman, Netherlands 71
13 0-0 ♘c7 14 ♖ad1 N 14 ♖fd1
♕e4 15 ♕d3 ♘e6 16 ♕xe4 fxe4 17
♘d2 f5 18 exf6 ♗xf6 19 c3 ♘d4!
20 cxd4 cxd4 21 ♘xe4 dxe3=
Klovan-Zaichik, Daugavpils 78 **♕c6**
14...♕xa2 15 c4 b6 16 ♕c2 +−;
14...♕e4 15 ♖d7 ♘e6 16 ♘d2! **15
♕d3 e6 16 c4 ♘a6 17 g4!?** 17 a3±
**♘b4 18 ♕b1 ♖fd8 19 gxf5 ♖xd1
20 ♕xd1 exf5!** 20...♕e4 21 ♗xc5
♘d3 22 fxe6! ♘xc5 23 exf7+ ♔h8
24 ♕d4 ♕g6+ 25 ♘g5 ♘e6 26 ♕e4 +−
**21 ♕b1! ♕g6+ 22 ♔f2 ♖d8 23 ♖d1
♖xd1 24 ♕xd1 ♗f8 25 a3 ♘c6 26
♕d5 b6 += 27 ♔e2?!** 27 ♔f1 ♘e7!
**28 ♕d7 ♕g2+ 29 ♗f2 ♘g6! 30 ♕xf5
♗h6= 31 e6! fxe6** 31...♘xf4+? 32
♕xf4! ♗xf4 33 e7! +− **32 ♕xe6+
♔g7 33 ♕d7+ ♔f6 34 ♕d6+ ♔g7 ½-½
Kapengut**

343 Hazai-Vadasz Hungary 78
**1 e4 d6 2 d4 ♘f6 3 ♘c3 g6 4 f4 ♗g7
5 ♘f3 0-0 6 ♗e3 ♘a6 7 e5 ♘g4 8 ♗g1
c5 9 h3 cxd4 10 ♕xd4 ♘h6 11 g4!?
♕a5?** 11...dxe5 12 ♕xd8 ♖xd8 13
♘xe5 ♘b4 **12 0-0-0 ♘b4** 12...♗e6
**13 a3 ♘c6 14 ♕d5 ♕xd5 15 ♘xd5
dxe5 16 ♘xe5 ♘xe5 17 ♘xe7+ ♔h8
18 fxe5 ♗e6 19 ♗h2 ♘xg4?? 20
hxg4 ♗xg4 21 ♖d3 ♖ae8 22 ♗d5
♗f5 23 ♖e3 ♗h6 24 ♗f4 ♗xf4 25
♘xf4 f6 26 e6 g5 27 e7 ♖f7 28 ♘d5
1-0 Haag**

344 Sigurjonsson-Fries Nielsen
Esbjerg 78
**1 e4 d6 2 d4 ♘f6 3 ♘c3 g6 4 f4 ♗g7
5 ♘f3 0-0 6 ♗e3 b6 7 ♗d3 ♗b7 8 f5!**

c5 9 fxg6 hxg6 10 d5 ♘bd7 11 0-0
♖e8? 11...♘g4 12 ♗g5 △ ♘xf7 a6
13 ♕e1 ♘f8 14 ♕h4 ♕d7 △ ♕g4
15 h3 △ ♖f3, ♖af1 e6

16 e5! dxe5 17 ♘ce4 ♘xe4 17...♘8h7
18 ♘xf6+ ♘xf6 19 ♖xf6 ♗xf6 20
♕h7+ ♔f8 21 ♖f1 ♕e7 22 d6! +−
18 ♖xf7 ♕xf7 19 ♘xf7 ♕xf7 20
dxe6+ ♖xe6 21 ♗xe4 ♗xe4 22 ♕xe4
+− ♖a7 23 ♖f1+ ♔g8 24 ♕d5 ♖ae7
25 ♗g5 ♖e8 26 ♕b7 △ ♖f7 e4 27
♖f7 ♗d4+ 28 ♔h2 e3 29 ♗h6 e2
30 ♖g7+ ♔h8 31 ♕f7 ♗e5+ 31...♖g1+
32 ♔h1 32 g3 ♗xg3+ 33 ♕g2 e1♘+
34 ♔xg3 1-0 Sigurjonsson

345 Spassky-Timman Tilburg 78
1 e4 d6 2 d4 ♘f6 3 ♘c3 g6 4 g3 ♗g7

5 ♗g2 0-0 6 ♘f3 ♗g4 7 ♗e3 ♘c6 8
h3 ♗xf3 9 ♕xf3 e5 10 dxe5 dxe5
11 0-0 ♘d4 12 ♕d1 ♕e7 13 ♘b1
h5! 14 ♘d2 14 h4 ♘g4 =+; 14 ♗g5
♖ad8 15 ♘d2 ♘e6 =/=+ h4 15 ♗xd4
exd4 16 gxh4 ♘h5∓ 17 ♕g4 ♕c5
18 ♕g5 ♕xc2 19 ♖fc1 ♕xb2 20 ♗f3
♗f6 21 ♕h6 ♗g7 22 ♕g5 ♖fe8 23
♘c4 ♕b4 24 ♗xh5 gxh5 25 ♖ab1
♕a4!? 27...♕e7 ∓/−+ 26 ♖xb7 ♕c6
27 ♔h2! ♖e6 27...♕xb7?? 28 ♖g1
♔f8 29 ♕xg7+ ♔e7 30 ♘e5 +− 28
♖g1 ♖g6 29 ♕d5 ♕xd5 30 exd5 ♖d8∓
31 ♖xg6 fxg6 32 ♖xc7 ♖xd5 33 ♖xa7
d3 34 ♘e3 d2 35 ♘d1 ♗h6 35...♖c5
36 ♖d7 ♗h6 37 ♘e3= 36 ♔g2 ♖e5
36...♖c5? 37 ♔f3 ♖c1 38 ♔e2=;
37 ♔f1?? ♖e5! −+ 37 ♖b7 ♖a5??
37...♖e1 38 ♖b1 ♗f8 39 a4 ♗a3 40
a5 ♗c1 41 a6 ♖xd1 42 a7 ♖g1+
43 ♔h2! ♖h1+ 44 ♔g2!=; 38...♗f4!
39 a4 ♗c7! △ ♗a5, ♔f7-e6-e5-d4-d3-c2
−+ 38 ♖b2 ♖a4 39 ♖b6 ♔f7 40 ♖d6
♖xa2 41 ♔f3 =+ ♖a1 42 ♔e2 ♖a4
43 ♘e3 ♖xh4 44 ♘f1 ♖xh3 45 ♘xd2
♗f4 46 ♘e4 ♔g7 46...♗xd6 47 ♘g5+
47 ♖d3 ♖h4 48 ♖d7+ ♔h6 49 ♔f3
♗e5 50 ♘g3 ♖f4+ 51 ♔g2 ♖g4 52
♔h3 ♔g5 53 ♖e7 ♔f6 54 ♖h7 ½-½
Miles

Games Index